W9-BXG-227

New Zealand's North Island

(Te Ika-a-Māui)

Bay of
Islands &
Northland
(p129)

Auckland
(p60)

Coromandel
Peninsula &
the Waikato
(p180)

Rotorua & the
Bay of Plenty
(p302)

The East
Coast
(p345)

Taupo & the
Ruapehu Region
(p270)

Taranaki &
Whanganui
(p233)

Wellington
Region
(p380)

Peter Dragicevich, Brett Atkinson, Anita Isalska, Sofia Levin

Contents

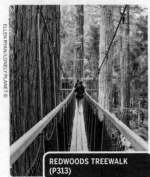

ELLEN RYAN/LONELY PLANET ©

REDWOODS TREEWALK
(P313)

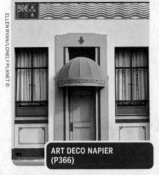

ELLEN RYAN/LONELY PLANET ©

ART DECO NAPIER
(P366)

Contents

Welcome to the North Island

Packing in cosmopolitan cities, authentic opportunities to experience Māori culture, and the country's bubbling volcanic heart, the North Island is an exceedingly versatile destination.

Volcanic Thrills

Welcome to one of the planet's youngest countries, at least in geological terms. Ascend the volcanic cones surrounding Auckland for super city views, before heading south to Rotorua for hot mud spa treatments and helicopter journeys to the jagged volcanic summit of Mt Tarawera. Journey due south to Lake Taupo, the legacy of one of the planet's biggest-ever volcanic eruptions, and now gateway to Tongariro National Park. Ski or snowboard on Mt Ruapehu's still-active slopes, or negotiate a steady path past Mt Ngauruhoe's brooding volcanic cone on the Tongariro Alpine Crossing.

Māori Culture

The influence of New Zealand's indigenous culture is more keenly felt in the North Island, where Māori make up a much higher percentage of the population. Across Te Ika-a-Māui (the island's Māori name) you're more likely to hear the Māori language being spoken, see main street *marae* (meeting houses), join in a *hāngi* (Māori feast), or catch a cultural performance with traditional Māori songs, dancing and a blood-curdling *haka* (war dance). Venture to the North Island's East Cape for the most authentic Māori experiences. Northland and Rotorua are also cultural hotspots.

Outdoor Experiences

New Zealand's South Island usually steals the attention, but the North Island also has a sublime combination of forests, mountains and beaches. In the latter, the North has a clear lead – particularly in subtropical Northland, the Coromandel Peninsula and the west coast, with its wild surf beaches. Tackle one of the Great Walks – one even offers a river journey by canoe or kayak – or spend a few hours wandering through the accessible wilderness of the Coromandel. Day trips from vibrant Auckland range from kayaking to dormant volcanoes, or canyoning and abseiling down forested waterfalls.

Food, Wine & Beer

Kiwi food was once a bland echo of a British Sunday lunch, but these days NZ chefs take inspiration from the New World, especially the Pacific with its abundance of seafood and diverse cuisines. Try some Māori faves: paua (abalone; a type of sea snail), kina (sea urchin) and kumara (sweet potato). Thirsty? NZ's cool-climate wineries have been collecting trophies for decades now, and the vineyard restaurants of Hawke's Bay are seriously good. The booming craft-beer scene also deserves some scrutiny. And with a firmly entrenched coffee culture, you're never far from an artfully prepared brew.

Why I Love the North Island

By Brett Atkinson, Writer

Born in Rotorua, and now a proud resident of Auckland, I've been exploring the North Island with friends and family for most of my life. Favourite places include the bush, beaches and hidden coves of the Coromandel Peninsula, the wine and food scenes of Hawke's Bay, and the rugged and remote volcanic landscapes of Tongariro National Park. For craft beer, coffee and culture, the national capital of Wellington is always appealing, and Auckland's growing ethnic diversity and cosmopolitan vibe makes me proud to live in NZ's most exciting city.

For more about our writers, see p480

Above: Cathedral Cove (p197), Hahei

New Zealand – North Island

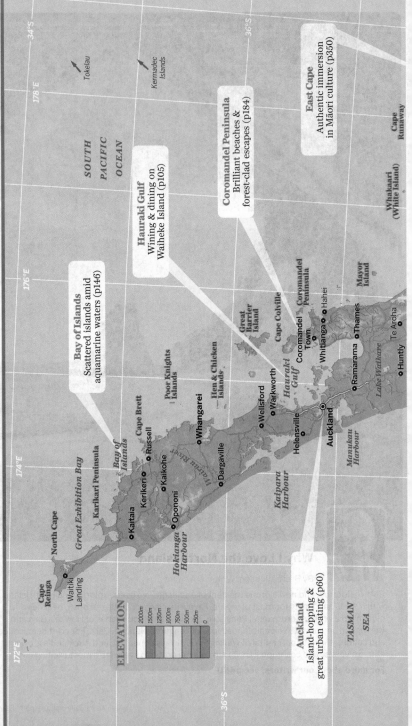

Bay of Islands
Scattered islands amid
aquamarine waters (p146)

Hauraki Gulf
Wining & dining on
Waiheke Island (p105)

Coromandel Peninsula
Brilliant beaches &
forest-clad escapes (p184)

East Cape
Authentic immersion
in Māori culture (p350)

Auckland
Island-hopping &
great urban eating (p60)

ELEVATION

2000m
1500m
1250m
1000m
750m
500m
250m
0

100 km
60 miles

*SOUTH
PACIFIC
OCEAN*

Tokelau

*Kermadec
Islands*

Cape Reinga
North Cape
Waitiki Landing
Great Exhibition Bay
Karikari Peninsula
Kaitaia
Kerikeri
*Bay of
Islands*
Cape Brett
Russell
Kaikohe
Opononi
*Hokianga
Harbour*
Waipoua River
Whangarei
Dargaville
Poor Knights
Islands
Hen & Chicken
Islands
Wellsford
Warkworth
Helensville
*Kaipara
Harbour*
*Hauraki
Gulf*
Great Barrier
Island
Cape Colville
Coromandel
Town
Coromandel
Peninsula
Auckland
*Manukau
Harbour*
Ramarama
Whitianga
Hahei
Thames
Lake Waikare
Te Aroha
Huntly
Mayor
Island
Whakaari
(White Island)
Cape
Runaway

*TASMAN
SEA*

172°E
174°E
176°E
178°E
34°S
36°S

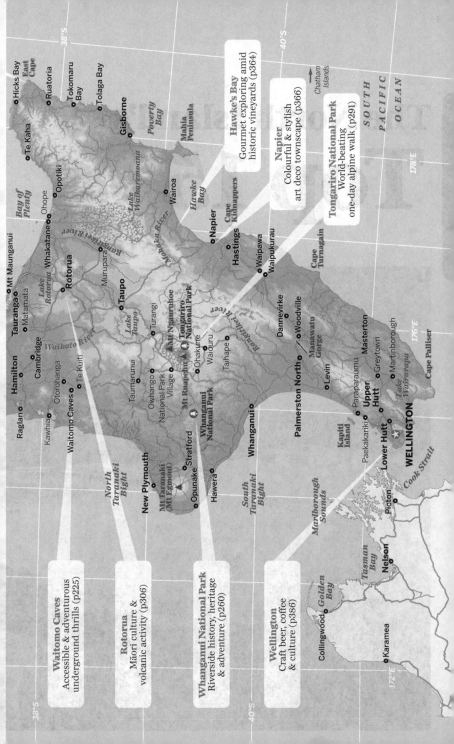

Waitomo Caves
Accessible & adventurous underground thrills (p225)

Rotorua
Māori culture & volcanic activity (p306)

Whanganui National Park
Riverside history, heritage & adventure (p260)

Wellington
Craft beer, coffee & culture (p386)

Hawke's Bay
Gourmet exploring amid historic vineyards (p364)

Napier
Colourful & stylish art deco townscape (p366)

Tongariro National Park
World-beating one-day alpine walk (p291)

SOUTH PACIFIC OCEAN

Chatham Islands

38°S

40°S

38°S

40°S

172°E   175°E   176°E   178°E

Hicks Bay
East Cape
Ruatoria
Te Kaha
Tokomaru Bay
Tolaga Bay
Opotiki
Ohope
Bay of Plenty
Whakatane
Mt Maunganui
Tauranga
Matamata
Lake Rotorua
Rotorua
Murupara
Gisborne
Poverty Bay
Lake Waikaremoana
Wairoa
Mahia Peninsula
Rangitaiki River
Mohaka River
Napier
Hawke Bay
Cape Kidnappers
Hastings
Waipawa
Waipukurau
Cape Turnagain
Raglan
Hamilton
Cambridge
Otorohanga
Kawhia
Waitomo Caves
Te Kuiti
Waikato River
Taupo
Lake Taupo
Turangi
Mt Ngauruhoe
Tongariro National Park
Dannevirke
Woodville
Taumarunui
Owhango
National Park Village
Ohakune
Mt Ruapehu
Waiouru
Taihape
Rangitikei River
Manawatu Gorge
Palmerston North
Masterton
Levin
Greytown
Martinborough
Lake Wairarapa
Cape Palliser
North Taranaki Bight
New Plymouth
Stratford
Mt Taranaki (Mt Egmont)
Opunake
Hawera
Whanganui National Park
Whanganui
South Taranaki Bight
Kapiti Island
Paraparaumu
Paekakariki
Upper Hutt
Lower Hutt
WELLINGTON
Cook Strait
Marlborough Sounds
Picton
Blenheim
Tasman Bay
Golden Bay
Collingwood
Nelson
Karamea

The North Island's
Top 15

Hauraki Gulf

1 A yachtie's paradise, the island-studded Hauraki Gulf (p104) is Auckland's aquatic playground, sheltering its harbour and east-coast bays, and providing ample excuse for the City of Sails' pleasure fleet to breeze into action. Despite the busy maritime traffic, the gulf has its own resident pods of whales and dolphins. Rangitoto Island is an icon of the city: its near-perfect volcanic cone provides the backdrop for many a tourist snapshot. With beautiful beaches, acclaimed wineries and upmarket eateries, Waiheke is Auckland's most popular island escape. Left: Waiheke Island (p105)

Urban Auckland

2 Held in the embrace of two harbours and built on the remnants of long-extinct volcanoes, Auckland (p60) isn't your average metropolis. It's regularly rated one of the world's most liveable cities, and with some recent regeneration projects, its star is in the ascendant. Auckland is also blessed with good beaches, flanked by wine regions, and it has a large enough population to support a thriving dining, drinking and live-music scene. Cultural festivals are celebrated with gusto in this ethnically diverse city, which has the world's largest Pacific Islander population. Right: Sky Tower (p67), Auckland

TROY WEGMAN/SHUTTERSTOCK ®

2

SAM DCRUZ/SHUTTERSTOCK

LUKAS BISCHOFF PHOTOGRAPHY/SHUTTERSTOCK ©

Waitomo Caves

3 Waitomo (p225) is a must-see – an astonishing maze of subterranean caves, canyons and rivers perforating the northern King Country limestone. Black-water rafting is the big lure here (similar to white-water rafting, but through a dark cave), plus glowworm grottoes, underground abseiling, and more stalactites and stalagmites than you'll ever see in one place again. Above ground, Waitomo township is a quaint conglomeration of businesses: a craft brewery, a cafe, a holiday park and some decent B&Bs. But don't linger in the sunlight – it's party time downstairs.

Geothermal Rotorua

4 The first thing you'll notice about Rotorua (p306) is the smell of sulphur, meaning this geothermal hot spot is a tad whiffy. But volcanic activity is what everyone comes to see, with gushing geysers, bubbling mud, steaming cracks in the ground, and boiling pools of mineral-rich water. Rotorua is definitely unique, a fact eagerly exploited by some commercially savvy local businesses. But you don't have to spend a fortune: there are plenty of affordable (and free) volcanic encounters to be had in parks and Māori villages, or just along the roadside.

Top right: Champagne Pool, Wai-O-Tapu Thermal Wonderland (p321)

Bay of Islands

5 Turquoise waters lapping in pretty bays, dolphins frolicking at the bows of boats, pods of orcas gliding gracefully by – the chances are these are the kinds of images that drew you to New Zealand in the first place, and these are exactly the kinds of experiences that the Bay of Islands (p146) delivers so well. Whether you're a hardened sea dog or a confirmed landlubber, there are myriad options to tempt you out on the water to explore the 150-odd islands that dot this beautiful bay.

PENG SHI/500PX ©

JACQUES VAN DINTEREN/GETTY IMAGES ©

Tongariro Alpine Crossing

6 At the centre of the North Island, Tongariro National Park presents an alien landscape of alpine desert punctuated by three smoking and smouldering volcanoes. The Tongariro Alpine Crossing (p291) offers the perfect taste of what the park has to offer, skirting the bases of two of the mountains and providing views of craters, brightly coloured lakes and the vast Central Plateau stretching out beyond. It's for these reasons that it's often rated as one of the world's best single-day wilderness walks.

Top: Emerald Lakes (p296), National Park Village

Wellington

7 One of the coolest little capitals in the world, windy Wellington (p386) lives up to the hype by keeping things hip, diverse and rootsy. It's long famed for a vibrant arts and music scene, fuelled by excellent espresso and more restaurants per head than New York...but a host of craft-beer bars have now elbowed in on the action. Edgy yet sociable, colourful yet often dressed in black, Wellington is big on the unexpected and unconventional. Erratic weather only adds zest to the experience.

Bottom: Wellington Harbour (p386)

FOTOS593/SHUTTERSTOCK ©

DMITRYSERBIN/SHUTTERSTOCK ©

Māori Culture

8 New Zealand's indigenous Māori culture is both accessible and engaging: join in a *haka* (war dance), chow down at a traditional *hāngi* (Māori feast cooked in the ground), carve a pendant from bone or *pounamu* (jade), learn some Māori language, or check out an authentic cultural performance with songs, dancing, legends, arts and crafts. Big-city and regional museums around the North Island are crammed with Māori artefacts and historical items, but Rotorua (p306) is perhaps the easiest place for travellers to engage with the living culture. Top: Tamaki Māori leader

Coromandel Peninsula

9 A beautiful finger of land that combines sweeping beaches, quirky and idiosyncratic coastal landscapes, and rugged bush-clad mountains, the Coromandel Peninsula (p184) is the perfect relaxing escape from Auckland. The area's hippie and alternative-lifestyle roots linger, with organic farms and various spiritual retreats. Well-marked, and sometimes challenging, trails criss-cross the peninsula's mountainous spine. Other options for active adventure include sea kayaking around Cathedral Cove, followed by a DIY natural spa pool at nearby Hot Water Beach. Above: Cathedral Cove (p197)

BANGKOKFLAME/SHUTTERSTOCK ©

BYVALET/SHUTTERSTOCK ©

12

TRAVELJUNKIE/SHUTTERSTOCK ©

Napier Art Deco

10 Geologically active NZ is known as the 'Shaky Isles' for good reason. In 1931 a magnitude 7.8 earthquake struck the North Island's east coast, nearly flattening the cities of Napier (p366) and Hastings. Reconstruction embraced the architectural fashions of the day, and now the twin cities are a showcase of art deco and Spanish mission design. Unlike the famous deco skyscrapers of Chicago or New York, this is architecture on a human scale – mainly houses and low-rise commercial buildings. Visit during February's art-deco weekend for the complete 1930s experience. Top left: Napier Municipal Theatre (p372)

Hawke's Bay Wine Country

11 Wine has been crafted in the Hawke's Bay (p364) region since 1851, with dozens of vineyards now joining famous longstanding local wineries such as Mission Estate and Church Road. The emphasis is on excellent Bordeaux-style reds and chardonnay, and many wineries also incorporate good vineyard restaurants. Farmers markets, craft breweries and other gourmet and artisan producers make it a magnet for foodie travellers, and smart lodge and B&B accommodation caters to them while taking advantage of gorgeous rural and coastal locations.

East Cape

12 Get right off the beaten track in NZ's easternmost region (p350), a twisting and turning coastal procession of isolated bays and coves, many punctuated during summer with the crimson blooms of the pohutukawa tree. Nowhere else in NZ is everyday Māori culture and society quite so evident, with quiet villages and *marae* (Māori meeting places) tucked into sleepy bays. Several East Cape tour operations are run by members of the local Ngāti Porou *iwi* (tribe), providing the opportunity for authentic and heartfelt interaction with travellers.

Whanganui National Park

13 After frantic jetboating or river rafting in other parts of the North Island, slow right down with a canoe or kayak trip down the history-rich Whanganui River in the gloriously isolated Whanganui National Park (p260). Snaking 329km from its source on Mt Tongariro to the Tasman Sea, it's the country's longest navigable river, tracking carefully through brooding native bush scattered with the remains of historical villages and trading stops. If you're more keen on a driving holiday, the spidery Whanganui River Rd is equally spectacular. Below: Canoeing on Whanganui River (p261)

Auckland's Pacific Island Culture

14 Around 195,000 residents of Polynesian descent (Samoa, the Cook Islands, Tonga, Niue, Fiji, Tokelau and Tuvalu) make Auckland the capital of the South Pacific. The city's professional sports teams showcase the best of Polynesian power, especially the NZ Warriors rugby league team. Immerse yourself in Pacific Island culture at the weekly Otara Market, or time your visit for March's annual Pasifika Festival (p83). Right: Tongan fans for sale at Pasifika Festival (p83)

JANETTEASCHE/GETTY IMAGES ©

KAREL LORIER/ALAMY STOCK PHOTO ©

CHAMELEONSEYE/SHUTTERSTOCK ©

Rugby

15 Rugby union is NZ's national game and governing preoccupation. If your timing's good, you might catch the revered national team (and reigning back-to-back world champions), the All Blacks, in action. The 'ABs' are resident gods: drop any of their names into a conversation and you'll win friends for life. Visit the New Zealand Rugby Museum (p265) in Palmerston North, watch some kids running around a suburban field on a Saturday morning, or yell along with the locals in a small-town pub as the big men collide on the big screen. Left: Sculpture of Charles John Monro by Sonny Hawkins, New Zealand Rugby Museum (p265)

Need to Know

For more information, see Survival Guide (p447)

Currency
New Zealand dollar ($)

Language
English, Māori

Visas
Citizens of 60 countries, including Australia, the UK, the US and most EU countries, don't need visas for NZ (length-of-stay allowances vary). See www.immigration.govt.nz.

Money
Credit cards are used for most purchases in NZ, and are accepted in most hotels and restaurants. ATMs are widely available in cities and larger towns.

Mobile Phones
European phones should work on NZ's network, but most American or Japanese phones will not. Buy a local SIM card and prepaid account for unlocked phones.

Time
New Zealand time (GMT/UTC plus 12 hours)

When to Go

Paihia
GO Feb–Apr

Auckland
GO Feb–Apr

Rotorua
GO Oct–Dec

Taupo
GO Jul–Oct (skiing)
or Feb–Apr

Wellington
GO Dec–Feb

High Season
(Dec–Feb)

➡ Summer: busy beaches, outdoor explorations, festivals and sporting events. December can be wet.

➡ Auckland empties out between Christmas and New Year.

➡ High season in the ski towns is winter (June to August).

Shoulder
(Mar–Apr)

➡ Prime travelling time: fine weather, short queues, kids in school and warm(ish) ocean.

➡ Long evenings sipping Kiwi wines and craft beers.

➡ Spring (September to November) is shoulder season too.

Low Season
(May–Aug)

➡ Head for the slopes of Mt Ruapehu for some brilliant southern-hemisphere skiing.

➡ No crowds, good accommodation deals and a seat in any restaurant.

➡ Warm-weather beach towns may be half asleep.

Useful Websites

100% Pure New Zealand (www.newzealand.com) Comprehensive official tourism site.

Department of Conservation (www.doc.govt.nz) DOC parks, trail conditions and camping info.

Lonely Planet (www.lonely planet.com/new-zealand) Destination information, hotel bookings, traveller forum and more.

Destination New Zealand (www.destination-nz.com) Event listings and info on all things NZ.

Te Ara (www.teara.govt.nz) Online encyclopedia of NZ.

Important Numbers

Regular NZ phone numbers have a two-digit area code followed by a seven-digit number. When dialling within a region, the area code is still required. Drop the initial 0 if dialling from abroad. If you're calling the police but don't speak English well, ask for Language Line, which may be able to hook you up with a translator.

NZ country code	☑64
International access code from NZ	☑00
Emergency (Ambulance, Fire, Police)	☑111
Directory Assistance (charges apply)	☑018

Exchange Rates

Australia	A$1	NZ$1.10
Canada	C$1	NZ$1.14
China	Y10	NZ$2.21
Euro zone	€1	NZ$1.72
Japan	¥100	NZ$1.29
Singapore	S$1	NZ$1.08
UK	UK£1	NZ$1.97
US	US$1	NZ$1.46

For current exchange rates, see www.xe.com.

Daily Costs

Budget: Less than $150

➡ Dorm beds or campsites: $25–40 per night

➡ Main course in a budget eatery: less than $15

➡ InterCity or Naked Bus pass: 15 hours or five trips $125–159

Midrange: $150–250

➡ Double room in a midrange hotel/motel: $110–200

➡ Main course in a midrange restaurant: $15–32

➡ Car rental: from $40 per day

Top end: More than $250

➡ Double room in an upmarket hotel: from $200

➡ Three-course meal in a classy restaurant: $80

➡ Domestic flight: from $100

Opening Hours

Opening hours vary seasonally depending on where you are. Most places close on Christmas Day and Good Friday.

Banks 9am–4.30pm Monday to Friday, some also 9am–noon Saturday

Cafes 7am–4pm

Post Offices 8.30am–5pm Monday to Friday; larger branches also 9.30am–noon Saturday

Pubs & Bars noon–late ('late' varies by region, and by day)

Restaurants noon–2.30pm and 6.30pm–9pm

Shops & Businesses 9am–5.30pm Monday to Friday and 9am to noon or 5pm Saturday

Supermarkets 8am–7pm, often 9pm or later in cities

Arriving on New Zealand's North Island

Auckland Airport Airbus Express buses run into the city every 10 to 30 minutes, 24 hours. Door-to-door shuttle buses run 24 hours (from $35). A taxi into the city costs $80 to $90 (45 minutes).

Wellington Airport Airport Flyer buses ($9) run into the city every 10 to 20 minutes from around 7am to 9pm. Door-to-door shuttle buses run 24 hours. A taxi into the city costs around $30 (20 minutes).

Entry & Exit Formulas

Disembarkation in New Zealand is generally a straightforward affair, with only the usual customs declarations and luggage-carousel scramble to endure. Under the Orwellian title of 'Advance Passenger Screening', documents that used to be checked after you touched down in NZ (passport, visa etc) are now checked before you board your flight – make sure all your documentation is in order so that your check-in is stress-free. There are no restrictions when it comes to foreign citizens entering NZ. If you have a current passport and visa (or don't require one), you should be fine.

For information on **getting around**, see p32

What's New

Stargazing on Great Barrier Island

Following its 2017 recognition as a Dark Sky Sanctuary, Great Barrier Island, 88km northeast of Auckland, now offers the opportunity for after-dark stargazing tours. Great Barrier is the only island in the world to be awarded Dark Sky Sanctuary status. (p116)

The Lighthouse

Designed by artist Michael Parekōwhai, Auckland's newest example of public art overlooks the harbour from Queens Wharf, and is a challenging and spectacular work blending commentary on sovereignty and colonisation. (p68)

Sevens Rugby in Hamilton

New Zealand's biggest annual sporting party comes to Hamilton in February for the NZ leg of the World Rugby Sevens. See NZ take on traditional foes Australia, Fiji and South Africa. (www.sevens.co.nz)

Zip-lining at Driving Creek Railway

Following an 18-minute journey on this narrow-gauge mountain railway in Coromandel Town, travel back down the forest-covered hill on an exciting series of eight zip-lines. (p189)

Expansion at Te Puia

Construction is well underway at Rotorua's Māori cultural centre for a new home for the national Māori carving and weaving schools, and a new exhibition space and *tā moko* (traditional tattoo) studio. (p307)

West End Precinct, New Plymouth

Centred around the former White Hart Hotel, this collection of cool cafes, restaurants and shops is an essential destination in New Plymouth. Highlights include the adjacent Govett-Brewster Art Gallery/Len Lye Centre and the carnivorous gourmet treats at Meat & Liquor. (p245)

Brew Union

This former warehouse is the best spot for a drink in Palmerston North. Look forward to 21 tap beers – some brewed on site – plus 45 gins and a great food menu. (p268)

Napier's Dining Scene

Recent openings have given Napier the most exciting restaurant scene in provincial NZ. New eating and drinking highlights in NZ's Art Deco capital include Bistronomy (p371), Greek National Cafe (p370) and Hapī (p370).

He Tohu Gallery at Wellington's National Library of New Zealand

A new space built to house three of NZ's most precious sets of political documents: the 1835 Declaration of Independence of the United Tribes of NZ, the 1840 Treaty of Waitangi and the 1893 Women's Suffrage Petition. (p392)

St Mary of the Angels

Reopened after a lengthy restoration and earthquake strengthening, this 1922 church in Wellington is looking simply divine. (p387)

For more recommendations and reviews, see lonelyplanet. com/new-zealand

If You Like...

Beaches

Karekare A classic black-sand West Auckland beach with wild surf. (p119)

Hahei The archetypal Coromandel beach, with fascinating Cathedral Cove and Hot Water Beach on its doorstep. (p197)

Gisborne The East Coast city is spoiled for choice with Waikanae, Midway and surfy Wainui. (p353)

Manu Bay New Zealand's most famous surf break (seen *Endless Summer?*) peels ashore south of Raglan. (p221)

Mangawhai Choose your mood: a terrific surf beach or the quiet waters of the estuary. (p136)

Ohope A long stretch of lovely sand and some hidden bays by the headland. (p341)

Whakaipo Bay A pretty spot to test your mettle in the frigid waters of Lake Taupo. (p281)

Cities

Auckland Sydney for beginners? We prefer 'Seattle minus the rain', infused with vibrant South Pacific culture. (p60)

Wellington All you'd expect in a capital, packed into what's really just a very big town. (p386)

Hamilton New Zealand's fourth-biggest city's bar scene, restaurants, museum and Waikato River all deserve a look. (p211)

New Plymouth Beyond New Plymouth's laid-back provincial charm is a winning selection of cosmopolitan museums and cafes. (p238)

Tauranga Fast-growing and go-ahead, with great beaches and thermal springs on its doorstep. (p326)

Napier An art-deco gem, great restaurants, and just maybe New Zealand's prettiest city. (p366)

Extreme Activities

SkyWalk & SkyJump, Auckland Sky Tower New Zealand's adrenaline-pumping extreme scene permeates even downtown Auckland. (p79)

Waitomo black-water rafting Rampage along an underground river in a wetsuit and a helmet with a torch attached. (p227)

Zorbing Bounce down a Rotorua hillside ensconced in a giant inflatable globe. (p313)

Skydiving Taupo is one of the world's best spots to leap from a perfectly good aircraft. (p279)

Sandboarding Blast your way down the massive dunes of Ninety Mile Beach. (p169)

Taupo Bungy Plummet towards the crystalline waters of the Waikato at one of NZ's prettiest bungy sites. (p279)

Festivals

Pasifika Festival Every March, Auckland's Western Springs is transformed into a slice of the tropical South Pacific. (p83)

WOMAD World music permeates New Plymouth's Bowl of Brooklands, one of NZ's best outdoor concert venues. (p242)

Whangamata Beach Hop This Coromandel surf town comes alive with music and classic car culture in March/April. (p201)

New Zealand Festival Biennial festival of the arts, held in Wellington in February/March in even-numbered years. (p397)

Highland Games Waipu's Scottish community attacks any New Year's Day hangovers with bagpipes and caber tossing. (p138)

Foodie Experiences

Auckland Top-notch restaurants and ethnic culinary enclaves make Auckland New Zealand's eating capital. (p87)

Bay of Plenty kiwifruit Pick up ripe and delicious kiwifruit from roadside stalls for as little as $1 per dozen. (p324)

Wellington Classy fine dining, casual cafes and authentic ethnic eateries line the capital's streets. (p386)

Hawke's Bay Combine dining in vineyard restaurants with exploring farmers markets and roadside stalls. (p364)

Māori Rotorua Tuck into a feast cooked in a *hāngi* (earth oven) on a Māori cultural tour. (p312)

Turangi trout Feast on your own catch in the trout-fishing capital of the world. (p289)

Galleries

Auckland Art Gallery Important European works and a strong New Zealand section, housed in an attractively renovated building. (p67)

Govett-Brewster Art Gallery New Plymouth's contemporary gallery has a striking metallic extension showcasing the work of Len Lye. (p239)

City Gallery A wonderful Wellington showcase for contemporary art, often hosting major international exhibitions. (p387)

Whangarei Art Museum An interesting permanent collection, serving the surprisingly artsy community of Northland's main centre. (p140)

Tauranga Art Gallery Historic and contemporary art housed in a converted bank building. (p326)

Wallace Arts Centre There's free entry to this wonderful mansion containing a cutting-edge private art collection. (p79)

History

Waitangi Treaty Grounds Site of the first signing of the treaty between Māori chiefs and the British Crown. (p154)

Top: Māori carving, Rotorua (p306)

Bottom: Kiwifruit growing in the Bay of Plenty (p329)

Te Papa Wellington's vibrant treasure-trove museum, where history speaks, sparkles and shakes. (p393)

Whanganui River Road Drive alongside the slow-curling river past Māori towns and the remnants of failed farms. (p260)

Russell New Zealand's rambunctious first capital is now a pretty harbourside village with historic sites aplenty. (p150)

One Tree Hill The terraces of historic Māori fortifications are clearly visible on Auckland's volcanic cones. (p77)

Buried Village Explore the remains of Te Wairoa, a village destroyed by the 1886 Mt Tarawera eruption. (p321)

Markets

Otara Flea Market Multicultural and edgy, Auckland's Saturday morning Otara Market brims with buskers, crafts, fashion and food. (p102)

River Traders Market Whanganui's riverside market is a Saturday-morning fixture, with up to 100 stalls. (p259)

Harbourside Market Wellington's obligatory produce pit stop with lots of artisan gourmet treats and a superb location. (p406)

La Cigale This French-influenced Auckland farmers market features an international array of stallholders. (p93)

Bay of Islands Farmers Market A Sunday-morning showcase of the beautiful produce grown in the subtropical north. (p161)

Gisborne Farmers Market Local producers sell everything from macadamia nuts to fresh fish. (p356)

Museums

Auckland Museum A classical Greek-temple design housing a superb collection of Māori and Pacific Islander artefacts. (p73)

Te Papa The country's biggest museum showcases NZ history, culture and geography. (p393)

Puke Ariki New Plymouth's snazzy waterfront museum is sprinkled with Māori, colonial and wildlife exhibits. (p238)

Te Kōngahu Museum of Waitangi Inside the Waitangi Treaty Grounds, this new museum tells the story of modern NZ's founding document. (p154)

Waipu Museum Interactive displays and holograms are all about this small town's Scottish heritage. (p138)

Waikato Museum An excellent museum that's especially strong on Māori history. (p212)

Māori Culture

Auckland A handful of excellent Māori tour operators showcase Auckland's indigenous culture and history. (p60)

Rotorua Catch a cultural performance and *hāngi* at one of several venues. (p306)

Footprints Waipoua Explore the staggeringly beautiful Waipoua Kauri Forest on Northland's west coast with a Māori guide. (p174)

Taiamai Tours Heritage Journeys Help paddle a *waka* (canoe) along the sleepy Waitangi River to Haruru Falls. (p156)

East Cape Beautifully carved meeting houses can be spotted all the way along the coastal highway. (p350)

Te Papa The national museum in Wellington has wonderful Māori displays and its own *marae* (meeting space). (p393)

Pubs, Bars & Beer

Wellington craft-beer scene Malthouse and Hashigo Zake are just two of around 20 craft-beer bars in the capital. (p403)

Hamilton Hood and Victoria Sts have great pubs and bars; don't miss Good George Brewing in Frankton. (p215)

Auckland The country's biggest city is fast developing as a hoppy hub. (p96)

Puhoi Pub New Zealand's only Bohemian-settled village contains this famously atmospheric 19th-century pub. (p125)

Horeke Hotel Reputedly the country's oldest pub, this Hokianga boozer has been pulling pints since 1826. (p173)

Wine Regions

Martinborough A small-but-sweet wine region a day trip from Wellington; easy cycling and easy-drinking pinot noir. (p413)

Waiheke Island Auckland's favourite weekend playground has a hot, dry microclimate: perfect for Bordeaux-style reds and rosés. (p105)

Hawke's Bay One of NZ's oldest and most established wine areas is still one of its best. (p364)

Matakana Matakana combines an expanding boutique vineyard scene, brilliant beaches and a great weekly farmers market. (p126)

Gisborne Chardonnay reigns supreme in the sunny farmland surrounding NZ's most easterly city. (p353)

West Auckland Sample the produce of the trailblazing Croatian families who kick-started New Zealand's wine industry. (p118)

Month by Month

January

New Zealand peels its eyes open after New Year's Eve, gathers its wits and gets set for another year. Great weather, cricket season in full swing and happy holidays for the locals.

🎉 Festival of Lights

New Plymouth's Pukekura Park is regularly dubbed a 'jewel', but the gardens really sparkle during this festival. It's a magical scene: pathways glow and trees are impressively lit with thousands of lights. Live music, dance and kids' performances too. (p242)

February

The sun is shining, the nights are long, and the sauv blanc and pale ale are chillin' in the fridge: this is prime party time across NZ. Book your festival tickets (and beds) in advance!

🎉 Waitangi Day

On 6 February 1840, the Treaty of Waitangi was signed between Māori and the British Crown. The day remains a public holiday across NZ, and in Waitangi itself (the Bay of Islands) there are guided tours, concerts, market stalls and family entertainment.

🎉 New Zealand Festival

This month-long spectacular happens in Wellington in February to March every even-numbered year, and is sure to spark your imagination. NZ's cultural capital exudes artistic enthusiasm with theatre, dance, music and visual arts, and there are international acts aplenty. (p397)

☆ Fringe NZ

Music, theatre, comedy, dance and visual arts in Wellington, but not the mainstream stuff from the New Zealand Festival. Fringe highlights the more unusual, emerging, controversial, low-budget and/or downright weird acts. (p397)

🎉 Splore

Explore Splore, a cutting-edge outdoor summer fest in Tapapakanga Regional Park, southeast of Auckland. Contemporary live music, performance and visual arts, safe swimming, pohutukawa trees and the company of very laid-back locals. Come here to chill out. (p83)

☆ New Zealand International Sevens

February sees the world's top seven-a-side rugby teams in Hamilton: everyone from heavyweights such as Australia and South Africa to minnows like the Cook Islands and Kenya. A great excuse for a party; fancy dress is encouraged.

🎉 Art Deco Weekend

In the third week of February, Napier, levelled by an earthquake in 1931 and rebuilt in high art-deco style, celebrates its architectural heritage with this high-steppin' fiesta, featuring music, food, wine, vintage cars and costumery. (p367)

March

March brings a hint of autumn, with harvest time in the vineyards and orchards, and long, dusky evenings with plenty of festivals plumping out the calendar. Locals unwind post tourist season.

✨ Te Matatini National Kapa Haka Festival

This engrossing Māori performing-arts competition (www.tematatini.co.nz) happens in early March in odd-numbered years in a different town each time. And it's not just the *haka* (war dance): expect traditional songs, dancing, storytelling and other performing arts.

☆ WOMAD

Local and international music, arts and dance performances fill New Plymouth's Bowl of Brooklands to overflowing. It's an evolution of the original world-music festival dreamed up by Peter Gabriel, who launched the inaugural UK concert in 1980. Perfect for families. (p242)

✨ Pasifika Festival

With around 140,000 Māori and notable communities of Tongans, Samoans, Cook Islanders, Niueans and Fijians, Auckland has the largest Pacific Islander community in the world. These vibrant island cultures come together at this annual fiesta in Western Springs Park. (p83)

April

April is when canny travellers hit NZ: the ocean is still swimmable and the weather still mild, with nary a tourist or queue in sight. Easter means pricey accommodation everywhere.

✨ National Jazz Festival

Every Easter Tauranga hosts the longest-running jazz fest in the southern hemisphere. The line-up is invariably impressive, and there's plenty of fine NZ food and wine to accompany the finger-snappin' sonics. (p328)

May

The nostalgia of autumn runs deep: party nights are long gone and another chilly Kiwi winter beckons. Thank goodness for the Comedy Festival! Farmers markets overflow with good-value and organic eating.

☆ New Zealand International Comedy Festival

Three-week laugh-fest in May, with venues across Auckland, Wellington and various regional centres. International gag-merchants line up next to home-grown talent.

June

It's the beginning of the ski season, so time to head to Mt Ruapehu. For everyone else, head north: the Bay of Plenty is always sunny, and is it just us or is Northland underrated?

✨ Matariki

Māori New Year is heralded by the rise of Matariki (aka the Pleiades star cluster) in May and the sighting of the new moon in June. Remem-

brance, education, music, film, community days and tree planting take place, mainly around Auckland, Wellington and Northland. (p397)

July

Wellington's good citizens clutch collars, shiver and hang out in bookshops and cafes. The All Blacks kick off the international rugby season, so find a pub and get cheering. Yes, even you Aussies.

☆ NZ International Film Festival

After separate film festivals in both Auckland and Wellington, a selection of flicks hits the road for screenings in regional North Island towns from July to November. Movie buffs in Masterton and Palmerston North get very excited – understandably so.

🏃 Russell Birdman

Birdman rallies are just so '80s... But they sure are funny! This one in Russell features the usual cast of costumed contenders propelling themselves off a jetty in pursuit of weightlessness. Bonus points if your name is Russell. (p151)

August

Land a good deal on accommodation pretty much anywhere except around Mt Ruapehu's ski scene. Winter is almost spent, but there's still not much happening outside. Music, great pubs and art are your saviours.

🎭 Taranaki International Arts Festival

Beneath the slopes of Mt Taranaki, August used to be a time of quiet repose. Not any more: this whizbang arts festival in New Plymouth now shakes the winter from the city with music, theatre, dance, visual arts and parades. (p242)

🎭 Jazz & Blues Festival

You might think that the Bay of Islands is all about sunning yourself on a yacht while dolphins splash saltwater on your stomach. In the depths of winter, this jazzy little festival (www.jazz-blues.co.nz) will give you something else to do.

🍷 Beervana

Attain beery nirvana at this annual craft-beef guzzle fest in Wellington (it's freezing outside – what else is there to do?). But seriously, the NZ craft-beer scene is booming – here's your chance to sample the best of it. (p397)

September

Spring has sprung! The amazing and surprising World of WearableArt Award Show is always a hit. And will someone please beat Canterbury in the annual ITM rugby cup final?

🎭 World of WearableArt

A bizarre (in the best possible way) two-week-long

Wellington event featuring amazing hand-crafted garments. (p397)

October

This post-rugby and pre-cricket season leaves sports fans twiddling their thumbs. Maybe it's time to head east to Gisborne? October is shoulder season, with reasonable accommodation rates, minimal crowds and no competition for good campsites.

🍷 First Light Wine & Food Festival

Around Labour Weekend – in the second half of the month – Gisborne's proud winemakers pair with local foodies and artisan producers to showcase the region's tasty goodies. There's lots of great music too. (p357)

November

Across the north of the north, NZ's iconic pohutukawa trees start to erupt with brilliant crimson blooms. The weather is picking up, and a few tourists are starting to arrive.

🎭 NZ Tattoo & Art Festival

The biggest tattoo-culture festival in Australasia attracts thousands of tatt fans to New Plymouth every November. It's quirky, edgy, sexy and hugely popular (not necessarily family viewing...). (p242)

🍷 Toast Martinborough

Bound for a day of boozy indulgence, wine-swilling Wellingtonians head over Rimutaka Hill and roll into upmarket Martinborough. The Wairarapa region produces some seriously good pinot noir: don't go home without trying some (as if you'd be so silly). (p415)

🏃 Lake Taupo Cycle Challenge

Feeling fit? Try cycling 160km around Lake Taupo and then talk to us. Held on the last Saturday in November, the event (https://cyclechallenge.com) is open to individuals and teams, and has been judged one of the world's six best recreational rides.

December

Summer! The crack of leather on willow resounds across the nation's cricket pitches and office workers surge towards the finish line. Everyone gears up for Christmas: avoid shopping centres like the plague.

🎭 Rhythm & Vines

Wine, music and song in sunny Gisborne for three days leading up to New Year's Eve. Top DJs, hip-hop acts, bands and singer-songwriters compete for your attention. Or maybe you'd rather just drink some chardonnay and kiss someone on the beach? (p357)

Itineraries

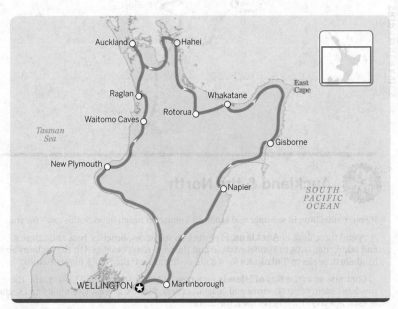

Auckland
Hahei
Raglan
Whakatane
Rotorua
Waitomo Caves
Tasman Sea
East Cape
New Plymouth
Gisborne
Napier
SOUTH PACIFIC OCEAN
WELLINGTON
Martinborough

2 WEEKS A Grand Circuit

Tracing a broad circuit around most of the North Island, this is an ideal route for travellers with time on their hands.

Kick off by exploring bustling **Auckland** before heading the long way around the Coromandel Peninsula, via Thames and Coromandel Town, to the legendary beach town of **Hahei**. Spend a day kayaking, visiting Cathedral Cove and digging a natural spa pool at nearby Hot Water Beach.

Continue south to **Rotorua**, the most dramatic of NZ's geothermal hot spots. Stop for the night at laid-back **Whakatane** before taking the winding coastal road right around isolated East Cape to beachy **Gisborne**. At **Napier**, pause to admire the art-deco architecture and acclaimed Hawke's Bay wineries. More wine awaits in **Martinborough**, a short hop from the nation's vibrant capital, **Wellington**.

After two nights in the capital, head north and then branch out west towards Whanganui and **New Plymouth**, a charming regional city with a brilliant art gallery, in the shadow of majestic Mt Taranaki. As you near the end of your North Island odyssey, take comfort that you've saved some highlights till last: the glowworm-lit magnificence of the **Waitomo Caves** and the chilled-out little surf town of **Raglan**.

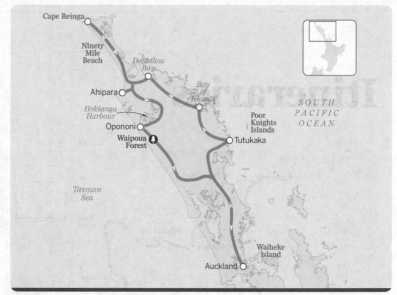

 Auckland & the North

If you're travelling in summer and fancy an unhurried beach holiday, this one's for you.

Spend three days in **Auckland**, exploring its volcanoes, beaches, bars and eateries, and taking day trips to Waiheke Island and the west-coast beaches. Hit the highway and head north to sleepy **Tutukaka** for a day's diving around the Poor Knights Islands.

Continue on to the **Bay of Islands** for a dose of Māori and colonial history, and the timeless charm of pretty coves and coastal scenery. Stay for at least two nights and spend at least one day cruising between the islands.

Drop by **Doubtless Bay** for another lazy beach day and to feast on fish and chips on the wharf at Mangonui. The following morning, take a long, leisurely drive up to **Cape Reinga** at the very tip of the country – the most sacred site in traditional Māori spirituality.

Venture south, skirting the windswept expanses of Ninety Mile Beach, before hitting **Ahipara**. Continue south via the Hokianga Harbour and stop for the night at **Opononi**. Allow yourself time to pay homage to the majestic trees of the **Waipoua Forest** before commencing the long, scenic drive back to Auckland.

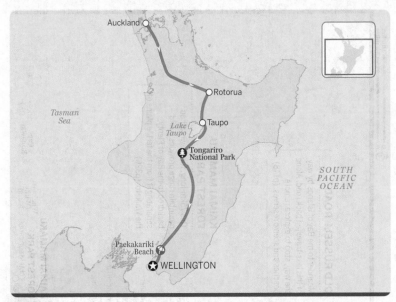

Central Highlights

This itinerary offers a short, sharp blast down the middle of the island, taking in NZ's two main cities and other highlights along the way.

After a couple of days in energetic and cosmopolitan **Auckland**, take a slow drive south, dropping in to briefly explore Hamilton and Cambridge en route to **Rotorua**. At your destination the classic combo of bubbling thermal activity and vibrant Māori culture awaits, and you can ease any travel aches with a lengthy soak in a hot spring.

Continue south to **Taupo** for jetboating thrills or the more relaxed appeal of trout fishing. If you're feeling brave, bungy jump from 47m above the Waikato River.

Follow the coves of Lake Taupo's picturesque eastern shore to **Tongariro National Park**, where there's good winter skiing, and the Tongariro Alpine Crossing, judged one of the world's best one-day walks.

Stop in at the National Army Museum at Waiouru and at the beach in Paekakariki before pushing on to **Wellington**. The nation's cute little capital has more than enough museums, galleries, bars and cafes to amuse you for a couple of days, and a good live-music scene to blast away the cobwebs at night.

Off the Beaten Track

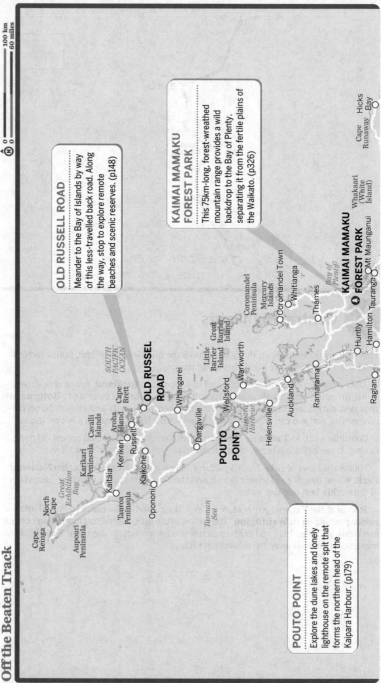

OLD RUSSELL ROAD

Meander to the Bay of Islands by way of this less-travelled back road. Along the way, stop to explore remote beaches and scenic reserves. (p148)

KAIMAI MAMAKU FOREST PARK

This 75km-long, forest-wreathed mountain range provides a wild backdrop to the Bay of Plenty, separating it from the fertile plains of the Waikato. (p326)

POUTO POINT

Explore the dune lakes and lonely lighthouse on the remote spit that forms the northern head of the Kaipara Harbour. (p179)

rush hours in places like Auckland, Tauranga and Wellington.

If you're flying into Auckland or Wellington, especially on a long flight, we'd highly recommend that you give yourself a day or two to recover and to see the sights (by public transport, taxi or Uber) before hiring a car.

Car Hire

It's easy to rent a car from any of the main centres, with the major international agencies having offices both at the airports and in the city centres. In most cases it's cheaper to hire from a local agency, where the cars may be a little older or slightly battered.

Driving Conditions

All major routes are sealed and well maintained, but in more remote, off-the-beaten-track areas you may strike some unsealed roads.

Famously, Northland has some beaches that are

gazetted as roads (notably Ninety Mile Beach and Ripiro Ocean Beach). However, driving on the sands isn't as easy as it looks, and vehicles regularly get stuck. Most rental insurance agreements won't cover you if you do, so these routes are best avoided unless you're travelling in a heavy-duty 4WD (a sedan equipped with a 4WD function won't cut it).

No Car?

Bus

Buses connect all of the major towns; however, services can be expensive, slow and infrequent. Various tour companies offer guided coach trips to the main destinations. The larger cities have extensive local bus networks.

Air

Aside from Auckland, the main air-travel hub,

there are airports in the Bay of Islands (Kerikeri), Gisborne, Great Barrier Island, Hamilton, Kapiti Coast, Napier, New Plymouth, Palmerston North, Rotorua, Taupo, Tauranga, Wellington, Whakatane, Whanganui and Whangarei. It's often possible to pick up a cheap domestic fare.

Train

The North Island's main trunk line from Auckland to Wellington is more of a scenic journey than an effective transport mode. Trains also connect Wellington to Palmerston North, the Kapiti Coast and the Wairarapa.

Bicycle

While plenty of people do it, New Zealand isn't the easiest country for cycle touring. Even on the North Island, the terrain is hilly and the traffic can be unforgiving and unaccommodating.

DRIVING FAST FACTS

➡ Drive on the left.

➡ All vehicle occupants must wear a seatbelt.

➡ Minimum age for a full licence is 18 years.

➡ Carry your licence at all times.

➡ Maximum speed 100km/h on motorways, 50km/h in built-up areas.

➡ Blood alcohol limit 50mg per 100ml (0.05%).

ROAD DISTANCES (KM)

	Auckland	Gisborne	New Plymouth	Taupo
Gisborne	490			
New Plymouth	360	570		
Taupo	280	330	300	
Wellington	640	530	350	375

Mt Taranaki (p246)

Plan Your Trip

Hiking on the North Island

Hiking (or 'tramping' as Kiwis call it) is the perfect opportunity for a close encounter with the North Island's natural beauty. There are thousands of kilometres of tracks here – some well marked (including three of New Zealand's celebrated 'Great Walks'), some barely a line on a map – plus an excellent network of huts enabling trampers to avoid lugging tents and (in some cases) cooking gear.

Hiking Books

The DOC publishes detailed books on the flora and fauna, geology and history of NZ's national parks, plus leaflets (50c to $2) detailing hundreds of NZ walking tracks.

Lonely Planet's *Hiking & Tramping in New Zealand* describes around 50 walks of various lengths and degrees of difficulty. Mark Pickering and Rodney Smith's *101 Great Tramps* has suggestions for two- to six-day tramps around the country. The companion guide, *202 Great Walks: the Best Day Walks in New Zealand,* by Mark Pickering, is handy for shorter, family-friendly excursions. New trampers should check out *Don't Forget Your Scroggin* by Sarah Bennett and Lee Slater – all about being safe and happy on the track. Bird's Eye Tramping Guides from Potton & Burton Publishing have fab topographical maps, and there are countless other books covering tramps and short urban walks around NZ – scan the bookshops.

Planning Your Tramp
When to Go

Mid-December–late January High season for tramping is during the school summer holidays, starting a couple of weeks before Christmas – avoid it if you can.

January–March The summer weather lingers into March: wait until February if you can, when tracks are less crowded.

June–August Winter is not the time to be out in the wild, especially at altitude – some paths close in winter because of snow and there are correspondingly lower levels of facilities and services.

Choosing Your Tramp

Select a track that suits your level of fitness and experience. If you're tramping with others, consider the ability of all group members. We've graded each tramp, from easy to demanding, to help you choose the most suitable ones for you. The Department of Conservation (DOC) website (www.doc.govt.nz) also grades tracks according to a national track standard. Talking to people who have recently completed a tramp is another great way to source information.

Many of NZ's most famous tracks are located in mountainous regions, and in winter these will be too dangerous or challenging to all but the most experienced trampers using specialised winter equipment. There are, however, tracks that can be completed in shoulder seasons or year-round (weather dependent).

If it's your first tramp, or you've just arrived in the country, the DOC's Day Hikes and Great Walks are an ideal introduction. Every one of them is incredibly scenic, well signposted and maintained, and (during the Great Walks season) they are monitored by hut wardens who will pass on weather reports, track-condition updates and advice. Regional i-SITE visitor information centres can also provide up-to-date information.

Track Classification

Tracks in NZ are classified according to various features, including level of difficulty. We loosely refer to the level of difficulty as easy, medium, hard or difficult. The widely used track classification system is as follows:

Short Walk Well formed; possibly allows for wheelchair access or constructed to 'shoe' standard (ie walking boots not required). Suitable for people of all ages and fitness levels.

Walking Track Easy and well-formed longer walks; constructed to 'shoe' standard. Suitable for people of most ages and fitness levels.

Easy Tramping Track or Great Walk Well formed; major water crossings have bridges and track junctions have signs. Light walking boots and average fitness required.

Tramping Track Requires skill and experience; constructed to 'boot' standard. Suitable for people of moderate physical fitness. Water crossings may not have bridges.

Route Requires a high degree of experience and navigation skills. Well-equipped, fit trampers only.

What to Bring

Primary considerations: your feet and your shoulders. Make sure your footwear is as tough as old boots and that your pack isn't too heavy. If you're camping or staying in huts without stoves, bring a camping stove. Also bring insect repellent to keep sandflies away, and don't forget your scroggin – a mixture of dried fruit and nuts (and sometimes chocolate) for munching en route.

First Aid

At least one person in your group should possess adequate first-aid knowledge and the skills to apply it. If possible, attend a course before heading into the outdoors or at least do some reading; the Mountain Safety Council's *New Zealand Outdoor First Aid* manual is comprehensive and can be purchased through their website (www.mountainsafety.org.nz), as is the St John online First Aid Library (www.stjohn.org.nz). A first-aid kit is a must for any tramp.

Go With Those in the Know

If possible tramp with someone else, or within a group, for safety in numbers (and, potentially, more fun). Hiking companions can be found by lingering around DOC visitors centres, or online through sites such as Meetup (www.meetup.com), Way-Wiser (www.waywiser.co.nz) or numerous tramping clubs affiliated with the Federated Mountain Clubs (www.fmc.org.nz).

Another great source of knowledge on the NZ tramping experience is the Mountain Safety Council, which produces a range of excellent resources, almost all of which are free. Its 29-part *Get Outdoors* video series on YouTube is highly recommended if you're considering any tramping in NZ. If you'd like to prepare for a specific trip, it has a range of activity-specific guides, as well as e-learning tools.

Maps

The topographical maps produced by Land Information New Zealand (LINZ) are a safe bet. Bookshops don't often have a good selection of these, but LINZ has map sales offices in major cities and towns, and DOC offices often sell LINZ maps for local tracks. Outdoor stores also stock them. The LINZ map series includes park maps (national, state and forest), dedicated walking-track maps, and detailed 'Topo50' maps (you may need two or three of these per track).

Emerald Lakes (p296), National Park Village

Online Resources

www.freewalks.nz Descriptions, maps and photos of long and short tramps all over NZ.

www.tramper.co.nz Articles, photos, forums and excellent track and hut information.

www.trampingnz.com Region-by-region track info with readable trip reports.

www.peakbagging.org.nz Find a summit and get up on top of it.

www.topomap.co.nz Online topographic maps of the whole country.

Intentions

Telling someone your plans, including setting a date and time for raising an alarm if you haven't returned, is an essential part of your pre-trip planning. There are several options available, and it's important you use a method that works for you and your trusted contact. This includes calling someone, leaving a written note, posting a personal message to someone on social media or using the outdoors intentions form at www.adventuresmart.org.nz/outdoors-intentions. Just remember to inform your trusted contact that you've returned safely to prevent the possibility of an unnecessary search.

ROB TUCKER/VENTURE TARANAKI TRUST ©

Hiking to Mt Taranaki via Egmont National Park (p247)

When you're on the track, write in the hut logbooks even if you're not staying there, as this acts like a breadcrumb trail and will help would-be rescuers locate and find you more quickly.

Responsible Tramping

If you went straight from the cradle into a pair of hiking boots, some of these tramping tips will seem ridiculously obvious; others you mightn't have considered. Online, the 'Leave No Trace' website (www.lnt.org) is a great resource for low-impact hiking, and the DOC site (http://freedomcamping.org) has plenty more responsible camping tips. When in doubt, ask DOC or i-SITE staff.

The ridiculously obvious:

➡ Time your tramp to avoid peak season: fewer people equals less stress on the environment and fewer snorers in the huts.

➡ Carry out all your rubbish. Burying rubbish disturbs soil and vegetation, encourages erosion, and animals will probably dig it up anyway.

➡ Don't use detergents, shampoo or toothpaste in or near watercourses (even if they're biodegradable).

➡ Use lightweight kerosene, alcohol or Shellite (white gas) stoves for cooking; avoid disposable butane gas canisters.

➡ Where there's a toilet, use it. Where there isn't one, dig a hole and bury your by-product (at least 15cm deep, 100m from any watercourse).

➡ If a track passes through a muddy patch, just plough straight on through – skirting around the outside increases the size of the bog.

You mightn't have considered:

➡ Wash your dishes 50m from watercourses; use a scourer, sand or snow instead of detergent.

➡ If you really need to scrub your bod, use biodegradable soap and a bucket, at least 50m from any watercourse. Spread the waste water around widely to help the soil filter it.

➡ If open fires are allowed, use only dead, fallen wood in existing fireplaces. Leave any extra wood for the next happy camper.

➡ Keep food-storage bags out of reach of scavengers by tying them to rafters or trees.

➡ Feeding wildlife can lead to unbalanced populations, diseases and animals becoming dependent on handouts. Keep your dried apricots to yourself.

Lake Waikaremoana (p348)

Great Walks

Three of NZ's nine official Great Walks are on the North Island, and one is actually a highly regarded river trip. Natural beauty abounds, but prepare yourself for crowds, especially during summer.

All three of the North Island's Great Walks are described in Lonely Planet's *Tramping in New Zealand,* and are detailed in pamphlets provided by DOC visitor centres.

To tramp these tracks you'll need to buy **Great Walk Tickets** before setting out. These track-specific tickets cover you for hut accommodation (from $22 to $70 per adult per night, depending on the track and season) and/or camping ($6 to $15 per adult per night). You can camp only at designated camping grounds. In the off-peak season (May to September), you can use **Backcountry Hut Passes** ($92 per adult, valid for six months) or pay-as-you-go **Backcountry Hut Tickets** (huts $5 to $15, camping $5) instead of Great Walk tickets on North Island Great Walks, except for the Lake Waikaremoana Track. We hear whispers of hut tickets being phased out over coming years: Backcounty Hut Passes are the way of the future.

There's a booking system in place for Great Walk huts and campsites. Trampers must book their chosen accommodation and specify dates when they purchase Great Walk Tickets. Bookings are required year-round for the Lake Waikaremoana Track. For the Tongariro Northern Circuit and the Whanganui Journey, bookings are required for the peak season only (October to April).

Bookings and ticket purchases can be made online (www.doc.govt.nz), by email (greatwalksbooking@doc.govt.nz), or via DOC offices close to the tracks. Bookings open mid-July each year.

Other Tracks

Of course, there are a lot more walks in the North Island than just the great ones! Try these selections on for size:

Cape Reinga Coastal Walkway A 50km, three-day, easy beach tramp (camping only) in Northland. A 132km six- to eight-day route is also possible.

TRACK SAFETY

Thousands of people tramp across NZ without incident, but every year a few folks meet their maker in the mountains. Some trails are only for the experienced, fit and well equipped – don't attempt these if you don't fit the bill. Ensure you are healthy and feel comfortable walking for sustained periods.

New Zealand's volatile climate subjects high-altitude walks to snow and ice, even in summer: always check weather and track conditions before setting off, and be ready for conditions to change rapidly. Consult a DOC visitor centre and let a responsible person know your hiking intentions before starting longer walks.

Also see www.mountainsafety.org.nz and www.metservice.co.nz for weather updates.

OLIVER STREWE/GETTY IMAGES ©

Top: Hiking in Te
Urewera (p361)

Bottom: Mt Ngauruhoe
(p293)

MATTEO COLOMBO/GETTY IMAGES ©

Mt Holdsworth–Jumbo Circuit A medium-to-hard, three-day tramp in Holdsworth Forest Park, scaling alpine Mt Holdsworth.

Pouakai Circuit A 25km, two- to three-day loop in the lowland rainforest, cliffs and subalpine forest at the foot of Mt Taranaki in Egmont National Park.

Tongariro Alpine Crossing A brilliant 19km, one-day, moderate tramp through Tongariro National Park.

Backcountry Huts

The DOC maintains more than 950 Backcountry Huts in NZ's national and forest parks. Hut categories comprise:

Basic huts Just a shed!

Standard huts No cooking equipment and sometimes no heating, but mattresses, water supply and toilets.

Serviced huts Mattress-equipped bunks or sleeping platforms, water supply, heating, toilets and sometimes cooking facilities.

Details about the hut services can be found on the DOC website. Backcountry Hut fees per adult, per night range from $5 to $15, with tickets bought in advance at DOC visitor centres (some huts can also be booked online: visit www.doc. govt.nz). Children under 10 can use huts for free; 11- to 17-year-olds are charged half price. If you do a lot of tramping,

DOC sells a six-month Backcountry Hut Pass applicable to most huts except Great Walk huts in peak season (October to April, during which time you'll need Great Walk tickets). In the low season (May to September), Backcountry Hut Tickets and Passes can also be used to procure a bunk or campsite on some Great Walks.

Depending on the hut category, a night's stay may use one or two tickets. Date your tickets and put them in the boxes provided at huts. Accommodation is on a first-come, first-served basis.

Conservation Campsites

The DOC also manages 220-plus 'Conservation Campsites' (often vehicle accessible) with categories as follows:

Basic campsites Basic toilets and water; free and unbookable.

Standard campsites Toilets and water supply, and perhaps barbecues and picnic tables; $6 to $13 and unbookable.

Serviced campsites Full facilities: flush toilets, tap water, showers and picnic tables. They may also have barbecues, a kitchen and laundry; $18; bookable via DOC visitor centres.

Children aged five to 17 pay half price for Conservation Campsites; kids four and under stay free.

NORTH ISLAND'S GREAT WALKS

WALK	DISTANCE	DURATION	DIFFICULTY	DESCRIPTION
Lake Waikaremoana Track	46km	3–4 days	Easy to medium	Lake views, bush-clad slopes and swimming in Te Urewera
Tongariro Northern Circuit	43km	3–4 days	Medium to hard	Through the active volcanic landscape of Tongariro National Park; see also Tongariro Alpine Crossing
Whanganui Journey	145km	5 days	Intermediate	Canoe or kayak down the Whanganui River in Whanganui National Park

Backcountry huts on the Tongariro Northern Circuit (p275)

Guided Walks

If you're new to tramping or just want a more comfortable experience than the DIY alternative, several companies can escort you through the wilds, usually staying in comfortable huts (showers!), with meals cooked and equipment carried for you.

Places on the North Island where you can sign up for a guided walk include Mt Taranaki, Lake Waikaremoana and Tongariro National Park. Prices for a four-night guided walk start at around $1800, and rise towards $2200 for deluxe guided experiences.

Trailhead Transport

Getting to and from trailheads can be problematic, except for popular trails serviced by public and dedicated trampers' transport. Having a vehicle only helps with getting to one end of the track (you still have to collect your car afterwards). If the track starts or ends down a dead-end road, hitching will be difficult.

Of course, tracks accessible by public transport are also the most crowded. An alternative is to arrange private transport, either with a friend or by chartering a vehicle to drop you at one end, then pick you up at the other. If you intend to leave a vehicle at a trailhead, don't leave anything valuable inside – theft from cars in isolated areas is a significant problem.

TE ARAROA

Epic! **Te Araroa** (www.teararoa.org. nz) is a 3000km tramping trail from Cape Reinga in NZ's north to Bluff in the south (or the other way around). The route links up existing tracks with new sections. Built over almost 20 years, mostly by volunteers, it's one of the longest hikes in the world: check the website for maps and track notes, plus blogs and videos from hardy types who have completed the end-to-end epic.

NARIJEDOM YAEMPONGSA/SHUTTERSTOCK ©

Snowboarding on Mt Ruapehu (p291)

Plan Your Trip

Skiing, Cycling & Scary Stuff

The North Island's astounding natural assets encourage even the laziest lounge lizards to drag themselves outside and get active. 'Extreme' sports are abundant and supremely well organised here. Mountaineering is part of the national psyche; skydiving, mountain biking, jetboating and rock climbing are well established; and pants-wetting, illogical activities like bungy jumping have become everyday pursuits. Just make sure you have travel insurance.

Top Extreme Sports

Top Anti-Gravity Activities

There are many locations for bungy jumping, but in Auckland you can make the leap of faith from the Sky Tower; the downhill thrills of zorbing take place in Rotorua; the sweep and swoosh of the Swoop and Shweeb is also in Rotorua

Top White-Water Rafting Trips

Tongariro River, Taupo; Kaituna River, Rotorua

Top Mountain-Biking Tracks

Ohakune Old Coach Road, Central Plateau; Redwoods Whakarewarewa Forest, Rotorua; 42 Traverse, Central Plateau

Top Surf Spots

Manu Bay, Raglan; Waikanae Beach, Gisborne; Mount Beach, Mt Maunganui

Skiing & Snowboarding

Global warming is triggering a worldwide melt, but NZ remains an essential southern-hemisphere destination for snow bunnies, with downhill skiing, cross-country (Nordic) skiing and snowboarding all passionately pursued. Heliskiing, where choppers lift skiers to the top of long, isolated stretches of virgin snow, also has its fans. The North Island ski season is generally June to October, though it can vary depending on annual weather conditions.

Where to Go

On the North Island, the volcanic landscape of Mt Ruapehu in Tongariro National Park showcases the Whakapapa and Turoa resorts, while club areas such as Tongariro's Tukino and Taranaki's Manganui are publicly accessible and usually less crowded and cheaper than the commercial fields.

Practicalities

New Zealand's commercial ski areas aren't generally set up as 'resorts' with chalets, lodges or hotels. Rather, accommodation and après-ski carousing are often in surrounding towns, connected with the slopes via daily shuttles. Many club areas have lodges you can stay at, subject to availability.

Visitor information centres in NZ and international Tourism New Zealand (www.newzealand.com) offices have info on the various ski areas, and can make bookings and organise packages. Lift passes cost anywhere from $70 to $120 per adult per day (half-price for kids). Lesson-and-lift packages are available in most areas. Ski/snowboard equipment rental starts at around $50 per day (cheaper for multiday hire).

Online Resources

www.mtruapehu.com The go-to website for information on Whakapapa and Turoa.

www.snow.co.nz Reports, cams and ski info across the country.

Mountain Biking

The North Island is laced with quality mountain-biking opportunities. Mountain bikes can be hired in Taupo and Rotorua, and both cities have bicycle repair shops.

Companies will take you up to the summit of Mt Ruapehu, so you can hurtle down without the grunt-work of getting to the top first. Rotorua's Redwoods Whakarewarewa Forest offers famously good mountain biking, as does the 42 Traverse near the township of National Park (close to Tongariro National Park). Other North Island options include Woodhill Forest, Waihi, Te Aroha, Te Mata Peak and Makara Peak in Wellington.

Some traditional tramping tracks are open to mountain bikes, but DOC has restricted access in many cases due to track damage and the inconvenience to walkers, especially at busy times. Never cycle on walking tracks in national parks unless it's permissible (check with DOC) – you risk heavy fines and the ire of hikers.

Resources include:

Classic New Zealand Mountain Bike Rides (www.kennett.co.nz) Details short and long rides all over NZ.

New Zealand Mountain Biker (www.nzmtbr. co.nz) A magazine that comes out every two months.

Cycle Touring

OK, so cruising around the country on a bicycle isn't necessarily 'extreme', but it is super popular in NZ, especially during summer. Most towns offer bike hire at either backpacker hostels or specialist bike shops, with bike repair shops found in bigger towns.

The New Zealand Cycle Trail (www. nzcycletrail.com) – known in Māori as Ngā Haerenga, 'the journeys' – is a national network of bike trails from Kaitaia to Bluff, featuring 23 'Great Rides', a similar concept to tramping's 'Great Walks'. Some sections/trails are still in the developmental stages,

White-water rafting on Kaituna River (p322)

but some stages are open: see the website for updates.

Cycling online resources:

Paradise Press (www.paradise-press.co.nz) Produces *Pedallers' Paradise* booklets by Nigel Rushton.

NORTH ISLAND SKI AREAS

Tongariro National Park

Whakapapa & Turoa On either side of Mt Ruapehu, these twin resorts comprise NZ's largest ski area. Whakapapa has 30 intermediate groomed runs, plus snowboarding, cross-country, downhill, a terrain park and the highest lift access in NZ. Drive from Whakapapa Village (6km; free parking), or shuttle-bus in from National Park Village, Taupo, Turangi or Whakapapa Village. Smaller Turoa has a beginners lift, plus snowboarding, downhill and cross-country skiing. There's free parking or shuttle-bus transport from Ohakune 17km away; the town has the North Island's liveliest post-ski scene.

Tukino Club-operated Tukino is on Mt Ruapehu's eastern side, 46km from Turangi. It's quite remote, 14km down a gravel road from the sealed Desert Rd (SH1), and you need a 4WD vehicle to get in. It's uncrowded, with mostly beginner and intermediate runs.

Taranaki

Manganui Offers volcano-slope, club-run skiing on the eastern slopes of spectacular Mt Taranaki in the Egmont National Park, 22km from Stratford (and a 25-minute walk from the car park). Ski off the summit when conditions permit: it's a sweaty two-hour climb to the crater, but the exhilarating 1300m descent compensates.

Cycling around Lake Taupo (p276)

White-Water Rafting, Kayaking & Canoeing

There are almost as many white-water rafting and kayaking possibilities as there are rivers in NZ, with no shortage of companies to get you into the rapids. Rivers are graded from I to VI, with VI meaning 'unraftable'. On the rougher stretches there's usually a minimum age limit of 12 or 13 years.

Popular North Island rafting rivers include the Rangitaiki, Wairoa, Motu, Mokau, Mohaka, Waitomo, Tongariro and Rangitikei. There are also the Kaituna Cascades near Rotorua, the highlight of which is the 7m drop at Okere Falls.

Canoeing is so popular on the North Island's Whanganui River that it's been designated one of NZ's Great Walks. You can also dip your paddle into Lake Taupo and Lake Rotorua. Some backpacker hostels close to canoe-friendly waters have Canadian canoes and kayaks for hire (some for free), and loads of commercial operators run guided trips.

Resources include:

New Zealand Rafting Association (www.nz-rafting.co.nz)

Whitewater NZ (www.rivers.org.nz)

New Zealand Kayak (www.kayaknz.co.nz)

Sea Kayaking

Sea kayaking is a fantastic way to see the coast and get close to wildlife you'd otherwise never see.

Highly rated sea-kayaking areas around the North Island include the Hauraki Gulf (particularly off Waiheke and Great Barrier Islands), the Bay of Islands and Coromandel Peninsula. Other North Island kayaking locations include Auckland's Waitemata Harbour, Hahei, Raglan and East Cape.

Useful resources:

Kiwi Association of Sea Kayakers (www.kask.org.nz)

Sea Kayak Operators Association of New Zealand (www.skoanz.org.nz)

Bungee jumping over the Waikato River (p279)

on a mini surfboard, can be attempted at Paihia, Tauranga, Mt Maunganui, Raglan and Wellington. You can tee up lessons at most of these places, too. Karikari Peninsula near Cape Reinga on NZ's northern tip is a kiteboarding mecca.

Bungy Jumping

Bungy jumping was made famous by Kiwi AJ Hackett's 1986 plunge from the Eiffel Tower, after which he teamed up with champion NZ skier Henry van Asch to turn the endeavour into a profitable enterprise. The South Island resort town of Queenstown is the spiritual home of bungy, but Taupo, Auckland and Rotorua on the North Island all offer the opportunity to leap bravely into the void on a giant rubber band.

Skydiving

Feeling confident? For most first-time skydivers, a tandem skydive will help you make the leap, even if common sense starts to get the better of you. Tandem jumps involve training with a qualified instructor, then experiencing up to 45 seconds of free fall before your chute opens. The thrill is worth every dollar (around $325/375 for a 10,000/12,000ft jump, extra for footage/photographs). The New Zealand Parachute Federation (www.nzpf.org) is the governing body.

Scuba Diving

New Zealand is prime scuba territory, with warm waters up north, brilliant sea life and plenty of interesting sites.

Around the North Island, get wet at the Bay of Islands Maritime and Historic Park, the Hauraki Gulf Maritime Park, the Bay of Plenty, Great Barrier Island, Goat Island Marine Reserve, the Alderman Islands, Te Tapuwae o Rongokako Marine Reserve near Gisborne, and Sugar Loaf Islands Marine Park near New Plymouth. The Poor Knights Islands near Whangarei are reputed to have the best diving in NZ (with the diveable wreck of the Greenpeace flagship *Rainbow Warrior* nearby).

Jet Boating

Hold onto your breakfast: passenger-drenching 360-degree spins ahoy!

On the North Island the Whanganui, Motu, Rangitaiki and Waikato Rivers are excellent for jetboating, and there are sprint jets at the Agrodome in Rotorua. Jetboating around the Bay of Islands in Northland is also de rigueur.

Parasailing & Kiteboarding

Parasailing (dangling from a modified parachute that glides over the water, while being pulled along by a speedboat/jet ski) is perhaps the easiest way for humans to achieve assisted flight. After a half-day of instruction you should be able to do limited solo flights. Tandem flights in the North Island happen at Te Mata Peak in Hawke's Bay.

Kiteboarding (aka kitesurfing), where a mini parachute drags you across the ocean

Top: Skydiving over Lake Taupo (p279)

Bottom: Surfer at Piha (p120)

Rock climbing in Whanganui Bay

Taupo, the Coromandel Peninsula, Waitomo, Pakiri, Ninety Mile Beach, Rotorua and the Bay of Plenty are top places on the North Island for an equine encounter.

For info and operator listings:

100% Pure New Zealand (www.newzealand.com)

True NZ Horse Trekking (www.truenz.co.nz/horsetrekking)

Auckland SPCA Horse Welfare Auxiliary Inc (www.horsetalk.co.nz)

Rock Climbing

Time to chalk up your fingers and don some natty little rubber shoes. On the North Island, popular rock-climbing areas include Auckland's Mt Eden Quarry; Whanganui Bay, Kinloch, Kawakawa Bay and Motuoapa near Lake Taupo; Mangatepopo Valley and Whakapapa Gorge on the Central Plateau; Humphries Castle and Warwick Castle on Mt Taranaki; and Piarere and Wharepapa South in the Waikato.

Climb New Zealand (www.climb.co.nz) has the low-down on the gnarliest overhangs around NZ, plus access and instruction info.

Expect to pay anywhere from $180 for a short, introductory, pool-based scuba course; and around $600 for a four-day, PADI-approved ocean-dive course. One-off organised boat- and land-based dives start at around $170.

Resources include:

New Zealand Underwater Association (www.nzu.org.nz)

Dive New Zealand (www.divenewzealand.com)

Horse Trekking

Unlike some other parts of the world where beginners' horses get led by the nose around a paddock, horse trekking in NZ lets you really get out into the countryside – on a farm, forest or beach. Rides range from one-hour jaunts (from around $60) to week-long, fully catered treks.

Caving

Caving (aka spelunking) opportunities abound in NZ's honeycombed karst (limestone) regions. On the North Island, you'll find local clubs and organised tours around Auckland, Waitomo and Whangarei.

Useful resources:

Wellington Caving Group (www.caving.org.nz)

Auckland Speleo Group (www.asg.org.nz)

New Zealand Speleological Society (www.caves.org.nz)

New Zealand lamb with porcini mushrooms

Plan Your Trip

Eat & Drink Like a Local

Eating in New Zealand is a highlight of any visit. You can be utilitarian if money is tight, or embrace NZ's full culinary bounty, from fresh seafood and gourmet burgers to farmers market fruit-and-veg and crisp-linen fine dining. Eateries range from fish and chip shops and pub bistros to retro cafes and ritzy dining rooms. Drinking here, too, presents boundless opportunities to have a good time with Kiwi coffee, craft beer and wine at the fore.

The Year in Food

Summer (December to February)

The Lunar New Year is celebrated with Asian food stalls and lanterns in Auckland. Māori cuisine is showcased at the Kawhia Kai Festival.

Autumn (March to May)

Waiheke Island and Wairarapa vineyards celebrate the harvest. Barbecues and hāngi (traditional earth-cooked) meals fill bellies during Te Kuiti's Great NZ Muster.

Winter (June to August)

The capital dishes up Wellington On A Plate.

Spring (September to November)

Bivalve botherers head to Whitianga for the annual Scallop Festival. Vegetarian Indian stalls proliferate at Diwali festivals in Auckland and Wellington. Paihia, Auckland, Gisborne and Martinborough host food and wine festivals.

Modern NZ

Once upon a time (yet not so long ago) NZ subsisted on a modest diet of 'meat and three veg'. Though small-town country pubs still serve their unchanging menu of roasted meats and battered fish, overall NZ's culinary sophistication has evolved dramatically. In larger towns, kitchens thrive on bending conventions and absorbing gastronomic influences from around the planet, all the while keeping local produce central to the menu.

LOCAL DELICACIES

Touring the menus of NZ, keep an eye out for these local delights: kina (sea urchin), paua (abalone; a type of sea snail), kumara (sweet potato, often served as chips), whitebait (tiny fish, often cooked into fritters or omelettes) and the humble kiwi fruit.

Immigration has been key to this culinary rise – particularly the post-WWII influx of migrants from Europe, Asia and the Middle East – as has an adventurous breed of local restaurant-goers and the elevation of Māori and Pacific Islander flavours and ingredients to the mainstream.

In order to wow the socks off increasingly demanding diners, restaurants must now succeed in fusing contrasting ingredients and traditions into ever more innovative fare. The phrase 'Modern NZ' has been coined to classify this unclassifiable technique: a melange of East and West, a swirl of Atlantic and Pacific Rim, and a dash of authentic French and Italian.

Traditional staples still hold sway (lamb, beef, venison, green-lipped mussels), but dishes are characterised by interesting flavours and fresh ingredients rather than fuss, clutter or snobbery. Spicing ranges from gentle to extreme, seafood is plentiful, and meats are tender and full flavoured. Enjoy!

Cafes & Coffee

Somewhere between the early 1990s and now, New Zealand cottoned onto coffee culture in a big way. Caffeine has become a nationwide addiction: there are Italian-style espresso machines in virtually every cafe, boutique roasters are de rigueur and, in urban areas, a qualified barista (coffee maker) is the norm. Wellington takes top billing as NZ's caffeine capital; its cafe and bean-roasting scene rivals the most vibrant in the world, and is very inclusive and family friendly.

Pubs, Bars & Beer

Kiwi pubs were once male bastions with dim lighting, smoky air and beer-soaked carpets – these days they're more of a family affair. Sticky floors and pie-focused menus still abound in rural parts of NZ, but pubs are generally where parents take their kids for lunch, friends mingle for sauv blanc and tapas, and locals of all ages congregate to roar at live-sports screenings. Food has become integral to the NZ pub experience, along with the inexorable

Top: Green-lipped mussels

Bottom: Brothers Beer (p96), Auckland

rise of craft beer in the national drinking consciousness.

Myriad small, independent breweries have popped up around the country in the last decade. Wellington, in particular, offers dozens of dedicated craft-beer bars, with revolving beers on tap and passionate bar staff who know all there is to know about where the beers have come from, who made them and what's in them. A night on the tiles here has become less about volume and capacity, more about selectivity and virtue.

Wine Regions

Like the wine industry in neighbouring Australia, the New Zealand version has European migrants to thank for its status and success – visionary visitors who knew good soils and good climate when they saw them, and planted the first vines. New Zealand's oldest vineyard – Mission Estate Winery (p377) in Hawke's Bay – was established by French Catholic missionaries in 1851 and is still producing top-flight wines today.

But it wasn't until the 1970s that things really got going, with traditional agricultural exports dwindling, Kiwis travelling more and the introduction of BYO ('bring your own' wine) restaurant licensing conspiring to raise interest and demand for local wines.

Since then, New Zealand's cool-climate wines have conquered the world, a clutch of key regions producing the lion's share of bottles.

Hawke's Bay The North Island's sunny East Coast is the cradle of the NZ wine industry and the second-largest producer – chardonnay and syrah are the mainstays. The Gisborne region a bit further north also produces terrific chardonnays, along with great pinot gris.

The Wairarapa Just an hour or two over the hills from Wellington, the Wairarapa region – centred on boutiquey Martinborough – is prime naughty-weekender territory, and produces winning pinot noir.

Lunch at Mission Estate Winery (p377)

Auckland & Around Vineyards established in the early 1900s unfurl across the countryside around Auckland, producing swell syrah and pinot gris to the north and chardonnay to the west. In the middle of the Hauraki Gulf, a short ferry ride from Auckland, Waiheke has a hot, dry microclimate that just happens to be brilliant for growing reds and rosés.

Vegetarians & Vegans

More than 10% of New Zealanders are vegetarian (more osn the North than the South Island), and numbers are rising. Most large urban centres have at least one dedicated vegetarian cafe or restaurant: see the Vegetarians New Zealand website (www.vegetarians.co.nz) for listings. Beyond this, almost all restaurants and cafes offer some vegetarian menu choices (although sometimes only one or two). Many eateries also provide gluten-free and vegan options.

Plan Your Trip

Travel with Children

New Zealand's a dream for family travel: kid-centric activities, family-friendly accommodation, a moderate climate and very few critters that can bite or sting. Cuisine is chilli-free and food servers are clued up on dietary requirements. Base yourself in a sizeable town for amenities galore and excursions within a short drive.

North Island for Kids

Fabulous wildlife parks, beaches, parks, snowy slopes and interactive museums proliferate across NZ. There are countless attractions and amenities designed specifically for kids, but families needn't stick to playgrounds and holiday parks. Kid-appropriate adventures, from surf schools to white-water rafting, are everywhere...if parents are brave enough, that is.

Admission Fees & Discounts

Kids' and family rates are often available for accommodation, tours, attraction entry fees, and air, bus and train transport, with discounts up to as much as 50% off the adult rate. Note that the definition of 'child' can vary from under 12 to under 18 years; toddlers (under four years old) usually get free admission and transport.

Eating Out

If you sidestep the flashier restaurants, children are generally welcome in NZ eateries. Cafes are kid-friendly, and you'll see families getting in early for dinner in pub dining rooms. Most places can supply high chairs. Dedicated kids' menus are common, but selections are usually uninspiring (pizza, fish fingers, chicken

Best Regions for Kids

Rotorua & the Bay of Plenty

Wow – bubbling volcanic mud, stinky gas, gushing geysers and Māori *haka* performances! Rotorua is hard to beat from a kid's perspective. And around the Bay of Plenty coast are beaut beaches and plenty of fish and chip shops.

Wellington Region

You need a compact city if you're walking around with kids. Wellington fits the bill, with a brilliant museum, a ratchety cable car, lots of cheery cafes and fab Kapiti Coast beaches less than an hour away.

Auckland Region

The big city has an abundance of child-friendly beaches and high-profile attractions such as Auckland Zoo and Kelly Tarlton's Sea Life Aquarium. There's even a dedicated children's theatre.

Northland

Beaches, beaches and more beaches. Northland is the perfect summertime destination, but even in winter it's usually a few degrees warmer than the rest of the country. Plus there are massive sand dunes to surf, and giant trees!

nuggets etc). If a restaurant doesn't have a kids' menu, find something on the regular menu and ask the kitchen to downsize it. It's usually fine to bring toddler food in with you. If the sun is shining, hit the farmers markets and find a picnic spot. New Zealand's restaurants are decent at catering for gluten-free and dairy-free diners – one less thing to worry about if kids follow a special diet.

Breastfeeding & Nappy Changing

Most Kiwis are relaxed about public breastfeeding and nappy changing: wrestling with a nappy (diaper) in the open boot of a car is a common sight! Alternatively, most major towns have public rooms where parents can go to feed their baby or change a nappy. Infant formula and disposable nappies are widely available.

Babysitting

For babysitters who have been fully interviewed, supplied child-care references and undergone a police check, try www.rockmybaby.co.nz (from $16 per hour). Alternatively look under 'baby sitting' in the *Yellow Pages* (www.yellow.co.nz).

Top Tips

➡ Book accommodation far in advance: many motels and hotels have adjoining rooms that can be opened up to form large family suites, but they are snapped up fast, especially in peak season.

➡ If you're planning to roam between locations, stock up on food in larger towns. There's much more choice, and prices in smaller food shops in remote locations can be sky high.

➡ Plan stops in advance if you're travelling by road. Distances can feel long but fortunately NZ is rich in gorgeous lookouts, roadside waterfalls and many towns have prominent public toilets, hurrah!

Children's Highlights
Getting Active

Whanganui Journey (p261) A slow-roaming canoe trip the kids will never forget.

Cape Reinga & Ninety Mile Beach (p168) Go sandboarding on gigantic dunes.

Redwoods Whakarewarewa Forest (p309) Big-timber mountain biking for older kids in Rotorua.

Beaches

Hahei Beach (p197) The classic NZ summer beach. On the Coromandel Peninsula.

Ngarunui Beach (p221) Learn to surf on gentle Waikato waves in view of lifeguards.

Mt Maunganui (p332) Sand and surf for the kids, cafes and bars for the oldies.

Hot Water Beach (p198) Dig your own hot pool in the Coromandel sand (but check the temperature).

Wildlife Encounters

Cape Palliser (p416) Sniff out the North Island's largest seal colony.

Zealandia, Wellington (p395) Twittering birds in the predator-free Wellington hills.

Kelly Tarlton's Sea Life Aquarium, Auckland (p73) Board a shark-shaped shuttle bus then watch stingrays swim overhead.

Culture with Kids

Te Papa, Wellington (p393) Earthquakes, Māori culture and molten magma.

Auckland Museum (p73) The Auckland volcanic field and a 25m *waka taua* (war canoe).

Hobbiton, Matamata (p209) Tours of hobbit holes and a drink in the Green Dragon Inn.

Puke Ariki, New Plymouth (p238) A mighty big shark plus Māori exhibits and more.

New Zealand Rugby Museum, Palmerston North (p265) Hands-on fun for mini–All Blacks.

MOTAT, Auckland (p75) Trains, planes and other transport marvels to goggle at.

But We're Hungry Now...

Mt Vic Chippery, Wellington (p403) Exceptional fish and (five kinds of!) chips.

Schoc Chocolates, Greytown (☑06-304 8960; www.schoc.co.nz; 177 Main St; truffles $2.50; ☺10am-4.30pm Mon-Fri, 10.30am-4.30pm Sat & Sun) Otherworldly chocs in the Wairarapa.

Hastings Farmers Market (p373) Fill a basket and have a picnic.

Gisborne Farmers Market (p356) Macadamia nuts, oranges, pastries...and all of it local.

Planning

For all-round information and advice, check out Lonely Planet's *Travel with Children*. Plan ahead by browsing Kidz Go! (www.kidzgo.co.nz) or pick up a free copy of its booklet from tourism info centres in Queenstown, Wanaka and Fiordland.

When to Go

New Zealand is a winner during summer (December to February), but summer is peak season and school-holiday time. Accommodation will be pricey and will require booking far ahead, especially for family-sized rooms. A better bet may be the shoulder months of March, April (sidestepping Easter) and November, when the weather is still good and there's less pressure on the tourism sector. Winter (June to August) is better again – chances are you'll have the whole place to yourselves! Except for the ski fields, of course, most of which are fully geared towards family snow-fun.

Accommodation

Many motels and holiday parks have playgrounds, games rooms and kids' DVDs, and often fenced swimming pools, trampolines and acres of grass (many have laundry facilities, too). Cots and high chairs aren't always available at budget and midrange accommodation, but top-end hotels supply them and some provide child-minding services. The bach (a basic holiday home) is a good-value option, while farmstays can be highly entertaining with the menagerie of animals on-site.

Many B&Bs promote themselves as blissfully kid-free, and most hostels focus on the backpacker demographic. But there are plenty of hostels (including YHA) that do allow kids.

What to Pack

Lots of layers New Zealand's weather can be fickle, even in summer. Pack beach gear for summer trips, but throw in a few thermal long-sleeve tops and jackets.

Sunhats, sunscreen and sunglasses Sunglasses for all, even in winter.

Food containers Farmers markets, beaches...NZ is primo picnic territory.

Insect repellent Itchy sandfly bites make grumpy children.

Getting Around

If your kids are little, check that your car-hire company can supply the right-sized car seat for your child, and that the seat will be properly fitted. Some companies legally require you to fit car seats yourself.

Most public transport – buses, trains, ferries etc – caters for young passengers, with discounted fares and a helping hand getting your stroller/nappy bag/shopping aboard.

Consider hiring a campervan for the whole trip. These formidable beasts are everywhere in NZ, kitted out with beds, kitchens, even toilets and TVs. Hire companies proliferate in major centres, with reasonable rates once you consider the savings on accommodation (and goodbye unpacking, repacking and leaving teddy in a hotel room).

Useful Websites

Kids Friendly Travel (www.kidsfriendlytravel.com) Directs you to baby equipment hire, accommodation listings and more.

LetsGoKids (http://letsgokids.co.nz) Download the NZ edition for family travel inspiration and money-saving vouchers.

Kidspot (www.kidspot.co.nz) The 'Family Fun' section has suggestions for child-friendly activities, road trips and more.

Kids New Zealand (www.kidsnewzealand.com) Listings of family-friendly cafes and activities.

Regions at a Glance

Auckland

Coastline
Eating & Drinking
Volcanoes

Beaches

From the calm, child-friendly bays facing the Hauraki Gulf to the black-sand surf beaches of the west coast, Auckland's water-lovers really are spoilt for choice.

Top-notch Venues

Auckland has some of the nation's best fine-dining and ethnic restaurants, a lively cafe and bar scene, and wine regions on three of its flanks.

Suburban Cones

Auckland is, quite literally, a global hot spot, with more than 50 separate volcanoes forming a unique topography. Take a hike up one of the landscape's dormant cones for a high, wide and handsome city panorama.

p60

Bay of Islands & Northland

Coastline
Wilderness
History

Beaches

Bay after beautiful bay lines Northland's east coast, making it a favourite destination for families, surfers and fishing enthusiasts. To the west, long windswept beaches stretch for dozens of kilometres, in places forming towering sand dunes.

Forests

Kauri forests once blanketed the entire north, and in the pockets where these giants remain, particularly in the Waipoua Forest, they're an imposing sight.

Colonial Sites

New Zealand was settled top down by both Māori and Europeans, with missionaries erecting the country's oldest surviving buildings in Kerikeri. In nearby Waitangi, the treaty that founded the modern nation was first signed.

p129

Coromandel Peninsula & the Waikato

Coastline
Towns
Caves

Beaches

Around Raglan you'll find safe swimming and world-class surf at legendary Manu Bay. Beaches on the Coromandel are extremely popular in summer, but splendid isolation can still be found.

Small-town Vibe

Smaller towns in the Waikato such as Te Aroha, Cambridge, Matamata and Raglan have great pubs, cafes and restaurants, and friendly locals. On the Coromandel the historic gold-rush roots of Thames and Coromandel Town are on display.

Waitomo Caves

Don't miss Waitomo Caves, NZ's most staggering cave complex. Black-water rafting along underground rivers is popular, or you can simply float through grottoes bedecked in glowworms.

p180

Taranaki & Whanganui

Nature
Cities
Coastline

Underrated Cities

New Plymouth, Whanganui and Palmerston North are mid-sized cities often overlooked by travellers. Visit and you'll find fantastic restaurants and bars, great coffee, wonderful museums and friendly folk.

National Parks

Whanganui National Park offers canoeing and kayaking amid the wilderness surrounding the Whanganui River. Near New Plymouth, Mt Taranaki (Egmont National Park) is a picture-perfect peak with fabulous tramping.

Beaches

South of New Plymouth are black-sand beaches and gnarly surf breaks. Whanganui offers remote, buffeted beaches, while south of Palmerston North, Horowhenua District has acres of empty brown sand.

p233

Taupo & the Ruapehu Region

Wilderness
Scenery
Outdoor Activities

Mountains

The three steaming, smoking, occasionally erupting volcanoes at the heart of the North Island are an imposing sight, with the focus on skiing in winter and tramping at other times.

Lake & Rivers

New Zealand's mightiest river has its origins in New Zealand's greatest lake. Aquatic pursuits in picturesque settings abound (kayaking, sailing and fishing). The water is famously chilly, but hot springs bubble up on the lakeside and riverbank.

Adrenaline

Skydiving, bungy jumping, white-water rafting, jet-boating, mountain biking, wakeboarding, parasailing, skiing – you want thrills? You got 'em. Add to this the buzz of hiking on an active volcano or three.

p270

Rotorua & the Bay of Plenty

Nature
Culture
Outdoor Activities

Thermal Activity

The landscape around Rotorua and Taupo is littered with geysers, steaming thermal vents, hot mineral springs and boiling mud pools. NZ's most active volcano, Whakaari (White Island), is 48km off the coast of Whakatane.

Māori Culture

Engage with Māori culture in Rotorua. A slew of companies offer cultural experiences for travellers, most involving a traditional dance and musical performance, a *haka* (war dance) and a *hāngi* (Māori earth-cooked feast).

Outdoor Action

Try paragliding, surfing, skydiving, zorbing, jetboating, blokarting (land-yachting), white-water rafting, mountain biking, kayaking... Or just have a swim at the beach.

p302

The East Coast

Coastline
Wine
Architecture

Coastal Scenery

Follow in the footsteps (or rather wake) of early Māori and James Cook along this stretch of coastline, home to the East Cape Lighthouse and Cape Kidnappers' gaggling gannet colony.

Wine Regions

Sip your way through Gisborne's bright chardonnays, then head to Hawke's Bay for seriously good Bordeaux-style reds and excellent winery dining at some of New Zealand's most historic vineyards.

Art Deco

Napier's art-deco town centre is a magnet for architecture lovers, the keenest of whom time their visit for the annual art-deco weekend, an extravaganza of music, wine, cars and costumes.

p345

Wellington Region

Arts
Eating & Drinking
Nightlife

Museums & Galleries

Crowbarred into the city centre is a significant collection of quality display spaces, including the highly interactive Te Papa museum and internationally flavoured City Gallery.

Cafe & Beer Culture

With more than a dozen roasters and scores of hip cafes, Wellington remains the coffee capital of New Zealand. The city also hosts a hip and happening craft-beer scene and great dining.

Bar-Hopping

Between the boho bars around Cuba St and Courtenay Pl's glitzy drinking dens, you should find enough to keep you entertained until sun-up. Live-music fans won't be disappointed.

p380

On the Road

Auckland

POP 1.57 MILLION

Best Places to Eat

➡ Cassia (p89)

➡ Azabu (p92)

➡ Tantalus Estate (p110)

➡ Sawmill Brewery (p127)

➡ Giapo (p88)

Best Places to Stay

➡ Hotel DeBrett (p84)

➡ Waiheke Dreams (p109)

➡ XSPOT (p117)

➡ Ascot Parnell (p86)

➡ Piha Beachstay – Jandal Palace (p120)

Why Go?

Paris may be the city of love, but Auckland is the city of many lovers, according to its Māori name, Tāmaki Makaurau. Those lovers so desired this place that they fought over it for centuries.

It's hard to imagine a more geographically blessed city. Its two harbours frame a narrow isthmus punctuated by volcanic cones and surrounded by fertile farmland. From any of its numerous vantage points you'll be surprised how close the Tasman Sea and Pacific Ocean come to kissing and forming a new island.

Whether it's the ruggedly beautiful west-coast beaches, or the glistening Hauraki Gulf with its myriad islands, the water's never far away. And within an hour's drive from the city's high-rise heart, there are dense tracts of rainforest, thermal springs, wineries and wildlife reserves. No wonder Auckland is regularly rated one of the world's top cities for quality of life and liveability.

When to Go

➡ Auckland has a mild climate, with the occasional chilly frost in winter and high humidity in summer.

➡ Summer months have an average of eight days of rain, but the weather is famously fickle, with 'four seasons in one day' possible at any time of the year.

➡ If you're after a big-city buzz, don't come between Christmas and New Year, when Aucklanders desert the city for the beach en masse; the sights remain open but many cafes and restaurants go into hibernation, some not surfacing again until well into January.

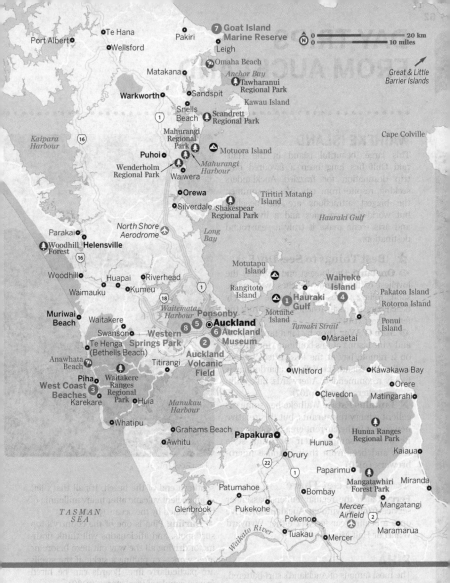

Auckland Highlights

❶ Hauraki Gulf (p104)
Visiting the island sanctuaries dotting this beautiful expanse.

❷ Auckland Volcanic Field (p67) Exploring fascinating volcanic mountains, lakes and islands.

❸ West Coast Beaches (p119) Treading the mystical and treacherous black sands of Karekare and Piha.

❹ Waiheke Island (p105)
Schlepping around world-class wineries and beaches.

❺ Ponsonby (p98) Trying out the cafes, restaurants and bars of Auckland's hippest inner-city suburb.

❻ Auckland Museum (p73)
Being awed by the Māori *taonga* (treasures) and moved, literally, in the eruption simulation and,

figuratively, in the war memorial galleries.

❼ Goat Island Marine Reserve (p127) Swimming with fish only a few steps from the beach at this pretty bay.

❽ Pasifika Festival (p83)
Soaking up the Polynesian vibe at this massive festival, held in March at Western Springs Park.

DAY TRIPS FROM AUCKLAND

WAIHEKE ISLAND

This large, beautiful island in the Hauraki Gulf has long been a favoured day-trip destination for frazzled Aucklanders seeking respite from city life. In summer, the biggest attractions are the beaches, but world-class wineries and a lively cafe and arts scene make it truly a year-round destination.

☆ Best Things to See/Do/Eat

◉ **Onetangi** The longest and arguably the loveliest of the island's beaches, with white sand, rolling waves and a couple of lively beach bars. It's easily reached by bus from the ferry wharf. (p105)

◉ **Man O' War** Drop by for a tapas platter and wine tasting at this boutique vineyard set on a remote bay at the less-visited 'bottom end' of the island; the Valhalla chardonnay is highly recommended. Afterwards, take a dip at the sheltered beach. (p107)

✕ **Tantalus Estate** Waiheke has some excellent winery restaurants, but this relative newcomer is the current cream of the crop. Be sure to sample their Bordeaux-style reds and beer from their inhouse microbrewery. (p110)

☆ How to Get There

Ferry Catch the regular Fullers passenger service from downtown Auckland or drive onto a Sealink car ferry at either Wynyard Wharf or Half Moon Bay.

PIHA

The most famous of Auckland's surf-battered, black-sand, west-coast beaches, Piha is perfect for surfing, rough-and-tumble swimming (between the flags only – it's one of the region's most dangerous beaches) and moody, wintry walks. The offshore drama is echoed by a magnificently rugged landscape dominated by large rock outcrops and imposing cliffs.

☆ Best Things to See/Do/Eat

◉ **Lion Rock** Perched majestically on the sands, this imposing outcrop dominates the

Lion Rock (p120)

southern end of the beach. It's all that's left of an ancient volcano after many millennia of being lashed by the ocean. (p120)

🏄 **Surfing** Piha is one of the country's top surf spots, and aficionados will think nothing of driving all the way out here before or after work – or pulling a sickie if the swells are particularly fine. Boards can be hired from a couple of local stores. (p120)

✕ **Piha Cafe** A top spot for a pre-surf pizza or post-surf beer. (p120)

☆ How to Get There

Car & Motorcycle There's no public transport to Piha, so it's best to hire a car for a day.

Shuttles Rapu offers a surf shuttle from central Auckland.

Tours Bush & Beach includes Piha in their day-walk itineraries, as do many other private tour companies.

LEIGH

Nestled at the far northern edge of the Auckland Region, little Leigh is worth visiting for two things: Goat Island Marine Reserve and the Leigh Sawmill Cafe. It can easily combined be on a day trip with a stop at the Waiwera thermal pools, Bohemian Puhoi or the wineries of Matakana.

☆ **Best Things to See/Do/Eat**

◉ **Goat Island Marine Reserve** In just over 40 years since it was declared a reserve, the marine population in the waters around Goat Island has exploded. Step out from the beach and you'll see plenty of fish; go deeper and put on googles and you'll see even more. (p127)

⚓ **Glass Bottom Boat Tours** An easy way to experience Goat Island's marine life without getting wet. (p128)

🍷 **Leigh Sawmill Cafe** After a day's splashing about, grab a crispy pizza and a beer in the garden bar. However this place really comes into its own as a live-music venue; check the website to see what's on. (p128)

☆ **How to Get There**

Car & Motorcycle There's no public transport, so consider hiring a car for the day. Head north on SH1 and either continue on the Northern Gateway Toll Road or take the scenic route through Orewa. Leave SH1 at Warkworth and follow the signs.

Base yourself in the centre of New Zealand's biggest city to explore all of the surrounding region, including the Hauraki Gulf islands and beautiful beaches to the west and north.

AUCKLAND'S BEACHES

HARBOUR BEACHES

Nestled within Auckland's central suburbs is a succession of small, sheltered bays. Other worthwhile contenders include **Orakei**, **Kohimarama**, **St Heliers** and nudie-friendly **Ladies Bay**.

☆ Mission Bay

The most famous of the city beaches, Mission Bay offers views to Rangitoto Island, a toddler-splash-friendly art-deco fountain, excellent people-watching and a bustling strip of cafes, bars and restaurants.

☆ Point Chevalier

It's only good for swimming an hour either side of high tide, but this is beach is beloved by locals for its child-friendly waveless waters, swimming pontoons and oodles of shade provided by a sheltering band of spectacular pohutukawa trees.

NORTH SHORE BEACHES

Fine swimming beaches stretch from North Head (p77) to Long Bay. The gulf islands shelter them from strong surf, making them safe for supervised children. Aim for high tide unless you fancy a lengthy walk to waist-deep water. **Cheltenham Beach** is a short walk from Devonport. Heading north there's **Narrow Neck**, **St Leonards** (popular with gay men and naturists), **Takapuna**, **Milford** and a succession of suburban beaches known collectively as the **East Coast Bays**.

☆ Takapuna

Takapuna is Auckland's answer to Bondi: it's the city's most popular beach, it's the closest ocean beach to the city centre, and it's backed by a busy town centre. There's a terrific cafe, the Takapuna Beach Cafe (p96), down the northern end should you get the hankering for lunch or an ice cream, and further options a couple of streets back.

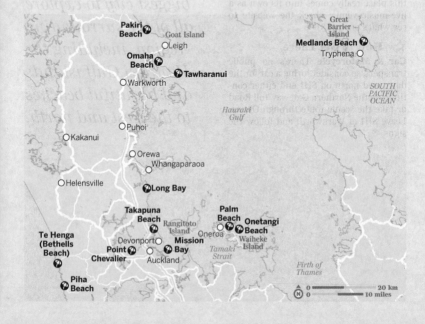

Proximity to the water is a defining feature of Auckland life and the city is blessed with huge diversity of beautiful beaches. Here are some of the best of them.

☆ Long Bay

The northernmost of Auckland's East Coast bays, Long Bay is a popular family picnic and swimming spot, attracting more than a million visitors a year. A three-hour-return coastal walk heads north from the sandy beach to the Okura River, taking in secluded Grannys Bay and Pohutukawa Bay (which attracts nude bathers).

WEST COAST BEACHES

The west coast's black sands and wild surf aren't for the fainthearted, but it's here that you'll find some of the most spectacular beaches in the country. They're also incredibly dangerous: swim between the flags. As well as the two listed here, check out **Karekare**, **Anawhata** and **Muriwai**.

☆ Piha

One of New Zealand's most famous beaches, Piha offers kilometres of black sand, reliable surfing and an exceptionally beautiful setting.

☆ Te Henga (Bethells Beach)

Aside from the super-clear waters and black sands of the main beach, there's a small, swimmable lake tucked among the dunes and an excellent little food-truck cafe for post-surf burgers and cake.

ISLAND BEACHES

All of the islands of the Hauraki Gulf have wonderful swimming spots, but the two largest – Waiheke and Great Barrier – have the longest, most spectacular beaches. Waiheke Islanders will argue the case between **Onetangi** and **Palm Beach** as the island's best beach, while others prefer the sheltered coves of **Little Oneroa** or isolated **Man O' War Bay**. You're more likely to get the beach to yourself on distant Great Barrier, especially in places like **Whangapoua**, **Kaitoke**, **Awana Bay** and **Harataonga**. If you've got access to a boat, explore the bays of Motutapu, Motuihe, Rotoroa, Rakino and Kawau Islands.

☆ Onetangi

There's plenty of space for sandcastles, frisbees, cricket and sun worshipping on the fine white sands of Waiheke's longest beach, with a couple of cafe-bars near at hand.

☆ Medlands

Remote Great Barrier Island has lots of gorgeous beaches and very few people. This spectacular stretch of white-sand gazes straight out across the vastness of the Pacific.

NORTH AUCKLAND BEACHES

The beautiful beaches of the increasingly built-up Hibiscus Coast stretch north from the Whangaparaoa Peninsula and include **Manly**, **Stanmore Bay**, **Red Beach**, **Orewa**, **Hatfields Beach** and **Waiwera**. North from here are a succession of regional parks, starting with **Wenderholm** and then **Mahurangi**, **Scandrett** and **Tawharanui**. Continuing north you'll pass the small beach settlements of **Omaha** and **Leigh**, before you hit **Goat Island Marine Reserve** (great for snorkelling) and the dazzling white sands of **Pakiri**.

☆ Tawharanui

A partly unsealed road leads to this 588-hectare reserve at the end of a peninsula. This is an open sanctuary for native birds, protected by a pest-proof fence, while the northern coast is a marine park (bring a snorkel). There are plenty of walking tracks (1½ to four hours) but the main attraction is Anchor Bay, one of the region's finest whitesand beaches. Camping is allowed at two sites near the beach.

☆ Pakiri

Blissful, remote Pakiri Beach, 12km past Goat Island (4km of the road is unsealed), is an unspoilt expanse of white sand and rolling surf – a large chunk of which is protected as a regional park. Pakiri Horse Riding (p128) has 60 horses available for superb bush-and-beach rides, along with accommodation scattered along the dunes.

AUCKLAND

POP 1.42 MILLION /

History

Māori occupation in the Auckland area dates back around 800 years. Initial settlements were concentrated on the Hauraki Gulf islands, but gradually the fertile isthmus beckoned and land was cleared for growing food.

Over hundreds of years Tamaki's many different tribes wrestled for control of the area, building *pā* (fortified villages) on the numerous volcanic cones. The Ngāti Whātua *iwi* (tribe) from the Kaipara Harbour took the upper hand in 1741, occupying the major *pā* sites. During the Musket Wars of the 1820s they were decimated by the northern tribe Ngāpuhi, leaving the land all but abandoned.

At the time the Treaty of Waitangi was signed in 1840, Governor Hobson had his base in the Bay of Islands. When Ngāti Whātua chief Te Kawau offered 3000 acres of land for sale on the northern edge of the Waitemata Harbour, Hobson decided to create a new capital, naming it after one of his patrons, George Eden (Earl of Auckland).

Beginning with just a few tents on a beach, the settlement grew quickly, and soon the port was busy exporting the region's produce, including kauri timber. However, it lost its capital status to centrally located Wellington after just 25 years.

Since the beginning of the 20th century Auckland has been New Zealand's fastest-growing city and its main industrial centre. Political deals may be done in Wellington, but Auckland is the big smoke in the land of the long white cloud.

In 2010 the municipalities and urban districts that made up the Auckland Region were merged into one 'super-city', and in 2011 the newly minted metropolis was given a buff and shine to prepare it for hosting the Rugby World Cup. The waterfront was redeveloped, the art gallery and zoo were given a makeover, and a swag of new restaurants and bars popped up – leaving a more vibrant city in the Cup's wake.

The years since then have seen Auckland maintain its impetuous growth and increasingly multicultural makeup – it is the preferred destination for new immigrants to NZ – and while housing prices and traffic snarls continue to frustrate residents, it's still thrillingly and energetically the only true international city in the country.

◉ Sights

Auckland is a city of volcanoes, with the ridges of lava flows forming its main thoroughfares and its many cones providing islands of green. As well as being by far the largest, it's also the most multicultural of NZ's cities. A sizeable Asian community rubs shoulders with the biggest Polynesian population of any city in the world.

The traditional Kiwi aspiration for a free-standing house on a quarter-acre section has resulted in a vast, sprawling city. The CBD was long ago abandoned to commerce, and inner-city apartment living has only recently caught on. While geography has been kind, city planning has been less so. Unbridled and ill-conceived development has left the centre of the city with plenty of architectural embarrassments. To get under Auckland's skin you're best to head to the streets of Victorian and Edwardian villas in hip inner-city suburbs such as Ponsonby, Grey Lynn, Kingsland and Mt Eden.

ESSENTIAL AUCKLAND

Eat amid the diverse and cosmopolitan scene of Ponsonby Central (p91).

Drink world-class craft beer at Hallertau (p121) or the Sawmill Brewery (p127).

Read *Under the Mountain* (1979) – Maurice Gee's teenage tale of slimy things lurking under Auckland's volcanoes.

Listen to *Melodrama* (2017) – The successful sophomore album from Devonport's very own Lorde.

Watch *The Piano* (1993) – Multiple Oscar winner filmed at Karekare Beach.

Celebrate Pasifika (p83)

Go Online www.aucklandnz.com; www.lonelyplanet.com/new-zealand/auckland

---

◉ City Centre

Civic Theatre THEATRE
(Map p70; ☎ 09-309 2677; www.aucklandlive.co.nz/venue/the-civic; cnr Queen & Wellesley Sts) The 'mighty Civic' (1929) is one of only seven 'atmospheric theatres' remaining in the world and a fine survivor from cinema's Golden Age. The auditorium has lavish Moorish dec-

AUCKLAND VOLCANIC FIELD

Some cities think they're tough just by living in the shadow of a volcano. Auckland's built on 50 of them and, no, they're not all extinct. The last one to erupt was **Rangitoto** about 600 years ago and no one can predict when the next eruption will occur. Auckland's quite literally a hot spot – with a reservoir of magma 100km below, waiting to bubble to the surface. But relax: this has only happened 19 times in the last 20,000 years.

Some of Auckland's volcanoes are cones, some are filled with water and some have been completely quarried away. Moves are afoot to register the field as a World Heritage site and protect what remains. Most of the surviving cones show evidence of terracing from when they formed a formidable series of Māori pā (fortified villages). The most interesting to explore are **Mt Eden** (p74), **One Tree Hill** (p77), **North Head** (p77) and **Rangitoto** (p105), but **Mt Victoria** (p77), **Mt Wellington** (Maungarei), **Mt Albert** (Owairaka), **Mt Roskill** (Puketāpapa), **Lake Pupuke**, **Mt Mangere** and **Mt Hobson** (Remuera) are all also worth a visit.

oration and a starlit southern-hemisphere night sky in the ceiling, complete with cloud projections and shooting stars. It's mainly used for touring musicals, international concerts and film-festival screenings.

Even if nothing is scheduled, try and sneak a peek at the foyer, an Indian indulgence with elephants and monkeys hanging from every conceivable fixture. Buddhas were planned to decorate the street frontage but were considered too risqué at the time – neoclassical naked boys were chosen instead!

★**Auckland Art Gallery**   GALLERY
(Map p70; ☑09-379 1349; www.aucklandart gallery.com; cnr Kitchener & Wellesley Sts; adult/ student/child $20/17/free; ⊙10am-5pm) Auckland's premier art repository has a striking glass-and-wood atrium grafted onto its 1887 French-chateau frame. It showcases the best of NZ art, along with important works by Pieter Bruegel the Younger, Guido Reni, Picasso, Cézanne, Gauguin and Matisse. Highlights include the intimate 19th-century portraits of tattooed Māori subjects by Charles Goldie, and the starkly dramatic text-scrawled canvasses of Colin McCahon.

Free 60-minute tours depart from the foyer daily at 11.30am and 1.30pm.

Albert Park   PARK
(Map p70; Princes St) Hugging the hill on the city's eastern flank, Albert Park is a charming Victorian formal garden overrun by students from the neighbouring University of Auckland during term time. The park was once part of the Albert Barracks (1847), a fortification that enclosed 9 hectares during the New Zealand Wars. A portion of the original barracks wall survives at the centre of the university campus.

University Clock Tower   ARCHITECTURE
(Map p70; 22 Princes St) The University Clock Tower is Auckland's architectural triumph. This stately 'ivory' tower (1926) tips its hat towards art nouveau (the incorporation of NZ flora and fauna into the decoration) and the Chicago School (the way it's rooted into the earth). It's usually open, so wander inside.

Old Government House   HISTORIC BUILDING
(Map p70; Waterloo Quadrant) FREE Built in 1856, this stately building was the colony's seat of power until 1865 when Wellington became the capital. The construction is unusual in that it's actually wooden but made to look like stone. It's now used by the University of Auckland, but feel free to wander through the lush gardens.

Sky Tower   TOWER
(Map p70; ☑09-363 6000; www.skycityauckland. co.nz; cnr Federal & Victoria Sts; adult/child $29/12; ⊙8.30am-10.30pm Sun-Thu, to 11.30pm Fri & Sat Nov-Apr, 9am-10pm May-Oct) The impossible-to-miss Sky Tower looks like a giant hypodermic giving a fix to the heavens. Spectacular lighting renders it space age at night and the colours change for special events. At 328m it is the southern hemisphere's tallest structure. A lift takes you up to the observation decks in 40 stomach-lurching seconds; look down through the glass floor panels if you're after an extra kick. Consider visiting at sunset and having a drink in the Sky Lounge Cafe & Bar.

The Sky Tower is also home to the Sky-Walk (p79) and SkyJump (p79).

St Patrick's Cathedral   CHURCH
(Map p70; ☑09-303 4509; www.stpatricks.org. nz; 43 Wyndham St; ⊙7am-7pm) Auckland's Catholic cathedral (1907) is one of the city's

Auckland

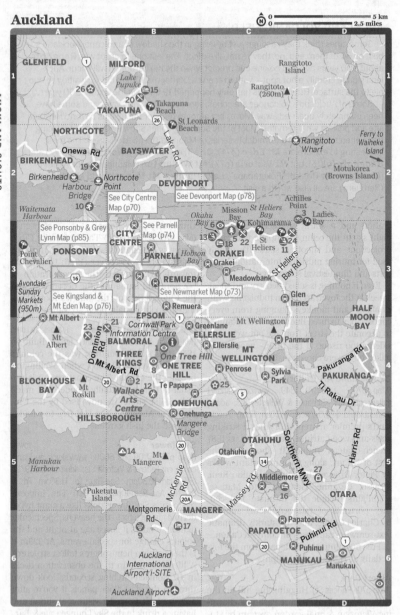

loveliest buildings. Polished wood and Belgian stained glass lend warmth to the interior of the majestic Gothic Revival church. There's a historical display in the old confessional on the left-hand side.

Lighthouse PUBLIC ART
(Map p70; Queens Wharf) Auckland's most recent installation of public art is this replica 'state house' – a form of public housing popular in NZ in the 1930s and 1940s – erected by artist Michael Parekōwhai at

Auckland

the end of Queens Wharf in early 2017. Māori-influenced *tukutuku* panels punctuate the exterior, while inside is a neon-lit, stainless-steel representation of British maritime explorer Captain James Cook. The house's idiosyncratic design is a commentary on sovereignty and colonialism. Best visited after dark.

◉ Viaduct Harbour & Wynyard Quarter

Once a busy commercial port, the Viaduct Harbour was given a major makeover for the 1999/2000 and 2003 America's Cup

yachting events. It's now a fancy dining and boozing precinct, and guaranteed to have at least a slight buzz any night of the week. Historical plaques, public sculpture and the chance to gawk at millionaires' yachts make it a diverting place for a stroll.

Connected to the Viaduct by a bascule bridge, Wynyard Quarter opened in advance of another sporting tournament, 2011's Rugby World Cup. With its public plazas, waterfront eateries, events centre, fish market and children's playground, it has quickly become Auckland's favourite new place to promenade. At the **Silo Park** area, down the western end, free outdoor Friday night movies and weekend markets have become summertime institutions. Most of Wynyard's better restaurants are set back from the water, on Jellicoe St.

New Zealand Maritime Museum   MUSEUM
(Map p70; ☎09-373 0800; www.maritime museum.co.nz; 149-159 Quay St; adult/child $20/10, incl harbour cruise $50/25; ⊙9am-5pm, free tours 10.30am & 1pm Mon-Fri) This museum traces NZ's seafaring history, from Māori voyaging canoes to the America's Cup. Recreations include a tilting 19th-century, steerage-class cabin and a 1950s beach store and bach (holiday home). 'Blue Water Black Magic' is a tribute to Sir Peter Blake, the Whitbread-Round-the-World and America's Cup–winning yachtsman who was murdered in 2001 on an environmental monitoring trip in the Amazon. Packages including an optional one-hour harbour cruise on a heritage boat are also available.

Auckland Fish Market   MARKET
(Map p70; ☎09-379 1490; www.aucklandfish market.co.nz; 22-32 Jellicoe St; ⊙7.30am-6pm) Early morning auctions combine with fish shops, cafes and restaurants, and a seafood-cooking school.

◉ Parnell & Newmarket

Parnell is one of Auckland's oldest areas, and amid the cafes, restaurants and fancy retailers are several heritage buildings. Neighbouring Newmarket is a busy shopping precinct known for its boutiques.

Auckland Domain   PARK
(Map p74; Domain Dr, Parnell; ⊙24hr) Covering about 80 hectares, this green swathe contains the Auckland Museum (p73), sports fields, interesting sculpture, formal

City Centre

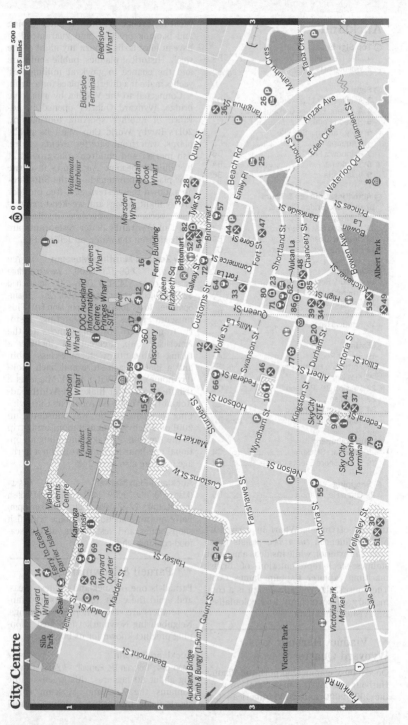

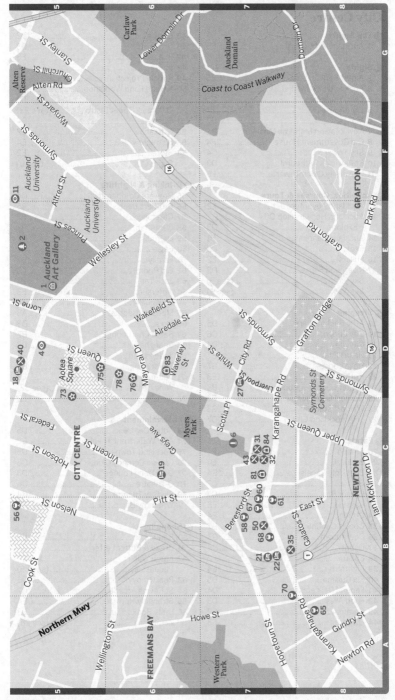

AUCKLAND

City Centre

gardens, wild corners and the **Wintergarden** (Map p74; Wintergarden Rd, Parnell; ⏲9am-5.30pm Mon-Sat, to 7.30pm Sun Nov-Mar, 9am-4.30pm Apr-Oct) FREE, with its fernery, tropical house, cool house, cute cat statue, coffee kiosk and neighbouring cafe. The mound in the centre of the park is all that remains of Pukekaroa, one of Auckland's volcanoes. At its humble peak, a totara tree surrounded by a palisade honours the first Māori king.

★**Auckland Museum**   MUSEUM
(Map p74; ☑09-309 0443; www.auckland museum.com; Auckland Domain, Parnell; adult/child $25/10; ⏲10am-5pm) This imposing neoclassical temple (1929), capped with an impressive copper-and-glass dome (2007), dominates the Auckland Domain and is a prominent part of the Auckland skyline, especially when viewed from the harbour. Admission packages can be purchased, which incorporate a highlights tour and a Māori cultural performance ($45 to $55).

The displays of Pacific Island and Māori artefacts on the museum's ground floor are essential viewing. Highlights include a 25m war canoe and an extant carved meeting house (remove your shoes before entering). There's also a fascinating display on Auckland's volcanic field, including an eruption simulation, and the upper floors showcase military displays, fulfilling the building's dual role as a war memorial. Auckland's main Anzac commemorations take place at dawn on 25 April at the cenotaph in the museum's forecourt.

Check the website for details of interesting, one-off local and international exhibitions.

Holy Trinity Cathedral   CHURCH
(Map p74; ☑09-303 9500; www.holy-trinity.org. nz; cnr St Stephens Ave & Parnell Rd, Parnell; ⏲10am-3pm) Auckland's Anglican cathedral is a hodgepodge of architectural styles, especially compared to **St Mary's Church** (Map p74; Parnell Rd, Parnell; ⏲10am-3pm) next door, a wonderful wooden Gothic Revival church with a burnished interior and interesting stained-glass windows (built 1886). Holy Trinity's windows are also notable, especially the rose window by English artist Carl Edwards, which is particularly striking above the simple kauri altar.

Parnell Rose Garden   GARDENS
(Map p74; 85-87 Gladstone Rd, Parnell) These formal gardens are blooming excellent from November to March. A stroll through

Newmarket

Dove-Myer Robinson Park leads to peaceful **Judges Bay** and tiny St Stephen's Chapel.

St Stephen's Chapel   CHURCH
(Map p74; Judge St) Tiny St Stephen's Chapel was built for the signing of the constitution of NZ's Anglican Church (1857).

◉ **Tamaki Drive**

This scenic, pohutukawa-lined road heads east from the city, hugging the waterfront. In summer it's a jogging/cycling/rollerblading blur.

A succession of child-friendly, peaceful swimming beaches starts at **Ohaku Bay**. Around the headland is **Mission Bay**, a popular beach with an electric-lit, art-deco fountain, historic mission house, restaurants and bars. Safe swimming beaches **Kohimarama** and **St Heliers** follow. Further east along Cliff Rd, the **Achilles Point Lookout** (Map p68; Cliff Rd, St Heliers) offers panoramic views and Māori carvings. At its base is **Ladies Bay**, popular with nudists.

Buses 767 and 769 from behind Britomart station follow this route, while buses 745 to 757 go as far as Mission Bay.

Kelly Tarlton's Sea Life Aquarium   AQUARIUM
(Map p68; ☑09-531 5065; www.kellytarltons. co.nz; 23 Tamaki Dr, Orakei; adult/child $39/22; ⏲9.30am-5pm) ✒ In this topsy-turvy aquarium sharks and stingrays swim over and around you in transparent tunnels that were once stormwater tanks. You can also enter the tanks in a shark cage with a snorkel ($124), or dive straight into the tanks ($265).

AUCKLAND SIGHTS

Parnell

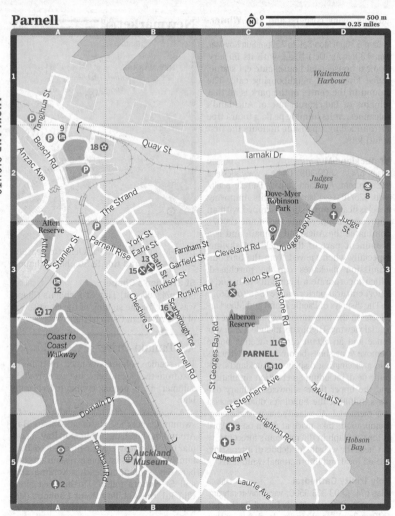

Other attractions include the Penguin Discovery tour (10.30am Tuesday to Sunday, $199 per person) where just four visitors per day can get up close with Antarctic penguins. For all tickets, there are significant discounts online, especially for midweek visits.

A free shark-shaped shuttle bus departs from 172 Quay St (opposite the Ferry Building (p104)) hourly on the half-hour from 9.30am to 3.30pm.

Bastion Point   PARK
(Map p68; Hapimana St, Orakei) Politics, harbour views and lush lawns combine on this pretty headland with a chequered history. An

elaborate cliff-top garden mausoleum honours Michael Joseph Savage (1872–1940), the country's first Labour prime minister, whose socialist reforms left him adored by the populace. Follow the lawn to a WWII gun embankment – one of many that line the harbour.

Mt Eden & Kingsland

★ Mt Eden   VOLCANO
(Maungawhau; Map p76; 250 Mt Eden Rd) From the top of Auckland's highest volcanic cone (196m) the entire isthmus and both harbours are laid bare. The symmetrical crater

Parnell

(50m deep) is known as Te Ipu Kai a Mataaho (the Food Bowl of Mataaho, the god of things hidden in the ground) and is considered highly *tapu* (sacred). Do not enter it, but feel free to explore the remainder of the mountain. The remains of *pā* terraces and food storage pits are clearly visible.

Until recently it was possible to drive right up to the summit but concerns over erosion have led to restricted vehicle access. Paths lead up the mountain from six different directions and the walk only takes around 10 minutes, depending on your fitness.

Eden Garden GARDENS
(Map p73; ☑ 09-638 8395; www.edengarden.co.nz; 24 Omana Ave; adult/child $10/free; ⊙9am-4pm) On Mt Eden's rocky eastern slopes, this mature garden is noted for its camellias, rhododendrons and azaleas.

◎ **Western Springs**

MOTAT MUSEUM
(Museum of Transport & Technology; Map p76; ☑ 09-815 5800; www.motat.org.nz; 805 Great North Rd, Western Springs; adult/child $19/10; ⊙10am-5pm)

This technology boffin's paradise is spread over two sites and 19 hectares. In the Great North Rd site look out for former Prime Minister Helen Clark's Honda 50 motorbike and the pioneer village. The Meola Rd site features the Aviation Display Hall with rare military and commercial planes. The two are linked by a vintage tram (free with admission, $1 otherwise), which passes Western Springs park and the zoo. It's a fun kids' ride whether you visit MOTAT or not.

Western Springs PARK
(Map p76; Great North Rd; ⊕) Parents bring their children to this picturesque park for the popular playground. It's a pleasant picnic spot and a good place to get acquainted with pukeko (swamp hens), ducks and pushy geese. This coastal lake was formed by a confluence of lava flows, where more than 4 million litres of spring water bubble up into the central lake daily. From the city, catch any bus heading west via Great North Rd (adult/child $5/3). By car, take the Western Springs exit from the North Western Motorway.

Until 1902 this was Auckland's main water supply.

Auckland Zoo ZOO
(Map p76; ☑ 09-360 3805; www.aucklandzoo.co.nz; Motions Rd; adult/child $28/12; ⊙9.30am-5pm, last entry 4.15pm) ⊘ At this modern, spacious zoo, the big foreigners tend to steal the attention from the timid natives, but if you can wrestle the kids away from the tigers and orang-utans, there's a well-presented NZ section. Called Te Wao Nui, it's divided into six ecological zones: Coast (seals, penguins), Islands (mainly lizards, including NZ's pint-sized dinosaur, the tuatara), Wetlands (ducks, herons, eels), Night (kiwi, naturally, along with frogs, native owls and weta), Forest (birds) and High Country (cheekier birds and lizards).

Frequent buses (adult/child $5.50/3) run from 99 Albert St in the city to bus stop 8124 on Great North Rd, where it is a 700m walk to the zoo's entrance.

◎ **Devonport**

With well-preserved Victorian and Edwardian buildings and loads of cafes, Devonport is an extremely pleasant place to visit and only a short ferry trip from the city. There are also two volcanic cones to climb and easy access to the first of the North Shore's beaches.

Kingsland & Mt Eden

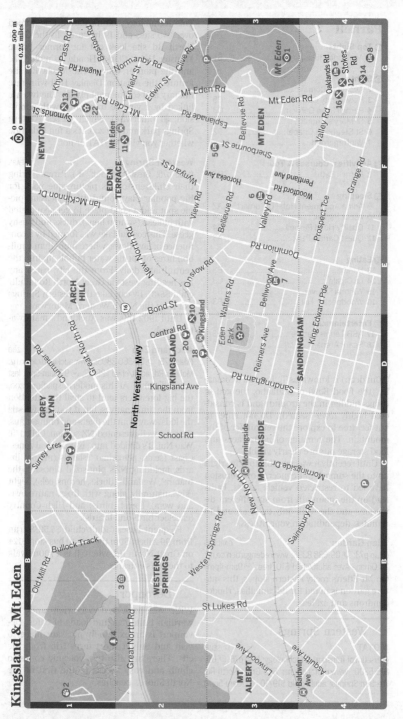

Kingsland & Mt Eden

◎ **Top Sights**
1 Mt Eden...G3

◎ **Sights**
2 Auckland Zoo A1
3 MOTAT..B2
4 Western Springs A1

🛏 **Sleeping**
5 Bamber House F3
6 Bavaria..F3
7 Eden Park B&B.....................................E3
8 Eden Villa G4
9 Oaklands Lodge G4

🍴 **Eating**
10 Atomic Roastery D2
11 Brothers Juke Joint BBQ...................F2
12 Frasers...G4
13 French Cafe...G1
14 Garden Shed G4
15 Tiger Burger C1
16 Zool Zool G4

🍷 **Drinking & Nightlife**
Citizen Park .... (see 10)
17 Galbraith's Alehouse G1
18 Neighbourhood D2
19 Pocket Bar & Kitchen C1
20 Portland Public House.......................D2

🎭 **Entertainment**
21 Eden Park D3
22 Power Station......................................G1

🛍 **Shopping**
Royal Jewellery Studio ....(see 18)

For a self-guided tour of historic buildings, pick up the *Old Devonport Walk* pamphlet from the **Visit Devonport** (p102) information centre. Bikes can be hired from the ferry terminal.

Ferries to Devonport (adult/child return $12/6.50, 12 minutes) depart from the Ferry Building at least every 30 minutes from 6.15am to 11.30pm (until 1am Friday and Saturday), and from 7.15am to 10pm on Sundays and public holidays. Some Waiheke Island and Rangitoto ferries also stop here.

Mt Victoria (Takarunga; Map p78; Victoria Rd) and **North Head** (Maungauika; Map p78; Takarunga Rd; ⊙6am-10pm) were Māori *pā* and they remain fortresses of sorts, with the navy maintaining a presence. Both have gun embankments and North Head is riddled with tunnels, dug at the end of the 19th century in response to the Rus-

sian threat, and extended during WWI and WWII. The gates are locked at night, but that's never stopped teenagers from jumping the fence for scary subterranean explorations.

Between the two, **Cambria Reserve** stands on the remains of a third volcanic cone that was largely quarried away.

Torpedo Bay Navy Museum MUSEUM
(Map p78; ☑09-445 5186; www.navymuseum.mil. nz; 64 King Edward Pde, Devonport; ⊙10am-5pm) **FREE** The navy has been in Devonport since the earliest days of the colony. Its history is on display at this well-presented and often moving museum, focusing on the stories of the sailors themselves.

◎ One Tree Hill

Looking at One Tree Hill, your first thought will probably be 'Where's the bloody tree?'. Good question. Up until 2000 a Monterey pine stood at the top of the hill. This was a replacement for a sacred totara that was chopped down by British settlers in 1852. Māori activists first attacked the foreign usurper in 1994, finishing the job in 2000.

After much consultation with local Māori and tree experts, a grove of six pohutukawa and three totara trees was planted on the summit in mid-2016. In an arboreal version of the *X-Factor,* the weaker performing trees will be eliminated, with only one tree left standing by 2026.

Auckland's most beloved landmark achieved international recognition in 1987 when U2 released the song 'One Tree Hill' on their acclaimed *The Joshua Tree* album. It was only released as a single in NZ, where it went to number one for six weeks.

★ **One Tree Hill** VOLCANO, PARK
(Maungakiekie; Map p68) This volcanic cone was the isthmus' key *pā* and the greatest fortress in the country. At the top (182m) there are 360-degree views and the grave of John Logan Campbell, who gifted the land to the city in 1901 and requested that a memorial be built to the Māori people on the summit. Nearby is the stump of the last 'one tree'. Allow time to explore surrounding **Cornwall Park** with its mature trees and historic Acacia Cottage (1841).

The Cornwall Park Information Centre (p102) has fascinating interactive displays illustrating what the *pā* would have looked like when 5000 people lived here.

Devonport

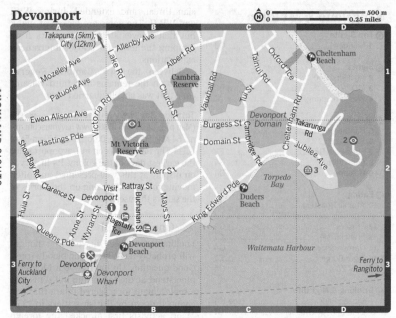

Devonport

◎ Sights
1 Mt Victoria B2
2 North Head D2
3 Torpedo Bay Navy Museum D2

⊟ Sleeping
4 Parituhu B3
5 Peace & Plenty Inn B3

⊗ Eating
6 Devon on the Wharf A3

Near the excellent children's playground, the **Stardome** (Map p68; ☑09-624 1246; www.stardome.org.nz; 670 Manukau Rd; shows adult/child from $12/10; ⊙10am-5pm Mon, to 9.30pm Tue-Thu, to 11pm Fri-Sun) FREE offers regular stargazing and planetarium shows that aren't dependent on Auckland's fickle weather (usually 7pm and 8pm Wednesday to Sunday, with extra shows on weekends).

To get to One Tree Hill from the the city take a train to Greenlane and walk 1km along Green Lane West. By car, take the Greenlane exit off the Southern Motorway and turn right into Green Lane West.

◎ South Auckland

Villa Maria   WINERY
(Map p68; ☑09-255 0666; www.villamaria.co.nz; 118 Montgomerie Rd, Mangere; ⊙9am-6pm Mon-Fri, to 4pm Sat & Sun) Clearly the roar of jets doesn't bother grapes, as NZ's most awarded winery is just 4km from the airport. The parklike grounds of Villa Maria are a green oasis in the encircling industrial zone. Short tours ($5) take place at 11am and 2pm. There's a charge for tastings ($5, refundable on purchase), but lingering over a lunch of wine and antipasto (platters $45 to $55, lunch $28 to $38) on the restaurant's terrace sure beats hanging around the departure lounge.

A series of concerts is held here every January and February featuring big international artists popular with the 40- to 50-something wine-swilling demographic.

Auckland Botanic Gardens   GARDENS
(Map p68; ☑09-267 1457; www.aucklandbotanic gardens.co.nz; 102 Hill Rd, Manurewa; ⊙8am-6pm Apr-Sep, to 8pm Oct-Mar) ♿ FREE This 64-hectare park has more than 10,000 plants (including threatened species), dozens of

WORTH A TRIP

HILLSBOROUGH

Housed in a gorgeous 1879 mansion with views to **One Tree Hill** (p77) and the Manukau Harbour, the **Wallace Arts Centre** (Map p68; ☑ 09-639 2010; www.tsbbankwallaceartscentre.org.nz; Pah Homestead, 72 Hillsborough Rd, Hillsborough; ⊗ 10am-3pm Tue-Fri, to 5pm Sat & Sun) is endowed with contemporary New Zealand art from an extensive private collection, which is changed every four to six weeks. Have lunch on the veranda at the excellent Homestead Cafe and wander among the magnificent trees in the surrounding park. The art is also very accessible, ranging from a life-size skeletal rugby ruck to a vibrant Ziggy Stardust painted on glass.

Bus 299 (Lynfield) departs every 15 minutes from Queen St (outside the **Civic Theatre**; p66) and heads to Hillsborough Rd ($5.50, 40 minutes).

themed gardens and an infestation of wedding parties. By car, take the Southern Motorway, exit at Manurewa and follow the signs. Otherwise take the train to Manurewa ($9, 43 minutes) and then walk along Hill Rd (1.5km).

🏃 Activities

Nothing gets you closer to the heart and soul of Auckland than sailing on the Hauraki Gulf. If you can't afford a yacht cruise, catch a ferry instead.

Trading on the country's action-packed reputation, Auckland has sprouted its own set of thrill-inducing activities. Look around for backpacker reductions or special offers before booking anything.

Extreme Sports

Auckland Bridge Climb
& Bungy   ADVENTURE SPORTS
(Map p68; ☑ 09-360 7748; www.bungy.co.nz; 105 Curran St, Westhaven; adult/child climb $125/85, bungy $160/130) 🌱 Climb up or jump off the Auckland Harbour Bridge.

SkyJump   ADVENTURE SPORTS
(Map p70; ☑ 0800 759 586; www.skyjump.co.nz; Sky Tower, cnr Federal & Victoria Sts; adult/child $225/175; ⊗ 10am-5.15pm) This thrilling 11-second, 85km/h base wire leap from the observation deck of the Sky Tower (p67) is more like a parachute jump than a bungy. Combine it with the SkyWalk in the Look & Leap package ($290).

SkyWalk   ADVENTURE SPORTS
(Map p70; ☑ 0800 759 925; www.skywalk.co.nz; Sky Tower, cnr Federal & Victoria Sts; adult/child $145/115; ⊗ 10am-4.30pm) The SkyWalk involves circling the 192m-high, 1.2m-wide outside halo of the Sky Tower (p67) without rails or a balcony. Don't worry, it's not completely crazy – there is a safety harness.

Auckland Adventure Jet   BOATING
(Map p70; ☑ 0800 255 538; www.aucklandadventurejet.co.nz; Pier 3A, Quay St; adult/child $98/58) Exciting 30-minute blasts around Auckland Harbour.

Walking

Visitor centres and public libraries stock the city council's *Auckland City's Walkways* pamphlet, which has a good selection of urban walks, including information on the Coast to Coast Walkway.

Coast to Coast Walkway   WALKING
(Map p68; www.aucklandcity.govt.nz) Heading right across the country from the Tasman to the Pacific (which is actually only 16km), this walk encompasses One Tree Hill (p77), Mt Eden (p74), the Domain (p69) and the university, keeping mainly to reserves rather than city streets.

Do it in either direction: starting from the Viaduct Basin and heading south, it's marked by yellow markers and milestones; heading north from Onehunga there are blue markers. Our recommendation? Catch the train to Onehunga and finish up at the Viaduct's bars. From Onehunga station, take Onehunga Mall up to Princes St, turn left and pick up the track at the inauspicious park by the motorway.

Kayaking

Auckland Sea Kayaks   KAYAKING
(Map p68; ☑ 0800 999 089; www.aucklandseakayaks.co.nz; 384 Tamaki Dr, St Heliers) 🌱 Guided trips (including lunch) to Rangitoto ($185, 6½ hours) and Motukorea (Browns Island; $135, four hours). Multiday excursions and sunset paddles are also available.

Fergs Kayaks   KAYAKING
(Map p68; ☑ 09-529 2230; www.fergskayaks.co.nz; 12 Tamaki Dr, Orakei; ⊗ 9am-5pm) Hires kayaks (per hour from $25), paddle boards ($30),

AUCKLAND FOR CHILDREN

All of the east-coast beaches (St Heliers, Kohimarama, Mission Bay, Okahu Bay, Cheltenham, Narrow Neck, Takapuna, Milford, Long Bay) are safe for supervised kids, while sights such as **Rainbow's End** (Map p68; ☑ 09-262 2030; www.rainbowsend.co.nz; 2 Clist Cres, Manukau; unlimited rides adult/child $57/46; ☺ 10am-5pm; ♿), **Kelly Tarlton's Sea Life Aquarium** (p73), **Auckland Museum** (p73) and **Auckland Zoo** (p75) are all firm favourites. **Parnell Baths** (Map p74; ☑ 09-373 3561; www.parnellbaths.co.nz; Judges Bay Rd, Parnell; adult/child $6.40/free; ☺ 6am-8pm Mon-Fri, 8am-8pm Sat & Sun Nov-Easter) has a children's pool, but on wintry days, head to the thermal pools at **Parakai** (p122) or Waiwera (p124).

For a spot of kid-oriented theatre, and a great family **restaurant** (p96) and children's playground, check out what's scheduled at **Whoa! Studios** (☑ 09-838 4553; https://whoastudios.co.nz; 8 Henderson Valley Rd, Henderson; tickets $25-30; ♿), an easy train journey west of the city in Henderson.

Baby-changing facilities are widespread, often in shopping malls and integrated within public toilets. City buses, trains and ferries offer convenient access for prams, and pavements are generally in good condition.

---

bikes ($20) and inline skates ($20). Guided kayak trips head to Devonport ($100, three hours, 8km) or Rangitoto ($160, six hours, 13km).

Surfing & Sailing

Rapu NZ Surf'n'Snow Tours　SURFING
(☑ 09-828 0426; www.rapuadventures.com; 1-/2-/5-/7-/14-day tour $120/199/800/1160/2154) One- or two-day surfing courses include transport, gear and two two-hour lessons each day, usually at Piha (others can tag along for the ride only for $50). Tours of five days or longer include accommodation (October to May only). Snow packages include transport to Mt Ruapehu.

Explore　BOATING
(Map p70; ☑ 0800 397 567; www.exploregroup.co.nz; Viaduct Harbour) ◈ Shoot the breeze for two hours on a genuine America's Cup yacht (adult/child $170/120), take a 90-minute cruise on a glamorous large yacht (adult/child $85/55) or tuck into a 2½-hour Harbour Dinner Cruise ($130/85).

☞ Tours

Cultural

Tāmaki Hikoi　CULTURAL
(☑ 021 146 9593; www.tamakihikoi.co.nz; 1/3hr $50/95) Guides from the Ngāti Whātua iwi (tribe) lead various Māori cultural tours, including walking and interpretation of sites such as Mt Eden (p74) and the Auckland Domain (p69).

TIME Unlimited　CULTURAL
(☑ 09-846 3469; www.newzealandtours.travel; adult/child from $195/97.50) ◈ Cultural, walking and sightseeing tours from a Māori perspective.

Food & Wine

Big Foody Food Tour　TOURS
(☑ 0800 366 386, 021 481 177; www.thebigfoody.com; per person $125-185) Small-group city tours, including visits to markets and artisan producers, and lots of tastings. A recent addition are hop-fuelled explorations of Auckland's burgeoning craft-beer scene.

Auckland Wine Trail Tours　TOURS
(☑ 09-630 1540; www.winetrailtours.co.nz) Small-group tours around west Auckland wineries and the Waitakere Ranges (half/full day $125/255); further afield to Matakana ($265); or a combo of the two ($265).

Fine Wine Tours　TOURS
(☑ 0800 023 111; www.insidertouring.co.nz) Tours of Kumeu, Matakana and Waiheke wineries, including a four-hour Kumeu tour ($199) and a six-hour tour including Muriwai Beach ($269).

Walking

Bush & Beach　WALKING
(☑ 09-837 4130; www.bushandbeach.co.nz) ◈ Tours including guided walks in the Waitakere Ranges and along west-coast beaches ($150 to $235); three-hour city minibus tours ($80); and food and wine tours in either Kumeu or Matakana (half/full day $235/325).

City Walk
City Centre Ramble

START ST KEVIN'S ARCADE, KARANGA-HAPE RD
END WYNYARD QUARTER
LENGTH 4.5KM; AROUND 3 HOURS

This walk aims to show you some hidden nooks and architectural treats in Auckland's somewhat scrappy city centre. Start among the restaurants and vintage boutiques of ❶ **St Kevin's Arcade** (p101) and take the stairs down to Myers Park. Look out for the reproduction of Michelangelo's ❷ **Moses** (Map p70; Myers Park) at the bottom of the stairs. Continue through the park, taking the stairs on the right just before the overpass to head up to street level.

Heading down Queen St, you'll pass the ❸ **Auckland Town Hall** (p100) and ❹ **Aotea Square** (p83), the civic heart of the city. On the next corner is the wonderful ❺ **Civic Theatre** (p66). Turn right on Wellesley St and then left onto Lorne St. Immediately to your right is ❻ **Khartoum Pl**, with tiling that celebrates NZ women's historic victory, becoming the first in the world to win the vote. Head up the stairs to the ❼ **Auckland Art Gallery** (p67).

Behind the gallery is ❽ **Albert Park** (p67). Cross through it and turn left into Princes St, where a row of ❾ **Victorian merchant's houses** faces the ❿ **University Clock Tower** (p67). Cut around behind the clock tower to ⓫ **Old Government House** (p67) and then follow the diagonal path back to Princes St. The attractive building on the corner of Princes St and Bowen Ave was once the city's main ⓬ **synagogue**.

Head down Bowen Ave and cut through the park past the ⓭ **Chancery precinct** to the ⓮ **High St** shopping strip. Take a left onto ⓯ **Vulcan Lane**, lined with historic pubs. Turn right onto Queen St and follow it down to the ⓰ **Britomart train station** (p104), housed in the former central post office. You're now standing on reclaimed land – the original shoreline was at Fort St. Detour to the nearby ⓱ **Britomart** precinct for good bars, restaurants and fashion boutiques.

From Britomart train station, turn left on Quay St and head to ⓲ **Viaduct Harbour**, bustling with bars and cafes, and then continue over the bridge to the rejuvenated ⓳ **Wynyard Quarter**.

Hiking New Zealand
TRAMPING

(☑ 0800 697 232; www.hikingnewzealand.com) Runs a wide range of 'hiking safaris' leaving from Auckland, including Far North ($1750, five days) and NZ Uncut ($7950, 13 days).

Scenic Flights & Cruises

Auckland Seaplanes
SCENIC FLIGHTS

(Map p70; ☑ 09-390 1121; www.aucklandseaplanes. com; 11 Brigham St, Wynyard Quarter; per person from $200) Flights in a cool 1960s floatplane that explore Auckland's harbour and islands.

Riverhead Ferry
CRUISE

(Map p70; ☑ 09-376 0819; www.riverheadferry. co.nz; Pier 3, Ferry Terminal; per cruise $35) Harbour and gulf cruises, including a 90-minute jaunt up the inner harbour to Riverhead, returning after two hours' pub time. Departure times depend on the tides. Check the website for details.

Fullers
CRUISE

(Map p70; ☑ 09-367 9111; www.fullers.co.nz; adult/ child $42/21; ☺ 10.30am & 1.30pm) Twice daily 1½-hour harbour cruises, including Rangitoto and a free return ticket to Devonport.

Bus Tours

Red Carpet Tours
TOURS

(☑ 09-410 6561; www.redcarpet-tours.com) 🗺 Tours with a *Lord of the Rings/Hobbit* focus ranging from six days ($3085) to 14 days ($7250) around all of Middle Earth. Discounts available for twin-share and triple-share bookings.

MĀORI AUCKLAND

Evidence of Māori occupation is literally carved into Auckland's volcanic cones. The dominant *iwi* (tribe) of the isthmus was Ngāti Whātua, but these days there are Māori from almost all of NZ's *iwi* living here.

For an initial taste of Māori culture, start at **Auckland Museum** (p73), where there's a wonderful Māori collection and a culture show. For a more personalised experience, take a tour with **TIME Unlimited** (p80), **Potiki Adventures** (p108) or Ngāti Whātua's **Tāmaki Hikoi** (p80), or visit the *marae* and recreated village at **Te Hana** (☑ 09-423 8701; www.tehana. co.nz; 307-308 SH1, Te Hana; adult/child $28.50/18.50; ☺ 9am-5pm Wed-Sun) 🗺.

Toru Tours
BUS

(☑ 027 457 0011; www.torutours.com; per person $79) The three-hour Express Tour will depart with just one booking – ideal for solo travellers.

Auckland Hop On, Hop Off Explorer
BUS

(Map p70; ☑ 0800 439 756; www.explorerbus. co.nz; adult/child per day $45/20) Two services – the red or blue route – take in the best of the waterfront, including attractions along Tamaki Drive (p73), or highlights including Mt Eden (p74) and the Auckland Zoo (p75). Red route buses depart from near Princes Wharf hourly from 10am to 3pm (more frequently in summer), and it's possible to link to the blue route at the Auckland Museum (p73).

🎊 Festivals & Events

Auckland Tourism's website (www.auckland-nz.com) has a thorough events calendar.

Silo Cinema & Markets
FILM

(www.silopark.co.nz; Silo Park, Wynyard Quarter; ☺ Dec-Easter) Classic movies screened outdoors on Friday nights, and markets with food trucks, DJs and craft stalls on Friday nights and Saturday and Sunday afternoons.

ASB Classic
SPORTS

(www.asbclassic.co.nz; ☺ Jan) Watch leading tennis players of both genders warm up for the Aussie Open; held early January at the ASB Tennis Centre (p101).

Movies in Parks
FILM

(www.moviesinparks.co.nz; ☺ Jan-Mar) Free movies on Friday and Saturday nights in various locations.

Music in Parks
MUSIC

(www.musicinparks.co.nz; ☺ Jan-Mar) Free gigs in various locations.

Auckland Anniversary Day Regatta
SPORTS

(www.regatta.org.nz; ☺ Jan) The 'City of Sails' lives up to its name; held Monday of the last weekend in January.

Laneway Festival
MUSIC

(http://auckland.lanewayfestival.com; Albert Park; ☺ Jan) International indie bands in a one-day festival on Anniversary Day (the Monday following the last weekend in January).

Auckland Pride Festival
LGBT

(www.aucklandpridefestival.org.nz; ☺ Feb) Two-week festival of music, arts, sport and culture celebrating the LGBT community.

Highlights include the Pride Parade, Pride Party and the Big Gay Out.

Splore
MUSIC
(www.splore.net; Tapapakanga Regional Park; ⊙mid-Feb) Three days of camping and music (generally of the dancey and soulful variety), held by the beach. Headliners include big-name international acts.

Lantern Festival
CULTURAL
(www.aucklandnz.com/lantern; Albert Park; ⊙Feb) Three days of Asian food, culture and elaborately constructed lantern tableaux in Albert Park to welcome the Lunar New Year (usually held in February).

Auckland Arts Festival
PERFORMING ARTS
(www.aucklandfestival.co.nz; ⊙Mar) Held over three weeks in March, this is Auckland's biggest celebration of the arts.

Auckland City Limits
MUSIC
(www.aucklandcitylimits.com; Western Springs Park; ⊙Mar) One-day festival featuring big-name international rock, indie and hip-hop acts.

Pasifika Festival
CULTURAL
(www.aucklandnz.com/pasifika; ⊙Mar) Western Springs (p75) park hosts this giant Polynesian party with cultural performances, and food and craft stalls; held over a weekend in early to mid-March.

Polyfest
CULTURAL
(www.asbpolyfest.co.nz; Sports Bowl, Manukau; ⊙mid-Mar) Massive Auckland secondary schools' Māori and Pacific Islands cultural festival.

Royal Easter Show
FAIR
(www.eastershow.co.nz; ASB Showgrounds, 217 Green Lane West; ⊙Mar/Apr) It's supposedly agricultural but most people attend for the funfair rides.

Auckland International Cultural Festival
CULTURAL
(www.facebook.com/culturalfestival; Mt Roskill War Memorial Park; ⊙late Mar or early Apr) One-day festival with ethnic food stalls and cultural displays and performances; late March or early April.

NZ International Comedy Festival
COMEDY
(www.comedyfestival.co.nz; ⊙Apr-May) Three-week laughfest with local and international comedians; late April to mid-May.

GABS
BEER
(Great Australasian Beer Spectacular; www.gabsfestival.com; ASB Showgrounds; ⊙late Jun) A dazzling array of craft beer, cider and street food combine at Auckland's brilliant version of one of the world's best beer festivals.

NZ International Film Festival
FILM
(www.nziff.co.nz; ⊙Jul) Art-house films for two weeks from mid-July, many in the beautiful Civic Theatre (p66).

Auckland Heritage Festival
CULTURAL
(www.heritagefestival.co.nz; ⊙Sep) Two weeks of (mainly free) tours of Auckland's neighbourhoods and historic buildings; from late September.

Diwali Festival of Lights
CULTURAL
(www.aucklandnz.com/diwali; Aotea Sq; ⊙mid-Oct) Music, dance and food from Auckland's Indian community in Aotea Sq.

Grey Lynn Park Festival
FAIR, MUSIC
(www.greylynnparkfestival.org; ⊙Nov) Free festival of arts and crafts, food stalls and live music in one of Auckland's more interesting inner suburbs; third Saturday in late November.

Santa Parade
CHRISTMAS
(www.santaparade.co.nz; ⊙Nov) The big guy in red parades along Queen St before partying in Aotea Square (Map p70); last Sunday of November.

Christmas in the Park
CHRISTMAS
(www.christmasinthepark.co.nz; ⊙mid-Dec) A huge concert and party in Auckland Domain (p69).

🛏 Sleeping

Auckland's city centre has plenty of luxury hotels, with several international chains. Any backpackers who leave with a bad impression have invariably stayed in crummy, noisy digs in the city centre. Not all of the cheap city accommodation is bad, but you'll find much better hostels in inner suburbs such as Ponsonby, Parnell, Freemans Bay and Mt Eden. Devonport has beautiful Edwardian B&Bs within a relaxing ferry ride of the city.

🛌 City Centre

Attic Backpackers
HOSTEL $
(Map p70; ☑09-973 5887; www.atticbackpackers. co.nz; 31 Wellesley St; dm $33-40, s/tw without bathroom $65/95; @ 🛜) Centrally located Attic

Backpackers features good facilities and an even better vibe. White walls and plenty of windows keep everything bright and fresh, and there's a rooftop area conducive to meeting other travellers.

YHA Auckland City HOSTEL $

(Map p70; ☑09-309 2802; www.yha.co.nz; 18 Liverpool St; dm $38-44, tw $99, d with/without bathroom $120/102; ☎) Struggle up one of the city's steepest streets to this big, impersonal tower block near the K Rd party strip. Refurbished in late 2016, the rooms are colourful, clean and well kept, and some have views and terraces.

Waldorf Celestion APARTMENT $$

(Map p70; ☑09-280 2200; www.celestion-waldorf.co.nz; 19-23 Anzac Ave; apt from $193; P@☎) A rash of Waldorfs have opened in recent years, all presenting similar symptoms: affordable, modern apartments in city-fringe locations. We prefer this one for its stylish crimson and charcoal colour palette.

City Lodge HOTEL $$

(Map p70; ☑09-379 6183; www.citylodge.co.nz; 150 Vincent St; s/d from $99/135; @☎) ✐ This YMCA-run and purpose-built tower caters well to the budget market. The tiny rooms and stamp-sized bathrooms make for clean and secure accommodation. There's also an industrial-style kitchen and comfy lounge.

★ Hotel DeBrett BOUTIQUE HOTEL $$$

(Map p70; ☑09-925 9000; www.hoteldebrett.com; 2 High St; r from $370; ☎) This hip historic hotel has been zhooshed up with stripy carpets and clever designer touches in every nook of the 25 extremely comfortable rooms. Prices include a continental breakfast, free unlimited wi-fi and a pre-dinner drink.

Adina Apartment Hotel Britomart APARTMENT $$$

(Map p74; ☑09-393 8200; www.adinahotels.com; 2 Tapora St; d/apt from $199/269; P☎) Handily located for concerts and events at Spark Arena (p100), eating and drinking in the Britomart (p90) precinct, and for harbour transport from the Ferry Building (p104), the Adina Britomart has colourful and modern suites and apartments with a touch of Scandi natural-wood style. There's a decent in-house bar and restaurant also.

CityLife HOTEL $$$

(Map p70; ☑09-379 9222; www.heritagehotels.co.nz/citylife-auckland; 171 Queen St; apt from $217; P☎☎) ✐ A worthy tower-block

hotel offering numerous apartments over dozens of floors, ranging from studios to three-bedroom suites. Facilities include a heated lap pool, gym and valet parking. The location couldn't be more central.

Waldorf Stadium APARTMENT $$$

(Map p70; ☑09-337 5300; www.stadium-apartments-hotel.co.nz; 40 Beach Rd; apt from $213; ☎) This large newish block has spacious (if generic) family-friendly apartments with double-glazing to keep out the road noise.

🛏 Ponsonby & Freemans Bay

Verandahs HOSTEL $

(Map p85; ☑09-360 4180; www.verandahs.co.nz; 6 Hopetoun St; dm $34-38, s $64, d $106, without bathroom $88; P@☎) Ponsonby Rd, K Rd and the city are an easy walk from this grand hostel, housed in two neighbouring villas overlooking the mature trees of Western Park. It's definitely one of Auckland's best backpacker hostels.

Ponsonby Backpackers HOSTEL $

(Map p85; ☑09-360 1311; www.ponsonby-backpackers.co.nz; 2 Franklin Rd, Ponsonby; dm $33-35, s/d without bathroom $60/82; P@☎) This elegant two-storey turreted villa has a friendly vibe, sunny rooms and a nice garden area. Central Auckland is a pleasant 20-minute walk away, and the buzz of Ponsonby Rd is right on your doorstep.

Brown Kiwi HOSTEL $

(Map p85; ☑09-378 0191; www.brownkiwi.co.nz; 7 Prosford St, Ponsonby; dm $32-35, s/d without bathroom $70/84; @☎) This low-key hostel is tucked away in a busy-by-day commercial strip, a stone's throw from Ponsonby's shopping and grazing opportunities. The garden courtyard is made for mooching.

Abaco on Jervois MOTEL $$

(Map p85; ☑09-360 6850; www.abaco.co.nz; 57 Jervois Rd, Ponsonby; r/ste from $145/205; P☎) Well positioned for cafes and buses, this neutral-toned motel has stainless-steel kitchens with dishwashers in the fancier units, and fridges and microwaves in the studios. The darker rooms downstairs are cheaper.

Great Ponsonby Arthotel B&B $$$

(Map p85; ☑09-376 5989; www.greatpons.co.nz; 30 Ponsonby Tce, Ponsonby; r $260-400; P☎) ✐ In a quiet cul-de-sac near Ponsonby Rd, this deceptively spacious Victorian villa has

Ponsonby & Grey Lynn

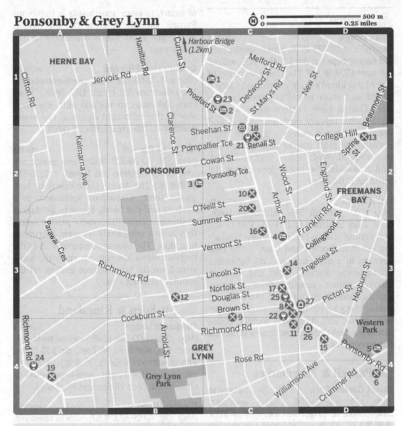

Ponsonby & Grey Lynn

🛏 Sleeping
1	Abaco on Jervois	C1
2	Brown Kiwi	C1
3	Great Ponsonby Arthotel	B2
4	Ponsonby Backpackers	C3
5	Verandahs	D4

✕ Eating
6	Azabu	D4
7	Bird on a Wire	C3
8	Blue Breeze Inn	C3
9	Cocoro	C3
10	Dizengoff	C2
11	Gypsy Caravan	C4
12	Lokanta	B3
13	New World	D2
	Ponsonby Central	(see 7)
14	Ponsonby Road Bistro	C3
15	Ponsonby Village International Food Court	D4
16	Prego	C3
17	Saan	C3
18	Sidart	C2
19	Siostra	A4
20	Unbakery	C2

🍷 Drinking & Nightlife
21	Annabel's	C2
22	Bedford Soda & Liquor	C3
23	Dida's Wine Lounge & Tapas Bar	C1
24	Freida Margolis	A4
25	SPQR	C3

🛍 Shopping
26	Karen Walker	D4
27	Women's Bookshop	D3
	Zambesi	(see 14)

gregarious hosts, impressive sustainability practices and great breakfasts.

Studio apartments open onto an attractive rear courtyard. Rates include breakfast.

Newton

Haka Lodge HOSTEL $
(Map p70; ☎09-379 4556; www.hakalodge.com; 373 Karangahape Rd; dm $31-41, r $139, without bathroom $109; 🛜) 🏊 The transformation of one of Auckland's dodgiest old pubs into a bright and shiny hostel is a modern miracle. Dorms have custom-made wooden bunks with privacy curtains, lockers and their own power points – making them perhaps the most comfortable bunkrooms in Auckland. Wi-fi is free and unlimited. And it couldn't be better located for the bustling K Rd scene.

Haka Hotel HOTEL $$
(Map p70; ☎09-281 3097; https://hakahotels. co.nz; 2 Day St; d from $161; P🛜) Part of the burgeoning Haka empire – also including excellent hostels and tours – this new opening in a quiet lane just off bohemian Karangahape features chic and modern accommodation ranging from compact studios through to one- and two-bedroom suites. Many rooms have balconies and harbour views, and mod cons include coffee machines and Chromecast functionality on flat-screen TVs.

Parnell & Newmarket

Quest Carlaw Park APARTMENT $$
(Map p74; ☎09-304 0521; www.quest carlawpark.co.nz; 15 Nicholls Lane; apt from $189; P@🛜) 🏊 It's in an odd spot but this set of smart, modern apartments is handy for Parnell, the city and the Domain, and if you've got a car, you're practically on the motorway.

Quality Hotel Parnell HOTEL $$
(Map p74; ☎09-303 3789; www.theparnell.co.nz; 10-20 Gladstone Rd; r from $167; P🛜) More than 100 motel rooms and units are available in this renovated complex. The newer north wing has great harbour views.

★ **Ascot Parnell** B&B $$$
(Map p74; ☎09-309 9012; www.ascotparnell. com; 32 St Stephens Ave, Parnell; r $295-375; P@🛜🏊) The Ascot's three luxurious bedrooms share a spacious apartment in a modern mid-rise block. You're in no danger of stumbling into the owners' private space; they have a completely separate apartment next door. The largest room grabs all of the harbour views but you can enjoy the same vista from the large terrace leading off the communal living area.

Mt Eden & Kingsland

Oaklands Lodge HOSTEL $
(Map p76; ☎09-638 6545; www.oaklandslodge. co.nz; 5a Oaklands Rd, Mt Eden; dm $30-38, s/d without bathroom $55/85; P@🛜) In a leafy cul-de-sac, this bright, well-kept hostel is close to Mt Eden village and city buses.

Bamber House HOSTEL $
(Map p76; ☎09-623 4267; www.bamberhouse. co.nz; 22 View Rd, Mt Eden; dm $32-36, r $100, without bathroom $85; P@🛜) 🏊 The original house here is a mansion of sorts, with some nicely maintained period trimmings and large grounds. The new prefab cabins have less character but come with en suites.

Bavaria B&B $$
(Map p76; ☎09-638 9641; www.bavariabandbho-tel.co.nz; 83 Valley Rd, Mt Eden; s/d from $130/180; P@🛜) This spacious villa offers large, airy, well-kept rooms, all of which have bathrooms, although some of them are closet sized. The communal TV lounge, dining room and deck all encourage mixing and mingling. A hot and cold buffet breakfast is included in the rates.

Eden Villa B&B $$$
(Map p76; ☎09-630 1165; www.edenvilla.co.nz; 16 Poronui St, Mt Eden; r $250; P) These pretty wooden villas are what Auckland's leafy inner suburbs are all about. This one has three

---

PASIFIKA IN AUCKLAND

There are nearly 195,000 Pacific Islanders (PI) living in Auckland, making it the world's principal Polynesian city. Samoans are by far the largest group, followed by Cook Islanders, Tongans, Niueans, Fijians, Tokelauans and Tuvaluans. The biggest PI communities can be found in South Auckland and pockets of West and Central Auckland.

Like the Māori renaissance of recent decades, Pasifika has become a hot commodity for Auckland hipsters. You'll find PI motifs everywhere: in art, architecture, fashion, homewares, movies and especially in music. The annual **Pasifika Festival** (p83) in March is a wonderful two-day celebration of Pacific culture.

comfortable en-suite bedrooms, a pleasantly old-fashioned ambience and charming hosts who prepare a good cooked breakfast. We prefer the room at the rear, which has the original bath-tub and views straight over the garden to Mt Eden (p74) itself.

Eden Park B&B B&B $$$
(Map p76; ☑09-630 5721; www.bedandbreak fastnz.com; 20 Bellwood Ave, Mt Eden; s/d $165/250; P🛜) The hallowed turf of Auckland's legendary Eden Park (p100) rugby ground is only a block away and, while the rooms aren't overly large, they mirror the Edwardian elegance of this fine wooden villa.

🛏 Devonport

Parituhu B&B $$
(Map p78; ☑09-445 6559; www.parituhu.co.nz; 3 King Edward Pde; r $140-160; P🛜) There's only one double bedroom (with its own adjoining bathroom) available in this relaxing and welcoming Edwardian waterfront bungalow. The well-travelled hosts are excellent company and know the city very well.

Peace & Plenty Inn B&B $$$
(Map p78; ☑09-445 2925; www.peaceand plenty.co.nz; 6 Flagstaff Tce; r $295-385; P🛜) 🌊 Stocked with antiques, this perfectly located, five-star Victorian house has romantic and luxurious en-suite rooms with TVs, flowers, free sherry/port and local chocolates.

🛏 South Auckland

Ambury Regional Park CAMPGROUND $
(Map p68; ☑09-366 2000; http://regionalparks. aucklandcouncil.govt.nz/ambury; 43 Ambury Rd, Mangere; sites per adult/child $15/6; P) A slice of country in suburbia, this regional park is also a working farm. Facilities are limited (a vault toilet, warm showers and not much shade) but it's handy to the airport, right on the water and dirt cheap.

Grange Lodge MOTEL $$
(Map p68; ☑09-277 8280; www.grangelodge. co.nz; cnr Grange & Great South Rds, Papatoetoe; apt $159-239; P🛜) If you've driven up from the south, consider staying at this friendly little suburban motel that's handy for the airport. From the Southern Motorway, take the East Tamaki Rd exit, turn right and right again onto Great South Rd.

Jet Park HOTEL $$
(Map p68; ☑09-275 4100; www.jetpark.co.nz; 63 Westney Rd, Mangere; r from $199; P@🛜🏊) 🌊 Located within the industrial area edging the airport, Jet Park has comfortable rooms and a vibe that exceeds that of the average midrange airport hotel. With departure screens in the lobby and free airport shuttles, there's no excuse for missing your flight.

🛏 Other Areas

Emerald Inn MOTEL $$
(Map p68; ☑09-488 3500; www.emerald inn.co.nz; 16 The Promenade, Takapuna; d/ste $200/285; P🛜🏊) Across the harbour bridge in Takapuna, the Emerald Inn is arrayed around a leafy courtyard and pool. It's just metres to Takapuna Beach, and there's plenty of good eating and drinking opportunities in the immediate area. Options range from studio units to one- and two-bedroom suites, and the friendly owners are packed with ideas of things to see and do.

Self-contained holiday villas and a cottage are just next door and enjoy views of Rangitoto Island.

Nautical Nook B&B $$
(Map p68; ☑09-521 2544; www.nauticalnook. co.nz; 23b Watene Cres, Orakei; s/d $108/162; P🛜) If you're a sailing buff you'll find a kindred spirit in Keith, who runs this cosy homestay with his wife, Trish. The lounge and terrace have views over the harbour, and the beach is close at hand.

Sofitel Viaduct Harbour HOTEL $$$
(Map p70; ☑09-909 9000; www.sofitel-auckland.com; 21 Viaduct Harbour Ave; d from $420; P🛜🏊) Auckland is one of the world's great harbour cities, so it makes perfect sense to stay beside the water. In close proximity to the restaurants and bars of Viaduct Harbour and the Wynyard Quarter, the Sofitel has classy rooms and suites arrayed around a central ornamental pool. Moored yachts bob nearby, and Auckland's 'City of Sails' moniker definitely rings true.

🍴 Eating

Because of its size and ethnic diversity, Auckland tops the country when it comes to dining options and quality. Lively eateries have sprung up to cater to the many Asian students, and offer inexpensive Japanese, Chinese and Korean staples. If you're on a budget, you'll fall in love with the city's food halls.

City Centre

Chuffed
CAFE $

(Map p70; ☑ 09-367 6801; www.chuffedcoffee. com; 43 High St; mains $6.50-18; ☺ 7am-4pm Mon-Wed, 7am-10pm Thu & Fri, 9am-10pm Sat, 9am-4pm Sun) Concealed in a lightwell at the rear of a building, this hip place, liberally coated in street art, is a definite contender for the inner-city's best cafe. Grab a seat on the indoor-outdoor terrace and tuck into cooked breakfasts, Wagyu burgers, lamb shanks or surprisingly flavour-packed toasted sandwiches. From Thursday to Saturday nights, cocktails and craft beers also feature.

Best Ugly Bagels
BAKERY, CAFE $

(Map p70; ☑ 09-366 3926; www.bestugly.co.nz; City Works Depot, 90 Wellesley St; filled bagels $6-14; ☺ 7am-3pm; ☑) Hand rolled, boiled and wood-fired, Best Ugly's bagels are a thing of beauty. Call into its super-hip bakery in a converted heavy-vehicle workshop and order one stuffed with pastrami, bacon, smoked salmon or a variety of vegetarian fillings. Or just ask for a cinnamon bagel slathered with cream cheese and jam. The coffee is killer, too.

Eighthirty
CAFE $

(Map p70; www.eighthirty.com; 35 High St; sandwiches $8-10; ☺ 7am-3.30pm Mon-Fri) Primarily a coffee roaster, Eighthirty's High St branch serves the inner-city's best coffee and a tasty array of fresh sandwiches, salads and sweet things. The dazzling white industrial decor is an interesting counterpoint to the wonderful heritage building in which it's housed.

Food Alley
FOOD HALL $

(Map p70; 9 Albert St; mains $9-19; ☺ 10.30am-10pm) There's Chinese, Indonesian, Indian, Thai, Vietnamese, Lebanese, Malaysian, Korean and Japanese all on offer at this no-frills food hall.

★ Giapo
ICE CREAM $$

(Map p70; ☑ 09-550 3677; www.giapo.com; 12 Gore St; ice cream $10-22; ☺ noon-10.30pm Sun-Thu, to 11.30pm Fri & Sat; ☑) ⬤ That there are queues outside this boutique ice-cream shop even in the middle of winter says a lot about the magical confections that it conjures up. Expect elaborate constructions of ice-cream art topped with all manner of goodies, as Giapo's extreme culinary creativity and experimentation combines with the science of gastronomy to produce quite possibly the planet's best ice-cream extravaganzas.

Odette's
MODERN NZ $$

(Map p70; ☑ 09-309 0304; www.odettes.co.nz; Shed 5, City Works Depot, 90 Wellesley St; dishes $19-40; ☺ 8am-3pm Sun & Mon, 7am-11pm Tue-Sat) Nothing about Odette's is run of the mill. Not the bubbly light fixtures or the quirky photography, and certainly not the menu. How about lamb meatballs with saffron mustard for brunch? Or wild mushrooms served with a truffle pancake and cashew cream? In the evening the more cafe-ish items are replaced with dishes for sharing. It gets hectic on weekends.

Depot
MODERN NZ $$

(Map p70; ☑ 09-363 7048; www.eatatdepot.co.nz; 86 Federal St; dishes $16-38; ☺ 7am-late) TV chef Al Brown's popular eatery offers first-rate comfort food in informal surrounds (communal tables, butcher tiles and a constant buzz). Dishes are designed to be shared, and a pair of clever shuckers serve up the city's freshest clams and oysters. It doesn't take bookings, so get there early or expect to wait.

Scarecrow
CAFE $$

(Map p70; ☑ 09-377 1333; www.scarecrow.co.nz; 33 Victoria St East; mains $16-32; ☺ 7am-5pm Mon, 7am-10pm Tue-Fri, 8am-5pm Sat & Sun; ☑) ⬤ Organic and vegan ingredients shine at this bustling cafe near Albert Park. Bentwood chairs add a Gallic ambience, and the menu veers towards European and Middle Eastern flavours. Try the shakshuka baked eggs or house-smoked fish cakes for brunch, or return at night for New Zealand lamb with labneh and hummus. A compact deli section sells local artisan food products.

Inti
SOUTH AMERICAN $$

(Map p70; ☑ 09-374 0981; www.inti.nz; cnr O'Connell & Chancery Sts; shared plates $14-36; ☺ noon-3pm Tue-Fri, 5pm-late Tue-Sat; ☑) ⬤ Welcome to one of Auckland's most interesting new restaurants where modern South American dishes are served in a spacious and elegant dining room. Chef Javier Carmona harnesses ingredients as diverse as alpaca, aji chillies, almonds and ants to create contemporary interpretations of classic Latin American street food. Come along with an open mind and prepare for a sublime culinary adventure.

Ela Cuisine
INDIAN $$

(Map p70; ☑ 09-379 2710; www.elacuisine.co.nz; 41 Elliott St; mains $15-25; ☺ 11.45am-2.45pm & 5-9.30pm; ☑) Tucked away at the rear of the

Elliott Stables food court, this excellent Indian eatery serves up lip-smacking curries (Kerala beef, coconut lamb shank, 'butterless' chicken etc) and *masala dosa* (stuffed pancakes), each accompanied by a generous serve of rice and salad. It's great value too.

Federal Delicatessen   AMERICAN $$

(Map p70; ☑ 09-363 7184; www.thefed.co.nz; 86 Federal St; mains $11-26; ⊘ 7am-late) Celebrity chef Al Brown's take on a New York Jewish deli serves up simple stuff like bagels and sandwiches, matzo-ball soup and lots of delicious comfort food to share (turkey meatloaf, spit-roasted chicken, New York strip steak). White butcher tiles, vinyl booth seating and waitstaff in 1950s uniforms add to the illusion.

Ima   MIDDLE EASTERN $$

(Map p70; ☑ 09-377 5252; www.imacuisine.co.nz; 53 Fort St; breakfast & lunch $10-24, dinner shared dishes $17-27; ⊘ 7am-11pm Mon-Fri, 8.30am-10pm Sat & Sun) Named after the Hebrew word for mother, Ima's menu features an array of Israeli, Palestinian, Yemeni and Lebanese comfort food, along with meat pies and sandwiches at lunchtime. Rustle up a group for Ima's excellent shared dinners and feast on whole fish, chicken *meschan* (a whole bird slow-cooked with herbs and spices and then grilled) or slow-cooked lamb shoulder.

Kimchi Project   KOREAN, CAFE $$

(Map p70; ☑ 09-302 4002; www.facebook.com/pg/thekimchiprojectnz; 20 Lorne St; snacks $12-18, mains $18-35; ⊘ 7am-10pm Sun-Thu, to midnight Fri & Sat) Begin with a brunch of matcha latte and yuzu muesli, or escape to the palm-fringed courtyard for Asian-inspired street food including spicy pulled-pork tacos, and *bao* (steamed buns) crammed with prawns. Packed with pork belly and topped with an egg, the kimchi fried rice is brilliant.

★ Cassia   INDIAN $$$

(Map p70; ☑ 09-379 9702; www.cassiarestaurant.co.nz; 5 Fort Lane; mains $32-40; ⊘ noon-3pm Wed-Fri, 5.30pm-late Tue-Sat) Occupying a moodily lit basement, Cassia serves modern Indian food with punch and panache. Start with a *pani puri,* a bite-sized crispy shell bursting with flavour, before devouring a decadently rich curry. The Delhi duck is excellent, as is the Goan-style snapper. Artisan gins and NZ craft beer are other highlights. Cassia was recently adjudged Auckland's best restaurant.

CAFE CULTURE

Aucklanders demand good coffee, so you never have to walk too far to find a decent cafe, especially in suburbs like Ponsonby, Mt Eden and Kingsland. Some double as wine bars or have gourmet aspirations, while others are content to fill their counters with fresh, reasonably priced snacks.

Masu   JAPANESE $$$

(Map p70; ☑ 09-363 6278; www.masu.co.nz; 90 Federal St; dishes $7-46, set lunch $40-65, set dinner $88-120; ⊘ noon-3pm & 5.30pm-late) Part of the SkyCity complex, Masu offers superb Japanese food – especially from the sushi bar and the robata grill – and the added attraction of refreshing cocktails made from *shochu* (Japanese liquor).

Grove   MODERN NZ $$$

(Map p70; ☑ 09-368 4129; www.thegrove restaurant.co.nz; St Patrick's Sq, Wyndham St; 9-/12-course degustation $99/145; ⊘ noon-3pm Thu & Fri, 6pm-late Mon-Sat) Romantic fine dining: the room is moodily lit, the menu encourages sensual experimentation and the service is effortless. If you can't find anything to break the ice from the extensive wine list, give it up mate – it's never going to happen.

O'Connell Street Bistro   EUROPEAN $$$

(Map p70; ☑ 09-377 1884; www.oconnellstbistro.com; 3 O'Connell St; mains $38-45; ⊘ 11.30am-3pm & 5-11pm Mon-Fri, 5-11pm Sat) O'Connell Street is a grown-up treat, with smart decor and wonderful food and wine, satisfying lunchtime power brokers and dinnertime daters alike. If you're dining before 7.15pm, a fixed-price menu is available (two/three courses $40/45).

Sugar Club   MODERN NZ $$$

(Map p70; ☑ 09-363 6365; www.thesugarclub.co.nz; Level 53, Sky Tower, Federal St; 3-/4-/5-course lunch $70/84/98, 3-/4-/5-/6-course dinner $95/113/125/135; ⊘ noon-2.30pm Wed-Sun, 5.30-9pm daily) It pays not to expect too much from restaurants stuck up towers, but when the executive chef is NZ's most famous culinary son, Peter Gordon, you can comfortably raise your expectations. Gordon's meticulously constructed, flavour-filled dishes compete with the stupendous views and come out on top.

Degustation menus are also available at lunch ($135) and dinner ($140).

✕ Britomart

Stretching for only a small grid of blocks above the train station, Britomart is a compact enclave of historic buildings and new developments that has been transformed into one of the city's best eating, drinking and shopping precincts. Most of Auckland's top fashion designers have recently decamped to the Britomart area from further uptown in High St.

Amano   ITALIAN $$

(Map p70; ☑ 09-394 1416; www.amano.nz; 66-68 Tyler St; mains $22-34; ☺ restaurant 7am-late, bakery 6.30am-6pm Mon-Sat, to 4pm Sun) ✈ Rustic Italian influences underpin this bistro-bakery in a repurposed warehouse in Auckland's Britomart precinct, but there's real culinary savvy evident in the open kitchen. Many dishes harness seasonal produce and ingredients from the owners' farm in West Auckland, and Amano effortlessly transitions from a buzzy caffeine-fuelled daytime cafe to a sophisticated evening bistro featuring New Zealand wines and craft beers.

The attached bakery has superb sourdough and wood-fired ciabatta sandwiches. Order an Italian meatball sandwich, grab a takeaway espresso and adjourn to a comfy bean bag in nearby Takutai Square.

Store   CAFE $$

(Map p70; ☑ 09-366 1864; www.thestorebritomart.nz; 5b Gore St; mains $15-26; ☺ 7am-3pm) With tables spilling into the fairylight- and flower-strewn space at the centre of Brit-

omart, this chic cafe is as fresh and effervescent as the sparkling water that arrives unbidden when you're seated. Seasonal vegetables and fruits feature prominently on an interesting and enticing menu spanning cooked breakfasts, pasta dishes, market fish and salt-beef sandwiches.

Ortolana   ITALIAN $$

(Map p70; www.ortolana.co.nz; 33 Tyler St; mains $25-35; ☺ 7am-11pm) Mediterranean and regional Italian flavours are showcased at this stylish restaurant. Dishes are as artfully arranged as they are delicious, and much of the produce comes from the owners' small farm in rural west Auckland. Some of the sweets come from its sister patisserie, the very fabulous Milse, next door. It doesn't take bookings.

Ebisu   JAPANESE $$$

(Map p70; ☑ 09-300 5271; www.ebisu.co.nz; 116-118 Quay St; large plates $34-40; ☺ noon-3pm Mon-Fri, 5.30pm-late daily) Ebisu specialises in *izakaya,* a style of drinking and eating that eschews Japanese formality, yet doesn't involve food being flung around the room or chugging along on a conveyor belt. This large bar gets it exactly right, serving exquisite plates designed to be shared. Look forward to Auckland's best selection of sake, including many rare and interesting varieties.

✕ Viaduct Harbour & Wynyard Quarter

Baduzzi   ITALIAN $$

(Map p70; ☑ 09-309 9339; www.baduzzi.co.nz; cnr Jellicoe St & Fish Lane, Wynyard Quarter; mains $16-36; ☺ 11.30am-late; ☑) This smart and sassy eatery does sophisticated spins on meatballs – try the crayfish ones – and other robust but elegant Italian dishes. Cosy up in the intimate booths, grab a seat at the bar, or soak up some Auckland sunshine outside.

Giraffe   MODERN NZ $$$

(Map p70; ☑ 09-358 1093; www.girafferestaurant.co.nz; Viaduct Harbour, 85/89 Customs St West; shared plates $15-32; ☺ 7am-late Mon-Fri, from 8am Sat & Sun) ✈ The latest opening from Simon Gault, one of NZ's most well-known chefs, Giraffe combines a stylish but casual harbourside dining room with an intensely local and seasonal menu. The restaurant was named by Gault's then 3½-year-old daughter, and the menu is packed with sophisticated and superior versions of comfort

---

ⓘ MARKETS & SUPERMARKETS

You'll find large supermarkets in most neighbourhoods: there's a particularly handy **Countdown** (Map p70; ☑ 09-275 2567; www.countdown.co.nz; 76 Quay St; ☺ 24hr) at the bottom of town and a **New World** (Map p85; ☑ 09-307 8400; www.newworld.co.nz; 2 College Hill, Freemans Bay; ☺ 7am-midnight) by Victoria Park. Self-caterers should consider the **Otara Flea Market** (p102) and **Avondale Sunday Markets** (www.avondalesundaymarkets.co.nz; Avondale Racecourse, Ash St; ☺ 5am-noon Sun) for cheap, fresh vegetables, and **La Cigale** (p93) for fancier fare and local artisan produce.

food such as pork and prawn Wellington, and roast chicken.

Local seafood takes a starring role with NZ oysters, mussels and fish often worked into the various plates designed for sharing.

✖ Ponsonby & Freemans Bay

Auckland's busiest restaurant-cafe-bar strip is so damn cool it has its own website (www. iloveponsonby.co.nz).

Bird on a Wire   FAST FOOD $
(Map p85; ☑09-378 6369; www.birdonawire.co.nz; Ponsonby Central, 136-146 Ponsonby Rd; mains $10-17; ☺7.30am-late) Tasty sandwiches and healthy burgers, seasonal salads and rotisserie chickens to take away. Select your baste of choice – Jamaican jerk or truffle butter, perhaps – and you're sorted.

Dizengoff   CAFE $
(Map p85; ☑09-360 0108; www.facebook.com/dizengoff.ponsonby; 256 Ponsonby Rd, Ponsonby; mains $8-22; ☺6.30am-4pm) This stylish shoebox crams in a disparate crowd of corporate and fashion types, Ponsonby denizens and travellers. There's a Jewish influence to the food, with tasty Israeli platters, chopped liver, bagels and chicken salads, along with tempting baking, heart-starting coffee and a great stack of reading material.

★ Saan   THAI $$
(Map p85; ☑09-320 4237; www.saan.co.nz; 160 Ponsonby Rd, Ponsonby; dishes $14-32; ☺4pm-late Mon & Tue, noon-late Wed-Fri, 11am-late Sat & Sun) Hot in both senses of the word, this super-fashionable restaurant focuses on the fiery cuisine of the Isaan and Lanna regions of northern Thailand. The menu is conveniently sorted from least to most spicy and split into smaller and larger dishes for sharing. Be sure to order the soft-shell crab.

Its Thai-style Bloody Mary cocktails and eggy noodle dishes for weekend brunch are a revitalising combo after a big night elsewhere along the Ponsonby strip.

Ponsonby Central   CAFE $$
(Map p85; www.ponsonbycentral.co.nz; 136-138 Ponsonby Rd, Ponsonby; mains $15-35; ☺7am-10.30pm Sun-Wed, to midnight Thu-Sat) Restaurants, cafes, bars and gourmet food shops fill this upmarket former warehouse space offering everything from Auckland's best pizza and Argentinean barbecue to Indo-Burmese curries partnered with zingy cocktails. It's a prime eating and drinking destination and offers

excellent dining options from breakfast right through to dinner. And if you're after the city's best gourmet burgers, look no further.

Unbakery   CAFE $$
(Map p85; ☑09-555 3278; www.littlebird organics.co.nz; 1a Summer St, Ponsonby; mains $13-21; ☺7am-4pm; ☑) ☑ Welcome to an 'unbakery', where virtually everything on the menu is prepared raw and uncooked, but is still very tasty and healthy. Put on your best Gwyneth Paltrow visage and tuck into dishes studded with acai berries, chia seeds and organic fruit; there are even bagels, risotto, tacos and delicious cakes. The juices and smoothies are also great.

Blue Breeze Inn   CHINESE $$
(Map p85; ☑09-360 0303; www.theblue breezeinn.co.nz; Ponsonby Central, 146 Ponsonby Rd, Ponsonby; mains $28-35; ☺noon-late) Regional Chinese flavours combine with a funky retro Pacific ambience at this so-hip-it-hurts eatery. The waitstaff are sassy, the rum cocktails are deliciously strong, and menu standouts include pork belly and pickled cucumber steamed buns, and cumin-spiced lamb.

★ Sidart   MODERN NZ $$$
(Map p85; ☑09-360 2122; www.sidart.co.nz; Three Lamps Plaza, 283 Ponsonby Rd, Ponsonby; 5-course lunch $65, 7-course dinner $145; ☺noon-2.30pm Fri, 6-11pm Tue-Sat) No one in Auckland produces creative degustations quite like Sid Sahrawat. It's food as art, food as science but, more importantly, food to fire up your taste buds, delight the brain, satisfy the stomach and put a smile on your face. The restaurant is a little hard to find, tucked away at the rear of what was once the Alhambra cinema.

On Tuesday nights, a special eight-course menu ($95) showcases new techniques, produce and flavours the kitchen has been working on. If you're a real foodie, check out the Chef's Table offering on the website.

Cocoro

JAPANESE $$$

(Map p85; ☑09-360 0927; www.cocoro.co.nz; 56a Brown St, Ponsonby; dishes $9-38, degustation menu $95-200; ◷noon-2pm & 5.30-10pm Tue-Sat) Japanese elegance infuses everything about this excellent restaurant, from the soft lighting and chic decor, to the delicate flavours of the artistically arranged food. At lunchtime it offers an affordable *donburi* rice bowl ($20 to $24) and a multiplate option ($39), while in the evening multicourse degustation menus showcase the chefs' skills.

Ponsonby Road Bistro

MODERN NZ $$$

(Map p85; ☑09-360 1611; www.ponsonbyroadbistro.co.nz; 165 Ponsonby Rd, Ponsonby; mains $34-36; ◷noon-12.30am Mon-Fri, 4pm-12.30am Sat) The service is first-rate at this modern, upmarket restaurant, which introduces Asian flavours to predominantly French- and Italian-style bistro dishes. Imported cheese and wine are a highlight, and the crispy-based pizzas make a delicious shared snack.

Prego

ITALIAN $$$

(Map p85; ☑09-376 3095; www.prego.co.nz; 226 Ponsonby Rd, Ponsonby; mains $26-40; ◷noon-midnight) This friendly and stylish Italian restaurant covers all the bases, with a fireplace in winter and a courtyard in summer. Speaking of bases, there's a popular pizza selection, top-notch pasta and a good selection of more substantial mains.

✕ Grey Lynn

Tiger Burger

BURGERS $

(Map p76; ☑027 847 5020; www.tigerburger.co.nz; 549 Great North Rd; burgers $13-15; ◷5pm-late Tue-Thu, noon-late Fri-Sun) Formerly starring at markets and food-truck pop-ups around town, Tiger Burger has graduated to a hip permanent space in the city-fringe suburb of Grey Lynn. What made its Korean-influenced burgers great – including pickled daikon, chilli mayo and juicy medium-rare beef – has effortlessly survived the transition, and Kiwi craft beers go exceedingly well with the Kimcheese fries.

Ponsonby Village International Food Court

FOOD HALL $

(Map p85; www.ponsonbyfoodcourt.co.nz; 106 Ponsonby Rd, Ponsonby; mains $9-20; ◷11am-10pm; ☑) Japanese, Malaysian, Chinese, Turkish, Thai, Lao and Indian flavours are all on offer here, and excellent Vietnamese and Indonesian. Beer and wine are well priced for a more expensive part of town.

★ Azabu

JAPANESE, PERUVIAN $$

(Map p85; ☑09-320 5292; www.azabuponsonby.co.nz; 26 Ponsonby Rd; mains & shared plates $16-35; ◷noon-late Wed-Sun, from 5pm Mon & Tue) Nikkei cuisine, an exciting blend of Japanese and Peruvian influences, is the focus at Azabu. Amid a dramatic interior enlivened by striking images of Tokyo, standout dishes include the tuna sashimi tostada, Japanese tacos with wasabi avocado, and king prawns with a jalapeño and ponzu dressing. Arrive early and enjoy a basil- and chilli-infused cachaça cocktail at Azabu's Roji bar.

Lokanta

GREEK, TURKISH $$

(Map p85; ☑09-360 6355; www.lokanta.nz; 137a Richmond Rd; mezze $7-19, mains $25-33; ◷4pm-late Tue-Sun) Featuring the cuisine of the eastern Mediterranean, unpretentious Lokanta is a laid-back alternative to the more trendy eateries along nearby Ponsonby Rd. Greek and Turkish flavours happily co-exist, and robust Greek wines partner well with hearty dishes including chargriiled octopus and roast goat with a barley risotto. The coconut and almond baklava introduces a tropical influence to the classic dessert.

Siostra

ITALIAN $$

(Map p85; ☑09-360 6207; www.siostra.co.nz; 472 Richmond Rd; dishes $17-29; ◷5-11pm Tue-Thu & Sat, noon-11pm Fri) Run by a charming pair of sisters, Siostra is the perfect little neighbourhood bistro, serving up hearty Italian fare with a modern sensibility. Highlights include the pork tortellini with cavolo nero and the excellent slow-cooked lamb shoulder.

Gypsy Caravan

MIDDLE EASTERN $$

(Map p85; ☑09-360 4075; www.gypsycaravan.co.nz; Lot 3, 130 Ponsonby Rd; mezze $14-20, mains $27-31; ◷noon-late Tue-Sun; ☑) Formerly a temporary pop-up eatery, the success of Gypsy Caravan has seen it graduate to being a permanent fixture along busy Ponsonby Rd. Seek out the hidden courtyard trimmed with billowing silk and vintage-style cushions, and combine Middle Eastern–inspired cocktails from the colourful drinks caravan with innovative shared plates like char-grilled tuna with kimchi and truffle-baked mushrooms in vine leaves.

✕ Newton

Karangahape Rd (K Rd) is known for its late-night clubs, but cafes and plenty of inexpensive ethnic restaurants are mixed in with the vintage clothing stores, second-hand boutiques, tattooists and adult shops.

Burger Bar BURGERS $
(Map p70; ✆09-300 6033; www.theburger barauckland.co.nz; St Kevins Arcade, 18/183 Karangahape Rd; burgers $9-14; ⊗noon-3pm Tue, to 9pm Wed & Thu, to 10pm Fri & Sat, to 5pm Sun) From the 'Why didn't we think of this first?' department, the Burger Bar's deliciously simple offering combines top burgers with the best of New Zealand craft beers. The compact eatery bakes its own buns, and sides include the best hand-cut chips and grilled kumara (sweet potato) slices in town. Essential board-game distractions include Monopoly and Battleship.

★Gemmayze St LEBANESE $$
(Map p70; ✆09-600 1545; www.facebook.com/gemmayzest; St Kevins Arcade, 15/183 Karangahape Rd; mezze & mains $18-34; ⊗6-11.30pm Tue-Sat, noon-3pm Thu & Fri; ✎) Located amid the restored heritage architecture of St Kevins Arcade, Gemmayze St presents a modern and stylish update on traditional Lebanese cuisine. Delicate mint, orange blossom and rosewater cocktails are prepared at the beaten copper bar, while shared tables encourage lots of sociable dining on mezze and expertly grilled meats. The $18 lunchtime selection of five mezze is excellent value.

Bestie CAFE $$
(Map p70; www.bestiecafe.co.nz; St Kevins Arcade, Karangahape Rd; mains $12-19; ⊗7.30am-3.30pm Mon-Fri, 9am-4pm Sat & Sun; ✎) ✿ One of the recently opened cafes and restaurants in revitalised St Kevins Arcade, Bestie is a perfect refuelling stop after trawling the arty and vintage shops along Karangahape Rd. Try and secure a table overlooking leafy Myers Park, and partner coffee or kombucha with signature dishes such as Bestie's ricotta doughnuts, or flatbread with chorizo, labneh and a chilli fried egg.

K'Road Food Workshop FOOD HALL $$
(Map p70; 309 Karangahape Rd; cookies $3.50, sandwiches $14-20; ⊗10.30am-9.30pm Tue-Fri, 11.30am-10.30pm Sat, 11.30am-4pm Sun) A tasty work-in-progress – new eateries are also scheduled to open – the K'Road Food Workshop combines an interesting mix of good-value gourmet flavours. Huge Argentinian-style steak sandwiches are served off a wood-fired grill at El Sizzling Lomito, while Moustache Milk & Cookie Bar dispenses chewy and gooey cookies crammed with white chocolate, macadamia nuts or Oreo chunks.

Coco's Cantina ITALIAN $$
(Map p70; ✆09-300 7582; www.cocoscantina. co.nz; 376 Karangahape Rd; mains $24-32; ⊗5pm-late Mon-Sat) Waiting for a table is sometimes part of the experience at this popular and bustling cantina, but propping up the bar is hardly a hardship – the ambience and drinks list see to that. The rustic menu is narrowly focused, seasonal and invariably delicious. If you're seated by 6pm on a Monday night, a bowl of pasta is just $13.

★French Cafe FRENCH $$$
(Map p76; ✆09-377 1911; www.thefrench cafe.co.nz; 210 Symonds St; 3-/4-/7 courses $110/135/160; ⊗noon-3pm Fri, 6pm-late Tue-Sat) The legendary French Cafe has been rated as one of Auckland's top restaurants for more than 20 years and it still continues to excel. The cuisine is nominally French-influenced, but chef Simon Wright sneaks in lots of tasty Asian and Pacific Rim touches. The service is impeccable.

✕ Parnell & Newmarket

Hansan VIETNAMESE $
(Map p73; ✆09-523 3988; www.hansan.co.nz; 55 Nuffield St, Newmarket; mains $11-17; ⊗11am-10pm) A branch of a small local chain serving good-value, authentic Vietnamese food.

La Cigale FRENCH, MARKET $
(Map p74; ✆09-366 9361; www.lacigale.co.nz; 69 St Georges Bay Rd, Parnell; cafe $8-19, bistro 2-/3 courses $38/50; ⊗market 9am-1.30pm Sat & Sun, cafe 9am-4pm Mon-Fri, to 2pm Sat & Sun, bistro 5pm-late Wed) Catering to Francophile foodies, this warehouse stocks French imports and has a patisserie-laden cafe. During the weekend farmers markets, this *cigale* (cicada) really chirps, with stalls laden with local artisan produce. On occasional Thursday evenings it becomes a food-truck stop, while on Wednesdays it's converted into a quirky evening bistro serving simple rustic dishes. Check the website for what's on.

AUCKLAND'S MULTICULTURAL MENU

Around 30% of New Zealanders live in Auckland, and the country's biggest city is also the most ethnically diverse. With immigration – especially from Asia – has come a cosmopolitan restaurant scene, and savvy Auckland foodies (and a few of the city's top chefs) keenly explore central fringe neighbourhoods for authentic tastes of the city's multicultural present and future.

Head to Dominion Rd in Balmoral (catch bus 267 from stop 7058 near the intersection of Queen and Wellesley Sts and get off at stop 8418) to be surrounded by Auckland's best Chinese food.

A few blocks west (catch bus 249 from stop 7022 in Victoria St East to stop 8316 on Sandringham Rd) are some of the city's best Indian and Sri Lankan restaurants. Our favourite is **Paradise** (Map p68; ☑09-845 1144; www.paradiseindianfood.co.nz; 591 Sandringham Rd, Sandringham; mains $12-18; ☺11.30am-9.30pm; ☑), specialising in the Mughlai cuisine you'd find on the streets of Hyderabad.

At the city's bustling night markets – held in a different suburban car park each night of the week – scores of stalls serve food from a diverse range of countries, from Argentina and Samoa, to Hungary and Turkey. Most convenient for travellers is the Thursday **Henderson Night Market** (www.aucklandnightmarket.co.nz; Waitakere Mega Centre, under Kmart; ☺5.30-11pm Thu). Catch a western line train from Britomart to Henderson and walk 650m to underneath the Kmart department store.

If you're in town around late March or early April, the **Auckland International Cultural Festival** (p83) offers a very tasty peek into the city's ethnically diverse future. Online, Cheap Eats (www.cheapeats.co.nz) scours Auckland for the city's best food for under $20.

Sip Kitchen
CAFE **$**

(Map p73; ☑021 377 037; www.facebook.com/SipKitchen; 12a Melrose St, Newmarket; snacks & mains $10-16; ☺8am-3.30pm Tue-Sat, 9am-3pm Sun; ☑) ✦ Relax and re-energise at this wholefood cafe a short walk from the best shopping precinct in Auckland. Organic teas and coffees are a speciality – try a beetroot or matcha latte – and nutrient-packed smoothies and cold-pressed juices are refreshing and fortifying. The counter food includes seasonal salads, best enjoyed as an overflowing selection on the Sip Nutrition Plate ($16.50).

Winona Forever
CAFE **$$**

(Map p74; ☑09-974 2796; www.facebook.com/winonaforevercafe; 100 Parnell Rd; mains $13-21; ☺7am-4.30pm Mon-Fri, 8am-4pm Sat & Sun) Some of Auckland's best counter food – including stonking cream doughnuts – partners with innovative cafe culture at this always-busy eatery near good shopping and art galleries along Parnell Rd. Local residents crowd in with travellers for coffee, craft beer and wine, and one of the cafe's signature dishes – the Ladyboy, a Thai-influenced eggs Benedict with grilled prawns.

Alluding to actor Winona Ryder, the cafe's name is both one of Johnny Depp's tattoos – now amended to 'Wino Forever' apparently – and a Vancouver indie rock band.

Woodpecker Hill
ASIAN, FUSION **$$**

(Map p74; ☑09-309 5055; www.woodpeckerhill.co.nz; 196 Parnell Rd, Parnell; large dishes $30-40; ☺noon-late) Marrying the flavours and shared dining style of Southeast Asian cuisine with an American approach to meat (smoky slow-cooked brisket, sticky short ribs etc), this odd bird has pecked out a unique place on the Auckland dining scene. The decor – a riotous mishmash of tartan, faux fur, copper bells and potted plants – is as eclectic as the food.

Han
KOREAN **$$**

(Map p74; ☑09-377 0977; www.hanrestaurant.co.nz; 100 Parnell Rd, Parnell; mains $20-34; ☺11am-2.30pm Tue-Sat, 5pm-late Wed-Sun) ✦ Korean flavours continue to influence Auckland's dining scene, and Han's evolution from a food truck to a standalone restaurant is testament to the innovation of chef Min Baek. Lunch is a more informal affair – think Korean-style burgers and healthy rice bowls – but the dinner menu really shines with modern dishes including beef short rib with beetroot and asparagus.

Tamaki Drive

Mission Bay Pavilion   SEAFOOD, MODERN NZ **$$**
(Map p68; 🗐09-930 7360; https://missionbay
pavilion.co.nz; 44 Tamaki Dr, Mission Bay; shared
plates $14-35; ⊘noon-late) 🍴 Mission Bay has
long been a mediocre dining destination,
but this recent opening in the heritage Mel-
anesian Mission building is definitely worth
the harbourside journey from the city along
Tamaki Dr. Seafood is highlighted in shared
plates including kingfish ceviche and Cloudy
Bay clams, and an Italian influence informs
other dishes such as grilled octopus, squid-
ink spaghetti and lamb shoulder.

St Heliers Bay Bistro   MODERN NZ **$$**
(Map p68; www.stheliersbaybistro.co.nz; 387 Tam-
aki Dr, St Heliers; brunch $16-27, dinner $27-34;
⊘7am-11pm) Head along Tamaki Dr to this
classy eatery with harbour views. No bookings are taken, but the switched-on crew
soon find space for diners. Look forward
to upmarket takes on the classics (pasta,
burgers, fish and chips), along with cooked
breakfasts, tasty salads and lots of Mediterranean influences. Excellent ice cream too –
best enjoyed walking along the beach.

Mt Eden & Kingsland

Zool Zool   RAMEN, JAPANESE **$**
(Map p76; 🗐09-630 4445; www.zoolzool.co.nz;
405 Mt Eden Rd, Mt Eden; snacks $9-18, ramen
$14-18; ⊘11.30am-2pm & 5.30-10pm Tue-Sun) A
co-production between two of Auckland's
most respected Japanese chefs, Zool Zool is
a stylish and modern take on a traditional
izakaya (Japanese pub). Some of the city's
best ramen noodle dishes are underpinned
by hearty and complex broths, and dishes
made for sharing over frosty mugs of Japanese beer include tempura squid, soft-shell
crab and panko-crumbed fried chicken.

Brothers Juke Joint BBQ   BARBECUE **$**
(Map p76; 🗐09-638 7592; www.jukejoint.co.nz;
5 Akiraho St, Mt Eden; snacks & mains $10-15;
⊘11.30am-10pm Tue-Sat, to 8pm Sun; 🐾) A spin-
off from central Auckland's excellent Brothers Beer (p96) craft beer bar, Juke Joint BBQ
serves up Southern US–style barbecue in a
hip renovated warehouse. Retro 1960s furniture underpins the decor and the compact
kids' play area is popular with local families on weekend afternoons. Brothers' own
brews are joined by the best from other Kiwi
breweries on the gleaming taps.

Atomic Roastery   CAFE **$**
(Map p76; 🗐0800 286 642; www.atomiccoffee.
co.nz; 420c New North Rd, Kingsland; snacks $9-
11; ⊘8am-3pm) Java hounds should follow
their noses to this, one of the country's best-
known coffee roasters. Tasty accompaniments include pies served in mini-frypans,
bagels, salads and cakes.

Kiss Kiss   THAI **$**
(Map p68; 🗐09-600 3076; www.kisskisseatery.
com; 1 Rocklands Ave, Balmoral; mains $17; ⊘5pm-
late Mon-Fri, 11am-late Sat & Sun; 🍴) Shared
tables and colourful wall art give this informal eatery a bohemian edge. Isaan classics
including chicken *laab*, *som tam* salad and
fiery northern Thai-style sausages go well
with craft beer, kombucha and Asian-inspired cocktails.

Garden Shed   BISTRO **$$**
(Map p76; 🗐09-630 3393; www.thegarden
shed.kiwi; 470 Mount Eden Rd, Mt Eden; mains
$18-33; ⊘11am-late Mon-Fri, from 9am Sat & Sun;
🍴) Overflowing with leafy plants, watering
cans and vintage gardening tools, the Gar-
den Shed is a convenient and relaxing spot
after exploring the view-friendly summit of
Mt Eden (p74) nearby. Tasty comfort food
includes buckwheat pancakes, spiced lamb
meatballs and hearty Mexican eggs, and the
diverse drinks selection incorporates zingy
artisan sodas, craft beer from around NZ
and a good wine list.

Frasers   CAFE **$$**
(Map p76; 🗐09-630 6825; cnr Mt Eden & Stokes
Rds, Mt Eden; mains $13-35; ⊘6am-11pm Mon-
Fri, 7am-11pm Sat & Sun) One of Mt Eden's
most loved cafes has been reborn after a
stylish makeover. The coffee and cakes are
still great – especially the baked New York
cheesecake – but now wine and craft beer
partner the concise menu of comfort-food
classics. Try the mushrooms on sourdough
for breakfast, or go for the veal schnitzel
with crispy potato gratin at dinner.

Devonport

Devon on the Wharf   TURKISH, CAFE **$$**
(Map p78; 🗐09-445 7012; www.devononthewharf.
nz; Devonport Wharf, Queens Pde; mezze $10-20,
mains $19-35; ⊘7am-11pm Mon-Fri, 8am-11pm Sat &
Sun; 🍴) From downtown Auckland, make the
short ferry journey to Devonport to visit this
laid-back cafe packed with Turkish influenc-
es. Combine harbour views with brunch op-
tions including *menemen* (baked eggs), or try

a mezze dinner selection of grilled haloumi, hummus and *lahmacun* (Turkish-style pizza). Levantine-inspired cocktails and a concise craft-beer selection are served at what is maybe Auckland's longest bar.

✕ Takapuna

Fortieth & Hurstmere   FOOD HALL
(Map p68; www.fortiethandhurstmere.co.nz; 40 Hurstmere Rd; ⊙hours vary) Easily reached by bus from midtown Auckland, this brick-lined laneway off Takapuna's main shopping street features cool eateries serving up everything from rotisserie chicken to super-healthy Hawaiian poke and acai bowls, and Colombian-style barbecue. Check the website for menus and opening times of the seven distinct operations covering options from cupcakes and coffee to superior wood-fired pizza and Auckland's best burgers.

Takapuna Beach Cafe   CAFE $$
(Map p68; ☑09-484 0002; www.takapuna beachcafe.co.nz; 22 The Promenade; mains $19-30; ⊙6.30am-6pm) Sophisticated cafe fare combined with excellent views of Takapuna Beach ensure that this cafe constantly buzzes. If you can't snaffle a table, grab an award-winning ice cream – our favourite is the salted caramel – and take a lazy stroll along the beach.

✕ Other Areas

Engine Room   MODERN NZ $$
(Map p68; ☑09-480 9502; www.engineroom. net.nz; 115 Queen St, Northcote; mains $32-35; ⊙noon-3pm Fri, 5.30-11pm Tue-Sat) One of Auckland's best restaurants, this informal eatery serves up lighter-than-air goat's-cheese soufflés, inventive mains and oh-my-God chocolate truffles. It's worth booking ahead and catching the ferry to Northcote Point; the restaurant is a further 1km walk away.

Grounds Eatery   CAFE $$
(☑09-393 8448; https://whoastudios.co.nz/the-grounds; 8-14 Henderson Valley Rd, Henderson; mains $20-33; ⊙9am-3pm Mon-Wed, to late Thu-Sun; ▣) ✔ Part of the Whoa! Studios (p80) complex in Henderson, the Grounds has pulled off the trick of being equally attractive to children and their parents. Handmade ice blocks, dumplings and creamy spaghetti bolognese keep the little ones happy, while Mum and Dad can partner roast duck pancakes or the Grounds' Wagyu burger with West Auckland wine and craft beer.

🍷 Drinking & Nightlife

Auckland's nightlife is quiet during the week – for some vital signs, head to Ponsonby Rd, Britomart or the Viaduct. Karangahape Rd (K Rd) wakes up late on Friday and Saturday; don't even bother staggering this way before 11pm.

🍷 City Centre

Brothers Beer   CRAFT BEER
(Map p70; ☑09-366 6100; www.brothersbeer. co.nz; City Works Depot, 90 Wellesley St; ⊙noon-10pm) This beer bar combines quirky decor with 18 taps crammed with Brothers' own brews and guest beers from NZ and further afield. Hundreds more bottled beers await chilling in the fridges, and bar food includes pizza. There are occasional movie and comedy nights, and beers are available to take away. The adjacent City Works Depot has other good eating options.

Gin Room   BAR
(Map p70; www.ginroom.co.nz; Level 1, 12 Vulcan Lane; ⊙5pm-midnight Tue & Wed, 5pm-2am Thu, 4pm-4am Fri, 6pm-4am Sat) There's a slightly disheveled colonial charm to this bar, discreetly tucked away above Auckland's oldest pub, which is completely in keeping with its latest incarnation as a gin palace. There are at least 50 ways to ruin mother here – ask the bar staff for advice – and that's not even counting the juniper-sozzled cocktails.

Vultures' Lane   PUB
(Map p70; ☑09-300 7117; www.vultureslane.co.nz; 10 Vulcan Lane; ⊙11.30am-late) With 22 taps, more than 75 bottled beers and sports on the TV, this pleasantly grungy historic pub is popular with the savviest of Auckland's craft-beer fans. Check the website for what's currently on tap, and also for news of regular tap takeovers from some of New Zealand's best brewers.

Jefferson   BAR
(Map p70; www.thejefferson.co.nz; basement, Imperial Bldg, Fort Lane; ⊙4pm-1am Mon-Thu, to 3am Fri & Sat) Lit by the golden glow of close to 600 different whisky bottles, this subterranean den is a sophisticated spot for a nightcap. There's no list – talk to the knowledgable bar staff about the kind of thing you're after (peaty, smooth, smokey, not too damaging to the wallet) and they'll suggest something.

LOCAL KNOWLEDGE

CARE FOR A CRAFT BEER?

Nelson, as the country's major hop-growing region, and bohemian Wellington both claim to be the 'craft beer capital of NZ', but while the southern centres have been debating the title over a few brews, Auckland's northern craft-beer scene has been fizzing and fermenting away to excellence. Driven by the sheer relative size of the market, there are now plenty of opportunities around Auckland for travelling beer fans to explore the diversity of the Kiwi beer scene.

In Auckland's rural hinterland both **Hallertau** (p121) and **Sawmill Brewery** (p127) offer award-winning beers with restaurant-worthy food, while across on Waiheke Island, three different craft breweries offer an alternative to the island's world-beating wines. For real island diversity, contrast rustic and relaxed **Boogie Van Brewing** (p111) with the stylish, brick-lined Alibi Brewing tasting room at **Tantalus Estate** (p110).

In the city, **Brothers Beer** (p96), **Galbraith's Alehouse** (p99) and **Vultures' Lane** (p96) are all essential destinations, while June's annual **GABS** (p83) festival is Auckland's very own version of the world-famous beer festival first launched in Melbourne, Australia.

Excellent Auckland region brewery names to look out for in restaurants and bars include 8 Wired, Behemoth, Liberty and Epic.

Brewers Co-operative CRAFT BEER
(Map p70; ☑ 09-309 4515; 128 Victoria St; ⊙ 11am-10pm) With 27 craft beers on tap, this corner bar is a good central-city option for an interesting brew and a feed of seafood and chips served the traditional way, in paper. It's popular with the after-work crowd on Friday evenings.

Mo's BAR
(Map p70; ☑ 09-366 6066; www.mosbar.co.nz; cnr Wolfe & Federal Sts; ⊙ 2pm-late Mon-Fri, 6pm-late Sat; 🛜) There's something about this tiny corner bar that makes you want to invent problems just so the bartender can solve them with soothing words and an expertly poured martini.

🍷 Britomart

Caretaker COCKTAIL BAR
(Map p70; www.caretaker.net.nz; Roukai Lane; ⊙ 5pm-3am) New York style infuses this cocktail bar concealed behind an old door inscribed with the title 'Caretaker'. The decor is equally eclectic, and a handful of tables and leather sofas means the bar always feels intimate and convivial. Choose from the very considered cocktail list, or just describe what you like and the bartenders will work their bespoke mixology magic.

Xuxu COCKTAIL BAR
(Map p70; ☑ 09-309 5529; www.xuxu.co.nz; cnr Galway & Commerce Sts; ⊙ noon-late Mon-Fri, 5pm-late Sat) A winning combination of Asian-tinged

cocktails and tasty dumplings. DJs kick in on weekends.

🍷 Viaduct Harbour & Wynyard Quarter

Dr Rudis MICROBREWERY
(Map p70; ☑ 021 048 7946; www.drrudis.co.nz; Viaduct Harbour, cnr Quay & Hobson Sts; ⊙ 7am-4am) Viaduct Harbour's best views – usually including a bevy of visiting super-yachts – combine with Dr Rudi's very own craft beers and a menu featuring wood-fired pizza and excellent seafood and barbecue platters designed to defeat even the hungriest group. There are also a couple of tenpin bowling lanes to get active on.

Signage is pretty subtle, so head up the escalators and follow your instincts.

Sixteen Tun CRAFT BEER
(Map p70; ☑ 09-368 7712; www.16tun.co.nz; 10-26 Jellicoe St, Wynyard Quarter; tasting 4/6/8 beers $12/18/24; ⊙ 11.30am-late) The glister of burnished copper perfectly complements the liquid amber on offer here in the form of dozens of NZ craft beers by the bottle and a score on tap. If you can't decide, go for a good-value tasting 'crate' of 200mL serves.

Jack Tar PUB
(Map p70; ☑ 09-303 1002; www.jacktar.co.nz; North Wharf, 34-37 Jellicoe St, Wynyard Quarter; ⊙ 8am-late) A top spot for a late-afternoon/early-evening drink and pub grub amid the relaxed vibe of the waterfront Wynyard Quarter.

🍸 Ponsonby & Freemans Bay

Along Ponsonby Rd, the line between cafe, restaurant, bar and club gets blurred. A lot of eateries also have live music or become clubs later on.

Annabel's
WINE BAR

(Map p85; www.annabelswinebar.com; 277 Ponsonby Rd; ⊗3-11pm) A self-described 'neighbourhood bar', Annabel's would also be right at home in the backstreets of Bordeaux or Barcelona. Cheese and charcuterie platters combine with a Eurocentric wine list, while Spanish beers and classic Negroni cocktails also help turn the South Pacific into the south of France. A thoroughly unpretentious affair; worth a stop before or after dining along Ponsonby Rd.

SPQR
BAR

(Map p85; ☑09-360 1710; www.spqrnz.co.nz; 150 Ponsonby Rd, Ponsonby; ⊗noon-late) Quite the best place to see and be seen on the Ponsonby strip, SPQR is a magnet for local scenesters who are quick to nab the tables on the footpath. Head inside for a more discreet assignation lit by the flattering glow of candles reflected in the burnished copper bar. The food is excellent too, especially the Roman-style thin-crust pizza.

Bedford Soda & Liquor
COCKTAIL BAR

(Map p85; ☑09-378 7362; www.bedfordsoda liquor.co.nz; Ponsonby Central, Richmond Rd, Ponsonby; ⊗noon-midnight) Candlelight and a semi-industrial fit-out set the scene for a New York–style bar devoted to the American drinking culture. The cocktails are pricey but worth it: some come wreathed in smoke, others in the alcoholic equivalent of a snow globe, while the 'salted caramel Malteaser whisky milkshake' is exactly as decadent as it sounds.

Dida's Wine Lounge & Tapas Bar
WINE BAR

(Map p85; ☑09-376 2813; www.didas.co.nz; 54 Jervois Rd, Ponsonby; ⊗noon-midnight) Great food and an even better wine list attract a grown-up crowd. There's an associated wine store, providore and cafe next door.

🍸 Grey Lynn

★Freida Margolis
BAR

(Map p85; ☑09-378 6625; www.facebook.com/freidamargolis; 440 Richmond Rd; ⊗4-11pm Sun-Wed, to 2am Thu-Sat) Formerly a butchers – look for the Westlynn Organic Meats sign – this corner location is now a great little neighbourhood bar with the ambience of the backstreets of Bogota. Loyal locals sit outside with their well-behaved dogs, supping on sangria, wine and craft beer, and enjoying eclectic sounds from the owner's big vinyl collection.

GAY & LESBIAN AUCKLAND

The Queen City (as it's known for completely coincidental reasons) has by far the country's biggest gay population, with the bright lights attracting gays and lesbians from all over the country. However, the even brighter lights of Sydney eventually steal many of the 30- to 40-somethings, leaving a gap in the demographic. There are very few gay venues and they only really kick off on the weekends. For the latest, see the monthly magazine *Express* (available from gay venues), or online at www.gayexpress.co.nz.

The big event on the calendar is the **Auckland Pride Festival** (p82). Also worth watching out for are the regular parties held by Urge Events (www.facebook.com/urgebar); the only reliably fun and sexy nights out for the over 30s, they book out quickly.

Venues change with alarming regularity, but these ones were the stayers at the time of writing:

Family (Map p70; ☑09-309 0213; 270 Karangahape Rd, Newton; ⊗9am-4am) Trashy, brash and extremely young, Family gets crammed on weekends, with drag hosts and dancing into the wee hours, both at the back of the ground-level bar and in the club downstairs.

Eagle (Map p70; ☑09-309 4979; www.facebook.com/the.eagle.bar; 259 Karangahape Rd, Newton; ⊗4pm-1am Mon, Tue & Sun, to 2am Wed & Thu, to 4am Fri & Sat) A cosy place for a quiet drink early in the evening, getting more raucous as the night progresses. Get in quick to put your picks on the video jukebox or prepare for an entire evening of Kylie and Taylor.

Centurian (Map p70; ☑09-377 5571; www.centuriansauna.co.nz; 18 Beresford St, Newton; before/after 3pm $25/30; ⊗11am-2am Sun-Thu, to 6am Fri & Sat) Gay men's sauna.

Pocket Bar & Kitchen BAR

(Map p76; ✆09-376 4309; www.pocketbarand kitchen.co.nz; 592 Great North Rd; ⏱4pm-late Tue-Thu, noon-late Fri-Sun) With its spacious and sunny beer garden, Pocket might have to start considering a new name. Colourful street art and a special area for chalk drawing create a family-friendly vibe on weekend afternoons, and later at night the cosy downstairs bar is the place to be. Craft beer, cocktails and a considered wine list combine with interesting bar snacks.

🍸 Newton

⭐**Madame George** BAR

(Map p70; ✆09-308 9039; www.facebook.com/ madamegeorgenz; 490 Karangahape Rd; ⏱5pm-late Tue-Sat) Two patron saints of cool – Elvis Presley and Al Pacino – look down in this compact space along Karangahape Rd. Shoot the breeze with the friendly bar staff over a craft beer or Auckland's best cocktails, or grab a shared table out front and watch the passing theatre of K Rd. It's just like hanging at your hippest mate's place.

Madame George also offers a classy food menu, either at the bar or in a cosy dining room out the back.

⭐**Lovebucket** COCKTAIL BAR, CRAFT BEER

(Map p70; ✆09-869 2469; www.lovebucket. co.nz; K'Road Workshop, 309 Karangahape Rd; ⏱4pm-late Tue-Sun) Lovebucket is a more sophisticated alternative to K Rd's often youthful after-dark vibe. Courtesy of shared ownership with the Hallertau Brewery in West Auckland, Lovebucket's craft-beer selection is one of Auckland's best – including barrel-aged and sour beers. Quirky cocktails and a well-informed wine list join interesting bar snacks such as cheeses, charcuterie and gourmet toasted sandwiches.

⭐**Galbraith's Alehouse** BREWERY

(Map p76; ✆09-379 3557; http://alehouse.co.nz; 2 Mt Eden Rd; ⏱noon-11pm) Brewing real ales and lagers on site, this cosy English-style pub in a grand heritage building offers bliss on tap. There are always more craft beers from around NZ and the world on the guest taps, and the food's also very good. From April to September, Galbraith's Sunday roast is one of Auckland's best.

Wine Cellar WINE BAR

(Map p70; www.facebook.com/winecellarstkevins; St Kevins Arcade, 183 Karangahape Rd, Newton; ⏱5pm-midnight Mon-Thu, to 1am Fri & Sat) Se-creted downstairs in an arcade, the Wine Cellar is dark, grungy and very cool, with regular live music in the neighbouring Whammy Bar (p100).

Shanghai Lil's COCKTAIL BAR

(Map p70; ✆022 096 5950; www.facebook.com/ lilsponsonby; 335 Karangahape Rd; ⏱5pm-late Wed-Sat) Recently relocated to the after-dark scene of Karangahape Rd, a louche old-world Shanghai vibe pervades this small bar, where the owner dispenses charm in a silk Mandarin jacket and octogenarian musicians tickle the ivories for satin-voiced jazz singers. It attracts a widely varied and eclectic crowd, with a healthy quotient of gay men in the mix.

Satya Chai Lounge BAR

(Map p70; ✆09-377 0007; 271 Karangahape Rd; ⏱5.30-10pm) Satya's South Indian restaurants are Auckland institutions, and their Karangahape Rd location has morphed into a raffish bar partnering craft beers – many from Wellington's iconic Garage Project brewery – with rustic and fiery Indian street food. Cocktails and a concise wine list complete the picture. There's no signage, so be brave and push the door open to the cosy interior.

Thirsty Dog PUB

(Map p70; ✆09-377 9190; www.facebook.com/ theThirstyDog; 469 Karangahape Rd; ⏱noon-3am Wed-Sat, to midnight Sun-Tue) This pub has a good beer selection and stacks of live music, along with comedy and poetry slams.

🍷 Mt Eden & Kingsland

Portland Public House BAR

(Map p76; www.facebook.com/theportlandpublic house; 463 New North Rd, Kingsland; ⏱4pm-midnight Mon-Wed, 4pm-2am Thu & Fri, noon-2am Sat, noon-midnight Sun) With mismatched furniture, cartoon-themed art, and lots of hidden nooks and crannies, the Portland Public House is like spending a few lazy hours at a hipster mate's place. It's also an excellent location for live music.

Citizen Park BEER GARDEN

(Map p76; ✆09-846 4964; www.citizenpark.co.nz; 424 New North Rd, Kingsland; ⏱11.30am-late) The easy, breezy beer garden vibe of Citizen Park makes it a top spot to meet friends over a few cold ones, before kicking on to a rugby match at nearby Eden Park (p100) or for dinner in the adjacent Kingsland restaurant strip. Lots of tap beers, punchy cocktails and a top wine list combine with a decent Mexican-accented menu.

Neighbourhood BAR
(Map p76; ☑ 09-846 3773; www.neighbour hood.co.nz; 498 New North Rd, Kingsland; ◷ noon-late; 🛜) With picture windows overlooking Eden Park (p100) and a front terrace that's pick-up central after dark, this upmarket pub is the place to be either side of rugby fixtures. DJs play on weekends.

☆ Entertainment

For listings, check the *New Zealand Herald's Time Out* magazine on Thursday and again in its Saturday edition. Tickets for most major events can be bought from **Ticketek** (☑ 0800 842 538; www.ticketek.co.nz), with an outlet at **SkyCity Theatre** (Map p70; ☑ 09-363 6000; www.skycity.co.nz; cnr Wellesley & Hobson Sts), and **Ticketmaster** (☑ 09-970 9700; www.ticketmaster.co.nz) at **Spark Arena** (Map p74; ☑ 09-358 1250; www.sparkarena.co.nz; Mahuhu Cres) and the **Aotea Centre** (Map p70; ☑ 09-309 2677; www.aucklandlive.co.nz; 50 Mayoral Dr). **iTicket** (☑ 0508 484 253; www.iticket.co.nz) handles a lot of smaller gig and dance party tickets.

Theatre & Comedy

ASB Waterfront Theatre THEATRE
(Map p70; ☑ box office 0800 282 849; www.asb waterfronttheatre.co.n; 138 Halsey St, Wynyard Quarter) The new ASB Waterfront Theatre is used by the Auckland Theatre Company and also for occasional one-off shows and concerts. There's a good selection of bars and restaurants in close proximity.

AUCKLAND TOP 10 PLAYLIST

Download these Auckland songs to your MP3 player:

➡ 'Me at the Museum, You in the Wintergardens' – Tiny Ruins (2014)

➡ '400 Lux' – Lorde (2013)

➡ 'Grey Lynn Park' – The Veils (2011)

➡ 'Auckland CBD Part Two' – Lawrence Arabia (2009)

➡ 'Forever Thursday' – Tim Finn (2008)

➡ 'Riverhead' – Goldenhorse (2004)

➡ 'A Brief Reflection' – Nesian Mystik (2002)

➡ 'Dominion Road' – The Mutton Birds (1992)

➡ 'Andy' – The Front Lawn (1989)

➡ 'One Tree Hill' – U2 (1987)

Q Theatre THEATRE
(Map p70; ☑ 09-309 9771; www.qtheatre.co.nz; 305 Queen St) Theatre by various companies and intimate live music. Silo Theatre (www.silotheatre.co.nz) often performs here.

Classic Comedy Club COMEDY
(Map p70; ☑ 09-373 4321; www.comedy.co.nz; 321 Queen St; ◷ 6.30pm-late) Stand-up performances most nights, with legendary late-night shows during the annual Comedy Festival (p83).

Live Music

Auckland Town Hall CLASSICAL MUSIC
(Map p70; ☑ 09-309 2677; www.aucklandlive.co.nz; 305 Queen St) This elegant Edwardian venue (1911) hosts the NZ Symphony Orchestra (www.nzso.co.nz) and Auckland Philharmonia (www.apo.co.nz), among others.

Whammy Bar LIVE MUSIC
(Map p70; www.facebook.com/thewhammybar; 183 Karangahape Rd, Newton; ◷ 8.30pm-4am Wed-Sat) Small, but a stalwart on the live indie music scene nonetheless.

Ding Dong Lounge LIVE MUSIC
(Map p70; ☑ 09-377 4712; www.dingdonglounge nz.com; 26 Wyndham St; ◷ 6pm-4am Wed-Fri, 8pm-4am Sat) Rock, indie and alternative sounds from live bands and DJs, washed down with craft beer.

Power Station LIVE MUSIC
(Map p76; www.powerstation.net.nz; 33 Mt Eden Rd, Eden Terrace) Midrange venue popular with up-and-coming overseas acts and established Kiwi bands.

Spectator Sports

Eden Park SPECTATOR SPORT
(Map p76; ☑ 09-815 5551; www.edenpark.co.nz; Reimers Ave, Mt Eden) This stadium hosts top rugby (winter) and cricket (summer) tests by the All Blacks (www.allblacks.com) and the Black Caps (www.blackcaps.co.nz), respectively. It's also the home ground of Auckland Rugby (www.aucklandrugby.co.nz), the Blues Super Rugby team (www.theblues.co.nz) and Auckland Cricket (www.aucklandcricket.co.nz). Catch the train from Britomart to Kingsland and follow the crowds.

Mt Smart Stadium SPECTATOR SPORT
(Map p68; ☑ 09-366 2048; www.mtsmart stadium.co.nz; 2 Beasley Ave, Penrose) Home ground for the Warriors rugby league team (www.warriors.kiwi), Auckland Football

Federation (www.aucklandfootball.org. nz) and Athletics Auckland (www.athletic-sauckland.co.nz). Also *really* big concerts.

ASB Tennis Centre SPECTATOR SPORT
(Map p74; www.tennisauckland.co.nz; 1 Tennis Lane, Parnell) In January the women's and men's ASB Classic (p82) is held here.

North Shore Events Centre SPECTATOR SPORT
(Map p68; ✍09-443 8199; www.nsevents centre.co.nz; Argus Pl, Wairau Valley) One of the two home courts of the NZ Breakers basketball team (www.nzbreakers.co.nz) and an occasional concert venue. The other home court is at Spark Arena (p100).

🛍 Shopping

Followers of fashion should head to the Britomart (p90) precinct, Newmarket's Teed and Nuffield Sts, and Ponsonby Rd. For vintage clothing and secondhand boutiques, try Karangahape Rd (K Rd) or Ponsonby Rd.

🛍 City Centre

★ Real Groovy MUSIC
(Map p70; ✍09-302 3940; www.realgroovy.co.nz; 369 Queen St; ⊙9am-7pm) Masses of new, secondhand and rare releases in vinyl and CD format, as well as concert tickets, giant posters, DVDs, books, magazines and clothes.

★ Unity Books BOOKS
(Map p70; ✍09-307 0731; www.unitybooks.co.nz; 19 High St; ⊙8.30am-7pm Mon-Sat, 10am-6pm Sun) The inner-city's best independent bookshop.

Strangely Normal CLOTHING
(Map p70; ✍09-309 0600; www.strangely normal.com; 19 O'Connell St; ⊙10am-6pm Mon-Sat, 11am-4pm Sun) Quality, NZ-made men's tailored shirts straight out of *Blue Hawaii* sit alongside hipster hats, sharp shoes and cufflinks.

Barkers' CLOTHING
(Map p70; ✍09-303 2377; www.barkersonline. co.nz; 1 High St; ⊙9am-7pm Mon-Sat, 10am-5pm Sun) This NZ menswear label has lifted its game and uncovered a cache of cool it never knew it had. Proof is this elegant concept store with its own cafe, upstairs 'groom room' and, of course, quality tailored clothes, artfully displayed.

Pauanesia GIFTS & SOUVENIRS
(Map p70; ✍09-366 7282; www.pauanesia.co.nz; 35 High St; ⊙9.30am-6.30pm Tue-Fri, 10am-5pm Sat-Mon) Homewares and gifts with a Polynesian and Kiwiana influence.

🛍 Britomart

Zambesi CLOTHING
(Map p70; ✍09-303 1701; www.zambesi.co.nz; 56 Tyler St; ⊙10am-6pm Mon-Fri, 11am-5pm Sat & Sun) Iconic NZ label much sought after by local and international celebs. Also in Ponsonby (Map p85; ✍09-360 7391; 169 Ponsonby Rd; ⊙10am-6pm Mon-Fri, 11am-5pm Sat & Sun) and Newmarket (Map p73; ✍09-523 1000; 38 Osborne St; ⊙10am-6pm Mon-Fri, 11am-5pm Sat & Sun).

Karen Walker CLOTHING
(Map p70; ✍09-309 6299; www.karenwalker.com; 18 Te Ara Tahuhu Walkway, Britomart; ⊙10am-6pm) Join Madonna and Kirsten Dunst in wearing Walker's cool (but pricey) threads. Also in Ponsonby Rd (Map p85; ✍09-361 6723; 128a Ponsonby Rd, Grey Lynn; ⊙10am-5.30pm Mon-Sat, 11am-4pm Sun) and Newmarket (Map p73; ✍09-522 4286; 6 Balm St, ⊙10am-6pm).

🛍 Newton

★ St Kevins Arcade SHOPPING CENTRE
(Map p70; www.stkevinsarcade.co.nz; 183 Karangahape Rd) Built in 1924, this historic, renovated shopping arcade has interesting stores selling vintage clothing and organic and sustainable goods. The arcade also has excellent cafes and restaurants.

Bread & Butter Letter ARTS & CRAFTS
(Map p70; ✍09-940 5065; www.breadandbutter letter.co.nz; 225 Karangahape Rd; ⊙10am-6pm Mon-Fri, 10am-5pm Sat, 11am-5pm Sun) Sells an excellent selection of arts, crafts, foodstuffs and homewares from local New Zealand designers. Bread & Butter Letter also offers retro and vintage Kiwiana products for sale.

🛍 Other Areas

★ Royal Jewellery Studio JEWELLERY
(Map p76; ✍09-846 0200; www.royal jewellerystudio.com; 486 New North Rd, Kingsland; ⊙10am-4pm Tue-Sun) Work by local artisans, including beautiful Māori designs and authentic *pounamu* (greenstone) jewellery.

⭐**Otara Flea Market**   MARKET

(Map p68; ☑09-274 0830; www.otaraflea market.co.nz; Newbury St; ☺6am-noon Sat) Held in the car park between the Manukau Polytech and the Otara town centre, this market has a palpable Polynesian atmosphere and is good for South Pacific food, music and fashion. Catch a train on the southern line to Papatoetoe and then switch to a bus to Otara.

Women's Bookshop   BOOKS

(Map p85; ☑09-376 4399; www.womensbook shop.co.nz; 105 Ponsonby Rd, Ponsonby; ☺10am-6pm Mon-Fri, to 5pm Sat & Sun) Excellent independent bookshop.

ⓘ Information

INTERNET ACCESS

Auckland Council offers free wi-fi in parts of the city centre, Newton, Ponsonby, Kingsland, Mt Eden and Parnell. All public libraries offer free wi-fi, and a few internet cafes catering to gaming junkies are scattered about the inner city.

MEDICAL SERVICES

Auckland City Hospital (☑09-367 0000; www.adhb.govt.nz; 2 Park Rd, Grafton; ☺24hr) The city's main hospital has a dedicated accident and emergency (A&E) service.

Starship Children's Health (☑09-307 4949; www.adhb.govt.nz; Park Rd, Grafton; ☺24hr) Has its own A&E department.

TOURIST INFORMATION

Auckland International Airport i-SITE (Map p68; ☑09-365 9925; www.aucklandnz.com; International Arrivals Hall; ☺6.30am-10.30pm)

Cornwall Park Information Centre (Map p68; ☑09-630 8485; www.cornwallpark.co.nz; Huia Lodge, Michael Horton Dr; ☺10am-4pm)

Karanga Kiosk (Map p70; ☑09-365 1290; cnr Jellicoe & Halsey Sts, Wynyard Quarter; ☺9.30am-4.30pm) Looking like a precariously stacked set of shipping containers, this volunteer-run centre dispenses information on goings on around the waterfront.

Princes Wharf i-SITE (☑09-365 9914; www. aucklandnz.com; ☺9am-5pm) Auckland's main official information centre, incorporating the **DOC Auckland Visitor Centre** (Map p70; ☑09-379 6476; www.doc.govt.nz; ☺9am-5pm Mon-Fri, extended hours Nov-Mar).

SkyCity i-SITE (Map p70; ☑09-365 9918; www.aucklandnz.com; SkyCity Atrium, cnr Victoria & Federal Sts; ☺9am-5pm)

Visit Devonport (Map p78; www.visitdevonport. co.nz; Victoria Rd; ☺9am-5pm Mon-Fri; ☎)

ⓘ Getting There & Away

AIR

Auckland is the main international gateway to NZ, and a hub for domestic flights. **Auckland Airport** (AKL; Map p68; ☑09-275 0789; www. aucklandairport.co.nz; Ray Emery Dr, Mangere) is 21km south of the city centre. It has separate international and domestic terminals, a 10-minute walk apart from each other via a signposted footpath; a free shuttle service operates every 15 minutes (5am to 10.30pm). Both terminals have left-luggage facilities, eateries, ATMs and car-rental desks.

The major domestic services flying to/from Auckland include the following:

Air New Zealand (☑09-357 3000; www.air-newzealand.co.nz) Flies to Kerikeri, Whangarei, Tauranga, Rotorua, Taupo, Gisborne, New Plymouth, Napier, Whanganui, Palmerston North, Kapiti Coast, Wellington, Nelson, Blenheim, Christchurch, Queenstown and Dunedin.

Air Chathams (☑09-257 0261; www.air-chathams.co.nz) Flies to Whakatane, Whanganui and the Chatham Islands.

Barrier Air (☑0800 900 600, 09-275 9120; www.barrierair.kiwi; adult/child from $99/94) Flies to Great Barrier Island (Claris and Okiwi) and Kaitaia.

FlyMySky (☑09-256 7025, 0800 222 123; www.flymysky.co.nz; adult/child one way $109/79) Flies to Claris, Great Barrier Island.

Jetstar (☑0800 800 995; www.jetstar.com) Flies to Wellington, Christchurch, Queenstown, Dunedin, Palmerston North, New Plymouth, Nelson and Napier.

BUS

Coaches depart from 172 Quay St, opposite the **Ferry Building** (p104), except for InterCity services, which depart from **SkyCity Coach Terminal** (Map p70; 102 Hobson St). Many southbound services also stop at the airport.

Go Kiwi (☑0800 446 549; www.go-kiwi.co.nz) offers daily Auckland City–Auckland Airport–Thames–Tairua–Hot Water Beach–Whitianga shuttles.

InterCity (☑09-583 5780; www.intercity. co.nz) has direct services to Kerikeri (from $37, 4½ hours, three daily), Hamilton (from $16, two hours, 16 daily), New Plymouth (from $35, 6¼ hours, daily), Taupo (from $25, five hours, five daily) and Wellington (from $29, 11 hours, four daily).

Naked Bus (www.nakedbus.com) travels along SH1 as far north as Paihia ($25, four hours) and as far south as Wellington (from $25, 11 hours), as well as heading to Tauranga ($15, 3½ hours), Rotorua ($18, 3¾ hours) and Napier (from $24, 12 hours). Some services are operated by ManaBus (www.manabus.com).

CAR, CARAVAN & CAMPERVAN
Hire

Auckland has many hire agencies around Beach Rd and Stanley St close to the city centre.

A2B (☑ 0800 545 000; www.a2b-car-rental.co.nz; 167 Beach Rd; ☺ 7am-7pm Nov-Apr, 7.30am-5pm May-Oct) Cheap older cars with no visible hire-car branding.

Apex Car Rentals (☑ 09-307 1063; www.apex-rentals.co.nz; 156 Beach Rd; ☺ 8am-5pm)

Budget (☑ 09-976 2270; www.budget.co.nz; 163 Beach Rd; ☺ 7am-6pm Mon-Fri, 8am-5pm Sat & Sun)

Escape (☑ 0800 216 171; www.escaperentals.co.nz; 61 The Strand; ☺ 9am-3pm) Eccentrically painted campervans.

Go Rentals (☑ 09-257 5142; www.gorentals.co.nz; Bay 4-10, Cargo Central, George Bolt Memoral Dr, Mangere; ☺ 6am-10pm)

Hertz (☑ 09-367 6350; www.hertz.co.nz; 154 Victoria St; ☺ 7.30am-5.30pm)

Jucy (☑ 0800 399 736; www.jucy.co.nz; 2-16 The Strand; ☺ 8am-5pm)

Kea, Maui & Britz (☑ 09-255 3910; www.maui.co.nz; 36 Richard Pearse Dr, Mangere; ☺ 8am-4.30pm)

NZ Frontiers (☑ 09-299 6705; www.newzealandfrontiers.com; 30 Laurie Ave, Papakura)

Omega (☑ 09-377 5573; www.omegarentals.com; 75 Beach Rd; ☺ 8am-5pm)

Quality (☑ 0800 680 123; www.qualityrental.co.nz; 8 Andrew Baxter Dr, Mangere; ☺ 8am-4pm)

Thrifty (☑ 09-309 0111; www.thrifty.co.nz; 150 Khyber Pass Rd; ☺ 8am-5pm)

Wilderness Motorhomes (☑ 09-255 5300; www.wilderness.co.nz; 11 Pavilion Dr, Mangere; ☺ 8am-5pm)

Purchase

Mechanical inspection services are on hand at secondhand car fairs, where sellers pay to display their cars.

Auckland Car Fair (☑ 09-529 2233; www.carfair.co.nz; Ellerslie Racecourse, Greenlane East; display fee $35; ☺ 9am-noon Sun) Auckland's largest car fair.

Auckland City Car Fair (☑ 09-837 7817; www.aucklandcitycarfair.co.nz; 27 Alten Rd; display fee $30; ☺ 8am-1pm Sat)

MOTORCYCLE

NZ Motorcycle Rentals (☑ 09-486 2472; www.nzbike.com; 72 Barrys Point Rd, Takapuna; per day $140-290) Guided tours of NZ also available.

TRAIN

Northern Explorer (☑ 0800 872 467; www.greatjourneysofnz.co.nz) trains leave from

Auckland Strand Station (Ngaoho Pl) at 7.45am on Monday, Thursday and Saturday and arrive in Wellington at 6.25pm. Stops include Hamilton (2½ hours), Otorohanga (three hours), Tongariro National Park (5½ hours), Ohakune (six hours), Palmerston North (8½ hours) and Paraparaumu (9¾ hours). Standard fares to Wellington range from $119 to $219.

ⓘ Getting Around

TO/FROM THE AIRPORT

Taxis usually costs $80 to $90 to the city, more if you strike traffic.

SkyBus (☑ 09-222 0084; www.skybus.co.nz; one way/return adult $18/32, child $6/12; ☎) runs bright-red buses between the terminals and the city, every 10 to 15 minutes from 5.15am to 7pm and at least half-hourly through the night. Stops include Mt Eden Rd or Dominion Rd, Symonds St, Queen St and Britomart. Reservations are not required; buy a ticket from the driver, the airport kiosk or online. Small discount if you book online.

Super Shuttle (☑ 09-522 5100; www.supershuttle.co.nz) is a convenient door-to-door shuttle charging $35 for one person heading between the airport and a city hotel; the price increases for outlying suburbs. Save money by sharing a shuttle.

A lengthier alternative is to catch the 380 bus to Onehunga ($3.50, 30 minutes, at least hourly 7am to 7.30pm), where you can catch a train to Britomart in the city centre ($5.50, 27 minutes, half-hourly 6am to 10pm).

BICYCLE

Auckland Transport (p104) publishes free cycle maps, available from public buildings such as stations, libraries and i-SITEs. Bikes can be taken on most ferries and trains for free (dependent on available space), but only folding bikes are allowed on buses.

Adventure Cycles (☑ 09-940 2453; www.adventure-auckland.co.nz; 9 Premier Ave, Western Springs; per day $30-40, per week $120-160, per month $260-350; ☺ 7.30am-7pm Thu-Mon) hires road, mountain and touring bikes, runs a buy-back scheme and does repairs.

CAR & MOTORCYCLE

Auckland's motorways jam badly at peak times, particularly the Northern and Southern Motorways. It's best to avoid them between 7am and 9am, and from 4pm to 7pm. Things also get tight around 3pm during term time, which is the end of the school day.

Expect to pay for parking in central Auckland from 8am to 10pm. Most parking meters are pay-and-display and take coins and credit cards;

display tickets inside your windscreen. City fringe parking is free on Sundays.

Prices can be steep at parking buildings. Better value are the council-run, open-air car parks near the old train station at 126 Beach Rd ($8 per day) and on Ngaoho Pl, off the Strand ($7 per day).

PUBLIC TRANSPORT

The **Auckland Transport** (☑ 09-366 6400; www.at.govt.nz) information service covers buses, trains and ferries, and has an excellent trip-planning feature.

Auckland's public transport system is run by a hodgepodge of different operators, but there is now an integrated AT HOP smartcard (www.athop.co.nz), which provides discounts of at least 20% on most buses, trains and ferries. AT HOP cards cost $10 (nonrefundable), so are really only worthwhile if you're planning an extended stay in Auckland. An AT HOP day pass costs $18 and provides a day's transport on most trains and buses and on North Shore ferries.

Bus

Bus routes spread their tentacles throughout the city and you can purchase a ticket from the driver. Some bus stops have electronic displays giving an estimate of waiting times, but be warned, they are often inaccurate.

Single-ride fares in the inner city are $3.50/2 (adult/child). If you're travelling further afield, there are fare stages from $5.50/3 to $11/6.

The most useful services are the environmentally friendly Link Buses that loop in both directions around three routes (taking in many of the major sights) from 7am to 11pm:

City Link (adult/child $1/50c, every seven to 10 minutes) Wynyard Quarter, Britomart, Queen St, Karangahape Rd.

Inner Link (adult/child $3.50/2, every 10 to 15 minutes) Queen St, SkyCity, Victoria Park, Ponsonby Rd, Karangahape Rd, Museum, Newmarket, Parnell and Britomart.

Outer Link (maximum $5.50, every 15 minutes) Art Gallery, Ponsonby, Herne Bay, Westmere, MOTAT 2, Pt Chevalier, Mt Albert, St Lukes Mall, Mt Eden, Newmarket, Museum, Parnell, University.

Ferry

Auckland's Edwardian baroque **Ferry Building** (Map p70; 99 Quay St) sits grandly at the end of Queen St. Ferry services are run by **Fullers** (☑ 09-367 9111; www.fullers.co.nz) (to Bayswater, **Birkenhead** (Map p68), **Devonport** (Map p78), Great Barrier Island, Half Moon Bay, **Northcote Point** (Map p68), Motuihe, Motutapu, Rangitoto and Waiheke) and **360 Discovery** (Map p70; ☑ 09-307 8005; www.fullers.co.nz) (to Coromandel, Gulf Harbour, Motuihe, Rotoroa and Tiritiri Matangi). Both leave from an adjacent pier.

Sealink (Map p70; ☑ 0800 732 546; www.sealink.co.nz) ferries to Great Barrier Island leave from Wynyard Wharf, along with some car ferries to Waiheke, but most of the Waiheke car ferries leave from Half Moon Bay in east Auckland.

Train

Auckland's train services are limited and infrequent but the trains are generally clean, cheap and on time – although any hiccup on the lines can bring down the entire network.

Impressive **Britomart train station** (Queen St) has food retailers, foreign-exchange facilities and a ticket office. Downstairs there are left-luggage lockers.

There are just four train routes. One heads west to Swanson, while the other three head south, terminating in Onehunga, Manukau and Pukekohe. Services are at least hourly from around 6am to 10pm (later on the weekends). Buy a ticket from machines or ticket offices at train stations. All trains have wheelchair ramps.

TAXI

Auckland's many taxis usually operate from ranks, but they also cruise popular areas. **Auckland Co-op Taxis** (☑ 09-300 3000; www.cooptaxi.co.nz) is one of the biggest companies. Cab companies set their own fares, so there's some variance in rates. There's a surcharge for transport to and from the airport and cruise ships, and for phone orders. Uber also operates in Auckland.

HAURAKI GULF ISLANDS

Stretching between Auckland and the Coromandel Peninsula, the Hauraki Gulf is dotted with *motu* (islands), and is as equally stunning as Northland's Bay of Islands. Some islands are only minutes from the city and make excellent day trips. Wine-soaked Waiheke and volcanic Rangitoto really shouldn't be missed. Great Barrier requires more effort (and cash) to get to, but provides an idyllic escape from modern life.

There are more than 50 islands in the Hauraki Gulf Marine Park, many administered by DOC. Some are good-sized islands, others are no more than rocks jutting out of the sea. They're loosely put into two categories: recreation and conservation. The recreation islands can easily be visited and their harbours are dotted with yachts in summer. The conservation islands, however, have restricted access. Permits are required to visit some, while others are closed refuges for the preservation of rare plants and animals, especially birds.

Rangitoto & Motutapu Islands

POP 75

Sloping elegantly from the Hauraki Gulf, 259m-high Rangitoto (www.rangitoto.org) is the largest and youngest of Auckland's volcanic cones. As recently as 600 years ago it erupted from the sea and was active for several years before settling down. Māori living on Motutapu (Sacred Island; www.motutapu.org.nz), to which Rangitoto is joined by a causeway, certainly witnessed the eruptions, as footprints have been found embedded in ash, and oral history details several generations living here before the eruption.

In contrast to Rangitoto, Motutapu is mainly covered in grassland, which is grazed by sheep and cattle. Archaeologically, this is a very significant island, with the traces of centuries of continuous human habitation etched into its landscape.

In 2011 both islands were officially declared predator-free after an extensive eradication program. Endangered birds such as takahe and tieke (saddleback) have been released and others such as kakariki and bellbirds have returned of their own volition.

🏃 Activities

Rangitoto makes for a great day trip. Its harsh scoria slopes hold a surprising amount of flora (including the world's largest pohutukawa forest) and there are excellent walks, but you'll need sturdy shoes and plenty of water. Although it looks steep, up close it's shaped more like an egg sizzling in a pan. The walk to the summit only takes an hour and is rewarded with sublime views. At the top a loop walk goes around the crater's rim. A walk to lava caves branches off the summit walk and takes 30 minutes return. There's an information board with walk maps at the wharf.

🛏 Sleeping

The only accommodation option on the islands is a basic **DOC campsite** (www.doc.govt.nz; Home Bay, Motutapu; sites per adult/child $8/4) at Home Bay, Motutapu. It's a three-hour walk from **Rangitoto Wharf** (Map p68); otherwise Fullers runs direct ferries to Home Bay on weekends and public holidays.

ℹ Getting There & Around

Fullers (📞 09-367 9111; www.fullers.co.nz; adult/child return $33/16.50) has ferry services to Rangitoto from Auckland's **Ferry Building**

MARINE MAMMALS

The gulf is a busy highway for marine mammals. Sei, minke and Bryde's whales are regularly seen in its outer reaches, along with orcas and bottlenose dolphins. You might even spy a passing humpback.

(p104) (adult/child return $33/16.50, 25 minutes, three daily on weekdays, four on weekends) and Devonport (two daily). It also operates the **Volcanic Explorer** (📞 09-367 9111; www.fullers.co.nz; adult/child incl ferry $68/34; ⊙ departs Auckland 9.15am & 12.15pm), a guided tour around the island in a canopied 'road train'. 'Early Bird' ferry tickets (adult/child $20/10) departing Auckland at 7.30am are available online if you're after a good deal.

Waiheke Island

POP 9200

Close to Auckland and blessed with its own warm, dry microclimate, Waiheke Island has long been a favourite escape for city dwellers and visitors alike. On the island's landward side, emerald waters lap at rocky bays, while its ocean flank has excellent sandy beaches.

While beaches are Waiheke's biggest drawcard, wine is a close second. There are around 30 boutique wineries scattered about, many with tasting rooms, swanky restaurants and breathtaking views. The island also boasts plenty of quirky galleries and craft stores, a lasting legacy of its hippyish past.

When you've had enough of supping, dining, lazing on the sand and splashing in the surf, there are plenty of other pursuits to engage in. A network of walking trails leads through nature reserves and past the clifftop holiday homes of the Auckland elite. The kayaking is excellent and there are ziplines to whizz along and clay pigeons to shoot.

👁 Sights

Beaches

Waiheke's two best beaches are **Onetangi**, a long stretch of white sand at the centre of the island, and **Palm Beach**, a pretty little horseshoe bay between Oneroa and Onetangi. Both have nudist sections; head west just past some rocks in both cases. **Oneroa** and neighbouring **Little Oneroa** are also excellent, but you'll be sharing the waters with moored yachts in summer. Reached by an unsealed road through farmland, **Man O' War Bay** is a sheltered beach that's excellent for swimming.

Waiheke Island

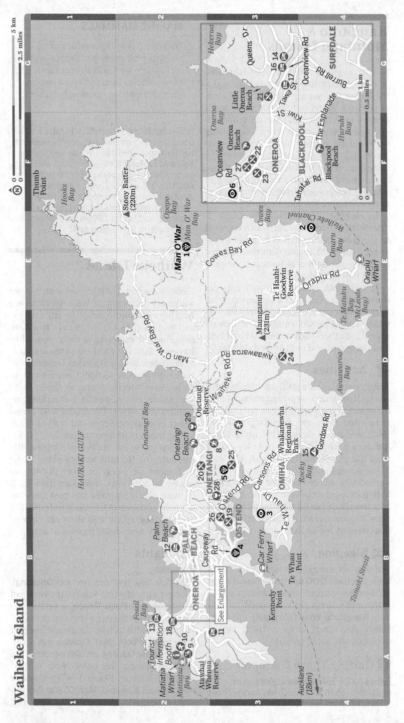

5 km

2.5 miles

G **F** **E** **D** **C** **B** **A**

SURFDALE

Queens Dr

Heketua Bay

16 14

Oceanview Rd

Burrell Rd

Little Oneroa Beach

21

Kiwi St

Tawa St

17

ONEROA

BLACKPOOL

1 km

0.5 miles

Oceanview Rd

Oneroa Bay

Oneroa Beach

27

22

The Esplanade

Huruhi Bay

23

Tahatai Rd

Blackpool Beach

6

Thumb Point

Hooks Bay

Stony Batter (220m)

Opopo Bay

Man O'War

1

Man O'War Bay

Cowes Bay

2

Waiheke Channel

Cowes Bay Rd

Te Haahi-Goodwin Reserve

Omaru Bay

Orapiu Rd

Orapiu Wharf

Maunganui (231m)

Te Matuku Bay (McLeods Bay)

Awaawaroa Rd

24

Avaawaroa Bay

HAURAKI GULF

Man O'War Bay Rd

Onetangi Bay

Onetangi Reserve

29

Waiheke Rd

Onetangi Beach

7

Whakanewha Regional Park

Gordons Rd

15

OMIHA

Rocky Bay

20

ONETANGI

28

8

25

5

19

Ostend Rd

Carsons Rd

Te Whau Dr

Palm Beach

26

OSTEND

3

PALM BEACH

12

Causeway Rd

4

Car Ferry Wharf

Te Whau Point

Tamaki Strait

Fossil Bay

Tourist Information

13

18

10

Matiatia Wharf

Booth

9

ONEROA

11

See Enlargement

Atawhai Whenua Reserve

Matiatia Bay

Kennedy Point

Auckland (18km)

Waiheke Island

Wineries

★ Man O' War
WINERY

(☑ 09-372 9678; www.manowarvineyards.co.nz; 725 Man O' War Bay Rd; ⊙ 11am-4pm Mon-Fri, to 6pm Sat & Sun Dec-Feb, 11am-4pm Mar-Nov) Settle in with a tapas platter and a glass of Man O' War's Valhalla Chardonnay at Waiheke's only beachfront tasting room. If the weather is good, go for a swim in beautiful Man O' War Bay.

Stonyridge
WINERY

(☑ 09-372 8822; www.stonyridge.com; 80 Onetangi Rd; tastings per wine $4-18; ⊙ 11.30am-5pm) 🍃 Waiheke's most famous vineyard is home to world-famous reds, an atmospheric cafe and the occasional dance party. Order a bottle of wine and a gigantic deli platter and retreat to one of the cabanas in the garden.

Goldie Estate
WINERY

(☑ 09-372 7493; www.goldieestate.co.nz; 18 Causeway Rd, Surfdale; tastings refundable with purchase $10; ⊙ noon-4pm Wed-Sun) Founded as Goldwater Estate in 1978, this is Waiheke's pioneering vineyard. The attached delicatessen sells well-stocked baskets for a picnic among the vines ($55 for two people).

Wild On Waiheke
WINERY, BREWERY

(☑ bookings for current week 09-372 3434, future and group bookings 09-372 4225; www.wildonwaiheke.co.nz; 82 Onetangi Rd; tastings per beer or wine $2-3; ⊙ 11am-4pm Thu-Mon, daily late Dec-Easter; 🏄) This winery and microbrewery offers tastings, archery, laser clay shooting, *pétanque*, a sandpit and a giant chessboard.

Art, Culture & History

The *Waiheke Art Map* brochure lists galleries and craft stores.

Connells Bay
GARDENS

(☑ 09-372 8957; www.connellsbay.co.nz; 142 Cowes Bay Rd; adult/child $30/15; ⊙ by appointment mid-Oct–mid-Apr) A pricey but excellent private sculpture park featuring a stellar roster of NZ artists. Admission is by way of a two-hour guided tour; book ahead.

Dead Dog Bay
GARDENS

(☑ 09-372 6748; www.deaddogbay.co.nz; 100 Margaret Reeve Lane; adult/child $10/free; ⊙ 9am-5pm) Wander steep pathways through privately owned rainforest, wetlands and gardens scattered with sculpture. Cash only.

Waiheke Island Artworks ARTS CENTRE
(2 Korora Rd, Oneroa) The Artworks complex houses the **Artworks Theatre** (☑09-372 2941; www.artworkstheatre.org.nz), the **Waiheke Island Community Cinema** (☑09-372 4240; www.waihekecinema.net; tickets adult/child $15/8), the attention-grabbing **Waiheke Community Art Gallery** (☑09-372 9907; www.waihekeartgallery.org.nz; ⊙10am-4pm) FREE and **Whittaker's Musical Museum** (☑09-372 5573; www.musical-museum. org; suggested donation $5; ⊙1-4pm, live shows 1.30pm Sat), a collection of antique instruments. This is also the place for free internet access, either on a terminal at the **Waiheke Library** (☑09-374 1325; www. aucklandlibraries.govt.nz; ⊙9am-6pm Mon-Fri, 10.30am-4pm Sat; 🛜) or on Artworks' wi-fi network.

🏃 Activities

The island's beautiful coastal walks (ranging from one to three hours) include the 3km **Cross Island Walkway** (from Onetangi to Rocky Bay). Other tracks traverse **Whakanewha Regional Park**, a haven for rare coastal birds and geckos, and the Royal Forest & Bird Protection Society's three reserves: **Onetangi** (Waiheke Rd), **Te Haahi-Goodwin** (Orapiu Rd) and **Atawhai Whenua** (Ocean View Rd).

Te Ara Hura is a 100km network of connected trails taking in coastline, forests, vineyard stops and historic places. Route markers indicate the way ahead on the island, and more information and detailed maps are available online at www.aucklandcouncil.govt.nz. Search for 'Waiheke Island Walkways'.

EcoZip Adventures ADVENTURE SPORTS
(☑09-372 5646; www.ecozipadventures.co.nz; 150 Trig Hill Rd; adult/child/family $119/79/317; ⊙9am-5pm) With vineyard, native bush and ocean views, EcoZip's three separate 200m zip-lines make for an exciting ride, and there's a gentle 1.5km walk back up through the bush after the thrills. Costs include free transfers from Matiatia Wharf (p111) or Oneroa if you don't have your own transport. Bookings are essential.

Ross Adventures KAYAKING
(☑09-372 5550; www.kayakwaiheke.co.nz; Matiatia Beach; half-/full-day trips $125/195, per 1/2/3/6hr $30/45/50/60) It's the fervently held opinion of Ross that Waiheke offers kayaking every bit as good as the legendary Abel Tasman

National Park. He should know – he's been offering guided kayak trips for 20 years. Experienced sea kayakers can comfortably circumnavigate the island in four days, exploring coves and sand spits inaccessible by land. Paddle boards also available for hire.

Waiheke Bike Hire CYCLING
(☑09-372 7937; www.waihekebikehire.co.nz; Matiatia; per day $35) Hires bikes from its base at the car park near the wharf.

🧭 Tours

Hike Bike Ako WALKING, CYCLING
(☑021 465 373; www.hikebikeako.co.nz; from $129; ⊙Nov-Mar) Explore the island with Māori guides on a walking or an e-biking tour, or a combination of both. Tours include pick up from the ferry, and a large dose of Māori legend, history and culture.

iWalkWaiheke WALKING
(☑021 960 690; www.iwalkwaiheke.co.nz; 11 Totara Rd, Onetangi; day walks per person $195) 🌿 Options include half- and full-day walks taking in the island's forests and beaches, and two-day/one-night walks including meals, accommodation and vineyard visits. Operator Vicki Angland has been resident on the island for more than 20 years, and walks recognise the framework of an eco policy reinforcing the island's environmental, cultural and conservation aspects.

Waiheke Island Wine Tours TOURS
(☑09-372 2140; www.waihekeislandwinetours. co.nz) Options include Views, Vines & Wines ($125 per person, six hours with a two-hour break for lunch at a restaurant of your choice), tailor-made Platinum Private Tours ($560 per couple) and Indulgence Two-Day Tours ($1100 per person including two nights' accommodation).

Potiki Adventures CULTURAL
(☑021 422 773; www.potikiadventures.co.nz; adult/child $150/80) Day-long island tours from a Māori cultural perspective, including beaches, a bush walk, a vineyard visit and demonstrations of traditional musical instruments and weaving.

Ananda Tours TOURS
(☑09-372 7530; www.ananda.co.nz) Wine tours ($120), gourmet wine and food tours ($185), and a wine connoisseurs' tour ($295) are among the options. Small-group, informal tours can be customised, including visits to artists' studios.

✦ Festivals & Events

Headland Sculpture on the Gulf　　ART
(www.sotg.nz; ⊙Feb) A 2.5km cliff-top sculpture walk, held for a month in February in odd-numbered years.

Waiheke Wine & Food Festival　FOOD & DRINK
(http://festival.waihekewine.co.nz; ⊙Mar/Apr) Four days of wine, food and music events. Seventeen different vineyards are involved, and shuttle buses travel between the different locations.

🛏 Sleeping

Waiheke is so popular in the summer holidays that many locals rent out their houses and bugger off elsewhere. You'll need to book ahead and even then there are very few bargains. Prices drop considerably in winter, especially midweek. For midrange accommodation, a good option is to book a holiday home through www.bookabach.co.nz or www.holidayhouses.co.nz.

★Fossil Bay Lodge　　　　CABIN $
(☑09-372 8371; www.fossilbay.net; 58 Korora Rd, Oneroa; s $60, d $85-90, tent $100-120, apt $130; ☎) Three cabins face the main building, which houses the communal toilets, kitchen and living area, and a compact self-contained upstairs apartment. 'Glamping' tents each have a proper bed and their own toilet, and one also includes a private outdoor kitchenette. Apart from the occasional squawking duck – or toddler from the adjacent Steiner kindergarten – it's a very peaceful place.

Hekerua Lodge　　　　　HOSTEL $
(☑09-372 8990; www.hekerualodge.co.nz; 11 Hekerua Rd, Oneroa; campsites $20, dm $32-35, s/d/tw $60/90/90; ☎▨) This secluded hostel is surrounded by native bush and has a barbecue, stone-tiled pool, spa pool, sunny deck, casual lounge area and its own walking track. It's far from luxurious, but it has a laid-back and social feel.

Poukaraka Flats Campsite　CAMPGROUND $
(☑09-301 0101; www.regionalparks.auckland council.govt.nz; Gordons Rd; sites per adult/child $15/6) In Whakanewha Regional Park, this pretty but basic waterfront camping ground has toilets, outdoor cold showers, gas barbecues and drinking water.

Tawa Lodge　　　　　GUESTHOUSE $$
(☑09-372 6675; www.pungalodge.co.nz; 15 Tawa St, Oneroa; r $110-120, apt $175-225; ☎) Between the self-contained two-person cottage at the front (our pick of the lot, due to the sublimely romantic views) and the apartment and house at the rear are three reasonably priced loft rooms sharing a small kitchen and bathroom.

Punga Lodge　　　　　　B&B $$
(☑09-372 6675; www.pungalodge.co.nz; 223 Oceanview Rd, Oneroa; r $155-170, units $155-200; @☎) Both the colourful en-suite rooms in the house and the self-contained garden units have access to decks looking onto a lush tropical garden. A renovation is overdue, but the welcome is warm and the hospitality extends to a free continental breakfast, afternoon tea and wharf transfers. There's also a private spa pool, if you fancy a soak.

★Waiheke Dreams　　RENTAL HOUSE $$$
(☑09-818 7129; www.waihekedreams.co.nz; 43 Tiri Rd, Oneroa; 1-/2-bedroom house $250/350) Dream a little dream of a luxurious, modern, spacious, open-plan, two-bedroom house on the crest of a hill with unsurpassed views over Oneroa Bay and the Hauraki Gulf – then pinch yourself and wake up with a smug smile in View43. Tucked at the rear is the considerably smaller one-bedroom CityLights, which glimpses Auckland's glimmer over the back lawn.

Enclosure Bay　　　　　B&B $$$
(☑09-372 8882; www.enclosurebay.co.nz; 9 Great Barrier Rd; r/ste $450/600; ☎) If you're going to shell out for a luxury B&B, you expect it to be special, and that's certainly what's offered here. Each of the three guest rooms have sumptuous views and balconies, and the owners subscribe to the nothing's-too-much-trouble school of hospitality.

Cable Bay Views　　　APARTMENT $$$
(☑09-372 2901; www.cablebayviews.co.nz; 103 Church Bay Rd; r $345; ☎) These three modern, self-contained studio apartments have stellar vineyard views and are handy to a couple of Waiheke's best vineyard restaurants. Check the website for good midweek and off-peak discounts.

✕ Eating

Waiheke has some excellent eateries and, if you're lucky, the views will be enough to distract from the hole being bored into your hip pocket. There's a supermarket in Ostend.

✕ Oneroa

Dragonfired PIZZA **$**
(📞 021 922 289; www.dragonfired.co.nz; Little Oneroa Beach; mains $12-16; ⏰ 10am-8pm Dec-Feb, 11am-7pm Fri-Sun Mar-Nov; 🍴) Specialising in 'artisan wood-fired food', this caravan by the beach serves the three Ps: pizza, polenta plates and pocket bread. It's easily Waiheke's best place for cheap eats.

Island Gelato ICE CREAM **$**
(📞 021 536 860; www.islandgelato.co.nz; 1 Oceanview Rd; ice cream from $5; ⏰ 8am-6.30pm daily, to 9pm Fri & Sat late Oct-Easter) Before school, after school, and on weekdays and weekends, Waiheke locals crowd Island Gelato's funky shipping container garden for delicious ice cream, coffee and bagels. Seasonal ice-cream flavours shine, including our favourite, the zingy kaffir-lime-and-coconut sorbet. You'll find all this irresistible goodness at the bottom end of Oneroa village.

Wai Kitchen CAFE **$$**
(📞 09-372 7505; www.waikitchen.co.nz; 1/149 Oceanview Rd; mains $17-26; ⏰ 8.30am-3.30pm, extended hours late Oct-Easter; 🖫) Why? Well firstly there's the lively menu that abounds with Mediterranean and Asian flavours. Then there's the charming service and the breezy ambience of this glassed-in wedge, facing the *wai* (water).

Oyster Inn SEAFOOD **$$**
(📞 09-372 2222; www.theoysterinn.co.nz; 124 Oceanview Rd; mains $27-36; ⏰ noon-late) The Oyster Inn is a popular destination for Auckland's smart set. They're attracted by the excellent seafood-skewed bistro menu, oysters and champagne, and a buzzy but relaxed vibe that's part bar and part restaurant. In summer, brunch on the veranda is a great way to ease into another Waiheke day.

✕ Ostend

Te Matuku Oysters SEAFOOD **$**
(📞 09-372 8600; www.tematukuoysters.co.nz; 17 Belgium St; ⏰ 9am-5pm) 🍴 Head to this combination seafood retailer and deli selling local gourmet produce for the freshest and best-value oysters on the island. Just $20 will get you 12 freshly shucked oysters. Enjoy with lemon juice and tabasco at the simple stand-up tables for a quintessential Waiheke experience. Mussels and clams are also for sale.

Annex CAFE **$**
(📞 09-372 9988; www.facebook.com/theannex waiheke; 10 Putiki Rd; snacks $5-12; ⏰ 9.30am-3pm Fri-Mon) 🍴 Framed by fruit trees, this 1920s-era wooden cottage makes for a perfect stop away from Waiheke's busier tourist spots. A superior range of teas and infusions are served either hot or cold in the relaxing rear courtyard, and snacks include sweet treats by the Little Tart Bakery – try its delicious cinnamon brioche – or excellent sourdough grilled-cheese sandwiches.

✕ Onetangi

Casita Miro SPANISH **$$**
(📞 09-372 7854; www.casitamiro.co.nz; 3 Brown St; tapas $9-19, ración $30-35; ⏰ noon-3pm Mon-Wed, to late Thu-Sun) A wrought-iron and glass pavilion backed with a Gaudí-esque mosaic garden is the stage for a very entertaining troupe of servers who will guide you through the menu of delectable tapas and *ración* (larger dishes), designed to be shared. In summer the sides open up, but otherwise, at busy times, it can get noisy.

★ **Tantalus Estate** MODERN NZ **$$$**
(📞 09-372 2625; www.tantalus.co.nz; 70-72 Onetangi Rd; mains $33-37; ⏰ 11am-4pm) 🍴 Up a winding driveway framed by grapevines, Waiheke's newest vineyard restaurant and tasting room channels an Iberian ambience, but the savvy and diverse menu effortlessly covers the globe. Secure a spot under rustic chandeliers crafted from repurposed tree branches, and enjoy a leisurely lunch imbued with Asian and Mediterranean influences.

Tantalus also crafts its own Rhone- and Bordeaux-style red wines, and makes craft beer on-site under the Alibi Brewing Company label. Check out its seasonal beers in the brick-lined Alibi Brewing tasting room downstairs. A concise menu of superior bar snacks is also available.

✕ Other Areas

Shed at Te Motu MODERN NZ **$$**
(📞 09-372 6884; www.temotu.co.nz/the-shed; 76 Onetangi Rd; shared plates small $16-21, large $29-42; ⏰ 11am-5pm daily, 6pm-late Fri & Sat Nov-Apr, reduced hours May-Oct) Secure a table shaded by umbrellas in the Shed's rustic courtyard for shared plates imbued with global influences and served by the restaurant's savvy and equally international waitstaff. Highlights

might include shiitake pancakes with kimchi and black garlic, or the wonderfully slow-cooked lamb shoulder partnered with a delicate biryani-spiced pilaf. Te Motu's standout wines are its stellar Bordeaux-style blends.

On Friday nights, the Shed offers a good value prix-fixe menu (two/three courses $45/55). Bookings are recommended for both lunch and dinner.

Poderi Crisci
ITALIAN $$
(☑09-372 2148; www.podericrisci.co.nz; 205 Awaawaroa Rd; lunch mains $25-33, dinner degustation $85; ⊘noon-5pm Sun, Mon & Thu, to 10pm Fri & Sat May-Sep, extended hours Oct-Apr) ✎ Poderi Crisci has quickly gained a sterling reputation for its food, particularly its legendary four-hour lunches on Sundays ($70 per person). Italian varietals and olives have been planted alongside the existing vines, and tastings are offered in the atmospheric cellar ($10, refunded upon purchase). It's definitely worth the drive into the winery's isolated valley, but book first.

Cable Bay
MODERN NZ $$$
(☑09-372 5889; www.cablebay.co.nz; 12 Nick Johnstone Dr; mezze $12-27, pizza $26-29, mains $42-45; ⊘11am-late; ☎) Impressive uber-modern architecture, interesting sculpture and beautiful views set the scene for this acclaimed restaurant. The food is sublime, but if the budget won't stretch to a meal, stop in for a wine tasting ($10 for five wines, refundable with a purchase, 11am to 5pm daily) or platters, pizza and shared plates at the Verandah bar.

Mudbrick
MODERN NZ $$$
(☑09-372 9050; www.mudbrick.co.nz; 126 Church Bay Rd; mains $47-49; ⊘11.30am-3.30pm & 6-10.30pm) ✎ The Hauraki Gulf is at its glistening best when viewed from Mudbrick's picturesque veranda. The pretty formal gardens make it popular with weddings, which periodically take over the restaurant (make sure you book ahead). The winery also offers tastings (from $10, 10am to 4pm). More informal dining is available at Archive (mains $34 to $45), a shaded bistro with garden views.

🍷 Drinking & Nightlife

You'll find bars in Oneroa and Onetangi, and pubs in Surfdale and Ostend.

Boogie Van Brewing
MICROBREWERY
(☑027 519 9737; www.facebook.com/Boogie VanBrewing; 29b Tahi Rd, Ostend; ⊘noon-5pm Fri-Sun) San Francisco expat Rick Paladi-no is enjoying island life at this compact microbrewery. Taproom hours are limited to Friday to Sunday afternoons, when Rick and his Kiwi partner Rochelle are on hand to guide tastings of their six core beers inspired by stoner rock. Given Rick's West Coast US roots, look forward to big and bold hop forward brews.

Charlie Farley's
BAR
(☑09-372 4106; www.charliefarleys.co.nz; 21 The Strand, Onetangi; ⊘8.30am-late) It's easy to see why the locals love this place when you're supping on a Waiheke wine or beer under the pohutukawa on the beach-gazing deck.

Shopping

Waiheke Wine Centre
WINE
(☑09-372 6139; www.waihekewinecentre.com; 153 Oceanview Rd, Oneroa; ⊘9.30am-7.30pm Mon-Thu, to 8pm Fri & Sat, from 10am Sun) Located in Oneroa's main street, this well-stocked and authoritative store features wine from all of Waiheke's vineyards, and is a good place to pick up information on wine destinations around the island. A special sampling system allows customers to purchase concise pours of various wines.

❶ Information

There is a convenient **tourist information booth** (Matiatia Wharf; ⊘9am-4pm) open for most arrivals at the ferry terminal at Matiatia Wharf. Online see www.tourismwaiheke.co.nz, www.waiheke.co.nz and www.aucklandnz.com.

❶ Getting There & Away

360 Discovery (☑09-307 8005; www.fullers. co.nz) You can pick up this tourist ferry at **Orapiu** on its limited voyages between Auckland and Coromandel Town. However, note that Orapiu is quite remote and not served by buses.

Fullers (☑09-367 9111; www.fullers.co.nz; return adult/child $36/12; ⊘5.20am-11.45pm Mon-Fri, 6.15am-11.45pm Sat, 7am-10.30pm Sun) Frequent passenger ferries from Auckland's Ferry Building to **Matiatia Wharf** (40 minutes), some via Devonport (adding an extra 10 minutes to the journey time).

SeaLink (☑0800 732 546; www.sealink. co.nz; return adult/child/car/motorcycle $37/20/175/72; ⊘6am-6pm) Runs **car ferries** to Kennedy Point, mainly from Half Moon Bay, east Auckland (45 to 60 minutes, at least hourly), but some leave from Wynyard Wharf in the city (60 to 80 minutes, three per day).

ⓘ Getting Around

BICYCLE

Various bicycle routes are outlined in the *Bike Waiheke!* brochure, usually available at the Matiatia Wharf. **Waiheke Bike Hire** (p108) hires mountain bikes from its base in the car park near the wharf.

Parts of Waiheke are quite hilly, so ease the load with a hybrid machine from **Onya Bikes** (☑ 022 050 2233; www.ecyclesnz.com; 124 Oceanview Rd, Oneroa; per day $60), combining pedalling with electric motors.

BUS

The island has bus services, starting from Matiatia Wharf and heading through Oneroa (adult/child $2/1, three minutes) on their way to all the main settlements, as far west as Onetangi (adult/child $5.50/3, 35 minutes). A day pass (adult/child $10/6) is available from the **Fullers** counter (p111) at Matiatia Wharf. Some services in the middle of the day can be as much as an hour apart, so to avoid lengthy waits at bus stops, consult a timetable from **Auckland Transport** (p104).

Another option is the **Waiheke Island Explorer** (www.fullers.co.nz; 1 day adult/child/ family incl ferry tickets $60/30/162, 2 day $90/45/243) bus, a hop-on, hop-off service covering 15 different stops around the island. A full circuit takes 90 minutes and attractions along the route include vineyards, beaches, activities and restaurants.

CAR, MOTORBIKE & SCOOTER

There are petrol stations in Oneroa and Onetangi.

Fun Rentals (☑ 09-372 8001; www.funrentals. co.nz; 14a Belgium St, Ostend; per day from $60) Includes free pick-ups and drop-offs to the ferries.

Island Scoot (☑ 021 062 5997; www.island scoot.nz; cnr Tui St & Mako Rd, Oneroa; per day $79; ⊙9am-6pm)

Rent Me Waiheke (☑ 09-372 3339; www.rent mewaiheke.co.nz; 14 Oceanview Rd, Matiatia; per day car/scooter $79/69)

Waiheke Auto Rentals (☑ 09-372 8998; www. waihekerentals.co.nz; Matiatia Wharf; per day car/scooter from $89/69)

Waiheke Rental Cars (☑ 09-372 8635; www. waihekerentalcars.co.nz; Matiatia Wharf; per day car/4WD from $79/109)

TAXI

Island Taxis (☑ 09-372 4111; www.islandtaxis. co.nz)

Waiheke Express Taxis (☑ 0800 700 789; www.waihekeexpresstaxis.co.nz)

Rotoroa Island

From 1911 to 2005 the only people to have access to this blissful little island on the far side of Waiheke were the alcoholics and drug addicts who came (or were sentenced) here to dry out, and the Salvation Army staff who cared for them. In 2011, 82-hectare Rotoroa (www.rotoroa.org.nz; adult/child $5/3) opened to the public for the first time in a century, giving visitors access to three sandy swimming beaches and the social history and art displays in the restored buildings of the former treatment centre.

⌘ Sleeping & Eating

There are three well-appointed, wildly retro holiday homes for rent, sleeping four ($375) to eight ($650) people, and excellent hostel accommodation in dorms (per person $35) in the former Superintendent's House.

You'll need to bring all of your food with you, as there's nothing available on the island. There are a couple of free gas barbecues for visitors to use.

ⓘ Getting There & Away

From Auckland the **360 Discovery** (☑ 09-307 8005; www.fullers.co.nz; adult/child from Auckland $52/30, from Orapiu $23/13) ferry takes 75 minutes, stopping at Orapiu on Waiheke Island en route. Services are infrequent and don't run every day. Prices include the island access fee.

Tiritiri Matangi Island

This magical, 220-hectare, predator-free island (www.tiritirimatangi.org.nz) is home to the tuatara (a prehistoric lizard) and lots of endangered native birds, including the very rare and colourful takahe. Other birds that can be seen include the bellbird, stitchbird, saddleback, whitehead, kakariki, kokako, little spotted kiwi, brown teal, New Zealand robin, fernbird and penguins; 78 different species have been sighted in total. The saddleback was once close to extinction, with just 150 left, but there are now up to 1000 on Tiritiri alone. To experience the dawn chorus in full flight, stay overnight at the **DOC bunkhouse** (☑ 09-425 7812; www.doc.govt.nz; adult/ child $30/20); book well ahead and ensure there's room on the ferry.

It's a good idea to book a guided walk ($5) with your ferry ticket; the guides know where all the really cool birds hang out.

Eating

You can get tea, coffee and drinking water from the visitor centre but there's no food available on the island. Bring everything you need and, if you're staying over, be sure to bring an extra day's food in case the ferry is cancelled.

ℹ Getting There & Away

360 Discovery (☑ 09-307 8005; www.fullers. co.nz; ☺ Wed-Sun) ferries depart for the island at 9am from Wednesday to Sunday, leaving the island at 3.30pm. The journey takes 70 minutes from Auckland's ferry terminal (adult/child return $70/40) or 20 minutes from Gulf Harbour ($55/32).

Kawau Island

POP 300

Kawau Island lies 50km north of Auckland off the Mahurangi Peninsula. There are few proper roads through the island – residents rely mainly on boats.

A set of short walks (10 minutes to two hours) are signposted from Mansion House, leading to beaches, the old copper mine and a lookout; download DOC's *Kawau Island Historic Reserve* map (www.doc.govt.nz).

Online, www.kawauisland.org.nz is also a good source of information, and features a list of self-contained rental accommodation.

◉ Sights

Mansion House HISTORIC BUILDING
(☑ 09-422 8882; www.doc.govt.nz; adult/child $4/2; ☺ noon-2pm Mon-Fri, noon-3.30pm Sat & Sun Sep-May) This impressive wooden manor was extended from an 1845 structure by Governor George Grey, who purchased the island in 1862. It houses a fine collection of Victoriana, including some of Grey's effects, and is surrounded by the original exotic gardens.

🛌 Sleeping & Eating

Beach House BOUTIQUE HOTEL $$$
(☑ 09-422 8850; www.kawaubeachhouse.co.nz; Vivian Bay; r/ste from $345/620) In the north of the island, on Kawau's best sandy beach, this upmarket complex has luxurious rooms facing the beach, a large paved courtyard, or in a cottage set back in the bush. It's a remote spot but it has its own restaurant (hotel guests only), so there's no need to go anywhere.

Mansion House Cafe CAFE $$
(☑ 09-422 8903; www.facebook.com/mansion housenz; 5 Schoolhouse Bay Rd; lunch $16-18; ☺ hours vary) If you haven't packed a picnic, this idyllically situated eatery serves tasty lunches, Devonshire teas with freshly baked scones, and hearty dinners.

ℹ Getting There & Away

Departing Sandspit several times daily, the Mansion House Cruise (adult/child $55/31) with **Kawau Cruises** (☑ 0800 111 616; www.kawaucruises.co.nz) allows plentiful time on the island before returning via an afternoon departure back to Sandspit. Check the website as summer and non-summer departure times vary. Another option is the Mail Run Cruise (adult/child $68/34, including barbecue lunch $95/50), which departs Sandspit at 10.30am and circles the island, delivering the post to 75 different wharves.

Great Barrier Island

POP 860

Great Barrier has unspoilt beaches, hot springs, old kauri dams, a forest sanctuary and a network of tramping tracks. Because there are no possums on the island, the native bush is lush.

Although only 88km and a 30-minute flight from Auckland, Great Barrier seems a world away. The island has no supermarket, no mains electricity supply (only private solar, wind and diesel generators) and no mains drainage (only septic tanks). Some roads are unsealed and petrol costs are high. Mobile-phone reception is improving but still limited and there are no banks, ATMs or street lights. Two-thirds of the island is publicly owned and managed by DOC.

Mid-December to mid-January is the peak season, so make sure you book transport, accommodation and activities well in advance.

History

Named Aotea (meaning cloud) by the Māori, and Great Barrier (due to its position at the edge of the Hauraki Gulf) by James Cook, this rugged and exceptionally beautiful place falls in behind South, North and Stewart as NZ's fourth-largest island (285 sq km). It closely resembles the Coromandel Peninsula to which it was once joined, and like the Coromandel it was once a mining, logging and whaling centre (although those industries have long gone).

Great Barrier Island

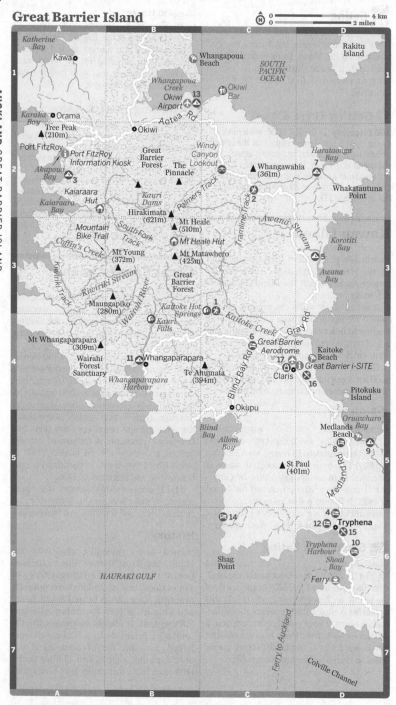

0   4 km
0   2 miles

Katherine Bay
Kawa
Rakitu Island

Whangapoua Beach
SOUTH PACIFIC OCEAN
Whangapoua Creek
13 Okiwi Airport
Okiwi Bar

Karaka Bay
Orama
Tree Peak (210m)
Port FitzRoy
Aotea Rd
Okiwi

Port FitzRoy Information Kiosk
Great Barrier Forest
The Pinnacle
Windy Canyon Lookout
Whangawahia (361m)
Harataonga Bay
7
Whakatautuna Point

Akapoua Bay
3
Kaiaraara Hut
Kauri Dams
Palmer's Track
2

Kaiaraara Bay
Hirakimata (621m)
Mt Heale (510m)
Tramline Track
Awana Stream
Korotiti Bay

Mountain Bike Trail
South Fork Track
Mt Heale Hut
Mt Matawhero (425m)
5
Awana Bay

Coffin's Creek
Mt Young (372m)
Great Barrier Forest
Kaitoke Hot Springs
1

Kiwiriki Track
Maungapiko (280m)
Waiahi River
Kaitoke Creek
Gray Rd

Kauri Falls

Mt Whangaparapara (309m)
11 Whangaparapara
Te Ahumata (394m)
6
Great Barrier Aerodrome
17
Claris
i
Great Barrier i-SITE
16
Kaitoke Beach

Wairahi Forest Sanctuary
Whangaparapara Harbour
Pitokuku Island

Okupu
Blind Bay Rd
Blind Bay
Allom Bay
Oruawharo Bay
Medlands Beach
8
9

St Paul (401m)
Medland Rd

14
4
12
Tryphena
15
10

Shag Point
Tryphena Harbour
Shoal Bay

HAURAKI GULF
Ferry

Ferry to Auckland

Colville Channel

Great Barrier Island

🕴 Activities

Water Sports
The beaches on the west coast are safe, but care needs to be taken on the surf-pounded eastern beaches. **Medlands Beach**, with its wide sweep of white sand, is one of the most beautiful and accessible beaches on the island. Remote **Whangapoua**, in the northeast, requires more effort to get to, while **Kaitoke**, **Awana Bay** and **Harataonga** on the east coast are also worth a visit.

Okiwi Bar has an excellent right-hand break, while Awana has both left- and right-hand breaks. Pohutukawa trees shelter the pretty bays around Tryphena.

Diving is excellent, with shipwrecks, pinnacles, lots of fish and more than 33m visibility at some times of the year.

Hooked on Barrier   BOATING, FISHING
(☑ 09-429 0740; www.hookedonbarrier.co.nz; 89 Hector Sanderson Rd; casual fishing trip per person $110, half-/full-day boat charter $800/1500) Hires out diving, snorkelling, fishing, surfing and kayaking gear, and runs tours and fishing, diving and sightseeing charters. Also wi-fi

access and a compact cafe dubbed Scoff & Tackle. Sightseeing cruises including lunch or dinner are $150 per person.

Hiking
The island's very popular walking tracks are outlined in DOC's free *Great Barrier Island (Aotea Island)* booklet. Before setting out, make sure you're properly equipped with water and food, and be prepared for both sunny and wet weather.

The most popular easy walk is the 45-minute **Kaitoke Hot Springs Track**, starting from Whangaparapara Rd and leading to natural hot springs in a bush stream. Check the temperature before getting in and don't put your head under the water.

Windy Canyon, which is only a 15-minute walk from Aotea Rd, has spectacular rock outcrops and affords great views of the island. From Windy Canyon, an excellent trail continues for another two to three hours through scrubby forest to Hirakimata (Mt Hobson; 621m), the highest point on the island, with views across the Hauraki Gulf and Coromandel. Near the top of the mountain are lush forests and a few mature kauri trees that survived the logging days. From Hirakimata it is 40 minutes south to **Mt Heale Hut** (☑ 09-379 6476; www.doc.govt. nz; dm per adult/child $15/7.50).

A more challenging tramp is the hilly **Tramline Track** (five hours), which starts on Aotea Rd and follows old logging tramlines to Whangaparapara Harbour. The initial stages of this track are not maintained and in some parts the clay becomes slippery after rain.

Of a similar length, but flatter and easier walking, is the 11km **Harataonga Coastal Walk** (five hours), which heads from Haraotaonga Bay to Whangapoua.

Many other trails traverse the forest, taking between 30 minutes and five hours. The **Aotea Track** combines bits of other paths into a three-day walk, overnighting in each of the huts. At the time of research, consideration was being given to making the Aotea Track one of NZ's Great Walks. Check the Department of Conservation website (www.doc. govt.nz) for the latest update and for detailed information on negotiating the Aotea Track.

Mountain Biking
With rugged scenery and relatively little traffic on the roads, mountain biking is a popular activity on the island. There's a designated 25km ride beginning on Blind Bay Rd,

STARGAZING SANCTUARY

Adjudged a Dark Sky Sanctuary by the International Dark-Sky Association in 2017 – one of only three regions in the world to enjoy such status – Great Barrier is quickly becoming regarded as one of the southern hemisphere's best places to observe the night sky.

Because there is no mains electricity or street lights on the island – all businesses and residents utilise solar power and batteries – light pollution is extremely minimal, and the Barrier's 88km ocean separation from Auckland means the city's far-reaching 'light dome' has no effect either.

Also because Great Barrier is almost 60% protected conservation land, future development is legislated to be minimal, and the entire island will be able to maintain this high standard of darkness and Dark Sky Sanctuary status in the future.

Just 30 minutes' flight from the country's international airport and in easy travelling proximity for the 1.42 million residents of Auckland, Great Barrier's stellar night sky is a significant tourism asset that the island's residents are keen to enhance and protect.

Okupu, winding beneath the Ahumata cliffs before crossing Whangaparapara Rd and beginning the 15km Forest Rd ride through beautiful forest to Port FitzRoy. Cycling on other DOC walking tracks is prohibited.

👉 Tours

Good Heavens OUTDOORS
(☑ 09-429 0876; www.goodheavens.co.nz; group tours per person $90, minimum 2 people private tours $400) 🌊 The Milky Way, constellations and other celestial attractions – sometimes including Saturn and Jupiter – are observed through telescopes and the naked eye, and Good Heavens' avid Dark Sky (p116) Ambassadors can even set up their sky-watching gear conveniently at your accommodation. Booking ahead is vital, preferably for your first night on the island to allow flexibility for weather conditions.

Crazy Horse Trike Tours SCENIC DRIVE
(☑ 09-429 0222, 0800 997 222; www.greatbarrier islandtourism.co.nz; per person from $75) Jump on the back of Steve Bellingham's custom-built motorised trike and let the friendly GB local drive you around the island. Options include two-hour sightseeing tours, beach visits, kayaking, hot springs and forest walks. Steve's a very entertaining source of information on interesting local stories and island history.

🛏 Sleeping

Unless you're camping (p118), Great Barrier isn't a cheap place to stay. At pretty much every price point you'll pay more than you would for a similar place elsewhere. In the low season, however, rates drop considerably.

Check accommodation and island information websites for packages including flights and car rental. Note that accommodation rates soar for around two weeks following Christmas and the island also gets very busy during this time.

**Medlands Beach
Backpackers & Villas** HOSTEL $
(☑ 09-429 0320; www.staymedlands.com; 9 Mason Rd; dm/d without bathroom $35/90, units from $250; 🐾) Chill out in the garden of this house on the hill, overlooking beautiful Medlands Beach. The backpackers area is simple, with a little double chalet for romantic budgeteers at a slight remove from the rest. The self-contained houses sleep up to seven.

Crossroads Lodge HOSTEL $
(☑ 09-429 0889; www.xroadslodge.com; 1 Blind Bay Rd; dm/s/d $40/60/90; @ 🐾) This low-key backpackers is 2km from the Great Barrier Aerodrome (p118) and Claris and close to forest walks and hot springs. Covered walkways connect the sleeping blocks to the main lodge, which has the kitchen, lounge and bathrooms.

Aotea Lodge APARTMENT $$
(☑ 09-429 0628; www.aotealodge.com; 41 Medland Rd, Tryphena; apt $130-220; 🐾) A well-tended, sunny garden surrounds these reasonably priced units, perched on the hill just above Tryphena. They range from a two-bedroom house to an unusual mezzanine unit loaded with bunks, and each has its own cooking facilities. Look forward to lots of bird life in the surrounding garden.

Tipi & Bob's Waterfront Lodge MOTEL $$
(☑09-429 0550; www.waterfrontlodge.co.nz; 38 Puriri Bay Rd; units $135-250; ☎) West of Tryphena, these smart motel-style units have some wonderful sea views and helpful owners. The cheapest room doesn't lend itself to cat swinging, but the rest are more than fit for the purpose. The complex includes a restaurant and bar; it's around 600m from Tryphena's cafe, pub and general store.

Sunset Waterfront Lodge MOTEL $$
(☑09-429 0051; www.sunsetlodge.co.nz; 5 Mulberry Grove Rd, Shoal Bay; units from $195) Gaze across the lawn to the sea from the attractive studio units, or fight over who's going to get the pointy room in the two-bedroom A-frame villas. There's a small shop and cafe next door.

★**XSPOT** APARTMENT $$$
(☑027 429 0877; www.xspot.co.nz; 21 Schooner Bay Rd, Tryphena; d $230; ☎⚡) ❤ Great Barrier's most spectacular accommodation option is also one of its more remote. A 25-minute drive from Tryphena – rent a 4WD vehicle – XSPOT is a spacious and stylish one-bedroom apartment with expansive windows offering jaw-dropping 270-degree views of the ocean. Equipped with a full kitchen and modern bathroom, it's the kind of place to linger amid spectacular marine vistas.

🍴 Eating & Drinking

In summer, most places open daily but for the rest of the year hours can be sporadic. A monthly guide to opening hours is on www.thebarrier.co.nz, but it pays to call ahead for an evening meal.

Self-caterers will find small stores in Tryphena, Claris, Whangaparapara and Port FitzRoy. Tryphena's **Stonewall Store** (☑09-429 0451; 82 Blackwell Dr; ⊙8.30am-6pm) has a good selection of wine, beer and local produce, and also operates a small market (from 10am Saturday).

Swallow BURGERS $
(☑09-429 0226; www.facebook.com/BurgerShack GBI; Main Rd, Claris; burgers $10-16; ⊙11am-7pm) Hands down the best burgers of the island with massive overflowing options including pork belly or beef, blue cheese and caramelised onions. Also wraps, seafood and Janene's Dreams icy treats handmade on the Barrier. During summer there's a couple of other food carts nearby selling juices and coffee.

Pah Beach Cafe CAFE $$
(☑09-429 0905; 82 Blackwell Dr, Tryphena; mains $15-23; ⊙8.30am-3pm & 5-7pm Sat & Sun; ☑) Pah Beach Cafe does the best impersonation of an Auckland cafe on the island with brunch classics including eggs Benedict and Mexican-style *huevos rancheros* eggs. Steak sandwiches and good counter food are the go for lunch, and its pies are deservedly famous on Great Barrier. Adjourn with the Kashmiri chicken pie ($8.50) to a spot on the nearby beach.

Tipi & Bob's PUB FOOD $$$
(☑09-429 0550; www.waterfrontlodge.co.nz; 38 Puriri Bay Rd, Tryphena; breakfast $16-20, dinner $39-44; ⊙7.30-10am & 5-10pm) Serving simple but satisfying meals in large portions, this popular haunt has an inviting deck overlooking the harbour. The steak and seafood combos are always good. There's also a cheaper menu in the bar.

★**Currach Irish Pub** IRISH PUB
(☑09-429 0211; www.currachirishpub.co.nz; 78 Blackwell Dr, Tryphena; mains $20-30; ⊙4pm-late Boxing Day–Easter, closed Wed Mar-Dec; ☎⚡) This excellent pub offers craft beer, seafood, steak and burgers, and is GB's main social centre. Wood-fired pizza combines with an alfresco salad bar, and there are regular live gigs with a Gaelic and folky bent. Sunday night quiz night is loads of fun, and a separate room features rotating exhibitions from local artists, all of it for sale.

Accommodation in renovated heritage rooms ($130 to $150) is available at the attached Innkeepers Lodge, and there's also a compact four-bed dorm ($35) with a full kitchen.

🔒 Shopping

Aotea Community Art Gallery ARTS & CRAFTS
(☑09-429 0580; www.gbicommunitygallery.org; 80 Hector Sanderson Rd, Claris; ⊙10am-4pm Dec-Feb, Thu-Tue Mar-Nov) This eclectic showcase for the island's artsy fraternity sells everything from paintings and sculpture to handmade soap and local honey.

ℹ Orientation

Tryphena is the main settlement, 4km from the ferry wharf at Shoal Bay. Strung out along several kilometres of coastal road, it consists of a few dozen houses and a handful of shops and accommodation places. From the wharf it's 3km to Mulberry Grove, and then another 1km over

ℹ DOC CAMPSITES

There are DOC campsites at **Harataonga Bay** (☑ 09-379 6476; www.doc.govt. nz; Harataonga Rd; sites per adult/child $13/6.50), **Medlands Beach** (☑ 09-379 6476; www.doc.govt.nz; Sandhills Rd; sites per adult/child $13/6.50), **Akapoua Bay** (☑ 09-379 6476; www.doc.govt.nz; Kaiaraara Bay Rd; sites per adult/child $13/6.50), **Whangapoua** (☑ 09-379 6476; www.doc. govt.nz; off Aotea Rd; sites per adult/child $13/6.50), **The Green** (☑ 09-379 6476; www.doc.govt.nz; Whangaparapara Harbour; sites per adult/child $13/6.50) and **Awana Bay** (☑ 09-379 6476; www.doc.govt.nz; off Aotea Rd; sites per adult/child $13/6.50).
All have basic facilities, including water, cold showers (except for the Green), toilets and a food-preparation shelter. You need to bring your own gas cooking stove as open fires are prohibited. Book in advance online.

the headland to Pah Beach and the **Stonewall Store** (p117).

The airport is at **Claris**, 12km north of Tryphena, a small settlement with a general store, bottle shop, laundrette, garage, pharmacy and cafe. **Whangaparapara** is an old timber town and the site of the island's 19th-century whaling activities. **Port FitzRoy** is the other main harbour on the west coast, a one-hour drive from Tryphena. These four main settlements have fuel available.

ℹ Information

INTERNET ACCESS

There's free wi-fi access at the **Great Barrier Aerodrome** (p118) at Claris and at **Hooked on Barrier** (p115).

TOURIST INFORMATION

The **Great Barrier i-SITE** (Destination Great Barrier Island; ☑ 09-420 0033; www.greatbarrier. co.nz; Claris airport; ⊙ 9am-3pm Mon-Sat; 🛜) at the Great Barrier Aerodrome at Claris also has a good range of Department of Conservation (DOC) information.

Go Great Barrier Island (☑ 0800 997 222; www.greatbarrierislandtourism.co.nz) offers a personal online planning service for island visits including all transport, rental cars and accommodation. Also runs tramper shuttles to tracks and arranges island tours by van or trike.

Port FitzRoy Information Kiosk (☑ 09-429 0848; www.thebarrier.co.nz; ⊙ 9am-3pm Mon-Sat) is a privately run kiosk that publishes the *Great Barrier Island Visitor Information Guide*.

ℹ Getting There & Away

AIR

FlyMySky (p102) flies at least three times a day between Claris' **Great Barrier Aerodrome** (Claris Airport) and Auckland. Cheaper flights are available if you travel to the island on a Sunday or leave on a Friday ($89), and there's a special return fare for flying one way and ferrying the other (adult/child $180/148).

Barrier Air (p102) departs from both Auckland Domestic Airport and North Shore Aerodrome 42 times a week for the 30-minute flight to Claris. Also occasional flights from both Auckland airports to **Okiwi**.

BOAT

SeaLink (☑ 0800 732 546, 09-300 5900; www.sealink.co.nz; adult/child/car one way $84/61/290, return $106/84/359) runs car ferries four days a week from Wynyard Wharf in Auckland to Tryphena's **Shoal Bay** (4½ hours) and once a week to Port FitzRoy (five hours). The last part of the crossing can get rough.

ℹ Getting Around

Most roads are narrow and windy but even small hire cars can handle the unsealed sections. Many of the accommodation places will pick you up from the airport or wharf if notified in advance.

Aotea Car Rentals (☑ 0800 426 832; www. aoteacarrentals.co.nz; Mulberry Grove, Shoal Bay) Rents cars (from $60), 4WDs (from $70) and vans (from $99).

Go Great Barrier Island (p118) Can arrange rental cars and tramper shuttles to island tracks.

Great Barrier Wheels (☑ 021 226 6055, 09-429 0062; www.greatbarrierwheels.co.nz; 67 Hector Sanderson Rd, Claris; ⊙ 8am-7pm Mon-Sat) Has a diverse range of cars from $60 to $85 per day. Also operates shuttle services from Claris to Tryphena ($25), Medlands ($25), Whangaparapara ($25) and Port FitzRoy ($30, minimum four passengers), as well as trampers' shuttles.

WEST AUCKLAND

West Auckland epitomises rugged: wild black-sand beaches, bush-shrouded ranges and mullet-haired, black-T-shirt-wearing 'Westies'. The latter is just one of several stereotypes of the area's denizens. Others include the back-to-nature hippie, the eccentric bohemian artist and the dope-smoking surfer dude, all attracted to a simple life at the edge of the bush.

Add to the mix Croatian immigrants, earning the fertile fields at the base of the Waitakere Ranges the nickname 'Dallie Valley' after the Dalmatian coast where most hailed from. These pioneering families planted grapes and made wine, founding one of New Zealand's major industries.

❶ Getting There & Away

There are regular buses as far as Titirangi and Helensville but no services to the west-coast beaches. The best options for the beaches are to rent a car or join a day tour from Auckland.

Titirangi

POP 3200

This little village marks the end of Auckland's suburban sprawl and is a good place to spot all manner of Westie stereotypes over a coffee, wine or cold beer. Once home to New Zealand's greatest modern painter, Colin McCahon, there remains an artsy feel to the place. Titirangi means 'Fringe of Heaven' – an apt name for the gateway to the Waitakere Ranges. This is the last stop for petrol and ATMs on your way west.

❍ Sights

Te Uru Waitakere
Contemporary Gallery GALLERY
(☑ 09-817 8087; www.teuru.org.nz; 420 Titirangi Rd; ☺ 10am-4.30pm) FREE This excellent art gallery is housed in a spectacular modern building on the edge of the village beside the heritage splendour of the former Hotel Titirangi. Rotating exhibitions and installations are sourced both from NZ and internationally, and the curator's remit could stretch from photography and sculpture to mixed media or video. The gallery also features a small shop selling interesting jewellery, pottery and gifts. Check the website for upcoming exhibitions.

✖ Eating

Deco Eatery MEDITERRANEAN $$
(☑ 09-817 2664; www.decoeatery.co.nz; Lopdell House, 418 Titirangi Rd; mains $16-30; ☺ 7am-late Mon-Fri, 7.30am-late Sat & Sun; ☑) Housed amid the heritage vibe of Lopdell House, Deco's decor channels a Turkish ambience, while the menu combines Anatolian classics with a broader Mediterranean focus. The restaurant is spacious and sunny, and a great stop before or after visiting the nearby surf beaches of Piha or Karekare.

Hardware Cafe CAFE $$
(☑ 09-817 5059; www.hardwarecafe.org.nz; 404 Titirangi Rd; brunch $11-20, dinner $18-30; ☺ 6am-4.30pm Mon-Thu, to 10pm Fri & Sat, to 6pm Sun) This popular licensed cafe serves cooked breakfasts and lunches, along with tempting counter food.

❶ Getting There & Away

The commuter-oriented bus 209 ($7, 45 minutes) travels from bus stop 7081 at 105 Albert St in central Auckland on Monday to Friday from 3pm to 6pm. For journeys at other times and on weekends, catch a bus or train to New Lynn and transfer to a Titirangi-bound bus there.

Karekare

Few stretches of sand have more personality than Karekare. Those prone to metaphysical musings inevitably settle on descriptions such as 'spiritual' and 'brooding'. Perhaps history has left its imprint: in 1825 it was

---

WAITAKERE RANGES

This 160-sq-km wilderness was covered in kauri until the mid-19th century, when logging claimed most of the giant trees. A few stands of ancient kauri and other mature natives survive amid the dense bush of the regenerating rainforest, which is now protected inside the Waitakere Ranges Regional Park. Bordered to the west by wildly beautiful beaches on the Tasman Sea, the park's rugged terrain is a spectacular sight.

Sadly the forest is facing a new threat, with the fungal disease kauri dieback (p###) already affecting many trees in the regional park. To prevent its further spread, the Auckland Council made the decision to close all tracks through the forested section of the park. However, you can still visit **Arataki** (☑ 09-817 0077; www.aucklandcouncil.govt.nz; 300 Scenic Dr; ☺ 9am-5pm) ✿ FREE, the park's impressive visitor centre, where they can advise on any non-forested tracks that remain open. The Māori carvings at the entrance depict the ancestors of the local Kawerau *iwi* and there are views over the rainforest from its rear deck. On the ground floor, the 12-minute *Dawn to Dusk* video offers an overview of the Ranges.

the site of a ruthless massacre of the local Kawerau *iwi* by Ngāpuhi invaders. Wild and gorgeously undeveloped, this famous beach has been the setting for on-screen moments both high- and low-brow, from Oscar winner *The Piano* to *Xena: Warrior Princess*.

From the car park the quickest route to the black-sand beach involves wading through a stream. Karekare rates as one of the most dangerous beaches in the country, with strong surf and ever-present rips, so don't even think about swimming unless the beach is being patrolled by lifeguards (usually only in summer). Pearl Jam singer Eddie Vedder nearly drowned here while visiting Neil Finn's Karekare pad.

Piha

POP 600

If you notice an Auckland surfer dude with a faraway look, chances are they're daydreaming about Piha. This beautifully rugged, iron-sand beach has long been a favourite for Aucklanders escaping from the city's stresses – whether for day trips, weekend teenage parties or family holidays.

Although Piha is popular, it's also incredibly dangerous, with wild surf and strong undercurrents, so much so that it's spawned its own popular reality TV show, *Piha Rescue*. If you don't want to inadvertently star in it, always swim between the flags, where lifeguards can provide help if you get into trouble.

Piha may be bigger and more populated than neighbouring Karekare, but there's still no supermarket, liquor shop, bank or petrol station, although there is a small general store that doubles as a cafe, takeaway shop and post office.

○ Sights

The view of the coast as you drive down Piha Rd is spectacular. Perched on its haunches near the centre of the beach is **Lion Rock** (101m), whose 'mane' glows golden in the evening light. It's actually the eroded core of an ancient volcano and a Māori *pā* site. A path at the south end of the beach takes you to some great lookouts. At low tide you can walk south along the beach and watch the surf shooting through a ravine in another large rock known as the **Camel**. A little further along, the waves crash through the **Gap** and form

a safe swimming hole. A small colony of little penguins nests at the beach's north end.

🏃 Activities

For surfboard hire, try **Piha Store** (☑09-812 8844; 26 Seaview Rd; snacks $3-10; ⊙7.30am-5.30pm) or Piha Surf Shop (p121).

🛏 Sleeping & Eating

★**Piha Beachstay – Jandal Palace** HOSTEL $
(☑09-812 8381; www.pihabeachstay.co.nz; 38 Glen Esk Rd; dm/s $40/79, d $140, without bathroom $89; @ ⓐ) 🍃 Attractive and ecofriendly, this wood-and-glass lodge has extremely smart facilities. It's 1km from the beach but there's a little stream at the bottom of the property and bush walks nearby. In winter an open fire warms the large communal lounge.

Piha Domain Motor Camp CAMPGROUND $
(☑09-812 8815; www.piha.co.nz/pihadomain-camp; 21 Seaview Rd; sites from $15, s/d cabin $50/60; ⓐ) Smack-bang on the beach, this camping ground is great for those seeking an old-fashioned, cheap-as-chips, no-frills family holiday. To keep unruly teens at bay, under 20-year-olds must be accompanied by parents. The cabins are tiny.

Black Sands Lodge APARTMENT $$
(☑021 969 924; www.pihabeach.co.nz; Beach Valley Rd; cabin $180, apt $240-280; ⓐ) These two modern conjoined apartments with private decks match their prime location with appealing touches, such as stereos and DVD players. The cabin is kitted out in a 1950s Kiwiana-bach style and shares a bathroom with the main house. Bikes and wi-fi are free for guests, and in-room massage and lavish dinners can be arranged on request.

Piha Cafe CAFE $$
(☑09-812 8808; www.facebook.com/thepiha cafe; 20 Seaview Rd; mains $14-28; ⊙8am-3pm Mon & Wed, to 9.30pm Thu-Sat, to 5pm Sun) 🍃 Big-city standards mesh seamlessly with sand-between-toes informality at this attractive ecofriendly cafe. Cooked breakfasts and crispy pizzas provide sustenance for a hard day's surfing. After the waves, head back for a cold beverage on the deck. Black Sands craft beer from nearby West Auckland is usually on tap; the pilsner is especially refreshing.

Shopping

West Coast Gallery   ARTS & CRAFTS
(☑09-812 8029; www.westcoastgallery.co.nz; Seaview Rd; ☺10am-5pm Wed-Sun) The work of more than 200 local artists is sold at this small not-for-profit gallery next to the Piha fire station.

Piha Surf Shop   SPORTS & OUTDOORS
(☑09-812 8723; www.pihasurf.co.nz; 122 Seaview Rd; ☺8am-5pm) A family run venture, with well-known surfboard designer Mike Jolly selling his wares and wife Pam selling cool T-shirts and a small range of crafts. Surfboards (per three hours/day $25/35), wetsuits ($8/18) and body boards ($15/25) can all be hired, and Mike can also hook you up with surfing locals for lessons.

❶ Getting There & Away

There's no public transport to Piha, but **Rapu** (☑021 550 546, 09-828 0426; www.rapu adventures.com; return from Auckland $50) provides shuttles from central Auckland when the surf's up. Piha is also often included in the daytrip itinerary of **Bush & Beach** (p80).

Te Henga (Bethells Beach)

Breathtaking Bethells Beach is reached by taking Te Henga Rd at the northern end of Scenic Dr in Auckland's western suburbs. It's a raw, black-sand beach with surf, windswept dunes and walks, such as the popular one over giant sand dunes to **Lake Wainamu** (starting near the bridge on the approach to the beach).

🛏 Sleeping & Eating

Wainamu Luxury Tents   B&B $$$
(☑022 384 0500, 09-810 9387; www.facebook. com/wainamu; d $200-250; ☺Oct-Jun) 🍃 Inspired by safari tents from Botswana and Māori *whare* (houses), these very comfortable tents combine quiet rural locations, recycled timber construction and a luxurious 'glamping' vibe. Cooking is done on barbecues, lighting from gas lamps and candles is practical and romantic, and outdoor baths also enhance the whole experience. Freerange eggs, fresh-baked bread and muesli combine in DIY breakfast packs.

Bethells Cafe   BURGERS, PIZZA $
(☑09-810 9387; www.facebook.com/thebethells cafe; Bethells Beach car park; mains $12-17; ☺5.30-9.30pm Fri, 10am-6pm Sat & Sun Nov-May, 10am-6pm Sun Jun-Oct) Less a cafe and more a food truck with an awning, Bethells Cafe does a roaring trade in burgers (beef and vegetarian), pizza, cakes and coffee. On Friday nights it's pretty much the perfect Kiwi beach scene, with live musicians entertaining the adults while the kids surf the sand dunes.

Kumeu & Around

West Auckland's main wine-producing area still has some vineyards owned by the original Croatian families who kick-started New Zealand's wine industry. The fancy eateries that have mushroomed in recent years have done little to dint the relaxed farmland feel to the region, but everything to encourage an afternoon's indulgence on the way back from the beach or the hot pools. Most cellars offer free tastings. Kumeu itself is a rapidly expanding dormitory suburb of West Auckland, but great wine, food and beer is nearby.

🏃 Activities

Coopers Creek   WINE
(☑09-412 8560; www.cooperscreek.co.nz; 601 SH16, Huapai; ☺10.30am-5.30pm) Buy a bottle, spread out a picnic in the attractive gardens and, from January to Easter, enjoy Sunday afternoon jazz sessions.

Kumeu River   WINE
(☑09-412 8415; www.kumeuriver.co.nz; 550 SH16; ☺11am-4.30pm Mon-Sat) Owned by the Brajkovich family, this winery produces one of NZ's best chardonnays, among other varietals.

🍴 Eating & Drinking

Tasting Shed   TAPAS $$
(☑09-412 6454; www.thetastingshed.com; 609 SH16, Huapai; dishes $14-29; ☺4-10pm Wed & Thu, noon-11pm Fri-Sun) Complementing its rural aspect with rustic chic decor, this slick eatery conjures up delicious dishes designed to be shared. It's not strictly tapas, as the menu strays from Spain and appropriates flavours from Asia, the Middle East, Croatia, Serbia, Italy and France.

Hallertau   BREWERY
(☑09-412 5555; www.hallertau.co.nz; 1171 Coatesville–Riverhead Hwy, Riverhead; share plates $9-24, mains $17-40; ☺11am-10pm) Hallertau offers tasting paddles ($12 to $14) of its craft beers served in its spacious and sociable *biergarten*, and inside on cosy tables near the bar. Regular guest beers,

good food, and occasional weekend DJs and live music make it popular with Auckland's hopheads. Our pick from the food menu are the beef *krokets*.

ⓘ Getting There & Away

From central Auckland, Kumeu is 25km up the Northwestern Motorway (SH16). Catch a bus to Westgate and then transfer to bus 122 or 125 to Kumeu.

Muriwai Beach

A rugged black-sand surf beach, Muriwai Beach's main claim to fame is the **Takapu Refuge gannet colony**, spread over the southern headland and outlying rock stacks. Viewing platforms get you close enough to watch (and smell) these fascinating seabirds. Every August hundreds of adult birds return to this spot to hook up with their regular partners and get busy – expect lots of outrageously cute neck-rubbing, bill-touching and general snuggling. The net result is a single chick per season; December and January are the best times to see the little ones testing their wings before embarking on an impressive odyssey (p122).

Nearby, a couple of short tracks will take you through beautiful native bush to a lookout that offers views along the 60km length of the beach.

🏃 Activities

Apart from surfing, Muriwai Beach is a popular spot for hang gliding, parapunting, kiteboarding and horse riding. There

---

THE GREAT GANNET OE

After honing their flying skills, young gannets get the ultimate chance to test them – a 2000km journey to Australia. They usually hang out there for several years before returning home, never to attempt the journey again. Once back in the homeland they spend a few years waiting for a piece of waterfront property to become available in the colony, before settling down with a regular partner to nest – returning to the same patch of dirt every year. In other words, they're your typical young New Zealander on their rite-of-passage Overseas Experience (OE).

---

are also tennis courts, a golf course and a cafe that doubles as a takeaway chippie. Wild surf and treacherous rips mean that swimming is safe only when the beach is patrolled (swim between the flags).

Helensville & Around

POP 2600

Heritage buildings, antique shops and cafes makes village-like Helensville a good whistle-stop for those taking SH16 north.

🏃 Activities

Tree Adventures OUTDOORS

(☏0800 827 926; www.treeadventures.co.nz; Restall Rd, Woodhill; ropes courses $19-42; ⊗9.30am-5.30pm) A set of high-ropes courses in Woodhill Forest, located 14km south of Helensville, consisting of swinging logs, nets, balance beams, Tarzan swings and a flying fox.

Woodhill Mountain Bike Park MOUNTAIN BIKING

(☏027 278 0969; www.bikeparks.co.nz; Restall Rd, Woodhill; adult/child $10/8, bike hire from $35; ⊗8am-5.30pm Thu-Tue, to 10pm Wed) Maintains many challenging tracks (including jumps and beams) within Woodhill Forest, 14km south of Helensville.

Parakai Springs SWIMMING, SPA

(☏09-420 8998; www.parakaisprings.co.nz; 150 Parkhurst Rd; adult/child $24/12; ⊗10am-9pm Sun-Thu, to 10pm Fri & Sat; 🖈) Aucklanders bring their bored children to Parakai, 2km northwest of Helensville, on wet wintry days as a cheaper alternative to Waiwera. It has large thermally heated swimming pools, private spas (per 30 minutes per person $5) and a couple of hydroslides.

ⓘ Information

Pick up free brochures detailing the *Helensville Heritage Trail* and *Helensville Riverside Walkway* at the **Visitor Information Centre** (☏09-420 7162; www.helensville.co.nz; 27 Commercial Rd; ⊗10am-3pm Mon-Fri).

ⓘ Getting There & Away

Bus 125x heads from 105 Albert St (bus stop 7081) in central Auckland to Helensville ($12.50, 1½ hours) from 3.20pm to 6.25pm Monday to Friday. For alternative journeys beyond this commuter-friendly service, you'll need to change buses at the Westgate shopping centre, around 20km west of central Auckland.

NORTH AUCKLAND

The Auckland supercity sprawls 90km north of the CBD to just past the point where SH16 and SH1 converge at Wellsford. The semirural area north of Auckland's suburban sprawl encompasses beautiful beaches, regional parks, tramping trails, quaint villages and wineries. Plus there are excellent opportunities for kayaking, snorkelling and diving. Consider visiting on a day trip from Auckland or as a way to break up your trip on the journey north.

Shakespear Regional Park

Shooting out eastward just before Orewa, the Whangaparaoa Peninsula is a heavily developed spit of land with a sizeable South African expat community. At its tip is this gorgeous 376-hectare regional park, its native wildlife protected by a 1.7km pest-proof fence.

Sheep, cows, peacocks and pukeko ramble over the grassy headland, while pohutukawa-lined **Te Haruhi Bay** provides great views of the gulf islands and the city. Walking tracks take between 40 minutes and two hours, exploring native forest, WWII gun embankments, Māori sites and lookouts. If you can't bear to leave, there's an idyllic beachfront **camping ground** (☑ 09-366 6400; www.aucklandcouncil.govt.nz; sites per adult/child $15/6) with flush toilets and cold showers.

ⓘ Getting There & Away

It's possible to get here via a tortuous 1½-hour bus trip from central Auckland (adult/child $9/5). An alternative is to take the 50-minute **360 Discovery** (☑ 09-307 8005; www.fullers.co.nz; adult/child $15/8) ferry service to Gulf Harbour, a Noddy-town development of matching townhouses, a marina, country club and golf course. Enquire at the ferry office about picking up a bus or taxi from here. Alternatively, walk or cycle the remaining 3km to the park. The ferry is a good option for cyclists wanting to skip the boring road trip out of Auckland; carry-on bikes are free.

Orewa

POP 7400

Orewa's main beach is a lovely expanse of sand, however, locals fear that the town is turning into New Zealand's equivalent of Queensland's Gold Coast. It is, indeed, very built up and high-rise apartment towers have begun to sprout, but unless they start

ⓘ WHICH MOTORWAY?

From Auckland, the multilane Northern Motorway (SH1) bypasses Orewa and Waiwera on the Northern Gateway Toll Road. It will save you about 10 minutes and you need to pay the **NZ Transport Agency** (☑ 0800 40 20 20; www.tollroad.govt.nz; per car & motorbike $2.30) online (in advance or within five days of your journey). If you don't pay the toll within the time frame, then you, or your rental-car company, will be charged an additional $5 administration fee.

Between Christmas and New Year, SH1 can be terribly gridlocked heading north between the toll road and Wellsford; winding SH16 through Kumeu and Helensville is a sensible alternative. The same is true if heading south in the first few days of the new year.

exporting retirees and replacing them with bikini-clad parking wardens, it's unlikely to reach the Gold Coast's extremes. Quieter and more compact **Hatfields Beach** is just 2km north over the hill.

⦿ Sights

Orewa Beach　　　BEACH
Orewa's 3km-long stretch of sand is its main drawcard. Being in the Hauraki Gulf, it's sheltered from the surf but still patrolled by lifeguards in the peak season.

Alice Eaves Scenic Reserve　　FOREST
(2 Old North Rd) Ten hectares of native bush with labelled trees, a *pā* site, a lookout and easy short walks.

⚡ Activities

Snowplanet　　SNOW SPORTS
(☑ 09-427 0044; www.snowplanet.co.nz; 91 Small Rd, Silverdale; day pass adult/child $69/49; ⊙10am-10pm Sun-Thu, 9am-midnight Fri & Sat) Snowplanet offers indoor skiing, snowboarding and tubing throughout the year. It's just off SH1, 8km south of Orewa.

Te Ara Tahuna Estuary Cycle & Walkway　　CYCLING, WALKING
Starting from South Bridge this 8km route loops around the estuary and includes explanations of the area's past as a centre for Māori food gathering.

🛏 Sleeping

Orewa Beach Top 10   HOLIDAY PARK **$**
(📞 09-426 5832; https://top10.co.nz; 265 Hibiscus
Coast Hwy; sites $44, units $70-130; @ 🛜) Taking
up a large chunk of the beach's south end,
this well-kept park has excellent facilities
but road noise can be a problem.

Orewa Motor Lodge   MOTEL **$$**
(📞 09-426 4027; www.orewamotorlodge.co.nz; 290
Hibiscus Coast Hwy; units $160-210; 🛜) One of
the motels lining Orewa's main road, this
refurbished complex has scrupulously clean
wooden units prettied up with hanging
flower baskets. There's also a spa pool.

Waves   MOTEL **$$$**
(📞 09-427 0888; www.waves.co.nz; cnr Hibiscus
Coast Hwy & Kohu St; units from $185; 🛜) This
complex offers spacious, self-contained apartments, and the downstairs units have gardens
and spa baths. It's only a few metres from the
beach.

🍴 Eating & Drinking

Casablanca   MEDITERRANEAN **$$**
(📞 09-426 6818; www.casablancacafenz.co.nz; 336
Hibiscus Coast Hwy; mains $16-29; ⊘11am-10pm
Mon-Fri, 9am-10pm Sat & Sun) Turkish, North
African and Mediterranean flavours fea-
ture at this buzzy cafe. Try the hearty baked
Moorish eggs and you'll be set for the next
chapter of your Kiwi road trip.

Coast   CRAFT BEER
(📞 09 421 1016; www.coastorewa.co.nz; 342 Hibis-
cus Coast Hwy; ⊘11am-11pm) Craft beer, cock-
tails and wine combine with good meals and
bar snacks – try the barbecued-duck tacos
– at this Orewa outpost of Auckland's Deep
Creek Brewing. Settle in for ocean views
from the upper deck, and look forward to
gigs from local musos most Friday and Sat-
urday nights. Deep Creek's seasonal Lupulin
Effect brews are always worth trying.

ℹ Getting There & Away

Direct buses head to Orewa from central Auck-
land (adult/child $12/7, 1¼ hours) and Waiwera
(adult/child $2.50/1.50, 12 minutes).

Waiwera

POP 285

This pleasant river-mouth village has a great
beach, but it's the *wai wera* (hot waters) that
attracts visitors. Warm mineral water bub-
bles up from 1500m below the surface to fill

the 19 pools of the Waiwera Thermal Resort.
Nearby, the 134-hectare Wenderholm Re-
gional Park incorporates bird life, beaches,
colonial history and walks.

👁 Sights & Activities

Wenderholm Regional Park   PARK
(📞 09-366 2000; www.aucklandcouncil.govt.nz; 37
Schishka Rd) Squeezed between the Waiwera
and Puhoi Rivers, the exquisite 134-hectare
Wenderholm Regional Park has a diverse
ecology, abundant bird life, beaches and
walks (30 minutes to 2½ hours). The Coul-
drey family were the original colonial settlers
of the Wenderholm area, and their **home-
stead** (www.aucklandcouncil.govt.nz; adult/child
$5/free; ⊘1-4pm Sat & Sun, daily Jan-Easter) dat-
ing from the 1860s is now a museum. The
camping ground (site per adult/child $15/6)
provides only tap water and toilets, and the
council also rents three comfortable self-
contained houses ($133 to $171).

Waiwera Thermal Resort   SWIMMING, SPA
(📞 09-427 8800; www.waiwera.co.nz; 21 Waiwera
Rd; adult/child $30/16; ⊘10am-8pm Fri-Sun; 🖼)
Warm water bubbles up from 1500m below
the surface to fill the numerous pools of this
thermal complex. There are big water slides,
barbecues, private tubs ($40) and a health
spa, or you can watch a flick in the movie
pool. It's lots of fun for families.

ℹ Getting There & Away

Bus 981 from Auckland's Fanshawe St heads to
Waiwera (adult/child $12.50/7, 1¼ hours) via
Orewa.

Puhoi

POP 450

Forget dingy cafes and earnest poets – this
quaint village is a slice of the real Bohemia.
In 1863 around 200 German-speaking immi-
grants from the present-day Czech Republic
settled in what was then dense bush.

👁 Sights & Activities

Church of Sts Peter & Paul   CHURCH
(www.holyname.org.nz; Puhoi Rd) The village's
pretty Catholic church dates from 1881 and
has an interesting tabernacle painting (a copy
of one in Bohemia), stained glass and statues.

Bohemian Museum   MUSEUM
(📞 09-422 0852; www.puhoihistoricalsociety.org.
nz; Puhoi Rd; adult/child $3.50/free; ⊘noon-3pm

Sat & Sun, daily Jan–Easter) Tells the story of the hardship and perseverance of the original Bohemian pioneers.

Puhoi River Canoe Hire   CANOEING, KAYAKING
(☑ 09-422 0891; www.puhoirivercanoes.co.nz; 84 Puhoi Rd; ⊙ Sep-Jun) Hires kayaks and Canadian canoes, either by the hour (kayak/canoe $25/50) or for an excellent 8km downstream journey from the village to Wenderholm Regional Park (single/double kayak $50/100, including return transport). Bookings are essential.

✖ Eating & Drinking

Puhoi Valley   CAFE $$
(☑ 09-422 0670; www.puhoivalley.co.nz; 275 Ahuroa Rd; mains $15-23; ⊙ 10am-4pm; 🖫) Renowned across NZ, Puhoi Valley cheese features heavily on the menu of this upmarket cheese shop and cafe, set blissfully alongside a lake, fountain and children's playground. In the summer there's music on the lawn, perfect with a gourmet ice cream.

★ Puhoi Pub   PUB
(☑ 09-422 0812; www.puhoipub.com; 5 Saleyards Rd; ⊙ 10am-10pm Mon-Sat, to 8pm Sun) There's character and then some in this 1879 pub, with walls completely covered in old photos, animal heads and vintage household goods.

ⓘ Getting There & Away

Puhoi is 1km west of SH1. The turn-off is 2km past the Johnstone Hills tunnel. There's no public transport.

Mahurangi & Scandrett Regional Parks

At the southern and eastern edges of the Mahurangi Peninsula northeast of Auckland, the Mahurangi Regional Park and Scandrett Regional Park are convenient as day trips from the city, or as a relaxing overnight stay in simple accommodation or at basic campsites. Walking tracks, coastal forests, sheltered beaches and Māori and colonial history all feature.

⊙ Sights

Mahurangi Regional Park   PARK
(☑ 09-366 2000; http://regionalparks.auckland council.govt.nz; 190 Ngarewa Dr, Mahurangi West) Straddling the head of Mahurangi Harbour, Mahurangi Regional Park is a boater's paradise incorporating areas of coastal forest,

pā sites and a historic homestead and cemetery. Its sheltered beaches offer prime sandy spots for a dip or picnic and there are loop walks ranging from 1½ to 2½ hours.

The park has three distinct fingers: Mahurangi West, accessed from a turn-off 3km north of Puhoi; Scott Point on the eastern side, with road access 16km southeast of Warkworth; and isolated Mahurangi East, which can only be reached by boat. Accommodation is available in four basic campsites (per adult/child $10/4) and four baches ($111 to $171), sleeping six to eight.

Scandrett Regional Park   PARK
(☑ 09-366 2000; http://regionalparks.auckland council.govt.nz; 114 Scandrett Rd, Mahurangi East) On the ocean side of the Mahurangi Peninsula, Scandrett Regional Park has a sandy beach, walking tracks, patches of regenerating forest, a historic homestead, *pā* sites and great views towards Kawau Island. Three baches (sleeping six to eight) are available for rent and there's room for campervans (per adult/child $8/4).

ⓘ Getting There & Away

You'll need your own transport to reach these parks. Some parts can only be reached by boat.

Warkworth
POP 5000

River-hugging Warkworth makes a pleasant pit stop, its cutesy main street retaining a village atmosphere. Increases in Auckland's real estate prices and better motorway access have seen the town grow in popularity in recent years, but it is still a laid-back spot near good beaches and wine country.

⊙ Sights & Activities

Dome Forest   FOREST
(SH1) Two kilometres north of Warkworth, a track leads through this regenerating forest to the Dome summit (336m). On a fine day you can see the Sky Tower from a lookout near the top. The summit walk takes about 1½ hours return, or you can continue for a gruelling seven-hour one-way tramp through the **Totora Peak Scenic Reserve**, exiting on Govan Wilson Rd.

Ransom Wines   WINE
(☑ 09-425 8862; www.ransomwines.co.nz; Valerie Close; tasting with purchase free, otherwise donation to Tawharanui Open Sanctuary $5; ⊙ 10am-4pm Tue-Sun) Well signposted from SH1, about

3km south of Warkworth, Ransom produces great food wines and showcases them with good-value tasting platters crammed with smoked meats and local cheeses.

Eating & Drinking

Chocolate Brown
CAFE $$
(☑ 09-422 2677; www.chocolatebrown.co.nz; 6 Mill Lane; mains $10-25; ☺ 8am-4pm) Decked out with quirky NZ-themed art – mostly for sale – this cafe serves excellent coffee, robust eggy breakfasts and delicious home-style baking. Definitely leave room for a few cacao-infused goodies from the chocolate shop next door; there are also plenty of gift packs for the folks back home.

Tahi Bar
CRAFT BEER
(☑ 09-422 3674; www.tahibar.com; 1 Neville St; ☺ 3.30pm-late Tue-Thu, noon-late Fri-Sun) Tucked down a quiet laneway, Tahi features nine ever-changing taps of New Zealand craft beer. It's an exceptionally friendly spot with decent platters and pub grub, and a rustic and sunny deck. Ask if any beers from award-winning and Warkworth-based 8 Wired Brewing are available.

Getting There & Away

InterCity (☑ 09-583 5780; www.intercity. co.nz) services pass through town, en route between Auckland and the Bay of Islands.

Matakana
POP 291

Around 15 years ago, Matakana was a nondescript rural village with a handful of heritage buildings and an old-fashioned country pub. Now the locals watch bemused as Auckland's chattering classes idle away the hours in stylish wine bars and cafes.

The reason for this transformation is the area's boutique wineries, which are developing a name for pinot gris, merlot, syrah and a host of obscure varietals. Local vineyards are detailed in the free *Matakana Coast Wine Country* (www.matakanacoast.com) and *Matakana Wine Trail* (www.matakanawine.com) brochures, available from the Matakana Information Centre (p127).

Also available at the centre is information on B&B accommodation, tours exploring the rural and coastal hinterland, and a growing array of local stores specialising in antiques and vintage furniture and homewares.

Sights & Activities

Brick Bay Sculpture Trail
GARDENS
(☑ 09-425 4690; www.brickbaysculpture.co.nz; Arabella Lane, Snells Beach; adult/child $12/8; ☺ 10am-5pm) After taking an hour-long artistic ramble through the beautiful grounds and native bush of Brick Bay Wines, recuperate with a wine tasting at the architecturally impressive cafe. Ask about the annual 'Folly' competition, where an up-and-coming New Zealand artist is funded to construct their winning design, which is subsequently installed at Brick Bay.

Omaha Beach
BEACH
The nearest swimming beach to Matakana, Omaha has a long stretch of white sand, good surf and ritzy holiday homes. It's the kind of place you might see a former NZ prime minister on the golf course, which is set a few genteel blocks back from the beach.

Blue Adventures
WATER SPORTS
(☑ 022 630 5705; www.blueadventures.co.nz; 331 Omaha Flats Rd, Omaha; lessons per hr from $59) Offers kitesurfing, paddle-boarding and wakeboarding lessons and rentals from Omaha and Orewa.

Matakana Bicycle Hire
CYCLING
(☑ 09-423 0076; www.matakanabicyclehire.co.nz; Matakana Country Park, 1151 Leigh Rd; half-/full-day hire from $30/40, tours from $110) Hire a bike to explore local vineyards and beaches. Pick up a *Matakana Trails* map from the information centre detailing routes to nearby Omaha and Port Wells.

Sleeping & Eating

BeauRegard Accommodation
COTTAGE $$
(☑ 021 803 378; www.beauregard.co.nz; 603 Matakana Rd; d incl breakfast $160-190; ❋ 🛜) Sitting in rural surroundings, a 4km drive from Matakana village, these three one-bedroom self-contained cottages are the ideal stylish haven for exploring the beaches and vineyards of the surrounding area. Each of the cottages has a Gallic name – Bel-Air, Voltaire or Bastille – and the French-Kiwi hosts have plenty of ideas for tasty discoveries at local markets and restaurants.

Charlie's Gelato Garden
ICE CREAM $
(☑ 09-422 7942; www.charliesgelato.co.nz; 17 Sharp Rd; ice cream $4-6, pizza slice/whole $5/18; ☺ 9am-5pm Nov-Mar, 10am-4pm Fri-Sun Apr-Oct) Superb sorbet and gelato made from fresh fruit and interesting ingredients – try the liquorice or

ginger-beer flavours – and excellent wood-fired pizzas during summer from Friday to Sunday.

Matakana   PUB FOOD **$$**
(☑ 09-422 7518; www.matakana.co.nz; 11 Matakana Valley Rd; mains $22-37; ⊙ 11.30am-1am) Matakana's heritage pub features stylish decor, local wines and craft beers, and decent bistro food, sometimes including Mahurangi oysters. An American-style smoker turns out good low 'n' slow barbecue – try the pork belly or the spicy ribs – and occasional DJs and live acts enliven the cool outdoor space. The pub quiz on Wednesdays is always a good time.

🍷 Drinking & Nightlife

⭐**Sawmill Brewery**   MICROBREWERY
(☑ 09-422 6555; www.sawmillbrewery.co.nz; 1004 Leigh Rd; ⊙ noon-10pm) Sawmill is recognised as one of the Auckland region's best craft breweries. Relax with a tasting rack of brews amid the rustic but hip decor, and order up a storm from the share-plates menu. It's all good, but we're partial to the citrusy Double IPA with goat hummus and cumin flatbreads.

Vintry   WINE BAR
(☑ 09-423 0251; www.vintry.co.nz; 2 Matakana Valley Rd; ⊙ 3-10pm)FPALORO In the **Matakana Cinemas** (☑ 09-422 9833; www.matakana cinemas.co.nz) complex, this wine bar serves as a one-stop cellar door for all the local producers. Beers from local craft breweries are on tap, and the same owners operate a riverside bistro downstairs serving breakfast, lunch and dinner.

🛍 Shopping

Matakana Village Farmers Market   MARKET
(www.matakanavillage.co.nz; Matakana Sq, 2 Matakana Valley Rd; ⊙ 8am-1pm Sat) This excellent farmers market lures plenty of Aucklanders up the highway.

ℹ Information

Matakana Information Centre (☑ 09-422 7433; www.matakanainfo.org.nz; 2 Matakana Valley Rd; ⊙ 10am-late) is in the foyer of the cinema complex.

ℹ Getting There & Away

Matakana village is a 10km drive northeast of Warkworth along Matakana Rd; there's no regular public transport. Ferries for Kawau Island leave from Sandspit, 8km east of Warkworth along Sandspit Rd.

Leigh
POP 390

Appealing little Leigh (www.leighbythesea. co.nz) has a picturesque harbour dotted with fishing boats, and a decent swimming beach at **Matheson Bay**.

Apart from the extraordinary Goat Island Marine Reserve (p127) on its doorstep, Leigh's other claim to fame is the legendary live-music venue Leigh Sawmill Cafe (p128), which sometimes sees surprisingly big names drop in to play a set or two.

👁 Sights

⭐**Goat Island
Marine Reserve**   WILDLIFE RESERVE
(www.doc.govt.nz; Cape Rodney to Okakari Point Marine Reserve, Goat Island Rd) Only 3km from Leigh, this 547-hectare aquatic area was established in 1975 as the country's first marine reserve. In less than 40 years the sea has reverted to a giant aquarium, giving an impression of what the NZ coast must have been like before humans arrived. You only need step knee-deep into the water to see snapper (the big fish with blue dots and fins), blue maomao and stripy parore swimming around.

Excellent interpretive panels explain the area's Māori significance (it was the landing place of one of the ancestral canoes) and provide pictures of the species you're likely to encounter.

There are **dive areas** all around Goat Island, which sits just offshore, or you can snorkel or dive directly from the beach. Colourful sponges, forests of seaweed, boarfish, crayfish and stingrays are common sights, and if you're very lucky you may see orcas and bottle-nosed dolphins. Visibility is claimed to be at least 10m, 75% of the time.

**Goat Island Marine
Discovery Centre**   AQUARIUM
(☑ 09-923 3645; www.goatislandmarine.co.nz; 160 Goat Island Rd; adult/child/family $9/7/20; ⊙ 10am-4pm Dec-Apr, Sat, Sun & public & school holidays May-Nov; ♿) Staffed by marine experts and graduate students from the University of Auckland, this centre is packed with interesting exhibitions on the ecosystem of the marine reserve, and is worth visiting before venturing into Goat Island's waters. The interactive displays and the tide pool full of marine creatures are great for children.

WORTH A TRIP

PAKIRI BEACH TREKS

Pakiri Horse Riding (☑ 09-422 6275; www.horseride-nz.co.nz; Rahuikiri Rd) has 60 horses available for superb bush-and-beach rides ranging from one hour ($80) to multiday 'safaris'. Accommodation is provided in basic but spectacularly situated beachside cabins (dorm/cabin $40/200) or in a comfortable four-bedroom house ($500) secluded among the dunes.

🏃 Activities

Goat Island Dive & Snorkel   DIVING
(☑ 09-422 6925; www.goatislanddive.co.nz; 142a Pakiri Rd; snorkel set hire adult/child $25/18, incl wetsuit $39/28) This long-standing operator offers guided snorkelling, PADI courses and dive trips in the Goat Island Marine Reserve (p127) and other key sites throughout the year. It also hires snorkelling and diving gear.

Glass Bottom Boat Tours   BOATING
(☑ 09-422 6334; www.glassbottomboat.co.nz; Goat Island Rd; adult/child $30/15; ☉ Sep-Apr) A glass-bottomed boat provides an opportunity to see the underwater life of Goat Island Marine Reserve (p127) while staying dry. Trips last 45 minutes and run from the beach (weather permitting). Go online or ring to check conditions and to book.

Octopus Hideaway   SNORKELLING
(☑ 021 926 212; www.theoctopushideaway.nz; 2 Seatoun Ave; ☉ 10am-6pm Tue-Sun) This crew hires snorkelling gear (adult/child $25/18, including wetsuit $38/26), and offers guided two-hour day ($75/55) and night ($90/70) snorkel expeditions.

Drinking & Nightlife

Leigh Sawmill Cafe   PUB
(☑ 09-422 6019; www.sawmillcafe.co.nz; 142 Pakiri Rd; ☉ 10am-late late Dec–mid-Feb, Thu-Sun mid-Feb–late Dec) This spunky little venue is a regular stop on the summer rock circuit, sometimes attracting surprisingly big names. The pizzas ($25) are thin and crunchy like they should be, and best enjoyed in the garden on a lazy summer's evening. It sometimes closes for private functions so it's wise to check its Facebook page before setting out.

If you imbibe too much of the good stuff from local wineries and craft breweries, there's accommodation inside the old sawmill shed, including basic backpacker rooms (from $25) and massive doubles with en suites ($125). Alternatively, you can rent the Cosy Sawmill Family Cottage (from $200, sleeps 10) or a stylish apartment ($200).

ⓘ Getting There & Away

You'll need your own wheels to get here.

Bay of Islands & Northland

Best Places to Eat

➡ Provenir (p158)

➡ Dune (p137)

➡ Sandbar (p137)

➡ Gables (p153)

➡ Cafe Bianca (p138)

Best Places to Stay

➡ Endless Summer Lodge (p172)

➡ Arcadia Lodge (p152)

➡ Old Oak (p166)

➡ Kahoe Farms Hostel (p165)

➡ Mangawhai Chalets (p137)

Why Go?

For many New Zealanders, the phrase 'up north' conjures up sepia-toned images of family fun in the sun, pohutukawa in bloom and dolphins frolicking in pretty bays. From school playgrounds to work cafeterias, owning a bach (holiday house) here is a passport to popularity.

Beaches are the main drawcard and they're here in profusion. Visitors from more crowded countries are sometimes flummoxed to wander onto beaches without a scrap of development or another human being in sight. The west coast shelters the most spectacular remnants of the ancient kauri forests that once blanketed the top of the country; the remaining giant trees are an awe-inspiring sight and one of the nation's treasures.

It's not just natural attractions that are on offer: history hangs heavily here. The site of the earliest settlements of both Māori and Europeans, Northland is unquestionably the birthplace of the nation.

When to Go

➡ Northland's beaches go crazy at New Year and remain busy throughout the January school holidays. Prices shoot up and accommodation can be in short supply.

➡ The long, lazy days of summer usually continue into February and March, making these the best months to visit.

➡ The 'winterless north' boasts a subtropical climate, most noticeable from Kerikeri upwards, which averages seven rainy days per month in summer, but 16 in winter.

➡ In winter the average highs hover around 16°C and the average lows around 7°C.

➡ Temperatures are often a degree or two warmer than Auckland, especially on the east coast.

Bay of Islands & Northland Highlights

1 Cape Reinga
(p168) Watching oceans collide while souls depart.

2 Waipoua Forest
(p176) Paying homage to the ancient kauri giants of this numinous forest.

3 Poor Knights Islands (p145)
Diving at one of New Zealand's, if not the world's, top spots.

4 Bay of Islands
(p146) Cruising northern waters and claiming your own island paradise among the many in this bay.

5 Ninety Mile Beach (p168) Surfing the giant sand dunes on this remote and seemingly endless stretch of sand.

6 Waitangi Treaty Grounds (p154) Delving into history and culture, both Māori and colonial.

7 Mangawhai Heads (p136) Soaking up the chilled-out surf-town vibe, honing your body-surfing skills and exploring the rolling dunes across the estuary.

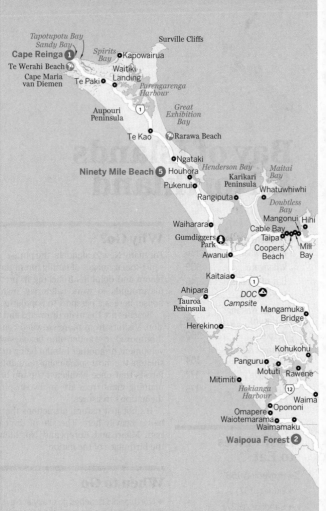

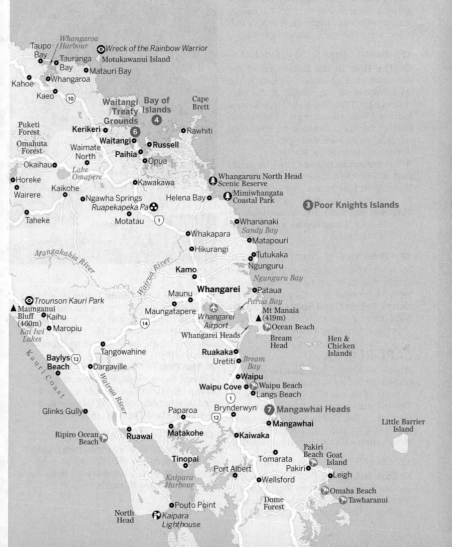

SOUTH PACIFIC OCEAN

Whangaroa Harbour
Taupo Bay
Tauranga Bay
Wreck of the Rainbow Warrior
Motukawanui Island
Whangaroa
Matauri Bay
Kahoe
Kaeo
10

Cape Brett

Puketi Forest
Waitangi Treaty Grounds
Bay of Islands 4
Omahuta Forest
Kerikeri
6
Waitangi
Rawhiti
Waimate North
Russell
Okaihau
Paihia
Lake Omapere
Opua
Horeke
Whangaruru North Head Scenic Reserve
Wairere
Kaikohe
Kawakawa
Helena Bay
Mimiwhangata Coastal Park
Taheke
Ngawha Springs
Ruapekapeka Pa
Motatau
1
Whananaki
Sandy Bay
3 Poor Knights Islands
Whakapara
Matapouri
Hikurangi
Tutukaka
Kamo
Ngunguru
Mangakahia River
Ngunguru Bay
Maunu
Whangarei
Pataua
Maungatapere
Wairua River
Pataua Bay
Mt Manaia (419m)
Trounson Kauri Park
Whangarei Airport
Ocean Beach
Maunganui Bluff (460m)
Kaihu
Whangarei Heads
Bream Head
Maropiu
Kai Iwi Lakes
Hen & Chicken Islands
Tangowahine
Ruakaka
Uretiti
Bream Bay
Baylys Beach 12
Dargaville
Waipu
Glinks Gully
Waipu Cove
Waipu Beach
Langs Beach
Paparoa
Brynderwyn
7 Mangawhai Heads
Wairua River
1
Little Barrier Island
Ripiro Ocean Beach
Ruawai
Matakohe
12
Mangawhai
Kaiwaka
Tinopai
Tomarata
Pakiri Beach
Goat Island
Port Albert
Pakiri
Wellsford
Leigh
Kaipara Harbour
Dome Forest
Omaha Beach
Tawharanui
North Head
Kaipara Lighthouse
Pouto Point

Kauri Coast

50 km
25 miles

DAY TRIPS FROM THE BAY OF ISLANDS

BAY CRUISE

Whether you're heading out on a yacht, a jet boat or a large commercial launch, a day trip on the emerald waters of the Bay of Islands is practically obligatory. As well as getting a closer look at the bay's 150 mainly untouched islands, you're likely to spot dolphins, whales and penguins along the way.

☆ **Best Things to See/Do/Eat**

◉ **The Hole in the Rock** One of the bay's most striking islands is Piercy Island (Motukōkako) off Cape Brett, at the bay's eastern edge. This steep-walled rock fortress features a vast natural arch – the famous Hole in the Rock. Provided the conditions are right, most boat tours will pass right through the heart of the island.

🚶 **Urupukapuka Island** Cruises inevitably land at this, the largest island in the bay. Take a short hike up the crest of the island for some blissful bay views. (p159)

✕ **Otehei Bay Café** This licensed cafe by the wharf on Urupukapuka caters to the daytime tour boats.

☆ **How to Get There**

There are literally dozens of boats primed to take visitors out on the bay every day of the week (weather permitting). The two big players, **Fullers Great Sights** and **Explore NZ**, both have trips to the Hole in the Rock, stopping at Urupukapuka on the way back.

CAPE REINGA

While it's a lengthy drive from the Bay of Islands (over 2½ hours each way), Cape Reinga is one of the essential sights of the north. This magical spot at the far northern tip of the island is heralded by the Māori people as the most spiritually significant place in the entire country. It's also incredibly beautiful.

☆ **Best Things to See/Do/Eat**

◉ **Cape Reinga** The Pacific Ocean and the Tasman Sea come crashing together at this dramatic point, where there's a real sense of standing at the end of the world. (p168)

The Hole in the Rock

◉ **Te Paki Giant Sand Dunes** Stop on your journey up or down the Aupouri Peninsula to clamber up and 'surf' down these giant dunes on Ninety Mile Beach. Bring your own boogie board, or rent one here in summer. (p168)

✕ **The Thai** Your journey to the Far North will take you through pretty Doubtless Bay. Take a brief detour on the way home to the cute harbourside village of Mangonui for Northland's best Thai food. (p167)

☆ **How to Get There**

Head north on SH10 to Awanui, then branch off to the north on SH1. There's no public transport up here, but various day tours depart from the Bay of Islands.

WAIPOUA FOREST

From the Bay of Islands it takes 90 minutes to reach the gargantuan trees of the Waipoua Forest, some of which have been holding court here for up to 3000 years. The drive will take you alongside the breathtaking Hokianga Harbour, with its immense sand dunes and tannin-tinted water.

☆ Best Things to See/Do/Eat

◉ **Tāne Mahuta** Named for the Māori god of the forest, this big lad takes up 244.5 cubic metres of space, dwarfing everything that enters into his presence. He's positioned conveniently close to the road in a very well signposted location. (p176)

🌴 **Footprints Waipoua** For an utterly mesmerising and unique experience of the forest, join one of these night-time tours, departing from Omapere. Māori guides introduce you to their culture and to the forest giants, reciting traditional *karakia* (prayers, incantations) before the trees. (p174)

🍴 **Landing Cafe** Enjoy the views over the Hokianga Harbour from the front deck while tucking into a meal at this Opononi cafe. It's by far the best food stop en route to the forest. (p175)

☆ How to Get There

Head west from Paihia (south from Kerikeri) and follow the signs to Kaikohe, then continue west on SH12 through Opononi and Omapere. Alternatively, join a **Fullers Great Sights** bus tour, departing from Paihia.

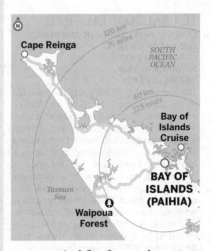

Aside from its own ample attractions, the Bay of Islands makes a good springboard for exploring the entire north. Russell is the prettiest bay town, but Paihia and Kerikeri make better bases for hitting the road.

HIKING IN NORTHLAND

TE PAKI COASTAL TRAIL

START TE PAKI STREAM (KAUAEPARAOA)
END KAPOWAIRUA
DURATION 3 DAYS
DISTANCE 42.5KM
DIFFICULTY EASY

The northern tip of NZ is a place pounded by the seas, whipped by winds and bathed in sunshine. It's a wild and powerful spot, where the strong and unforgiving currents of the Tasman Sea and Pacific Ocean sweep along the shorelines before meeting in a fury of foam just west of Cape Reinga.

Providing trampers with a front-row seat to nature's beauty and drama here is Te Paki Coastal Track, which meanders between spectacular beaches, coastal forest, wetlands and towering dunes. Once described as a 'desert coast', Ninety Mile Beach is one of NZ's longest beaches and is almost concrete-hard below the high-tide line – which makes for easy (if at times

footsore) tramping – and is bordered much of the way by sand dunes up to 6km wide and rising in places to 143m in height. The tramp then climbs to Cape Reinga, site of the famous lighthouse, but also a sacred Māori site, before following cliff tops and descending to idyllic, sandy beaches.

The DOC maintains four camping grounds along the track. The tramp can be extended by starting in Ahipara, 83km south of Te Paki Stream (Kauaeparaoa) at the southern end of Ninety Mile Beach, adding three or four days to the journey. You can also join it at Waipapakauri (69km south of Te Paki Stream), Hukatere (51km) or the Bluff (19km) – the 32km portion from Hukatere to the Bluff (a famous spot for surf fishing) is ruler-straight. Keep in mind, however, that you'll encounter cars and tour buses daily on Ninety Mile Beach until you pass Te Paki Stream.

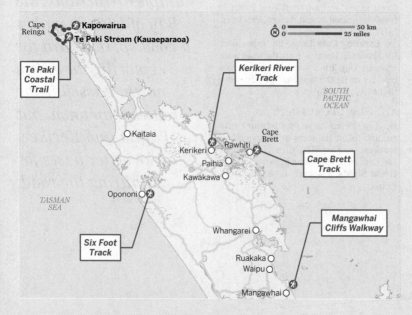

There are excellent tracks scattered all throughout the Northland region, ranging from easy riverside strolls right through to arduous multiday hikes.

CAPE BRETT TRACK
START/END RAWHITI
DURATION 2 DAYS
DISTANCE 33KM
DIFFICULTY MODERATE

A scenic underscore to the Bay of Islands, Cape Brett is a gossamer-thin strip of land that famously ends beside the Hole in the Rock, the most popular tourist attraction in the area.

But while boats and helicopters hurry to the Hole in the Rock, the Cape Brett Track winds slowly along the tops of the cape, always climbing or descending, and peeling open views of the Bay of Islands before coming to its coup de grâce moment – as you step through a small saddle just beyond the turn-off to Deep Water Cove, the land plummets away into the Pacific Ocean and the full cliff-lined drama of Cape Brett is revealed. It's a spectacular couple of days on foot, aided by the opportunity to stay a night inside a former lighthouse keepers' cottage, in one of the finest coastal regions in New Zealand.

Between Rawhiti and the Deep Water Cove junction, the track crosses private, Māori-owned land. To cover track maintenance along this section, a permit fee of $40 is charged to tramp the track. You'll pay the fee online when you book your stay at the Cape Brett Hut. Bookings and the permit payment can also be made in person at the Bay of Islands i-SITE (p158) in Paihia.

MANGAWHAI CLIFFS WALKWAY
START/END MANGAWHAI HEADS
DURATION 2-3 HOURS RETURN
DISTANCE 10KM RETURN
DIFFICULTY EASY

This short track affords extensive views of sea and land on the beautiful coast heading north from Mangawhai Heads. It can be walked as a loop with a return along the beach at low tide – otherwise you'll come and go via the cliffs. This is part of Te Araroa, the national walking track. Ask at the Mangawhai visitor information centre (p138) for the *Tracks and Walks* brochure detailing other walks in the area.

SIX FOOT TRACK
START/END THE END OF MOUNTAIN RD, OPONONI
DURATION 3 HOURS RETURN
DISTANCE 7KM RETURN
DIFFICULTY MODERATE

Leading from the end of a country road to a remote DOC hut, this short hike takes in native bush, waterfalls and views over the Hokianga district. View it as a teaser for the longer, more difficult walks that start from the hut and explore the Waima Forest and Ranges.

KERIKERI RIVER TRACK
START KERIKERI BASIN
END RAINBOW FALLS ROAD
DURATION 1 HOUR
DISTANCE 3.5KM
DIFFICULTY EASY

This popular walking track meanders through beautiful native bush lining the Kerikeri River. Along the way you'll pass broad Wharepuke Falls, the Fairy Pools swimming holes and the Rainbow Falls, where even on dim days the 27m drop conjures dancing rainbows.

WHANGAREI DISTRICT

To truly experience this area you'll need to get wet, and scores of beaches offer opportunities for swimming, surfing or just splashing about. The hotspots heave with Kiwi holidaymakers at peak times, but even then it's possible to find isolated stretches of sand where your footprints are the only ones.

North of Whangarei, the Tutukaka Coast is one of the planet's top three coastlines, according to *National Geographic Traveler* magazine, and the late Jacques Cousteau rated the neighbouring Poor Knights Islands as one of the world's best dive sites.

Mangawhai

POP 2400

Mangawhai village sits at the base of a gorgeous horseshoe estuary, but it's the surf beach at Mangawhai Heads, 5km further on, that's the real treat.

Various Māori tribes inhabited the area before the 1660s, when Ngāti Whātua became dominant. In 1807 Ngāti Whātua defeated Ngāpuhi in a major battle, letting the survivors escape. One of them was Hongi Hika, who in 1825 returned, armed with muskets obtained from Europeans. The ensuing bloodbath all but annihilated Ngāti Whātua and the district became *tapu* (sacred, taboo). British squatters moved in and were rewarded with land titles by the

government in the 1850s. Ceremonies were only performed to lift the *tapu* in the 1990s.

These days Mangawhai is benefiting from improved traffic links with Auckland, and new housing subdivisions are expanding the spread of the area. Down on the surf beach, though, it's still a quintessential laid back New Zealand beach town.

◉ Sights & Activities

★ **Mangawhai Heads**   BEACH
(Wintle St) Mangawhai's main claim to fame is the surf beach at the northern head of its large estuary. The large beach-side car park fills up quickly in peak season.

Just across the water a narrow spit of sand stretches for kilometres to form the estuary's south head, sheltering a seabird sanctuary. A short kayak across the estuary will bring you to this beautiful, empty expanse of dunes and its long, sublime, usually deserted beach. Take care to avoid endangered dotterels and fairy terns nesting in the sand.

Mangawhai Museum   MUSEUM
(☑09-431 4645; www.mangawhai-museum.org.nz; Molesworth Dr, Mangawhai Heads; adult/child $12/3; ☑10am-4pm) One of regional New Zealand's best museums, this spectacular building on the main road linking Mangawhai village to Mangawhai Heads is packed with interesting displays on the area's history and environment. Check out the roof shaped like a stingray (Mangawhai means 'stream of the rays'). There's also a sun-drenched cafe worthy of a stop.

Te Whai Bay Wines   VINEYARD
(☑09-945 0580; www.tewhaibaywines.co.nz; 367 King Rd; ☑11am-5pm Oct-Apr) Handcrafted wines include chardonnay, pinot gris and Bordeaux-style reds, and the beautiful vineyard is a great spot for a shared antipasto platter to enhance the pleasant illusion of being in a southern hemisphere version of Tuscany. It pays to call ahead to check it's open. Ask at Mangawhai's Visitor Information Centre about other local vineyards.

Wined About Bike Tours   CYCLING
(☑09-945 0580; www.winedabout.co.nz; per person $50) Three different self-guided tour options include all the good things in life: Art & Chocolate, Wineries & Olives or a Freestyle Ride exploring Mangawhai village and nearby beaches. Pick-ups are included in the prices, both before and after riding.

ESSENTIAL NORTHLAND

Eat fresh Orongo Bay oysters.

Drink Northland craft beer at Mangawhai's Wood Street Freehouse (p137).

Read *The House of Strife* (1993), Maurice Shadbolt's riveting novel set during the Northland War.

Listen to *Cape Reinga Way* (2011) by The Nukes, ukuleles heading to the afterlife.

Watch *Land of the Long White Cloud* (2009), fishing philosophers on Ninety Mile Beach.

Celebrate Waitangi Day (p156).

Go green sing to the trees with Footprints Waipoua (p174).

Online www.northlandnz.com; www.kauricoast.com.

🛏 Sleeping

Mangawhai Heads
Holiday Park   HOLIDAY PARK $
(☑09-431 4675; www.mangawhaiheadsholiday
park.co.nz; 2 Mangawhai Heads Rd; sites from $18,
unit with/without bathroom from $105/65; 🛜)
With an absolute waterfront location on the
sandy expanse of Mangawhai's estuary, this
laid-back combo of campsites, units and cabins is a retro slice of Kiwiana holiday style.
Visit in summer for a vibrant halo of red
blooms from groves of ancient pohutukawa
trees. It's a family-friendly place, with an expectation of no noise after 10.30pm.

Mangawhai Backpackers:
The Coastal Cow   HOSTEL $
(☑09-431 5246; www.facebook.com/mangawhai
backpackers; 299 Molesworth Dr, Mangawhai
Heads; dm $20, s $55-89, d & tw $68-95, f $102-
136) The rooms at this unassuming house-
style hostel have been spruced up with a
splash of pale-blue paint. Bathrooms are
shared and there's a pleasant barbecue
area on the back deck. Family rooms sleep
up to four people.

★ Mangawhai Chalets   CHALET $$
(☑09-431 5029; www.mangawhaichalets.co.nz;
252 Molesworth Dr, Mangawhai Heads; units
from $130; ❄🛜) There's a Cape Cod feel
to the three stylishly decked out cedar
chalets positioned in the lavender-filled
garden behind the main house. All of the
units have fridges and there's a communal kitchen with a barbecue and a stove
in the open-sided 'clubhouse', should the
cooking urge take you.

Mangawhai Lodge   B&B $$
(☑09-431 5311; www.seaviewlodge.co.nz; 4 Heather
St, Mangawhai Heads; s/d $185/195, apt $185-250;
🛜) 🍃 This hillside lodge has smartly fur-
nished rooms opening onto a picture-perfect
wraparound veranda with terrific sea views.
Choose between two classic B&B rooms and
two apartments with kitchenettes.

🍴 Eating

Mangawhai Village Market   MARKET $
(☑09-431 2195; 45 Moir St, Mangawhai village;
⊙9am-1pm Sat) Held in the library hall, this
is a good place to stock up on organic produce (including wine and olive oil), peruse
local crafts and fill up on food-truck fare.
Another market is held on Sunday mornings in the Mangawhai Heads Domain from
mid-October to Easter.

★ Dune   CAFE $$
(☑09-431 5695; www.facebook.com/thedune
mangawhai; 40 Moir St, Mangawhai village; mains
$19-28; ⊙9am-9pm Wed-Sun, extended summer)
🍃 Despite the name, Mangawhai's best eatery is nowhere near the sands. Situated in the
heart of the village, Dune is half bar, half cafe
–with sunny outdoor tables arrayed around
both. The food is excellent, including a deliciously smoky brisket, gourmet pizza and lots
of yummy vegetable side dishes. Much of the
produce is sourced from the owners' family
farms.

★ Sandbar   CAFE, BISTRO $$
(☑09-431 5587; www.sandbarmangawhai.co.nz;
Fagan Pl, Mangawhai Heads; mains brunch $12-19,
lunch $18-22, dinner $31-33; ⊙9am-3pm daily &
6-10pm Fri & Sat, extended summer; 🔧) Polished
concrete floors and a living wall set a quietly
stylish scene for a daytime cafe and night-
time bistro. Evening meals are sophisticated
and deftly constructed, featuring the likes
of fresh fish, Scotch fillet, merino lamb and
wonderfully fluffy gnocchi with wild mushrooms and truffle oil.

Frog & Kiwi   FRENCH $$
(☑09-431 4439; www.frogandkiwirestaurant.co.nz;
The Hub, 6 Molesworth Dr, Mangawhai village; mains
brunch $12-25, dinner $32-35; ⊙8.30am-2.30pm
& 6-10pm) This relaxed eatery does a mixture of French and Kiwi cafe fare by day
and more refined French classics at night. A
five-course degustation menu (with/without
wine matches $119/93) is also available, but
you'll need to book 24 hours in advance.

🍷 Drinking & Nightlife

Mangawhai Tavern   PUB
(☑09-431 4505; www.mangawhaitavern.co.nz; 2
Moir St, Mangawhai village; ⊙11am-late) One of
the country's oldest pubs – established in
1865, but twice burnt down since then – the
tavern's harbourside location is a top spot for
an afternoon beer. There's live music most
Saturday nights and Sunday afternoons, and
across the Christmas–New Year period some
of NZ's top bands rock the outside stage. The
meals are also very good.

Wood Street Freehouse   BAR
(☑09-431 4051; www.woodstreetfreehouse.co.nz;
12 Wood St, Mangawhai Heads; mains $18-26, shared
plates $10-12; ⊙4pm-late Mon-Fri, from noon Sat &
Sun; 🔧) Craft beer has arrived in Mangawhai
at this buzzing bar/cafe, including a good
selection from Northland brewers. Excellent

WORTH A TRIP

KAIWAKA KAI

If you're feeling peckish on the route between Auckland and Whangarei or the Kauri Coast, stop for *kai* (food) at Kaiwaka.

It's an unusual spot for a Dutch-style delicatessen, but the **Kaiwaka Cheese Shop** (☑09-431 2195; www.cheese-shop. co.nz; 1957 SH1, Kaiwaka) has long been an essential stop for travelling foodies seeking some luxury additions to their holiday provisions. Dutch dominates but you'll also find British and NZ cheese, and a good selection of wine and tasty snacks.

Another great option is **Cafe Bianca** (☑09-431 2327; 1956 SH1, Kaiwaka; mains $7-20; ⊙9am-3.30pm Thu-Tue; 🕏). Beyond the rough wooden exterior is a corrugated-iron-lined speakeasy where staff dressed as flappers deliver cooked breakfasts, gourmet burgers and seafood chowder to bemused road-weary patrons seated at Edwardian tables. Try the beef burger – it's surprisingly light and exceedingly delicious.

food includes burgers, gourmet pizzas and shared plates – the truffle and parmesan fries are addictive. They also host regular family-friendly movie nights.

ℹ️ Information

Visitor Information Centre (☑09-431 5090; www.mangawhai.co.nz; Molesworth Dr, Mangawhai Heads; ⊙9am-6pm daily Jan & Feb, 2-5pm Fri, 11am-5pm Sat, 11am-1pm Sun Mar-Dec) Staffed sporadically but there are information boards outside. Ask about opportunities to visit local vineyards and olive groves.

ℹ️ Getting There & Away

Mangawhai is around 80 minutes by car from Auckland. There is no regular public transport.

Waipu & Bream Bay

POP 1680

Waipu is a sleepy rural town with a fascinating history, giggle-inducing name and a couple of excellent swimming beaches nearby at **Waipu Cove** and **Langs Beach**.

Waipu's original 934 British settlers came from Scotland via Nova Scotia (Canada) between 1853 and 1860. These canny Scots had

the good sense to eschew frigid Otago, where so many of their kindred settled, for sunnier northern climes. Only 10% of current residents are direct descendants but there's a big get together every year, when the **Highland Games** (www.waipugames.co.nz; ⊙1 Jan), established in 1871, take place in Caledonian Park.

Bream Bay has miles of blissfully deserted beach, blighted only slightly by a giant oil refinery at the north end. At **Uretiti**, a stretch of beach south of a DOC campsite is unofficially considered 'clothing optional'. Over New Year the crowd is evenly split between Kiwi families, serious European nudists and gay guys from Auckland and Northland.

⊙ Sights & Activities

There are excellent walks in the area, including the 3km **Waipu Coastal Trail**, which heads south from Waipu Cove to Ding Bay via the Pancake Rocks. The 2km **Waipu Caves Track** starts near the entrance to a large cave containing glow-worms and limestone formations; bring a torch and sturdy footwear.

Waipu Museum   MUSEUM
(☑09-432 0746; www.waipumuseum.co.nz; 36 The Centre, Waipu; adult/child $10/5; ⊙9.30am-4.30pm) In this fascinating little museum Waipu's Scottish heritage comes to life through holograms, a short film and interactive displays. Fun fact: church services were still being held in Scots Gaelic in Waipu right up until 1907.

🛏️ Sleeping

Camp Waipu Cove   HOLIDAY PARK $
(☑09-432 0410; www.campwaipucove.com; 869 Cove Rd, Waipu Cove; sites/r from $38/45, unit with/without bathroom from $120/70) Set beside a blissful stretch of beach with views to craggy islands, this well-kept campground has a range of simple cabins, motel-style units, bunk rooms and tent and campervan sites. Facilities include a colourful and clean toilet block, communal kitchen, playground, giant chess set and TV room. Native birds flitter around in profusion.

Waipu Wanderers Backpackers   HOSTEL $
(☑09-432 0532; www.waipu-hostel.co.nz; 25 St Marys Rd, Waipu; dm/s/d $33/49/70; 🕏) There are only three rooms at this friendly backpackers in Waipu township, set behind a lovely old house lined with citrus trees; bathrooms are shared. Look forward to free cereal and toast, and fruit in season.

DOC Uretiti Campsite
CAMPGROUND **$**

(☎09-432 1051; www.doc.govt.nz; SH1, Uretiti; sites per adult/child $13/6.50) At Uretiti, there is a DOC campsite with hot showers and stellar beach views amid rolling sand dunes.

Waipu Cove Resort
MOTEL **$$**

(☎09-432 0348; www.waipucoveresort.co.nz; 891 Cove Rd, Waipu Cove; units $120-220; 🛜🏊) Nestled behind sand dunes, this complex is more like a modern motel than a resort, although it does have it's own spa and swimming pools, and the arcing sprawl of the beach is just metres away.

✖ Eating

Little Red
CAFE **$**

(www.facebook.com/blackshedwaipu.co.nz; 7 Cove Rd; snacks $4-7; ⊗8am-3pm Nov-Easter) Good coffee, artisan icy treats, organic soft drinks and kombucha (fermented sweet tea), and homestyle baking – all served from a funky red shipping container. Grab a spot on one of the colourful Cape Cod–style chairs out the front and tuck into brioche and brownies.

Cove
CAFE **$$**

(☎09-432 0234; www.thecovecafe.co.nz; 910 Cove Rd, Waipu Cove; breakfast $12-19, mains $22-35; ⊗7am-late Dec-Mar, 9am-9pm Thu-Mon Apr-Oct) This heritage cottage near Waipu covers all the bases, from coffee and breakfast bagels to pizza, gourmet burgers, craft beer and healthy smoothies, and the deck is a very pleasant spot to celebrate exploring NZ. The baking is particularly tempting.

McLeod's Pizza Barn
PIZZA **$$**

(☎09-432 1011; www.facebook.com/mcleodspizzabarn; 2 Cove Rd, Waipu; pizzas $13-29, mains $20-27; ⊗11.30am-9pm Wed-Sun Apr-Nov, daily Dec-Mar) The flavour combinations may seem almost as odd as a Scots-named pizzeria, but the crispy-based pizzas are delicious. Try the Gumdigger, with smoked salmon, asparagus, blue-vein cheese and pesto, and wash it down with a craft beer from Waipu's very own McLeod's Brewery. Other crowd-pleasing menu options include burgers, lamb shanks and pasta dishes.

Waipu Cafe Deli
CAFE **$$**

(☎09-432 0990; www.facebook.com/waipu.cafe.deli; 29 The Centre, Waipu; mains $12-19; ⊗8am-3pm) Enticing salads, sandwiches, cooked breakfasts, pasta, muffins and organic fairtrade coffee are served at this attractive little cafe on Waipu's main drag.

ℹ Information

Tourist brochures and internet access are available at the **Waipu Museum** (p138).

ℹ Getting There & Away

BUS

InterCity (☎09-583 5780; www.intercity.co.nz) has three or four coaches a day to and from Auckland (from $23, 2½ hours), Whangarei (from $18, 25 minutes), Kawakawa (from $28, 1½ hours), Paihia (from $25, 1¾ hours) and Kerikeri (from $25, 2¼ hours).

Mana Bus (☎09-367 9140; www.manabus.com), in association with Naked Bus, has two or three daily coaches to and from Auckland (from $17, two hours), Warkworth (from $15, one hour), Whangarei ($10, 45 minutes), Kawakawa ($14, 1¾ hours) and Paihia ($14, two hours).

CAR & MOTORCYCLE

Waipu Cove can be reached by a particularly scenic route that heads from Mangawhai Heads through Langs Beach. Otherwise, turn off SH1 38km south of Whangarei.

Whangarei

POP 56,400

Northland's only city is surrounded by natural beauty, and its compact town centre offers plenty of rainy-day diversions. There's a thriving artistic community, some good walks, and interesting cafes and bars.

⊙ Sights

⊙ Town Basin

This attractive riverside marina is home to museums, galleries, cafes, shops, public art and an information centre. It's a great place for a stroll, with a marked **Art Walk** and **Heritage Trail**. An **artisans' fair** (www.artisansfair.org.nz) is held on Saturdays from late October to Easter under the shade of the pedestrian bridge.

Clapham's National Clock Museum
MUSEUM

(☎09-438 3993; www.claphamsclocks.com; Lower Dent St, Town Basin; adult/child $10/4; ⊗9am-5pm) This charming collection of 1600 ticking, gonging and cuckooing timepieces is more interesting than you'd imagine. There are all manner of kooky and kitschy items displayed alongside the more august specimens, such as the venerable 1690 English-built grandfather clock.

Whangarei

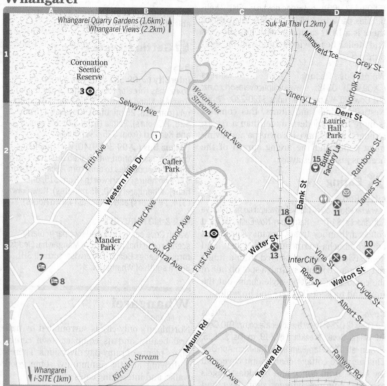

Whangarei Art Museum GALLERY
(☑ 09-430 4240; www.whangareiartmuseum.co.nz; The Hub, 91 Dent St, Town Basin; ☺10am-4pm) FREE Whangarei's public gallery has an interesting permanent collection, but the two large gallery spaces usually house temporary exhibitions by local and regional artists.

Te Kākano ARCHITECTURE
(www.yeswhangarei.co.nz; Town Basin) Fans of the late Austrian-born architect Friedensreich Hundertwasser will instantly recognise his influence in this colourful, irregularly shaped, one-room shed. The name means 'the seed' and this building has been planted here to represent the Hundertwasser Art Centre that is scheduled to be completed in 2020 on a site nearby.

Hundertwasser designed the building in 1993, but the decision to go ahead with the $21 million project was only confirmed after a district-wide referendum in 2015. When completed it will be the only major Hundertwasser building in the southern hemisphere – not withstanding the Kawakawa Public Toilets (p159) – and one of only around 30 in the world. It's expected to display original Hundertwasser artworks on loan from Vienna, along with a gallery devoted exclusively to contemporary Māori art.

◉ Other Areas

Botanica GARDENS
(☑ 09-430 4200; www.wdc.govt.nz; First Ave; ☺9am-4pm) FREE Native ferns, tropical plants and cacti are displayed in this little council-run fernery and conservatory, set on the edge of cute **Cafler Park**. The park encloses the Waiarohia Stream and includes a rose garden and a scented garden.

Quarry Arts Centre ARTS CENTRE
(☑ 09-438 1215; www.quarryarts.org; 21 Selwyn Ave; ☺9.30am-4.30pm) FREE An eccentric village of artists' studios and co-operative

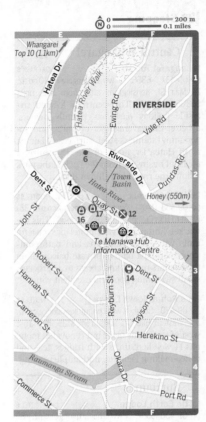

galleries where you can often pick up well-priced art and craft.

Whangarei Quarry Gardens　GARDENS
(☏09-437 7210; www.whangareigardens.org.nz; 37a Russell Rd, Kensington; admission by donation; ⊙9am-5pm) 🅿 Green-fingered volunteers have transformed this old quarry into a blissful park with a lake, waterfalls, pungent floral aromas, wild bits, orderly bits and lots of positive energy. Plus there's a visitor centre and an excellent cafe. To get here, take Rust Ave, turn right into Western Hills Dr and then left into Russell Rd.

Whangarei Falls　WATERFALL
(Otuihau; Ngunguru Rd, Glenbervie) Short walks around these 26m-high falls provide views of the water cascading over the edge of an old basalt lava flow. The falls can be reached on the Tikipunga bus ($3, no service on Sundays), leaving from Rose St in the city.

AH Reed Memorial Kauri Park　FOREST
(www.wdc.govt.nz; Whareora Rd) 🅿 FREE A grove of immense 500-year-old kauri trees has been preserved in this lush tract of native bush, where a cleverly designed boardwalk leads you effortlessly up into the canopy. To get here, head north on Bank St and turn right into Whareora Rd.

Abbey Caves　CAVE
(Abbey Caves Rd) FREE Abbey Caves is an undeveloped network of three caverns full of glow-worms and limestone formations, 6km east of town. Grab a torch, strong shoes, a mate for safety and prepare to get wet. The surrounding reserve is a forest of crazily shaped rock extrusions. Ask at the i-SITE (p144) about an information sheet for the caves.

Kiwi North　MUSEUM
(☏09-438 9630; www.kiwinorth.co.nz; 500 SH14, Maunu; adult/child $20/5; ⊙10am-4pm) 🅿 Five kilometres west of Whangarei, this complex includes 19th-century buildings and a museum displaying Māori and colonial artefacts. A gecko and kiwi house offers a rare chance to see the country's feathery fave in a darkened nocturnal house.

Whangarei Native Bird
Recovery Centre   BIRD SANCTUARY
(☑09-438 1457; www.nbr.org.nz; 500 SH14, Maunu; ⊙1-4.30pm Mon & Fri, 10am-4.30pm Tue-Thu) ⊘ FREE This avian hospital nurses sick and injured birds back to health. Take a walk around the outdoor aviaries and say hi to the talking tui for us.

🏃 Activities & Tours

The free *Hatea River Walk & Surrounds* brochure, available from the i-SITE (p144), has maps and detailed descriptions of some excellent local tracks. The **Hatea River Walk** follows the river from the Town Basin to the falls (90 minutes each way, or return on bus 303A). Longer tracks head through **Parihaka Reserve**, which is just east of the Hatea River and encompasses the remnants of a volcanic cone (241m) and a major *pā* (fortified village) site.

The city is spread out for inspection from the lookout at the top, which is accessible by car. Other tracks head through **Coronation Scenic Reserve**, an expanse of bush immediately west of the centre that includes two *pā* sites and abandoned quarries.

Skydive Ballistic Blondes   SKYDIVING
(☑0800 695 867; www.skydiveballisticblondes. co.nz; 10 Domain Road, Onerahi; skydive $199-380) Not only is this the oddest-named skydiving outfit in the country, it's also the only one licensed to land on the beach (Ocean Beach, Ruakaka or Paihia).

Pacific Coast Kayaks   KAYAKING
(☑09-436 1947; www.nzseakayaking.co.nz; hire 4/8hr $60/80, tours $40-150) Hires kayaks and offers guided paddles to various locations in the Whangarei region. Pick ups and drop offs are free from the Whangarei suburb of Onerahi, and charged for locations such as Tutukaka ($50), Matapouri ($60) and Whangaroa ($130).

Pupurangi Hire & Tour   CULTURAL
(☑09-438 8117; www.hirentour.co.nz; Jetty 1, Riverside Dr) Various hour-long tours of Whangarei, all with a Māori flavour, including *waka* (canoe) trips on the river ($35). Also hires kayaks (per hour $17), *waka* ($25), aquacycles ($17) and bikes ($15).

🛏 Sleeping

Central Whangarei

Whangarei Top 10   HOLIDAY PARK $
(☑09-437 6856; www.whangareitop10.co.nz; 24 Mair St, Kensington; sites from $22, units $68-160; ☎) ⊘ This centrally located riverside holiday park has friendly owners, a better-than-average set of units, and super-shiny stainless-steel surfaces. Mair St is off Hatea Dr, north of the city centre; a pleasant bushwalk from the back of the park follows the river to the Town Basin.

Lodge Bordeaux   MOTEL $$
(☑09-438 0404; www.lodgebordeaux.co.nz; 361 Western Hills Dr; apt from $195; ❄🛜🏊) This up-market European-styled motel has tasteful units with stellar kitchens and bathrooms (most with spa baths), private balconies on the upstairs rooms, and access to a barbecue, small swimming pool and excellent wine.

BK's Pohutukawa Lodge   MOTEL $$
(☑09-430 8634; www.pohutukawalodge.co.nz; 362 Western Hills Dr; units from $125; 🛜) Just west of town, this older but renovated motel has 14 well-kept units with fridges, tea- and coffee-making facilities, and ample parking.

Surrounds

Little Earth Lodge   HOSTEL $
(☑09-430 6562; www.littleearthlodge.co.nz; 85 Abbey Caves Rd; s/d/tr from $67/78/96; 🛜) Set on a farm 6km from town and right next to Abbey Caves, Little Earth makes most other hostels look downright shabby in comparison. Forget dorm rooms crammed with nasty, spongy bunks: settle down in a proper cosy bed with nice linen. Resident critters include miniature horses and alpacas, and there's a free-standing cabin available.

Whangarei Falls Holiday Park &
Backpackers   HOSTEL, HOLIDAY PARK $
(☑09-437 0609; www.whangareifalls.co.nz; 12 Ngunguru Rd, Glenbervie; sites/dm from $25/32, s/d $60/72; 🛜🏊) Located 5km from central Whangarei, but a short walk from Whangarei Falls, this holiday park has good-value cabins, some with small kitchenettes but none with private bathrooms. It's also part of the YHA network and has a 10-bed dorm with bunks, along with smaller backpackers rooms.

Lupton Lodge
B&B $$

(☑ 09-437 2989; www.luptonlodge.co.nz; 555 Ngunguru Rd, Glenbervie; s/d/ste/apt from $145/190/290/310; 🛱 🅿) The rooms are spacious, luxurious and full of character in this historic homestead (1896), peacefully positioned in farmland 5km past Whangarei Falls in the direction of Tutukaka. Wander the orchard, splash around the pool or shoot some snooker in the guest lounge. Also available is a stylish apartment in a renovated barn.

✖ Eating

Whangarei has a solid selection of eating options in the central city and around the Town Basin area. Ethnic restaurants cluster in the pedestrians-only Quality St Mall, and there are a couple of restaurants that are worthy of a short detour to the suburbs.

Whangarei Growers' Market
MARKET

(www.facebook.com/thewhangareigrowersmarket; 17 Water St; ⏱ 6am-10am Sat) Stock up on local produce at this farmers market.

La Familia
CAFE $

(☑ 09-438 8404; www.lafamilia.nz; 84 Cameron St; mains $11-17, pizza $14-19; ⏱ 7am-4pm Tue-Sat, 9am-3pm Sun) Versatility rules at this cosy corner location. Good pastries, bagels, counter food and coffee segue in to robust mains and pizzas for lunch. There's a compact wine list and a good selection of beers.

Quay
CAFE, BISTRO $$

(☑ 09-430 2628; www.thequaykitchen.co.nz; 31 Quayside, Town Basin; mains $14-20, dinner $29-35, pizza $21-25; ⏱ 9am-10pm) Sit out on the wraparound veranda of this beautiful riverside villa or take a table in the stylish, hollowed-out interior. The menu shuffles from cooked breakfasts to pizza and bistro-style meals in the evening.

Fat Camel
ISRAELI $$

(☑ 09-438 0831; 12 Quality St; mains $10-25; ⏱ 9am-9pm) In a pedestrian laneway lined with ethnic eateries, this little Israeli cafe stands out for its pita pockets and platters laden with falafels, salads and grilled meat. For something a little different try the *malawach*, a Yemeni flaky pastry-like pancake served with salad and dips. The coffee's good, too.

Suk Jai Thai
THAI $$

(☑ 09-437 7287; www.sukjai.co.nz; 93 Kamo Rd, Kensington; mains $17-35; ⏱ 11.30am-2.30pm Tue-Sat & 5-10pm daily; 🍽) It's well worth a trip to the suburbs to seek out this cheerful and relaxed restaurant, popular with Thai expats for its authentic flavours, gutsy approach to spice, and desserts such as banana with sticky coconut rice. To find it head north on Bank St and veer left onto Kamo Rd.

Pimarn Thai
THAI $$

(☑ 09-430 0718; www.pimarnthai.co.nz; 12 Rathbone St; mains $18-24; ⏱ 11am-2.30pm Mon-Sat, from 5pm daily; 🍽) As gaudy as every good Thai restaurant should be, Pimarn features all of Thailand's blockbuster dishes, including an excellent *yum talay* (spicy seafood salad).

TopSail
BISTRO $$$

(☑ 09-436 2985; www.topsail.co.nz; 206 Beach Rd, Onerahi; mains $40-44; ⏱ 6pm-late Wed-Sat) Located upstairs in the Onerahi Yacht Club, around 10km from central Whangarei, TopSail serves superlative French-style bistro classics and lots of fresh Northland seafood and NZ produce such as Fiordland venison. If you're in the mood for something upmarket, it's definitely a worthwhile destination and just a 15-minute taxi ride from town. Bookings are recommended.

🍷 Drinking & Nightlife

Old Stone Butter Factory
BAR

(☑ 09-430 0044; www.thebutterfactory.co.nz; 8 Butter Factory Lane; ⏱ 11am-late Tue-Sat) This cool basement bar hosts lots of live gigs from touring Kiwi bands along with the occasional poetry night or gay mixer. As the hours dissolve, DJs kick in. Burgers and pizza are good value, and the sunny courtyard is ideal for a coffee, craft beer or wine.

Frings
PUB

(☑ 09-438 4664; www.frings.co.nz; 104 Dent St; ⏱ 11am-8pm Sun, Tue & Wed, 11am-11.45pm Thu-Sat) This popular pub brews its own beers, and has a terrace, wood-fired pizzas, and lots of live music including Thursday jam nights. Grab a seat on the deck shaped like the prow of a ship.

🛍 Shopping

You can often pick up well-priced art and craft at Quarry Arts Centre (p140).

Bach
ARTS & CRAFTS

(☑ 09-438 2787; www.thebach.gallery; Town Basin; ⏱ 9.30am-4.30pm) Co-op store representing over 100 Northland artisans.

Burning Issues Gallery
ARTS & CRAFTS

(☑ 09-438 3108; www.burningissuesgallery.co.nz; 8 Quayside, Town Basin; ⊙10am-5pm) Glass art, ceramics and jewellery.

Tuatara Design Store
ARTS & CRAFTS

(☑ 09-430 0121; www.tuataradesignstore.com; 29 Bank St; ⊙ 9.30am-5.30pm Mon-Fri, 8am-3.30pm Sat) Māori and Pasifika design, art and craft.

ℹ Information

DOC Whangarei Office (☑ 09-470 3300; www.doc.govt.nz; 2 South End Ave, Raumanga; ⊙8am-4.35pm Mon-Fri) Located just off SH1 around 2km south of central Whangarei.

Te Manawa Hub Information Centre (☑ 09-430 1188; www.whangareinz.com; 91 Dent St, Town Basin; ⊙9am-5pm; 🛜) Central branch of the i-SITE, in the foyer of the Whangarei Art Museum.

Whangarei i-SITE (☑ 09-438 1079; www. whangareinz.com; 92 Otaika Rd (SH1); ⊙9am-5pm) Information, cafe, toilets and showers.

ℹ Getting There & Away

AIR

Whangarei Airport (WRE; ☑ 09-436 0047; www.whangareiairport.co.nz; Handforth St, Onerahi; 🛜) is at Onerahi, 6km southeast of the city centre. **Air New Zealand** (☑ 0800 737 000; www.airnewzealand.co.nz) flies to/from Auckland. Taxis into town cost around $25. Bus route 2 ($3) stops at the airport at least hourly until around 6.30pm on weekdays, but only until 1.30pm on Saturdays; there are no Sunday services.

BUS

Long distance coaches stop at the **Hub**, in the Town Basin.

InterCity (p139) has three or four buses a day to/from Auckland (from $31, three hours), Waipu (from $18, 25 minutes), Paihia (from $12, 1¼ hours) and Kerikeri (from $12, 1¾ hours).

Mana Bus (p139) has two or three services a day to/from Auckland (from $20, 2¾ hours), Waipu ($10, 45 minutes) and Paihia ($12, 1¼ hours).

West Coaster (☑ 021 380 187; www.dargaville. co.nz; one way $10) links Dargaville and Whangarei twice daily on weekdays.

ℹ Getting Around

City Link Whangarei (www.citylinkwhangarei. co.nz, cash fare per adult/child $3/2) operates buses on seven routes, all departing from Rose St. The most useful are routes 2 (to the airport), 3 (Whangarei Falls) and 6 (Kiwi North). Services are reduced on Saturdays and there are no buses on Sundays.

Whangarei Heads

Whangarei Heads Rd winds 35km along the northern reaches of the harbour to the Heads' entrance, passing mangroves and picturesque pohutukawa-lined bays. There are great views from the top of **Mt Manaia** (419m), a sheer rock outcrop above McLeod Bay, but prepare for a lung- and leg-busting 1½-hour climb.

Bream Head caps off the craggy finger of land. A five-hour one-way walking track from **Urquharts Bay** to **Ocean Beach** passes through the **Bream Head Scenic Reserve** and lovely **Smugglers Bay** and **Peach Cove**.

Magnificent **Ocean Beach** stretches for miles on the other side of the headland. There's decent surfing to be had and lifeguards patrol the beach in summer. A detour from **Parua Bay** takes you to glorious **Pataua**, a small settlement that lies on a shallow inlet linked to a surf beach by a footbridge.

🏃 Activities

Bream Head Coast Walks
TRAMPING

(☑09-434 0571; www.coastwalks.nz; 395 Ody Rd; 2/3 nights $435/535; ⊙Oct-May) Enjoyed across two or three days, this self-guided walking network traverses farmland, public walkways and stunning coastal scenery. Accommodation is in a luxury lodge and excellent food is included. The lodge is used as a base for each night after undertaking a variety of walks in the area. Track notes are included and pick-ups from Whangarei can be arranged.

🛏 Sleeping & Eating

Kauri Villas
B&B $$

(☑09-436 1797; www.kaurivillas.com; 73 Owhiwa Rd, Parua Bay; apt/ste from $195/220; 🛜🐾) Perched on a hill with views back over the harbour to Whangarei, this pretty blue-trimmed villa has a charming old-world feel and two massive suites, each with two bedrooms and a sitting room. There's also a self-contained apartment across the lawn, sleeping up to 10 people.

Ara Roa
RENTAL HOUSE $$$

(☑027 320 0770; www.araroa.nz; Harambee Rd, Taiharuru; d $325-950; 🛜🐾) This collection of five different architecturally striking properties dotted around a coastal peninsula ranges from the two-bedroom Te Huia – with sunset views and a bush track where kiwi are often heard after dark – to the gorgeous one-bedroom Glasshouse at the very end of the peninsula. Two-bedroom Aria has its own lap pool.

Parua Bay Tavern PUB FOOD $$
(☑09-436 5856; www.paruabaytavern.co.nz; 1034 Whangarei Heads Rd; mains $15-28; ☻11.30am-late Wed-Sun) A magical spot on a summer's day, this friendly pub is set on a thumb-shaped peninsula, with a sole pohutukawa blazing red against the green water. Grab a seat on the deck, a cold beverage and a decent pub meal, including good burgers and pizza.

ⓘ Getting There & Away

There's no public transport on this winding ocean-fringed drive.

Tutukaka Coast

At the **Poor Knights Islands**, colourful underwater scenery combines with two decommissioned navy ships to provide a perfect playground for divers. Dive boats depart from the bustling marina at **Tutukaka**, a small fishing settlement 28km northeast of Whangarei.

From Tutukaka the road heads slightly inland, popping out 10km later at the golden sands of **Matapouri**. A blissful 20-minute coastal walk leads from here to **Whale Bay**, fringed with giant pohutukawa trees.

Continuing north from Matapouri, the wide expanse of **Sandy Bay**, one of Northland's premier surf beaches, comes into view. Long-boarding competitions are held here in summer. The road then loops back to join SH1 at Hikurangi. A branch leading off from this road doubles back north to the coast at **Whananaki**, where there are glorious beaches and the Otamure Bay DOC campsite (p146).

🏃 Activities

Tutukaka's dive crews cater to both first-timers and experienced divers. There are some excellent walks along the coast; ask about options at the Whangarei i-SITE (p144).

★Dive! Tutukaka DIVING
(☑0800 288 882; www.diving.co.nz; Marina Rd; 2 dives incl gear $289) 🚣 Dive courses include a three-day PADI open-water course. For non-divers, the **Perfect Day Ocean Cruise** (www.aperfectday.co.nz, $189) includes lunch and snacks, snorkelling in the marine reserve, kayaking through caves and arches, paddle boarding, and sightings of dolphins (usually) and whales (occasionally). Cruises run from November to May, departing at 11am and returning at 4pm.

Check the website for upcoming initiatives, including a six-room dive lodge, and multi-day dive trips on the RV *Acheron*, a live-aboard expedition-style research vessel.

Yukon Dive DIVING
(☑09-434 4506; www.yukon.co.nz; Marina Rd; 2 dives incl full gear $290) An owner-operator offering dive trips for a maximum of 12 people at a time. Trips for non-divers incorporating snorkelling and kayaking are also available ($190).

O'Neill Surf Academy SURFING
(☑09-434 3843; www.oneillsurfacademy.co.nz; 2hr/day from $80/135) Offers group and private two-hour surfing lessons, and longer Day Tripper options incorporating morning and afternoon lessons. Weekend and four-day surf tours around Northland, including camping, are also available (from $350).

Tutukaka Surf SURFING
(☑021 227 0072; www.tutukakasurf.co.nz; Marina Rd; 2hr lesson from $75; ☻shop 9am-5pm daily Nov-Feb, 10am-5pm Fri-Mon Mar-Oct) Runs surf lessons in Sandy Bay, 10km northwest of Tutukaka, at 9.30am most days in summer and on the weekends otherwise. Private lessons can also be arranged. They also hire surfboards (per day $45) and stand-up paddle boards (per day $20) from their Tutukaka store.

MARINE RICHES AT THE POOR KNIGHTS

Established in 1981, the Poor Knights marine reserve is rated as one of the world's top-10 diving spots. The islands are bathed in a subtropical current from the Coral Sea, so varieties of tropical and subtropical fish not seen in other NZ waters can be observed here. The waters are clear, with no sediment or pollution problems. The 40m to 60m underwater cliffs drop steeply to the sandy bottom and are a labyrinth of archways, caves, tunnels and fissures that attract a wide variety of sponges and colourful underwater vegetation. Schooling fish, eels and rays are common (including manta rays in season).

The two main volcanic islands, Tawhiti Rahi and Aorangi, were home to the Ngāti Wai tribe, but since a raiding-party massacre in 1825 the islands have been *tapu* (forbidden). Even today the public is barred from the islands, in order to protect their pristine environment. Not only do tuatara and Buller's shearwater breed here, but there are unique species of flora, such as the Poor Knights lily.

🛏 Sleeping & Eating

DOC Otamure Bay Campsite CAMPGROUND $

(☑ 09-433 8402; www.doc.govt.nz; Rockell Rd, Whananaki; sites per adult/child $13/6.50) This scenic campsite is located near a sandy beach with plenty of shade from well-established pohutukawa trees. Expect cold showers, drinking water and little else.

Pacific Rendezvous MOTEL $$$

(☑ 09-434 3847; www.pacificrendezvous.co.nz; 73 Motel Rd, Tutukaka; apt from $229) Perfectly situated for spectacular views on the manicured, lawn-covered southern head of Tutukaka Harbour, this is a great choice for families and small groups. The multiroom units are all individually owned and decorated.

Schnappa Rock CAFE $$

(☑ 09-434 3774; www.schnapparock.co.nz; Marina Rd, Tutukaka; mains brunch $14-23, dinner $25-36; ⊙ 8am-late Oct-May, closed Sun night Jun-Sep) 🍴 Filled with expectant divers in the morning and those capping off their perfect day in the evening, this cafe-restaurant-bar is often buzzing. Top NZ bands sometimes play on summer weekends.

❶ Getting There & Away

Whangarei Coastal Commuter (☑ 0800 435 355; www.coastalcommuter.co.nz; one way/return per person $25/40) runs a daily shuttle for travellers on dive trips, leaving Whangarei in the morning and returning in the afternoon.

MĀORI NORTHLAND

Known to Māori as Te Tai Tokerau, this region has a long and proud Māori history and today has one of the country's highest percentages of Māori people. Along with East Cape, it's a place where you might hear Māori being spoken. In mythology the region is known as the tail of the fish of Māui.

Māori sites of particular significance include **Cape Reinga** (p168), the **Waitangi Treaty Grounds** (p154), **Ruapekapeka Pā** (p159) and, in the Waipoua Forest, **Tāne Mahuta** (p176).

Māori cultural experiences are offered by many local operators, including **Footprints Waipoua** (p174), **Ahikaa Adventures** (p169), **Sand Safaris** (p169) and **Rewa's Village** (p160). Many businesses catering to travellers are owned or run by Māori individuals or *hapū* (subtribal) groups.

BAY OF ISLANDS

The Bay of Islands ranks as one of NZ's top summertime destinations. Lingering shots of its turquoise waters and 150 undeveloped islands feature heavily in the country's tourist promotions. Most of the action here is out on the water, whether that be yachting, big-game fishing, kayaking, diving or cruising around in the company of whales and dolphins.

It's also a place of enormous historical significance. Māori knew it as Pēwhairangi and settled here early in their migrations. As the site of NZ's first permanent British settlement (at Russell), it is the birthplace of European colonisation in the country. It was here that the Treaty of Waitangi was drawn up and first signed in 1840; the treaty remains the linchpin of race relations in NZ today.

🏃 Activities

The Bay of Islands offers some fine subtropical diving, made even better by the sinking of the 113m navy frigate HMNZS *Canterbury* in Deep Water Cove near Cape Brett. Local operators also head to the wreck of the *Rainbow Warrior* off the Cavalli Islands, about an hour north of Paihia by boat. Both offer a colourful feast of pink anemones, yellow sponges and abundant fish life.

There are plenty of opportunities for kayaking, sailing or cruising around the bay, either on a guided tour or by renting and going it alone. Note that some boat companies do not operate during the winter months.

There are some good walks in the area, including an easy 5km track that follows the coast from Opua to Paihia.

Bay of Islands Kayaking KAYAKING

(☑ 021 272 3353; www.bayofislandskayaking.co.nz; tours $80-150) Rents sea kayaks and organises guided expeditions to Haruru Falls (p154) and the outer islands.

Great Escape Yacht Charters BOATING

(☑ 09-402 7143; www.greatescape.co.nz; 4 Richardson St, Opua) Offers introductory sailing lessons (two-day course $445) and longer options.

Flying Kiwi Parasail PARASAILING

(☑ 09-402 6068; www.parasailnz.com; solo $115, tandem per adult/child $95/65) Departs from both Paihia and Russell wharves for NZ's highest parasail (1200ft/366m).

Bay of Islands

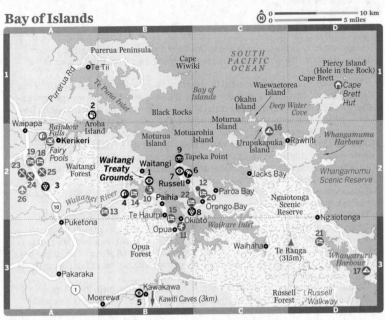

Bay of Islands

☞ Tours

Where do you start? First by praying for good weather, as torrential rain or choppy seas could exclude some options. The Bay of Islands i-SITE (p158) and accommodation operators can book tours.

OLD RUSSELL ROAD

The quickest route to Russell takes SH1 to Opua and then crosses by ferry. If you're coming from the south, the old Russell Rd is a snaking scenic alternative that adds about half an hour to the trip.

The turn-off is easy to miss, located 6km north of Hikurangi at Whakapara (look for the sign to Oakura). After 13km stop at the **Gallery & Cafe** (☑ 09-433 9934; www.galleryhelenabay.co.nz; 1392 Russell Rd, Helena Bay; mains $10-20; ☀10am-4pm), high above **Helena Bay**, for fair-trade coffee, scrummy cake, amazing views, and interesting Kiwiana art and craft.

Near Helena Bay an unsealed detour leads 8km to **Mimiwhangata Coastal Park** (☑ 09-433 6554; www.doc.govt.nz; 453 Mimiwhangata Rd, Helena Bay) FREE, which features sand dunes, pohutukawa trees, jutting headlands and picturesque beaches. Here, DOC-managed accommodation includes an eight-person lodge (per week $945), a simple but comfortable cottage (per week $630), and a beach house (per week $630), all of which sleep seven to eight people. Basic camping (per adult/child $13/6.50) is available at secluded Waikahoa Bay.

Back on Russell Rd, **The Farm** (☑ 09-433 6894; www.thefarm.co.nz; 3632 Russell Rd, Whangaruru; sites/dm $15/20, r with/without bathroom $80/60) is a rough-and-ready backpackers that rambles through various buildings, including an old woolshed. The rooms are basic and it's a popular park-up spot for campervans, but off season it's a chilled-out rustic escape. Best of all, you can arrange a horse trek ($50, two hours), dirt biking (from $50), kayaking and fishing.

At an intersection shortly after The Farm, Russell Rd branches off to the left for an unsealed, winding section traversing the **Ngaiotonga Scenic Reserve**. Unless you're planning to explore the forest (there are two short walks: the 20-minute Kauri Grove Nature Walk and the 10-minute Twin Bole Track), you're better off veering right onto the sealed Rawhiti Rd.

After 2.6km, a side road leads to the **Whangaruru North Head Scenic Reserve**, which has beaches, walking tracks and fine scenery. A loop route from DOC's sheltered **Puriri Bay Campsite** (☑ 09-433 6160; www.doc.govt.nz; Whangaruru North Rd, Whangaruru; sites per adult/child $13/6.50) leads up to a ridge, offering a remarkable coastal panorama.

If you want to head directly to Russell, continue along Rawhiti Rd for another 7km before veering left onto Manawaora Rd, which skirts a succession of tiny idyllic bays before reconnecting with Russell Rd.

Otherwise take a detour to isolated **Rawhiti**, a small Ngāpuhi settlement where life still revolves around the *marae* (traditional meeting place). Rawhiti is the starting point for the tramp to **Cape Brett**, a tiring eight-hour, 16.3km walk to the top of the peninsula, where overnight stays are possible in DOC's **Cape Brett Hut** (☑ 09-407 0300; www.doc.govt.nz; dm adult/child $15/7.50). The hut must be booked in advance. An access fee is charged for crossing private land (adult/child $40/20), which you can pay at the **Bay of Islands i-SITE** (p158). Another option is to take a water taxi to Cape Brett lighthouse from Russell or Paihia and walk back.

A shorter one-hour walk leads through Māori land and the **Whangamumu Scenic Reserve** to Whangamumu Harbour. There are more than 40 ancient Māori sites on the peninsula and the remains of an unusual whaling station.

Boat

Options include sailing boats, jetboats and large launches. Boats leave from either Paihia or Russell, calling into the other town as their first stop.

The best way to explore the bay is under sail. Either help crew the boat (no experience required), or just spend the afternoon island-hopping, sunbathing, swimming, snorkelling, kayaking and fishing.

The Rock

CRUISE

(☑ 0800 762 527; www.rocktheboat.co.nz; dm/d/f $268/650/894) A former vehicle ferry that's now a floating hostel, the *Rock* has dorms, private rooms and a bar. The cruise departs at 5pm and includes a barbecue and seafood dinner, then time spent island-hopping, fishing, kayaking, snorkelling and swimming the following day. It's also possible just to do the overnight portion (adult/child $208/178) or the daytime cruise ($128/98).

R Tucker Thompson
BOATING

(☑ 09-402 8430; www.tucker.co.nz; ☺ Nov-Mar) Run by a charitable trust with an education focus, the *Tucker* is a majestic tall ship offering day sails (adult/child $149/75, including a barbecue lunch) and late-afternoon cruises (adult/child $65/33).

Phantom
BOATING

(☑ 0800 224 421; www.yachtphantom.com; day sail $110) A fast 50ft racing sloop, known for its wonderful food. Allows BYO (bring your own) beer and wine.

She's a Lady
BOATING

(☑ 0800 724 584; www.sailingbayofislands.com; day sail $97) Day sails include lunch, fishing, snorkelling and paddling a see-through-bottomed kayak.

Fullers Great Sights
CRUISE

(☑ 09-402 7421; www.dolphincruises.co.nz; Maritime Building, Marsden Rd, Paihia) The four-hour Hole in the Rock Cruise (adult/child $107/54) heads out to the famous sea arch and stops at Urupukapuka Island on the way back. The full-day Cream Trip (adult/child $129/65, November to April only) follows the mail route around the bay. Boats stop at Russell wharf for pick-ups on all trips.

Explore NZ
CRUISE

(☑ 09-402 8234; www.exploregroup.co.nz; cnr Marsden & Williams Rds, Paihia) Explore's four-hour Discover the Bay cruise (adult/child $149/90 including barbecue lunch) heads to the Hole in the Rock and stops at Urupukapuka Island.

Ecocruz
CRUISE

(☑ 0800 432 627; www.ecocruz.co.nz; dm/d $725/1700; ☺ departs 8am Tue & Fri Oct-May) Three-day/two-night sailing cruise aboard the 72ft ocean-going yacht *Manawanui*. Prices include accommodation, food, kayaking, sustainable fishing and snorkelling.

Gungha II
BOATING

(☑ 0800 478 900; www.bayofislandssailing.co.nz; day sail $110) A 65ft ocean yacht with a friendly crew, departing from both Russell and Paihia; lunch included.

Carino
CRUISE

(☑ 09-402 8040; www.sailingdolphins.co.nz; Paihia Wharf; adult/child $124/80) This 50ft

catamaran offers day cruises with an island stopover and snorkelling; a barbecue lunch is available for $6.

Bus

It's cheaper and quicker to take trips to Cape Reinga from Ahipara, Kaitaia or Doubtless Bay, but if you're short on time, various long day trips (10 to 12 hours) leave from the Bay of Islands. They all drive one way along Ninety Mile Beach, stopping to sandboard on the dunes.

Fullers Great Sights (p149) runs regular bus tours and backpacker-oriented versions, both stopping at Puketi Forest. The standard, child-friendly version (adult/child $150/75) includes an optional lunch at Houhora. It also runs **Awesome NZ** (☑ 0800 486 877; www.awesomenz.com; Maritime Building, Marsden Rd, Paihia; tour $130) tours, with louder music, more time sandboarding, and stops for a snack at Taipa and to devour fish and chips at Mangonui.

Explore NZ's (p149) Dune Rider tour (adult/child $150/110) also gives you the chance to sample Mangonui's feted fish and chips.

Transport options to the Hokianga and Waipoua Forest are limited, so a day trip makes sense if you don't have your own car or if you're time starved. Fullers' Giants & Glow Worms (adult/child $129/65) takes in Tāne Mahuta (p176) and the Kawiti Caves (p159) on an eight-hour tour with local Māori guides.

> ### TWIN COAST CYCLE TRAIL – POU HERENGA TAI
>
> This cycle route stretches from the Bay of Islands clear across the country to the Hokianga Harbour. OK, so that's only 87km, but as far as we're concerned that still gives you boasting rights when you get home. The complete route takes two days and travels from Opua to Kawakawa, Kaikohe, Okaihau and Horeke before finishing at Mangungu Mission Station.
>
> The most popular day ride is the 14km section from **Kaikohe** to **Okaihau** which passes through an abandoned rail tunnel before skirting **Lake Omapere**.
>
> The trail is well described at www.twincoastcycletrail.kiwi.nz, which includes details of bike hire and shuttle transport.

Total Tours FOOD & DRINK
(☑0800 264 868; www.totaltours.co.nz; tours $80)
Departing from Paihia, these bus or van tours
head into the countryside around Kerikeri for
a half-day Wine, Food and Craft tour or a half
day devoted to just wine. Customised tours
taking in the Kawiti Caves and Kawakawa
Hundertwasser toilets can be arranged.

⚝ Festivals & Events

**Bay of Islands Country
Rock Festival** MUSIC
(☑09-404 1063; www.country-rock.co.nz; festival
pass $60; ☺May) Country-rock bands jangle
and twang from stages in Paihia and Russell
over the second weekend in May.

**Bay of Islands Jazz
& Blues Festival** MUSIC
(☑09-404 1063; www.jazz-blues.co.nz; festival
pass $60; ☺Aug) Local and international acts
take to stages in Paihia and Russell over the
second weekend in August.

Russell

POP 720

Although it was once known as the hellhole of the Pacific, those coming to Russell
for debauchery will be sadly disappointed:
they've missed the orgies on the beach by 180
years. Instead they'll find a historic town with
gift shops and B&Bs, and, in summer, you can
rent kayaks and dinghies along the Strand.

History

Before it was known as a hellhole, or even as
Russell, this was Kororāreka (Sweet Penguin),
a fortified Ngāpuhi village. In the early 19th
century the tribe permitted it to become Aotearoa's first European settlement. It quickly
became a magnet for rough elements, such
as fleeing convicts, whalers and drunken sailors. By the 1830s dozens of whaling ships at a
time were anchored in the harbour. In 1839
Charles Darwin described it as full of 'the very
refuse of society' in his book *The Voyage of
the Beagle* (originally known as *Narrative of
the Surveying Voyages of His Majesty's Ships
Adventure and Beagle*).

In 1830 the settlement was the scene of
the so-called Girls' War, when two pairs of
Māori women were vying for the attention
of a whaling captain called Brind. A chance
meeting between the rivals on the beach led
to verbal abuse and fighting. This minor
conflict quickly escalated as family members

rallied around to avenge the insult and harm
done to their respective relatives. Hundreds
were killed and injured over a two-week period before missionaries managed to broker
a peace agreement.

After the signing of the Treaty of Waitangi in 1840, Okiato (where the car ferry now
leaves from) was the residence of the governor and the temporary capital. The capital
was officially moved to Auckland in 1841 and
Okiato, which was by then known as Russell,
was eventually abandoned. The name Russell ultimately replaced Kororāreka.

◎ Sights

Pompallier Mission HISTORIC BUILDING
(☑09-403 9015; www.pompallier.co.nz; 5 The
Strand; adult/child $10/free; ☺10am-4pm) Built
in 1842 to house the Catholic mission's
printing press, this rammed-earth building
is the mission's last remaining building in
the western Pacific, and NZ's oldest factory.
Over its seven years of operation, a staggering 40,000 books were printed here in
Māori. Admission includes extremely interesting hands-on tours that lead you through
the entire bookmaking process, from the
icky business of tanning animal hides for
the covers, to setting the type and stitching
together the final books.

Russell Museum MUSEUM
(☑09-403 7701; www.russellmuseum.org.nz; 2
York St; adult/child $10/free; ☺10am-4pm) This
small museum has a well-presented Māori
section, a large 1:5 scale model of Captain
Cook's *Endeavour,* and a 10-minute video
on the town's history.

Christ Church CHURCH
(www.oldchurch.org.nz; Church St) English nat-
uralist Charles Darwin made a donation
towards the cost of building of this, the
country's oldest surviving church (1836). The
graveyard's biggest memorial commemorates
Tamati Waka Nene, a powerful Ngāpuhi chief
from the Hokianga who sided against Hōne
Heke in the Northland War. The church's
wooden exterior has musket and cannonball
holes dating from the 1845 battle.

Maiki HILL
(Flagstaff Rd) Overlooking Russell, this is the
hill where Hōne Heke (p152) chopped down
the flagpole four times. You can drive up,
but the view justifies a climb. Take the track
west from the boat ramp along the beach at
low tide, or head up Wellington St.

Russell

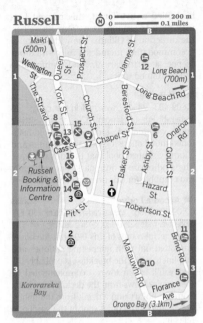

Tapeka Point   VIEWPOINT, BEACH
North of Russell, on the other side of Mai-ki hill, Tapeka Rd heads down to a sandy beach in the shadow of a craggy headland. A *pā* once stood at the top of the hill. Follow the pathway for views stretching to the far northern reaches of the Bay of Islands.

Long Beach   BEACH
(Oneroa; Long Beach Rd) About 1.5km behind Russell (an easy walk or cycle) is this placid, child-friendly beach. Turn left (facing the sea) to visit **Donkey Bay**, a small cove that is an unofficial nudist beach.

Omata Estate   WINERY
(☏ 09-403 8007; www.omata.co.nz; 212 Aucks Rd; ☺ 11am-6pm Oct-May, by appointment Jun-Sep) With a growing reputation for red wines – especially its old-growth syrah – Omata Estate is one of Northland's finest wineries. To complement the tastings and sea views, shared platters ($40) are available. The winery is on the road from Russell to the car ferry at Okiato.

☞ Tours

Russell Nature Walks   ECOTOUR
(☏ 027 908 2334; www.russellnaturewalks.co.nz; 6080 Russell Whakapara Rd; adult/child from $55/25) ✐ Located in privately owned native forest 2.5km south of Russell, guided day and night tours provide the opportunity to see native birds, including the weka and tui, and insects such as the weta. Glowworms softly illuminate night tours, and after dark there's the opportunity to hear (and very occasionally see) kiwi. Walks last 1½ to two hours.

Russell Mini Tours   BUS
(☏ 09-403 7866; www.russellminitours.com; cnr The Strand & Cass St; adult/child $30/15; ☺ tours 11am, midday, 1pm & 2pm year-round, also 10am, 3pm & 4pm Oct-Apr) Minibus tour around historic Russell with commentary.

✯ Festivals & Events

Tall Ship Race   SAILING
(www.russellboatingclub.org.nz; ☺ Jan) Held in Russell on the first Saturday after New Year's Day.

Russell Birdman   SPORTS
(www.russellbirdman.co.nz; Russell Wharf; ☺ Jul) Lunatics with various flying contraptions jump off Russell wharf into frigid waters.

Coastal Classic   SAILING
(www.coastalclassic.co.nz; ☺ Oct) New Zealand's largest yacht race, from Auckland to Russell, held on Labour Weekend in October.

🛏 Sleeping

Wainui   HOSTEL **$**
(☑09-403 8278; www.wainuilodge-russell-nz.com; 92d Te Wahapu Rd; dm/s/d $29/54/68; 🛜) Hard to find but worth the effort, this modern bush retreat with direct beach access has only two rooms that share a pleasant communal space. It's 5km from Russell on the way to the car ferry; you wouldn't want to stay here without your own wheels. Take Te Wahapu Rd and then turn right into Waiaruhe Way.

Pukeko Cottage   HOSTEL **$**
(☑09-403 8498; http://pukekocottageback packers.co.nz; 14 Brind Rd; dm/r $30/60; 🛜) More like staying at a mate's place than a hostel, this homey house has just two bedrooms for rent and a caravan in the back garden. The bathroom and kitchen is shared with Barry, the music-loving artist owner.

Russell Top 10   HOLIDAY PARK **$$**
(☑09-403 7826; www.russelltop10.co.nz; 1 James St; sites from $25, unit with/without bathroom from $150/100; @🛜) This leafy and extremely well-maintained holiday park has a small store, good facilities, wonderful hydrangeas, tidy cabins and excellent self-contained units with decks, coffee machines and views over the bay.

Russell-Orongo Bay Holiday Park   HOLIDAY PARK **$$**
(☑09-403 7704; www.russellaccommodation. co.nz; 5960 Russell Rd; sites from $42, unit with/without bathroom from $125/85; 🛜⛵) 🍃 Surrounded by 14 acres studded with bird-filled native forest, this relaxed holiday park is around 3km from Russell in the direction of Okiato. The wide range of accommodation includes a fully kitted-out teepee, a retro caravan and comfortable self-contained units.

Motel Russell   MOTEL **$$**
(☑09-403 7854; www.motelrussell.co.nz; 16 Matauwhi Rd; units from $120; 🛜⛵) Sitting amid well-tended gardens, this old-fashioned motel offers a good range of units and a kidney-shaped pool that the kids will love. The studios are a little dark, but you really can't quibble for this price in central Russell.

⭐ **Arcadia Lodge**   B&B **$$$**
(☑09-403 7756; www.arcadialodge.co.nz; 10 Florance Ave; r/ste $220/330; ⊙Sep-Jun; 🛜) 🍃 The characterful rooms of this 1890 hillside house are kitted out with interesting antiques and fine linen, while the breakfast is probably the best you'll eat in town – complemented by spectacular views from the deck. Grab a book from the library and a drink from the honesty bar, and find a quiet spot in the garden to relax in.

Duke of Marlborough Hotel   HISTORIC HOTEL **$$$**
(☑09-403 7829; www.theduke.co.nz; 35 The Strand; r $150-280; 🛜) Holding NZ's oldest pub licence, the Duke boasts about 'refreshing rascals and reprobates since 1827', although the building has burnt down twice since then. The upstairs accommodation ranges from small, bright rooms in a 1930s extension, to snazzy, spacious doubles facing the water.

HŌNE HEKE & THE NORTHLAND WAR

Just five years after he had been the first signatory to the Treaty of Waitangi, Ngāpuhi chief Hōne Heke was so disaffected that he planned to chop down Kororāreka's flagstaff, a symbol of British authority, for the fourth time. Governor FitzRoy was determined not to let that happen and garrisoned the town with soldiers and marines.

On 11 March 1845 the Ngāpuhi staged a diversionary siege of the town. It was a great tactical success, with Chief Kawiti attacking from the south and another party attacking from Long Beach. While the troops rushed off to protect the township, Hōne Heke felled the Union Jack on **Maiki** (p150) for the fourth and final time. The British were forced to evacuate to ships lying at anchor. The captain of the HMS *Hazard* was wounded severely in the battle and his replacement ordered the ships' cannons to be fired on the town; most of the buildings were razed. The first of the New Zealand Wars had begun.

In the months that followed, British troops (united with Hokianga-based Ngāpuhi) fought Heke and Kawiti in several battles. During this time the modern *pā* (fortress) was born, effectively the world's first sophisticated system of trench warfare. It's worth stopping at **Ruapekapeka Pā** (p159), south of Kawakawa, to see how impressive these fortifications were. Eventually Heke, Kawiti and George Grey (the new governor) made their peace, with no side the clear winner.

Hananui Lodge & Apartments MOTEL $$$

(☑09-403 7875; www.hananui.co.nz; 4 York St; units $155-250; 🐾) Choose between sparkling motel-style units in the trim waterside lodge or apartments in the newer block across the road. The pick of the bunch are the upstairs waterfront units with views straight over the beach.

Commodore's Lodge MOTEL $$$

(☑09-403 7899; www.commodoreslodgemotel. co.nz; 28 The Strand; units from $200; 🐾🐾) Being the envy of every passer-by makes up for the lack of privacy in the front apartments that face the waterfront promenade. Spacious, nicely presented units are the order of the day here, along with a small pool and hot tub, and free kayaks and bikes.

Bellrock Lodge APARTMENT $$$

(☑09-403 7422; www.bellrocklodge.co.nz; 22 Chapel St; unit $350; 🐾🐾) Each of Bellrock's four self-contained units has it's own terrace offering awe-inspiring views over the bay. The rooms are pleasantly furnished but it's the outlook rather than the ambience which justifies the price. It's a short walk down to the town centre but you'll certainly work off any dinner calories on the steep climb back.

🍴 Eating & Drinking

Newport Chocolates CAFE $

(☑09-403 8888; www.newportchocolates.co.nz; 1 Cass St; chocolates around $3; ⊙10am-6pm Tue-Thu, 10am-7.30pm Fri & Sat) The delicious artisan chocolates are all handmade on-site, with flavours including raspberry, lime and chilli, and, our favourite, caramel and sea salt. It's also a top spot for divinely decadent hot chocolate and refreshing frappes.

Hell Hole CAFE $

(☑022 175 7847; www.facebook.com/hellhole coffee; 19 York St; snacks $6-12; ⊙7am-5pm Jan & Feb, 8am-3pm Mar, Apr, Nov & Dec) Bagels, baguettes and croissants all feature with the best coffee in town at this compact spot one block back from the waterfront. Beans are locally roasted, and organic soft drinks and artisan ice blocks all combine to make Hell Hole a hugely popular place.

Delish FAST FOOD $

(☑09-403 8829; 4 Cass St; snacks $3-6; ⊙7.30am-4pm) In the depths of winter, this humble coffee counter is the prime local gathering point and the best bet for your morning cuppa and muffin. In summer it does a steady trade in ice-cream cones, smoothies and milkshakes.

★Gables CONTEMPORARY $$

(☑09-403 7670; www.thegablesrestaurant.co.nz; 19 The Strand; mains lunch $22-28, dinner $27-35; ⊙noon-3pm & 5.30-10pm Wed-Mon) Serving an imaginative take on Kiwi classics (lamb, beef, seafood), the Gables occupies an 1847 building on the waterfront built using whale vertebrae for foundations. Ask for a table by the windows for maritime views and look forward to top-notch local produce, including oysters and cheese.

Duke of Marlborough Hotel PUB FOOD $$

(☑09-403 7829; www.theduke.co.nz; 35 The Strand; mains lunch $20-32, dinner $25-37; ⊙11.30am-9pm) There's no better spot in Russell to while away a few hours, glass in hand, than the Duke's sunny deck. Thankfully the upmarket bistro food matches the views, plus there's an excellent wine list and a great selection of NZ craft beers.

Hōne's Garden PIZZA $$

(☑022 466 3710; www.facebook.com/hones garden; 10 York St; pizza $18-25; ⊙noon-10pm Wed-Mon Nov-Apr) Head out to Hōne's pebbled courtyard for wood-fired pizza (with 11 different varieties), cold craft beer on tap and a thoroughly easy-going Kiwi vibe. An expanded menu features tasty wraps and healthy salads. Antipasto platters are good for groups and indecisive diners.

Duke of Marlborough Tavern PUB

(☑09-403 7831; www.duketavern.co.nz; 19 York St; mains $19-24; ⊙noon-11pm Tue-Sat, to 6pm Sun Mar-Nov, noon-late daily Dec-Feb) Not be confused with the historic hotel of the same name on the waterfront, this cosy locals' tavern dates only from 1976. Pub quiz on a Tuesday night is always good fun, and there are pool tables and well-priced pub meals.

ℹ Information

Russell Booking & Information Centre (☑09-403 8020; www.russellinfo.co.nz; Russell Wharf; ⊙8am-5pm, extended summer)

ℹ Getting There & Away

The quickest way to reach Russell by car is via the car ferry (car/motorcycle/passenger $13/5.50/1), which runs every 10 minutes from Opua (5km from Paihia) to Okiato (8km from Russell), between 6.50am and 10pm. Buy your tickets on board. If you're travelling from the south, a scenic alternative is the coastal route via Russell Rd.

On foot, the easiest way to reach Russell is on a **passenger ferry** from Paihia (adult/child return $12/6). They run from 7am to 9pm (until 10pm October to May), generally every 30 minutes, but hourly in the evenings. Buy your tickets on board or at the **i-SITE** (p158) in Paihia.

Paihia, Waitangi & Haruru

POP 2532

The birthplace of NZ (as opposed to Aotearoa), Waitangi inhabits a special but somewhat complex place in the national psyche – aptly demonstrated by the mixture of celebration, commemoration, protest and apathy that accompanies the nation's birthday (Waitangi Day, 6 February).

It was here that the long-neglected and much-contested Treaty of Waitangi was first signed between Māori chiefs and the British Crown, establishing British sovereignty or something a bit like it, depending on whether you're reading the English or Māori version of the document. If you're interested in getting to grips with NZ's history and race relations, this is the place to start.

Joined to Waitangi by a bridge, Paihia would be a fairly nondescript coastal town if it wasn't the main entry point to the Bay of Islands. If you're not on a tight budget, catch a ferry to Russell, which is prettier but much quieter.

◉ Sights

★ **Waitangi Treaty Grounds**   HISTORIC SITE
(☑ 09-402 7437; www.waitangi.org.nz; 1 Tau Henare Dr, Waitangi; adult/child $50/free; ◷ 9am-5pm)
🖈 Occupying a headland draped in lawns and bush, this is NZ's most significant historic site. Here, on 6 February 1840, after much discussion, the first 43 Māori chiefs signed the Treaty of Waitangi with the British Crown; eventually, over 500 chiefs would sign it. Admission incorporates a guided tour and spirited cultural performance, and entry to the **Museum of Waitangi**, the **Whare Rūnanga** (carved meeting house) and the historic **Treaty House**.

Opened in 2016, **Te Kōngahu Museum of Waitangi** is a modern and comprehensive showcase of the role of the treaty in the past, present and future of Aotearoa New Zealand. It provides a warts-and-all look at the early interactions between Māori and Europeans, the events leading up to the treaty's signing, the long litany of treaty

breaches by the Crown, the wars and land confiscations that followed, and the protest movement that led to the current process of redress for historic injustices. Many *taonga* (treasures) associated with Waitangi were previously scattered around NZ, and this excellent museum is now a safe haven for a number of key historical items. One room is devoted to facsimiles of all the key documents, while another screens a fascinating short film dramatising the events of the initial treaty signing.

The **Treaty House** was shipped over as a kit-set from Australia and erected in 1834 as the four-room home of the official British Resident James Busby. It's now preserved as a memorial and museum containing displays about the house and the people who lived here. Just across the lawn, the magnificently detailed **Whare Rūnanga** was completed in 1940 to mark the centenary of the treaty. The fine carvings represent the major Māori tribes. It's here that the cultural performances take place, starting with a *haka pōwhiri* (challenge and welcome) and then heading inside for *waiata* (songs) and spine-tingling *haka* (war dances).

Near the cove is the 35m, 6-tonne *waka taua* (war canoe) **Ngātokimatawhaorua**, also built for the centenary. A photographic exhibit details how it was fashioned from gigantic kauri logs. There's also an excellent gift shop selling Māori art and design, with a carving studio attached.

Tours leave on the hour from 10am to 3pm. Admission is discounted to $25 for NZ residents upon presentation of a passport or driver's licence.

St Paul's Anglican Church   CHURCH
(36 Marsden Rd, Paihia) The characterful St Paul's was constructed of Kawakawa stone in 1925, and stands on the site of the original mission church, a simple *raupo* (bulrush) hut erected in 1823. Look for the native birds in the stained glass above the altar – the kotare (kingfisher) represents Jesus (the king plus 'fisher of men'), while the tui (parson bird) and kereru (wood pigeon) portray the personalities of the Williams brothers (one scholarly, one forceful), who set up the mission station here.

Haruru Falls   WATERFALL
(Haruru Falls Rd, Haruru) A walking track (one way 1½ hours, 5km) leads from the Treaty Grounds along the Waitangi River to these attractive horseshoe falls. Part of

Paihia

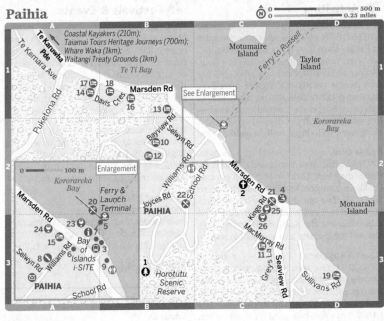

Paihia

◉ Sights
1 Opua Forest	B3
2 St Paul's Anglican Church	C2

✈ Activities, Courses & Tours
3 Awesome NZ	B3
4 Bay Beach Hire	C2
5 Carino	B3
6 Explore NZ	A3
7 Fullers Great Sights	A3
8 Paihia Dive	A3
9 Salt Air	B3
Tango Jet Ski Tours	(see 5)

⌂ Sleeping
10 Abri Apartments	B2
11 Admiral's View Lodge	C3
12 Allegra House	B2
13 Breakwater Motel	B1
14 Cap'n Bob's Beachhouse	A1
15 Haka Lodge	A3
16 Paihia Beach Resort & Spa	B1
17 Seabeds	A1
18 Seaspray Suites	B1
19 Tarlton's Lodge	D3

⊗ Eating
Bay of Islands Farmers Market	(see 6)
20 Charlotte's Kitchen	A2
21 El Cafe	C2
22 Legends	B2
Provenir	(see 16)

☕ Drinking & Nightlife
23 Alongside	A3
24 Bay of Islands Swordfish Club	A3
25 Kings Road Bar & Brasserie	C2
26 Pipi Patch	C3

the path follows a boardwalk through the mangroves. Otherwise you can drive here, turning right off Puketona Rd onto Haruru Falls Rd.

Opua Forest   FOREST
(www.doc.govt.nz) Just behind Paihia, this regenerating forest has walking trails ranging from 10 minutes to five hours. A few large trees have escaped axe and fire, including some big kauri. Information on Opua Forest walks is available from the i-SITE (p158), including the 1.5km **Paihia School Road Track** (about 30 minutes each way) leading to a lookout. You can also drive into the forest by taking Oromahoe Rd west from Opua.

☆ Activities

Bay Beach Hire
KAYAKING, BOATING

(☑ 09-402 6078; www.baybeachhire.co.nz; Marsden Rd, Paihia; ⊙9am-5pm) Hires kayaks (from $15 per hour), sailing catamarans ($50 first hour, $40 per additional), mountain bikes ($75 per day), boogie boards ($10/25 per hour/day), stand-up paddleboards ($25 per hour), fishing rods (from $10 per day), wetsuits and snorkelling gear (both $20 per day). Also offers kayaking tours, including a twilight paddle ($69).

Paihia Dive
DIVING

(☑ 09-402 7551; www.divenz.com; 7 Williams Rd, Paihia; dives from $249; ⊙7.45am-5.30pm daily Oct-May, 8.30am-5pm Mon-Fri, to 1.30pm Sat Jun-Sep) This five-star PADI dive crew offers combined reef and wreck trips to either the *Canterbury* or the *Rainbow Warrior*. They also sell fishing gear and snorkelling sets.

Coastal Kayakers
KAYAKING

(☑ 0800 334 661; www.coastalkayakers.co.nz; Te Karuwha Pde, Paihia) Runs guided tours (half-/full day $89/139, minimum two people) and multiday adventures. Kayaks (half-/full day $40/60) can also be rented for independent exploration.

☞ Tours

Taiamai Tours
Heritage Journeys
CULTURAL, CANOEING

(☑ 09-405 9990; www.taiamaitours.co.nz; 2½hr tour $135; ⊙departs 9am Tue, Thu, Sat & Sun Oct-Apr) Paddle a traditional 12m carved *waka* (canoe) from the Waitangi bridge to the Haruru Falls. The Ngāpuhi hosts wear traditional garb, and perform the proper *karakia* (incantations) and share stories. The price includes admission to the Waitangi Treaty Grounds (p154).

Salt Air
SCENIC FLIGHTS

(☑ 09-402 8338; www.saltair.co.nz; Marsden Rd, Paihia) Scenic flights include a five-hour light aircraft and 4WD tour to Cape Reinga and Ninety Mile Beach ($425), and helicopter flights out to the Hole in the Rock ($250). Another tour even lands on the famed island (from $399) where visitors are welcomed by a local Māori guide.

Tango Jet Ski Tours
BOATING

(☑ 0800 253 8754; www.tangojetskitours.co.nz; Paihia Wharf, Marsden Rd, Paihia; tours from $160-460) Led by a guide, zip around the bay on your own jet ski; longer trips go all the way to the Hole in the Rock. Prices are per ski, which can take up to two people.

☆ Festivals & Events

Waitangi Day
CULTURAL

(Waitangi Treaty Grounds; ⊙6 Feb) Various ceremonial events at Waitangi Treaty Grounds on 6 February, including speeches, a naval salute and an annual outing for the huge *waka taua* (war canoe) Ngātoki-matawhaorua. The day then continues with food, music and cultural performances.

Bay of Islands Beast
SPORTS

(www.thebeast.co.nz; ⊙Jul) Held in July, the Beast is billed as a 7km 'run, walk, crawl' event, featuring around 1000 participants in costume trudging along muddy tracks.

It! Bay of Islands
Food & Wine Festival
FOOD & DRINK

(www.paihianz.co.nz; Village Green, 60 Marsden Rd; adult/child $55/15; ⊙Oct) A day of food, wine and well-known Kiwi musicians in Paihia.

⊨ Sleeping

⊨ Paihia

Seabeds
HOSTEL $

(☑ 09-402 5567; www.seabeds.co.nz; 46 Davis Cres; dm/s/d $28/69/89; ☎) Offering comfortable, friendly, stylish budget digs in a converted motel, Seabeds is one of Paihia's best hostels. Little design touches give it a stylish ambience, and it's in a quieter location than most of Paihia's more social hostels along Kings Rd. Best of all, all of the rooms have their own bathrooms.

Haka Lodge
HOSTEL $

(☑ 09-402 5637; www.hakalodge.com; 76 Marsden Rd; dm/r from $29/99; ☎) Located above good restaurants and across the road from the wharf, it's impossible to be more central than Haka Lodge. It also scores points for its modern and colourful decor, and appealing shared spaces with huge flat-screen TVs and unlimited wi-fi access. Accommodation ranges from excellent dorms to private rooms with en suites and TVs.

Cap'n Bob's Beachhouse
HOSTEL $

(☑ 09-402 8668; www.capnbobs.co.nz; 44 Davis Cres; dm/s/d/apt from $30/60/76/110; ☎) This small backpackers is a home-like place, with sea views from the verandah, and more than a touch of easy-going charm. There's a studio apartment with its own bathroom and kitchen; all the other rooms use the communal facilities.

Beachside Holiday Park HOLIDAY PARK $
(☑09-402 7678; www.beachsideholiday.co.nz; 1290 Paihia Rd (SH11); sites from $20, units with/without bathroom from $100/75; ☎) Wake up at the water's edge at this small, sheltered camping ground, south of Paihia township. The angular lemon cabins have 1970s charm, and there are kayaks for hire.

Abri Apartments APARTMENT $$
(☑09-402 8003; www.abriapartments.co.nz; 10-12 Bayview Rd; apt $165-185; ☎) Choose between one of two free-standing pole houses, set within subtropical gardens, or a spacious one-bedroom suite under the owners' home. All three offer wonderful bay views and kitchen facilities, and there's a free guest laundry too.

Breakwater Motel MOTEL $$
(☑09-402 7558; www.breakwatermotel.co.nz; 1 Bayview Rd; unit $145-195; ☀☎) Located by the little headland that breaks up the Paihia strip, this older motel has been renovated within an inch of its life. The units are tidy and modern, and each has its own kitchen. Best of all are the Waterfront Suites, with balconies and patios facing the sea.

Seaspray Suites MOTEL $$
(☑09-402 0013; www.seaspray.co.nz; 138 Marsden Rd; unit from $179; ☎) One of the best of the phalanx of motels and apartments lining the Paihia waterfront, Seaspray Suites has modern, self-contained one- and two-bedroom options, some with sea-view balconies or private courtyards.

Admiral's View Lodge MOTEL $$
(☑09-402 6236; www.admiralsviewlodge.co.nz; 2 MacMurray Rd; unit from $129; ☀@☎) This hillside lodge offers natty units with balconies just begging for a relaxed sunset gin and tonic. Some have spa baths and bay views.

Allegra House B&B $$$
(☑09-402 7932; www.allegra.co.nz; 39 Bayview Rd; r $260-290, apt $305; ☀☎) Offering quite astonishing views of the bay from an eyrie high above the township, Allegra has three handsome B&B rooms and a spacious self-contained apartment. Best of all is the top room, with its large rooftop terrace. If you feel the need for a singalong, there's a guest lounge with a piano.

Tarlton's Lodge B&B $$$
(☑09-402 6711; www.tarltonslodge.co.nz; 11 Sullivans Rd; r $320-350; ☎) Striking architecture combines with modern decor in this hilltop B&B with expansive bay views. All three suites have their own outdoor spa, perfect for a romantic stay. Look forward to excellent breakfasts.

Paihia Beach Resort & Spa RESORT $$$
(☑09-402 0111; www.paihiabeach.co.nz; 130 Marsden Rd; r from $488; ☀☎☀) All of the stylish and modern rooms in this mid-sized resort have sea views. An elegant downstairs piazza includes a swimming pool and Paihia's best fine dining restaurant Provenir (p158). Luxury spa services are also available. Check online for pamper and romance packages – or escape the romance with a golf getaway.

🛏 Haruru

Baystay B&B B&B $$
(☑09-402 7511; www.baystay.co.nz; 93a Yorke Rd; r $165-185; ☀@☎) Enjoy valley views from the spa pool of this slick, gay-friendly establishment. Yorke Rd is off Puketona Rd, just before the falls. Minimum stay of two nights; no children under 12 years.

Bay of Islands Holiday Park HOLIDAY PARK $$
(☑09-402 7646; www.bayofislandsholidaypark.co.nz; 678 Puketona Rd; sites from $34, units with/without bathroom $147/68; @☎☀) Under tall trees by a set of shallow rapids on the Waitangi River, 7km down Puketona Rd, this holiday park has excellent cabins, units and shady campsites.

🍴 Eating

El Cafe LATIN AMERICAN $
(☑09-402 7637; www.facebook.com/elcafepaihia; 2 Kings Rd, Paihia; mains $11-15; ⏱8am-4pm; ☎) This excellent Chilean-owned cafe has the best coffee in town and terrific breakfast burritos, tacos and baked-egg dishes, such as spicy *huevos rancheros*. The Cuban pulled-pork sandwich is truly a wonderful thing. The fruit smoothies are also great on a warm Bay of Islands day.

Bay of Islands Farmers Market MARKET $
(www.bayofislandsfarmersmarket.co.nz; Village Green, Paihia; ⏱1-4.30pm Thu) Stock up on local fruit, vegetables, pickles, preserves, honey, fish, smallgoods (small meat products), eggs, cheese, bread, wine and oil, straight from the producer.

Charlotte's Kitchen CONTEMPORARY $$
(☑09-402 8296; www.charlotteskitchen.co.nz; Paihia Wharf, 69 Marsden Rd, Paihia; mains lunch $16-27, dinner $20-35; ⏱11.30am-late Mon-Fri,

8am-late Sat & Sun) Named after an escaped Australian convict who was NZ's first white female settler, this hip restaurant/bar occupies a cheeky perch on the main pier. Bits of Kiwiana decorate the walls, while the menu takes a swashbuckling journey around the world, including steamed pork buns, quesadillas, Cubano sandwiches and a particularly delicious Asian-style broth with pork dumplings.

Whare Waka CAFE $$
(☑ 09-402 7437; www.waitangi.org.nz; Waitangi Treaty Grounds, 1 Tau Henare Dr, Waitangi; mains $13-19; ☺ 8am-4pm) Located beside a pond studded with ducks, backed by bush and overlooking the Treaty Grounds (p154), the Whare Waka (Boathouse) is a top spot for good cafe fare during the day, and to return to for a *hāngi* (earth-oven-cooked) dinner and concert on Tuesday, Thursday and Sunday evenings from December to March.

Legends PUB FOOD $$
(☑ 09-402 6037; www.kravecateringpaihia.co.nz; 1 Joyces Rd, Paihia; mains $16-27; ☺ 5-10pm) When locals are after a substantial, old-fashioned, good-value meal (think burgers, fish and chips, fried seafood platters and a roast of the day), they head to this no-nonsense restaurant at the Paihia Ex-Servicemen's Club. Drinks can be ordered separately from the bar, but mind that you return your plates and glasses before you leave to avoid a telling off.

★**Provenir** CONTEMPORARY $$$
(☑ 09-402 0111; www.paihiabeach.co.nz; Paihia Beach Resort, 130 Marsden Rd, Paihia; mains $30-40; ☺ 8-10am & 6pm-late) A concise seasonal menu of main dishes showcases regional NZ produce and local seafood (including plump oysters from nearby Orongo Bay), underpinned by subtle Asian influences and one of Northland's best wine lists. Desserts are extraordinarily creative and well worth leaving room for.

🍷 Drinking & Nightlife

Alongside BAR
(☑ 09-402 6220; www.alongside35.co.nz; 69 Marsden Rd, Paihia; ☺ 8am-10pm) Quite possibly the biggest deck in all of Northland extends over the water, and a versatile approach to entertaining begins with coffee and bagels for breakfast before the inevitable transformation of Alongside into a very enjoyable bar. There are bar snacks and meals on offer, and lots of comfy lounges ready for conversations fuelled by cocktails or cold beer.

Kings Road Bar & Brasserie BAR
(☑ 09-402 6080; 14 Kings Rd, Paihia; ☺ 11.30am-midnight; 🛜) Slink into this low-lit bar for a cosy beverage on one of the couches or a crack at the free pool table.

Pipi Patch BAR
(☑ 09-402 7111; www.facebook.com/basebay ofislands; 18 Kings Rd; ☺ 5pm-late) The party hostel has the party bar: a popular spot with large video screens and a decent terrace. You'll be shuffled inside at midnight to keep the neighbours happy – although most of them are backpackers who'll be here anyway.

Bay of Islands Swordfish Club BAR
(Swordy; ☑ 09-402 7773; www.swordfish.co.nz; Level 1, 96 Marsden Rd, Paihia; ☺ 4pm-late) Great views, cold beer and tall tales abound at this brightly lit club bar where creatures from the deep protrude from every available surface. Decent burgers, steaks and seafood are also served.

ℹ️ Information

Bay of Islands i-SITE (☑ 09-402 7345; www.northlandnz.com; 69 Marsden Rd, Paihia; ☺ 8am-5pm Mar-Dec, to 7pm Jan & Feb) Information and bookings.

ℹ️ Getting There & Away

All **buses** (Maritime Building, Paihia) serving Paihia stop at the Maritime Building by the wharf.

InterCity (p139) has three or four coaches a day to and from Auckland (from $29, four hours), Waipu (from $25, 1¾ hours), Whangarei (from $12, 1¼ hours), Kawakawa (from $15, 20 minutes) and Kerikeri (from $15, 20 minutes).

Mana Bus (p139), in association with Naked Bus, has two daily coaches to and from Auckland ($34, four hours), Warkworth ($27, three hours), Waipu ($14, two hours), Whangarei ($12, 1¼ hours) and Kawakawa (from $7, 20 minutes).

Ferries (Paihia Wharf) depart regularly for Russell, and there are seasonal services to Urupukapuka Island.

ℹ️ Getting Around

For bike rental, visit **Bay Beach Hire** (p156).

Urupukapuka Island

The largest of the bay's islands, Urupukapuka is a tranquil place criss-crossed with walking trails and surrounded by aquamarine waters. Native birds are plentiful thanks to a conservation initiative that has rendered this and all of the neighbouring islands predator free; check that there aren't any rats, mice or ants stowing away on your boat or in your gear before leaving the mainland.

🛏 Sleeping

DOC Campsites   CAMPGROUND **$**
(www.doc.govt.nz; sites per adult/child $13/6.50) There are DOC campsites at Cable, Sunset and Urupukapuka Bays. They have water supplies, cold showers (except Sunset Bay) and composting toilets; bring food, a stove and fuel. Bookings are required year-round.

ℹ Getting There & Away

Explore NZ (p149) runs ferries to Otehei Bay (adult/child $35/20) from Paihia and Russell; they're supposedly year-round, although they can be irregular in winter. Most of the scheduled bay cruises moor at Otehei Bay for a little island time.

Bay of Islands Kayaking (p146) can arrange kayaking trips and camping gear for the island. Note that it does not rent to solo kayakers, so you'll need to find a friend.

Kawakawa

POP 1220

Kawakawa would be just another ordinary, economically challenged Northland town if it weren't for a couple of extraordinary features in its modest town centre: an architecturally significant public toilet and a steam train that runs along the main street. There are also a pair of important Māori sites hidden within the surrounding farmland that are fascinating in their own right and well worth a detour.

◉ Sights & Activities

Kawakawa Public Toilets   NOTABLE BUILDING
(58 Gillies St) It's rare that public toilets are a town's claim to fame but Kawakawa's were designed by Austrian-born artist and eco-architect Friedensreich Hundertwasser, who lived near Kawakawa in an isolated house without electricity from 1973 until his death in 2000. The most photographed toilets in NZ are typical Hundertwasser – lots of organic, wavy lines decorated with ceramic mosaics and brightly coloured bottles, and with grass and plants on the roof.

Other examples of his work can be seen in Vienna and Osaka.

Kawiti Caves   CAVE
(☑ 09-404 0583; www.kawiticaves.co.nz; 49 Waiomio Rd; adult/child $20/10; ⊗ 8.30am-4pm) Explore these glowworm-illuminated limestone caverns on a 30-minute subterranean tour led by direct descendants of Ngāti Hine chief Kawiti, who fought the British at Ruapekapeka Pā during the first of the New Zealand wars.

Ruapekapeka Pā   HISTORIC SITE
(www.ruapekapeka.co.nz; Ruapekapeka Rd) FREE
For 10 days in January 1846, 1600 British troops bombarded 500 Māori warriors hunkered down in a *pā* (fortress) composed of trenches, tunnels and wooden palisades on this lonely hillside. Ruapekapeka translates as 'the bat's nest' but by the time the British broke through, the bats had already flown, leaving them (not for the first time) with an empty *pā*. This stalemate was to be the final battle of the Northland War; following this the parties made peace.

Detailed information boards explain the battle and the layout of the fortress. A track heads from the car park through beautiful native bush to a carved gate leading up to the *pā*, where the trenches can easily be seen. At the top there's a memorial in the form of a *pou* (carved post).

Ruapekapeka is reached by a 5km unsealed road signposted from SH11, 15km south of Kawakawa.

Bay of Islands Vintage Railway   RAIL
(☑ 09-404 0684; www.bayofislandsvintagerailway.org.nz; Gilies St; adult/child $20/5; ⊗ 10.45am, noon, 1.15pm, 2.30pm Fri-Sun, daily school holidays) Take a 50-minute spin down the main street of Kawakawa to Taumarere and back in a carriage pulled by either Gabriel the steam engine or a vintage diesel engine.

ℹ Getting There & Away

InterCity (p139) coaches stop at Kawakawa junction, with three or four services daily to and from Auckland (from $37, 3¾ hours), Waipu (from $28, 1½ hours), Whangarei (from $14, 50 minutes), Paihia (from $15, 20 minutes) and Kerikeri (from $17, 50 minutes).

Mana Bus (p139), in association with Naked Bus, has two daily coaches to and from Auckland ($34, four hours), Warkworth ($27, 2¾ hours), Waipu ($14, 1¾ hours), Whangarei ($12, one hour) and Paihia (from $7, 20 minutes).

ABC Shuttles & Tours (☑ 022 025 0800; www.abcshuttle.co.nz; tours from $40) run tours from Paihia to Kawakawa and the caves ($40 not including cave admission).

Kerikeri

POP 6500

Kerikeri means 'dig dig', which is apt, as lots of digging goes on around the area's fertile farmland. Famous for its oranges, Kerikeri also produces kiwifruit, vegetables and wine. If you're looking for some back-breaking, poorly paid work that the locals aren't keen to do, your working holiday starts here.

A snapshot of early Māori and British interaction is offered by a cluster of historic sites centred on the picturesque river basin. In 1819 the powerful Ngāpuhi chief Hongi Hika allowed Reverend Samuel Marsden to start a mission under the shadow of his Kororipo Pā. There's an ongoing campaign to have the area recognised as a Unesco World Heritage Site.

◉ Sights

★ Kerikeri Mission Station HISTORIC BUILDING

(☑ 09-407 9236; www.historic.org.nz; 246 Kerikeri Rd; museum $8, house tour $8, combined $10; ◎ 10am-4pm) Two of the nation's most significant buildings nestle side by side on the banks of Kerikeri Basin. Start at the **Stone Store**, NZ's oldest stone building (1836). Upstairs there's an interesting little museum, while downstairs the shop sells Kiwiana gifts as well as the type of goods that used to be stocked here in the 19th century. Tours of neighbouring **Kemp House** depart from here. Built by the missionaries in 1822, this humble yet pretty wooden Georgian-style house is NZ's oldest building.

The house is encircled by heritage gardens and the mature fruit trees scattered all around the river basin are the remnants of the mission's original orchard. In summer, the Honey House Cafe operates from a neighbouring cottage.

Kororipo Pā HISTORIC SITE

(Kerikeri Rd) FREE Just up the hill from Kerikeri Mission Station is a marked historical walk, which leads to the site of Hongi Hika's *pā* (fortress) and village. Little remains aside from the terracing that once supported wooden palisades. Huge war parties once departed from here, terrorising much of the North Island and slaughtering thousands during the Musket Wars. The role of missionaries in arming Ngāpuhi remains controversial. The walk emerges near the cute wooden St James Anglican Church (1878).

Rewa's Village MUSEUM

(☑ 09-407 6454; www.rewasvillage.co.nz; 1 Landing Rd; adult/child $10/5; ◎ 10am-4pm) If you had a hard time imagining nearby Kororipo Pā in its original state, take the footbridge across the river to this mock-up of a traditional Māori fishing village. Opening hours can be hit and miss, and it's in need of some maintenance.

Aroha Island WILDLIFE RESERVE

(☑ 09-407 5243; www.arohaisland.co.nz; 177 Rangitane Rd; ◎ 9.30am-5.30pm) FREE Reached via a permanent causeway through the mangroves, this 12-hectare island provides a haven for the North Island brown kiwi and other native birds, as well as a pleasant picnic spot for their nonfeathered admirers. It has a visitor centre, kayaks for rent (from $22), and you can also arrange after-dark walks to spy kiwi in the wild (adult/child $40/15) can also be arranged. You've got around a 50% chance of seeing a kiwi, and booking ahead is essential.

🛏 Sleeping

Aroha Island CAMPGROUND $

(☑ 09-407 5243; www.arohaisland.co.nz; 177 Rangitane Rd; sites/units from $20/125) Kip among the kiwi on the eco island of love (*aroha*). There's a wide range of reasonably priced options, from the peaceful campsites with basic facilities by the shelly beach, to a whole house. The entire island, indoors and out, is nonsmoking.

Wharepuke Subtropical Accommodation CABIN $$

(☑ 09-407 8933; www.accommodation-bay-of-islands.co.nz; 190 Kerikeri Rd; cabins $180; 🖥) Best known for its food and lush gardens, Wharepuke also rents five self-contained one-bedroom cottages hidden among the palms. They have the prefabricated look of holiday-park cabins, but are a step up in terms of fixtures and space.

Pagoda Lodge LODGE, CAMPGROUND $$

(☑ 09-407 8617; www.pagoda.co.nz; 81 Pa Rd; sites/safari tent/caravan from $40/120/130, unit with/without bathroom from $145/110; ◎ Nov-Mar; 🖥) Built in the 1930s by an oddball Scotsman with an Asian fetish, this lodge features pagoda-shaped roofs grafted onto wooden cottages. The property descends to the river and is dotted with Buddhas, gypsy caravans, and safari tents with proper beds, or you can pitch your own. Take Cobham Rd, turn left into Kerikeri Inlet Rd, then left into Pa Rd.

Kerikeri

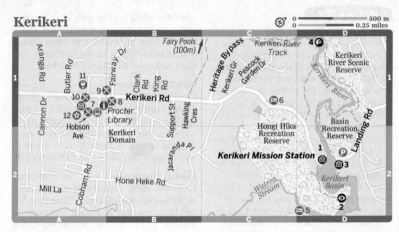

Kerikeri

◎ Top Sights
1 Kerikeri Mission Station........................D2

◎ Sights
2 Kororipo Pā...D2
3 Rewa's Village.....................................D2
4 Wharepuke Falls D1

⨺ Sleeping
5 Pagoda Lodge D2
6 Wharepuke Subtropical
   Accommodation C1

⨯ Eating
7 Bay of Islands Farmers Market..............A1

8 Cafe Jerusalem....................................B1
CC's Cafe Cinema ....(see 12)
9 Fishbone..A1
Food at Wharepuke.........................(see 6)
Village Cafe ....(see 8)
10 Ziezo..A1

◎ Drinking & Nightlife
11 La Taza Del Diablo.............................A1

◎ Entertainment
12 Cathay Cinemas.................................A1

Kauri Park   MOTEL **$$**
(☏09-407 7629; www.kauripark.co.nz; 512 Kerikeri Rd; units from $130; ☎☒) Hidden behind tall trees on the approach to Kerikeri, this well-priced motel has a mixture of units of varying layouts. The premium suites are extremely comfortable, but all options are spacious and stylishly furnished.

Relax a Lodge   HOMESTAY **$$**
(☏09-407 6989; www.relaxalodge.co.nz; 1574 Springbank Rd (SH10); s/d $55/70, cottages $120-145; ☎) Located in an orange grove, 4km out of town, this quiet rural retreat has tidy backpacker rooms in the main house (bathrooms are shared) and attractive self-contained cottages, sleeping two to four people, dotted around the property.

Moon Gate Villa   B&B **$$$**
(☏09-929 5921; www.moongatevilla.com; 462 Kerikeri Rd; ste $339-369, cottage $299; ☎☒) A stream-like water feature flows through the centre of this modern house, set amidst tropical foliage on the approach to Kerikeri. The larger of the two suites has a huge spa bath, while the other has an extra single room attached for parties of three. There's also a compact self-contained cottage in the garden and a solar-powered swimming pool.

⨯ Eating & Drinking

⨯ Town Centre

Bay of Islands Farmers Market   MARKET **$**
(www.bayofislandsfarmersmarket.co.nz; Hobson Ave; ◷8.30am-noon Sun) On a Sunday morning the car park behind the post office is lined with tents selling everything from gourmet sausages to oversized carrots. Grab a coffee and graze on the free samples.

WORTH A TRIP

TE WAIMATE MISSION

Set in verdant farmland 18km south-west of Kerikeri, **Te Waimate Mission** (☑09-405 9734; www.tewaimatemission.co.nz; 344 Te Ahu Ahu Rd, Waimate North; adult/child $10/5; ☺10am-5pm Fri-Tue Nov-Apr, to 4pm Sat-Mon May-Oct) holds several claims to fame. It's NZ's second-oldest house (built in 1831) and the site of the country's first European-style farm. Many of the exotic trees surrounding it are amongst the oldest of their kind in the country, and Charles Darwin stayed here in 1835. Inside, the story of the mission station and its inhabitants are outlined in displays in rooms dotted with items of original furniture.

The complex also includes the wooden St John the Baptist Church and an 1877 Sunday school building.

Fishbone CAFE $
(☑09-407 6065; www.fishbonecafe.co.nz; 88 Kerikeri Rd; mains $10-17; ☺8am-4pm Mon-Fri, 8.30am-2pm Sat & Sun) After 20 years, Fishbone is no longer the coolest kid in town but they're still a reliable coffee and brunch spot. Grab a shady table out the front for a summer wine.

Ziezo BISTRO $$
(☑09-407 9511; 55 Kerikeri Rd; mains $20-29; ☺5pm-late Thu-Sun) This stylish bistro certainly brightens up Kerikeri's retail-focused main street, and the food is equally interesting. Ziezo is the Dutch equivalent of *voila* ('here it is!') and, alongside classic bistro dishes, a subtle Netherlander influence reveals itself in beef rendang (the classic curry from former colony Indonesia) and Dutch apple pie.

Cafe Jerusalem ISRAELI $$
(☑09-407 1001; www.cafejerusalem.co.nz; Village Mall, 85 Kerikeri Rd; mains $17-20; ☺10am-late Mon-Sat) Northland's best falafels, lamb shawarma (kebab) and mezze platters, all served with a smile and a social vibe. Most mains come with rice, pita bread, tabouleh and a salad. Try the *shakshuka* (baked eggs in a spicy tomato sauce) for a hearty brunch.

Village Cafe CAFE $$
(☑09-407 4062; www.facebook.com/thevillagecafe kerikeri; Village Mall, 85 Kerikeri Rd; mains $12-20; ☺8am-4pm Mon-Fri, 8.30am-2pm Sat & Sun) This cute little cafe is popular with locals for good coffee, freshly prepared counter food, and a relaxed menu of brunch and lunch dishes. Grab a table outside in the Northland sunshine, and order the hearty potato hash.

CC's Cafe Cinema CAFE $$
(☑09-407 9121; www.cafecinema.co.nz; 27-29 Hobson Ave; mains brunch $8-17, dinner $20-30; ☺9am-3pm Mon, to late Tue-Sun) Excellent coffee, meals and snacks are served in this cool cafe beside the local cinema. A Movie Meal Deal including one main dish and a cinema ticket is $36.

Food at Wharepuke THAI, EUROPEAN $$$
(☑09-407 8936; www.foodatwharepuke.co.nz; 190 Kerikeri Rd; mains $30-40; ☺11am-10pm Tue-Sat) With one foot in Europe, the other in Thailand and its head in the lush vegetation of Wharepuke Subtropical Gardens, this is Kerikeri's most unusual and inspired eatery. On Friday nights it serves popular Thai banquets (three courses $48). Adjacent is the interesting Wharepuke Print Studio & Gallery.

✕ Surrounds

Old Packhouse Market MARKET $
(☑09-401 9588; www.theoldpackhousemarket.co.nz; 505 Kerikeri Rd; ☺8am-1.30pm Sat) Local artisans, winemakers and farmers sell their goodies at this market in an old fruit-packing shed on the outskirts of town. On a Saturday morning it's the best place in town to have a leisurely breakfast.

★ Rusty Tractor CAFE $$
(☑09-407 3322; www.rustytractorcafe.co.nz; 582 Kerikeri Rd; mains breakfast $17-20, lunch $20-26; ☺8am-4pm; 🛜🛝) As decadent breakfasts go, Rusty Tractor's doughnuts with crème fraiche and berries takes some beating. There are healthier options, too, and the coffee's up with the best in Kerikeri. Otherwise, treat yourself to a glass of wine while the kids play on the rocketship slide on the back lawn.

Marsden Estate CONTEMPORARY $$
(☑09-407 9398; www.marsdenestate.co.nz; 56 Wiroa Rd; mains breakfast $16-18, lunch $28-38; ☺10am-4pm; 🛝) The interior of this winery restaurant is large and featureless so opt for the covered terrace at the rear, which has wonderful views over the vines and a pretty pond. Cooked breakfasts give way to sophisticated lunches that match prime local produce with flavours from all over the world.

Ake Ake

BRITISH, FRENCH $$$

(☑09-407 8230; www.akeakevineyard.co.nz; 165 Waimate North Rd; mains $30-36; ☺noon-3pm & 6-9pm Mon-Sat, noon-3pm Sun, tastings 10am-4.30pm; 🖭) 🖋 At this upmarket winery restaurant, the rural setting is complemented by hearty but sophisticated country fare such as lamb shanks, wild game pie, confit duck and steak. The Sunday roasts are legendary. After lunch, work off some of the calories on the 1km self-guided trail through the vineyard. Free overnight parking is available for customers with self-contained vehicles.

🍸 Drinking & Entertainment

La Taza Del Diablo

BAR

(☑09-407 3912; www.facebook.com/eltazadel diablo; 3 Homestead Rd; ☺11.30am-late Wed-Sun; 🛜) This Mexican-style bar is about as energetic and raffish as buttoned-down Kerikeri gets with a decent selection of tequila, Mexican beers and, just maybe, Northland's best margaritas. Tacos, enchiladas and chimichangas all feature on the bar snacks menu, and occasional live gigs sometimes raise the roof in this genteel town.

Cathay Cinemas

CINEMA

(☑09-407 4428; www.cathaycinemas.co.nz; 27 Hobson Ave; adult/child $15/9) Hollywood blockbusters and art-house flicks.

ℹ️ Information

Procter Library (6 Cobham Rd; ☺8am-5pm Mon-Fri, 9am-2pm Sat; 🛜) Tourist brochures and free internet access.

ℹ️ Getting There & Away

AIR

Bay of Islands (Kerikeri) Airport (KKE; ☑09-407 6133; www.bayofislandsairport.co.nz; 218 Wiroa Rd) is 8km southwest of town. Air New Zealand flies from Auckland to Kerikeri. **Super Shuttle** (☑0800 748 885; www.supershuttle. co.nz; Kerikeri Airport) provides shuttles between Kerikeri Airport and Bay of Islands destinations such as Kerikeri ($12) and Paihia ($27).

BUS

InterCity (p139) buses leave from a **stop** (9 Cobham Rd) at 9 Cobham Rd, opposite the library. Destinations include Auckland (from $29, 4½ hours, three daily), Whangarei (from $12, 1¾ hours, three daily), Paihia (from $15, 20 minutes, three daily), Mangonui ($28, one hour, daily) and Kaitaia ($37, 1¾ hours, daily). **Hokianga Link** (☑021 405 872; www.buslink. co.nz) offers a weekly minibus service between Kerikeri and Omapere, which expands to twice weekly in summer.

Puketi & Omahuta Forests

Inland from Kerikeri, the Puketi and Omahuta Forests form a continuous expanse of native rainforest. Logging in Puketi was stopped in 1951 to protect not only the remaining kauri but also the endangered kokako bird. Keep an eye out for this rare charmer (grey with a blue wattle) on your wanders.

The forests are reached by several entrances and contain a network of walking tracks varying in length from 15 minutes (the wheelchair-accessible Manginangina

---

KERIKERI ARTISANS

You'd be forgiven for thinking that everyone in Kerikeri is involved in some small-scale artisanal enterprise, given the bombardment of craft shops on the way into town. A little further afield, a handful of vineyards are doing their best to stake Northland's claim as a wine region. The little-known red grape chambourcin has proved particularly suited to the region's subtropical humidity, along with pinotage and syrah.

Look out for the *Art & Craft Trail* and *Wine Trail* brochures. Here are our tasty recommendations:

Ake Ake (p163) Wine tastings (usually $8) are free with lunch or a purchase of wine.

Cottle Hill (☑09-407 5203; www.cottlehill.co.nz; 28 Cottle Hill Dr; tastings $5, free with purchase; ☺10am-5pm daily Nov-Mar, Wed-Sun Apr-Oct) Wine, port, grappa and liquors.

Get Fudged & Keriblue Ceramics (☑09-407 1111; www.keriblueceramics.co.nz; 1691 SH10; ☺9am-5pm) An unusual pairing of ceramics and big, decadent slabs of fudge.

Makana Confections (☑09-407 6800; www.makana.co.nz; 504 Kerikeri Rd; ☺9am-5.30pm) Artisan chocolate factory with a cafe attached.

Marsden Estate (p162) Wine tastings and lunch on the terrace.

Kauri Walk) to two days (the challenging Waipapa River Track); see the DOC website (www.doc.govt.nz) for other walks.

Tours

Adventure Puketi ECOTOUR
(☑09-401 9095; www.forestwalks.com; 476 Puketi Rd; tours $65-155) ✒ Adventure Puketi leads guided ecowalks through the forest, including night-time tours to seek out the nocturnal wildlife. It also offers very comfortable B&B accommodation on the edge of the forest. Check the website for packages incorporating tours and accommodation.

🛏 Sleeping

Sleeping is restricted to a **DOC campsite** (☑09-407 0300; www.doc.govt.nz; Waiare Rd; sites per adult/child $8/4) ✒ and 18-bunk hut, and also B&B accommodation with Adventure Puketi (p164). Most travellers visit from Paihia or Kerikeri.

❶ Getting There & Away

There is no public transport. Most travellers visit from Paihia or Kerikeri.

THE FAR NORTH

Here's your chance to get off the beaten track, even if that sometimes means onto unsealed roads. The far-flung Far North always plays second fiddle to the Bay of Islands for attention and funding, yet the subtropical tip of the North Island has more breathtaking coastline per square kilometre than anywhere apart from the offshore islands. While the 'winterless north' may be a popular misnomer, summers here are long and leisurely. Note that parts of the Far North are noticeably economically depressed and in places could best be described as gritty.

Matauri & Tauranga Bays

It's a short detour from SH10, but the exceptionally scenic loop route leading inland to these awesome beaches is a world away from the glitzy face presented for tourists in the Bay of Islands.

Matauri Bay is a long, sandy surf beach, 18km off SH10, with the 17 **Cavalli Islands** scattered offshore. On top of the headland above the park is a monument to the *Rainbow Warrior;* the Greenpeace ship's under-water resting place among the nearby islands is a popular dive site.

Back on the main road, the route heads west, passing through pleasant **Te Ngaere** village and a succession of little bays before the turn-off to **Tauranga Bay**, a smaller beach where the sand is a peachy pink colour.

🏃 Activities

Northland Sea Kayaking KAYAKING
(☑09-405 0381; www.northlandseakayaking.co.nz; half-/full-day tours $90/115) Down a private road leading from Tauranga Bay, Northland Sea Kayaking leads kayak explorations of this magical coastline of coves, sea caves and islands. Accommodation is available in conjunction with tours for $35 extra per person.

🛏 Sleeping

Matauri Bay Holiday Park HOLIDAY PARK $
(☑09-405 0525; www.matauribayholidaypark. co.nz; Matauri Bay Rd; sites/units from $20/60) Taking up the north end of the beach, this holiday park has only a handful of cabins but plenty of space to pitch a tent or park a campervan. There's also a shop selling groceries, booze and petrol.

Tauranga Bay Holiday Park HOLIDAY PARK $$
(☑09-405 0436; www.taurangabay.co.nz; 51 Tauranga Bay Beach Rd; sites from $20, cabins with/without bathroom $125/85; @ 🐾) Tauranga Bay Holiday Park has well-maintained accommodation on the picturesque beachfront, but it lacks trees and bears the brunt of the weather. A charge per night of $60 for campsites and a seven-night minimum stay applies from mid-December to the end of January.

❶ Getting There & Away

There is no public transport to these areas.

Whangaroa Harbour

Just around the headland from Tauranga Bay is the narrow entrance to Whangaroa Harbour. The small fishing village of **Whangaroa** is 6km from SH10 and calls itself the 'Marlin Capital of NZ'.

There are plenty of charter boats for game-fishing (December to April); prices start at around $1200 a day. If you're planning to hook a monster, insist on it being released once caught – striped marlin and swordfish are among NZ's least-sustainable fishing options.

On the other side of the harbour's north head is **Taupo Bay**, a surf beach that attracts a loyal Kiwi contingent in summer. On easterly swells, there are quality right-handers to surf at the southern end of the bay, by the rivermouth. It's reached by an 11km road signposted from SH10.

🏃 Activities

An excellent 20-minute hike starts from the car park at the end of Old Hospital Rd and goes up **St Paul's Rock** (213m), which dominates Whangaroa village. At the top you have to use a wire cable to pull yourself up, but the views make it worth the effort.

The **Wairakau Stream Track**, heading north to Pekapeka Bay, begins near the church hall on Campbell Rd in Totara North on the other side of the bay. It's an extremely beautiful, undeveloped stretch and you can cool off in swimming holes along the way. The two-hour (5.6km) hike passes through forest, an abandoned farm and around a steep-walled estuary before arriving at DOC's **Lane Cove Hut** (🏠 09-407 0300; www.doc.govt.nz; adult/child $15/7.50) 🏊.

🛏 Sleeping & Eating

⭐ **Kahoe Farms Hostel** HOSTEL **$**
(🏠 09-405 1804; www.kahoefarms.co.nz; 1266 SH10; dm $32, r with/without bathroom from $116/86; 🛜) On SH10, 10km north of the turn-off to Whangaroa, this hostel has a deservedly great reputation – for its comfortable accommodation, bucolic setting and home-cooked Italian food, but mostly for its welcoming owners. The backpackers' cottage is great, but slightly up the hill there's an even more impressive villa with excellent-value en-suite rooms.

Marlin PUB FOOD **$$**
(🏠 09-405 0347; www.marlinhotel.co.nz; 578 Whangaroa Rd; mains $14-28; ⏰ noon-1am Sun, 9am-1am Mon-Sat) A friendly local pub with good honest tucker served from the attached cafe. Inside there are a few impressive wall-mounted game fish that definitely didn't get away.

BAY OF ISLANDS & NORTHLAND WHANGAROA HARBOUR

THE BOMBING OF THE RAINBOW WARRIOR

On the morning of 10 July 1985, New Zealanders awoke to news reporting that a terrorist attack had killed a man in Auckland Harbour. The Greenpeace flagship *Rainbow Warrior* had been sunk at its anchorage at Marsden Wharf, where it was preparing to sail to Moruroa Atoll near Tahiti to protest against French nuclear testing.

A tip-off from a Neighbourhood Watch group eventually led to the arrest of two French foreign intelligence service (DGSE) agents, posing as tourists. The agents had detonated two mines on the boat in staggered explosions – the first designed to cause the crew to evacuate and the second to sink her. However, after the initial evacuation, some of the crew returned to the vessel to investigate and document the attack. Greenpeace photographer Fernando Pereira was drowned below decks following the second explosion.

The arrested agents pleaded guilty to manslaughter and were sentenced to 10 years' imprisonment. In response, the French government threatened to embargo NZ goods from entering the European Economic Community – which would have crippled NZ's economy. A deal was struck whereby France paid $13 million to NZ and apologised, in return for the agents being delivered into French custody on a South Pacific atoll for three years. France eventually paid over $8 million to Greenpeace in reparation – and the bombers were quietly freed before their sentence was served.

Initially French President François Mitterrand denied any government involvement in the attack, but following an inquiry he eventually sacked his Defence Minister and the head of the DGSE, Admiral Pierre Lacoste. On the 20th anniversary of the attack, *Le Monde* newspaper published a report from Lacoste dating from 1986, declaring that the president had personally authorised the operation.

The bombing left a lasting impact on NZ, and French nuclear testing at Moruroa ceased for good in 1996. The wreck of the *Rainbow Warrior* was re-sunk near Northland's Cavalli Islands, where, today, it can be explored by divers. The masts were bought by the **Dargaville Museum** (p178) and overlook the town. The memory of Fernando Pereira endures in a peaceful bird hide in Thames, while a memorial to the boat sits atop a Māori *pā* site at Matauri Bay, north of the Bay of Islands.

❶ Information

Boyd Gallery (☑ 09-405 0230; www.whanga-roa.co.nz; 537 Whangaroa Rd; ☺ 8am-7pm) General store and tourist information office.

❶ Getting There & Away

There is no public transport to Whangaroa Harbour. Buses usually drop off at SH10 in nearby Kahoe, immediately west of the harbour and 15km from Whangaroa village.

Doubtless Bay

POP 1662

The bay gets its unusual name from an entry in Cook's logbook, where he wrote that the body of water was 'doubtless a bay'. No kidding, Cap'n. It's a big bay at that, with a string of pretty swimming beaches heading towards the Karikari Peninsula.

The main centre, **Mangonui** (meaning 'Big Shark'), retains a fishing-port feel, despite cafes and gift shops now infesting its well-labelled line of historical waterfront buildings. They were constructed in the days when Mangonui was a centre of the whaling industry (1792–1850) and exported flax, kauri wood and gum.

The popular holiday settlements of **Coopers Beach**, **Cable Bay** and **Taipa** are restful pockets of beachside gentrification.

◉ Sights & Activities

Grab the free *Heritage Trail* brochure from the visitor information centre (p167) for a 3km self-guided walk that takes in 22 historic sites. Other walks lead to attractive **Mill Bay**, west of Mangonui, and **Rangikapiti Pā Historic Reserve**, which has ancient Māori terracing and a spectacular view of Doubtless Bay – particularly at sunrise and sunset. A walkway runs from Mill Bay to the *pā* (fortified village site), but you can also drive nearly to the top.

Butler Point Whaling Museum   MUSEUM
(☑ 09-406 0006; www.whalingmuseumbutler point.com; Marchant Rd, Hihi; adult/child $25/5; ☺ by appointment) This small private museum is set in lovely gardens at Hihi, 15km northeast of Mangonui. The centrepiece is a still-lived-in Victorian homestead built by retired whaling captain, William Butler, who settled here in 1838, had 13 children and became a trader, farmer, magistrate and Member of Parliament. Visits must be prearranged and start with a guided tour of the house, after which you're welcome to wander around the grounds for as long as you like.

⌂ Sleeping

Mangonui Waterfront Apartments Motel   APARTMENT $$
(☑ 09-406 0347; www.mangonuiwaterfront.co.nz; 88 Waterfront Dr, Mangonui; apt $120-250; ☏) Character radiates from the kauri boards of these apartments that occupy a set of historic houses on the Mangonui waterfront. Each is different, ranging from a small bedsit to a two-bedroom unit with a full kitchen sleeping up to five people. Best of all is one-bedroom Tahi, with French doors opening onto the best balcony in Mangonui.

Puketiti Lodge   GUESTHOUSE $$
(☑ 09-406 0369; www.puketitilodge.co.nz; 53 Puketiti Dr; r $150; ☺ Nov-Mar; @☏) You'll need a car to get here, but the views from the generously proportioned deck more than justify the distance from the water. The two spacious rooms each have a double bed and a set of bunks, and there's a communal kitchen and lounge too. Turn inland at Midgley Rd, 6km south of Mangonui village, just after the Hihi turn-off.

★Old Oak   HISTORIC HOTEL $$$
(☑ 09-406 1250; www.theoldoak.co.nz; 66 Waterfront Dr, Mangonui; s/d/ste from $175/225/275; ※☏) This atmospheric 1861 kauri inn is now an elegant boutique hotel with top-notch furnishings in its six rooms and suites. It oozes personality, not least because the building is reputedly haunted.

Ramada Resort Reia Taipa Beach   RESORT $$$
(☑ 09-406 0656; www.ramadataipa.co.nz; 22 Taipa Point Rd, Taipa; apt from $270; ※☏※) Renovated accommodation and a warm welcome combine at this long-standing resort, which offers a choice between beachfront and poolside studio units and apartments. There's also an on-site restaurant, a tennis court and a spa pool.

✕ Eating

Mangonui Fish Shop   FISH & CHIPS $
(☑ 09-406 0478; 137 Waterfront Dr, Mangonui; mains $8-16; ☺ 10am-7pm; ☏) Locals dismiss this place as overpriced and full of tourists, but there's no denying the appeal of downing fish-and-chips and a cold beer on the deck jutting over the water. They also sell smoked fish and seafood salads.

The Thai
THAI $$

(☑09-406 1220; www.thethaimangonui.co.nz; 80 Waterfront Dr, Mangonui; mains $21-27; ☺5-11pm Tue-Sun; ☑) Northland's best Thai restaurant serves zingy dishes with intriguing names such as Angry Pig, Kiwi Chick and Mangonui Showtime, and there's also a good range of Isaan (northeastern Thai) dishes to go with a frosty Singha beer. Actually, make that one of New Zealand's best Thai restaurants.

Little Kitchen on the Bay
CAFE $$

(☑09-406 1644; www.facebook.com/littlekitchen nz; 118 Waterfront Dr, Mangonui; mains $12-20; ☺8am-3pm) With a terrace facing the water and a sun-drenched interior, this cute cafe serves Mangonui's best coffee, excellent counter food and good mains. Menu options include burgers, pies, toasted sandwiches, curries, sticky pork belly and laksa.

Waterfront Cafe & Bar
CAFE $$

(☑09-406 0850; 1 Thomas St, Mangonui; brunch $15-22, dinner $26-34, pizza $16-26; ☺8.30am-9pm) Waterfront has water views and old-world charm, although the service can be hit and miss. A pizza menu kicks in at lunch and extends into dinner, when it supplements bistro dishes.

🔒 Shopping

Exhibit A
ARTS & CRAFTS

(☑09-406 2333; www.mangonuigallery.co.nz; 124 Waterfront Dr, Mangonui; ☺10am-4.30pm Sep-Jun, to 3pm Sat & Sun Jul & Aug) This co-op gallery showcases Far North artists in a historic courthouse building.

Flax Bush
ARTS & CRAFTS

(☑09-406 1510; www.flaxbush.co.nz; 50 Waterfront Dr, Mangonui; ☺10am-5pm) Pasifika- and Māori-inflected craft, jewellery and gifts, including items made of flax, wood and shell.

Mangonui Craft Market
MARKET

(Mangonui Memorial Hall, 132 Waterfront Dr, Mangonui; ☺9am-2pm Sat) Everything from local olive oil, home baking and jams through to carved kauri and country-style homewares.

ℹ Information

Doubtless Bay Visitor Information Centre
(☑09-406 2046; www.doubtlessbay.co.nz; 118 Waterfront Dr, Mangonui; ☺10am-5pm Mon-Sat Jan-Apr, to 3pm May-Dec) Excellent source of local information.

ℹ Getting There & Away

InterCity (p139) stops here daily, en route between Kerikeri ($28, one hour) and Kaitaia ($25, 40 minutes).

Far North Link (☑09-408 1092; www.buslink. co.nz) has a weekday service to Kaitaia ($5, one hour), timed around office hours.

Both buses stop outside Wilton's Garage in Mangonui, outside the sports store in Coopers Beach, opposite the shop in Cable Bay and outside the Z petrol station in Taipa.

Karikari Peninsula

The oddly shaped Karikari Peninsula bends into a near-perfect right angle. The result is beaches facing north, south, east and west in close proximity, so if the wind's annoying you or you want to catch some surf, a sunrise or a sunset, just swap beaches.

Despite its natural assets, the sun-baked peninsula has largely escaped development, with farmers well outnumbering tourist operators. There's no public transport and you won't find a lot of shops or eateries either. However change is in the air.

In 2017 plans to turn Carrington Resort into the country's biggest tourist complex were announced. Locals were concerned about the scale of the proposal but, at the time of research, plans had yet to be finalised.

⦿ Sights & Activities

Tokerau Beach is the long, sandy stretch forming the western edge of Doubtless Bay. Neighbouring **Whatuwhiwhi** is smaller and more built-up, facing back across the bay. Lovely **Maitai Bay**, with its twin coves, is a great spot for swimming – the water is sheltered enough for the kids, but with enough swell to body surf. It's located at the lonely end of the peninsula down an unsealed road.

Rangiputa faces west at the elbow of the peninsula; the pure white sand and crystal-clear sheltered waters come straight from a Pacific Island daydream. A turn-off on the road to Rangiputa takes you to remote **Puheke Beach**, a long, windswept stretch of snow-white sand dunes forming Karikari's northern edge.

Karikari Estate
WINERY

(☑09-408 7222; www.karikariestate.co.nz; Maitai Bay Rd; tastings $15; ☺11am-4pm Sun-Thu, to 8.30pm Fri & Sat Nov-Mar) Part of the Carrington Resort complex, impressive Karikari Estate produces wines of all hues and has a cafe attached. While the wine tastings are shamelessly overpriced, at least the sublime views are free.

Airzone Kitesurf School KITESURFING
(☑ 021 202 7949; www.kitesurfnz.com; 1-/2-/3-day course $195/380/560; ☉Nov-Mar) The unique set-up of Karikari Peninsula makes it one of the world's premium spots for kitesurfing. Learners get to hone their skills on flat water before heading to the surf, while the more experienced can chase the wind around the peninsula.

🛏 Sleeping

Karikari Lodge HOSTEL $
(☑ 09-406 7378; www.karikarilodge.co.nz; 26 Inland Rd, Whatuwhiwhi; dm/r/cabin $35/65/80; 🛜) More like a family-run homestay than a backpackers hostel, this Pasifika-themed place has only three bedrooms, shared bathrooms and a separate cabin in the garden. Perks include free use of kayaks, boogie boards, surfboards and stand-up paddle boards. There's also a full kitchen and barbecue facilities if you get lucky while fishing.

Whatuwhiwhi Top 10 Holiday Park HOLIDAY PARK $
(☑ 09-408 7202; www.whatuwhiwhitop10.co.nz; 17 Whatuwhiwhi Rd; sites from $40, unit with/without bathroom from $100/75; 🛜) Sheltered by hills and overlooking the beach, this friendly complex has a great location, good facilities, free barbecues and a playground. It also offers dive air fills and kayaks for hire.

DOC Maitai Bay Campsite CAMPGROUND $
(www.doc.govt.nz; Maitai Bay Rd; sites per adult/child $13/6.50; 🚲 A large first-in, first-served (no bookings) camping ground at the peninsula's most beautiful beach, with flush toilets, drinking water and cold showers.

Carrington Resort RESORT $$$
(☑ 09-408 7222; www.carrington.co.nz; 109 Matai Bay Rd; r/villa from $215/315; 🛜🍽) There's something very Australian-looking about this hilltop lodge, with its wide verandas and gum trees, tempered by Māori and Pacific design in the spacious rooms and villas. The view over the golf course to the dazzling white beach is exquisite. The resort has its own upmarket restaurant along with a seasonal cafe in its vineyard across the road.

❶ Getting There & Away

There is no public transport to the Karikari Peninsula.

Cape Reinga & Ninety Mile Beach

Māori consider Cape Reinga (Te Rerenga Wairua) the jumping-off point for souls as they depart on the journey to their spiritual homeland. That makes the Aupouri Peninsula a giant diving board, and it even resembles one – long and thin, it reaches 108km to form NZ's northern extremity. On its west coast Ninety Mile Beach (Ninety Kilometre Beach would be more accurate) is a continuous stretch lined with high sand dunes, flanked by the Aupouri Forest.

◉ Sights

★**Cape Reinga** VIEWPOINT
(Far North Rd) State Highway 1 terminates at this dramatic headland where the waters of the Tasman Sea and Pacific Ocean meet, breaking together into waves up to 10m high in stormy weather. Cape Reinga is the end of the road both literally and figuratively: in Māori tradition the spirits of the dead depart the world from here, making it the most sacred site in all of Aotearoa. Out of respect, you're requested to refrain from eating or drinking in the vicinity.

The actual departure point is believed to be the 800-year-old pohutukawa tree clinging to the rocks on the small promontory of Te Rerenga Wairua (Leaping Place of the Spirits) far below; to those in corporeal form, access is forbidden.

From the car park it's a rolling 1km walk to the lookout, passing the Cape Reinga Lighthouse along the way. Information boards detail the area's ecology, history and cultural significance. Little tufts of cloud sometimes cling to the ridges, giving sudden spooky chills even on hot days.

Contrary to expectation, Cape Reinga isn't actually the northernmost point of the country; that honour belongs to the inaccessible Surville Cliffs which can be spotted to the right in the distance. In fact, it's much closer to the westernmost point, Cape Maria van Diemen, immediately to the left.

★**Te Paki Giant Sand Dunes** DUNES
(www.doc.govt.nz; Te Paki Stream Rd) A large chunk of the land around Cape Reinga is

part of the Te Paki Recreation Reserves managed by DOC. It's public land with free access; leave the gates as you found them and don't disturb the animals. There are 7 sq km of giant sand dunes on either side of the mouth of Te Paki Stream. During summer, Ahikaa Adventures (p169) are on hand to rent sandboards ($15) for those wishing to clamber up and toboggan back down.

Great Exhibition Bay
BEACH

On the east coast, Great Exhibition Bay has dazzling snow-white silica dunes. There's no public road access, but some tours pay a *koha* (donation) to cross Māori farmland or approach the sand by kayak from Parengarenga Harbour.

Ngā-Tapuwae-o-te-Mangai
TEMPLE

(6576 Far North Rd, Te Kao) With its two domed towers (Arepa and Omeka, alpha and omega) and the Rātana emblem of the star and crescent moon, you could be forgiven for mistaking this temple for a mosque. Rātana is a Māori Christian sect with more than 50,000 adherents, formed in 1925 by Tahupō-tiki Wiremu Rātana, who was known as 'the mouthpiece of God'. The temple is built on land where Rātana once stood, and the name translates as 'the sacred steps of the mouthpiece'.

You'll pass it at Te Kao, 46km south of Cape Reinga.

Gumdiggers Park
MUSEUM

(09-406 7166; www.gumdiggerspark.co.nz; 171 Heath Rd, Waiharara; adult/child $13/6; ⊙9am-4.30pm Nov-Apr) Kauri forests covered this area for 100,000 years, leaving ancient logs and the much-prized gum (used for making varnish and linoleum) buried beneath. Digging it out was the region's main industry from the 1870s to the 1920s. In 1900 around 7000 gumdiggers were digging holes all over Northland, including at this site. Start with the 15-minute video, and then walk on the bush tracks, leading past gumdiggers' huts, ancient kauri stumps, huge preserved logs and holes left by the diggers.

🏃 Activities

Natives
OUTDOORS

(09-409 8482; www.natives.co.nz) 🌿 The local Ngāti Kuri people, guardians of the sacred spaces around the Cape, have come up with a unique way of funding reforestation. For $35 you can assuage your carbon guilt by planting a native tree or bush of your choice, or letting the staff plant it for you.

Te Paki Coastal Track
TRAMPING

From Cape Reinga, a walk along **Te Werahi Beach** to **Cape Maria van Diemen** (a five-hour loop) takes you to the westernmost point of New Zealand. This is one of many sections of the three- to four-day (48km) coastal track from Kapowairua to Te Paki Stream that can be tackled individually.

Beautiful **Tapotupotu Bay** is a 2½-hour (3km) walk east of Cape Reinga, via Sandy Bay. From Tapotupotu Bay it's a 5½-hour (9km) walk to the Pandora campsite on the western edge of **Spirits Bay**, one of NZ's most spectacular beaches. From here it's a further 3km to the Kapowairua campsite at the eastern end of the beach. Both bays are also accessible by road.

Olly Lancaster (09-409 7500; return $20) offers shuttles to and from the track from his base in Paua, around 30km shy of the cape, storing your vehicle at his house (you can also camp there).

👉 Tours

Petricevich Cape Reinga Tours
ADVENTURE

(09-408 2411; www.capereingatours.co.nz; adult/child $55/30) 🌿 Visit Cape Reinga and the Te Paki dunes and zoom along Ninety Mile Beach in the Dune Rider bus. Sandboarding is included. Pick-up points include Mangonui, Kaitaia and Ahipara.

Far North Outback Adventures
ADVENTURE

(09-409 4586; www.farnorthtours.co.nz; price on application) Flexible, day-long 4WD tours from Kaitaia/Ahipara, including morning tea and lunch. Options include visits to remote areas such as Great Exhibition Bay.

Sand Safaris
ADVENTURE

(09-408 1778; www.sandsafaris.co.nz; adult/child $50/30) 🌿 Coach trips from Ahipara, Kaitaia and Awanui, including sandboarding and a picnic lunch in Tapotupotu Bay.

Harrisons Cape Runner
ADVENTURE

(0800 227 373; www.harrisonscapereingatours.co.nz; adult/child $50/25) Day trips in a 4WD truck-like bus along Ninety Mile Beach to Cape Reinga that include sandboarding and a picnic lunch in Tapotupotu Bay. They depart Kaitaia at 9am daily, returning at 5pm.

Ahikaa Adventures
CULTURAL

(09-409 8228; www.ahikaa-adventures.co.nz; Te Paki Stream Rd; tours $70-190) Māori culture permeates these tours, which can include sandboarding, kayaking, snorkelling, fishing and pigging out on traditional *kai* (food) cooked in a *hāngi* (earth oven).

🛌 Sleeping

There are few good accommodation options on the peninsula itself. The DOC has basic but spectacularly positioned sites at **Rarawa Beach** (www.doc.govt.nz; Rarawa Beach Rd; sites per adult/child $8/4) 🏖️, **Kapowairua** (www.doc.govt.nz; Spirits Bay Rd; sites per adult/child $8/4) 🏖️ and **Tapotupotu Bay** (www.doc.govt.nz; Tapotupotu Rd; sites per adult/child $8/4) 🏖️. Only water, flush toilets and cold showers are provided. Bring a cooker, as fires are not allowed, and plenty of repellent to ward off mosquitoes and sandflies. 'Freedom/Leave No Trace' camping is allowed along the Te Paki Coastal Track.

North Wind Lodge Backpackers HOSTEL $
(☑09-409 8515; www.northwind.co.nz; 88 Otaipango Rd, Henderson Bay; dm/s/tw/d $30/60/66/80; ☺Sep-May) Six kilometres down an unsealed road on the Aupouri Peninsula's east side, this unusual turreted house offers a homey environment and plenty of quiet spots on the lawn to sit with a beer and a book. It's within walking distance of a beautiful beach.

🍴 Eating

Eating options are few and far between. Their are a couple of decent options in Pukenui or you could try the friendly fishing club at Houhora.

ℹ️ Getting There & Away

Apart from numerous tours, there's no public transport past Pukenui – and even this is limited to Thursday-only buses from Kaitaia ($5, 45 minutes) operated by **Far North Link** (p167).

As well as Far North Rd (SH1), rugged vehicles can travel along Ninety Mile Beach itself. However, cars have been known to hit soft sand and be swallowed by the tides – look out for unfortunate vehicles poking through the sands. Check tide times before setting out; avoid it 2½ hours either side of high tide. Watch out for 'quicksand' at Te Paki Stream – keep moving. Many car-rental companies prohibit driving on the sands; if you get stuck, your insurance won't cover you.

It's best to fill up with petrol before hitting the Aupouri Peninsula.

Kaitaia
POP 4890

Nobody comes to the Far North to hang out in this provincial town, but it's a handy stop if you're after a supermarket, a post office or an ATM. It's also a jumping-off point for tours to Cape Reinga and Ninety Mile Beach.

👁️ Sights

Te Ahu Centre ARTS CENTRE
(☑09-401 5200; www.kaitaianz.co.nz; Cnr South Rd & Matthews Ave) This civic and community centre features a cinema, theatre, tourist information centre, gallery and the **Te Ahu Heritage** (☑09-408 9454; www.teahuheritage.co.nz; adult/child $7/free; ☺8.30am-5pm Mon-Fri) exhibits of the Far North Regional Museum. Artefacts include kauri gum, carved greenstone weapons and wood carvings dating to the 14th century. There's also a cafe, and free wi-fi at the library. The centre's foyer is circled by a series of *pou* (carved posts) featuring the different cultures – Māori, British, Croatian etc – that have had a major impact in the local area.

Each of the parts of the centre have their own opening hours.

Okahu Estate Winery WINERY
(☑09-408 2066; www.okahuestate.co.nz; 520 Okahu Rd; ☺10am-5pm daily Jan & Feb, noon-5pm Thu-Sat Mar-Aug & Oct-Dec) Just south of town, off the road to Ahipara, Kaitaia's only winery offers free tastings and sells local produce, including the famous Kaitaia Fire chilli sauce.

🛌 Sleeping & Eating

Loredo Motel MOTEL $$
(☑09-408 3200; www.loredomotel.co.nz; 25 North Rd; units from $120; 🛜🏊) Opting for a breezy Spanish style, this tidy motel has well-kept units set among palm trees and lawns, with a swimming pool.

Gecko Cafe CAFE $
(☑09-408 1160; 71 Commerce St; mains $9-18; ☺7am-3pm Mon-Fri, 8am-1.30pm Sat) Morning queues of locals attest to the Gecko having the best coffee in town (they roast their own), and the food's pretty good, too. Kick off another day on the road with mushrooms and chorizo, or grab a mussel-fritter burger for lunch.

Beachcomber BISTRO $$
(☑09-408 2010; www.beachcomber.net.nz; 222 Commerce St; mains lunch $19-36, dinner $25-38; ☺11am-2.30pm Mon-Fri & 5-9pm Mon-Sat; 🚗♿)

NGĀTI TARARA

As you're travelling around the north you might notice the preponderance of road names ending in '-ich'. Then there's the trilingual signage in the Kaitaia and Dargaville museums. *Haere mai, dobro došli* and welcome to one of the more peculiar ethnic conjunctions in the country.

From the end of the 19th century, men from the Dalmatian coast of what is now Croatia started arriving in NZ looking for work. Many ended up in Northland's gumfields. Anglo-NZ society wasn't particularly welcoming to the new immigrants, particularly during WWI, as they were travelling on Austrian passports. Not so the small Māori communities of the north. Here they found an echo of Dalmatian village life, with its emphasis on extended family and hospitality, not to mention a shared history of injustice at the hands of colonial powers.

The Māori jokingly named them Tarara, as their rapid conversation in their native tongue sounded like 'ta-ra-ra-ra-ra' to Māori ears. Many Croatian men married local *wahine* (women), founding clans that have left several of today's famous Māori with Croatian surnames, such as singer Margaret Urlich and former All Black Frano Botica. You'll find large Tarara communities in the Far North, Dargaville and West Auckland.

This Pacific-themed family restaurant is easily the best dinner option in Kaitaia, with a wide range of seafood, meat and vegetarian fare, and a well-stocked salad bar. Save room for the pavlova of the day.

ℹ Information

Far North i-SITE (☑ 09-408 9450; www.northlandnz.com; Te Ahu Centre, cnr Matthews Ave & South Rd; ⊙ 8.30am-5pm) An excellent information centre with advice for all of Northland.

ℹ Getting There & Away

AIR
Kaitaia Airport (KAT; ☑ 021 818 314; Quarry Rd, Awanui) is 6km north of town. **Barrier Air** (☑ 09-275 9120; www.barrierair.kiwi; Kaitaia Airport) flies to and from Auckland (one hour).

BUS
Far North Link (p167) has services to Ahipara ($3.50, 15 minutes) and Doubtless Bay ($5, one hour) on weekdays, and to Pukenui ($5, 45 minutes) on Thursdays.

InterCity (p139) buses depart daily from the Te Ahu Centre (p170) and head to Kerikeri ($37, 1¾ hours) via Doubtless Bay ($25, 40 minutes).

Ahipara

POP 1060

All good things must come to an end, and Ninety Mile Beach does at this spunky beach town. A few holiday mansions have snuck in, but mostly it's just the locals keeping it real, rubbing shoulders with visiting surfers.

The area is known for its huge sand dunes and massive kauri gumfield, where 2000 people once worked. Sandboarding and quad-bike rides are popular activities on the dunes above Ahipara and further around the Tauroa Peninsula.

◉ Sights & Activities

Shipwreck Bay   BEACH
(Te Kōhanga; Wreck Bay Rd) The best surfing is at this small cove at Ahipara's western edge, so named for shipwrecks still visible at low tide.

Ahipara Viewpoint   VIEWPOINT
(Gumfields Rd) This spectacular lookout on the bluff behind Ahipara is reached by an extremely rough road leading off the unsealed Gumfields Rd, which starts at the western end of Foreshore Rd.

Ahipara Treks   HORSE RIDING
(☑ 09-408 2532; www.taitokerauhoney.co.nz/ahipara-horse-treks; 11 Foreshore Rd; 1hr/2hr $65/85) Offers beach canters, including some farm and ocean riding (when the surf permits).

Ahipara Adventure   ADVENTURE SPORTS
(☑ 09-409 2055; www.ahiparaadventure.co.nz; 15 Takahe Rd) Hires sand toboggans ($15 per half day), surfboards ($40 per half day), body boards ($20 per half day), stand-up paddleboards ($50 per half day), blokarts for sand yachting ($80 per hour) and quad-bikes ($115 per hour).

NZ Surfbros SURFING
(📞 021 252 7078; www.nzsurfbros.co.nz; 27 Kaka St; 2hr lesson $60) Rents boards and offers surfing lessons and five-day surf tours (from $599 including accommodation, meals and transport from Auckland).

🛏 Sleeping

⭐**Endless Summer Lodge** HOSTEL $
(📞 09-409 4181; www.endlesssummer.co.nz; 245 Foreshore Rd; dm/r from $30/86; 🛜) Across from the beach, this superb kauri villa (1880) has been beautifully restored and converted into an exceptional hostel. There's no TV, which encourages bonding around the long table and wood-fired pizza oven on the vine-covered back terrace. Body boards and sandboards can be borrowed and surfboards can be hired.

Ahipara Holiday Park HOLIDAY PARK $
(📞 0800 888 988; www.ahiparaholidaypark. co.nz; 168 Takahe Rd; sites/dm/tw/d from $18/28/75/85, unit with/without bathroom from $105/75; 🛜) There's a large range of accommodation on offer at this holiday park, including cabins, motel units and a worn but perfectly presentable YHA-affiliated backpackers' lodge. The communal hall has an open fire and colourful murals.

GEMS Seaside Lodge APARTMENT $$
(📞 027 820 9403; www.gemsseasidelodge.co.nz; 14 Kotare St; apt from $150; 🛜) Who cares if it's a bit bourgeois for Ahipara? These two upmarket, self-contained apartments have watery views and there's direct access to the beach. The bottom floor is a spacious studio, while the upper floor apartment has two bedrooms and two bathrooms.

🍴 Eating

North Drift Cafe CAFE $
(📞 09-409 4093; www.facebook.com/north driftcafe; 250 Ahipara Rd; mains $9-20; ⊙8am-2.30pm) Start the day with a cooked breakfast and Ahipara's best coffee on the sunny front deck of this relaxed little cafe. Come back at lunch for a burger, fish and chips, or Cajun chicken tacos. In summer, they reopen at 5pm for dinner from Thursday through to Sunday.

Bidz Takeaways FISH & CHIPS $
(📞 09-409 4727; www.facebook.com/bidztake aways; 7 Takahe Rd; meals $7-14; ⊙10am-8pm) Longstanding Bidz sells fresh fish, and the best fish, chips and burgers in town. There's also a small grocery store attached.

ℹ Getting There & Away

Far North Link (p167) has a weekday bus to Kaitaia ($3.50, 15 minutes), departing Ahipara early in the morning and returning in the evening.

HOKIANGA

The Hokianga Harbour stretches out its skinny tentacles to become the fourth-biggest in the country. Its ruggedly beautiful landscape is painted in every shade of green and brown. The water itself is rendered the colour of ginger ale by the bush streams that feed it.

Of all the remote parts of Northland, this is the pocket that feels the most removed from the mainstream. Pretension has no place here. Isolated, predominantly Māori communities nestle around the harbour's many inlets, as they have done for centuries. Discovered by legendary explorer Kupe, it's been settled by Ngāpuhi since the 14th century. Hippies arrived in the late 1960s and their legacy is a thriving little artistic scene.

Many of the roads remain unsealed, and, while tourism dollars are channelled eastward to the Bay of Islands, this truly fascinating corner of the country remains remarkably undeveloped, just as many of the locals like it.

Kohukohu

POP 165

Quick, someone slap a preservation order on Kohukohu before it's too late. There can be few places in NZ where a Victorian village full of interesting kauri buildings has been so completely preserved with hardly a modern monstrosity to be seen. During the height of the kauri industry it was a busy town with a sawmill, shipyard, two newspapers and banks. These days it's a very quiet backwater on the north side of Hokianga Harbour, 4km from the Rawene car ferry (p174).

◎ Sights

Village Arts GALLERY
(📞 09-405 5827; www.villagearts.co.nz; 1376 Kohukohu Rd; ⊙10am-3pm) A sophisticated surprise in such a small place, this gallery fills a restored heritage building with ever-changing exhibitions – mainly from Hokianga artists.

🛏 Sleeping & Eating

Tree House HOSTEL $
(☑ 09-405 5855; www.treehouse.co.nz; 168 West Coast Rd; sites/dm/s/d from $20/32/64/82; ☎) 🌿 One of the country's very best hostels, the Tree House has dorm rooms in the wood-lined main building and brightly painted little cottages set among the surrounding fruit and nut trees. Bathrooms are shared and there's a communal kitchen and dining space. This quiet retreat is 2km from the ferry terminus (turn sharp left as you come off the ferry).

Koke Cafe CAFE $
(☑ 09-405 5808; 1374 Kohukohu Rd; mains $8-16; ⊙8am-4pm Wed-Sun, extended in summer) Set up on the street-side terrace of the Kohukohu Hotel, this little cafe serves decent coffee and food, including bagels, gourmet pies, pork sandwiches, burgers and cooked breakfasts.

Kohukohu Hotel PUB
(☑ 09-405 5808; 1376 Kohukohu Rd; ⊙noon-6pm Sun-Wed, to 10pm Thu-Sat) A classic Kiwi pub with harbour views, good-value bistro meals and a friendly welcome from the occasional wisecracking local.

❶ Getting There & Away

There's no public transport, so you'll need your own vehicle. Look forward to the scenic **ferry crossing** (p174) across the harbour to slightly less sleepy Rawene.

Horeke & Around

Tiny Horeke was NZ's second European settlement after Russell. A Wesleyan mission operated here from 1828 to 1855, while in 1840, 3000 Ngāpuhi gathered here for what was the single biggest signing of the Treaty of Waitangi. Nowadays its an all-but-forgotten hamlet, with pig-hunting dogs usually outnumbering people on the dusty streets.

The rustic **Horeke Hotel** (☑ 09-401 9133; www.horekehotel.nz; 2118 Horeke Rd; ⊙1pm-late Wed-Sun, bistro 5.30-8pm Thu-Sun) is reputedly New Zealand's oldest pub – the first cold one was poured back in 1826 – and the garden bar rocks with live music on occasional weekends during summer.

Horeke is also the western end point of the Pou Herenga Tai Twin Coast Cycle Trail (p149).

OFF THE BEATEN TRACK

MOTUTI

Catholicism arrived in Aotearoa in the form of well-respected French bishop Jean Baptiste Pompallier, who celebrated NZ's first Mass at Totara Point shortly after landing in the Hokianga in 1838. His remains were interred beneath the altar of **St Mary's Catholic Church** (Hata Maria; www.hokiangapompallier.org.nz; Motuti Rd, Motuti) in 2002, after an emotional 14-week pilgrimage full of Māori ceremony brought them back from France. You'll find it in the rural hamlet of Motuti, 22km west of Kohukohu.

◉ Sights

Wairere Boulders Nature Park PARK
(☑ 09-401 9935; www.wairereboulders.co.nz; McDonnell Rd; adult/child/family $15/5/35, cash only; ⊙to 5pm/7pm winter/summer) 🌿 At Wairere, massive basalt rock formations have been eroded into odd fluted shapes by the acidity of ancient kauri forests. Allow 40 minutes for the main loop track; expect a few dips and climbs. An additional track leads through rainforest to a platform at the end of the boulder valley (1½ hours). The park is signposted from SH1 and Horeke; the last 3km are unsealed.

Māngungu Mission HISTORIC BUILDING
(☑ 09-405 9734; www.mangungumission.co.nz; Motukiore Rd; adult/child $10/free; ⊙11am-3pm Sat-Mon Dec-Feb) Completed in 1839, this sweet wooden cottage contains relics of the missionaries who once inhabited it, and of Horeke's shipbuilding past. In the grounds there's a large stone cross and a simple wooden church. Māngungu is 1km down the unsealed road leading along the harbour from Horeke village.

🛏 Sleeping

Horeke Hotel PUB $$
(☑ 09-401 9133; www.horekehotel.nz; 2118 Horeke Rd; r $130-150) Simple but clean accommodation in the local pub. All three room have en suites and harbour views.

❶ Getting There & Away

There is no public transport, so the only way to get here is by bike or car. The main sealed approach to town is Rangiahua Rd, heading south from SH1. Horeke Rd, heading north from SH12, is rough and unsealed.

Rawene

POP 471

Founded shortly after nearby Horeke, Rawene was NZ's third European settlement. A surprising number of historic buildings (including six churches!) remain from a time when the harbour was considerably busier than it is now. Information boards outline a heritage trail of the main sights.

There's an ATM in the 4 Square grocery store, and you can get petrol here.

◉ Sights

Clendon House   HISTORIC BUILDING

(☑ 09-405 7874; www.clendonhouse.co.nz; Clendon Esplanade; adult/child $10/free; ◷ 10am-4pm Sun May-Oct, Sat & Sun Nov-Apr) This pretty cottage was built in the bustling 1860s by James Clendon, a trader, shipowner and magistrate. After his death, his 34-year-old half-Māori widow Jane was left with a brood of kids and a whopping £5000 debt. She managed to clear the debt and her descendants remained in the house until 1972. It's now administered by Heritage New Zealand.

No 1 Parnell   GALLERY

(☑ 09-405 7520; www.no1parnell.weebly.com; 1 Parnell St; ◷ 9am-4.30pm) Occupying a century-old corner building originally built as a grocery store, this upmarket commercial gallery exhibits interesting work by local artists alongside some from further afield. There's a sun-filled cafe attached.

🛏 Sleeping & Eating

Rawene Holiday Park   HOLIDAY PARK $$

(☑ 09-405 7720; www.raweneholidaypark.co.nz; 1 Marmon St West; sites from $18, unit with/without bathroom $130/65; 🛜🌊) Tent sites shelter in the bush at this nicely managed park. The cabins range from basic units where you'll need to bring your own linen (or pay extra to hire a set) to fully made-up units with kitchenettes. There's only one en-suite unit.

Boatshed Cafe   CAFE $

(☑ 09-405 7728; www.facebook.com/boatshed caferawene; 8 Clendon Esplanade; mains $8.50-15; ◷ 8.30am-4pm) You can eat overlooking the water in Hokianga's best cafe, which occupies a historic boat shed near the car ferry. It's a cute place with excellent food and a gift shop that sells local art and crafts.

ⓘ Getting There & Away

A **car ferry** (☑ 09-405 2602; www.fndc.govt.nz; car/campervan/motorcycle $20/40/5, passenger $2; ◷ 7.30am-8pm) heads to the northern side of the Hokianga, docking 4km south of Kohukohu at least hourly. You can buy your ticket for this 15-minute ride on board. It usually leaves Rawene on the half-hour and the north side on the hour.

You can request a pick-up by the **Hokianga Link** (p163) minivan by calling the **Opononi i-SITE** (p175). Services head between Opononi (30 minutes) and Kerikeri (one hour) on Thursdays, as well as Tuesdays in summer.

Opononi & Omapere

POP 414

Although they were once separate villages, Opononi and Omapere have now merged into one continuous coastal community spread along a beautiful stretch of coast near the south head of Hokianga Harbour. The water's much clearer here and good for swimming, and views are dominated by the mountainous sand dunes across the water at North Head. If you're approaching Omapere from the south, the view of the harbour is nothing short of spectacular.

◉ Sights & Activities

Arai-te-uru
Recreation Reserve   NATURE RESERVE

(Signal Station Rd, Omapere) Covering the southern headland of the Hokianga Harbour, this reserve offers magnificent views over the harbour and along the wild west coast. A short walk leads to the site of an old signal station built to assist ships making the treacherous passage into the Hokianga. It closed in 1951 due to a decline in ships entering the harbour. A track also heads down to pretty little **Martin's Bay**.

This is also the start of the 10.6km **Waimamakau Coastal Track**, a three-hour walk (each way) along the coast to Waimamakau Beach Rd at the mouth of the Waimamakau River.

Footprints Waipoua   CULTURAL

(☑ 09-405 8207; www.footprintswaipoua.co.nz; Copthorne, 334 SH12, Omapere; adult/child $95/35) 🌿 Led by Māori guides, this four-hour twilight tour into Waipoua Forest is a fantastic introduction to both the culture and the forest giants. Tribal history and stories are shared, and mesmerising *karakia* (prayers, incantations) are recited before the gargantuan trees.

Daytime tours ($80) are also available, but the twilight tours amplify the sense of spirituality.

Hokianga Express ADVENTURE

(☑ 021 405 872; hkexpress@xtra.co.nz; Opononi Jetty; adult/child $27/17; ⊞) Take a boat ride across to the north side of the harbour and attack the giant sand dunes armed with a boogie board for a swift descent; at high tide you can skim straight out over the water. The boat departs daily in summer (weather permitting) and on demand at other times, but bookings are essential regardless.

Hokianga Bone Carving Studio COURSE

(☑ 09-405 8061; hokiangabonecarvingstudio@gmail.com; 15 Akiha St, Omapere; class incl lunch $60) Book in for a day course in Jim Taranaki's ocean-facing studio and learn how to create your own Māori-inspired bonecarving.

🛏 Sleeping

Globetrekkers Lodge HOSTEL $

(☑ 09-405 8183; www.globetrekkerslodge.com; 281 SH12, Omapere; dm/s/d $29/54/70; ☏) Unwind in casual style at this homey hostel with harbour views and bright dorms. Private rooms don't have their own bathrooms but there are plenty of thoughtful touches, such as writing desks, mirrors, art and fluffy towels. There's a stereo but no TV, encouraging plenty of schmoozing in the grapevine-draped barbecue area.

Copthorne Hotel & Resort HOTEL $$

(☑ 09-405 8737; www.millenniumhotels.com; 336 SH12, Omapere; r/apt from $135/189; ☏⛱) This blissfully positioned beachfront resort consists of a hodgepodge of buildings from different eras. Some are luxurious and some dated, but the beds are comfy throughout. However, pricey add-ons for breakfast and wi-fi detract from the appeal. The original Victorian villa at its centre is an attractive spot for a summer's drink or a brasserie-style meal ($27 to $29).

Opononi Hotel HOTEL $$

(☑ 09-405 8858; www.opononihotel.com; 19 SH12; r $130-150; ☏) The rooms at the old Opononi pub aren't huge but the white-paint and blonde-wood makeover has left them quietly stylish. Try to grab one of the front two rooms – they're a bit bigger and have the best views. Otherwise aim for those facing away from the pub for a slightly quieter stay.

Kokohuia Lodge B&B $$$

(☑ 021 779 927; www.kokohuialodge.co.nz; 101 Kokohuia Rd, Omapere; r $320; ☏) 🌿 Luxury and eco-friendly practices combine at this B&B, nestled in regenerating native bush high above the silvery dune-fringed expanse of the Hokianga Harbour. Solar energy and organic and free-range produce all feature, but there's no trade-off for luxury in the modern and stylish accommodation.

Hokianga Haven APARTMENT $$$

(☑ 09-405 8285; www.hokiangahaven.co.nz; 226 SH12, Omapere; r $220; ☏) Fall asleep only steps from the beach in this spacious self-contained studio apartment tucked underneath a modern house. An additional queen room is available for friends or family travelling together. Alternative healing therapies can be arranged.

🍴 Eating & Drinking

Flounder is a local speciality – if you see it on the menu, order it. While there are several places to eat, the quality is hit and miss. By far the best is the cafe attached to the tourist office in Opononi. There's a decent fish-and-chip shop in Opononi, and sit-down meals can be had in the pub and the resort.

Landing Cafe CAFE $

(☑ 09-405 8169; www.thelandingcafe.co.nz; 29 SH12, Opononi; mains $10-15; ⊙ 9am-3pm; ☏) Stylish Kiwiana decor combines with good coffee at this appealing place attached to the tourist office. Grab a table on the expansive deck and tuck into scrambled eggs with smoked salmon while gazing over the water. It's head and shoulders above other local eateries.

Opononi Hotel PUB

(☑ 09-405 8858; www.opononihotel.com; 19 SH12; mains $13-36) Try and score an outside table at this friendly local pub so that you can take in the improbable views of Opononi's massive sand dunes just across the harbour. There are regular live gigs in summer and it's a good place to watch the rugby.

ℹ Information

Opononi i-SITE

(☑ 09-405 8869; www.hokiangatourism.org.nz; 29 SH12; ⊙ 8.30am-5pm) Excellent information office with a good range of local souvenirs.

ℹ Getting There & Away

A **Hokianga Link** (p163) minivan heads between Omapere and Kerikeri ($15, 1½ hours) on Thursdays. From December to March they also operate on Tuesdays.

Waiotemarama & Waimamaku

The neighbouring Waiotemarama and Waimamaku villages, nestled between the Hokianga Harbour and the Waipoua Forest, are the first of many tiny rural communities scattered along this underpopulated stretch of SH12.

🏃 Activities

Labyrinth Woodworks OUTDOORS
(☑ 09-405 4581; www.nzanity.co.nz; 647 Waiotemarama Gorge Rd; maze adult/child $4/3; ⊙ 9am-5pm) Crack the code in the outdoor maze by collecting letters to form a word. The puzzle museum and retro board games are also interesting. Nearby walks lead to a waterfall and magnificent kauri trees.

🍴 Eating

Morrell's Cafe CAFE $
(☑ 09-405 4545; 7235 SH12, Waimamaku; mains $11-17; ⊙ 9am-3pm) This cafe and craft shop occupies a former cheese factory. It's the last good eatery before Dargaville so drop in for coffee, an eggy breakfast or a freshly baked scone.

ℹ Getting There & Away

There is no public transport to Waiotemarama and Waimamaku.

KAURI COAST

Apart from the odd bluff and river, this coast is basically unbroken and undeveloped for the 110km between the Hokianga and Kaipara Harbours. The main reason for coming here is to marvel at the kauri forests, one of the great natural highlights of NZ. If you're a closet tree hugger you'll need 8m-long arms to get them around some of the big ones here.

There are few stores or eateries and no ATMs north of Dargaville, so stock up beforehand. Trampers should check DOC's website (www.doc.govt.nz) for walks in the area.

Waipoua Forest

The highlight of Northland's west coast, this superb forest sanctuary – established in 1952 after much public pressure – is the largest remnant of the once-extensive kauri forests of northern NZ. The forest road (SH12) stretches for 18km and passes some huge trees – a kauri can reach 60m in height and have a trunk more than 5m in diameter.

Control of the forest has been returned to Te Roroa, the local *iwi* (tribe), as part of a settlement for Crown breaches of the Treaty of Waitangi. Te Roroa runs the **Waipoua Forest Visitor Centre** (☑ 09-439 6445; www.teroroa.iwi.nz/visit-waipoua; 1 Waipoua River Rd; ⊙ 9am-2pm daily Nov-Mar, Wed-Sun Apr-Oct), cafe and campground near the south end of the park.

◉ Sights

★ **Te Matua Ngahere** LANDMARK
From the Kauri Walks car park, a 20-minute walk leads past the **Four Sisters**, a graceful stand of four tall trees fused together at the base, to Te Matua Ngahere (the Father of the Forest). At 30m, he has a significant presence. Reinforced by a substantial girth – he's the fattest living kauri (16.4m) – the tree presides over a clearing surrounded by mature trees resembling mere matchsticks in comparison. It's estimated that he could be up to 3000 years old.

A 30-minute (one way) path leads from near the Four Sisters to **Yakas**, the seventh-largest kauri.

★ **Tāne Mahuta** LANDMARK
Near the north end of the park, not far from the road, stands mighty Tāne Mahuta, named for the Māori forest god. At 51.5m, with a 13.8m girth and wood mass of 244.5 cubic metres, he's the largest kauri alive, and has been holding court here for somewhere between 1200 and 2000 years. He's easy to find and access, with a well-labelled car park (complete with coffee cart) on the highway.

Lookout VIEWPOINT
(Lookout Rd) For a bird's-eye view over the canopy, head to the forest lookout, near the very south end of the park. You can either drive to it (the road is well signposted but quite rough and not suitable for campervans), or take the 2.5km Lookout Track from the visitor centre.

🛏 Sleeping

Waipoua Forest Campground CAMPGROUND $
(☑ 09-439 6445; www.teroroa.iwi.nz/visit-waipoua; 1 Waipoua River Rd; sites/units from $15/20) Situated next to the Waipoua River and the visitor centre, this peaceful camping ground offers hot showers, flush toilets and a kitchen. The cabins are extremely spartan, with unmade squab beds (bring your own linen or hire it).

Waipoua Lodge   B&B $$$
([☎] 09-439 0422; www.waipoualodge.co.nz; 4748 SH12; ste $625; [⊛]) [♥] This fine old villa at the southern edge of the forest has four luxurious, spacious suites, which were originally the stables, the woolshed and the calf-rearing pen. Decadent dinners ($95) are available.

❶ Getting There & Away

There is no public transport to Waipoua Forest. If you don't have a car, consider taking a tour from Omapere with **Footprints Waipoua** (p174) or from Paihia with **Fullers Great Sights** (p149).

Trounson Kauri Park

This 586-hectare stand of old-growth forest has been subject to active predator eradication since 1995 and has become an important mainland refuge for threatened native bird species. An easy half-hour (1.8km) loop walk leads from the picnic area by the road, passing through beautiful forest with streams, some fine kauri stands, a couple of fallen trees, and two pairs of trees with conjoined trunks known as the Four Sisters.

The neighbouring holiday park runs **guided night walks** (adult/child $30/20), which explain the flora and nocturnal wildlife that thrives here. You might even catch a rare glimpse of a brown kiwi in the wild.

🛏 Sleeping

Kauri Coast Top 10 Holiday Park   HOLIDAY PARK $
([☎] 09-439 0621; www.kauricoasttop10.co.nz; 7 Opouteke Rd; sites from $44, units with/without bathroom from $114/90; [⊛]) Set beside the Kaihu River, 2km from SH12, this excellent holiday park has attractive motel units and a brace of tidy cabins, with or without their own bathrooms and kitchens. As well as their famed guided night walks, there's a swimming hole and an adventure playground with a flying fox and trampoline.

DOC Trounson Kauri Park Campsite   CAMPGROUND $
(www.doc.govt.nz; Trounson Park Rd; sites from $30) A step-up from most DOC campsites, this one has both powered and unpowered sites, and a communal kitchen, flush toilets and hot showers.

❶ Getting There & Away

There is no public transport to Trounson Kauri Park. If you're approaching by car from the north,

---

WORTH A TRIP

KAI IWI LAKES

These three trout-filled freshwater dune lakes nestle together near the coast, 12km off SH12. The largest, **Taharoa**, has blue water fringed with sandy patches. **Lake Waikere** (meaning 'rippling waters') is popular with water-skiers, while **Lake Kai Iwi** ('food for the tribe') is good for kayaking and swimming, as it's off-limits to motorised craft. A half-hour walk leads from the lakes to the coast and it's another two hours to reach the base of volcanic **Maunganui Bluff** (460m); the hike up and down it takes five hours.

The largest of the two campsites at the side of Lake Taharoa is **Kai Iwi Lakes Campground** ([☎] 09-439 0986; www.kaiiwicamp.nz; Domain Rd; adult/child $15/8). Pine Beach has flush toilets and coin-operated hot showers ($2 for three minutes). More sites are available at Promenade Point (cold showers only).

---

it's easier to take the second turn-off to the park, near Kaihu, which avoids a rough unsealed road.

Baylys Beach

Baylys Beach is a village of brightly coloured baches (holiday cottages) and a few new mansions, 12km from Dargaville. It lies on 100km-long Ripiro Ocean Beach, a surf-pounded stretch of coast that has been the site of many shipwrecks.

The beach is a gazetted highway: you can drive along the sand at low tide, although it is primarily for 4WDs. Despite being NZ's longest drivable beach, it's less well known and hence less travelled than Ninety Mile Beach. Ask locals about conditions and check your car-rental agreement before venturing onto the sand: you probably won't be covered by insurance and if you don't know what you're doing, you're very likely to get stuck. Quad bikes can be hired at the holiday park.

🏃 Activities

Baylys Beach Horse Treks   HORSE RIDING
([☎] 027 697 9610; www.baylysbeachhorsetreks.webs. com; 1hr/2hr beach ride $70/125) Offers half-hour riding lessons ($25) and horse treks along the broad expanse of Baylys Beach. The minimum age for beach rides is 14, unless the

child is experienced. Younger children can take an hour-long paddock ride ($40).

Sleeping

Baylys Beach Holiday Park　　HOLIDAY PARK **$**
(📞 09-439 6349; www.baylysbeach.co.nz; 24 Seaview Rd; sites $20, units with/without bathroom from $90/80; 🛜) This midsized camping ground has attractive cream-and-green units scattered around a lawn circled by pohutukawa trees. Options range from basic cabins to a self-contained cottage sleeping six. They also rent quad bikes and take bookings for horse treks.

Sunset View Lodge　　B&B **$$**
(📞 021 231 4114; www.sunsetviewlodge.co.nz; 7 Alcemene Lane; r $175-195; ☉ Jul-May; 🛜🐾) If gin-in-hand sunset gazing is your thing, this large, modern B&B fits the bill. The upstairs rooms have terrific sea views and all of them have decks. Children are not permitted.

ℹ Getting There & Away

There is no public transport to Baylys Beach. Most travellers visit from Dargaville or en route to/from the Waipoua Forest.

Dargaville

POP 4250

When a town proclaims itself the 'kumara capital of NZ' (it produces two-thirds of the country's sweet potatoes), you should know not to expect too much. Founded in 1872 by timber merchant Joseph Dargaville, this once-important river port thrived on the export of kauri timber and gum. Once the forests were destroyed, it declined, and today it's a quiet backwater servicing the agricultural Northern Wairoa area.

◉ Sights

Dargaville Museum　　MUSEUM
(📞 09-439 7555; www.dargavillemuseum.co.nz; Harding Park; adult/child $15/5; ☉ 9am-4pm) The hilltop Dargaville Museum is more interesting than most regional museums. There's a large gumdigging display, plus maritime, Māori and musical-instrument sections, and a neat model railway. Outside, the masts of the *Rainbow Warrior* are mounted at a lookout near a *pā* site, and there's a recreation of a gumdiggers' camp.

Kumara Box　　FARM
(📞 09-439 7018; www.kumarabox.co.nz; 503 Pouto Rd; kumara show $20, train ride $10; ☉ by prior book-ing) To learn all about kumara, book ahead for Kumara Ernie's show. It's surprisingly entertaining, usually involving a journey by home-built tractor-train through the fields to 'NZ's smallest church'. There's also an extensive shell collection, and a communal kitchen and bathroom facilities for campervanners looking for a park for the night ($12).

Sleeping & Eating

Dargaville has motels and a hostel, and there are further options at nearby Baylys Beach. Campervans can stay at the Dargaville Museum car park for $15 per night and at Kumara Box farm for $12.

Greenhouse Backpackers　　HOSTEL **$**
(📞 09-439 6342; greenhousebackpackers@ihug. co.nz; 15 Gordon St; dm/r $30/74; @🛜) This converted 1921 schoolhouse has classrooms partitioned into a large bunk-free dorm and a communal lounge, both painted with colourful murals. Better still are the cosy units in the back garden.

Riverside Produce Market　　MARKET **$**
(Kapia St; ☉ noon-4pm Thu) Local produce and crafts.

Raan Ahaan Thai Aroi Dee　　THAI **$$**
(📞 09-439 1081; www.raanahaanthaiaroideee.com; 57 Victoria St; mains $15-17; ☉ 11.30am-2pm & 5.30-9pm Tue-Fri, 5-9.30pm Sat & Sun; 🛜🍴) Don't be put off by the fluorescent lighting and the lunch-bar feel; this unassuming restaurant is one of Dargaville's best. The Northern Thai cuisine – prepared by actual Thai chefs – is as authentic as you could hope for given the town's distance from specialist suppliers.

Blah, Blah, Blah...　　CAFE **$$**
(📞 09-439 6300; 101 Victoria St; breakfast $10-19, lunch $10-20, dinner $22-35; ☉ 9am-3.30pm Sun & Mon, to 8pm Tue-Sat; 🛜) The number-one eatery and best bar in central Dargaville has a garden area, hip music, deli-style snacks, and beer, wine and cocktails. The global menu includes excellent breakfasts, pizza and steak.

Aratapu Tavern　　TEX-MEX **$$**
(📞 09-439 5923; www.aratapu.com; 701 Pouto Rd; mains $15-22; ☉ noon-late Tue-Sun; 🛜) This welcoming country pub, around 7km from Dargaville on the road to Poutu Point, is deservedly famous for its lamb shanks, but also of flavour-packed interest is the Tex-Mex food, including tacos and burritos, prepared by the bubbly Texan co-owner. There's occasional live music in the garden bar on Saturdays.

🛍 Shopping

The Woodturners Studio ARTS & CRAFTS
(☑09-439 4975; www.thewoodturnersstudio.co.nz;
4 Murdoch St; 9am-6pm daily Sep-Jun, 10am-5pm
Tue-Sun Jul & Aug) Visit master woodturner
Rick Taylor at his workshop and store. Items
crafted from millennia-old kauri – prehistoric
timber recovered from local swamps – include
bowls, platters and treasure boxes.

ℹ Information

DOC Te Tai Kauri/Kauri Coast Office (☑09-
439 3450; www.doc.govt.nz; 150 Colville Rd;
⊙8am-4.30pm Mon-Fri) An area office rather
than an visitor centre, but a good source of
Northland tramping and camping information.
Visitor Information Centre (☑09-439 4975;
www.kauriinfocentre.co.nz; 4 Murdoch St;
⊙9am-6pm Sep-Jun, 10am-5pm Tue-Sun Jul &
Aug; ☎) Operates from the Woodturners Studio.
Books accommodation and tours.

ℹ Getting There & Away

West Coaster (p144) shuttle buses link Dargaville
with Whangarei twice daily on weekdays.

   Te Wai Ora Coachlines (☑027 482 2950; www.
tewaioracoachlines.com; adult/child $50/40)
runs shuttles linking Dargaville to Auckland (three
hours) via Warkworth and Matakohe, departing
Auckland on a Friday evening and returning from
Dargaville on a Sunday evening.

Matakohe

POP 400

Apart from its rural charms, the key reason
for visiting Matakohe is the superb Kauri
Museum. The museum shop stocks mementoes
crafted from kauri wood and gum.

   Facing the museum is the tiny kauri-built
Matakohe Pioneer Church (1867), which
served both Methodists and Anglicans, and
acted as the community's hall and school.
Nearby, you can wander through a historic
school house (1878) and post office/telephone
exchange (1909).

◎ Sights

Kauri Museum MUSEUM
(☑09-431 7417; www.kau.nz; 5 Church Rd; adult/child
$25/8; ⊙9am-5pm) 🅟 The giant cross-sections
of trees at this superb museum are astounding
in themselves, but the entire industry is
brought to light through life-sized reproductions
of a pioneer sawmill, boarding house,
bushman's hut and Victorian home – along
with photos, artefacts, and fabulous furniture
and marquetry. The Gum Room holds a weird

OFF THE BEATEN TRACK

POUTO POINT

A narrow spit descends south of Dargaville,
bordered by the Tasman Sea and
Wairoa River, and comes to an abrupt halt
at the entrance of NZ's biggest harbour,
the Kaipara. It's an incredibly remote
headland, punctuated by dozens of petite
dune lakes and the lonely **Kaipara
Lighthouse** (built from kauri in 1884).
Less than 10km separates Kaipara Harbour's
north and south heads, but if driving
between the two you'd cover 267km.

   A 4WD is ideal for the 71km stretch of
beach from Glinks Gully near Dargaville.
The DOC's *Pouto Hidden Treasures* is
a helpful guide for motorists,; it can be
downloaded at www.doc.govt.nz.

and wonderful collection of kauri gum, the
amber substance that can be carved, sculpted
and polished to a jewel-like quality.

🛏 Sleeping

Matakohe Holiday Park HOLIDAY PARK $
(☑09-431 6431; www.matakoheholidaypark.co.nz;
66 Church Rd; sites $38, units with/without bathroom
from $120/65) 🅟 This well-kept little park has
modern amenities, plenty of space, a playground
and good views of Kaipara Harbour.
Accommodation ranges from basic cabins
without bathrooms to self-contained two-bedroom
motel units.

Matakohe House B&B $$
(☑09-431 7091; matakohebnb@gmail.com; 24
Church Rd; r $170-180; ☎) This B&B inhabits a
pretty villa near the Kauri Museum. The simply
furnished rooms open onto a wrap-around
veranda and offer winning touches such as
complimentary port and chocolates. There's
also a small kitchen for making hot beverages
and a communal lounge with a piano.

Petite Provence B&B $$
(☑09-431 7552; www.petiteprovence.co.nz; 703c Tinopai
Rd; s/d $130/170; ☎) This attractive B&B,
owned by a Kiwi-French couple, is a popular
weekender for Aucklanders so book ahead. A
continental breakfast is included in the rates
and three-course dinners are $45 per person.

ℹ Getting There & Away

Te Wai Ora Coachlines (p179) runs a bus to
Dargaville leaving Auckland on Friday night and
returning on Sunday night. This service stops at
Matakohe's Kauri Museum on request.

Coromandel Peninsula & the Waikato

Best Places to Eat

➡ Hayes Common (p215)

➡ Madame Woo (p214)

➡ Refinery (p205)

➡ Rock-It Kitchen (p219)

➡ Port Road Project (p201)

Best Places to Stay

➡ Earthstead (p210)

➡ Solscape (p218)

➡ Bow St Studios (p219)

➡ Out in the Styx (p209)

➡ Aroha Mountain Lodge (p207)

Why Go?

Verdant rolling hills line New Zealand's mighty Waikato River, and adrenaline junkies can surf at Raglan, or undertake extreme underground pursuits in the extraordinary Waitomo Caves.

But this is also Tainui country. In the 1850s this powerful Māori tribal coalition elected a king to resist the loss of land and sovereignty. The fertile Waikato was forcibly taken from them, but they retained control of the rugged King Country to within a whisper of the 20th century.

To the northeast, the Coromandel Peninsula juts into the Pacific, forming the Hauraki Gulf's eastern boundary. The peninsula's east coast has some of the North Island's best white-sand beaches, and the muddy wetlands and picturesque stony bays of the west coast have long been a refuge for alternative lifestylers. Down the middle, the mountains are criss-crossed with walking tracks, allowing trampers to explore large tracts of isolated bush studded with kauri trees.

When to Go

➡ Beachy accommodation in Waihi, Whitianga, Whangamata and Raglan peaks during the summer holidays from Christmas until the end of January. New Year's Eve in particular can be very busy.

➡ Balmy February and March are much quieter around the Coromandel Peninsula with settled weather and smaller crowds. Rainfall peaks in the mountainous Coromandel region from May to September.

➡ The Waikato region can see summer droughts, but the southern area around Taumarunui is often wetter and colder.

➡ If you avoid the height of school summer holidays (Christmas to January), accommodation is plentiful in the Waikato region.

➡ Raglan's surf breaks are popular year-round.

Coromandel Peninsula & the Waikato Highlights

❶ Far North Coromandel (p192) Travelling remote gravel roads under a crimson canopy of ancient pohutukawa trees.

❷ Te Whanganui-A-Hei Marine Reserve (p194) Kayaking around hidden islands, caves and bays.

❸ Karangahake Gorge (p204) Penetrating the mystical depths of the dense bush.

❹ Hahei Beach (p197) Watching the offshore islands glow in the dying haze of a summer sunset.

❺ Waitomo Caves (p225) Seeking subterranean stimulation and trying black-water rafting.

❻ Raglan (p217) Hitting the surf (and then the pub) at this unhurried surf town.

❼ Sanctuary Mountain Maungatautari (p209) Tramping through an inland island paradise.

❽ Hobbiton Movie Set Tours (p209) Channelling your inner Bilbo or Frodo at this fascinating film set.

HIKING IN THE COROMANDEL

COROMANDEL WALKWAY

START/END STONY BAY
DURATION 6–7 HOURS
DISTANCE 20KM (12.4 MILES)
DIFFICULTY MODERATE
SUMMARY A REMOTE AND WILD COASTAL WALK NEAR THE NORTHERN TIP OF THE COROMANDEL PENINSULA, COMBINING THICK FOREST, DRAMATIC COASTLINE AND VIEWS OF THE HAURAKI GULF ISLANDS.

Despite being just 60 straight-line kilometres from Auckland, and 100km by road from Thames, there's a remoteness to the Coromandel Peninsula's northern tip that mere distances can't portray. Forming a boundary between the Pacific Ocean and Hauraki Gulf, here there's a real sense of the wild as the sea storms ashore on Poley Bay, and Sugar Loaf and its entourage of rocks stand like petrified waves. With rugged coastline, unruly seas and gorgeous sections of bush, the Coromandel Walkway is a fitting crown for the peninsula, and if the stunning drive up the Coromandel to get here doesn't create expectation, you're not paying attention.

There are DOC campgrounds at both ends of the trail, so you may want to linger for a while either side of your tramp, or you can throw on the backpack and turn it into a two-day tramp, staying the night at Fletcher Bay.

The walkway can be tramped in either direction, but the dramatic surprise of rising to the main lookout point above Shag Bay is enhanced if you walk from Stony Bay, having not yet sighted the coast around Poley Bay and Sugar Loaf.

If you're looking for a shorter tramp, the most spectacular section of the walkway is between Stony Bay and Poley Bay.

The postcard-perfect Coromandel Peninsula is criss-crossed with walking tracks, allowing trampers to explore large tracts of untamed bush where kauri trees once towered and are starting to do so again.

KAUAERANGA KAURI TRAIL

START/END KAUAERANGA VALLEY RD
DURATION 2 DAYS
DISTANCE 14KM (8.7 MILES)
DIFFICULTY MODERATE
SUMMARY A TRAMP UP THE POPULAR KAUAERANGA VALLEY, FEATURING HISTORIC LOGGING TRAILS AND REGENERATING FORESTS. A SIDE TRIP TO THE LOFTY PINNACLES GIVES SPECTACULAR VIEWS TO BOTH COASTS.

The 719 sq km of rugged, forested reserves that make up the Coromandel Forest Park are spread across the Coromandel Peninsula. There are more than 30 tramps through the forest park, with the most popular area being the Kauaeranga Valley, which cuts into the Coromandel Range behind Thames.

A logging boom took place in the Coromandel Range during the late 19th century, when stands of massive kauri were extracted. Today, the Kauaeranga Valley is filled with remnants of its lumbering past: packhorse trails, tramway clearings and many old kauri dams. Dancing Camp Dam (close to Pinnacles Hut) has been partly restored. Many of these dams are now inaccessible and/or unrecognisable, with the exception of Dancing Camp Dam.

The **DOC Kauaeranga Visitor Centre** (Department of Conservation; ✆07-867 9080; www.doc. govt.nz; Kauaeranga Valley Rd; ⊗8.30am-4pm) has interesting displays about the kauri forest and its history. Maps and conservation resources are available for purchase and staff dispense advice. The centre is 14km off SH25; it's a further 9km along a gravel road to the start of the trails.

Pinnacles Hut ($15) must be booked in advance year-round; DOC hut passes and tickets are not valid. The hut has gas stoves, a solid fuel heater, running water, mattresses, a barbecue and solar-powered lighting. The old hut is now used as a residence for a permanent hut warden.

There are eight self-registration Scenic campsites (per person $13) around the valley, all in appealing settings with water supply and toilets. There are also Backcountry campsites ($5) near Pinnacles Hut, at Billygoat Basin and Moss Creek.

KARANGAHAKE GORGE

START/END KARANGAHAKE HALL
DURATION 5–6 HOURS
DISTANCE 16.5KM (10.3 MILES)
DIFFICULTY EASY
SUMMARY COMBINING NATURAL AND HUMAN HISTORY, THIS TRAMP THROUGH A FORMER GOLD-RICH GORGE REVEALS DRAMATIC VIEWS AND A UNIQUE WALK THROUGH MINING REMNANTS.

As SH2 journeys between Auckland and Tauranga it passes through the dramatic Karangahake Gorge, creating one of the most scenic short stretches of road on the North Island. Running along the opposite bank of the gorge, which is cut by the Ohinemuri River, is a network of walking trails that are even more beautiful.

This tramp follows a shared hiking/cycling trail through the most beautiful stretch of the gorge, branching off onto hiking-only trails that explore the remnants of the gorge's gold-rush days, at one point even burrowing through tunnels carved by miners.

The tramp is a NZ rarity – predominantly flat – with a quirky cafe stop at the turnaround point. By tramping standards, this is about as civilised as it gets.

The most spectacular section is the lower gorge and Windows area, so if you only have half a day, walk the Railway Tunnel Loop, which passes through the lower gorge and back through the tunnel, taking in the Windows along the way. Note that the section of the Windows Walk through the lower Waitawheta Gorge can sometimes close due to rockfall or instability of the cliffs.

COROMANDEL PENINSULA

Although relatively close to the big cities of Auckland, Hamilton and Tauranga, the Coromandel Peninsula offers easy access to splendid isolation. Its dramatic, mountainous spine bisects it into two very distinct parts.

When Auckland shuts up shop for Christmas and New Year, it heads to the spectacular white-sand beaches of the east coast. The cutesy historic gold-mining towns on the western side escape the worst of the influx, their wetlands and rocky bays holding less appeal for the masses.

History

This whole area – including the peninsula, the islands and both sides of the gulf – was known to the Māori as Hauraki. Various *iwi* (tribes) held claim to pockets of it, including the Pare Hauraki branch of the Tainui *iwi* and others descended from Te Arawa and earlier migrations. Polynesian artefacts and evidence of moa-hunting have been found, pointing to around 1000 years of continuous occupation.

The Hauraki *iwi* were some of the first to be exposed to European traders. The region's proximity to Auckland, safe anchorages and ready supply of valuable timber initially lead to a booming economy. Kauri logging was big business on the peninsula. Allied to the timber trade was shipbuilding, which took off in 1832 when a mill was established at Mercury Bay. Things got tougher once the kauri around the coast became scarce and the loggers had to penetrate deeper into the bush for timber. Kauri dams, which used water power to propel the huge logs to the coast, were built. By the 1930s virtually no kauri remained and the industry died.

Gold was first discovered in NZ near Coromandel Town in 1852. Although this first rush was short-lived, more gold was discovered around Thames in 1867 and later in other places. The peninsula is also rich in semiprecious gemstones, such as quartz, agate, amethyst and jasper. A fossick on any west-coast beach can be rewarding.

Despite successful interactions with Europeans for decades, the Hauraki *iwi* were some of the hardest hit by colonisation. Unscrupulous dealings by settlers and government to gain access to valuable resources resulted in the Māori losing most of their lands by the 1880s. Even today there is a much lower Māori presence on the peninsula than in neighbouring districts.

ESSENTIAL WAIKATO

Eat Coromandel bivalves – mussels, oysters and scallops are local specialities.

Drink local Blue Fridge Brewery craft beer at Luke's Kitchen & Cafe (p194).

Read *The Penguin History of New Zealand* (2003) by the late Michael King, a former Opoutere resident.

Listen to The native bird life at Sanctuary Mountain Maungatautari (p209).

Watch passing schools of fish while snorkelling near Hahei (p197).

Celebrate at the annual Whangamata Beach Hop (p201).

Go green with off-the-grid tepees at Solscape (p218).

Online www.thecoromandel.com, www.hamiltonwaikato.com, www.king country.co.nz

---

Miranda

It's a pretty name for a settlement on the swampy Firth of Thames, just an hour's drive from Auckland. The two reasons to come here are splashing around in the thermal pools and bird-watching.

This is one of the most accessible spots for studying waders or shorebirds all year round. The vast mudflat is teeming with aquatic worms and crustaceans, which attract thousands of Arctic-nesting shorebirds over the winter – 43 species of wader have been spotted here. The two main species are the bartailed godwit and the lesser or red knot, but it isn't unusual to see turnstones, sandpipers and the odd vagrant red-necked stint. One godwit tagged here was tracked making an 11,570km nonstop flight from Alaska. Shorthaul travellers include the pied oystercatcher and the threatened wrybill from the South Island, and banded dotterels and pied stilts.

Coromandel Peninsula

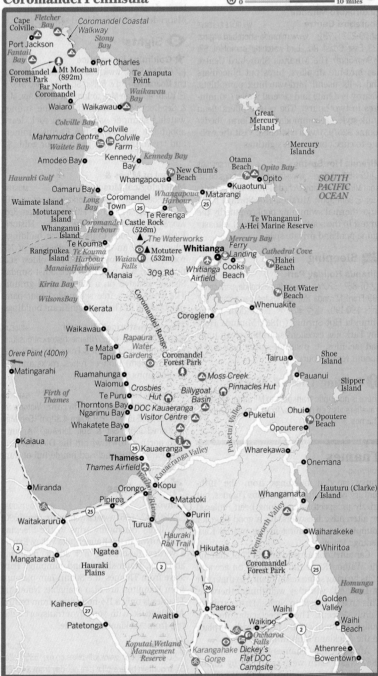

⊙ Sights & Activities

Pukorokoro Miranda
Shorebird Centre WILDLIFE RESERVE

(☑09-232 2781; www.miranda-shorebird.org.nz; 283 East Coast Rd; bird-watching pamphlet $2; ☺9am-5pm) The Miranda Shorebird Centre has bird-life displays, hires out binoculars and sells useful bird-watching pamphlets. Nearby is a hide and several walks (30 minutes to two hours). The centre offers clean bunk-style accommodation (dorm beds/ rooms $25/95) with a kitchen. Visit the website to check out recent sightings.

Miranda Hot Springs HOT SPRINGS

(☑07-867 3055; www.mirandahotsprings.co.nz; Front Miranda Rd; adult/child $14/7, private spa extra $15; ☺9am-9pm) Miranda Hot Springs has a large thermal swimming pool (reputedly the largest in the southern hemisphere), a toasty sauna pool and private spas.

🛏 Sleeping

Miranda Holiday Park HOLIDAY PARK $

(☑07-867 3205; www.mirandaholidaypark.co.nz; 595 Front Miranda Rd; campsites per person $27, units $90-190; @⊛☎☒) 🛥 Next door to the Miranda Hot Springs (p186), Miranda Holiday Park has excellent sparkling-clean units and facilities, its own hot-spring pool and a floodlit tennis court.

ⓘ Getting There & Away

There is no public transport to Miranda. Most travellers visit en route to/from Auckland and Thames.

Thames

POP 7060

Dinky wooden buildings from the 19th-century gold rush still dominate Thames, but grizzly prospectors have long been replaced by alternative lifestylers. It's a good base for tramping or canyoning in the nearby Kauaeranga Valley.

Captain Cook arrived here in 1769, naming the Waihou River the 'Thames' 'on account of its bearing some resemblance to that river in England'; you may well think otherwise. This area belonged to Ngāti Maru, a tribe of Tainui descent. Their spectacular meeting house, Hotunui (1878), holds pride of place in the Auckland Museum.

After opening Thames to gold miners in 1867, Ngāti Maru were swamped by 10,000 European settlers within a year. When the initial boom turned to bust, a dubious system of government advances resulted in Māori debt and forced land sales.

⊙ Sights

★ Goldmine Experience MINE

(☑07-868 8514; www.goldmine-experience.co.nz; cnr Moanataiari Rd & Pollen St; adult/child $15/5; ☺10am-4pm Jan-Mar, to 1pm Sat & Sun Apr, May & Sep-Dec) Walk through a mine tunnel, watch a stamper battery crush rock, learn about the history of the Cornish miners and try your hand at panning for gold ($2 extra).

School of Mines &
Mineralogical Museum MUSEUM

(☑07-868 6227; www.historicplaces.org.nz; 101 Cochrane St; adult/child $10/free; ☺11am-3pm Jan & Feb, Wed-Sun Mar-Dec) The Historic Places Trust runs tours of these buildings, which house an extensive collection of NZ rocks, minerals and fossils. The oldest section (1868) was part of a Methodist Sunday School, situated on a Māori burial ground. The Trust has a free self-guided tour pamphlet taking in Thames' significant buildings.

Thames Historical Museum MUSEUM

(☑07-868 8509; http://thameshistoricalmuseum. weebly.com; cnr Cochrane & Pollen Sts; adult/child $5/2; ☺1-4pm) Pioneer relics, rocks and old photographs of the town.

Butterfly Forest GARDENS

(☑07-868 8080; www.butterfly.co.nz; Victoria St; adult/child $15/7; ☺9.30am-4.30pm Sep-May, 10.30am-3.30pm Sat & Sun Jun-Aug) Around 3km north of town within the Dickson Holiday Park is this enclosed jungle full of hundreds of exotic flappers.

🏃 Activities

Canyonz OUTDOORS

(☑0800 422 696; www.canyonz.co.nz; trips $390) 🛥 All-day canyoning trips to the Sleeping God Canyon in the Kauaeranga Valley. Expect a vertical descent of over 300m, requiring abseiling, water-sliding and jumping. Trips leave from Thames at 8.30am; 7am pick-ups from Hamilton are also available. Note that Thames is only a 1½-hour drive from central Auckland, so with your own transport a day trip from Auckland is possible.

JollyBikes CYCLING

(☑07-867 9026; www.jollybikes.co.nz; 535 Pollen St; mountain bike/e-bike hire per day from $45/80;

Thames

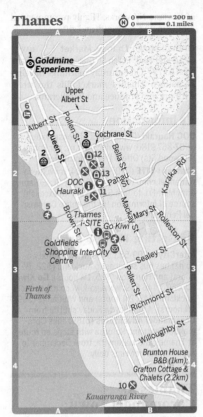

N 0 ——— 200 m
0 ——— 0.1 miles

Firth of Thames

Brunton House B&B (1km); Grafton Cottage & Chalets (2.2km)

Kauaeranga River

⏱9.30am-5pm Mon-Fri, to 2pm Sat) Rents out mountain bikes and e-bikes, does repairs and has plenty of information on tackling the Hauraki Rail Trail.

Karaka Bird Hide BIRD-WATCHING

🏁 FREE Built with compensation funds from the *Rainbow Warrior* bombing, this hide can be reached by a boardwalk through the mangroves just off Brown St.

▣ Sleeping

Sunkist Guesthouse B&B $

(☏07-868 8808; www.sunkistguesthouse.nz; 506 Brown St; s/d & tw $75/95; @🛜) Formerly the Lady Bowen Hotel, this character-filled 1860s heritage building offers singles, twins and doubles, and a sunny garden. Breakfast is included and all rooms share bathrooms. The well-equipped kitchen is ideal for

self-catering meals, and there's a pleasant outdoor barbecue area.

Brunton House B&B B&B $$

(☏07-868 5160; www.bruntonhouse.co.nz; 210 Parawai Rd; r from $160; @🛜⛲) This impressive two-storey kauri villa (1875) has a modern kitchen and bathrooms, while staying true to the building's historic credentials (there are no en suites). Guests can relax in the grounds, by the pool, in the designated lounge or on the upstairs terrace. During summer, lawn tennis is an option on the property's own grass court.

Grafton Cottage & Chalets CHALET $$

(☏07-868 9971; www.graftoncottage.co.nz; 304 Grafton Rd; units $140-220; @🛜⛲) Most of these attractive wooden chalets perched on a hill have decks with awesome views. The hospitable hosts provide free internet access and breakfast, as well as use of the pool, spa and barbecue areas.

Cotswold Cottage B&B $$

(☏07-868 6306; www.cotswoldcottage.co.nz; 46 Maramarahi Rd; r $185-225; 🛜) ⍉ Looking over the river and racecourse, 3km southeast of town, this pretty villa features luxuriant linen and an outdoor spa pool. The comfy rooms all open onto a deck.

✕ Eating & Drinking

Cafe Melbourne CAFE $
(☑07-868 3159; www.facebook.com/cafe melbournegrahamstown; 715 Pollen St; mains $13-20; ⊙8am-5pm Mon-Thu, to 9pm Fri, 9am-4pm Sat & Sun) Stylish and spacious, this cafe definitely channels the cosmopolitan vibe of a certain Australian city. Shared tables promote a convivial ambience, and the menu travels from ricotta pancakes to beef sliders and fish curry for lunch. It's in a repurposed building called the Depot where you'll also find a juice bar and a deli with artisanal bread and takeaway salads.

Coco Coffee Bar CAFE $
(☑07-868 8616; 661 Pollen St; snacks from $5; ⊙6.45am-2pm Mon-Sat) Occupying a corner of an old villa, this chic little cafe serves excellent coffee and enticing pastries and cakes.

Wharf Coffee House & Bar CAFE $
(☑07-868 6828; www.facebook.com/thewharf coffeehouseandbar; Shortland Wharf, Queen St; snacks & mains $10-18; ⊙9am-3pm Mon & Tue, to 7pm Wed, Sat & Sun, to 9pm Thu & Fri) Perched beside the water, this rustic wood-lined pavilion does great fish and chips. Grab a table outside with a beer or a wine to understand why the Wharf is a firm local favourite. The smoked seafood platter is especially good.

Nakontong THAI $$
(☑07-868 6821; www.nakontong.com; 728 Pollen St; mains $16-21; ⊙11am-2.30pm Mon-Fri, 5-10pm daily; ☑) Although the bright lighting may not induce romance, the tangy Thai dishes will provide a warm glow at this long-established and popular local eatery.

Junction Hotel PUB
(☑07-868 6008; www.thejunction.net.nz; 700 Pollen St; ⊙10am-late) Serving thirsty gold diggers since 1869, the Junction is the archetypal slightly rough-around-the-edges, historic, small-town pub. Live music attracts a younger crowd on the weekends, while families head to the corner-facing Grahamstown Bar & Diner for hearty pub grub of bar snacks, pizza and mains ($15 to $33).

🔒 Shopping

★Bounty Store ARTS & CRAFTS
(☑07-868 8988; www.facebook.com/bountystore; 754 Pollen St; ⊙9.30am-5pm Tue-Fri, 9.30am-2pm & 5-6pm Sat) Excellent arts and crafts shop with loads of local products and a quirky selection of Kiwiana NZ works. Highly recommended for distinctive souvenirs and gifts.

Grahamstown Thames Market MARKET
(☑07-868 9841; Pollen St, Grahamstown; ⊙8am-noon Sat) 🌿 On Saturday mornings the Grahamstown Thames market fills the street with organic produce and handicrafts.

ℹ Information

DOC Hauraki (Department of Conservation; ☑07-867 9180; www.doc.govt.nz; cnr Pahau & Kirkwood Sts) Offers track information.
Thames i-SITE (☑07-868 7284; www.theco romandel.com/thames; 200 Mary St; ⊙9am-4pm Mon-Fri, to 1pm Sat & Sun) An excellent source of information for the entire Coromandel Peninsula.

ℹ Getting There & Away

InterCity (☑09-583 5780; www.intercity. co.nz) has bus services to Auckland ($22, 1½ hours) and Hamilton ($25, 1¾ hours). **Go Kiwi** (☑0800 446 549; www.go-kiwi.co.nz) services Auckland ($49, 2¼ hours) and Whitianga ($39, 1¾ hours). A Monday to Friday shuttle from **Coromandel Adventures** (p189) links Coromandel Town and Rotorua with stops en route at Thames and Matamata; from December to April this service runs daily.

Thames to Coromandel Town

From Thames, narrow SH25 snakes along the coast past pretty little bays and rocky beaches. Sea birds are plentiful, and you can fish, dig for shellfish and fossick for quartz, jasper and even gold-bearing rocks. The landscape turns crimson when the pohutukawa (often referred to as the 'New Zealand Christmas tree') blooms in December.

A handful of stores, motels, B&Bs and camping grounds are scattered around the picturesque bays. At **Tapu** turn inland for a mainly sealed 6km drive to the **Rapaura Water Gardens** (☑07-868 4821; www.rapaura watergardens.co.nz; 586 Tapu-Coroglen Rd; adult/child $15/6; ⊙9am-5pm) 🌿, combining water, greenery and sculpture.

From **Wilsons Bay** the road heads away from the coast and negotiates several hills and valleys before dropping down to Coromandel Town, 55km from Thames. The view looking towards the island-studded Coromandel Harbour is exquisite.

DRIVING CREEK RAILWAY

A lifelong labour of love for its conservationist owner, the late Barry Brickell, this unique **train** (✐ 07-866 8703; www.dcrail.nz; 380 Driving Creek Rd; adult/child $35/13; ⊗ 10.15am, 11.30am, 12.45pm, 2pm, 3.15pm & 4.30pm, additional times summer) runs up steep grades, across four trestle bridges, along two spirals and a double switchback, and through two tunnels, finishing at the 'Eye-full Tower'. The one-hour trip passes artworks and regenerating native forest. Booking ahead is recommended in summer.

Every night in summer a special 7pm departure (adult/child $50/13) includes a barbecue (BYO food, drinks, plates and utensils) at the 'Eye-full Tower'.

At the time of research, a zip-line was planned, with a series of eight zip-line stations leading down through the native forest to the Copeland Stream where gold was first discovered in New Zealand.

✖ Eating

Waiomu Beach Cafe   CAFE $$
(✐ 07-868 2554; www.facebook.com/waiomubeach cafe; 622 Thames Coast Rd, Waiomu Bay; mains $11-25; ⊗ 7am-5pm) Just north of Te Puru, stop at the colourful Waiomu Beach Cafe for hearty breakfasts, gourmet pizza, freshly squeezed juices and healthy salads. Locally brewed craft beer from around the peninsula is also available.

❶ Getting There & Away

Driving your own vehicle is recommended around this spectacular and winding coastal road. **Coromandel Adventures** runs shuttles linking Thames and Coromandel Town.

Coromandel Town

POP 1480

Crammed with heritage buildings, Coromandel Town is a thoroughly quaint little place. Its natty cafes, interesting art stores, excellent sleeping options and delicious smoked mussels could keep you here longer than you expected.

Gold was discovered nearby at Driving Creek in 1852. Initially the local Patukirikiri *iwi* (tribe) kept control of the land and received money from digging licences. After initial financial success the same fate befell them as the Ngāti Maru in Thames. By 1871, debt had forced them to sell all but 778 mountainous acres of their land. Today fewer than 100 people remain who identify as part of this *iwi*.

Note that Coromandel Town is just one part of the entire Coromandel Peninsula, and its location on the peninsula's west coast means it is not a good base for visiting Cathedral Cove and Hot Water Beach on the peninsula's east coast.

◎ Sights & Activities

Many historic sites are featured in the Historic Places Trust's *Coromandel Town* pamphlet, available at the Coromandel Town Information Centre (p191).

Coromandel Mining &
Historic Museum   MUSEUM
(✐ 07-866 8987; 841 Rings Rd; adult/child $5/free; ⊗ 10am-4pm mid-Dec–Jan, 10am-1pm Sat & Sun Feb–mid-Dec) Small museum with glimpses of pioneer life.

Coromandel Goldfield
Experience   SCENIC DRIVE
(www.dcrail.nz) Illuminating the story of the Coromandel Goldfields, this new experience combines a journey by electric mine train to Copeland's Stream where gold was first discovered in NZ in 1853 with a visit to a historic Stamper Battery and panning for gold. Check the website for prices and departure times.

Mussel Barge Snapper Safaris   FISHING
(✐ 07-866 7667; www.musselbargesafaris.co.nz; adult/child $60/30) Fishing trips with a local flavour and lots of laughs. Pick-up available. Trips only leave with a minimum of eight participants.

Coromandel Adventures   DRIVING
(✐ 0800 462 676; www.coromandeladventures. co.nz; 90 Tiki Rd; tours adult/child from $75/45) Various tours around Coromandel Town and the peninsula, plus shuttles to Whitianga. Also runs a handy shuttle service linking Coromandel Town to Rotorua via Thames, Paeroa, Te Aroha, Matamata and Tirau. The shuttle runs Monday to Friday from May to November and daily from December to April.

🛏 Sleeping

Coromandel Town has a good range of accommodation, from hostels to motels and B&Bs. Enquire at Coromandel Accommodation Solutions about renting a house at one of the nearby beaches.

Tui Lodge   HOSTEL $
(📞07-866 8237; www.coromandeltuilodge.co.nz; 60 Whangapoua Rd; campsite per person $20, dm $29-32, r $70-90; @🛜) Pleasantly rural but still just a short walk to town, Coromandel's best backpackers has plenty of trees, free bikes, fruit (in season) and straight-up rooms. The pricier ones have en suites.

Coromandel Motel &
Holiday Park   HOLIDAY PARK $
(📞07-866 8830; www.coromandeltop10.co.nz; 636 Rings Rd; campsites from $46, units $90-185; @🛜🏊) Well kept and welcoming, with nicely painted cabins, attractive units and manicured lawns – it gets busy in summer, so book ahead. Also hires bikes ($20 per day). The spotless cabins with shared bathrooms are good value for backpackers.

Anchor Lodge   MOTEL, HOSTEL $
(📞07-866 7992; www.anchorlodgecoromandel. co.nz; 448 Wharf Rd; dm $31, d $75, units $145-370; @🛜🏊) This upmarket backpacker-motel combo has its own gold mine, glow-worm cave, small heated swimming pool and spa. The 2nd-floor units have harbour views.

Hush Boutique
Accommodation   RENTAL HOUSE $$
(📞07-866 7771; www.hushaccommodation.co.nz; 425 Driving Creek Rd; cabins from $125; 🛜) 🅿 Four rustic but stylish private cabins with en-suite bathrooms are scattered throughout native bush at this easygoing spot. Natural wood creates a warm ambience. Located beside a peaceful stream, the alfresco area with a barbecue and full cooking facilities is

a top spot to catch up with fellow travellers. The adjacent Hush House accommodates up to six ($355).

Green House   B&B $$
(📞07-866 7303; www.greenhousebandb.co.nz; 505 Tiki Rd; r $195; @🛜) Good old-fashioned hospitality with three smartly furnished rooms on offer. The property has been refurbished, and guests enjoy sea views and a rural outlook.

Jacaranda Lodge   B&B $$
(📞07-866 8002; www.jacarandalodge.co.nz; 3195 Tiki Rd; s $90, d $155-185; 🛜) 🅿 Located among 6 hectares of farmland and rose gardens, this two-storey cottage is a relaxing retreat. Look forward to excellent breakfasts from the friendly owners, Judy and Gerard, often using produce – plums, almonds, macadamia nuts and citrus fruit – from the property's spray-free orchard. Some rooms share bathrooms.

Little Farm   APARTMENT $$
(📞07-866 8454; www.abbeycourtmotelandthelittle farm.com; 750 Tiki Rd; r $100-150; 🛜) Overlooking a private wetland reserve at the rear of a fair-dinkum farm, these comfortable units offer plenty of peace and quiet. The largest has a full kitchen and superb sunset views.

Driving Creek Villas   COTTAGE $$$
(📞07-866 7755; www.drivingcreekvillas.com; 21a Colville Rd; villas $345; 🛜) This is the posh, grown-up's choice – three spacious, self-contained, modern, wooden villas with plenty of privacy. The Polynesian-influenced interior design is slick and the bush setting, complete with bubbling creek, sublime.

🍴 Eating & Drinking

Driving Creek Cafe   VEGETARIAN $
(📞07-866 7066; www.drivingcreekcafe.nz; 180 Driving Creek Rd; mains $9-20; ⏱9am-5pm Tue-Sun; 🛜🍴) 🅿 Vegetarian, vegan, gluten-free, organic and fair-trade delights await at this funky mudbrick cafe. The food is beautifully presented, fresh and healthy. Once sated, the kids can play in the sandpit while the adults check their email on the free wi-fi. Don't miss ordering a terrific juice or smoothie, and try the buckwheat blinis or a tasty felafel wrap.

Coromandel Smoking Co   SEAFOOD $
(📞07-866 8757; www.corosmoke.co.nz; 70 Tiki Rd; fish & seafood $5-15; ⏱9am-5pm) Smoked fish and seafood for cooking and snacking.

ℹ COROMANDEL ACCOMMODATION SOLUTIONS

This **booking service** (📞07-866 8803; www.accommodationcoromandel.co.nz; 265 Kapanga Rd; units & apt $129-250; 🛜) for cottages and rental houses around the Coromandel region; an excellent opportunity for coastal scenery. It also has three stylish apartments centrally located in Coromandel Town.

★ **Wharf Road** CAFE, VEGETARIAN **$$**

(☑07-866 7538; www.facebook.com/pg/
wharfroad; 24 Wharf Rd; mains $12-18; ⊙8am-
3pm; ⊘) ✐ Bringing cosmopolitan cool
to Coromandel Town, Wharf Road offers
the opportunity to ease into another day
equipped with excellent coffee, interesting
brunch dishes such as avocado bagels or
Turkish eggs with chilli butter, and an easy-
going soundtrack of loping Kiwi reggae.
Lunch amid the wood-lined space is equally
popular, with wine and craft beer balanc-
ing super-healthy organic and vegetarian
bowls.

Coromandel Mussel Kitchen SEAFOOD **$$**

(☑07-866 7245; www.musselkitchen.co.nz; cnr
SH25 & 309 Rd; mains $15-26; ⊙9am-3pm mid-
Sep–early Jun) This cool cafe-bar sits among
fields 3km south of town. Mussels are served
with Thai- and Mediterranean-tinged sauc-
es or grilled on the half-shell. In summer
the garden bar is perfect for a mussel-fritter
stack and a frosty craft beer from MK Brewing Co, the on-site microbrewery. Smoked
and chilli mussels and bottles of the beers
are all available for takeaway.

Pepper Tree MODERN NZ **$$**

(☑07-866 8211; www.peppertreerestaurant.co.nz;
31 Kapanga Rd; mains lunch $16-28, dinner $25-
36; ⊙10am-9pm; ☏⊘) Coromandel Town's
most upmarket option dishes up generously
proportioned meals with an emphasis on
local seafood. On a summer's evening, the
courtyard tables under the shady tree are
the place to be.

Umu CAFE **$$**

(☑07-866 8618; www.facebook.com/umu
cafe; 22 Wharf Rd; breakfast $11-18, lunch $12-25,
dinner $14-32; ⊙9am-9pm; ☏) Classy cafe
fare including pizza, counter food (tarts
and quiches around $7), superb coffee and
tummy-taming breakfasts. Craft beer from
Hamilton's Good George is refreshing after
a day's adventuring.

Star & Garter Hotel PUB

(☑07-866 8503; www.starandgarter.co.nz; 5
Kapanga Rd; ⊙11am-late) Making the most of
the simple kauri interior of an 1873 building, this smart pub has pool tables, decent
sounds and a roster of live music and DJs
on the weekends. The beer garden is smartly
clad in corrugated iron.

WORTH A TRIP

COROMANDEL OYSTER COMPANY

Briny-fresh mussels, scallops, oysters
and cooked fish and chips and flounder.
Coming from Thames you'll find **Coromandel Oyster Company** (☑07-866
8028; www.freshoysters.co.nz; 1611 Tiki Rd;
snacks & meals $5-25; ⊙10am-5.30pm)
on the hill around 7km before you reach
Coromandel Town. Ask if the excellent
chowder is available.

🛍 **Shopping**

Source ARTS & CRAFTS

(☑07-866 7345; 31 Kapanga Rd; ⊙10am-4pm) Creative showcase of more than 30 local artists.

ℹ **Information**

The **Coromandel Town Information Centre**
(☑07-866 8598; www.coromandeltown.co.nz;
85 Kapanga Rd; ⊙10am-4pm; ☏) has good
maps and local information. Pick up the Historic
Places Trust's *Coromandel Town* pamphlet here.

ℹ **Getting There & Away**

The best way to Coromandel Town from Auckland is on a **360 Discovery** (☑0800 360 3472;
www.360discovery.co.nz) ferry (one way/
return $60/95, two hours, daily in summer,
Saturday and Sunday other seasons), which
makes a stop at Orapiu on Waiheke Island en
route. The ferry docks at Hannafords Wharf, Te
Kouma, from where free buses shuttle passengers the 10km into Coromandel Town. It's also
possible to book same-day return trips visiting
Coromandel destinations like the **Driving
Creek Railway** (p189).

There's no charge for carrying your bike on a
360 Discovery ferry. Touring cyclists can avoid
Auckland's traffic fumes and treacherous roads
completely by catching the ferry at Gulf Harbour
to Auckland's ferry terminal and then leapfrog-
ging directly to Coromandel Town.

Leaving from a **stop** (Woollams Ave) near the
Coromandel Town Information Centre (p191),
InterCity (☑09-583 5780; www.intercity.co.nz)
has buses linking Coromandel Town to Hamilton
($40, 3½ hours) and **Go Kiwi** (☑0800 446 549;
www.go-kiwi.co.nz) heads to Auckland ($59, 4½
hours). **Coromandel Adventures** (p189) runs
a shuttle from Coromandel Town to Rotorua
(Monday to Friday from May to November and
daily from December to April), with a key stop in
Matamata for **Hobbiton** (p209).

Far North Coromandel

Supremely isolated and gobsmackingly beautiful, the rugged tip of the Coromandel Peninsula is well worth the effort required to reach it. The best time to visit is summer, when the gravel roads are dry, the pohutukawa trees are in their crimson glory and camping's an option (there isn't much accommodation up here).

◉ Sights & Activities

The tiny settlement of Colville is a remote rural community populated by alternative lifestylers. There's not much here except for the quaint Colville General Store (p193) and the Hereford 'n' a Pickle cafe.

Three kilometres north of Colville the sealed road turns to gravel and splits to straddle each side of the peninsula. Following the west coast, ancient pohutukawa shade turquoise waters and stony beaches. The small DOC-run Fantail Bay Campsite (☑07-866 6685; www.doc.govt.nz; Port Jackson Rd; adult/child $13/6.50) is 23km north of Colville. Another 7km brings you to the beachfront DOC Port Jackson Campsite (☑07-866 6932; www.doc.govt.nz; Port Jackson Rd; adult/child $13/6.50).

There's a spectacular lookout about 4km further on. Great Barrier Island is only 20km away, looking every part the extension of the Coromandel Peninsula that it once was. The road stops at Fletcher Bay – a magical land's end. Although it's only 37km from Colville, allow an hour for the drive. There's another DOC campsite (☑07-866 6685; www.doc.govt.nz; Fletcher Bay; adult/child $13/6.50) here, as well as Fletcher Bay Backpackers.

At Stony Bay, where the east coast road terminates, there's another DOC campsite (☑07-866 6822; www.doc.govt.nz; Stony Bay; adult/child $13/6.50, bach $80) and a small DOC-run bach (holiday home) that sleeps five. Heading south there are a couple of nice beaches peppered with baches on the way to the slightly larger settlement of Port Charles, where you'll find Tangiaro Kiwi Retreat.

Another 8km brings you to the turn-off leading back to Colville, or you can continue south to Waikawau Bay, where there's a large DOC campsite (☑07-866 1106; www.doc.govt.nz; Waikawau Beach Rd, Waikawau Bay; adult/child $15/6.50) that has a summer-only store. The road then winds its way south past Kennedy Bay before cutting back to come out near the Driving Creek Railway (p189).

Coromandel Discovery WALKING
(☑07-866 8175; www.coromandeldiscovery.co.nz; 39 Whangapoua Rd, Coromandel Town; adult/child $135/75) If you're not keen on walking the return leg of the Coromandel Coastal Walkway, Coromandel Discovery will drive you from Coromandel Town up to Fletcher Bay and pick you up from Stony Bay four hours later. Ask about other tours exploring Cathedral Cove and Hot Water Beach.

🛏 Sleeping

Mahamudra Centre RETREAT $
(☑07-866 6851; www.mahamudra.org.nz; RD4, Main Rd, Colville; campsite/dm/s/tw $18/28/50/80) The Mahamudra Centre is a serene Tibetan Buddhist retreat with a stupa, meditation hall and regular meditation courses. It offers simple accommodation in a parklike setting.

Fletcher Bay Backpackers HOSTEL $
(☑07-866 6685; www.doc.govt.nz; Fletcher Bay; dm $26) The Fletcher Bay Backpackers is a simple affair that has four rooms with four bunks in each. Bring sheets and food. It's 37km from Colville.

Colville Farm LODGE $$
(☑07-866 6820; www.colvillefarmholidays.co.nz; 2140 Colville Rd; d $50-100; @ 🛜) The 1260-hectare Colville Farm has a range of interesting accommodation, including bare-basics bush lodges and self-contained houses. Guests can try their hands at farm work (including milking) or go on horse treks ($40 to $150, one to five hours).

Tangiaro Kiwi Retreat COTTAGE $$$
(☑07-866 6614; www.kiwiretreat.co.nz; 1299 Port Charles Rd, Port Charles; units $220-350; 🛜) Located in Port Charles, Tangiaro Kiwi Retreat offers eight one- or two-bedroom self-contained wooden cottages, each pair sharing a barbecue. There's a bush-fringed spa, an in-house massage therapist ($75 per hour) and, in summer, a cafe and licensed restaurant. The 20km road down to Port Charles from the intersection of Port Charles Rd and Waikawau Rd is winding and unsealed.

✖ Eating

Hereford 'n' a Pickle CAFE $
(☑07-866 6937; www.facebook.com/hereford.n.a.pickle; Colville Town; pies $4-6; ☺9am-4pm, reduced hours Apr-Oct; 🛜) Good coffee, fresh-fruit ice cream, and pies made from meat

from local Hereford cattle are the standouts at this rustic self-described 'farm shop' that also boasts free wi-fi and sunny outdoor seating. Sausages and smoked meats are available to take away, along with loads of other local produce including fresh juices, jams and pickles.

Colville General Store DELI $
(☏07-866 6805; Colville Rd, Colville; ☺8.30am-5pm; ☏) ✎ The quaint Colville General Store sells just about everything from organic food to petrol (warning: this is your last option for either). The attached cafe serves up delicious vegan and vegetarian snacks and locally roasted coffee, but opening hours can be haphazard.

Coromandel Town to Whitianga

309 Road

There are two routes from Coromandel Town southeast to Whitianga. The main road is the slightly longer but quicker SH25, which enjoys sea views and has short detours to pristine sandy beaches. The other is the less-travelled but legendary 309 Rd, an unsealed, untamed route through deep bush. Starting 3km south of Coromandel Town, the 309 Rd cuts through the Coromandel Range for 21km (most of which is unsealed but well maintained), rejoining SH25 7km south of Whitianga.

Highlights include a quirky water park, and just 2km further west there's a two-minute walk through bush to the 10m-high **Waiau Falls**. A further 500m on, an easy 10-minute bush walk leads to an amazing **kauri grove**. This stand of 600-year-old giants escaped the carnage of the 19th century, giving a majestic reminder of what the peninsula once looked like. The biggest tree has a 6m circumference.

◎ Sights

Waterworks PARK
(☏07-866 7191; www.thewaterworks.co.nz; 471 309 Rd; adult/child $25/20; ☺10am-6pm Nov-Mar, to 4pm Apr-Oct; ☏) ✎ The Waterworks, 5km east along the 309 Rd from SH25, is a wonderfully bizarre park filled with whimsical water-powered amusements made from old kitchen knives, washing machines, bikes and toilets.

🛏 Sleeping

★ **Wairua Lodge** B&B $$$
(☏07-866 0304; www.wairualodge.co.nz; 251 Old Coach Rd; r $195-275) Wairua Lodge is a peaceful B&B with charming hosts, nestled in the bush towards the Whitianga end of the 309 Rd. There's a riverside swimming hole on the property, barbecue, spa and romantic outdoor bath-tub.

State Highway 25

SH25 starts by climbing sharply to an incredible lookout before heading steeply down. The turn-off at Te Rerenga follows the harbour to **Whangapoua**. There's not much at this beach except for holiday homes and a pleasant holiday park. Walk along the rocky foreshore for 30 minutes to the remote, beautiful and often-deserted and undeveloped **New Chum's Beach**, regarded as one of the most beautiful in the country. Be ready to take your shoes off and wade through a lagoon to get there, and consult the map near the beach store in Whangapoua before you start walking.

Continuing east on SH25 you soon reach Kuaotunu, a more interesting holiday village on a beautiful stretch of white-sand beach, with a cafe-gallery, a store and an ancient petrol pump. From Kuaotunu it's a short drive to Otama Beach and Opito.

◎ Sights

Heading off the highway at Kuaotunu takes you (via an unsealed road) to one of Coromandel's best-kept secrets. First the long stretch of **Otama Beach** comes into view – deserted but for a few houses and farms. Continuing along the narrowing road, the sealed road finally starts again and you reach **Opito**, a hidden-away enclave of 250 flash properties (too smart to be called baches), of which only 16 have permanent residents. From this magical beach, you can walk to the Ngāti Hei *pā* (fortified village) site at the far end.

🛏 Sleeping & Eating

Whangapoua Holiday Park HOLIDAY PARK $
(☏07-866 5215; www.whangapouaholidaypark.co.nz; 1266 Whangapoua Rd, Whangapoua; campsites from $20, cabins $75-105; ☺mid-Oct–Apr) This holiday park has cosy cabins and leafy campsites with well-maintained kitchen and ablution blocks.

Leighton Lodge
B&B $$

(☑ 07-866 0756; www.leightonlodge.co.nz; 17 Stewart Pl, Opito; s $160-190, d $200-220; @) One of the 'real' residences in Opito houses the delightful folks of Leighton Lodge. This smart B&B has chatty owners, an upstairs room with a view-hungry balcony and a self-contained flat downstairs. Say 'hi' to Fern, the owners' very friendly labrador.

Kuaotunu Bay Lodge
B&B $$$

(☑ 07-866 4396; www.kuaotunubay.co.nz; SH25; d $310; ☎) An elegant B&B set among manicured gardens, offering a small set of spacious sea-gazing rooms.

★ Luke's Kitchen & Cafe
CAFE, PIZZA $$

(☑ 07-866 4420; www.lukeskitchen.co.nz; 20 Blackjack Rd, Kuaotunu; mains & pizza $15-28; ☺cafe & gallery 8.30am-3.30pm, restaurant & bar 11am-10pm, shorter restaurant hours Apr-Oct) Luke's Kitchen & Cafe has a rustic surf-shack ambience, cold brews including local craft beer from the tiny Blue Fridge Brewery, and excellent wood-fired pizza. Occasional live music, seafood and creamy fruit smoothies make Luke's an essential stop. Adjacent is Luke's daytime cafe and gallery with very good coffee, homebaked goodies and eclectic local art for sale.

❶ Getting There & Away

The best way to explore the meandering roads is by car. Kuaotunu is also a stop on **Go Kiwi** (p196) shuttles linking Matarangi and Auckland.

Whitianga

POP 4700

Whitianga's big attractions are the sandy beaches of Mercury Bay and the diving, boating and kayaking opportunities afforded by the craggy coast and nearby **Te Whanganui-A-Hei Marine Reserve**. The pretty harbour is a renowned base for game fishing (especially marlin and tuna between January and March).

The legendary Polynesian explorer and seafarer Kupe is believed to have landed near here sometime around AD 950. The name Whitianga is a contraction of Te Whitianga a Kupe (Crossing Place of Kupe).

❍ Sights

Buffalo Beach stretches along Mercury Bay, north of Whitianga Harbour. A five-minute **passenger ferry** (☑ 021 025 10169; www.whitiangaferry.co.nz; adult/child/bicycle $5/3/1.50; ☺7.30am-7.30pm & 8.30-10.30pm) ride will take you across the harbour to **Ferry Landing**. From here you can walk to local sights like **Whitianga Rock Scenic & Historical Reserve**, a park with great views over the ocean, and the **Shakespeare Cliff Lookout**. Further afield are Hahei Beach (13km), Cathedral Cove (15km) and Hot Water Beach (18km, one hour by bike). Look forward to relatively flat terrain if you're keen on riding from Ferry Landing to these other destinations. Cathedral Cove Shuttles (p198) runs a handy service.

Lost Spring
SPRING

(☑ 07-866 0456; www.thelostspring.co.nz; 121a Cook Dr; per 90min/day $40/70; ☺9.30am-6pm Sun-Fri, to 8pm Sat) This expensive but intriguing Disney-meets-Polynesia thermal complex comprises a series of hot pools in a lush jungle-like setting complete with an erupting volcano. It's the ideal spot to relax in tropical tranquillity, with a cocktail in hand. There's also a day spa and cafe. Children under 14 must be accompanied by an adult in the pools.

Mercury Bay Museum
MUSEUM

(☑ 07-866 0730; www.mercurybaymuseum.co.nz; 11a The Esplanade; adult/child $7.50/2; ☺10am-4pm) A small but interesting museum focusing on local history – especially Whitianga's most famous visitors, Kupe and Cook.

🏃 Activities

Fishing charters start at around $500 and head into the thousands. If you snag an overfished species, consider releasing your catch.

Bike Man
CYCLING

(☑ 07-866 0745; thebikeman@xtra.co.nz; 16 Coghill St; per day $25; ☺9am-5pm Mon-Fri, to 1pm Sat) Rent a bike to take across on the ferry (p194) and journey to Hahei and Hot Water Beach.

☞ Tours

There are a baffling number of tours to **Te Whanganui-A-Hei Marine Reserve**, where you'll see interesting rock formations and, if you're lucky, dolphins, fur seals, penguins and orcas. Some are straight-out cruises while others offer optional swims and snorkels.

Windborne
BOATING

(☑ 027 475 2411; www.windborne.co.nz; day sail $95; ☺Dec-Apr) Day sails in a 19m 1928 schooner from December to April, and also departures to the Mercury Islands ($150) in February and March.

Whitianga

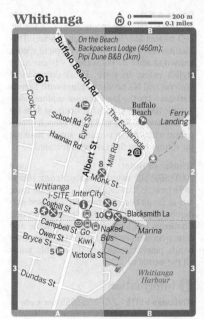

On the Beach
Backpackers Lodge (460m);
Pipi Dune B&B (1km)

Buffalo Beach Rd
Cook Dr
School Rd
Eyre St
The Esplanade
Buffalo Beach
Ferry Landing
Hannan Rd
Albert St
Mill Rd
Monk St
Whitianga i-SITE
InterCity
Coghill St
Campbell St
Go Kiwi
Naked Bus
Blacksmith La
Marina
Owen St
Bryce St
Victoria St
Dundas St
Whitianga Harbour

Ocean Leopard BOATING
(☑0800 843 8687; www.oceanleopardtours.co.nz; adult/child $90/50; ⊙10.30pm, 1.30pm & 4pm) Two-hour trips taking in coastal scenery, naturally including Cathedral Cove (p197). The boat has a handy canopy for sun protection. A one-hour Whirlwind Tour (adult/child $60/35) is also on offer.

Glass Bottom Boat BOATING
(☑07-867 1962; www.glassbottomboatwhitianga.co.nz; adult/child $95/50) Two-hour bottom-gazing tours exploring the Te Whanganui-A-Hei Marine Reserve.

Whitianga Adventures BOATING
(☑0800 806 060; www.whitianga-adventures.co.nz; adult/child $75/45) A two-hour Sea Cave Adventure in an inflatable.

Cave Cruzer BOATING
(☑0800 427 893; www.cavecruzer.co.nz; adult/child 1hr $60/35, 2hr $80/45) Tours on a rigid-hull inflatable.

✦ Festivals & Events

Scallop Festival FOOD & DRINK
(☑07-867 1510; www.scallopfestival.co.nz; ⊙Sep) One-day showcase of food, entertainment and more than a few people's favourite bivalves.

🛏 Sleeping

Turtle Cove HOSTEL $
(☑07-867 1517; www.turtlecove.co.nz; 14 Bryce St; dm $29-30, d $77-198; @☎) Colourful shared areas and a spacious modern kitchen make Turtle Cove one of the best hostels in the Coromandel Peninsula and Waikato area. The largest dormitories have only six beds, making Turtle Cove more like a friendly homestay than a rip-roaring party palace. The team at reception is unfailingly helpful with plenty of ideas on how to maximise your time.

On the Beach Backpackers Lodge HOSTEL $
(☑07-866 5380; www.coromandelbackpackers.com; 46 Buffalo Beach Rd; dm $27, d & tw $80-115, f $160; @) Brightly painted and beachside, this large YHA-affiliate has a wide range of rooms, including some with sea views and en suites. It provides free kayaks, boogie boards and spades (for Hot Water Beach). Bikes ($20) are also available if you're keen to catch the ferry and cycle to Hahei.

Beachside Resort MOTEL $$
(☑07-867 1356; www.beachsideresort.co.nz; 20 Eyre St; units $195-225; ☎⊠) Attached to the sprawling Oceans Resort, this modern motel has tidy units with kitchenettes and balconies on the upper level. Despite the name, it's set back from the beach but it does have a heated pool.

Pipi Dune B&B B&B $$
(☑07-869 5375; www.pipidune.co.nz; 5 Pipi Dune; r $180; ☎) This attractive B&B in a quiet cul-de-sac has guest lounges, kitchenettes, laundries

and free wi-fi. To get here, head north on Cook Dr, turn left onto Surf St and then take the first right.

Within the Bays
B&B $$$

(☑07-866 2848; www.withinthebays.co.nz; 49 Tarapatiki Dr; r $275-325; @🖵) It's the combination of charming hosts and incredible views that make this B&B set on a hill overlooking Mercury Bay really worth considering. It's extremely well set up for guests with restricted mobility – there's even a wheelchair-accessible bush track on the property. Find it 5km from Whitianga town.

✕ Eating & Drinking

Coghill House
CAFE $

(☑07-866 0592; www.thecog.co.nz; 10 Coghill St; mains $10-18; ⊗8am-3pm) Get an early start on the sunny terrace of this side-street cafe, where good counter food is partnered with huge pancake stacks and plump tortilla wraps. Look forward to the best coffee in town, too.

Blue Ginger
SOUTHEAST ASIAN $$

(☑07-867 1777; www.blueginger.co.nz; 1/10 Blacksmith Lane; shared plates $9-14, mains $22-28; ⊗11am-2pm Tue-Fri, 5pm-late Tue-Sat) Southeast Asian flavours infuse the menu at this relaxed spot with shared tables. Highlights include Indonesian-style beef rendang, pad thai noodles and a great roast-duck red curry. Beer and wine is not served.

Salt Restaurant & Bar
MODERN NZ, SEAFOOD $$

(☑07-866 5818; www.salt-whitianga.co.nz; 2 Blacksmith Lane; shared plates $12-30, mains $25-39; ⊗4pm-late Mon-Thu, from noon Fri-Sun) Views of the Whitianga marina – including the sleepy ferry crossing to Ferry Landing – provide the backdrop for relaxed but stylish dining at this restaurant attached to Whitianga Hotel (p196). In summer the place to be is out on the deck, combining local wines with pan-seared fish with Cloudy Bay clams or Coromandel oysters from the raw bar.

Mercury Bay Estate
BISTRO $$

(☑07-866 4066; www.mercurybayestate.co.nz; 761a Purangi Rd, Cooks Beach; platters $18-48, wine tasting $10-18; ⊗10am-5pm Mon-Fri, 9am-6pm Sat & Sun) Repurposed timber and corrugated iron feature at this rustic but chic vineyard en route from Ferry Landing to Cooks Beach. Seafood, cheese and charcuterie platters team well with wines such as the excellent Lonely Bay chardonnay. Local artwork is also for sale. It's 35km from Whitianga town.

Poivre & Sel
FRENCH $$$

(☑07-866 0053; www.poivresel.co.nz; 2 Mill Rd; 2-/3 courses $58/76; ⊗5pm-late Tue-Sat) This Mediterranean-style villa – complete with a garden shaded by palm trees – is the most stylish eatery in town. Local Coromandel seafood and NZ produce shines with French flavours – try the bouillabaisse seafood soup – while the restaurant's bar opens at 5pm for combinations ($20 to $30) of French champagne with cheese or garlic snails. Booking for dinner from 6pm is recommended.

Whitianga Hotel
PUB

(☑07-866 5818; www.whitiangahotel.co.nz; 1 Blacksmith Lane; ⊗11am-late) Good-value pub food, lots of frosty beers on tap and a relaxed garden bar equal a classic Kiwi pub experience. Challenge the locals on the pool table and return on weekend nights for DJs and cover bands playing songs you'll probably know all the words to.

ℹ Information

Whitianga i-SITE (☑07-866 5555; www.whitianga.co.nz; 66 Albert St; ⊗9am-5pm Mon-Fri, to 4pm Sat & Sun) has information and internet access. Hours are extended in summer.

ℹ Getting There & Away

InterCity (☑07-348 0366; www.intercity.co.nz) links Whitianga to Thames ($25, 90 minutes, twice daily) for onward transfer to Auckland and Hamilton. **Go Kiwi** (☑07-866 0336; www.go-kiwi.co.nz) links Whitianga to Thames ($39, 90 minutes, one daily) and Auckland ($64, 3½ hours, one daily). This service also loops around Hot Water Beach and Hahei; check the website for timings. **Naked Bus** (https://nakedbus.com) also services Whitianga.

Coroglen & Whenuakite

The blink-and-you'll-miss-them villages of Coroglen and Whenuakite are on SH25, south of Whitianga and west of Hot Water Beach. Along this route are a few interesting diversions, including a good craft brewery (p197) and a weekly **farmers market** (☑07-866 3315; www.facebook.com/coroglenfarmersmarket; SH25, Coroglen; ⊗9am-1pm Sun late Oct–early Jun).

🏃 Activities

Rangihau Ranch
HORSE RIDING

(☑07-866 3875; www.rangihauranch.co.nz; Rangihau Rd, Coroglen; rides per hr $60) The folks at Rangihau Ranch will lead you on horseback up a historic packhorse track, through beautiful bush to spectacular views. Accommodation in a quaint rural cottage ($150) is also available.

🛏 Sleeping

Seabreeze Holiday Park HOLIDAY PARK **$**
(☑ 07-866 3050; www.seabreezeholidaypark.co.nz; 1043 SH25, Whenuakite; campsite per person $19-25, dm $34, unit $85-170; 🛜) A friendly and grassy park with the bonus of an on-site craft brewery. What's not to like?

🍴 Eating & Drinking

Colenso CAFE **$**
(☑ 07-866 3725; www.colensocafe.co.nz; SH25, Whenuakite; mains $10-19; ⊘10am-4pm) Better than your average highway stop, Colenso has excellent fair-trade coffee, scones, cakes and light snacks, as well as a shop selling homewares and gifts. Try the delicious macadamia nut brittle.

Hot Water Brewing Co CRAFT BEER
(☑ 07-866 3830; www.hotwaterbrewingco.com; Sea Breeze Holiday Park, 1043 SH25, Whenuakite; ⊘11am-late) Hot Water Brewing Co is a modern craft brewery with lots of outdoor seating. Standout brews include the hoppy Kauri Falls Pale Ale and the robust Walker's Porter. OK bar snacks and pizza are available.

Coroglen Tavern PUB
(☑ 07-866 3809; www.coroglentavern.co.nz; 1937 SH25, Coroglen; ⊘10am-late) The legendary Coroglen Tavern is the archetypal middle-of-nowhere country pub that attracts big-name Kiwi bands in summer.

ℹ Getting There & Away

InterCity (p188) buses linking Thames to Whitianga stop at Whenuakite and Coroglen.

Hahei

POP 270

A legendary Kiwi beach town, little Hahei balloons to 7000 people in summer but is nearly abandoned otherwise – apart from the busloads of tourists doing the obligatory stop-off at Cathedral Cove. It's a charming spot and a great place to unwind for a few days, especially in the quieter months. It takes its name from Hei, the eponymous ancestor of the Ngāti Hei people, who arrived in the 14th century on the Te Arawa canoe. Online, see www.hahei.co.nz.

⦿ Sights

Cathedral Cove BEACH
Beautiful Cathedral Cove, with its famous gigantic stone arch and natural waterfall shower, is best enjoyed early or late in the day – avoiding the worst of the hordes. From the Cathedral Cove car park, around 2km north of Hahei, it's a rolling walk of 30 to 40 minutes. On the way there's rocky **Gemstone Bay**, which has a snorkelling trail where you're likely to see big snapper, crayfish and stingrays, and sandy **Stingray Bay**.

If you walk from Hahei Beach (p197) directly to Cathedral Cove, it will take about 70 minutes. Another option is the 10-minute **Cathedral Cove Water Taxi** (☑ 027 919 0563; www.cathedralcovewatertaxi.co.nz; adult one way/return $15/30, child $10/20; ⊘every 30min).

If you're driving, you're best leaving your car at the **Hahei Park N'Ride Car Park** at the entrance to Hahei village, as over the peak summer months, the Cathedral Cove car park (and the cove itself) can be exceptionally busy. You can either walk the 2km to the Cathedral Cove car park from Hahei, or, from 10am to 6pm, catch a Go Kiwi (p196) shuttle ($5).

Hahei Beach BEACH
Long, lovely Hahei Beach is made more magical by the view to the craggy islands in the distance. From the southern end of Hahei Beach, it's a 15-minute walk up to **Te Pare**, a *pā* (fortified village) site with splendid coastal views.

🏃 Activities

Hahei Beach Bikes CYCLING
(☑ 021 701 093; www.haheibeachbikes.co.nz; bike hire half/full day $35/45) Friendly owner Jonny provides maps with key points of interest and a spade for digging a spa pool at Hot Water Beach. Most times of the year bikes can be picked up from the **Hahei Holiday Park** (41 Harsant Ave), but Jonny can also deliver bikes to travellers arriving at Ferry Landing off the ferry from Whitianga, or to Hahei village.

Cathedral Cove Sea Kayaking KAYAKING
(☑ 07-866 3877; www.seakayaktours.co.nz; 88 Hahei Beach Rd; half/full day $115/190; ⊘8.45am & 1.30pm, additional departures Dec & Jan) This outfit runs guided kayaking trips around the rock arches, caves and islands in the Cathedral Cove (p197) and Mercury Bay area. The Remote Coast Tour heads the other way when conditions permit, visiting caves, blowholes and a long tunnel.

Hahei Explorer
ADVENTURE

(☎07-866 3910; www.haheiexplorer.co.nz; adult/child $95/50) Hour-long jetboat rides touring the coast.

Cathedral Cove Dive & Snorkel
DIVING

(☎07-866 3955; www.hahei.co.nz/diving; 48 Hahei Beach Rd; dives from $99) Offers daily dive trips and rents out scuba gear, snorkelling gear ($25) and boogie boards ($20). A Discover Scuba half-day beginner course costs $240 including all the gear. Check out its website for recommendations on where to snorkel in the area.

🛏 Sleeping

Tatahi Lodge
HOSTEL, MOTEL $

(☎07-866 3992; www.tatahilodge.co.nz; Grange Rd; dm $33, r $84-130, units from $175; @🛜) A wonderful place where backpackers are treated with at least as much care and respect as the lush, bromeliad-filled garden. The dorm rooms and excellent communal facilities are just as attractive as the pricier motel units.

The Church
COTTAGE $$

(☎07-866 3533; www.thechurchhahei.co.nz; 87 Hahei Beach Rd; cottages $150-230; 🛜) 🍴 Set within a subtropical garden, these beautifully kitted out, rustic timber cottages have plenty of character. The switched-on owners are really welcoming and have loads of ideas on what to do and see around the area.

Purangi Garden Accommodation
COTTAGE $$

(☎07-866 4036; www.purangigarden.co.nz; Lees Rd; d $180-200) On a quiet cove on the Purangi River, this relaxing spot has accommodation ranging from comfortable chalets through to larger houses and a spacious, self-contained yurt. Well-established gardens and rolling lawns lead to the water – perfect for swimming and kayaking – and don't be surprised if the friendly owners drop off some organic fruit or freshly baked bread.

🍴 Eating & Drinking

During the peak of summer holidays, New Zealand and international holidaymakers swamp Hahei's cafes and restaurants. But come off-season, the area really does have a 'gone fishing' vibe. The local store remains open and the eateries take it in turns so that there's usually one option open every evening.

The Church
MEDITERRANEAN $$

(☎07-866 3797; www.thechurchbistro.co.nz; 87 Hahei Beach Rd; mains $30-35; ⊙3pm-late, reduced hours Mar-Oct) This charming wooden church is Hahei's swankiest eatery. A concise menu of European-influenced mains includes a French-style soup crammed with local seafood, and braised chicken pot pie with pancetta and peas in a madeira sauce. Definitely leave room for excellent desserts and try and book ahead – especially over summer – as the heritage dining room is relatively compact.

★ Pour House
PUB

(☎07-866 3354; www.coromandelbrewingcompany.co.nz; 7 Grange Rd; ⊙5pm-late Mon-Fri, noon-late Sat & Sun May-Nov, from noon daily Dec-Apr) Home base for the Coromandel Brewing Company, this pub and bistro regularly features around five of its beers in a modern ambience. Platters of meat, cheese and local seafood combine with decent pizzas in the beer garden. Our favourite brew is the Code Red Irish Ale.

❶ Getting There & Away

In the absolute height of summer school holidays the council runs a bus service from the Cooks Beach side of Ferry Landing to Hot Water Beach, stopping at Hahei. Ask at the **Whitianga i-SITE** (p196).

Go Kiwi (p196) runs a daily service linking Hahei and Hot Water Beach to Auckland and Whitianga.

Cathedral Cove Shuttles (☎027 422 5899; www.cathedralcoveshuttles.co.nz; from $15; 🚐) offers a convenient transport service from Ferry Landing to nearby beaches and attractions. Service is by request via phone or text.

From Ferry Landing to Hahei is around 10km. Bikes can be rented from **Hahei Beach Bikes** (p197), with pick-up at **Hahei Holiday Park** (p197).

❶ Getting Around

Go Kiwi (p196) runs a shuttle bus ($5) from 10am to 6pm linking the **Hahei Park N'Ride Car Park** (p197) to the **Cathedral Cove** (p197) car park. **Cathedral Cove Water Taxi** (p197) offers services along the coast from Hahei Beach to the cove.

Hot Water Beach

Justifiably famous, Hot Water Beach is quite extraordinary. For two hours either side of low tide, you can access an area of sand in front of a rocky outcrop at the middle of the beach where hot water oozes up from beneath the surface. Bring a spade, dig a hole and, voila, you've got a personal spa pool. Surfers stop off before the main beach to access some decent breaks. The headland between the two beaches still has traces of a Ngāti Hei *pā* (fortified village).

Sights & Activities

Moko Artspace GALLERY
(07-866 3367; www.moko.co.nz; 24 Pye Pl; 10am-5pm) Near Hot Water Beach, Moko is full of beautiful things – art, sculpture, jewellery – with a modern Pasifika/Māori bent.

Hot Water Beach Store OUTDOORS
(07-866 3006; Pye Pl; 9am-5pm) Spades ($5) can be hired from the Hot Water Beach Store, which has a cafe attached.

Sleeping & Eating

Hot Water Beach

Top 10 Holiday Park HOLIDAY PARK $
(07-866 3116; www.hotwaterbeachtop10.co.nz; 790 Hot Water Beach Rd; campsites from $25, dm $30, units $90-165; @) Bordered by tall bamboo and gum trees, this is a very well-run holiday park with everything from grassy campsites through to a spacious and spotless backpackers lodge and stylish villas with arched ceilings crafted from NZ timber.

Hot Waves CAFE $$
(07-866 3887; 8 Pye Pl; mains $12-26; 8.30am-4pm Mon-Thu & Sun, to 8.30pm Fri & Sat) In summer everyone wants a garden table at this excellent cafe. For a lazy brunch, try the eggs Benedict with smoked salmon or a breakfast burrito. It also hires spades for the beach ($5). Ask about occasional Friday-night music sessions.

Getting There & Away

Cathedral Cove Shuttles (027 422 5899; www.cathedralcoveshuttles.co.nz; per person depending on destination $4-40; 9am-late Dec-Feb, to 10.30pm Mar-Nov) and **Go Kiwi** (p196) both stop here. It's also a popular destination for cyclists leaving from Ferry Landing across the water from Whitianga. Look forward to a rolling ride of around 18km from Ferry Landing to Hot Water Beach.

Tairua & Pauanui
POP 1270

Tairua and its twin town Pauanui sit either side of a river estuary that's perfect for windsurfing or for little kids to splash about in. Both have excellent surf beaches (Pauanui's is

BEACH SAFETY
Hot Water Beach has dangerous rips, especially directly in front of the main thermal section. It's one of the four most dangerous beaches in New Zealand in terms of drowning numbers, although this may be skewed by the huge number of tourists that flock here. Regardless, swimming here is *not* safe if the lifeguards aren't on patrol.

probably a shade better) and both are ridiculously popular in the summertime, but that's where the similarity stops. While Tairua is a functioning residential town (with shops, ATMs and a choice of eateries), Pauanui is an upmarket refuge for Aucklanders. Friendly Tairua knows how to keep it real.

Sights & Activities

Various operators offer fishing charters and sightseeing trips. Enquire at the information centre (p200).

Paaku MOUNTAIN
Around seven million years ago Paaku was a volcanic island, but now it forms the northern head of Tairua's harbour. Ngāti Hei had a *pā* here before being invaded by Ngāti Maru in the 17th century. It's a steep 15-minute walk to the summit from the top of Paku Dr, with the pay-off being amazing views over Tairua, Pauanui and the Alderman Islands. Plaques along the way detail Tairua's colonial history; only one is devoted to its long Māori occupation.

Sleeping

Tairua Backpackers & Beach Villa B&B HOSTEL $
(07-864 8345; www.tairuabackpackers.com; 200 Main Rd; dm $30, s $74-83, d $83-93, f $117-140; @) Rooms are homely and casual at this estuary-edge hostel in a converted house, and the dorm scores great views. Guests can help themselves to fishing rods, kayaks, sailboards and bikes. When we last dropped by the switched-on managers were completing a colourful top-to-toe renovation. Highly recommended.

Pacific Harbour Lodge HOTEL $$
(07-864 8581; www.pacificharbour.co.nz; 223 Main Rd; chalets $170-220; @) This 'island-style' resort in the town centre has spacious self-contained chalets, with natural

wood and Gauguin decor inside and a South Seas garden outside. Discount packages are usually available online.

Sunlover Retreat
B&B $$$

([☎] 07-864 9024; www.sunlover.co.nz; 20 Ridge Rd; d $320-350; [☎]) Enjoy stunning views of Paaku (p199) and Tairua at this stylish B&B high above the harbour. Two of the three suites have private outdoor balconies, and huge picture windows provide plenty of light and space. Decor is chic, modern and dotted with quirky NZ art, and guests receive a warm welcome from Rover, the Sunlover Retreat labradoodle.

✖ Eating

Manaia Kitchen & Bar
CAFE $$

([☎] 07-864 9050; www.manaiakitchenbar.co.nz; 228 Main Rd; mains breakfast $12-18, lunch $17-24, dinner $24-32; [☉] 9am-late Thu-Tue) With courtyard seating for lazy summer brunches and a burnished-copper bar to prop up later in the night, Manaia is the most cosmopolitan spot on the Tairua strip. Interesting menu options include fish tacos and calamari with spicy harissa, and Tairua's most authentic pizzas are prepared by an Italian chef. There's occasional live music and DJs on Friday nights.

Old Mill Cafe
CAFE $$

([☎] 07-864 9390; www.theoldmillcafetairua.com; 1 The Esplanade; mains $15-25; [☉] 8am-4pm Thu-Sun) With colourful walls, elegant veranda furniture and harbour views, the Old Mill Cafe serves interesting cafe fare like Spanish baked eggs for breakfast and Thai prawn curry for lunch. Quite possibly the Coromandel's best muffins too.

❶ Information

Tairua Information Centre ([☎] 07-864 7575; www.thecoromandel.com/tairua; 223 Main Rd; [☉] 9am-5pm) has maps and can help with accommodation and transport bookings.

❶ Getting There & Away

InterCity (www.intercity.co.nz), Naked Bus (www.nakedbus.com) and Go Kiwi (www.go-kiwi.co.nz) all run bus services to Tairua.

Tairua and Pauanui are connected by a **passenger ferry** ([☎] 027-497 0316; $5; [☉] daily Dec & Jan), which departs around every hour from 10am to 4pm across the peak of summer and holiday weekends. In other months the ferry offers a water taxi service.

Opoutere

File this one under Coromandel's best-kept secrets. Apart from a cluster of houses there's nothing for miles around. Swimming can be dangerous, especially near Hikinui Islet, which is close to the beach. On the sand spit is the **Wharekawa Wildlife Refuge**, a breeding ground for the endangered New Zealand dotterel.

🛏 Sleeping

Copsefield
B&B $$

([☎] 07-865 9555; www.copsefield.co.nz; 1055 SH25; r $120-200; [☎]) Copsefield is a peaceful country-style villa set in attractive, lush gardens with a spa and riverside swimming hole. The main house has three attractive B&B rooms, while cheaper accommodation is offered in a separate bach-style cottage.

❶ Getting There & Away

With a change in Hikuai, it's possible to catch the **Go Kiwi** ([☎] 0800 446 549; www.go-kiwi.co.nz) Auckland–Whitianga shuttle to Opoutere.

Whangamata

POP 3560

When Auckland's socially ambitious flock to Pauanui, the city's young and free head to Whangamata to surf, party and hook up. It can be a raucous spot over New Year, when the population swells to more than 40,000. It's a true summer-holiday town, but in the off-season there may as well be tumbleweeds rolling down the main street.

🏃 Activities

Besides fishing (game-fishing runs from January to April), other activities include snorkelling near Hauturu (Clarke) Island, and surfing, orienteering and mountain biking. There are also excellent walks.

Walking

The **Wentworth Falls** walk takes 2½ hours (return); it starts 3km south of the town and 4km down the unsealed Wentworth Valley Rd. A further 3km south of Wentworth Valley Rd is Parakiwai Quarry Rd, at the end of which is the **Wharekirauponga** walk, a sometimes muddy 10km return track (allow 3½ to four hours) to a mining camp, battery and waterfall that passes unusual hexagonal lava columns and loquacious bird life.

Kiwi Dundee Adventures TRAMPING
(☑ 07-865 8809; www.kiwidundee.co.nz) ✎ Styl-
ing himself as a local version of Crocodile
Dundee, Doug Johansen offers informative
one- to 16-day wilderness walks and guided tours in the Coromandel Peninsula and
countrywide.

Water Sports
A popular destination for kayaking and
paddle boarding is **Whenuakura** (Donut
Island). Note that in an effort to boost the
islands' status as wildlife sanctuaries, it's not
permitted to land on them. Boating around
the islands is allowed.

SurfSup WATER SPORTS
(☑ 021 217 1201; www.surfsup.nz; 1 Wharf Rd; half-/
full-day surfboard hire $30/50, kayak from $40/60,
1/2hr paddle board $20/30) Paddle-boarding
and surfing lessons are available, and kayaking and paddle-boarding tours to Whenuakura (Donut Island) run daily from December to March.

☆ Festivals & Events

Whangamata Beach Hop CULTURAL
(www.beachhop.co.nz; ☉ late Mar-early Apr)
This annual celebration of retro American culture – expect hot rods, classic cars,
motorbikes and rock and roll music – is a
great time to be in town. Dust off the classic white T-shirt and leather jacket combo,
pile high the beehive hairdo, but definitely
book accommodation if you're planning on
attending.

🛏 Sleeping

Surf n Stay NZ HOSTEL $
(☑ 07-865 8323; http://surfnstaynewzealand.com;
227 Beverly Tce; dm $34-36, s $60, d $120; 🛜) In
a quiet street a block from the waves, this
hostel owned by a friendly Kiwi-Brazilian
couple has dorms and private rooms that
are clean and comfortable. Cooked breakfast
included. There's also the option of surfing
and paddle-boarding lessons (from $70),
hire of paddle boards, surfboards and kayaks (from $20), and longer surf camps, some
incorporating yoga.

Breakers MOTEL $$
(☑ 07-865 8464; www.breakersmotel.co.nz; 324
Hetherington Rd; units $185-245; 🛜🏊) Fac-
ing the marina on the Tairua approach to
Whangamata, this newish motel features
an enticing swimming pool, and spa pools
on the decks of the upstairs units.

OFF THE BEATEN TRACK

WENTWORTH VALLEY CAMPSITE
More upmarket than most DOC camping grounds, **Wentworth Valley
Campsite** (☑ 07-865 7032; www.doc.
govt.nz; 474 Wentworth Valley Rd; adult/
child $13/6.50) is accessed from the
Wentworth Falls (p200) walk and has
toilets, showers and gas barbecues.

Southpacific Accommodation MOTEL $$
(☑ 07-865 9580; www.thesouthpacific.co.nz; 249
Port Rd; units $150-180; @🛜) This hard-to-
miss, corner-hogging complex consists of a
cafe and warmly decorated, self-contained
motel units. Facilities are clean and modern.
Bikes and kayaks are available for hire.

🍴 Eating & Drinking

Soul Burger BURGERS $
(☑ 07-865 8194; www.soulburger.co.nz; 441 Port
Rd; burgers $11-17; ☉ 5pm-late Wed-Sun, daily Dec-
Feb) Serving audacious burgers with names
like Soul Blues Brother and Vegan Vibe, this
hip corner joint is also licensed so you can
have an ice-cold beer with your burger.

★ Port Road Project CAFE $$
(☑ 07-865 7288; www.facebook.com/portroad
project; 719 Port Rd; mains $15-25; ☉ 8am-3pm Thu-
Mon, longer hours Dec-Feb; 🍷) ✎ Sleek Scandi
style makes the new Port Road Project a
standout in sleepy Whanga. Join the locals
on the sunny, shared tables and partner the
all-day menu with fine coffee, Hamilton craft
beer and cider, and a good wine list. Ask about
occasional evening openings – especially over
summer – offering innovative shared plates
or feasts from the American-style barbecue.

Argo Restaurant MODERN NZ $$
(☑ 07-865 7157; www.argorestaurant.co.nz; 328
Ocean Rd; mains $26-35; ☉ 5-9.30pm Mon, Thu &
Fri, 2-10pm Sat & Sun, daily late Dec-early Feb; 🛜)
Whangamata's classiest restaurant offers a
concise and evolving menu of bistro classics
that might feature twice-cooked pork belly or
confit duck leg. Starters to look for include
sautéed scallops and prawns or fresh oysters.
The airy deck is perfect for a few lazy afternoon tipples of NZ craft beer or wine. During
the height of summer, hours are extended.

Lincoln PUB
(☑ 07-865 6338; www.facebook.com/thelincoln
whangamata; 501 Port Rd; ☉ 5pm-late Tue-Fri,

11am-late Sat) Part pub, part bistro, part cafe and all-round good times feature at this versatile spot on Whangamata's main drag. DJs kick in on summer weekends.

ℹ Information

Whangamata Info Plus (☑ 07-865 8340; www.thecoromandel.com/whangamata; 616 Port Rd; ☺ 9am-5pm Mon-Fri, 9.30am-3.30pm Sat & Sun) is staffed by a friendly and well-informed team.

ℹ Getting There & Away

Go Kiwi (☑ 0800 446 549; www.go-kiwi.co.nz) has a shuttle service to Auckland ($75, 3½ hours, one daily) and to other parts of the Coromandel region.

Waihi & Waihi Beach

POP 4527 & 1935

Gold and silver have been dragged out of Waihi's Martha Mine, New Zealand's richest, since 1878. The town formed quickly thereafter and blinged itself up with grand buildings and an avenue of impressive phoenix palms.

After closing down in 1952, open-cast mining restarted in 1988, and proposals to harness the potential of other nearby mines forecast mining to continue to around 2020. Another more low-key bonanza is also taking place, with Waihi an integral part of the excellent Hauraki Rail Trail (p203).

While Waihi is interesting for a brief visit, it's Waihi Beach where you'll want to linger. The two places are as dissimilar as surfing is from mining, separated by 11km of farmland. The long sandy beach stretches 9km to Bowentown, on the northern limits of Tauranga Harbour, where you'll find sheltered beaches such as beautiful **Anzac Bay**. There's a popular 45-minute walk north through bush to pristine **Orokawa Bay**.

◉ Sights

Waihi's main drag, Seddon St, has interesting sculptures, information panels about Waihi's golden past and roundabouts that look like squashed daleks. Opposite the visitor centre (p203), the skeleton of a derelict **Cornish Pumphouse** (1904) is the town's main landmark, atmospherically lit at night. From here the **Pit Rim Walkway** has fascinating views into the 250m-deep **Martha Mine**.

The *Historic Hauraki Gold Towns* pamphlet (free from the visitor centre) outlines walking tours of both Waihi and Paeroa.

★**Gold Discovery Centre** MUSEUM
(☑ 07-863 9015; www.golddiscoverycentre.co.nz; 126 Seddon St, Waihi; adult/child $25/13; ☺ 9am-5pm, to 4pm Apr-Nov) Waihi's superb Gold Discovery Centre tells the area's gold-mining past, present and future through interactive displays, focusing on the personal and poignant to tell interesting stories. Holograms and short movies both feature, drawing visitors in and informing them through entertainment. Good luck in taking on the grizzled miner at 'virtual' Two-Up (a gambling game using coins).

Waihi Arts Centre & Museum MUSEUM
(☑ 07-863 8386; www.waihimuseum.co.nz; 54 Kenny St, Waihi; adult/child $5/3; ☺ 10am-3pm Thu & Fri, noon-3pm Sat-Mon, reduced hours Apr-Nov) The Waihi Arts Centre and Museum has an art gallery and displays focusing on the region's gold-mining history. Prepare to squirm before the collection of miners' chopped-off thumbs preserved in glass jars.

Athenree Hot Springs HOT SPRINGS
(☑ 07-863 5600; www.athenreehotsprings.co.nz; 1 Athenree Rd, Athenree; adult/child $7/5.50; ☺ 10am-7pm) ⚑ In cooler months, retreat to these two small but blissful outdoor hot pools, hidden within a **holiday park** (campsite from $54, unit $85-175; @ � 🛏) ⚑.

🏃 Activities

Waihi Bicycle Hire CYCLING
(☑ 07-863 8418; www.waihibicyclehire.co.nz; 25 Seddon St, Waihi; bike hire half/full day from $30/40; ☺ 8am-5pm) Bike hire and loads of information on the Waihi end of the Hauraki Rail Trail. Fun tandems and efficient e-bikes are both available.

Goldfields Railway RAIL
(☑ 07-863 8251; www.waihirail.co.nz; 30 Wrigley St, Waihi; adult/child return $20/12, bikes per route extra $2; ☺ departs Waihi 10am, 11.45am & 1.45pm Sat, Sun & public holidays) Vintage trains depart Waihi for a 7km, 30-minute scenic journey to Waikino. It's possible to take bikes on the train so they can be used to further explore the Karangahake Gorge section of the Hauraki Rail Trail. The timetable varies seasonally so check the website.

Waihi Gold Mine Tours TOURS
(☑ 07-863 9015; www.golddiscoverycentre.co.nz/tours; Gold Discovery Centre, 126 Seddon St, Waihi; adult/child $34/17; ☺ 10am & 12.30pm, additional tours Dec-Feb) To get down into the

Waikato & King Country

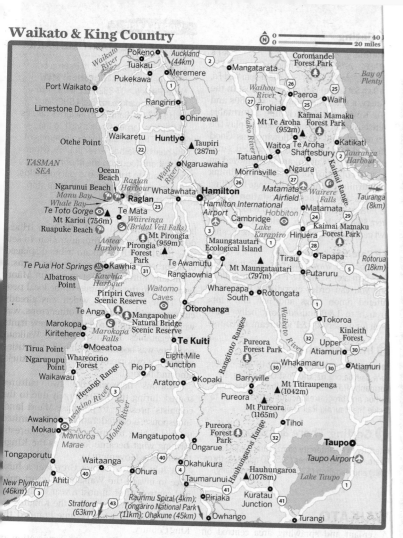

spectacular Martha Mine, join a 1½-hour Waihi Gold Mine Tour departing from the Gold Discovery Centre.

🛏 Sleeping

The best place to be located is near the ocean at Waihi Beach or pretty Bowentown.

Bowentown Beach
Holiday Park   HOLIDAY PARK $
(☎ 07-863 5381; www.bowentown.co.nz; 510 Seaforth Rd, Waihi Beach; campsites from $50, units $85-195; @🕾) Having nabbed a stunning stretch of sand, this impressively maintained holiday park makes the most of it with first-rate motel units and camping facilities.

Beachfront B&B   B&B $$
(☎ 07-863 5393; www.beachfrontbandb.co.nz; 3 Shaw Rd, Waihi Beach; r $140) True to its name with absolute beachfront and spectacular sea views, this comfortable downstairs flat has a TV, fridge and direct access to the surf. It's also just a short stroll to an excellent oceanfront cafe.

Waihi Beach Lodge   B&B $$$
(☎ 07-863 5818; www.waihibeachlodge.co.nz; 170 Seaforth Ave, Waihi Beach; d $295; 🕾) A short stroll from the beach, this accommodation features colourful and modern rooms, and a studio apartment with its own kitchenette. Legendary breakfasts are often served on the sunny deck. Ask friendly owners Greg and Ali how they're going with their homemade honey and limoncello, and look forward to sampling both. Chatty Greg is a great source of local information.

🍴 Eating

Ti-Tree Cafe & Wine Bar   CAFE $
(☎ 07-863 8668; 14 Haszard St, Waihi; mains $12-20; ⊙6.30am-2.30pm Mon-Fri, 8am-2.30pm Sat & Sun; 🕾) Housed in a cute little wooden building with punga-shaded outdoor seating, Ti-Tree serves fair-trade organic coffee, cooked breakfasts and delicious fruit sorbets and ice cream during summer. Occasional live music on Sunday afternoons.

★ Surf Shack   CAFE $$
(☎ 07-863 4353; www.surfshackcafe.co.nz; 123 Emerton Rd, Waihi Beach; mains $10-22; ⊙9am-2.30pm Wed-Sun; 🗐) On the outskirts of Waihi Beach, the Surf Shack is definitely worth a detour for its plate-filling salads and quite possibly the best burgers in New Zealand. Other menu highlights include snacks inspired by

the street food of Mexico, Greece and Southeast Asia, and the drinks list combining NZ craft beer, kombucha and organic cold-press juices ticks all the boxes.

Flatwhite   CAFE $$
(☎ 07-863 1346; www.flatwhitecafe.co.nz; 21 Shaw Rd, Waihi Beach; mains brunch $13-24, dinner $23-39; ⊙8am-10pm; 🕾) Funky, licensed and right by Waihi Beach, Flatwhite has a lively brunch menu, decent pizzas and flash burgers. Our favourite off the dinner menu is the dukkah-rubbed salmon with harissa yoghurt. The best place to sit is on the spacious deck or oceanfront lawn as you combine a frosty beer or chilled white wine with brilliant Pacific views.

ℹ Information

Waihi i-SITE (☎ 07-863 9015; www.waihi.org.nz; 126 Seddon St, Waihi; ⊙9am-5pm, to 4pm Apr-Nov) has local information and houses the interesting **Gold Discovery Centre** (p202), a modern and interactive showcase of the gold-flecked past, present and future of the Waihi region. There's also a good **information centre** (www.waihibeachinfo.co.nz; Wilson Rd, Waihi Beach; ⊙10am-3pm). It's volunteer-run, so hours can be flexible.

HAURAKI RAIL TRAIL

The Hauraki Rail Trail, which runs from Thames south to Paeroa, and then further south to Te Aroha, or east to Waihi, is growing in popularity due to its proximity to the bigger cities of Auckland and Hamilton. Two- and three-day itineraries are most popular, but shorter sections of the trail can be very rewarding too. The spur from Paeroa east through the Karangahake Gorge via Waikino to Waihi is spectacular as it skirts a picturesque river valley. The key centres of Thames, Paeroa, Te Aroha and Waihi have an expanding range of related services including bike hire, shuttles and accommodation.

See www.haurakirailtrail.co.nz for detailed information including trail maps and recommendations for day rides. At the time of research, planning was underway to extend the trail west from Kopu around the Firth of Thames via Miranda to Kaiaua. Check the website for the latest.

---

ase for tramping or 'taking the waters' in the wn's therapeutic thermal springs (p206). 's also the southern trailhead on the Haura Rail Trail. The sleepy main street is good r trawling for quirky antiques and vintage othing and accessories. Many of the town's tractions are arrayed around Te Aroha's afy hillside Domain.

⊙ Sights & Activities

Aroha Museum   MUSEUM
07-884 4427; www.tearoha-museum.com; Te ha Domain; adult/child $5/2; ⊙11am-4pm Nov-r, noon-3pm Apr-Oct) In the town's ornate

former thermal sanatorium (aka the 'Treasure of Te Aroha'). Displays include quirky ceramics, old spa-water bottles, historical photos and an old printing press.

Te Aroha Mineral Spas   SPA
(☎ 07-884 8717; www.tearohamineralspas.co.nz; Boundary St, Te Aroha Domain; 30min session adult/child $19/11; ⊙10.30am-9pm Mon-Fri, to 10pm Sat & Sun) In the Edwardian Hot Springs Domain, this spa offers private tubs, massage, beauty therapies and aromatherapy. Also here is the temperamental Mokena Geyser – the world's only known soda geyser – which

Getting There & Away

Waihi is serviced by **InterCity** (p216) buses, which head to Hamilton ($33, 2½ hours), Tauranga ($19, one hour) and Thames ($15, 50 minutes).

Karangahake Gorge

The road between Waihi and Paeroa, through the bush-lined ramparts of the Karangahake Gorge, is one of the best short drives in the country. Walking and biking tracks take in old Māori trails, historic mining and rail detritus, and dense bush. In Māori legend the area is said to be protected by a *taniwha* (supernatural creature). The local *iwi* managed to keep this area closed to miners until 1875, aligning themselves with the militant Te Kooti.

Sights

Victoria Battery Tramway & Museum
HISTORIC SITE
(☎ 027 351 8980; www.vbts.org.nz; Waikino; ☉10am-3pm Wed, Sun & public holidays) Across the river from the Waikino train station, the Victoria Battery Tramway & Museum is the former site of the biggest quartz-ore processing plant in Australasia. There's a dinky tram ride and regular guided tours of the underground kilns.

Sleeping & Eating

Falls Retreat
COTTAGE $$
(☎ 07-212 8087; www.fallsretreat.co.nz/accommodation; 25 Waitawheta Rd; d $150) Falls Retreat has two accommodation options. Rose Cottage features a cosy bedroom upstairs, a lounge with a log fire downstairs and a self-contained kitchenette. French doors lead out onto a private patio. Incorporating a mezzanine bedroom, the more private and romantic Waterfall Cabin has views of Owharoa Falls. A cooked breakfast at both is an additional $30 per couple.

★ Bistro at the Falls Retreat
CAFE $$
(☎ 07-863 8770; www.fallsretreat.co.nz; 25 Waitawheta Rd; pizzas $24-26, mains $30-40; ☉11am-10pm Wed-Sun; ▣) The Bistro at the Falls Retreat (p204) is located in a wooden cottage under a shaded canopy of trees. Gourmet pizzas and rustic meat dishes emerge from the wood-fired oven on a regular basis, and there's a great little playground for the kids. An excellent wine and craft beer list keeps the older patrons entertained.

Ohinemuri Estate Winery
CAFE $$
(☎ 07-862 8874; www.ohinemuri.co.nz; Moresby St; mains $16-33, shared platters $45; ☉10am-4pm Wed-Sun) Ohinemuri Estate Winery has Latvian-influenced architecture and serves excellent lunches – shared platters, seafood, soups and vegetarian dishes all feature. You'd be right if you thought it was an unusual site for growing grapes – the fruit is imported from other regions. Tastings are $5, refundable with purchase.

If you imbibe too much, snaffle the chalet-style hut ($135 per night) and revel in the charming atmosphere of this secluded place.

Waikino Station Cafe
CAFE $
(☎ 07-863 8640; www.facebook.com/waikinostationcafe; SH2; mains $10-20; ☉10am-3pm Mon-Fri, 9.30am-4pm Sat & Sun) The Waikino terminus of the Goldfields Railway (p202) has a friendly cafe with good burgers and counter food. Bikes can be hired here for $45 if you're keen to explore the scenic Karangahake Gorge section of the Hauraki Rail Trail.

Getting There & Away

Goldfields Railway (p202) trains link Waihi to Waikino from where it is an interesting and mainly flat bike ride on a very scenic spur of the Hauraki Rail Trail through the Karangahake Gorge. Otherwise this route is best driven.

Paeroa

POP 3980

Paeroa is the birthplace of Lemon & Paeroa (L&P), an icon of Kiwiana that markets itself as 'world famous in New Zealand'. Ironically, the fizzy drink is now owned by Coca-Cola Amatil and produced in Auckland. Still, generations of Kiwi kids have pestered their parents to take this route just to catch a glimpse of the giant L&P bottles. See www.paeroa.org.nz for the full story of this iconic Kiwi tipple. For fans of yesteryear, Paeroa's main street has a few excellent vintage and antique shops.

Sights

Paeroa Museum
MUSEUM
(☎ 07-862 8942; 37 Belmont Rd; adult/child $2/1; ☉noon-3pm Tue-Fri) This small museum has a grand selection of Royal Albert porcelain and other pioneer and Māori artefacts – look in the drawers.

Eating

★ Refinery
CAFE $
(☎ 07-862 7678; www.the-refinery.co.nz; 5 Willoughby St; snacks $8-14; ☉8.30am-4pm Wed-Fri, from 9am Sat & Sun) Get pleasantly lost in the Refinery, a spacious showcase of 1960s and 1970s Kiwiana style including a turntable where customers are encouraged to play the vinyl records that fill overflowing bins. Good coffee and food (especially the grilled sandwiches – try the Cuban) are best enjoyed on the retro collection of old sofas and dining room furniture filling this heritage building.

There's stylish **accommodation** (☎07-862 7678; www.the-refinery.co.nz; 5 Willoughby St; d from $99; ▣) here too. Welcome to a true Kiwi gem and one of the country's best cafes.

L&P Cafe, Bar & Brasserie
CAFE $$
(☎ 07-862 6753; www.lpcafe.co.nz; SH2; mains $11-20; ☉8am-late) At the L&P Cafe, Bar & Brasserie you can order everything from L&P-battered onion rings and fish and chips through to L&P-braised pork belly. Leave room for dessert of L&P ice cream. Of course.

Information

Paeroa Information Centre (☎ 07-862 6999; www.paeroa.org.nz; Old Post Office Bldg, 101 Normanby Rd; ☉9am-5pm Mon-Fri) has information and brochures including one on how to tackle the Hauraki Rail Trail.

Getting There & Away

InterCity (www.intercity.co.nz) runs buses to Paeroa linking to Thames ($15, 30 minutes, three daily) and Hamilton ($25, five hours, one daily).

WAIKATO

A verdant and sprawling area centred on the city of Hamilton, the Waikato region is renowned throughout New Zealand as dairy farming country. Highlights for travellers include the excellent restaurants, bars and cafes of its biggest (only) city, the surf and cafe scene at laid-back Raglan, and the Middle Earth vibe of the extremely popular Hobbiton (p209) film set near Matamata. To escape the Tolkien fans, take a trip off the beaten track to the excellent Sanctuary Mountain Maungatautari (p209).

History

By the time Europeans started to arrive, this region – stretching as far north as Auckland's Manukau Harbour – had long

WORTH A TRIP

HISTORICAL MARITIME PARK

Around 3km northwest of Paeroa on SH2, the excellent **Historical Maritime Park** (☎ 07-862 7121; www.historicalmaritimepark.co.nz; 6894 SH2; adult/child $5/2; ☉10am-3pm) includes details of Captain James Cook's visit to the Firth of Thames and his explorations of the nearby Waihou River in 1769. Other exhibitions focus on the importance of river trade to the Coromandel goldfield. The museum is definitely worth a stop while travelling north or south.

been the homeland of the Waikato tr descended from the Tainui migration. tling this land, the Waikato tribes disp or absorbed tribes from earlier migrati

Initially European contact was on terms and to the advantage of the loca ple. Their fertile land, which was al cultivated with kumara and other crop well suited to the introduction of new and vegetables. By the 1840s the Wa economy was booming, with bulk qua of produce exported to the settlers in land and beyond.

Relations between the two cu soured during the 1850s, largely due colonists' pressure to purchase Māori In response, a confederation of tribes to elect a king to safeguard their int forming what became known as the tanga (King Movement).

In July 1863 Governor Grey sent force to invade the Waikato and exer nial control. After almost a year of fi known as the Waikato War, the King treated south to what became bran King Country.

The war resulted in the confisca 3600 sq km of land, much of which v en to colonial soldiers to farm and def 1995 the Waikato tribes received a full apology for the wrongful invasion and cation of their lands, as well as a $170 package, including the return of land Crown still held.

Te Aroha

POP 3800

Te Aroha has a great vibe. You could that it's got 'the love', which is the litera ing of the name. Tucked under the e the bush-clad Mt Te Aroha (952m), it'

blows its top around every 40 minutes, shooting water 3m into the air (the most ardent eruptions are between noon and 2pm). Book ahead for spas and treatments.

Swim Zone Te Aroha SWIMMING
(☑ 07-884 4498; www.swimzonepools.co.nz; Boundary St, Te Aroha Domain; adult/child $6/4; ☺ 10am-5pm) Outdoor heated freshwater pools, a thermal bathhouse and a pool for toddlers.

Mt Te Aroha TRAMPING, MOUNTAIN BIKING
Trails up Mt Te Aroha start at the top of the domain. It's a 45-minute climb to Bald Spur/Whakapipi Lookout (350m), then another 2.7km (two hours) to the summit. Ask at the i-SITE (p207) about mountain-bike trails.

🛏 Sleeping

Te Aroha Holiday Park HOLIDAY PARK $
(☑ 07-884 9567; www.tearohaholidaypark.co.nz; 217 Stanley Rd; campsites from $20, on-site vans s/d $30/45, cabins & units $65-110; @ 🕸 🥽) Wake up to a bird orchestra among the oaks at this site equipped with a grass tennis court, gym and hot pool, 2km southwest of town.

★ Aroha Mountain Lodge LODGE, B&B $$
(☑ 07-884 8134; www.arohamountainlodge.co.nz; 5 Boundary St; s/d/cottage $135/145/320) Spread over two lovely Edwardian villas on the hillside above town, the plush Mountain Lodge offers affordable luxury (*sooo* much nicer than a regulation motel) and optional breakfast ($20 per person). The self-contained Chocolate Box sleeps six to eight.

Te Aroha Motel MOTEL $$
(☑ 07-884 9417; www.tearohamotel.co.nz; 108 Whitaker St; units $129-140; 🕸) Old-fashioned but reasonably priced and tidy units with kitchenettes, right in the centre of town.

🍴 Eating

Domain Cottage Cafe CAFE $
(☑ 07-884 9222; Whitaker St, Te Aroha Domain; snacks & mains $8-22; ☺ 9am-3pm Tue-Sun) Very pleasant daytime cafe in the heritage surroundings of the Te Aroha Domain. Definitely worthy of a stop for coffee and cake even if you're only passing through town. The stonking lamb sandwich is perfect after hiking or biking on nearby Mt Te Aroha.

Ironique CAFE $$
(☑ 07-884 8489; www.ironique.co.nz; 159 Whitaker St; mains $10-35; ☺ 8am-4pm Mon-Wed, to late Thu-Sun) Come for a coffee and a restorative breakfast of eggs Benedict after tackling the Hauraki Rail Trail, or pork belly or pumpkin risotto for dinner. Don't overlook venturing to the quiet courtyard out the back for a few drinks.

ℹ Information

Ask about walking trails on **Mt Te Aroha** and other local sights at **Te Aroha i-SITE** (☑ 07-884 8052; www.tearohanz.co.nz; 102 Whitaker St; ☺ 9.30am-5pm Mon-Fri, to 4pm Sat & Sun).

MĀORI WAIKATO

The Waikato and King Country region remains one of the strongest pockets of Māori influence in New Zealand. This is the heartland of the Tainui tribes, descended from those who disembarked from the Tainui *waka* (canoe) in Kawhia in the 14th century. Split into four main tribal divisions (Waikato, Hauraki, Ngāti Maniapoto and Ngāti Raukawa), Tainui are inextricably linked with the Kīngitanga (King Movement), which has its base in Ngaruawahia.

The best opportunities to interact with Māori culture is Ngaruawahia's Regatta Day and Koroneihana celebrations. Interesting *taonga* (treasures) are displayed at museums in Hamilton and Te Awamutu.

Reminders of the Waikato Land War can be found at Rangiriri, Rangiaowhia and Orakau. See www.thewaikatowar.co.nz to download maps, audio files and a smartphone app covering various locations of the fighting from 1863 to 1864.

Dozens of *marae* (meeting house) complexes are dotted around the countryside – including at Awakino, and at Kawhia, where the Tainui *waka* is buried. You won't be able to visit these without permission, but you can get decent views from the gates. Some regional tours include an element of Māori culture, including **Ruakuri Cave** (p225) at Waitomo.

Although it has a long and rich Māori history, the nearby Coromandel Peninsula doesn't offer many opportunities to engage with the culture. Historic *pā* (fortified village) sites are dotted around, with the most accessible being **Paaku** (p199). There are others at Opito Beach, Hahei and Hot Water Beach.

ℹ Getting There & Away

Te Aroha is on SH26, 21km south of Paeroa and 55km northeast of Hamilton. Waikato Regional Council's **Busit!** (☑ 0800 4287 5463; www. busit.co.nz) runs to/from Hamilton (adult/child $8.40/4.20, one hour, weekdays at 5.15pm). Te Aroha is also a stop on Monday to Friday shuttle services provided by **Coromandel Adventures** (p189) linking Coromandel Town and Rotorua.

Matamata

POP 7800

Matamata was just one of those pleasant, horsey country towns you drove through until Peter Jackson's epic film trilogy *The Lord of the Rings* put it on the map. During filming, 300 locals got work as extras (hairy feet weren't a prerequisite).

Following the subsequent filming of *The Hobbit*, the town has now ardently embraced its Middle Earth credentials, including a spooky statue of Gollum, and given the local information centre an appropriate extreme makeover.

Most tourists who come to Matamata are dedicated Hobbit-botherers. For everyone else there's a great cafe, avenues of mature trees and undulating green hills.

◉ Sights & Activities

Wairere Falls
WATERFALL

About 15km northeast of Matamata are the spectacular 153m Wairere Falls, the highest on the North Island. From the car park it's a 45-minute walk through native bush to the lookout or a steep 1½-hour climb to the summit.

Firth Tower
MUSEUM, HISTORIC BUILDING

(☑ 07-888 8369; www.firthtower.co.nz; Tower Rd; grounds free, buildings adult/child $10/5; ☺ grounds 10am-4pm daily, buildings 10am-4pm Thu-Mon) Firth Tower was built by Auckland businessman Josiah Firth in 1882. The 18m concrete tower was then a fashionable status symbol; now it's filled with Māori and pioneer artefacts. Ten other historic buildings are set around the tower, including a school room, church and jail. It's 3km east of town.

Opal Hot Springs
HOT SPRINGS

(☑ 0800 800 198; www.opalhotsprings.co.nz; 257 Okauia Springs Rd; adult/child $8/4, 30min private spas $10/5; ☺ 9am-9pm) Opal Hot Springs isn't nearly as glamorous as it sounds, but it does have three large thermal pools. Turn off just

north of Firth Tower and follow the road for 2km. There's a holiday park here, too.

🛏 Sleeping

Matamata Backpackers
HOSTEL $

(☑ 07-880 9745; www.matamatabackpackers. co.nz; 61 Firth St; dm/r $28/70; ☏) Handily located a short walk from the bus departure point to Hobbiton (p209), this well-run and welcoming 2017 opening offers the best value beds around town. Colourful bed linen enlivens the simply decorated dorms and private rooms, and hostel facilities include spacious shared common areas.

Broadway Motel & Miro Court Villas
MOTEL $$

(☑ 07-888 8482; www.broadwaymatamata.co.nz; 128 Broadway; d $115-185, 2-bedroom apt $290; @ 🖨) This sprawling family-run motel complex has spread from a well-maintained older-style block to progressively newer and flasher blocks set back from the street. The nicest are the chic apartment-style Miro Court villas.

🍴 Eating & Drinking

Workman's Cafe Bar
CAFE $$

(☑ 07-888 5498; 52 Broadway; mains $12-33; ☺ 7.30am-10pm Wed-Sun) Truly eccentric (old transistor radios dangling from the ceiling, a wall full of art-deco mirrors, Johnny Cash on the stereo), this funky eatery has built itself a reputation that extends beyond Matamata. It's also a decent bar later at night.

Redoubt Bar & Eatery
PUB

(☑ 07-888 8585; www.redoubtbarandeatery.co.nz; 48 Broadway; ☺ 11am-1am) Look forward to thin-crust pizzas named after *LOTR* characters, a winning salmon and hash stack, occasional movie nights in the adjacent laneway, and live music most weekends. It's also a mini-shrine to all things sporty and Matamata-related, and a few interesting tap beers definitely hit the spot.

ℹ Information

Matamata i-SITE (☑ 07-888 7260; www. matamatanz.co.nz; 45 Broadway; ☺ 9am-5pm) is housed in a wonderful Hobbit gatehouse. Hobbiton tours leave from here.

ℹ Getting There & Away

Matamata is on SH27, 20km north of Tirau. **InterCity** (☑ 09-583 5780; www.intercity.co.nz) runs to Cambridge ($15, 40 minutes, two daily), Hamilton ($15, one hour, three daily), Rotorua ($28, one hour, two daily) and Tauranga ($25, one hour, two daily). **Naked Bus** (☑09-979 1616; https://nakedbus.com) offers similar services, plus a bus to Auckland ($17, 3½ hours, two daily).

Coromandel Adventures (p189) runs a Monday to Friday shuttle service from Coromandel Town to Rotorua, stopping at Matamata en route.

Maungatautari

Can a landlocked volcano become an island paradise? Inspired by the success of pest eradication and native species reintroduction in Auckland's Hauraki Gulf, pest-proof fencing has been installed around the three peaks of Maungatautari (797m) to create the impressive Sanctuary Mountain Maungatautari.

Hiking through the mountain's pristine native forest (around six hours) is a popular activity, and shorter guided tours are available from the visitor centre. Fauna-related attractions include two only-in-NZ species: the tuatara and the kiwi. Accommodation and trailhead transport can be provided by Out in the Styx.

◉ Sights

Sanctuary Mountain
Maungatautari　　　WILDLIFE RESERVE, FOREST
(☑07-870 5180; www.sanctuarymountain.co.nz; 99 Tari Rd, Pukeatua; adult/child $20/8) A community trust has erected 47km of pest-proof fencing around the triple peaks of Maungatautari (797m) to create the impressive Sanctuary Mountain Maungatautari. This atoll of rainforest dominates the skyline between Te Awamutu and Karapiro and is now home to its first kiwi chicks in 100 years. There is also a 'tuatarium', where New Zealand's iconic reptile the tuatara can be seen. The main entrance is at the visitor centre at the sanctuary's southern side.

Guided tours (adult/child $37/16) leaving from the visitor centre from Tuesday to Sunday include an afternoon wetlands tour, and morning and afternoon departures explore the bird and insect life of the sanctuary's Southern Enclosure. Online or phone bookings for guided tours must be made at least 24 hours in advance. Guided night walks are also available.

⌂ Sleeping

Out in the Styx　　　LODGE, HOSTEL $$$
(☑07-872 4505; www.styx.co.nz; 2117 Arapuni Rd, Pukeatua; dm/s/d $125/185/320) Out in the

HOBBITON

Due to copyright, all the movie sets around NZ were dismantled after the filming of *The Lord of the Rings*, but Hobbiton's owners negotiated to keep their hobbit holes, which were then rebuilt for the filming of *The Hobbit*. **Hobbiton Movie Set Tours** (☑0508 446 224 866, 07-888 1505; www.hobbitontours.com; 501 Buckland Rd, Hinuera; adult/child tours $84/42, dinner tours $195/152.50; ☺tours 10am-4.30pm) include a drink at the wonderful Green Dragon Inn. Free transfers leave from the Matamata i-SITE (p208) – check timings on the Hobbiton website. Booking ahead is strongly recommended. The popular Evening Dinner Tours on Sunday and Wednesday include a banquet dinner.

To get to Hobbiton with your own transport, head towards Cambridge from Matamata, turn right into Puketutu Rd and then left into Buckland Rd, stopping at the Shire's Rest Cafe.

Styx is near the southern end of the Maungatautari (p209) guided day- and night-walk options. The three stylishly furnished rooms are especially nice, plus there are bunk rooms and a spa for soothing weary legs. Prices include a four-course dinner and breakfast.

Drop-off and pick-up services ($10 per person, minimum $40) are available if you wish to walk across the mountain (around six hours).

❶ Getting There & Away

There is no public transport. Most travellers visit from Te Awamutu, Hamilton or Cambridge. See www.sanctuarymountain.co.nz for the best way to approach the sanctuary from these centres.

Cambridge

POP 15,200
The name says it all. Despite the rambunctious Waikato River looking nothing like the Cam, the good people of Cambridge have done all they can to assume an air of English gentility with village greens and tree-lined avenues.

Cambridge is famous for the breeding and training of thoroughbred horses. Equine references are rife in public sculpture, and plaques boast of past Melbourne

Cup winners. It's also an emerging dining destination, with some excellent eateries worth the short drive from Hamilton.

◉ Sights

Jubilee Gardens GARDEN, MONUMENT

(Victoria St) Apart from its Spanish Mission town clock, Jubilee Gardens is a whole-hearted tribute to the 'mother country'. A British lion guards the cenotaph, with a plaque that reads 'Tell Britain ye who mark this monument faithful to her we fell and rest content'. Across the road in leafy Victoria Sq, a farmers market (p211) is held every Saturday morning.

Cambridge Museum MUSEUM

(☑07-827 3319; www.cambridgemuseum.org.nz; 24 Victoria St; by donation; ⊙10am-4pm Mon-Fri, to 2pm Sat & Sun) In a former courthouse, the quirky Cambridge Museum has plenty of pioneer relics, a military history room and a range of local history displays.

Lake Karapiro LAKE

(☑07-827 4178; www.waipadc.govt.nz; Maungatautari Rd) Eight kilometres southeast of Cambridge, Lake Karapiro is the furthest downstream of a chain of eight hydroelectric power stations on the Waikato River. It's an impressive sight, especially when driving across the top of the 1947 dam. The 21km-long lake is also a world-class rowing venue.

🏃 Activities

Te Awa CYCLING, WALKING

(The Great New Zealand River Ride; www.te-awa.org.nz) The Te Awa cycling and walking path meanders for 70km along the Waikato River, from Ngaruawahia north of Hamilton, to Horahora south of the city. It's a flat and scenic route. Highlights include riding from the Avantidrome in Cambridge – a training hub for NZ's elite cycling athletes – south to the shores of Lake Karapiro. See the website for details.

Boatshed Kayaks KAYAKING

(☑07-827 8286; www.theboatshed.net.nz; The Boatshed, 21 Amber Lane; single/double kayak 3hr $20/40, paddle board 2hr $40; ⊙9am-5pm Wed-Sun) Boatshed Kayaks has basic kayaks and paddle boards for hire. You can paddle to a couple of waterfalls in around an hour. There are also guided kayak trips (adult/child $110/75) at twilight to see a glow-

worm canyon up the nearby Pokewhaenua stream; bookings are essential. See the website for other guided kayaking on Lake Karapiro and the Waikato River.

Waikato River Trails CYCLING, WALKING

(www.waikatorivertrails.com) The 103km Waikato River Trails track is part of the Nga Haerenga, New Zealand Cycle Trail (www.nzcycletrail.com) project. Winding south and east from near Cambridge – beginning at the Pokaiwhenua Bridge – the trails pass Lake Karapiro (p210) and go into the South Waikato area to end at the Atiamuri Dam.

Heritage & Tree Trail WALKING

This self-guided Cambridge walking tour includes the Waikato River, the 1881 St Andrew's Anglican Church (look for the Gallipoli window) and leafy Te Koutu lake. Grab a map at the Cambridge i-SITE (p211).

🛏 Sleeping

Cambridge Coach House B&B, CABIN $$

(☑07-823 7922; www.cambridgecoachhouse.co.nz; 3796 Cambridge Rd, Leamington; ste from $165, cottage from $175; 🐾⚛) This farmhouse accommodation is a beaut spot to relax amid Waikato's rural splendour. There are two stylish suites and a self-contained cottage. Flat-screen TVs and heat pumps are convenient additions, and guests are welcome to fire up the barbecue in the leafy grounds. It's a couple of kilometres south of town, en route to Te Awamutu.

Cambridge Mews MOTEL $$

(☑07-827 7166; www.cambridgemews.co.nz; 20 Hamilton Rd; d $160-200; 🐾) All the spacious units in this chalet-style motel are immaculately maintained and have double spa baths and decent kitchens. It's a 10-minute walk to town.

★ Earthstead B&B $$$

(☑07-827 3771; www.earthstead.co.nz; 3635 Cambridge Rd, Monvale; d $219-419; 🐾) 🍃 In a rural setting a short drive south of Cambridge, Earthstead has two units – Earth House and Cob Cottage – constructed using ecofriendly and sustainable adobe-style architecture, and two other options with an elegant European vibe. Fresh and organic produce from Earthstead's compact farm is used for breakfast, including eggs, honey and freshly baked sourdough bread.

✕ Eating & Drinking

Cambridge Farmers Market MARKET $
(www.waikatofarmersmarkets.co.nz; ⊙8am-noon
Sat) Local flavours abound at this excellent
weekly market held in the leafy surroundings of Victoria Sq.

Paddock CAFE $
(✐07-827 4232; www.paddockcambridge.co.nz;
46a Victoria St; snacks & mains $9-18; ⊙8am-5pm
Mon-Thu, to 8pm Fri & Sat, to 4pm Sun) Free-range
this and organic that punctuate the menu at
this cool slice of culinary style that looks like
it's dropped in from Auckland or Melbourne.
Distressed timber furniture and a vibrant
and colourful mural enliven Paddock's corner location, and artisan sodas and healthy
smoothies – try the banana, date and cinnamon – partner well with gourmet bagels and
burgers.

Alpha Street Kitchen & Bar MODERN NZ $$
(✐07-827 5596; www.alphast.co.nz; 47 Alpha St;
mains $23-43; ⊙11am-late Tue-Sun; ✐) Former-
ly the National Hotel, this heritage space is
now one of the Waikato's best new restau-
rants. Sit outside for a leisurely lunch of
miso smoked salmon or sophisticated spins
on lamb or venison for dinner. The shared
plates dishes – think tempura oyster sliders
or chorizo and potato croquettes – also work
very well as bar snacks.

Alpino cucina e vino ITALIAN $$
(✐07-827 5595; www.alpino.co.nz; 43 Victoria St;
pizzas $19-26, mains $29-38; ⊙11.30am-9.30pm
Wed-Sun) In a heritage former post office,
the stylish and elegant yet informal and
approachable Alpino cucina e vino is one
of the best restaurants in the Waikato region. The main menu focuses on excellent
pasta, hearty Italian-style mains – try the
rosemary and parmesan risotto with a confit duck leg – and top-notch wood-fired pizza that's also available for takeaway.

Onyx CAFE $$
(✐07-827 7740; www.onyxcambridge.co.nz; 70
Alpha St; pizzas $20-24, mains $17-32; ⊙9am-
late) All-day Onyx occupies a lofty space,
with onyx-black furnishings and warm-
toned timber floors. Wood-fired pizzas are
the mainstay, plus salads, tortillas, sand-
wiches, steaks, cakes, organic coffee, NZ
wines and local beer from Good George
Brewing (p216) in Hamilton.

Good Union PUB
(✐07-834 4040; www.goodunion.co.nz; 98 Victo-
ria St; ⊙11am-late) Hamilton's Good George
Brewing (p216) empire has now spread to
this Cambridge venue in a colourful and
characterful former church. Secure a spot
in the interesting heritage interior, or grab a
place on the huge outdoor deck and partner
Good George's excellent beers and ciders with
pizza, tacos and hearty main dishes. Visit on a
weekend afternoon for occasional live music.

ℹ Information

Cambridge i-SITE (✐07-823 3456; www.
cambridge.co.nz; cnr Victoria & Queen Sts;
⊙9am-5pm Mon-Fri, 10am-4pm Sat & Sun; ☎)
has free **Heritage & Tree Trail** (p210) and town
maps, plus internet access.

ℹ Getting There & Away

Being on SH1, 22km southeast of Hamilton, Cam-
bridge is well connected by bus. Waikato Regional
Council's **Busit!** (✐0800 4287 5463; www.busit.
co.nz) heads to Hamilton ($6.70, 40 minutes,
seven daily weekdays, three daily weekends).

InterCity (✐09-583 5780; www.intercity.co.nz)
services numerous destinations including the
following:

DESTINATION	PRICE ($)	DURATION	FREQUENCY (DAILY)
Auckland	19-47	2½hr	12
Hamilton	16	30min	8
Matamata	15-20	30min	2
Rotorua	15-36	1¼hr	5
Wellington	29-70	8½hr	3

Naked Bus (✐09-979 1616; https://nakedbus.
com) runs services to the same destinations:

DESTINATION	PRICE ($)	DURATION	FREQUENCY (DAILY)
Auckland	15	2½hr	6
Hamilton	13	30min	5
Matamata	25	2¼hr	1
Rotorua	15	1¼hr	4
Wellington	51	9½hr	1

Hamilton
POP 206.400
Landlocked cities in an island nation are
never going to have the glamorous appeal of
their coastal cousins. Rotorua compensates
with boiling mud and Taupo has its lake, but

Hamilton, despite the majestic Waikato River, is more prosaic.

The city definitely has an appeal, with vibrant bars and excellent restaurants and cafes around Hood and Victoria Sts. You're guaranteed to eat really well after visiting highlights like the Hamilton Gardens.

The great grey-green Waikato River rolls right through town, but the city's layout largely ignores its presence: unless you're driving across a bridge you'll hardly know it's there. Thankfully, work has begun on a development to provide access from the CBD to riverside walking trails.

Most people blast along SH1 between Auckland and Hamilton in about 1½ hours, but if you're keen to meander, the upper Waikato has some interesting diversions including Ngaruawahia, where you will find **Turangawaewae Marae** (☑07-824 5189; 29 River Rd).

◉ Sights

Waikato River   RIVER, PARK
Bush-covered walkways run along both sides of the river and provide the city's green belt. Jogging paths continue to the boardwalk circling **Lake Rotoroa**, west of the centre. **Memorial Park** is closer to town and has the remains of PS *Rangiri-ri* – an iron-clad, steam-powered gunboat from the Waikato War – embedded in the river bank. At the time of research, improved walking access was being developed from Victoria St, Hamilton's main shopping thoroughfare.

★ Waikato Museum   MUSEUM
(☑07-838 6606; www.waikatomuseum.co.nz; 1 Grantham St; by donation; ⊙10am-5pm) FREE The excellent Waikato Museum has several main areas: an art gallery; interactive science galleries; Tainui galleries housing Māori treasures, including the magnificently carved *waka taua* (war canoe), *Te Winikawaka;* and a Waikato River exhibition. The museum also runs a rigorous program of public events. Admission is charged for some displays, and there is a full schedule of one-off and visiting exhibitions.

ArtsPost   GALLERY
(www.waikatomuseum.co.nz/artspost; 120 Victoria St; ⊙10am-5pm) FREE This contemporary gallery and gift shop is housed in a grand, former post office. It focuses on the best of local art: paintings, glass, prints, textiles and photography.

Riff Raff   MONUMENT
(www.riffraffstatue.org; Victoria St) One of Hamilton's more unusual public artworks is a life-sized statue of *Rocky Horror Picture Show* writer Richard O'Brien, aka Riff Raff, the time-warping alien from the planet Transsexual. It looks over a small park on the site of the former Embassy Theatre where O'Brien worked as a hairdresser, though it's hard to imagine 1960s Hamilton inspired the tale of bisexual alien decadence. Opposite the statue, the bright red 'Frankenfurter's Lab' actually conceals recently installed public toilets.

Classics Museum   MUSEUM
(☑07-957-2230; www.classicsmuseum.co.nz; 11 Railside Pl, Frankton; adult/child $20/8; ⊙7am-3pm Mon-Fri, 8am-4pm Sat & Sun) Travel in time amid this collection of more than 100 classic cars from the first half of the 20th century. Even if you're not a motorhead, you'll still be dazzled by the crazy Amphicar and the cool Maserati and Corvette sports cars. The museum is just off SH1, northwest of central Hamilton.

★ Hamilton Gardens   GARDENS
(☑07-838 6782; www.hamiltongardens.co.nz; Cobham Dr; guided tour adult/child $15/8; ⊙enclosed gardens 7.30am-5pm, info centre 9am-5pm, guided tours 11am Sep-Apr) FREE Spread over 50 hectares southeast of the city centre, Hamilton Gardens incorporates a large park, cafe, restaurant and extravagant themed enclosed gardens. There are separate Italian Renaissance, Chinese, Japanese, English, American and Indian gardens complete with colonnades, pagodas and a mini Taj Mahal. Equally interesting are the sustainable Productive Garden Collection, fragrant herb garden and precolonisation Māori Te Parapara garden. Look for the impressive *Nga Uri O Hinetuparimaunga* (Earth Blanket) sculpture at the main gates.

Recent additions include a Tudor-style garden and a tropical garden with more than 200 different warm-climate species. Booking ahead for the guided tours is recommended. To get to the gardens, catch bus 29 (adult/child $3.30/2.20) from the Hamilton Transport Centre (p217).

Hamilton Zoo   ZOO
(☑07-838 6720; www.hamiltonzoo.co.nz; 183 Brymer Rd; adult/child/family $23/11/66, tours extra; ⊙9am-4.30pm, last entry 3pm) Hamilton Zoo houses 500-plus species including wily and curious chimpanzees. Guided-tour options include Eye2Eye and Face2Face opportunities

Hamilton

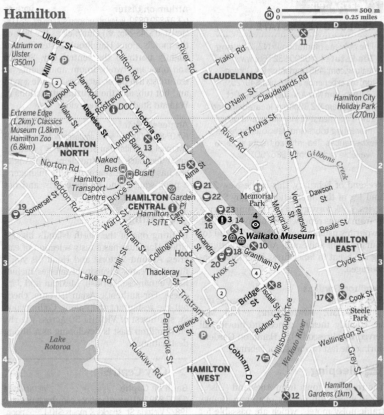

N 0 ——————— 500 m
0 ——————— 0.25 miles

Hamilton

to go behind the scenes to meet various animals, plus daily Meet the Keeper talks from the critters' caregivers. The zoo is 8km northwest of Hamilton city centre.

★☆ Festivals & Events

New Zealand Rugby Sevens   SPORTS
(www.sevens.co.nz; ⊙ early Feb) Held at Hamilton's Stadium Waikato across the first

ZEALONG TEA ESTATE

The only tea plantation in NZ, **Zealong Tea Estate** (☑ 0800 932 566; www.zealong.com; 495 Gordonton Rd, Gordonton; tea experience adult/child $49/25; ⊗ 10am-5pm Nov-Apr, Tue-Sun May-Oct, tours 9.30am & 2.30pm) is located around 10km northeast of Hamilton, and offers interesting tours and delicious high-tea experiences. Tea-infused treats are also available (adult/child $85/60).

weekend of February, this is the New Zealand leg of the international Rugby Sevens Series. Look forward to lots of running rugby from teams representing many countries. Favourites usually include New Zealand (of course...), Fiji and South Africa, and attending the event in fancy dress is definitely encouraged.

Hamilton Gardens Arts Festival PERFORMING ARTS
(☑ 07-859 1317; www.hgaf.co.nz; ⊗ Feb) Music, comedy, theatre, dance and movies, all served up alfresco in the Hamilton Gardens during the last two weeks of February.

🛏 Sleeping

The road into town from Auckland (Ulster St) is lined with dozens of unremarkable, traffic-noisy motels, which are passable for short stays. Hotels in the city centre have regular online discounts and provide good access to cafes, restaurants and bars.

★ **City Centre B&B** B&B $
(☑ 07-838 1671; www.citycentrebnb.co.nz; 3 Anglesea St; r $90-125; @ 🕿 ⊠) At the quiet riverside end of a central city street (just five minutes' walk to the Victoria and Hood Sts action), this sparkling self-contained apartment opens onto a swimming pool. There's also a bedroom available in a wing of the main house. Self-catering breakfast is provided. Minimum stay of two nights.

Backpackers Central HOSTEL $
(☑ 07-839 1928; www.backpackerscentral.co.nz; 846 Victoria St; dm $30, s $49, r $82-125; @ 🕿) Well-run hostel with dorms and singles on one floor, doubles and family rooms on another – some with en-suite bathrooms and all with access to a shared kitchen and lounge. Worth considering as an alternative to a motel room if you're travelling as a couple or in a group.

Atrium on Ulster MOTEL $$
(☑ 07-839 0839; www.atriumonulster.co.nz; 281 Ulster St; d $145-245; 🕿) Our pick as the best of the motels along Hamilton's Ulster St strip slightly north of the central city. Studios and one- and two-bedroom apartments all feature stylish decor, facilities include a gym and hot tub, and the sporting attractions at Waikato Stadium are very close.

Anglesea Motel MOTEL $$
(☑ 07-834 0010; www.angleseamotel.com; 36 Liverpool St; units from $150; @ 🕿 ⊠) Getting great feedback from travellers, the Anglesea has plenty of space, friendly managers, a pool, squash and tennis courts, and not un-stylish decor.

🍴 Eating

Befitting one of the North Island's biggest cities, Hamilton has a tasty selection of eateries. Around Victoria and Hood Sts you'll find the greatest diversity of eateries, including Vietnamese, Turkish, Mexican and Japanese. For authentic Asian flavours, check out the restaurant strip along Collingwood St, southwest of Victoria St. Across the river, Hamilton East is developing as a dining destination.

🍴 City Centre

Banh Mi Caphe VIETNAMESE $
(☑ 07-839 1141; www.facebook.com/banhmicaphe; 198/2 Victoria St; snacks & mains $10-17; ⊗ noon-late Tue-Sat) Fresh spring rolls, Vietnamese *banh mi* (sandwiches) and steaming bowls of *pho* (noodle soup) all feature at this hip spot channelling the backstreets of Hanoi.

★ **Madame Woo** MALAYSIAN $$
(☑ 07-839 5605; www.madamwoo.co.nz/hamilton; 6 Sapper Moore-Jones Pl; mains $26-32; ⊗ 11am-late; 🍴) 🍴 The authentic flavours of Malaysian street food are served in this high-ceilinged space just off Victoria St. Partner Asian-inspired cocktails or craft beer with Madame Woo's signature hawker rolls crammed with pork or chicken, or order up a feast of punchy curries and zingy salads. Service is excellent, and it's a crime to not order Portuguese-style egg tarts for dessert.

Gothenburg TAPAS $$
(☑ 07-834 3562; www.gothenburg.co.nz; ANZ Centre, 21 Grantham St; shared plates $8-27; ⊗ 9am-11pm Mon-Fri, 11.30am-late Sat) Showcasing a scenic riverside spot with high ceilings and a summer-friendly deck,

Gothenburg is one of our favourite Hamilton restaurants. The menu of shared plates effortlessly spans the globe – try the pork and kimchi dumplings or the potato gnocchi with blue cheese and candied walnuts – and the beer list features rotating taps from Scandinavian breweries and local Waikato craft brewers.

Hazel Hayes CAFE $$
(07-839 1953; www.hazelhayes.co.nz; 587 Victoria St; mains $10-24; 7am-4pm Mon-Fri, 8am-2pm Sat) This mash-up of country kitchen decor showcases inventive cafe fare. Free-range and organic options punctuate the short, focused menu, and both the service and coffee are very good. Try the homemade hash browns with salmon or bacon and a rich hollandaise sauce and you'll definitely be set for the day.

River Kitchen CAFE $$
(07-839 2906; www.theriverkitchen.co.nz; 237 Victoria St; mains $14-19; 7am-4pm Mon-Fri, 8am-3pm Sat & Sun;) River Kitchen does things with simple style: cakes, gourmet breakfasts and fresh seasonal lunches (angle for the salmon hash), and a barista who knows his beans. It's the kind of place you visit for breakfast, come back to for lunch, then consider for breakfast the next day.

Chim Choo Ree MODERN NZ $$$
(07-839 4329; www.chimchooree.co.nz; 14 Bridge St; mains $36-38; 11.30am-2pm Mon-Fri, 5pm-late Mon-Sat) In a heritage building beside the river, Chim Choo Ree focuses on small plates such as tuna tartare with rugby grapefruit, goat curd tortellini, and confit pork belly, plus larger, equally inventive mains using duck, lamb, venison and snapper. Local foodies wash it all down with a great wine list and flavourful NZ craft beers. A six-course tasting menu is $100.

Palate MODERN NZ, FUSION $$$
(07-834 2921; www.palaterestaurant.co.nz; 20 Alma St; mains $34-38; 11.30am-2pm Tue-Fri, 5.30pm-late Tue-Sat) Simple, sophisticated Palate has a well-deserved reputation for lifting the culinary bar across regional NZ. The innovative menu features highlights such as beef-cheek ravioli with smoked mushroom and a blue-cheese pudding. The wine selection is one of Hamilton's finest, local craft breweries are well supported with seasonal brews on offer, and a good-value express lunch is $25 for two courses.

✕ Hamilton East & Claudelands

Duck Island Ice Cream ICE CREAM $
(07-856 5948; www.duckislandicecream.co.nz; 300 Grey St; ice cream from $4.50; 11am-6pm Tue-Thu & Sun, to 9pm Fri & Sat;) A dazzling array of ever-changing flavours – how does rhubarb and Szechuan peppercorn or blackberry, sage and honey sound? – make Duck Island one of NZ's best ice-cream parlours. The sunny corner location is infused with a hip retro vibe, and the refreshing house-made sodas and ice-cream floats are other worthy reasons to cross the river to Hamilton East.

Hamilton Farmers Market MARKET $
(022 639 1995; www.waikatofarmersmarkets.co.nz; Brooklyn Rd, Claudelands; 8am-noon Sun) Located northeast across the river in Claudelands, this farmers market is a veritable Sunday-morning feast of local cheeses, baked goods and produce. A piping hot and flaky treat from the Raglan Pie Co is a pretty good way to kick off the day.

★ Hayes Common CAFE $$
(027 537 1853; www.hayescommon.co.nz; cnr Plunket Tce & Jellicoe Dr, Hamilton East; mains $21-34; 8am-11pm Wed-Sat, to 4pm Sun & Tue;) Journey across to Hamilton East to this bustling new opening in a former garage. Thoroughly unpretentious, Hayes Common's versatile menu stretches from acai bowls for breakfast through to dukkah fried eggs or a jerk-chicken burger for lunch. Dinner options including lamb with harissa are equally cosmopolitan, and the wine list and local craft beers on tap will ensure you linger.

Rocket Espresso CAFE $$
(07-856 5616; www.rocketespressobar.co.nz; 385 Grey St; mains $11-23; 7am-4pm Mon-Fri, 8.30am-3pm Sat & Sun;) Part of the emerging dining scene across the river in Hamilton East, Rocket Espresso lures caffeine fiends to gather at communal tables strewn with foodie magazines and newspapers. The concise menu ranges from excellent counter food through to robust mains including spicy Mexican scrambled eggs and vegetable fritters with smoked salmon and poached eggs for lunch.

🍷 Drinking & Nightlife

The blocks around Victoria and Hood Sts make for a boozy bar-hop, with weekend live music and DJs. The city also has a good craft-beer scene worth exploring. Friday is the big night of the week.

Craft
CRAFT BEER

(☏07-839 4531; www.facebook.com/craftbeer hamilton; 15 Hood St; ⊘3pm-late Wed-Fri, from 1pm Sat) Fifteen rotating taps of amber goodness flow at Craft, which is plenty to keep the city's craft-beer buffs coming back. Brews from around NZ make a regular appearance, with occasional surprising additions from international cult breweries. Quiz night kicks off most Wednesdays at 7pm, and decent sliders and wood-fired pizza could well see you making a night of it.

Local Taphouse
BAR

(☏07-834 4923; www.facebook.com/thelocal taphouse; Sky City, 346 Victoria St; ⊘11am-10pm) Part of Hamilton's Sky City eating and drinking precinct, the Local Taphouse features locally sourced beers from the nearby regions of Waikato, Bay of Plenty and Coromandel. Food is served, including hearty pots of mussels and gourmet burgers. Other adjacent Sky City options include a Spanish tapas and grill restaurant, a good daytime cafe and an elegant after-dark cocktail bar.

SL28
CAFE

(☏07-839 6422; www.facebook.com/sl28.coffee; 298 Victoria St; ⊘7.30am-4pm Mon-Fri) Hamilton java-hounds and CBD desk jockeys in need of the city's best coffee make tracks to this specialist coffee bar. If you know the difference between your Chemex and your cold brew and you're searching for a shot of Sumatran single origin, here's where to come.

Little George
CRAFT BEER

(☏07-834 4345; www.facebook.com/littlegeorge popupbar; 15 Hood St; ⊘4pm-1am Tue-Thu, 3pm-3am Fri, 5.30pm-3am Sat) The more central sibling to Good George Brewing (p216) , Little George is an excellent bar along Hood St's nightlife strip. Beers from Good George are regularly featured, but guest taps also showcase other Kiwi craft breweries. Good bar snacks are available, and a local food truck is usually on hand from 4pm to 9pm on Thursdays. Taco Tuesdays are also good value.

Good George Brewing
BREWERY

(☏07-847 3223; www.goodgeorge.co.nz; 32a Somerset St, Frankton; tours incl beer $22; ⊘11am-late, tours from 6pm Tue-Thu) Channelling a cool industrial vibe, the former Church of St George is now a shrine to craft beer. Order a flight of five beers ($15), and partner the hoppy heaven with wood-fired pizzas ($22) or main meals ($25 to $34). Our favourite brews are the citrusy American Pale Ale and the zingy Drop Hop Cider. Tours must be booked ahead.

Check online for lots of weekly beer and food specials, and look forward to tasty seasonal brews from Good George's sour beer program.

Wonderhorse
COCKTAIL BAR, CRAFT BEER

(☏07-839 2281; www.facebook.com/wonder horsebar; 232 Victoria St; ⊘5pm-3am Wed-Sat) Tucked away around 20m off Victoria St, Wonderhorse regularly features craft beers from niche local brewers including Shunters Yard and Brewaucracy. Vintage vinyl is often spinning on the turntable, and sliders and Asian street eats combine with killer cocktails at one of Hamilton's best bars.

🛈 Information

MEDICAL SERVICES
Anglesea Clinic (☏07-858 0800; www.angle-seamedical.co.nz; cnr Anglesea & Thackeray Sts; ⊘24hr)

Waikato Hospital (☏07-839 8899; www. waikatodhb.govt.nz; Pembroke St; ⊘24hr)

TOURIST INFORMATION
Hamilton i-SITE (☏0800 242 645, 07-958 5960; www.visithamilton.co.nz; cnr Caro & Alexandra Sts; ⊘9am-5pm Mon-Fri, 9.30am-3.30pm Sat & Sun; 🛜) can help organise accommodation, activities and transport bookings and has free wi-fi right across Garden Pl. DOC's Hamilton **branch** (Department of Conservation; ☏07-858 1000; www.doc.govt. nz; Level 5, 73 Rostrevor St; ⊘8am-4.30pm Mon-Fri) has maps and brochures on walking tracks, campsites and DOC huts.

🛈 Getting There & Away

AIR
Hamilton International Airport (HIA; ☏07-848 9027; www.hamiltonairport.co.nz; Airport Rd) is 12km south of the city. **Air New Zealand** (☏0800 737 000; www.airnewzealand.co.nz) has regular direct flights from Hamilton to Christchurch, Palmerston North and Wellington.

Super Shuttle (☏0800 748 885, 07-843 7778; www.supershuttle.co.nz; one way $30) offers a door-to-door service into the city. **Aerolink Shuttles** (☏0800 151 551; www.aerolink. nz; one way $80) also has airport services, while **Raglan Scenic Tours** (☏021 0274 7014, 07-825 0507; www.raglanscenictours.co.nz) links the airport with Raglan. A **taxi** (p217) costs around $55. **InterCity** (☏09-583 5780; www.intercity. co.nz) runs a direct bus from Hamilton to Auckland airport.

BUS

All buses arrive at and depart from the **Hamilton Transport Centre** (📞 07-834 3457; www.hamilton.co.nz; cnr Anglesea & Bryce Sts; 🛜).

Waikato Regional Council's **Busit!** (📞 0800 4287 5463; www.busit.co.nz; city routes adult/child $3.30/2.20) coaches serve the region, including Ngaruawahia, Cambridge, Te Awamutu and Raglan.

InterCity (p216) services numerous destinations including the following:

DESTINATION	PRICE ($)	DURATION	FREQUENCY (DAILY)
Auckland	12-32	2hr	11
Cambridge	10-22	25min	9
Matamata	10-18	50min	4
Ngaruawahia	10-21	20min	9
Rotorua	14-35	1½hr	5
Te Aroha	10	1hr	2
Te Awamutu	10-15	35min	3
Wellington	30-75	5hr	3

Naked Bus (https://nakedbus.com) services run to the following destinations (among many others):

DESTINATION	PRICE ($)	DURATION	FREQUENCY (DAILY)
Auckland	17-19	2hr	5
Cambridge	15	30min	5-7
Matamata	20	1hr	1
Ngaruawahia	15	30min	5
Rotorua	10	1½hr	4-5
Wellington	25-45	9½hr	1-2

TRAIN

Hamilton is on the **Northern Explorer** (📞 0800 872 467; www.greatjourneysofnz.co.nz) route between Auckland (from $49, 2½ hours) and Wellington (from $119, 9½ hours) via Otorohanga (from $59, 45 minutes). Trains depart Auckland on Monday, Thursday and Saturday and stop at Hamilton's **Frankton train station** (Fraser St), 1km west of the city centre; there are no ticket sales here – see the website for ticketing details.

🛈 Getting Around

Hamilton's **Busit!** network services the city centre and suburbs daily from around 7am to 7.30pm (later on Friday). All buses pass through **Hamilton Transport Centre**. Busit! also runs a free CBD shuttle looping around Victoria, Liverpool, Anglesea and Bridge Sts every 10 minutes (7am to 6pm weekdays).

Victoria St is the city's main shopping area and parking can be difficult to secure. You'll have more luck finding parking a few blocks to the west.

For a taxi, try **Hamilton Taxis** (📞 07-847 7477, 0800 477 477; www.hamiltontaxis.co.nz).

Alternatively, you can rent a car from **RaD Car Hire** (📞 07-839 1049; www.radcarhire.co.nz; 383 Anglesea St; ⏱ 7.30am-5pm Mon-Fri, 8am-noon Sat).

Raglan

POP 2740

Laid-back Raglan may well be New Zealand's perfect surfing town. It's small enough to have escaped mass development, but big enough to exhibit signs of life including good eateries and a bar that attracts big-name bands in summer. Along with the famous surf spots to the south, the harbour just begs to be kayaked upon. There's also an excellent arts scene, with several galleries and shops worthy of perusal.

👁 Sights & Activities

Old School Arts Centre　　ARTS CENTRE, GALLERY
(📞 07-825 0023; www.raglanartscentre.co.nz; Stewart St; ⏱ 10am-2pm Mon-Fri) **FREE** A community hub, the Old School Arts Centre has changing exhibitions and workshops, including weaving, carving, yoga and storytelling. Movies screen here regularly during summer ($15); grab a snack and a beer to complete the experience. The hippie/artsy **Raglan Creative Market** happens out the front on the second Sunday (10am to 2pm) of the month.

Raglan Rock　　ROCK CLIMBING, CAVING
(📞 0800 724 7625; www.raglanrock.com; climbing half-day $120, caving & canyoning $120) Full instruction and all equipment for climbing on the limestone cliffs of nearby Stone Valley, or the exciting Stupid Fat Hobbit climb and abseil above Raglan Harbour. Caving options include Stone Valley and the more challenging Rattlesnake. Canyoning is also available – ask about after-dark canyoning trips taking in a glowworm-illuminated waterfall. Minimum two people.

Waihine Moe Sunset Harbour Cruise　　CRUISE
(📞 07-825 7873; www.raglanboatcharters.co.nz; Raglan Wharf; adult/child $49/29; ⏱ Thu-Sun late Dec-Mar) Two-hour sunset cruises, including a few drinks, around Raglan Harbour on the *Wahine Moe*. Ninety-minute morning harbour cruises ($30/15 per adult/child) leaving

Raglan

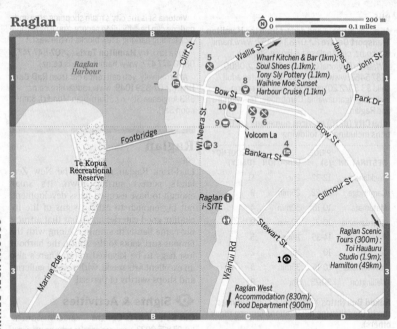

Raglan

◉ Sights
1 Old School Arts Centre	C3

🛏 Sleeping
2 Bow St Studios	B1
3 Raglan Backpackers	C2
4 Raglan Sunset Motel	C2

🍴 Eating
5 Aloha Sushi	C1
6 Pantry	C1
7 Shack	C1

🍷 Drinking & Nightlife
8 Harbour View Hotel	C1
9 Raglan Roast	C1
10 Yot Club	C1

🛍 Shopping
Jet Collective	(see 7)

from Raglan's Bow St jetty are also available on the smaller *Harmony* vessel. Complimentary pick-ups are included.

🛏 Sleeping

Solscape HOSTEL, CABIN **$**
(☑ 07-825 8268; www.solscape.co.nz; 611 Wainui Rd; campsites per person $20, caboose dm/d $30/80, tepees per person $40, cottage d $100-220; @ 🛜)
🌱 With a hilltop location fringed by native bush, Solscape's ecofriendly accommodation includes tepees, bell tents, rammed-earth domes, railway carriages and stylish eco-baches. There's room for tents and campervans, and simpler cottages are also avail-

able. Environmental impact is minimised with solar energy, and organic produce from the permaculture garden is used for guest meals in the Conscious Kitchen cafe.

Raglan Backpackers HOSTEL **$**
(☑ 07-825 0515; www.raglanbackpackers.co.nz; 6 Wi Neera St; vehicle sites per person $19, dm $29-31, s $59, tw & d $78; @) This laid-back hostel is right on the water, with sea views from some rooms. Other rooms are arranged around a garden courtyard or in a separate building. There are free bikes and kayaks for use, and surfboards for hire, or take a yoga class, strum a guitar or drip in the sauna. No wi-fi – it 'ruins the vibe'.

★ Bow St Studios   APARTMENT $$

(☑07-825 0551; www.bowstreet.co.nz; 1 Bow St; studios $155-245, cottages $175-195; ☎) With a waterfront location right in town, Bow St has self-contained studios and a historic cottage. The cool and chic decor is stylish and relaxing. The property is surrounded by a subtropical garden and shaded by well-established pohutukawa trees.

Hidden Valley   COTTAGE $$

(☑07-825 5813; www.hiddenvalleyraglan.com; SH23, Te Uku; d $195-245) Located on 12 hectares of native forest 3km from Raglan, Hidden Valley features two individual chalets, both with private spa pools. The Tree Tops chalet is nestled beside a stand of kahikatea (NZ white pine), while the Mountain View chalet looks out towards Mt Karioi. Decor is stylish and modern with fully self-contained kitchens. Check online for good midweek discounts.

Raglan Sunset Motel   MOTEL $$

(☑07-825 0050; www.raglansunsetmotel.co.nz; 7 Bankart St; d $165-180; ☎) A block from Bow St's shops and restaurants with spacious and modern units. The owners also have self-contained apartments (doubles from $165) and beach houses (four people $300) available. See www.ourbeachhouse.co.nz for information on these properties.

✗ Eating

Food Department   CAFE $

(☑07-282 0248; www.facebook.com/fooddepartmentraglanroast; 45 Wainui Rd; pizza slices $6, whole pizza $18-24; ⊙8am-8.30pm Thu-Mon, to 5pm Tue & Wed) Pizza by the slice and interesting gelato – our favourite is the cinnamon and rice – reinforce the authentic Italian credentials of the Food Department. The scattering of mismatched retro furniture is good for the first coffee of the day, and comfort food like lasagna can be purchased to eat in or take away. Also a great place for a leisurely brunch.

Aloha Sushi   JAPANESE $

(☑07-825 7440; www.facebook.com/AlohaSushiRaglan; 4 Wallis St; sushi $1.60-2, mains $10-23; ⊙10am-8pm Wed-Mon; ✍) Rolled-to-order sushi, udon noodles and *donburi* rice bowls, all with a touch of hip Hawaiian-Japanese surfer style. Check out the great selection of surfing and rock-music posters, and set yourself up for the day with a super-healthy bowl of salmon and avocado poke.

★ Rock-It Kitchen   CAFE $$

(☑07-825 8233; www.rockitraglan.co.nz; 248 Wainui Rd; mains $20-35; ⊙9am-3pm Sun-Thu, to late Fri & Sat; ✍) ✦ Around 3km from town adjacent to surf beaches, Rock-It Kitchen combines rustic decor – it's housed in an old woolshed – with the area's best food. NZ wines and beer from west Auckland's Hallertau brewery combine with Scotch fillet steak and truffle potato mash for dinner, and the all-day breakfast of kumara hash cakes is popular with hungry surfers.

During summer, the outdoor tables are the place to be, and if the tide's right, it's even possible to steer a kayak way up the Wainui estuary from Raglan.

Shack   INTERNATIONAL $$

(☑07-825 0027; www.theshackraglan.com; 19 Bow St; mains $15-21; ⊙8am-4pm; ☎✍) ✦ Brunch classics – try the chickpea-and-corn fritters – and interesting mains such as kimchi fried rice and slow-roasted lamb shoulder feature at Raglan's best cafe. A longboard strapped to the wall, wobbly old floorboards, up-tempo tunes and international staff serving Kiwi wines and craft beers complete the picture. Healthy options include an acai bowl crammed with fruit, granola and local coconut yoghurt.

Pantry   CAFE $$

(☑07-825 8405; 23 Bow St; mains $15-20; ⊙8am-4pm daily, 5-9pm Thu-Sat; ✍) ✦ Previously dubbed the Raglan Social Club, this spacious and sunny location on the main street reopened in October 2017 as the Pantry. Look forward to excellent counter food – including fresh salads prepared daily – and Thursday to Saturday dinner specials (eat in or take away), including tacos and gourmet burgers. Imported beer and cider both available on tap.

There are also plenty of vegetarian and vegan options.

⛻ Drinking & Nightlife

Wharf Kitchen & Bar   BAR, CAFE

(☑07-825-0010; www.thewharfkitchenbar.co.nz; 43 Rose St; ⊙9.30am-late) Recently opened near the town's wharf, this is the best place to combine a wine or cold beer with afternoon sunshine or a Raglan sunset. Inside, the decor mixes Raglan's heritage with a maritime vibe, and a good food menu includes plump mussels, fish tacos and snapper ceviche. Shared platters ($38 to $55) are good for groups or hungry couples.

HORSING AROUND RAGLAN

Tramping, surfing, paddle boarding and kayaking are all popular ways to explore the stellar blend of forest and ocean scenery around Raglan, but horse riding is also highly regarded. Two well-established operators offer excursions ranging from beach rides – even riding bareback into the shallows of the ocean – through to farm rides and negotiating forested paths. Check out **Surf & Turf** (✆027 435 2648; www.raglanhorseriding.co.nz; 3953B SH23; from $65) for the best opportunities to blend equine and ocean action, and hook up with **Wild Coast Ruapuke** (✆07-825 0059; www.wildcoast.co.nz; 1549 Whaanga Rd, Ruapuke; from $130) 🏇 for exciting combinations of bush, beach and farm scenery around Mt Karioi.

Raglan Roast CAFE
(✆07-825 8702; www.raglanroast.co.nz; Volcom Lane; coffee $4-5; ◷7am-5pm, shorter hours Mar-Nov) Hole-in-the-wall coffee roaster with the best brew in town. Stop by for a cup, a cookie and a conversation. Don't leave town without buying a few fragrant bags of coffee for life on the road. The adjacent noticeboard is a good spot to catch up on the latest goings-on around town.

Yot Club BAR
(✆07-825 8968; www.facebook.com/YOTClub Raglan; 9 Bow St; free-$25; ◷8pm-late Wed-Sat, 4pm-late Sun) Raucous, nocturnal bar with DJs and touring bands.

Harbour View Hotel PUB
(✆07-825 8010; www.harbourviewhotel.co.nz; 14 Bow St; ◷11am-late) Classic old pub with main-street drinks on the shaded veranda. Decent pizza too and occasional live music on weekends and during summer.

🛍 Shopping

★ **Toi Hauāuru Studio** ART
(✆021 174 4629, 07-825 0244; www.toihauauru.com; 4338 Main Rd; ◷10am-5pm Wed-Sun) Run by local artist Simon Te Wheoro, this excellent gallery/shop is located 2km from Raglan on the road from Hamilton. Contemporary artwork and sculpture with a Māori influence and *pounamu* (greenstone) carvings are for sale. Simon is also skilled in the Māori art of *ta moko* (tattoo) – if you're keen for one, get in touch via the website.

Quirky local surfwear and colourful Māori *hei tiki* (pendants) make affordable and interesting souvenirs.

Tony Sly Pottery ARTS & CRAFTS
(✆0800 825 037; www.tonyslypottery.com; Raglan Wharf, 90 Wallis St; ◷9am-5pm) Subtle and natural colours and a mix of rustic and more modern designs feature at this store and workshop at Raglan Wharf.

Jet Collective ARTS & CRAFTS
(✆07-825 8566; www.jetcollective.co.nz; 19a Bow St; ◷10am-4pm Wed-Mon) Funky gallery-shop showcasing 100% Raglan artists with everything from music CDs and mixed media pieces through to retro Kiwiana-inspired work. It's also a good spot to drop in and chat with the friendly team about Raglan's growing and diverse arts scene.

Soul Shoes SHOES
(✆07-825 8765; www.soulshoes.co.nz; Raglan Wharf, Wallis St; ◷10am-5pm) World famous in Raglan since 1973, Soul Shoes' range of handmade leather footwear has been joined by equally cool satchels, backpacks and bags. It also has an outlet (open Thursday to Monday) on Volcom Lane in central Raglan.

ⓘ Information

Raglan i-SITE (✆07-825 0556; www.raglan.org.nz; 13 Wainui Rd; ◷9am-5pm Tue-Thu, to 6.30pm Fri & Sat, to 5.30pm Sun & Mon) has Department of Conservation (DOC) brochures, plus information about accommodation and activities including kitesurfing and paddle boarding. Check out the attached museum, especially the exhibition on the history of Raglan's surfing scene.

West Coast Health Centre (✆07-825 0114; 12 Wallis St; ◷9am-5pm Mon-Fri)

ⓘ Getting There & Away

Raglan is 48km west of Hamilton along SH23. Unsealed back roads connect Raglan to Kawhia, 50km south; they're slow, winding and prone to rockslides, but scenic and certainly off the beaten track. Head back towards Hamilton for 7km and take the Te Mata/Kawhia turn-off and follow the signs; allow at least an hour.

Waikato District Council's **Busit!** (✆0800 4287 5463; www.busit.co.nz; adult/child $9/5.60) heads between Hamilton and Raglan (one hour) four times daily on weekdays and twice daily on weekends.

Raglan Scenic Tours (✆07-825 0507; www.raglanscenictours.co.nz; 7a Main Rd; 2½hr Raglan sightseeing tour adult/child $60/20) runs a Raglan–Hamilton shuttle bus (one way $42.50) and direct transfers to/from Auckland International Airport.

ⓘ Getting Around

For a cab, call **Raglan Taxi** (☑ 027 825 8159).

South of Raglan

South of Raglan, the North Island's west coast unfurls with a series of excellent surf beaches. Whale Bay and Manu Bay draw board riders from around the world, and for non-surfers, there are scenic walking opportunities around Mt Karioi and Mt Pirongia.

◎ Sights

Mt Karioi   MOUNTAIN
(Sleeping Lady) In legend, Mt Karioi (756m), the Sleeping Lady (check out that profile), is the sister to Mt Pirongia. At its base (8km south of Whale Bay), **Te Toto Gorge** is a steep cleft in the mountainside, with a vertigo-inducing lookout perched high over the chasm. Starting from the Te Toto Gorge car park, a strenuous but scenic track goes up the western slope. It takes 2½ hours to reach a lookout point, followed by an easier hour to the summit.

From the eastern side, the **Wairake Track** is a steeper 2½-hour climb to the summit, where it meets the Te Toto Track.

Waireinga   WATERFALL
(Bridal Veil Falls) Just past Te Mata (a short drive south of the main Raglan–Hamilton road) is the turn-off to the 55m-high Waireinga, 4km from the main road. From the car park, it's an easy 10-minute walk through mossy native bush to the top of the falls (not suitable for swimming). A further 10-minute walk leads down to the bottom. Lock your car: theft is a problem here.

Mt Pirongia   MOUNTAIN
(www.mtpirongia.org.nz) The main attraction of the 170-sq-km Pirongia Forest Park is Mt Pirongia, its 959m summit clearly visible from much of the Waikato. The mountain is usually climbed from Corcoran Rd (three to five hours, one way) with tracks to other lookout points. Interestingly, NZ's tallest known kahikatea tree (66.5m) grows on the mountainside. There's a six-bunk DOC hut near the summit if you need to spend the night: maps and information are available from Hamilton DOC (p216).

🏃 Activities

The surf spots near Raglan – Indicators, Whale Bay and Manu Bay – are internationally famous for their point breaks. Bruce Brown's classic 1964 wave-chaser film *The Endless Summer* features Manu Bay.

Ngarunui Beach   SURFING, SWIMMING
Less than 1km south of **Ocean Beach**, Ngarunui Beach is great for grommets learning to surf. On the cliff top is a clubhouse for the volunteer lifeguards who patrol part of the black-sand beach from late October until April. This is the only beach with lifeguards, and is the best ocean beach for swimming.

Manu Bay   SURFING
A 2.5km journey from Ngarunui Beach will bring you to Manu Bay, a legendary surf spot said to have the longest left-hand break in the world. The elongated uniform waves are created by the angle at which the Tasman Sea swell meets the coastline (it works best in a southwesterly swell).

Whale Bay   SURFING
Whale Bay is a renowned surf spot 1km west of Manu Bay. It's usually less crowded than Manu Bay, but from the bottom of Calvert Rd you have to clamber 600m over the rocks to get to the break.

🛏 Sleeping

Karioi Lodge   HOSTEL $
(☑ 07-825 7873; www.karioilodge.co.nz; 5b Whaanga Rd, Whale Bay; dm/d $33/79; @ 🐾) 🐾
Deep in native bush, Karioi Lodge offers a sauna, mountain bikes, bush and beach walks, sustainable gardening, tree planting and the **Raglan Surf School** (☑ 07-825 7873; www.raglansurfingschool.co.nz; 5b Whaanga Rd, Whale Bay; rental per hr surfboards from $20, body boards $5, wetsuits $5, 3hr lesson incl transport from Raglan $89). There are no en suites, but the rooms are clean and cosy. Campervan travellers can stay for $18 per person in forested surroundings with access to Karioi's bathroom and kitchen facilities.

Sleeping Lady Lodgings   LODGE $$
(☑ 07-825 7873; www.sleepinglady.co.nz; 5b Whaanga Rd; lodges $175-280) Sleeping Lady Lodgings is a collection of very comfortable self-contained houses all with ocean views.

ⓘ Getting There & Away

There is no public transport. Tours are available with **Raglan Scenic Tours** (p220).

Te Awamutu

POP 9800

Deep into dairy-farming country, Te Awamutu (which means 'The River Cut Short'; the Waikato beyond this point was unsuitable for large canoes) is a pleasant rural service centre. With a blossom-tree-lined main street and a good museum, TA (aka Rose Town) makes a decent overnighter.

◎ Sights & Activities

★ Te Awamutu Museum
MUSEUM

(☑ 07-872 0085; www.tamuseum.org.nz; 135 Roche St; by donation; ◷ 10am-4pm Mon-Fri, to 2pm Sat) Te Awamutu Museum has a superb collection of Māori *taonga* (treasures) and an excellent display on the Waikato War. The highlight is the revered *Te Uenuku* ('The Rainbow'), an ancient Māori carving estimated to be up to 600 years old. If you're a fan of the Finn brothers from Crowded House and Split Enz, videos, memorabilia and a scrapbook are available on request – Te Awamutu is their home town.

Rose Garden
GARDENS

(cnr Gorst Ave & Arawata St; ◷ 24hr) FREE The Rose Garden has 2500 bushes and 51 varieties with fabulously fruity names such as Lady Gay and Sexy Rexy. The roses usually bloom from November to May.

🛏 Sleeping & Eating

Rosetown Motel
MOTEL $$

(☑ 0800 767 386, 07-871 5779; www.rosetownmotel. co.nz; 844 Kihikihi Rd; d $130-150; ⊗⊠) The older-style units at Rosetown have kitchens, new linen and TVs, and share a spa. A solid choice if you're hankering for straight-up, small-town sleeps.

Walton St Coffee
CAFE $

(☑ 022 070 6411; www.facebook.com/walton streetcollective; 3 Walton St; snacks & meals $6-15; ◷ 7am-3pm Tue-Fri, 8.30am-1pm Sat) 🍴 In a rustic building with exposed beams and retro furniture, this combo of cafe, gallery and performance space is Te Awamutu's top spot for coffee. The menu has a strong focus on organic and gluten-free options. Try the Buddha Bowl, a changing concoction of fresh seasonal veggies and the grain of the day, topped with a cashew and herb dressing.

Fahrenheit Restaurant & Bar
MODERN NZ, PIZZA $$

(☑ 07-871 5429; www.fahrenheitrestaurant.co.nz; 13 Roche St; mains $18-37; ◷ 11am-late) The decor is a tad stark at this spacious upstairs eatery, but a friendly local welcome and plenty of Waikato sunshine easily counter any misgivings about ambience. Shared tapas plates, good pizza, and a decent wine and beer list are all reasons to dine at lunch; for a more high-end experience, order the Sichuan spiced duck for dinner.

In summer, the best place to be is outside on Fahrenheit's slim deck overlooking Te Awamutu's (occasionally) bustling main drag.

Red Kitchen
CAFE $$

(☑ 07-871 8715; www.redkitchen.co.nz; 51 Mahoe St; mains $14-21; ◷ 7am-5.30pm Mon-Fri, 7.30am-2.30pm Sat) Excellent coffee, counter food, cosmopolitan brunches and lunches, and food store all feature at this sunny spot. Try the macadamia and cranberry muesli or the creamy mushrooms on ciabatta. Pick up gourmet TV dinners from Monday to Friday – actually really good – and fire up the motel microwave for your evening meal.

ⓘ Information

Te Awamutu i-SITE (☑ 07-871 3259; www. teawamutuinfo.co.nz; 1 Gorst Ave; ◷ 9am-5pm Mon-Fri, to 2.30pm Sat & Sun) has plenty of local information.

ⓘ Getting There & Away

Te Awamutu is on SH3, halfway between Hamilton and Otorohanga (29km either way). The regional bus service **Busit!** (☑ 0800 4287 5463; www.busit.co.nz) is the cheapest option for Hamilton (adult/child $6.70/4.50, 50 minutes, eight daily weekdays, three daily weekends). Three daily **InterCity** (☑ 09-583 5780; www. intercity.co.nz) services connect Te Awamutu with Auckland ($23, 2½ hours) and Hamilton ($11, 30 minutes).

KING COUNTRY

Holding good claim to the title of New Zealand's rural heartland, this is the kind of no-nonsense place that raises cattle and All Blacks. A bastion of independent Māoridom, it was never conquered in the war against the King Movement. The story goes that King Tawhiao placed his hat on a large map of NZ and declared that all the land it covered would remain under his *mana* (authority), and the region was effectively off-limits to Europeans until 1883.

The Waitomo Caves are the area's major drawcard. An incredible natural phenomenon in themselves, they also feature lots of adrenaline-inducing activities.

Kawhia

POP 670

Along with resisting cultural annihilation, low-key Kawhia (think mafia with a K) has avoided large-scale development, retaining its sleepy fishing-village vibe. There's not much here except for the general store, a couple of takeaways and a petrol station. Even Captain Cook blinked and missed the narrow entrance to the large harbour when he sailed past in 1770.

◎ Sights & Activities

Kayaks can be hired from Kawhia Beachside S-Cape and Kawhia Motel.

Kawhia Regional Museum & Gallery
MUSEUM, GALLERY

(☑07-871 0161; www.facebook.com/Museum Kawhia; Omimiti Reserve, Kawhia Wharf; by gold coin donation; ⊙11am-4pm, reduced hours Mar-Nov) Kawhia's modest waterside museum has local history, nautical and Māori artefacts, and regular art exhibitions. It doubles as the visitor information centre.

Maketu Marae
HISTORIC SITE

(www.kawhia.maori.nz; Kaora St) From Kawhia Wharf, a track extends along the coast to Maketu Marae, which has an impressively carved meeting house, Auaukiterangi. Two stones here – Hani and Puna – mark the burial place of the Tainui waka (a 14th-century ancestral canoe). You can't see a lot from the road, but the marae is private property and shouldn't be entered without permission. Email the Maketu Marae Committee for access.

The Tainui waka made its final landing at Kawhia. The expedition leaders – Hoturoa, the chief/captain, and Rakataura, the tohunga (priest) – searched the west coast until they recognised their prophesised landing place. Pulling into shore, they tied the waka to a pohutukawa tree, naming it Tangi te Korowhiti. This unlabelled tree still stands on the shoreline between the wharf and Maketu Marae. The waka was then dragged up onto a hill and buried: sacred stones were placed at either end to mark its resting place, now part of the marae.

Ocean Beach
BEACH, HOT SPRING

(Te Puia Rd) Four kilometres west of Kawhia is Ocean Beach and its high, black-sand dunes. Swimming can be dangerous, but one to two hours either side of low tide you can find the **Te Puia Hot Springs** in the sand – dig a hole for your own natural hot pool.

⨆ Sleeping & Eating

Kawhia Beachside S-Cape
HOLIDAY PARK $

(☑07-871 0727; www.kawhiabeachsidescape.co.nz; 225 Pouewe St; campsites from $40, cabins $65-110, units $135-165; ⊛) This water's edge campground looks shabby from the road but has comfortable cottages, plus cabins and camping with shared bathrooms. Two-hour kayak hire is $10 per person.

Kawhia Motel
MOTEL $$

(☑07-871 0865; www.kawhiamotel.co.nz; cnr Jervois & Tainui Sts; d $129-159; ⊛) These six perkily painted, well-kept, old-school motel units are right next to the shops. Kayaks and bikes are available for hire.

Rusty Snapper
CAFE $$

(☑07-871 0030; www.facebook.com/rusty snapperkawhia; 64 Jervois St; mains $12-24; ⊙10am-4pm, extended hours Jan & Feb) Freshly baked scones, slices and cakes combine with the best coffee in town, and if you're after fish and chips or fresh, seasonal seafood, the Rusty Snapper's a top spot too. Local oysters and whitebait fritters often feature.

ℹ Information

ℹ Getting There & Away

Kawhia doesn't have a bus service. Take SH31 from Otorohanga (58km) or explore the scenic but rough road to Raglan (50km, 22km unsealed).

Otorohanga

POP 2700

Otorohanga's main street is festooned with images of cherished Kiwiana icons: sheep, gumboots, jandals, No 8 wire, All Blacks, pavlova and the beloved Buzzy Bee children's toy. The town's Kiwi House is also well worth a visit.

◉ Sights

Otorohanga Kiwi House & Native Bird Park   ZOO

(☏ 07-873 7391; www.kiwihouse.org.nz; 20 Alex Telfer Dr; adult/child $24/8; ⊘9am-5pm, kiwi feedings 10.30am,1.30pm & 3.30pm daily) This bird barn has a nocturnal enclosure where you can see active kiwi energetically digging with their long beaks, searching for food. This is one of the only places where you can see a great spotted kiwi, the biggest of the three kiwi species. Brown kiwi are also on display, and there's a breeding program for these birds here. Other native birds on show include kaka, kea, morepork and weka.

Ed Hillary Walkway   MEMORIAL

As well as the Kiwiana decorating the main street, the Ed Hillary Walkway (running off Maniapoto St) has information panels on the All Blacks, Marmite and, of course, Sir Ed.

✖ Eating & Drinking

Ō Cafe   CAFE $$

(☏ 07-873 8714; www.facebook.com/Cafe.Otorohanga; 35 Maniapoto St; mains $12-20; ⊘7.30am-3.30pm) Otorohanga's newest and most cosmopolitan cafe is a goodie, with big shared tables, lots of natural light, and a versatile menu stretching from breakfast classics and home-style baking through to hearty lunch options. We can personally recommend the lamb burger with zingy beetroot relish.

The attached gift shop sells a few eclectic examples of local arts and crafts.

Thirsty Weta   PUB, CRAFT BEER

(☏ 07-873 6699; www.theweta.co.nz; 57 Maniapoto St; ⊘10am-2am; ☏) Hearty meals including pizza, steak, burgers and quesadillas (mains $12 to $38). Later on a pub-meets-wine-bar ambience kicks off as the local musos plug in. It's one of just a handful of places you'll find craft beers on tap from the local King Country Brewing Co (p228). Our favourite is the well-balanced pale ale.

ℹ Information

Otorohanga i-SITE (☏ 07-873 8951; www.otorohanga.co.nz; 27 Turongo St; ⊘9am-5pm Mon-Fri year-round, 10am-2pm Sat Oct-Apr; ☏) has free wi-fi and local information.

THE KĪNGITANGA

The concept of a Māori people is a relatively new one. Until the mid-19th century, New Zealand was effectively comprised of many independent tribal nations, operating in tandem with the British from 1840.

In 1856, faced with a flood of Brits, the Kīngitanga King Movement formed to unite the tribes to better resist further loss of land and culture. A gathering of leaders elected Waikato chief Pōtatau Te Wherowhero as the first Māori king, hoping that his increased *mana* (prestige) could achieve the cohesion that the British had under their queen.

Despite the huge losses of the Waikato War and the eventual opening up of the King Country, the Kīngitanga survived – although it has no formal constitutional role. A measure of the strength of the movement was the huge outpouring of grief when Te Arikinui Dame Atairangikaahu, Pōtatau's great-great-great-granddaughter, died in 2006 after 40 years at the helm. Although it's not a hereditary monarchy (leaders of various tribes vote on a successor), Pōtatau's line continues to the present day with King Tūheitia Paki.

ℹ Getting There & Away

BUS

InterCity (✆ 09-583 5780; www.intercity.co.nz) buses run from Otorohanga to Auckland ($20 to $42, 3¼ hours, three daily), Te Awamutu ($10 to $21, 30 minutes, three daily), Te Kuiti ($10 to $21, one hour, three daily) and Rotorua ($25 to $53, 2½ hours, two daily).

Naked Bus (✆ 0900 625 33; https://nakedbus.com) runs one bus daily to Waitomo Caves at 5pm ($13, 20 minutes). Other departures include Hamilton ($16, one hour) and New Plymouth ($22, 3¼ hours).

Caves Shuttle & Taxi Service (✆ 07-873 9083; www.cavesshuttlewaitomo.co.nz; adult/child $15/8; ⊙ from Waitomo 10.30am & 6pm, from Otorohanga 10am & 5pm) is a convenient service linking Otorohanga and Waitomo with scheduled departures or on demand. Book through local information centres or accommodation providers. Transport to Auckland or Hamilton airport is also available.

TRAIN

Otorohanga is on the **Northern Explorer** (✆ 0800 872 467; www.greatjourneysofnz.co.nz) train route between Auckland (from $59, 3¼ hours) and Wellington (from $139, nine hours) via Hamilton (from $59, 50 minutes); it also stops at Palmerston North, Ohakune and National Park. Southbound trains run on Monday, Thursday and Saturday, and northbound trains return from Wellington to Auckland on Tuesday, Friday and Sunday.

Waitomo Caves

POP 500

Even if damp, dark tunnels are your idea of hell, head to Waitomo anyway. The limestone caves and glowing bugs here are one of the North Island's premier attractions.

The name Waitomo comes from *wai* (water) and *tomo* (hole or shaft): dotted across this region are numerous shafts dropping into underground cave systems and streams. There are 300-plus mapped caves in the area: the three main caves – Glowworm, Ruakuri and Aranui (p226) – have been bewitching visitors for over 100 years.

Your Waitomo experience needn't be claustrophobic: the electrically lit, cathedral-like Glowworm Cave is far from squeezy. But if it's tight, gut-wrenching, soaking-wet, pitch-black excitement you're after, Waitomo can oblige.

There's no petrol in town, but there's an ATM at **Kiwi Paka** (✆ 07-878 3395; www.waitomokiwipaka.co.nz; Hotel Access Rd; dm/s/d $35/65/75, chalet s/d/tw/q $95/100/110/150; @🛜). It's best to stock up on cash, groceries and petrol in either Te Kuiti or Otorohanga though.

◉ Sights

Waitomo Caves
Visitor Centre   VISITOR CENTRE
(✆ 0800 456 922; www.waitomo.com; Waitomo Caves Rd; ⊙ 9am-5pm) The big-three Waitomo Caves are all operated by the same company, based at the spectacular Waitomo Caves Visitor Centre (near the Glowworm Cave. Various combo deals are available, including a Triple Cave Combo (adult/child $97/44), and other deals incorporate exciting underground thrills with the Legendary Black Water Rafting Company (p227). Check the website. For the cave tours, try to avoid the large tour groups, most of which arrive between 10.30am and 2.30pm.

★ **Glowworm Cave**   CAVE
(✆ 0800 456 922; www.waitomo.com/waitomo-glowworm-caves; adult/child $51/23; ⊙ 45min tours half-hourly 9am-5pm) The guided tour of the Glowworm Cave, which is behind the visitor centre, leads past impressive stalactites and stalagmites into a large cavern known as the **Cathedral**. The highlight comes at the tour's end when you board a boat and swing off onto the river. As your eyes grow accustomed to the dark you'll see a Milky Way of little lights surrounding you – these are the glowworms. Book your tour at the visitor centre.

The acoustics are so good that Dame Kiri Te Kanawa and the Vienna Boys Choir have given concerts here.

Ruakuri Cave   CAVE
(✆ 0800 782 587, 07-878 6219; www.waitomo.com/ruakuri-cave; adult/child $74/29; ⊙ 2hr tours 9am, 10am, 11am, 12.30pm, 1.30pm, 2.30pm & 3.30pm) Ruakuri Cave has an impressive 15m-high spiral staircase, bypassing a Māori burial site at the cave entrance. Tours lead through 1.6km of the 7.5km system, taking in caverns with glowworms, subterranean streams and waterfalls, and intricate limestone structures. Visitors have described it as spiritual – some claim it's haunted – and it's customary to wash your hands when leaving to remove the *tapu* (taboo). Book tours at the visitor centre, or at the departure point, the Legendary Black Water Rafting Company (p227).

Waitomo Caves

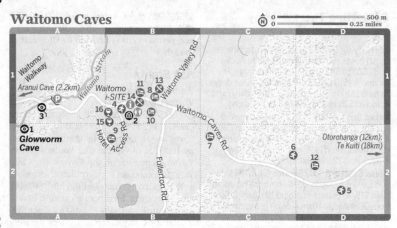

Waitomo Caves

◉ Top Sights
1 Glowworm Cave.....................................A2

◉ Sights
2 Waitomo Caves Discovery
  Centre...B1
3 Waitomo Caves Visitor
  Centre...A1

◉ Activities, Courses & Tours
4 CaveWorld...B1
5 Legendary Black Water
  Rafting Company................................D2
  Spellbound....................................(see 14)
6 Waitomo Adventures............................C2

◉ Sleeping
7 Abseil Inn..C2
8 Huhu Chalet...B1
9 Kiwi Paka..B2
10 Waitomo Caves Guest Lodge................B1
11 Waitomo Top 10 Holiday Park..............B1
12 YHA Juno Hall Waitomo.......................D2

◉ Eating
13 Huhu..B1
14 Waitomo General Store.........................B1

◉ Drinking & Nightlife
15 King Country Brewing Company...........B1
16 Tomo..B1

Aranui Cave   CAVE
(☏ 0800 456 922; www.waitomo.com/aranui-cave;
adult/child $50/23; ☉ 1hr tours depart 9am-4pm)
Three kilometres west from the Glowworm
Cave (p225) is Aranui Cave. This cave is dry
(hence no glowworms) but compensates
with an incredible array of limestone formations. Thousands of tiny 'straw' stalactites
hang from the ceiling. Book tours at the visitor centre (p225), from where there is transport to the cave entrance. A 15-minute bush
walk is also included.

Waitomo Caves Discovery Centre   MUSEUM
(☏ 07-878 7640; www.waitomocaves.com; 21
Waitomo Caves Rd; adult/child $5/free; ☉ 8.45am-
5pm) **FREE** Adjoining the Waitomo i-SITE
(p229) the Waitomo Caves Discovery Centre
has excellent exhibits explaining how caves
are formed, the flora and fauna that thrive
in them, and the history of Waitomo's caves
and cave exploration.

🏃 Activities

The Waitomo i-SITE (p229) has free pamphlets on walks in the area. The walk from
Aranui Cave to Ruakuri Cave (p225) is an excellent short path. From the Waitomo Caves
Visitor Centre (p225), the 5km, three-hour-
return **Waitomo Walkway** takes off through
farmland, following Waitomo Stream to the
Ruakuri Scenic Reserve, where a 30-min-
ute return walk passes by a natural limestone tunnel. There are glowworms here
at night – drive to the car park and bring a
torch to find your way.

Glowing Adventures   CAVING
(☏ 0508 445 694, 07-878 7234; www.glowing.co.nz;
1199 Oparure Rd; per person $159) 🖉 Located on
a family farm, the Waitomo region's newest
subterranean option operates small-group
tours (maximum eight people) through
more remote and unmodified caves. Tours

involve clambering over boulders, up hills and through underground streams, so a moderate level of fitness and adventure is required. Glowworms are aplenty, and you'll spend around two hours of the three-hour tour underground.

Kiwi Cave Rafting
CAVING

(☑ 0800 228 372, 07-873 9149; www.blackwater raftingwaitomo.co.nz; 95 Waitomo Caves Rd) These small-group expeditions ($250, five hours) start with abseil training, followed by a 27m descent into a natural cave, and then a float along a subterranean river on an inner-tube. After some caving, a belayed rock climb up a 20m cliff brings you to the surface. Book directly online with Kiwi Cave Rafting for a significant discount.

Dundle Hill Walk
TRAMPING

(☑ 07-878 7640; www.dundlehillwalk.co.nz; adult/ child $75/35) The self-guided privately run Dundle Hill Walk is a 27km, two-day/one-night loop walk through Waitomo's bush and farmland, including overnight bunkhouse accommodation high up in the bush.

Spellbound
CAVING

(☑ 0800 773 552, 07-878 7622; www.glowworm. co.nz; 10 Waitomo Caves Rd; adult/child $75/26; ☺ 3hr tours 10am, 11am, 2pm & 3pm) Spellbound is a good option if you don't want to get wet, are more interested in glowworms than an 'action' experience, and want to avoid the big groups in the main caves. Small-group tours access parts of the heavily glowworm-dappled Mangawhitiakau cave system, 12km south of Waitomo (and you still get to ride on a raft!).

Legendary Black Water Rafting Company
CAVING

(☑ 0800 782 5874; www.waitomo.com/black-water-rafting; 585 Waitomo Caves Rd) The Black Labyrinth tour ($142, three hours) involves floating in a wetsuit on an inner tube down a river through Ruakuri Cave (p225). The highlight is leaping off a small waterfall and then floating through a long, glowworm-covered passage. The trip ends with showers, soup and bagels in the cafe. There's also the more adventurous Black Abyss tour ($246, five hours).The latter includes a 35m abseil into Ruakuri Cave, a flying fox and more glowworms and tubing.

Minimum ages apply for all tours, and there are occasional discounts if you prebook online. Check the website for combo deals also incorporating entry to the other Waitomo caves.

Waitomo Adventures
CAVING

(☑ 0800 924 866, 07-878 7788; www.waitomo.co.nz; 654 Waitomo Caves Rd) Waitomo Adventures offers various cave adventures, with a substantial 20% discount for advance online bookings at least 12 hours prior. The Lost World trip ($405/580, four/seven hours) combines a 100m abseil with walking, rock climbing, wading and swimming. Haggas Honking Holes ($275, four hours) includes three waterfall abseils, rock climbing and a subterranean river. TumuTumu Toobing ($215, four

---

GLOWWORM MAGIC

Glowworms are the larvae of the fungus gnat. The larva glowworm has luminescent organs that produce a soft, greenish light. Living in a sort of hammock suspended from an overhang, it weaves sticky threads that trail down and catch unwary insects attracted by its light. When an insect flies towards the light it gets stuck in the threads – the glowworm just has to reel it in for a feed.

The larval stage lasts from six to nine months, depending on how much food the glowworm gets. When it has grown to about the size of a matchstick, it goes into a pupa stage, much like a cocoon. The adult fungus gnat emerges about two weeks later.

The adult insect doesn't live very long because it doesn't have a mouth. It emerges, mates, lays eggs and dies, all within about two or three days. The sticky eggs, laid in groups of 40 or 50, hatch in about three weeks to become larval glowworms.

Glowworms thrive in moist, dark caves but they can survive anywhere if they have the requisites of moisture, an overhang to suspend from and insects to eat. Waitomo is famous for its glowworms but you can see them in many other places around New Zealand, both in caves and outdoors.

When you come upon glowworms, don't touch their hammocks or hanging threads, try not to make loud noises and don't shine a light right on them. All of these things will cause them to dim their lights. It takes them a few hours to become bright again, during which time the grub will go hungry. The glowworms that shine most brightly are the hungriest.

hours) is a walking, climbing, swimming and tubing trip. St Benedict's Cavern ($215, three hours) includes abseiling and a subterranean flying fox.

CaveWorld CAVING
(☑0800 228 338, 07-878 6577; www.caveworld. co.nz; cnr Waitomo Caves Rd & Hotel Access Rd) CaveWorld runs the Tube It black-water rafting trip ($139, two hours) through glow-worm-filled Te Anaroa. Also available is the Footwhistle Glowworm Cave Tour ($59, one hour), incorporating a stop in a forest shelter for a mug of restorative *kawakawa* tea, a natural tonic made with leaves from an indigenous bush plant. Twilight Footwhistle tours are $65.

🛏 Sleeping

Waitomo Top 10 Holiday Park HOLIDAY PARK $
(☑07-878 7639, 0508 498 666; www.waitomopark. co.nz; 12 Waitomo Caves Rd; campsites from $44, cabins & units $95-190; @🛜🌊) This lovely holiday park in the heart of the village has spotless facilities, modern cabins and plenty of outdoor distractions to keep the kids busy. The cabins are a good alternative to dorm accommodation for friends travelling together, and renovated communal bathrooms are spotless.

YHA Juno Hall Waitomo HOSTEL $
(☑07-878 7649; www.junowaitomo.co.nz; 600 Waitomo Caves Rd; campsites from $17, dm $30, d with/without bathroom $84/74; @🛜🌊) A slick purpose-built hostel 1km from the village with a warm welcome, a warmer wood fire in the woody lounge area, and an outdoor pool and tennis court.

Huhu Chalet RENTAL HOUSE $$
(www.airbnb.com; 10 Waitomo Caves Rd; d $150) Concealed in a quirky pyramid structure that was once part of an advertising sign, Huhu Chalet has a cosy mezzanine bedroom upstairs, and a vibrant (red!) and modern bathroom and living space downstairs. With its simple wooden walls and a scattering of retro furniture, there's a warm Kiwiana vibe to the chalet, and Waitomo's best restaurant is literally metres away.

Waitomo Caves Guest Lodge B&B $$
(☑07-878 7641, 0800 465 762; www.waitomo cavesguestlodge.co.nz; 7 Waitomo Village Rd; s/d incl breakfast $100/150; 🛜) Bag your own cosy little hillside en-suite cabin at this central operation with a sweet garden setting. The top cabins have valley views. Large continental

breakfasts, friendly and helpful owners, and the on-site managerial skills of Thomas the cat are also big ticks.

Abseil Inn B&B $$
(☑07-878 7815; www.abseilinn.co.nz; 709 Waitomo Caves Rd; d $140-180; 🛜) A *veeery* steep driveway takes you to this delightful B&B with four themed rooms, great breakfasts and witty hosts. The biggest room has a double bath and valley views.

🍴 Eating

Waitomo General Store CAFE $
(☑07-878 8613; www.facebook.com/waitomo generalstore; 15 Waitomo Caves Rd; snacks & mains $8-18; ⊙8.30am-4pm Mar-Nov, to 8.30pm Dec-Feb; 🛜) The Waitomo General Store cafe has pre- and post-caving sustenance including hearty burgers, good coffee and tap beer. Fire up the free wi-fi on the sunny deck.

★Huhu MODERN NZ $$
(☑07-878 6674; www.huhucafe.co.nz; 10 Waitomo Caves Rd; mains $15-32; ⊙noon-late; 🛜) Huhu combines expansive terrace views and contemporary NZ food. Sip a Kiwi wine or craft beer – including brews from the local King Country Brewing Co – or graze the menu of delights including slow-cooked lamb, smoked salmon and roast duck. Downstairs is a small King Country Brewing beer bar that's open mainly in summer. For lunch, try the moreish buttermilk chicken.

🍷 Drinking & Nightlife

Tomo PUB
(☑07-878 8448; Hotel Access Rd; ⊙11am-late) The welcoming Tomo is Waitomo's pub and home turf for the King Country Brewing Co. A frosty pale ale teamed with a fish burger, chowder or the massive pork ribs could be just the thing after a busy day underground. Served on the sunny deck, of course. Keep an eye out for the pub's very friendly resident black cat.

King Country Brewing Company BREWERY
(☑021 498 665; www.kingcountrybrewingco.co.nz; Tomo, Hotel Access Rd; ⊙11am-late) This craft brewery based at Tomo (p228) pub brews pilsner, IPA, pale ale, wheat beer and cider. Due to contractual issues with bigger breweries, not all the beers are on tap at the pub, but they are all available in Waitomo at Huhu (p228). You'll also find them at Thirsty Weta in Otorohanga.

ℹ Information

Waitomo i-SITE (📞 0800 474 839, 07-878 7640; www.waitomocaves.com; 21 Waitomo Caves Rd; ⊙ 9am-5.30pm) has internet access and a post office, and is a booking agent for tours.

ℹ Getting There & Away

Naked Bus (📞 0900 625 33; https://naked-bus.com) runs one bus daily to Waitomo Caves village at 5pm ($13, 20 minutes). Other departures include Hamilton ($16, one hour) and New Plymouth ($22, 3¼ hours).

Caves Shuttle & Taxi Service (p225) links Otorohanga and Waitomo with scheduled departures or on demand. Book through local information centres or accommodation providers. Shuttles depart Otorohanga at 10am and 5pm, and Waitomo at 10.30am and 6pm. Transport to Auckland or Hamilton airport is also available.

Waitomo Wanderer (📞 0800 000 4321, 03-477 9083; www.travelheadfirst.com) operates a daily return service from Rotorua or Auckland, with optional caving, glowworm and tubing add-ons. It'll even integrate Hobbiton into the mix if you're a JRR Tolkien or Sir Peter Jackson fan.

South from Waitomo to Taranaki

This obscure route heading west of Waitomo on Te Anga Rd is a slow but fascinating alternative to SH3 if Taranaki's your goal. Only 12km of the 111km route remains unsealed, but it's nearly all winding and narrow. Allow around two hours (not including stops) and fill up with petrol.

◎ Sights

The **Mangapohue Natural Bridge Scenic Reserve**, 26km west of Waitomo, is a 5.5-hectare reserve with a giant natural limestone arch. It's a five-minute walk to the arch on a wheelchair-accessible pathway.

About 4km further west is **Piripiri Caves Scenic Reserve**, where a five-minute walk leads to a large cave containing fossils of giant oysters. Bring a torch and be prepared to get muddy after heavy rain. Steps wind down into the gloom...

The impressively tiered, 30m **Marokopa Falls** are 32km west of Waitomo. A short track (15 minutes return) from the road leads to the bottom of the falls.

Just past Te Anga you can turn north to Kawhia, 59km away, or continue southwest to **Marokopa** (population 1560), a small black-sand village on the coast. The whole Te Anga/Marokopa area is riddled with caves.

The road heads south to **Kiritehere**, through idyllic farmland to **Moeatoa** then turns right (south) into Mangatoa Rd. Now you're in serious backcountry, heading into the dense **Whareorino Forest**. For trampers, there's the 16-bunk, DOC-run **Leitch's Hut** (📞 07-878 1050; www.doc.govt.nz; per adult $5).

At **Waikawau** take the 5km detour along the unsealed road to the coast near **Ngarupupu Point**, where a 100m walk through a dank tunnel opens out on an exquisitely isolated stretch of black-sand beach. Think twice about swimming here as there are often dangerous rips in the surf.

The road then continues through another twisty 28km, passing lush forest and the occasional farm before joining SH3 east of Awakino.

🏃 Activities

Walks in the **Tawarau Forest**, 20km west of the Waitomo Caves, are outlined in DOC's *Waitomo & King Country Tracks* booklet ($1, available from DOC in Hamilton or Te Kuiti), including a one-hour track to the Tawarau Falls from the end of Appletree Rd.

ℹ Getting There & Away

There's no public transport to Marokopa, but it's a very scenic drive here in your own vehicle.

Te Kuiti

POP 4380

Cute Te Kuiti sits in a valley between picturesque hills. Welcome to the shearing capital of the world, especially if you visit for the annual Great New Zealand Muster (p230). It's also the birthplace of the late Sir Colin Meads, one of NZ's most iconic All Blacks.

◎ Sights

Sir Colin Meads Statue   STATUE
(Rora St) This statue commemorates the late Sir Colin Meads, a legendary captain of the All Blacks, and regarded as one of New Zealand's finest rugby players. Nicknamed 'Pinetree', and a lifelong resident of Te Kuiti and the King Country, Sir Colin's laconic and pragmatic demeanour means he's also fondly remembered as the quintessential Kiwi – a 'good bugger' in local parlance.

Te Kuititanga-O-Nga-Whakaaro   MONUMENT
(The Gathering of Thoughts & Ideas; Rora St) Te Kuititanga-O-Nga-Whakaaro is a beautiful pavilion of etched-glass, *tukutuku* (woven

flax panels) and wooden carvings that celebrates the town's history.

Big Shearer
LANDMARK

(Rora St) The 7m-high, 7½-tonne Big Shearer statue is at the southern end of town.

✨ Festivals & Events

Great New Zealand Muster
CULTURAL, FOOD & DRINK

(www.waitomo.govt.nz/events/the-great-nz-muster; ⊙ late Mar/early Apr) The highlight of the Great New Zealand Muster is the legendary Running of the Sheep, when 2000 woolly demons stampede down Te Kuiti's main street. The festival includes sheep-shearing championships, a parade, Māori cultural performances, live music, barbecues, *hāngi* and market stalls.

🛏 Sleeping & Eating

Waitomo Lodge Motel
MOTEL $$

(⌨ 07-878 0003; www.waitomo-lodge.co.nz; 62 Te Kumi Rd; units $130-175; 🛜) At the Waitomo end of Te Kuiti, this motel's modern rooms feature contemporary art, flat-screen TVs and little decks overlooking Mangaokewa Stream from the units at the back. A couple of resident animals include Willow the friendly terrier.

Stoked Eatery
CAFE $$

(⌨ 07-878 8758; www.stokedeatery.co.nz; Te Kuiti Railway Station, 2 Rora St; mains $17-38; ⊙ 10am-late) This busy restaurant and bar in the former railway station celebrates a great location on the station platform with a relaxed ambience and a menu of hearty fare. Servings are very generous; standouts include lamb shanks or the buttermilk-fried chicken. A decent wine list and local craft beer on tap make Stoked a good option for a drink too.

ℹ Information

Te Kuiti DOC (Department of Conservation; ⌨ 07-878 1050; www.doc.govt.nz; 78 Taupiri St; ⊙ 8am-4.30pm Mon-Fri) is the area office for the surrounding Maniapoto region.

Te Kuiti i-SITE (⌨ 07-878 8077; www.waitomo.govt.nz; Rora St; ⊙ 9am-5pm Mon-Fri, 10am-2pm Sat & Sun, closed weekends May-Oct; 🛜) has internet access and visitor information.

ℹ Getting There & Away

InterCity (⌨ 09-583 5780; www.intercity.co.nz) buses run daily to the following destinations (among others): Auckland ($24 to $49, 3½ hours, three daily), Mokau ($14 to $29, two hours, one daily), New Plymouth ($15 to $29,

2½ hours, one daily), Otorohanga ($10 to $21, 20 minutes, three daily) and Taumarunui ($10 to $21, 1¼ hours, one daily).

Naked Bus (⌨ 09-979 1616; https://nakedbus.com) runs to Hamilton ($16, 1½ hours, two daily), New Plymouth ($16, 2¼ hours, one daily) and Otorohanga ($11, 20 minutes, two daily).

Pio Pio, Awakino & Mokau

From Te Kuiti, SH3 runs southwest to the coast before following the rugged shoreline to New Plymouth. Detour at Pio Pio (population 400) to Hairy Feet Waitomo, one of New Zealand's newest Middle Earth themed attractions.

Along this scenic route the sheep stations sprout peculiar limestone formations before giving way to lush native bush as the highway winds along the course of the Awakino River. This river spills into the Tasman at Awakino (population 60), a small settlement where boats shelter in the estuary while locals find refuge at the rustic **Awakino Hotel** (⌨ 06-752 9815; www.facebook.com/AwakinoHotel; SH3, Awakino; meals $13-22; ⊙ 11am-10pm Sun-Thu, to midnight Fri & Sat).

Five kilometres further south, as Mt Taranaki starts to emerge on the horizon, is the village of Mokau (population 400). It offers a fine black-sand beach and good surfing and fishing. From August to November the Mokau River (the second-longest on the North Island) spawns whitebait and subsequent swarms of territorial whitebaiters.

◎ Sights & Activities

A little south of Awakino the impressive **Maniaroa Marae** dominates the cliff above the highway. This important complex houses the anchor stone of the Tainui *waka*, which brought this region's original people from their Polynesian homeland. You can get a good view of the intimidatingly carved meeting house, **Te Kohaarua**, from outside the fence – don't cross into the *marae* unless someone invites you.

Hairy Feet Waitomo
FILM LOCATION

(⌨ 07-877 8003; www.hairyfeetwaitomo.co.nz; 1411 Mangaotaki Rd, Pio Pio; tours adult/child $50/25; ⊙ tours 10am & 1pm) Detour at Pio Pio northwest to the Mangaotaki valley and Hairy Feet Waitomo, one of NZ's most interesting Middle-earth–themed film location attractions. Scenes from *The Hobbit* were filmed here with a background of towering limestone cliffs.

Tainui Historical Society Museum   MUSEUM
(📞 06-752 9072; www.mokaumuseum.nz; SH3, Mokau; by donation; ⊙ 10am-4pm) Mokau's interesting Tainui Historical Society Museum has old photographs and artefacts from when this once-isolated outpost was a coal and lumber shipping port for settlements along the river. The adjacent art gallery featuring local artists was added during a 2016 renovation.

Mokau River Tours   BOATING
(📞 0800 665 282; www.mokauriver.co.nz; adult/child $60/10) Mokau River Tours operates a three-hour river cruise on the MV *GlenRoyal,* including a stop upriver in an old camping ground in the forest.

🛏 Sleeping & Eating

Mokau Motel   MOTEL $$
(📞 06-752 9725; www.mokaumotels.co.nz; SH3, Mokau; s/d/ste from $100/115/130; 🛜) Above the village, the Mokau Motel offers fishing advice, self-contained units and three luxury suites.

Fat Pigeon Cafe   CAFE $
(📞 07-877 8822; www.theowlsnest.co.nz/fat-pigeon-cafe.html; 41 Moa St, Pio Pio; mains $12-19; ⊙ 7.30am-4pm Mon-Sat, 8am-4pm Sun) The Fat Pigeon offers good-value mains such as pulled-pork tacos, and huge freshly baked muffins and bagels crammed with salmon and cream cheese.

Whitebait Inn   CAFE $$
(📞 06-752 9713; www.whitebaitinn.co.nz; 55 North St, Mokau; snacks & mains $12-27; ⊙ 7.30am-6.30pm) A great place to try the local speciality of whitebait is this classic Kiwi diner. Look for the quirky statue of the whitebait fisherman on the roof before tucking into tasty fritters or an omelette stuffed into a fresh slice of fluffy white bread. Add a squeeze of lemon juice and salt and pepper and you're good to go.

ⓘ Getting There & Away

InterCity (www.intercity.co.nz) buses run from Te Kuiti to Mokau (from $14, one hour, one daily) as part of a bus service linking Auckland to New Plymouth.

Taumarunui

POP 5140
Taumarunui on a cold day can feel a bit miserable, but this town in the heart of the King Country has potential. The main reason to stay here is to kayak on the Whanganui River or as a cheaper base for skiing in Tongariro National Park. There are also some beach walks and cycling tracks around town.

For details on the Forgotten World Hwy between Taumarunui and Stratford, contact Eastern Taranaki Experience (p248). Details on canoeing and kayaking on the Whanganui River can be obtained from Whanganui National Park (p261).

⊙ Sights

Across the Ongarue River on the western edge of town, **Te Peka Lookout** is a good vantage point.

Hakiaha Street   STREET
At the street's eastern end is **Hauaroa Whare**, a beautifully carved house. At the western end, **Te Rohe Potae** memorialises King Tawhiao's assertion of his *mana* (authority) over the King Country in a sculpture of a top hat on a large rock.

🏃 Activities & Tours

The 3km **Riverbank Walk** along the Whanganui River runs from Cherry Grove Domain, 1km south of town, to Taumarunui Holiday Park.

Forgotten World Adventures   TOURS
(📞 0800 7245 2278; www.forgottenworld adventures.co.nz; 9 Hakiaha St; half-/1-/2-day tours from $125/230/595; ⊙ booking office 9am-2pm) Ride the rails on quirky, converted former golf carts along the railway line linking Taumarunui to the tiny hamlet of Whangamomona in the Taranaki region. The most spectacular trip takes in 20 tunnels. Other options include a rail and jetboat combo and a longer two-day excursion covering the full 140km from Taumarunui to Stratford (including an overnight stay in Whangamomona).

Forgotten World Jet   ADVENTURE
(📞 0800 7245 2278, 07-895 7181; www.fwj.co.nz; Cherry Grove Domain; 1/2hr from $105/205) High-octane jetboat trips on the Whanganui River. Longer eight-hour adventures take in the spectacular Bridge to Nowhere, and trips incorporating rail journeys with Forgotten World Adventures (p231) are also available.

🛏 Sleeping & Eating

Taumarunui Holiday Park   HOLIDAY PARK $
(📞 07-895 9345; www.taumarunuiholidaypark.co.nz; SH4; campsites from $18, cabins & cottages $55-90; ◉🛜) On the banks of the Whanganui River, 4km east of town, this shady camping ground offers safe river swimming and clean facilities.

PUREORA FOREST PARK

Fringing the western edge of Lake Taupo, the 780-sq-km Pureora Forest is home to New Zealand's tallest totara tree. Logging was stopped in the 1980s after a long campaign by conservationists, and the subsequent regeneration is impressive. Tramping routes through the park include tracks to the summits of **Mt Pureora** (1165m) and the rock pinnacle of **Mt Titiraupenga** (1042m). A 12m-high tower, a short walk from the Bismarck Rd car park, provides a canopy-level view of the forest for bird-watchers.

Awhina Wilderness Experience (www.facebook.com/AwhinaWildernessExperience) offers five-hour walking tours with local Māori guides through virgin bush to the summit of Titiraupenga, their sacred mountain. Cyclists can ride the spectacular **Timber Trail** from Pureora village in the north of the forest southwest for 85km to Ongarue. Two days is recommended. Accommodation and shuttle transport is available at **Pa Harakeke** (☑07-929 8708; www.paharakeke.co.nz; 138 Maraeroa Rd; d $150) ✍, an interesting Māori-operated initiative near Pureora village.

For shuttles and bike hire, contact **Epic Cycle Adventures** (☑022 023 7958; www.thetimbertrail.nz; 9 Rata St, Manunui; bike & shuttle from $105) in Taumarunui. See www.the-timbertrail.com and www.thetimbertrail.nz for maps, shuttle and bike hire information and route planning.

Accommodation includes three DOC campsites (www.doc.govt.nz; adult/child $8/4), with self-registration boxes, and a couple of interesting lodges and chalets. To stay overnight in one of the three standard DOC huts you'll need to buy hut tickets in advance, unless you have a Backcountry Hut Pass. Hut tickets, maps and information are available from DOC.

The friendly owners have lots of ideas on what to see and do.

Twin Rivers Motel   MOTEL **$$**
(☑07-895 8063; www.twinrivers.co.nz; 23 Marae St; units $90-215; ☏) The 12 units at Twin Rivers are spick and span. Bigger units sleep up to seven.

Copper Tree Cafe   CAFE **$$**
(☑07-896 7442; 75 Hakiaha St; mains $14-24; ⊗9am-4pm Mon-Wed, 9am-9pm Thu & Fri, 10am-4pm Sat & Sun) A switched-on young couple have enlivened this main-street cafe. Hearty quiche and homemade pies are served with chips and salad, while eggs Benedict partners with good coffee for brunch. At the time of research, the friendly owners were opening for dinner on Thursday and Friday nights too.

ⓘ Information

Taumarunui i-SITE (☑07-895 7494; www.visitruapehu.com; 116 Hakiaha St; ⊗8.30am-5.30pm) has internet access.

ⓘ Getting There & Away

Taumarunui is on SH4, 81km south of Te Kuiti and 41km north of National Park township. **InterCity** (☑0508 353 947; www.intercity.co.nz) buses head to Auckland (from $30, 4½ hours) via Te Kuiti and to Palmerston North (from $33, 4½ hours) via National Park.

Owhango

POP 210

A pint-sized village where all the street names start with 'O', Owhango makes a cosy base for walkers, mountain bikers (the **42 Traverse** ends here) and skiers who don't want to fork out to stay closer to the slopes in Tongariro National Park. Take Omaki Rd for a two-hour loop walk through virgin forest in **Ohinetonga Scenic Reserve**.

🛏 Sleeping

Blue Duck Station   LODGE, HOSTEL **$**
(Map p262; ☑07-895 6276; www.blueduckstation.co.nz; RD2, Whakahoro; dm $45, d $100-195) ✍
Overlooking the Retaruke River 36km southwest of Owhango (take the Kaitieke turn-off 1km south of town), this ecosavvy place is actually various lodges, offering accommodation from dorms in old shearers' quarters to a self-contained family cottage sleeping eight. The owners are mad-keen conservationists, restoring native-bird habitats and historic buildings. Activities include bush tours, horse riding, kayaking and mountain biking.

ⓘ Getting There & Away

Owhango is 14km south of Taumarunui on SH4. All the **InterCity** (☑0508 353 947; www.intercity.co.nz) buses that stop in Taumarunui also stop here.

Taranaki & Whanganui

Best Places to Eat

➜ Monica's Eatery (p244)

➜ Social Kitchen (p244)

➜ Saigon Corner (p267)

➜ Opunake Fish, Chips and More (p252)

➜ Citadel (p258)

Best Places to Stay

➜ One Burgess Hill (p243)

➜ Ducks & Drakes (p242)

➜ Ahu Ahu Beach Villas (p251)

➜ Tivoli Homestay (p243)

➜ King & Queen Hotel Suites (p242)

Why Go?

Halfway between Auckland and Wellington on New Zealand's underappreciated west coast, Taranaki (aka 'the 'Naki') is the country's Texas, with oil and gas streaming in from offshore rigs. But in New Plymouth free galleries, a provincial museum and dining hot spots attract young families and retirees from Auckland craving a slower pace without compromising lifestyle. Travellers are following suit.

Behind the city the stunning Mt Taranaki demands to be photographed, if not visited. The volcanic terrain is responsible for the area's black-sand beaches, lapped up by surfers and holidaymakers during summer.

Further east the history-rich Whanganui River curls its way through Whanganui National Park down to Whanganui city, a 19th-century river port ageing with grace and embracing its local arts scene. Palmerston North, the Manawatu region's main city, is a students' town courtesy of caffeinated Massey University literati. Beyond the city, the region blends rural grace with yesterday's pace.

When to Go

➜ In January and February, cruise the 105km-long Surf Highway 45 and find your favourite black-sand beach – surf's up in summer!

➜ Powder snow and picture-perfect runs on Mt Taranaki make July the ideal time to visit.

➜ In December the crowds arrive to see the lights in Pukekura Park at the annual Festival of Lights.

Taranaki & Whanganui Highlights

1 Mt Taranaki (p247) Hiking up or around this massive cone.

2 New Zealand Rugby Museum (p265) Flexing your All Blacks spirit in Palmerston North.

3 Surf Highway 45 (p250) Riding big breaks along this surf-battered coast.

4 New Plymouth (p238) Savouring experimental art at the dazzling Len Lye Centre and bouncing from bean to bean at the city's cafes.

5 New Zealand Glassworks (p254) Watching a glass-blowing demonstration in Whanganui.

6 Whanganui National Park (p260) Redefining serenity on a Whanganui River canoe or kayak trip – or taking on an extreme jetboating adventure.

7 Whanganui River Road (p260) Traversing River Road by car or bike – it's all about the journey, not how fast you get there.

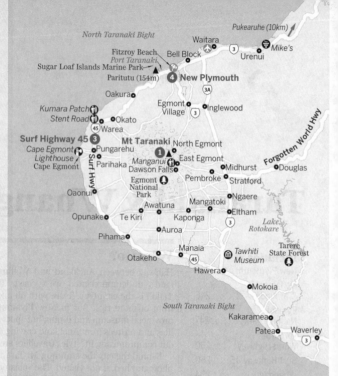

North Taranaki Bight

Pukearuhe (10km)

Waitara

Fitzroy Beach
Port Taranaki
Sugar Loaf Islands Marine Park
Paritutu (154m) **4 New Plymouth**

Bell Block

Mike's
Urenui

Oakura

Egmont Village

Inglewood

Kumara Patch
Stent Road
Okato
Warea

Surf Highway 45 3
Cape Egmont
Lighthouse
Cape Egmont

Pungarehu
Parihaka
Dawson Falls

Mt Taranaki North Egmont
1
Manganui
East Egmont
Pembroke

Midhurst
Stratford

Douglas

Oaonui

Egmont National Park

Awatuna

Mangatoki
Ngaere

Eltham

Lake Rotokare

Opunake
Te Kiri
Kaponga

Pihama

Auroa

Tarere State Forest

Manaia
Tawhiti Museum

Otakeho

Hawera

Mokoia

South Taranaki Bight

Kakaramea

Patea
Waverley

Forgotten World Hwy

TASMAN SEA

N
0   40 km
0   20 miles

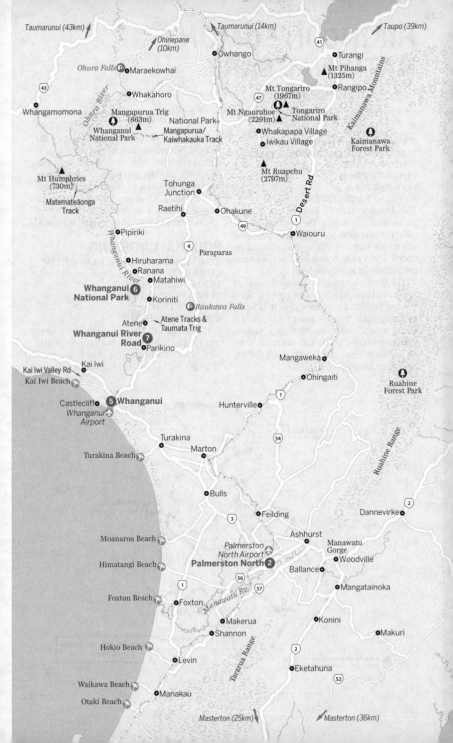

HIKING IN EGMONT NATIONAL PARK

POUAKAI CIRCUIT

START/END EGMONT NATIONAL PARK
VISITOR CENTRE
DURATION 2 DAYS
DISTANCE 25KM
DIFFICULTY MODERATE

The Pouakai Circuit features spectacular views from the top of the Pouakai Range, which at one time was a volcano of similar size to Mt Taranaki. Natural erosion has reduced it to a rugged area of high ridges and rolling hills of subalpine bush.

The track also passes through the mighty Ahukawakawa Swamp, a unique wetland formed around 3500 years ago. It is home to many plant species, some of which are found nowhere else on the planet. Sedges, sphagnum moss, herbs and red tussock are all common here, along with small orchids and other flowering plants.

This loop can be tramped in either direction, but trampers can also walk it in a day, leaving the route at Pouakai Hut and following the Mangorei Track (a two-hour tramp) to the end of Mangorei Rd – this is the Pouakai Crossing. This road leads to New Plymouth, a mostly downhill walk of 15km (there's usually little traffic this far up).

POUAKAI CROSSING

START EGMONT NATIONAL PARK VISITOR
CENTRE
END MANGOREI RD
DURATION 7½–9½ HOURS
DISTANCE 17KM
DIFFICULTY MODERATE

If the Tongariro Alpine Crossing is widely regarded as the best day walk in New Zealand, the Pouakai Crossing is its heir apparent. This walk is another volcanic highlights

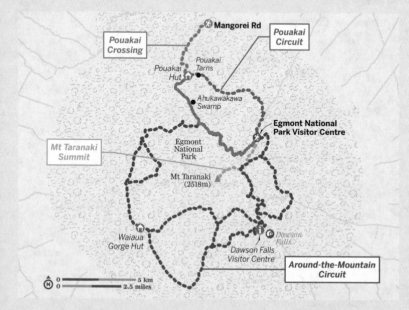

Tramping here is dominated by volcanic Mt Taranaki – think, Mt Fuji with a Kiwi accent. The mountain is laced with tramping routes, from a contender for the title of NZ's best day hike, to a lap around the volcano and a summit climb.

reel, taking in spectacular cliffs, a waterfall, the primeval Ahukawakawa Swamp and the (hopefully) mirror-perfect Pouakai Tarns.

It's a walk that packs plenty of panoramic punch without the need to lug a heavy pack filled with overnight gear. It's also a great option for those staying in New Plymouth, allowing you a grand day out with a debrief back among the bright lights of the city. Its relatively low altitude means it can also be walked much of the year, though it's worth checking in with Egmont National Park Visitor Centre before you leave to make sure the track's OK.

Starting at the visitor centre, the track follows the first day of the Pouakai Circuit as far as Pouakai Hut before heading down Mangorei Track to the road, where you can be collected by shuttle bus for the return trip to New Plymouth. It's a full-on day, but a hugely satisfying one.

Ahukawakawa Swamp

AROUND THE MOUNTAIN CIRCUIT

START/END EGMONT NATIONAL PARK VISITOR CENTRE
DURATION 5 DAYS
DISTANCE 49–53KM
DIFFICULTY MODERATE TO DEMANDING

The Around the Mountain Circuit (AMC) is exactly what the name on the tin suggests – a spectacular loop around Taranaki on a backcountry track for experienced trampers through stunted subalpine forest and spectacular volcanic scenery.

The track can be started at either the Egmont National Park Visitor Centre or Dawson Falls. Trampers starting at Dawson Falls often go directly to Waiaua Gorge Hut via the upper level tracks on the first day. Note that high- and low-level tracks exist for some sections of the track, giving you the chance to climb high in good weather, or stay low and safe in bad. It's important to remember that there are lots of rivers along the track, and not many bridges. Rivers can become

dangerous to cross after heavy rain. If in doubt, wait it out.

MT TARANAKI SUMMIT

START/END EGMONT NATIONAL PARK VISITOR CENTRE
DURATION 8–10 HOURS
DISTANCE 12.6KM
DIFFICULTY MODERATE TO DEMANDING

Taranaki is the most climbed mountain in New Zealand, and in ideal summer conditions most fit trampers can make it to the summit, but you need to be prepared – a long list of people have been killed on its slopes. It's an ascent of around 1570m – a big day out – so don't take it lightly whatever the conditions. You must check the forecast, and be prepared to turn tail and retreat if the weather deteriorates (check in with the Egmont National Park Visitor Centre for up-to-date information before you set out.

NEW PLYMOUTH

POP 74,200

Dominated (in the best possible way) by Mt Taranaki and surrounded by lush farmland, New Plymouth is the only international deep-water port in this part of New Zealand. Like all port towns, the world washes in and out on the tide, leaving the locals buzzing with a global outlook. The city has a bubbling arts scene (with two superb free galleries), some fab cafes and a rootsy, outdoorsy focus. Surf beaches and Mt Taranaki (Egmont National Park) are just a short hop away.

History

Local Māori *iwi* (tribes) have long contested Taranaki lands. In the 1820s they fled to the Cook Strait region to escape Waikato tribes, who eventually took hold of the area in 1832. Only a small group remained at Okoki Pā (in today's New Plymouth). When European settlers arrived in 1841, the coast of Taranaki seemed deserted and there was little opposition to land claims. The New Zealand Company bought extensive tracts from the remaining Māori.

When other members of local tribes returned after years of exile, they fiercely objected to the land sale. Their claims were upheld by Governor FitzRoy, but the Crown gradually acquired more land from Māori, and European settlers sought the fertile soil. Settlers forced the government to abandon negotiations with Māori, and war erupted in 1860. By 1870 more than 500 hectares of Māori land had been confiscated.

Ensuing economic growth was largely founded on dairy farming. The 1959 discoveries of natural gas and oil in the South Taranaki Bight have kept the province economically healthy in recent times.

ESSENTIAL TARANAKI & WHANGANUI

Eat In one of Palmerston North's hip George St eateries.

Drink third-wave coffee from Ozone Coffee Roaster's Bean Store (p245).

Read *Came a Hot Friday*, a 1964 novel by Ronald Hugh Morrieson, born in Hawera, about two conmen who cheat bookmakers throughout the country.

Listen to the rockin' album *Back to the Burning Wreck* by Whanganui riff-monsters the Have.

Watch *The Last Samurai*, co-starring Tom Cruise (though Mt Taranaki should get top billing).

Go Green by paddling a stretch of the Whanganui River, an awe-inspiring slice of NZ wilderness.

Online www.visit.taranaki.info, www.whanganuinz.com, www.manawatunz.co.nz

⊙ Sights

◎ City Centre

★ Puke Ariki   MUSEUM
(☑ 06-759 6060; www.pukeariki.com; 1 Ariki St; ⊘ 9am-6pm Mon, Tue, Thu & Fri, to 9pm Wed, to 5pm Sat & Sun) FREE Translating as 'Hill of Chiefs', Puke Ariki is home to the i-SITE (p246), a museum, a library, a cafe and Arborio (☑ 06-759 1241; www.arborio.co.nz; Puke Ariki Museum, 65 St Aubyn St; breakfast & lunch $10-26, dinner $21-38; ⊘ 9am-late; ☏) restaurant. The excellent museum has an extensive collection of Māori artefacts, plus colonial, mountain geology and wildlife exhibits (we hope the shark suspended above the lobby isn't to scale).

Wind Wand   SCULPTURE
(Puke Ariki Landing, St Aubyn St; ⊘ 24hr) FREE The wonderfully eccentric Wind Wand at Puke Ariki Landing was designed by Len Lye – the artist who has put this town on the map in modern times. This 45m-high kooky kinetic sculpture is a truly beloved icon of bendy pole-ness. Look for it all lit up at night.

★ Len Lye Centre   GALLERY
(☑ 06-759 6060; www.lenlyefoundation.com; 42 Queen St; ⊘ 10am-5pm; ♿) FREE 'Great art goes 50-50 with great architecture', so said Len Lye, the world-beating NZ artist (1901–80) to whom this contemporary-art gallery is dedicated. And indeed, the architecture is amazing: an interlocking facade of tall, mirror-clad concrete flutes, inside which is a series of galleries linked by ramps housing Lye's works – kinetic, noisy and surprising. It also has a cinema, kids' art sessions and the broader Govett-Brewster Art Gallery (p239) next door. Don't miss it.

New Plymouth

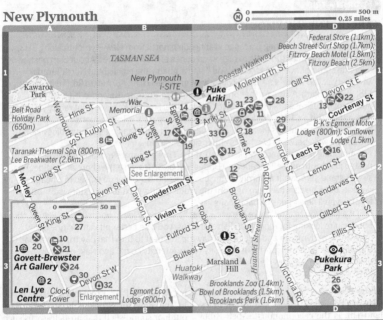

New Plymouth

★ **Govett-Brewster Art Gallery** GALLERY
(☐ 06-759 6060; www.govettbrewster.com; 42 Queen St; ☺10am-5pm) FREE Adjacent to the superb Len Lye Centre, this is arguably the country's best regional art gallery, present-ing contemporary – and often experimental and provocative – local and international shows. Pop into the wonderful Monica's Eatery (p244) next door for a bite.

WORTH A TRIP

AROUND NEW PLYMOUTH

There are some interesting places to visit heading north from New Plymouth along SH3, with various seaward turn-offs to high sand dunes and surf beaches. About 5km past riverside summer hot spot **Urenui**, you'll find arguably the highlight of North Taranaki – a brewery called **Mike's** (☑ 06-752 3676; www.mikesbeer.co.nz; 487 Mokau Rd, Urenui; pizzas $18; ☉10am-5pm). A little further on is the turn-off to **Pukearuhe** and **White Cliffs**, huge precipices resembling their Dover namesakes. From Pukearuhe boat ramp, you can tackle the **White Cliffs Walkway**, a three-hour loop walk with mesmerising views of the coast and mountains (Taranaki and Ruapehu). The tide can make things dicey along the beach: walk between two hours either side of low tide.

Continuing north towards Mokau, stop at the **Three Sisters** rock formation sign-posted just south of the Tongaporutu Bridge – you can traverse the shore at low tide. Two sisters stand somewhat forlornly off the coast: their other sister collapsed in a heap last decade, but a new sis is emerging from the eroding cliffs. Next to the sisters is **Elephant Rock** – you'll never guess what it looks like.

If it's food you're after, there are a few beachy takeaway joints north of New Plymouth, but if you're looking for more than fish and chips, you'll be better off in the city – bunk down in New Plymouth and treat it as a day trip. It's best to turn that day trip into a road trip with your own transport, but InterCity (www.intercity.co.nz) and Naked Bus (www.nakedbus.com) services ply the SH3.

Kibby Carillon MONUMENT
(Marsland Hill, Robe St) **FREE** On top of Marsland Hill is the cacophonous 37-bell Kibby Carillon, a huge automated glockenspiel-like device that tolls out across the New Plymouth rooftops.

New Plymouth Observatory OBSERVATORY
(☑ 021 071 3315; www.sites.google.com/site/astronomynp; Marsland Hill, Robe St; adult/child/family $5/3/10; ☉ 7.30-9.30pm Tue Mar-Oct, 8.30-10pm Tue Nov-Feb) Atop Marsland Hill (great views!) is this wee observatory, with one of the most powerful public-access telescopes in NZ.

◉ Brooklands

★**Pukekura Park** GARDENS
(☑ 06-759 6060; www.pukekura.org.nz; Liardet St; ☉daylight hr) **FREE** The pick of New Plymouth's parks, Pukekura has 49 hectares of gardens, playgrounds, trails, streams, waterfalls, ponds and display houses. **Rowboats** (per half-hour $15, summer only) meander across the main lake (full of arm-sized eels), next to which the **Tea House** (☑06-758 7205; www.pukekura.org.nz; Pukekura Park, Liardet St; dishes $8-19; ☉9am-4pm; ♠) serves light meals. The technicolored Festival of Lights (p242) draws the summer crowds here, as does the impeccably mowed **cricket oval**.

Brooklands Park PARK
(☑ 06-759 6060; www.newplymouthnz.com; Brooklands Park Dr; ☉ daylight hrs) **FREE** Adjoining Pukekura Park, Brooklands Park is home to the Bowl of Brooklands, a world-class outdoor sound-shell that hosts festivals such as WOMAD (p242), and old-school rockers including Fleetwood Mac. Park highlights include a 2000-year old puriri tree, a 300-variety rhododendron dell and the farmy (and free!) **Brooklands Zoo** (☑06-759 6060; www.newplymouthnz.com; Brooklands Park, Brooklands Park Dr; ☉9am-5pm; ♠) **FREE**.

◉ Surrounds

Te Rewa Rewa Bridge BRIDGE
(☑06-759 5150; www.visit.taranaki.info; Te Rewa Rewa Bridge; ☉24hr) Just past the Fitzroy Golf Course and accessible via Fitzroy Seaside Park or Peringa Park, this 83m-long bridge crosses Waiwhakaiho River and extends the Coastal Walkway by 4km, a 12.7km path along the ocean stretching from Pioneer Park at Port Taranaki to the eastern side of Bell Block Beach. Resembling a whale skeleton, visit on a clear day for an iconic Taranaki photo opportunity of Mt Taranaki framed by the bridge.

Paritutu Rock HILL
(Centennial Dr; ☉daylight hrs) **FREE** Just west of town is Paritutu, a steep-sided, craggy hill over 150m tall whose name translates as 'Rising Precipice'. 'Precipice' is right – it's a seriously knee-trembling, 15-minute scramble to the top, the upper reaches over bare rock with a chain to grip on to. If you can ignore your inner screams of common sense,

you can see for miles around at the summit: out to the Sugar Loaves, down across the town and out to Mt Taranaki beyond. If the weather is unfavourable, it's best (and safest!) to save it for another day.

Tupare HISTORIC BUILDING
(📞 0800 736 222; www.tupare.info; 487 Mangorei Rd, New Plymouth; ⊙ 9am-5pm Apr-Oct, to 8pm Nov-Mar, tours 11am Fri-Mon Oct-Mar) FREE Tupare is a Tudor-style house designed by the renowned architect James Chapman-Taylor. It's as pretty as a picture, but the highlight of this 7km trip south of New Plymouth will likely be the rambling 3.6-hectare garden surrounding it. Bluebells and birdsong under the boughs – picnic paradise.

Hurworth Cottage HISTORIC BUILDING
(📞 04-472 4341; www.historic.org.nz; 906 Carrington Rd, New Plymouth; adult/child/family $5/2/10; ⊙ by appointment) This 1856 cottage, 8km south of New Plymouth, was built by four-time NZ prime minister Harry Atkinson. The cottage is the sole survivor of a settlement abandoned at the start of the Taranaki Land Wars. It's a rare window into the lives of early settlers.

Taranaki Aviation, Transport & Technology Museum MUSEUM
(TATATM; 📞 06-752 2845; http://tatatm.tripod.com/museum; cnr SH3 & Kent Rd, New Plymouth; adult/child/family $7/2/16; ⊙ 10.30am-4pm Sat & Sun, school & public holidays) Around 9km south of New Plymouth is this roadside museum, with ramshackle displays of old planes, trains, automobiles and general household miscellany. Run by volunteer enthusiasts, the collection is always growing, thanks to donations. Many of the displays are interactive. Don't miss the chance to sit in the cockpit of the Harvard training plane!

Pukeiti GARDENS
(📞 0800 736 222; www.pukeiti.org.nz; 2290 Carrington Rd, New Plymouth; ⊙ 9am-5pm) FREE This sprawling garden, 23km south of New Plymouth, is home to masses of rhododendrons and azaleas. The flowers bloom between September and November, but it's worth a visit any time. Take a garden walk (45 minutes to two hours), or entertain the kids with the self-guided Treehouse Trail adventure. There's a cafe here, too.

🏃 Activities

Hiking

The New Plymouth i-SITE (p246) stocks the *Taranaki: A Walker's Guide* booklet,

which includes coastal, local reserve and park walks. The excellent **Coastal Walkway** (11km) from Bell Block to Port Taranaki gives you a surf-side perspective on New Plymouth and crosses the much-photographed Te Rewa Rewa Bridge (p240). The **Huatoki Walkway** (5km), following Huatoki Stream, is a rambling walk into the city centre. Alternatively, the *New Plymouth Heritage Trail* brochure, taking in historic hot spots, is a real blast from the past.

If you wish to tackle the mountain (p247) itself, whether a short loop or a multiday tramp, **Top Guides Taranaki** (📞 0800 448 433; www.topguides.co.nz; half-/full-day tramps per person from $99/299) and **Taranaki Tours** (📞 06-757 9888; www.taranakitours.com; per person from $145) run shuttle services between New Plymouth and Egmont National Park.

Surfing

New Plymouth's black, volcanic-sand beaches are terrific for surfing. Close to the eastern edge of town are **Fitzroy Beach** and **East End Beach** (allegedly the cleanest beach in Oceania). There's also decent surf at **Back Beach**, near Paritutu (p240), at the western end of the city. Otherwise, head south along Surf Hwy 45.

Beach Street Surf Shop SURFING
(📞 06-758 0400; 39 Beach St; 1hr lessons per person from $100; ⊙ 10am-5pm Mon-Fri, to 3pm Sat & Sun; 🖐) Close to Fitzroy Beach, this surf shop offers lessons, gear hire (surfboard/SUP/wetsuit per hour $15/25/10) and surf advice (see its Facebook page for the low-down on local breaks).

Other

Taranaki Thermal Spa SPA
(📞 06-759 1666; www.pureone.co.nz/taranaki-thermal-spa.html; 8 Bonithon Ave; treatments from $13; ⊙ 10am-7.30pm Tue-Fri, 2-8pm Sat & Sun Dec-Apr, 10am-9pm Tue-Sun May-Nov) The warm mineral water filling the tanks at Taranaki Thermal Spa was discovered during the search for oil in 1906. Private baths are filled on arrival and there's a suite of massage and beauty therapies available, although not on Sundays. An absolute tonic.

Chaddy's Charters BOATING
(📞 06-758 9133; www.chaddyscharters.co.nz; Ocean View Pde, Lee Breakwater; trips adult/child $40/15; ⊙ 8am-4pm Sep-Jun, 9am-4pm Jul & Aug; 🖐) Take a trip out to visit the Sugar Loaf Islands with Chaddy: expect at least four laughs a minute during a one-hour

SUGAR LOAF ISLANDS MARINE PARK

A refuge for 10,000 sea birds and home to a breeding colony of NZ fur seals, these rugged **islets** (☑06-759 0350; www.doc.govt.nz; ⊙24hr) (Ngā Motu in Māori) are eroded volcanic remnants, 1km offshore. Most seals come here from June to October, but some stay all year round. A popular diving spot, visibility can reach up to 20m in summer and autumn. The i-Site (p246) at Puke Ariki (p238) can point you in the direction of kayak hire and guides, or take a tour (p241).

bob around on the swell. Departs daily from Lee Breakwater, tide and weather permitting. You can also hire kayaks (single/double per hour $15/30), bikes ($10 per hour) and stand-up paddleboards ($30 per hour). Winter opening hours vary with the weather.

✨ Festivals & Events

Festival of Lights   CULTURAL
(☑06-759 6060; www.festivaloflights.nz; ⊙Dec-Feb) Complete with live music, 1000 light installations and costumed characters roaming the undergrowth, this colourful display illuminates Pukekura Park (p240) from mid-December to early February.

★WOMAD   MUSIC, CULTURAL
(World of Music, Arts & Dance; ☑0800 484 253; www.womad.co.nz; ⊙Mar) A diverse array of local and international artists perform at the **Bowl of Brooklands** (☑06-759 6060; www.npeventvenues.nz; Brooklands Park Dr; ⊙performance days only) each March. Hugely popular, with music fans trucking in from across NZ. Camping sites available to purchase online.

NZ Tattoo & Art Festival   CULTURAL
(www.nztattooart.com; ⊙Nov) This saucy skin fest attracts thousands of ink fans over a busy weekend in November. Get yourself a new 'badge', or check out the BMX stunt riders or the burlesque gyrators.

Taranaki International Arts Festival   ART
(☑06-759 8412; www.taft.co.nz; ⊙Aug & Sep) The regional big-ticket arts fest: theatre, dance, music, visual arts, parades and plenty of food and wine.

🛏 Sleeping

🛌 City Centre

★Ducks & Drakes   HOSTEL, HOTEL $
(☑06-758 0404; www.ducksanddrakes.co.nz; 48 Lemon St; hostel dm/s/d from $32/68/90, hotel r from $130; ☜) The hostel here occupies a labyrinthine 1920s heritage building with bright feature walls and fancy timberwork brimming with character. Upstairs rooms are the pick: secluded, quiet and catching the morning sun. Next door is a pricier hotel wing with snazzy studios and one-bedroom suites, to which the owner escapes when his teenage daughter has friends over.

State Hotel   BOUTIQUE HOTEL $$
(☑06-75 75162; www.thestatehotel.co.nz; 162 Devon St E; s $140, d from $155; ☜) The 15 moderately sized rooms here are attractively furnished with lush grey blankets, patterned cushions and flamingo wallpaper for extra flair – one of the owners is an interior designer. Bathrooms are practical but tiny, and there's a shared lounge area with comfortable chairs and big windows. The restaurants that share the building are worth a visit.

Metrotel   MOTEL $$
(☑06-222 0036; www.themetrotel.co.nz; 22 Gill St; d $130-160, 2-bedroom ste $255; ℗☜) Opened 2017, there are hints of history in the original 1920s warehouse walls. Rooms are simple but slick whether boasting a pop of colour, exposed light bulbs or couches half-upholstered in animal print. Two-bedroom mezzanine rooms have high ceilings, wheelchair-accessible studios have wooden decks and two-bedroom studios a separate kitchen and lounge.

Dawson Motel   MOTEL $$
(☑06-758 1172, 0800 581 177; www.thedawsonmotel.co.nz; 16 Dawson St; d from $150, 1-/2-bedroom units from $200/250; ℗☜) Opened in 2011, the handsome, corporate Dawson is a sharp-looking, two-storey number – all white, red and black inside – with sea and mountain views from top-floor rooms. The location is primo: a five-minute walk into town and 100m to the Coastal Walkway.

★King & Queen Hotel Suites   BOUTIQUE HOTEL $$$
(☑06-757 2999, 0800 574 683; www.kingandqueen.co.nz; cnr King & Queen Sts; d from $179, ste from $219-440; ℗@☜) This regal hotel occupies the corner of King and Queen Sts (get it?) in the cool West End Precinct. Run by unerringly

professional staff, each suite features antique Moroccan and Euro furnishings, lustrous black tiles, hip art, leather couches and touches of industrial chic. Guests can borrow free bikes, and there are chargeback facilities set up with some of New Plymouth's top cafes, bars and restaurants.

Nice Hotel BOUTIQUE HOTEL $$$
(☑06-758 6423; www.nicehotel.co.nz; 71 Brougham St; d from $250, 3-bedroom ste $500; 🛜) A high-class hotel from top to tail – 'nice' is the understatement of the decade. In fact it's New Plymouth's oldest timber building (1870, ask to see the original snug 'library'). Rooms feature luxury furnishings, fancy wallpaper, designer bathrooms and *objets d'art* collected by the eccentric owner. It also has a three-bedroom villa (three-night minimum stay) and a fantastic in-house restaurant, Table (p244).

Waterfront Hotel HOTEL $$$
(☑0508 843 9283, 06-769 5302; www.waterfront.co.nz; 1 Egmont St; d/f from $240/390; 🅿@🛜) Sleek and snazzy, Waterfront is the place to stay if the boss is paying. Within walking distance of the major sites, the minimalist studios are pretty flash, while the penthouses steal the show with big TVs and little balconies. It's got terrific views from some – but not all – rooms, and certainly from the curvy-fronted bar-restaurant, Salt.

🛏 Surrounds

Belt Road Holiday Park HOLIDAY PARK $
(☑06-758 0228, 0800 804 204; www.beltroad.co.nz; 2 Belt Rd; campsites from $23, cabins $75-145; 🛜) 🐾 Set among grassy lawns studded with pohutukawa trees, this holiday park sits atop a bluff overlooking the Tasman Sea, about a 15-minute walk from town. The half-dozen best cabins have million-dollar views and there's a play area for the kids, complete with a trampoline.

⭐One Burgess Hill MOTEL, APARTMENTS $$
(☑06-757 2056; www.oneburgesshill.co.nz; 1 Burgess Hill Rd; d from $146, 1-/2-bedroom ste from $186/255; 🛜) Completely exceeding motel expectations, lovely One Burgess Hill is a complex of 15 stylish units on a green hillside, about 5km south of central New Plymouth (en route to Mt Taranaki). Slick interior design, nifty kitchens, wood heaters and private valley views offer a departure from usual drive-in motels. Upstairs rooms have baths by the bed overlooking the Waiwhakaiho River.

BK's Egmont Motor Lodge MOTEL $$
(☑0800 115 033, 06-758 5216; www.bksegmontmotorlodge.co.nz; 115 Coronation Ave; d from $140, 1-/2-/3-bedroom units from $165/210/220; 🅿🛜) Opposite the racecourse and a short roll downhill into town, low-slung BK's has 18 ground-floor units and oceans of parking. Rooms are comfortable and clean with photographs of New Plymouth hanging on the walls, and the owner is more than happy to show you around before you commit. Spend a little extra on a spa room.

Fitzroy Beach Motel MOTEL $$
(☑06-757 2925, 0800 757 2925; www.fitzroybeachmotel.co.nz; 25 Beach St; 1-/2-bedroom units from $160/200, extra person $20; 🛜) This quiet motel is just 200m from Fitzroy Beach and has been thoroughly redeemed with a major overhaul and extension. Highlights include a calming colour palette, quality carpets, double glazing, lovely bathrooms, big TVs and an absence of poky studio-style units (all are one- or two-bedroom). Free bikes, too.

Tivoli Homestay B&B $$$
(☑06-751 1206; www.tivolihomestay.co.nz; 22 Scott St, Moturoa; d $229; 🅿🛜) About 5km west of the town centre and 1km from Paritutu Rock (p240) is this charismatic, three-room B&B with friendly owners. Aside from serving one of the best breakfasts in New Plymouth, the upstairs common spaces (including an outdoor deck and fairytale-like turret) boast views over Mt Taranaki, across the Central Plateau and out to sea.

🍴 Eating

🍴 City Centre

Ms White Pizza & Beer Garden PIZZA $
(www.mswhite.co.nz; White Hart Courtyard, 47 Queen St; pizza $13-19; ⏰4-10pm Mon & Tue, 11am-10pm Wed, Thu & Sun, to 11pm Fri & Sat; 🍴) Sharing a fairy-light-draped courtyard with Snug Lounge (p245), Ms White serves traditional wood-fired Italian pizza and more than 40 varieties of craft beer from an outdoor kitchen. Choose from pizza *rosse* bases with tomato sauce and mozzarella or pizza *bianche* with olive oil in place of tomato. Look out for $10 Monday specials and be sure to use the hashtag: #pizzawillneverbreakyourheart.

 TARANAKI & WHANGANUI NEW PLYMOUTH

Public Catering Co. CAFE $

(☑ 06-759 7090; www.publiccatering.co.nz; White Hart courtyard, 43a Queen St; $6-10; ⊙8am-3.30pm Mon-Sat, 9am-3pm Sun) Another White Hart Precinct gem, this cafe is a front for a gourmet catering company. The cabinet flaunts doughnuts, pies and Reuben sandwiches, while hot meat rolls and the soup are winners on a cold day. There's one communal table in the textural space – all decorative concrete blocks and exposed piping – but if it's warm, opt for gelato in the courtyard.

Deluxe Diner DINER $

(☑ 06-757 5300; www.deluxediner.co.nz; 36 Leach St; $8-19; ⊙10am-9pm Tue-Thu, to 10pm Fri, 9am-10pm Sat, to 9pm Sun; ♿) This diner attracts mainly families and those nostalgic for the 1950s. Order at the counter (pancake stacks for breakfast and a burger or hot dog later on) and take a seat in the red-vinyl booths. The memorabilia collection includes a jukebox, neon signs and Elvis posters. Ask about the Deluxe Loaded Donut if you're counting memories, not calories.

Chaos CAFE $

(☑ 06-759 8080; www.chaoscafe.co.nz; 36 Brougham St; mains $12-18; ⊙7.30am-2pm Mon-Fri, 8.30am-2pm Sat, 9am-1.30pm Sun; ☎♿♿) Not so much chaotic as endearingly kooky, Chaos is a dependable spot for a coffee and a zingy brunch. Cabinet food is labelled according to whether it's gluten-free, dairy-free or vegan, while dishes with names like 'mental lentil' (fragrant lentils served with poached eggs, house labneh and bruschetta) are hard to beat. Look for the graffiti-covered side wall.

★ Social Kitchen LATIN AMERICAN $$

(☑ 06-757 2711; www.social-kitchen.co.nz; 40 Powderham St; share plates $30-55; ⊙noon-late; ☎) Inside what was once the Salvation Army Citadel, this trendy restaurant is filled with neon charm and taxidermy. Hanging meat and pigs' heads are displayed like art, but you can avoid them in the courtyard strung with colourful festoon lights. Arrive hungry and share flavour-packed Spanish sausage and Waitoa free-range chicken cooked in a Mibrasa charcoal oven.

Swing by for 'slow cooked Sundays', a great value option that includes the chef's selection of small and large seasonal plates for $25.

★ Monica's Eatery MODERN NZ $$

(☑ 06-759 2038; www.monicaseatery.co.nz; cnr King & Queen Sts; breakfast $13-19, lunch $15-39,

dinner $23-40; ⊙6.30am-late; ☎♿) Beside the Govett-Brewster Art Gallery (p239) and Len Lye Centre (p238), this all-day diner is homely despite its contemporary interior. Perhaps it's seeing handmade pappardelle lowered into bowls through the open kitchen, or the upbeat soundtrack that swings between Bill Withers and the Supremes. It's quite possibly the staff, who advise holding onto warm house focaccia for 'sauce mopping'. Whatever it is, we feel at home at here.

Kathakali SOUTH INDIAN $$

(☑ 06-758 8848; www.kathakali.co.nz; 39a Devon St E; mains $17-22; ⊙noon-2pm & 5-10pm Tue-Sun; ♿) Wander upstairs from Devon St to this local favourite where staff know regulars by name. The menu delivers all sorts of South Indian delights, from must-order *dosa* (savoury pancakes) with coconut chutney and *sambar* (lentil soup), to mixed vegetable korma with coconut and ground cashews. Somehow, Kerala doesn't seem so far away.

Table INTERNATIONAL $$$

(☑ 06-758 6423; www.nicehotel.co.nz; 71 Brougham St; mains $35-42; ⊙5.30-9pm; ☎) ♪ Worth visiting for a fancier dinner, Table at Nice Hotel (p243) consists of a lush dining space with opulent furniture, a New York–style bar (open 3pm until late) and an outdoor area complete with a fireplace. The menu takes inspiration from around the world, but you can sense the Kiwi touch in wild venison ragout pappardelle and Manuka honey panna cotta.

Prohibition BURGERS $$

(☑ 06-758 1236; www.facebook.com/prohibition nz; 41 Brougham St; burgers $15-18, mains $16-27; ⊙11am-3pm & 5-9.30pm; ♿♿) With a dozen gourmet burgers with names like 'My Dark Twisted Crantasy' and 'The Boss', this burger bar is the epitome of cool. There are also smaller plates and mains like 24-hour braised lamb shoulder, alongside a menu of local craft beer. Take a seat on the mezzanine level and admire the tattoo art plastered on the walls.

Portofino ITALIAN $$

(☑ 06-757 8686; www.portofino.co.nz; 14 Gill St; mains $20-39; ⊙5pm-late Tue-Sun) Thick-accented Italian staff scream – or more accurately, gesture – authenticity at this discreet family-run restaurant. One of a dozen locations in the North Island, this stalwart has been keeping locals and travellers happy for years with old-fashioned Italian pasta and pizza, just like nonna used to make. Ingredients are a mix of market fresh and European imports.

Frederic's
PUB FOOD $$

(☑06-759 1227; www.frederics.co.nz; 34 Egmont St; plates $14-21, mains $19-30; ⊙noon-midnight; 🛜) Freddy's is a happening gastro-bar with quirky interior design (rusty medieval chandeliers, peacock-feather wallpaper and religious icon paintings), serving tacos, burgers and heartier fare from a tick-the-box bar menu. Order a local craft beer and, depending on the weather, enjoy it wrapped in a cosy blanket or on the sunny, faux-lawn sidewalk tables.

Meat & Liquor
AMERICAN $$$

(☑06-7591 227; www.meatandliquor.co.nz; 34a Egmont St; mains $26-45; ⊙noon-2pm Thu & Fri, 5-11pm daily; 🛜) Follow the glow of red neon past Frederic's (p245) bar and up the stairs to the dining room, where tea towels replace napkins and butcher's paper sits in for tablecloths. Leave vegetarian pals at home and share 400g cuts of sustainable beef, local lamb rump and pork. We love the built-in bar and catchy slogan: 'fine cuts nice drop'.

✕ Surrounds

Federal Store
CAFE $$

(☑06-757 8147; www.thefederalstore.com; 440 Devon St E; mains $12-19; ⊙7am-4.30pm Mon-Fri, 8.30am-4.30pm Sat & Sun; 🖋🖰) Super-popular and crammed with retro furniture, Federal conjures up a 1950s corner-store vibe. Switched-on staff in dinky headscarves take your coffee requests at the counter as you queue beneath colourful bunting, keeping you buoyant until your southern fried chicken bagel, shashuka or eggs Benedict arrives. Cakes, tarts and premade counter food are also available. Kid-friendly.

Bach on Breakwater
CAFE $$

(☑06-769 6967; www.bachonbreakwater.co.nz; Ocean View Pde, Lee Breakwater; mains $12-25; ⊙9.30am-4pm Wed-Fri, to 5pm Sat & Sun; 🖋) Constructed from weighty recycled timbers, this cool cafe-bistro in the Lee Breakwater precinct looks like an old sea chest washed up after a storm. The all-day brunch menu ranges from a vegan version of a big breakfast to New Yorker french toast slathered in peanut butter. Vegans, vegetarians and gluten-free diets can follow the handy colour-coded cabinet.

🍷 Drinking & Nightlife

★ Snug Lounge
COCKTAIL BAR

(☑06-757 9130; www.snuglounge.co.nz; cnr Devon St W & Queen St; small plates $9-19; ⊙4pm-late Mon-Sat, noon-late Sun) Located inside the iconic former White Hart Hotel, this savvy bar on the downtown fringe is the classiest place in town for a drink – unlike its predecessor. Dress to be seen, order a Tropical Botanical (gin, coconut and mint) and act like you own the town. An excellent selection of Japanese share plates will ensure you stay vertical.

Escape Coffee
COFFEE

(☑07-373 6024; www.escapecoffee.nz; 15 Liardet St; snacks $3-5, food $8-12; ⊙6.30am-4pm Mon-Fri, 8am-2pm Sat) Inside this old wool warehouse is a counter selling raw snacks and coffee (roasted out the back in a shipping container). There's a fridge loaded with ready-made chia puddings, bircher muesli and juices, alongside an organic fruit box paid for by donation. Sit by the indoor skate bowl, browse through streetwear or eat your fill after a yoga class upstairs.

Bean Store
COFFEE

(Bean Store by Ozone Coffee; ☑06-757 5404; www.ozonecoffee.co.nz; 47a King St; dishes $5-12; ⊙7am-3.30pm Mon-Fri, 7am-2pm Sat, 8am-2pm Sun) In a converted warehouse with steel beams and exposed timber is New Plymouth's best coffee spot. The Ozone roastery out the back supplies other cafes and a tiled counter supports a grey La Marzocco machine with matching jugs. Hungry? There's a tiny breakfast menu and vibrant counter food. Grab a coffee-tamper table number and find a seat.

Hour Glass
BAR

(☑06-758 2299; www.facebook.com/thehourglass49; 49 Liardet St; tapas $4-10, mains $32-35; ⊙4pm-late Tue-Sat) On an unremarkable rise of Liardet St is this late-night tapas and craft-beer bar, with richly brocaded crimson drapes, straight-backed wooden chairs and interesting timber panelling. Plenty of craft beers, killer cocktails and even named lockers for expensive bottles if you're a regular. Check the Facebook page for tastings and informal jam sessions.

🔒 Shopping

Kina
ARTS, JEWELLERY

(☑06-759 1201; www.kina.co.nz; 101 Devon St W; ⊙9am-5.30pm Mon-Fri, 9.30am-4pm Sat, 11am-4pm Sun) Fabulous Kiwi crafts, jewellery, bath and beauty products plus art and design, as well as regular gallery exhibitions in a lovely shopfront on the main drag. It's the perfect spot to pick up a meaningful NZ souvenir.

TARANAKI & WHANGANUI NEW PLYMOUTH

Kathmandu SPORTS & OUTDOORS
(☑06-769 5581; www.kathmandu.com.au; 10 Gill
St; ☺9am-5.30pm Mon-Fri, to 5pm Sat, 10am-4pm
Sun) From waterproof clothing and solid
hiking shoes to sleeping bags and hiking
accessories, you're probably already familiar
with Kathmandu for a reason.

Macpac SPORTS & OUTDOORS
(☑0800 622 722, 06-758 7209; www.macpac.com.
au; 28 Devon St W; ☺9am-5.30pm Mon-Fri, to 5pm
Sat, 10am-4pm Sun) Visit to start your Taranaki tramp prepared with camping and tramping gear galore.

❶ Information

DOC (Department of Conservation; ☑06-759
0350; www.doc.govt.nz; 55a Rimu St; ☺8am-
4.30pm Mon-Fri) Info on regional national
parks, tramping and camping.

New Plymouth i-SITE (☑06-759 6060; www.
taranaki.co.nz; Puke Ariki, 1 Ariki St; ☺9am-
6pm Mon, Tue, Thu & Fri, to 9pm Wed, to 5pm
Sat & Sun, closed public holidays) In the Puke
Ariki building, with a fantastic interactive
tourist-info database.

Phoenix Urgent Doctors (☑06-759 4295;
www.phoenixdoctors.co.nz; 95 Vivian St;
☺8.30am-8pm) Doctors by appointment and
urgent medical help.

Taranaki Base Hospital (☑06-753 6139; www.
tdhb.org.nz; 23 David St, Westown; ☺24hr)
Accident and emergency.

❶ Getting There & Away

AIR

New Plymouth Airport (☑0800 144 129; ww-
w.newplymouthairport.com; Airport Dr) is 11km
east of the centre off SH3. **Scott's Airport
Shuttle** (☑0800 373 001, 06-769 5974; www.
npairportshuttle.co.nz; per person $18-28,
per 2 people $22-32) operates a door-to-door
shuttle to/from the airport.

Airlines include the following:

Air New Zealand (☑06-357 3000, 0800 737
000; www.airnewzealand.co.nz) Daily direct
flights to/from Auckland, Wellington and
Christchurch, with onward connections.

Singapore Airlines (www.singaporeair.com)
Flies between New Plymouth, Christchurch and
Auckland.

Virgin Australia (www.virginaustralia.com)
Flies the same routes as Air New Zealand.

BUS

Services run from the **Bus Centre** (cnr Egmont
& Ariki Sts) in central New Plymouth. Standard
fares (ie, no refund) are the cheapest option.

InterCity (www.intercity.co.nz) services
include the following:

DESTINATION	COST	TIME (HR)	FREQUENCY (DAILY)
Auckland	from $43	6	2
Hamilton	from $33	3½-4	4
Palmerston North	from $28	4	1
Wellington	from $29	7	1
Whanganui	from $23	2½	1

Naked Bus (www.nakedbus.com) services
ply similar routes and sometimes link up with
other operators. Visit the website for routes
and fares.

❶ Getting Around

BICYCLE

Cycle Inn (☑06-758 7418; www.cycleinn.
co.nz; 133 Devon St E; per 2hr/day $10/20;
☺8.30am-5pm Mon-Fri, 9am-4pm Sat, 10am-
2pm Sun) rents out bicycles, as does **Chaddy's
Charters** (p241) at Lee Breakwater.

BUS

Citylink (☑0800 872 287; www.taranakibus.
info; tickets adult/child $3.70/2.30) services
run Monday to Friday around New Plymouth,
as well as north to Waitara and south to
Oakura. Buses depart from the **Bus Centre**.

CAR

For cheap car hire, try **Rent-a-Dent** (☑06-757
5362, 1800 14 18 22; www.rentadent.co.nz;
592 Devon St E; ☺8am-5pm Mon-Fri, to noon
Sat).

MT TARANAKI &
AROUND

Mt Taranaki sure looks good for
120,000-years old. A point of reference
everywhere you go, it's responsible for
the fertile plains – and the unpredictable
weather. Appreciated by both Māori *iwi*
with a spiritual connection and travellers
with wi-fi connection, those who come
prepared can appreciate the views from
the top.

Hiking can be dangerous as the conditions change quickly, but it's just as beautiful from the bottom in the surrounding
towns of Inglewood and Stratford.

Egmont National Park

A near-perfect 2518m volcanic cone dominating the landscape, Mt Taranaki is a magnet to all who catch his eye. According to Māori, Taranaki travelled from the North Island's volcanic plateau after he lost a battle with Mt Tongariro over the beautiful Mt Pihanga. Geologically, Taranaki is the youngest of three large volcanoes – including Kaitake and Pouakai – that stand along the same fault line. With the last eruption more than 350 years ago, experts say that the mountain is overdue for another go. But don't let that put you off – it's an absolute beauty and the highlight of any visit to the region, although trampers should check in with DOC information centres before attempting a climb as it's notoriously dangerous.

Access points for the mountain are North Egmont, Dawson Falls and East Egmont. There are DOC centres at North Egmont (p248) and Dawson Falls (p248); for accommodation and supplies head to Stratford or Inglewood.

🏃 Activities

Due to its accessibility, Mt Taranaki ranks as the 'most climbed' mountain in NZ. Nevertheless, tramping on this mountain is dangerous and should not be undertaken lightly. It's crucial to get advice before departing and to leave your intentions with a Department of Conservation (DOC) visitor centre or i-SITE.

Most walks are accessible from North Egmont, Dawson Falls or East Egmont. Check out DOC's collection of detailed walk pamphlets ($1 to $1.50 each, or free if you print it off the web) or the free *Taranaki: A Walker's Guide* booklet for more info – although there are rumours the printed booklet might soon be discontinued.

The meatiest hikes (p236) – including the **Pouakai Circuit**, **Pouakai Crossing**, **Mt Taranaki Summit** and **Around-the-Mountain Circuit** – depart from North Egmont. Short, easy walks from here include the **Ngatoro Loop Track** (40 minutes), **Veronica Loop** (two hours) and **Nature Walk** (15-minute loop).

East Egmont has the **Potaema Track** (wheelchair accessible; 30 minutes return) and **Stratford Plateau Lookout** (10 minutes return). A longer walk is the steep **Enchanted Track** (two to three hours return).

At Dawson Falls you can do several short walks, including **Wilkies Pools Loop** (1¼ hours return), whose new bridge provides an outlook back up towards the mountain and across the pools, or the excellent but challenging hike to **Fanthams Peak** (five hours return), which is snowed-in during winter. The **Kapuni Loop Track** (one-hour loop) runs to the impressive 18m **Dawson Falls** themselves. You can also see the falls from the visitor centre via a 10-minute walk to a viewpoint.

The **York Road Loop Track** (up to three hours), accessible from York Rd north of Stratford, is a fascinating walk following part of a disused railway line.

You can tramp without a guide from January through to April when snowfalls are low, but at other times inexperienced climbers can check with DOC for details of local clubs and guides. It costs around $300 per day to hire a guide.

Manganui Ski Area SKIING
(www.skitaranaki.co.nz; off Pembroke Rd, East Egmont; daily lift passes adult/child $50/35) From Stratford take Pembroke Rd up to Stratford

TARANAKI & WHANGANUI EGMONT NATIONAL PARK

MĀORI TARANAKI & WHANGANUI

Ever since Mt Taranaki fled here to escape romantic difficulties, the Taranaki region has had a turbulent history. Conflicts between local *iwi* (tribes) and invaders from the Waikato were followed by two wars with the government – first in 1860–61, and then again in 1865–69. Then there were massive land confiscations and an extraordinary passive-resistance campaign at Parihaka.

A drive up the Whanganui River Rd takes you into traditional Māori territory, passing the Māori villages of Atene, Koriniti, Ranana and Hiruharama along the way. In Whanganui itself, run your eyes over amazing indigenous exhibits at the **Whanganui Regional Museum** (p254), and check out the superb Māori carvings in **Putiki Church** (p256).

Over in Palmerston North, **Te Manawa** (p265) museum has a strong Māori focus, while the **New Zealand Rugby Museum** (p265) pays homage to Māori All Blacks, without whom the team would never have become back-to-back Rugby World Cup winners.

ⓘ DECEPTIVE MOUNTAIN

Mt Taranaki might look small compared to mountains overseas, but this unassuming mountain has claimed more than 80 lives. The microclimate changes fast: from summery to whiteout conditions almost in an instant. There are also precipitous bluffs and steep icy slopes.

There are plenty of short walks here, safe for much of the year, but for adventurous trampers January to March is the best time to go. Take a detailed topographic map (the Topo50 1:50,000 Mt Taranaki or Mt Egmont map is good) and consult a DOC officer for current conditions. You must register your tramping intentions with Dawson Falls or North Egmont DOC visitor centres on the mountain, New Plymouth i-SITE (p246) or online via www.adventuresmart.org.nz.

Plateau, from where it's a 1.5km (20-minute) walk to the small Manganui Ski Area. The Stratford i-SITE (p250) has daily weather and snow reports; otherwise check the webcam online. There's also shared-facilities ski-lodge accommodation here (adult/child/family $45/15/100), but to stay there you need a group of 10, with at least five adults. For up-to-date information and speedy responses, check the Facebook page: www.facebook.com/Manganui.

🛏 Sleeping

Several DOC huts are scattered about the mountain wilderness, and are accessible via tramping tracks. Most cost $15 per night (Syme costs $5); purchase hut tickets in advance from DOC. BYO cooking, eating and sleeping gear. Bookings are not accepted – it's first come, first served.

On the road-accessible slopes of the mountain you'll find a hostel, two DOC-managed bunkhouses and some interesting lodges.

Camphouse HOSTEL $
(06-756 0990; www.doc.govt.nz; Egmont Rd, North Egmont; per adult/child $25/10, exclusive use $600) Bunkhouse-style accommodation behind the North Egmont Visitor Centre in a historic 1860 corrugated-iron building, complete with gun slots in the walls (through which settlers fired at local Māori during the Taranaki Land Wars). Enjoy endless horizon views from the porch. Sleeps 32 in four rooms, with communal facilities.

★ Ngāti Ruanui Stratford Mountain House LODGE $$
(06-765 6100, 027 588 0228; www.stratford mountainhouse.co.nz; Pembroke Rd; d/f from $155/195;) This efficiently run lodge on the Stratford side of the big hill (15km from the SH3 turn-off and 3km to the Manganui Ski Area) has eight motel-style chalets, a twin room and a family room for four up a short, foresty path. Spa baths are a blessing on chilly nights, as is the fireplace in the mod, European-style restaurant (breakfast and lunch mains $12 to $39, dinner $31 to $42). Accommodation and meal packages also available (from $345).

ⓘ Information

Dawson Falls Visitor Centre (06-443 0248; www.doc.govt.nz; Manaia Rd, Dawson Falls; 9am-4pm Thu-Sun, daily school holidays) On the southeastern side of the mountain, fronted by an awesome totem pole.

MetService (www.metservice.com) Mountain weather updates.

North Egmont Visitor Centre (06-756 0990; www.doc.govt.nz; Egmont Rd, North Egmont; 8am-4pm, reduced winter hr) Current and comprehensive national park info, and definitive details on tramping and huts.

ⓘ Getting There & Away

There are three main entrance roads to Egmont National Park, all of which are well signposted. The closest to New Plymouth is North Egmont: turn off SH3 at Egmont Village, 12km south of New Plymouth, and follow Egmont Rd for 14km. From Stratford, turn off at Pembroke Rd and continue for 15km to East Egmont and the Manganui Ski Area. From the southeast, Manaia Rd leads up to Dawson Falls, 23km from Stratford.

There are no public buses to the national park, but there are a few shuttle/tour operators who will take you there for around $40/60 one way/return (usually cheaper for groups).

Eastern Taranaki Experience (06-765 7482, 027 4717136, 027 246 6383; www.easterntaranaki.co.nz; 5 Verona Place, Stratford; per person incl lunch from $210) Mountain shuttle services as well as tours and accommodation. Based in Stratford.

Taranaki Tours (p241) New Plymouth to North Egmont return – good for day walks.

Top Guides Taranaki (p241) Mountain shuttle services, with pick-up points around New Plymouth. Picks up from accommodation between 7am and 7.20am. Mountain guides also available.

Inglewood

POP 3250

Handy to Mt Taranaki on SH3, the little main-street town of Inglewood is a useful stop for supermarket supplies or a casual bite to eat.

◉ Sights

Fun Ho! National Toy Museum   MUSEUM
(☑06-756 7030; www.funhotoys.co.nz; 25 Rata St; adult/child $7/3.50; ⊙10am-4pm; ⊛) Inglewood's cute Fun Ho! National Toy Museum exhibits (and sells) old-fashioned sand-cast toys. It doubles as the local visitor information centre. Good for big kids and hobbyists, too! Everybody shout, 'Fun Ho!'.

🛏 Sleeping & Eating

Inglebrook Villa & Gardens   B&B $$
(☑027 271 8354, 06-756 6062; www.inglebrook. co.nz; 87 Rata St; s/d incl breakfast $140/170; ☎) This early 1907 property is set on 300 sq metres of manicured trees and gardens with a lush outlook from the only room, the Garden Suite, which boasts double french doors and a patio. Love the timber-clad bathroom and brick fireplace in the lounge. Add $10 for a cooked breakfast. Sofa bed available in the lounge ($60 extra)

Funkfish Grill   SEAFOOD, BURGERS $$
(☑06-756 7287; 32 Matai St; takeaways $8-19, mains $19-32; ⊙4-9pm) In need of a refurb, funky Funkfish is still one of the better options in Inglewood, serving fish and chips and burgers. Doubles as a bar at night. Swap fries for kumara chips.

ⓘ Getting There & Away

InterCity (www.intercity.co.nz) and Naked Bus (www.nakedbus.com) services between New Plymouth and Whanganui pass through Inglewood. If you want to linger and/or explore Mt Taranaki, your own vehicle will be your closest ally.

Stratford

POP 8991

A gateway town to Mt Taranaki and 40km southeast of New Plymouth on SH3, Stratford plays up its connection to namesake Stratford-upon-Avon, Shakespeare's birthplace, by naming its streets after bardic characters. The town is also home to NZ's first (and

last) **glockenspiel clock**, which chimes four times a day (10am, 1pm, 3pm and 7pm). More impressive is the **Carrington Walkway**, accessible through the memorial gate at King Edward Park, which hugs the Pātea Stream and takes you across bridges and through farmland and a rhododendron dell.

◉ Sights

Taranaki Pioneer Village   MUSEUM
(☑06-765 5399; www.pioneervillage.co.nz; SH3; adult/child $12/5; ⊙10am-4pm; ⊛) About 1km south of Stratford on SH3, the Taranaki Pioneer Village is a 4-hectare outdoor museum housing 40 historic buildings, with many dating back to the early 1850s. It's very bygone-era and even a little spooky! The Pioneer Express Train is a good way to see it if your feet need a rest ($5 or $3 with entry fee). There's a cafe here, too.

Percy Thomson Gallery   GALLERY
(☑06-765 0917; www.percythomsongallery.org.nz; Prospero Pl, 56 Miranda St; ⊙10.30am-4pm Mon-Fri, to 3pm Sat & Sun) FREE Right next door to Stratford i-SITE, this progressive community gallery (named after the former mayor) displays eclectic local, regional and national art shows. New exhibitions every three to four weeks.

🛏 Sleeping

Stratford Kiwi Motels & Holiday Park   HOLIDAY PARK $
(☑06-765 6440; www.stratfordholidaypark.co.nz; 10 Page St; campsites/dm/cabins/units from $20/32/70/110; ☎) A trim caravan park offering one-room cabins, backpackers' bunks and newer studio motel units (the pick of the bunch). Neat little hedges separate campervan sites and three-wheel pedal go-karts are available to zoom around in for $5 per hour.

Regan House   B&B $$
(☑022 412 3354, 06-765 4189; www.reganhouse. co.nz; 193 Regan St; s/d incl breakfast $100/150; ℗☎) With only two suites available in this early 1900s house (one when family is staying), Regan House is a peaceful alternative to Stratford's limited, more commercial accommodation. Absurdly comfortable beds, manicured gardens and a generous cooked breakfast using eggs from the property's farm make this feel like home, sweet home. Located at the start of the Forgotten World Hwy.

TARANAKI & WHANGANUI INGLEWOOD

Amity Court Motel MOTEL $$
(☑ 06-765 4496, 0800 496 313; www.amitycourt
motel.co.nz; 35 Broadway N; d/apt from $140/224;
🛜) All stone-clad columns, jaunty roof an-
gles, timber louvres and muted cave-colours,
Amity Court Motel ups the town's accommo-
dation standings. The two-bedroom apart-
ments are a good set-up for families, while
couples should ask for room 12 with the hot
tub on the balcony. Electric car-charging sta-
tion on-site.

ℹ Information

Stratford i-SITE (☑ 0800 765 6708, 06-765
6708; www.stratford.govt.nz; Prospero Pl,
Broadway S, Stratford; ☉ 8.30am-5pm Mon-Fri,
10am-3pm Sat & Sun) All the local low-down,
plus good advice on walks on Mt Taranaki.
Down an arcade off the main street.

ℹ Getting There & Away

Both InterCity (www.intercity.co.nz) and Naked
Bus (www.nakedbus.com) services between
New Plymouth and Whanganui rumble through
Stratford. If you're heading up Mt Taranaki or
along the Forgotten World Hwy, you'll need your
own vehicle.

Forgotten World Highway

The remote 150km road between Stratford
and Taumarunui (SH43) has become known
as the Forgotten World Hwy. The drive winds
through hilly bush country, passing Māori
pā (fortified villages), abandoned coal mines
and memorials to those long gone. Just a
short section (around 12km) is unsealed

**THE WHANGAMOMONA
REPUBLIC**
••
Whangamomona became a republic in
1988 after redrawn council boundaries
saw residents booted from Taranaki. Un-
happy with the arrangement, 'Whanga'
went out on its own. As a result, the
local pub will stamp your passport for a
$2 donation to the community, or you
can buy a Whangamomona passport for
$5. It also means a president is elected
every two years. Although the president
at the time of writing is John Herlihy, Tai
the Poodle and Billy Gumboot the Goat
have also held office, although there's
speculation that Billy ate his challeng-
ers' ballots.

---

road. Allow four hours and plenty of stops,
and fill up with petrol at either end (there's
no petrol along the route itself). Pick up the
Forgotten World Highway pamphlet from
i-SITEs or DOC visitor centres in the area.

◉ Sights

Whangamomona VILLAGE
(SH43) The town of Whangamomona (popu-
lation 40) is a highlight. This quirky village
declared itself an independent republic in
1989 after disagreements with local coun-
cils. The town celebrates Republic Day in
January every odd-numbered year with a
themed extravaganza. Don't miss the grand
old Whangamomona Hotel (p250), a pub of-
fering simple accommodation and big coun-
try meals.

🛏 Sleeping

Whangamomona Hotel PUB $$
(☑ 06-762 5823; www.whangamomonahotel.co.nz;
6018 Forgotten World Hwy, Whangamomona; s/d
$120/150, lodge $175; ☉ 9am-late) In the middle
of Whangamomona is the unmissable grand
old Whangamomona Hotel. Built in 1912 after the original burnt down, it's a pub offering simple accommodation and big country
meals (breakfast and lunch $12 to $20, dinner $18 to $35). Accommodation plus meal
packages also available ($145 per person). A
new lodge has just been built 50m from the
property with private bathroom facilities.

This is where you come to get your passport stamped ($2 gold coin community
donation) and to grab a Whangamomona
passport ($5).

ℹ Getting There & Away

If you're not driving, try a tour through the area
by **Eastern Taranaki Experience** (p248) or
Taranaki Tours (p241). See also **Forgotten
World Adventures** (p231) in Taumarunui.

SURF HIGHWAY 45

Sweeping south from New Plymouth around
the coastline to Hawera, the 105km-long
SH45 is known as Surf Highway 45. But
don't take the name as gospel: while there is
an abundance of black-sand beaches along
the way, the road snakes inland through
green paddocks and farmland, too. Pick up
the *Surf Highway 45* brochure at visitor
centres.

Oakura

POP 1380

From New Plymouth, the first cab off the rank is laid-back Oakura, 15km southwest on SH45. For a town with not much more than a souvenir shop, petrol station and family medical centre, Oakura has a disproportionately high number of decent places to eat on your way through. Its broad sweep of beach is hailed by waxheads for its right-hander breaks, but it's also great for families (take sandals – that black sand gets scorching hot!).

Sleeping

Oakura Beach Holiday Park HOLIDAY PARK $
(06-752 7861; www.oakurabeach.com; 2 Jans Tce; campsites from $22, cabins $75-150; @) Wedged between the cliffs and the sea, this better-than-average beachside park caters best to caravans, but self-contained units C11 and C12 have uninterrupted ocean views. Simple, elevated cabins and absolute beachfront spots for pitching a tent. Take the walk from the park through the native reserve to the Gaerloch shipwreck and try to imagine it in its former 345-ton glory.

Ahu Ahu Beach Villas BOUTIQUE HOTEL $$$
(06-752 7370; www.ahu.co.nz; 321 Ahu Ahu Rd; d & f $210-295, 2-bedroom lodge from $450;) Pricey on the pocket but with priceless views. Set on a knoll overlooking the ocean, these luxury, architecturally designed villas are superbly eccentric, with huge recycled timbers, bottles cast into walls, century-old lichen-covered French tile roofs and polished-concrete floors with inlaid paua shell. The lodge sleeps four and is the place for sunset drinks.

Eating

High Tide CAFE $
(www.facebook.com/hightideoakura; 1136b SH45; lunch $9-15, pastries $3-5; 7am-2pm) Formerly a food caravan on Oakura Beach, High Tide grew so popular it moved to permanent digs. It's super-fresh cabinet nosh only here (try the smoked-salmon bagel or a French pastry), and the coffee is the best in town. Staff are all smiles while local artwork, indoor festoon lights and patterned cushions add a charming boho surf vibe.

Panda Peeking ASIAN $
(06-752 7823; www.facebook.com/peekingpanda. oakura; 1151 SH45; small plates $6-14; 3.30-11pm Thu & Fri, noon-11pm Sat & Sun) Plenty of timber, foliage and conical straw light fittings lend a tropical feel to this Asian fusion restaurant. Owned by the same people behind Hour Glass (p245) and **Polpetta** (06-759 8323; www.facebook.com/polpettanp; 170 Devon St E; mains $14-24; 5-10pm Tue-Sat;), this time steamed bao buns, dumplings and other delights are on the menu. We love the outdoor area at the front, boxed in by wooden slats.

Black Sand Pizzeria & Bistro PIZZA, BREAKFAST $$
(06-752 7806; www.facebook.com/black sandOK; 1 Tasman Pde; pizza $15-20; 9am-late Tue-Sun summer, 5pm-late Thu & Fri, 9am-late Sat & Sun winter;) Reliable Black Sand is right on the beach and shares a building with the surf club. It's a surprising location to stumble upon authentic Napoli-style pizzas – all thin-based and blistered crusts – but these wood-fired beauties made in a custom Italian oven give the rest of Taranaki a run for its margherita. Bistro food, breakfast and beer on tap are also available.

Cafe Mantra INDIAN $$
(06-752 7303; www.cafemantra.co.nz; 1131 SH45; mains $17-25; 10am-2pm Tue-Fri, 9am-2pm Sat & Sun, 4.30pm-late daily) European dishes, authentic Indian mains and wood-fired pizzas – is there anything Mantra doesn't do? This roadside, mostly Indian cafe is Bollywood kitsch meets boardrider shtick. Skewered lamb kebab and chicken tikka are crowd-pleasers, but save room for pistachio and mango kulfi (Indian ice cream).

Getting There & Away

Oakura is a short drive south of New Plymouth – an easy day trip. Local SouthLink buses (www.taranakibus.info) run here once on Fridays ($3), en route to Opunake and Hawera further south.

Okato & Around

Between Oakura and Opunake, SH45 veers inland through Okato, with detours to sundry beaches along the way. There are legendary surf spots at **Stent Rd** (Stent Rd, Warea; 24hr), just south of Warea, and **Kumara Patch** (Komene Rd, Okato; 24hr), west of Okato. Near Pungarehu, Cape Egmont is home to a historic **lighthouse** (Cape Rd, Pungarehu; 24hr) FREE and associated **museum** (06-763 8507, 06-763 8489; www.southtaranaki.com; Bayly Rd, Warea; by donation; 11am-3pm Sat-Mon).

PARIHAKA – BEACON OF PEACE

From the mid-1860s Parihaka, a small Māori settlement east of SH45 near Pungarehu, became the centre of a peaceful resistance movement, one which involved not only other Taranaki tribes, but Māori from around the country. Its leaders, Te Whiti-o-Rongomai and Tohu Kākahi, were of both Taranaki and Te Āti Awa descent.

After the Land Wars, confiscation of tribal lands was the central problem faced by Taranaki Māori, and under Te Whiti's leadership a new approach to this issue was developed: resisting European settlement through nonviolent methods.

When the government started surveying confiscated land on the Waimate Plain in 1879, unarmed followers of Te Whiti, wearing the movement's iconic white feather in their hair, obstructed development by ploughing troughs across roads, erecting random fences and pulling survey pegs – all in good humour. Nevertheless, many were arrested and held without trial on the South Island. The protests continued and intensified. Finally, in November 1881, the government sent a force of more than 1600 troops to Parihaka. Its inhabitants were arrested or driven away, and the village was later demolished. Te Whiti and Tohu were arrested and imprisoned until 1883. In their absence Parihaka was rebuilt and the ploughing campaigns continued into the 1890s.

In 2006 the NZ government issued a formal apology and financial compensation to the tribes affected by the invasion and confiscation of Parihaka lands.

🛏 Sleeping & Eating

Stony River Hotel
PUB $$

(☑ 06-752 4454; www.stonyriverhotel.co.nz; 2502 SH45, Okato; tw/d/tr incl breakfast $110/120/170; 🛜) This lemon-yellow highway hotel dates back to 1875, when mailmen on horses would stop to rest on their way north. There are bright, super-tidy, country-style en-suite rooms upstairs and a restaurant downstairs (mains $17 to $34), serving weekend lunches and dinner Wednesday to Sunday. The corner rooms have the best views. Don't miss Wednesday schnitzel nights with live oom-pah tunes.

★ Cafe Lahar
CAFE $

(☑ 06-752 4865; 64 Carthew St, Okato; mains $10-22; ☺ 8.30am-3pm Tue, to 4pm Wed & Thu, to 11pm Fri-Sun) Relaxed Lahar occupies an angular, black-trimmed timber box in Okato (hard to miss – there's not much else here). It's a lofty space with spinning fans, some tempting couches out the front and a menu ranging from pork sausages and beans, to tandoori chicken salad and pizzas on Friday, Saturday and Sunday nights. Good coffee and live music now and then.

ℹ Getting There & Away

Once a week on Fridays, SouthLink buses (www.taranakibus.info) from New Plymouth run through Okato ($4) on the way to Opunake.

Opunake

POP 1335

A sleepy summer town, Opunake is Taranaki's surfie epicentre, but it also has a sheltered family beach. There's not much happening on the main strip, but you can't go wrong grabbing some seriously good fish and chips and catching a film at the restored **Everybody's Theatre** (☑ 027 383 7926; www.everybodystheatre.co.nz; 72 Tasman St; adult/child $10/8; ☺ screenings 1pm & 7pm Wed & Sat, 7pm Fri & Sun).

🛏 Sleeping & Eating

Opunake Beach Holiday Park
HOLIDAY PARK $

(☑ 0800 758 009, 06-761 7525; www.opunakebeach nz.co.nz; 1 Beach Rd; d campsites/cabins/cottages $44/75/110; @🛜) Opunake Beach Holiday Park is a mellow spot behind the black-sand beach surf beach. Sites are grassy, the camp kitchen is big, the amenities block is cavernous and the waves are just a few metres away.

★ Opunake Fish, Chips and More
FISH & CHIPS $

(☑ 06-761 8478; www.facebook.com/Opunakefish chipsandmore; 61 Tasman St; fish & chips $3.50-10; ☺ 11am-8pm) This is as good as fish and chips gets. With a lengthy history (open since the 1960s), hand-cut chips, a range of fish (including fresh catches of the day), smiling local owners and gluten-free options, one meal here and you'll instantly feel part of the Opunake community.

🛒 Shopping

Pihama Lavender Farm ARTS & CRAFTS
(☑ 06-761 7012; www.pihamalavender.com; 3510 South Rd; ☺ 10am-5pm Sat & Sun) Technically in Pihama, 7km east from Opunake, this 2-hectare lavender farm in a former dairy farm is home to a local gallery and gift store. On the third Sunday of each month there's a farmers market. If you're passing in January when the flowers are in full bloom, book the two-bedroom, Dutch-influenced Punehu Stream Cottage ($140 per night).

ℹ️ Information

Opunake Library (☑ 0800 111 323; www. opunakenz.co.nz; 43 Tasman St; ☺ 9am-5pm Mon-Fri, 9.30am-1pm Sat; 🛜) Doubles as the local visitor information centre, with a couple of internet terminals and free 24-hour wi-fi in the forecourt.

ℹ️ Getting There & Away

Local SouthLink buses (www.taranakibus.info) run from New Plymouth to Opunake on Fridays ($6).

Hawera

POP 11,750

Don't expect much urban virtue from agricultural Hawera, the largest town in South Taranaki. Still, it's a good pit stop to pick up supplies, grab a coffee, visit the info centre, stretch your legs or bed down for a night. If you ain't nothin' but a hound dog, don't miss Elvis.

👁️ Sights

⭐ KD's Elvis Presley Museum MUSEUM
(☑ 06-278 7624, 027 498 2942; www.elvismuseum. co.nz; 51 Argyle St; admission by donation; ☺ by appointment) Elvis lives! At least he does at Kevin D Wasley's astonishing museum, which houses more than 10,000 of the King's records and a mind-blowing collection of Elvis memorabilia collected over nearly 60 years. 'Passion is an understatement', says KD, who's grey hair is slicked back and on theme. Admission is by appointment – phone ahead.

Waihi Beach BEACH
(☑ 0800 111 323, 06-278 8599; www.southtaranaki. com; Denby Rd) You can access Waihi Beach by turning into Denby Rd and descending the steep gravel track from the carpark. At low tide you can walk to Ohawe Beach (or do it in the reverse direction). All black sand, rock pools and rugged cliffs. If you look closely,

you'll spot fossils embedded in the marine terraces. Check the tides before you go and pack a picnic.

Tawhiti Museum MUSEUM
(☑ 06-278 6837; www.tawhitimuseum.co.nz; 401 Ohangai Rd; adult/child $15/5; ☺ 10am-4pm Fri-Sun Feb-May & Sep-Dec, daily Jan, Sun only Jun-Aug) The excellent Tawhiti Museum houses a collection of exhibits, dioramas and creepily lifelike human figures modelled on people from the region. A large collection of tractors pays homage to the area's rural heritage; there's also a bush railway and a 'Traders & Whalers' boat ride (extra charges for both). It's near the corner of Tawhiti Rd, 4km north of town.

Hawera Water Tower TOWER, VIEWPOINT
(☑ 06-278 8599; www.southtaranaki.com; 55 High St; adult/child/family $2.50/1/6; ☺ 8.30am-4pm Mon-Fri, 10am-2pm Sat & Sun & public holidays) The austere, 55m Hawera Water Tower is one of few noteworthy attractions in quiet Hawera. Grab the key from the neighbouring i-SITE (p254), ascend the 215 steps, then scan the horizon for signs of life (you can see the coast and Mt Taranaki on a clear day).

🛏️ Sleeping & Eating

Park Motel MOTEL $$
(☑ 06-278 7275; www.theparkmotel.co.nz; 61 Waihi Rd; d $140, 1-/2-bedroom apt $155/170; 🅿️) These 18 basic but clean rooms across the road from King Edward Park and an aquatic centre make up our pick of the motels in Hawera. Consists of studio units and one- and two-bedroom apartments; room number 8 may have a spa bath, but all rooms come with homemade cookies.

Tairoa Lodge B&B $$$
(☑ 06-278 8603; www.tairoa-lodge.co.nz; 3 Puawai St; s/d $165/215, cottage d $245, extra adult/child $50/30, all incl breakfast; 🛜🍴) Set on grassy lawns, gorgeous old Tairoa is a photogenic 1875 Victorian manor house on the eastern outskirts of Hawera, with three guest rooms and two outlying cottages (two and three bedrooms). Lashings of heritage style, bird-filled gardens (often full of wedding parties, too) and big cooked breakfasts await at the end of the bamboo-lined driveway.

Someday CAFE $$
(☑ 06-278 6097; www.facebook.com/someday cafehawera; 90 Princes St; dishes $9-19; ☺ 7am-5pm Mon-Fri, 9am-3pm Sat; 🛜) In a town short

on decent places to eat, you can almost hear Someday cafe sigh at its surroundings. Around 20 can fit on the mid-century chairs and at the industrial communal table, where locals chat over cake and the best coffee around for miles and all-day brunch (try the generous ploughman's platter). Just passing through? Don't stop anywhere else.

At the time of writing, Someday had plans to open for dinner, license application pending.

ℹ Information

South Taranaki i-SITE (☑ 06-278 8599; www. southtaranaki.com; 55 High St; ⊙ 8.30am-5pm Mon-Fri, 10am-3pm Sat & Sun; ☎) has the local low-down. Extended summer weekend hours.

ℹ Getting There & Away

Unlike the rest of SH45, Hawera is serviced by InterCity and Naked Bus, before/after the inland run to Stratford and New Plymouth. Local South-Link buses (www.taranakibus.info) from New Plymouth also service Hawera, via Opunake on SH45 (once on Fridays only) or Stratford on the inland route (once daily Monday to Friday).

WHANGANUI

POP 42,150

Before Whanganui was Whanganui, it was Petre, a town built at the mouth of the river in 1940. As one of New Zealand's oldest towns (and the fifth-largest until 1936), it's an amalgamation of Māori culture, heritage buildings – take a 60-minute self-guided tour with the free Whanganui Heritage Guide from the i-SITE (p259) – and a thriving local art community.

Despite the occasional flood, the wide Whanganui River is the lifeblood of the town, with regular markets, scenic walkways and old port buildings being turned into glass-art studios. There are few more appealing places to while away a sunny afternoon than the dog-free zone beneath Victoria Ave's leafy canopy.

History

Māori settlement along the Whanganui River (the people of Te Ātihaunui-a-Papārangi) dates back more than 40 generations. So when Andrew Powers, the first European on the river, arrived in 1831, you can understand why the Māori didn't want to exchange Pākehā gifts for their land – although Whanganui's

European settlement didn't take off until 1840, when the New Zealand Company could no longer satisfy Wellington's land demands.

Seven years of conflict ensued, with thousands of government troops occupying the Rutland Stockade in Queens Park. Ultimately, the struggle was settled by arbitration; during the Taranaki Land Wars, the Whanganui Māori assisted the Pākehā.

By the 1900s, Whanganui was booming thanks to agricultural industries and the river tourists trade.

◉ Sights

★ **New Zealand Glassworks**   GALLERY
(☑ 06-927 6803; www.nzglassworks.com; 2 Rutland St; ⊙ 10am-4.30pm) FREE The pick of Whanganui's many glass studios. Watch glass-blowers working, check out the gallery, take a one-day glass-blowing course ($290, four people max) or a 30-minute 'Make a Paperweight' lesson ($80), or just hang out and warm up on a chilly afternoon.

★ **Waimarie Centre**   MUSEUM
(☑ 0800 783 2637, 06-347 1863; www.waimarie. co.nz; 1a Taupo Quay; cruises adult/child/family $45/15/90; ⊙ 10am-3pm Oct-Apr; ☎) FREE The historical displays are interesting, but everyone's here for the PS *Waimarie*, the last of the Whanganui River paddle steamers. In 1900 it was shipped out from England and paddled the Whanganui until it sank ingloriously at its mooring in 1952. Submerged for 41 years, it was finally raised, restored, then relaunched on the first day of the 21st century. It now offers two-hour tours up the river, boarding at 10.30am. Book in advance.

★ **Sarjeant on the Quay**   GALLERY
(☑ 06-349 0506; www.sarjeant.org.nz; 38 Taupo Quay; ⊙ 10.30am-4.30pm) FREE The elegant old neoclassical Sarjeant Gallery building in Queens Park is closed for earthquake-proofing. Until that work is finished, this estimable art collection is housed on Taupo Quay. There's not as much room here as up on the hill, so exhibits are limited (but revolving). There's more on show above the Whanganui i-SITE (p259) across the road. Fab gift shop, too, with lots of Whanganui glass.

Whanganui Regional Museum   MUSEUM
(☑ 06-349 1110; www.wanganui-museum.org.nz; 62 Ridgway St; ⊙ 10am-4.30pm) FREE When we visited, the original Queens Park museum was closed for earthquake strengthening but open for business on Ridgway St. Here you'll

Whanganui

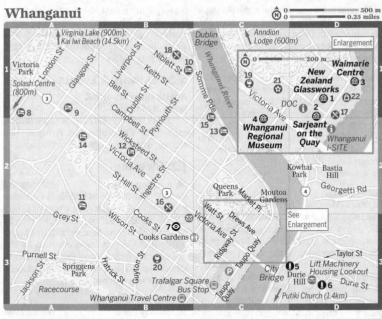

Whanganui

get a glimpse of one of NZ's better natural-history museums, including Māori exhibits, some vicious-looking *mere* (greenstone clubs) and colonial and wildlife installations.

Durie Hill Elevator   TOWER, VIEWPOINT
(☎0800 92 64 26; www.visitwhanganui.nz; Anzac Pde; adult/child one way $2/1; ◷8am-6pm Mon-

Fri, 10am-5pm Sat & Sun) Across City Bridge from downtown Whanganui, this elevator was built with grand visions for Durie Hill's residential future. Beyond an entrance lined with Māori carvings, a tunnel burrows 213m into the hillside, from where a 1919 elevator rattles 65.8m to the top.

At the summit you can climb the 176 steps of the War Memorial Tower and scan the horizon for Mt Taranaki and Mt Ruapehu. There's another lookout atop the lift machinery housing (just 41 steps).

Ward Observatory
OBSERVATORY

(☑ 06-349 0508, 027 245 8066; www.whanganuinz. com; Cooks Gardens, St Hill St; per person/family $2/5; ☺ 8-10pm Fri, weather dependent) Established in 1903, astro-geeks will be delighted to know that this 24cm telescope is the largest unmodified refractor operating in NZ. Roll up on Friday nights to gaze at galaxies far, far away.

Putiki Church
CHURCH

(St Paul's Memorial Church; ☑ 06-349 0508; www.visitwhanganui.nz; 20 Anaua St; per person $10; ☺ service 9am Sun, tours 2pm Thu-Sun or by arrangement) Across the City Bridge from town and 1km towards the sea is the Putiki Church (aka St Paul's Memorial Church). It's unremarkable externally, but just like the faithful pew-fillers, it's what's inside that counts: the interior is magnificent, completely covered in Māori carvings and *tukutuku* (wall panels). Show up for Sunday service, or get some inside knowledge on a guided tour organised via the i-SITE (p259).

Virginia Lake
LAKE

(Rotokawau; ☑ 0800 92 64 26; www.visitwhanganui. nz; 110 Great N Rd, St Johns Hill; ☺ 24hr; ♿) A couple of kilometres northwest of the centre, Virginia Lake is the perfect place for a stroll (around the lake or the woodland walk). Aside from the ducks, there's an aviary with cheeky cockatoos (9am to 4pm), the Winter Gardens (9am to 5pm), a sculpture garden, a playground and a cafe.

🏃 Activities & Tours

Wanganui Horse Treks
HORSE RIDING

(☑ 06-345 3285, 021 930 950; www.facebook. com/wanganuihorsetreks; 78 Wikitoria Rd, Wanganui Airport; 1/1½hr rides $80/120) Climb onto an agreeable horse and ride around the beaches and dunes at South Beach and Kai Iwi, a short drive southwest and northwest of Whanganui central respectively. A little cheaper if you can lasso a group of three friends together. Call for times, directions and bookings. Giddy-up!

Wanganui City Guided Walking Tours
WALKING

(☑ 06-349 3258; www.visitwhanganui.nz; 31 Taupo Quay; per person $10; ☺ 10am & 2pm Sat & Sun

Oct-Apr) Sign up for a 90-minute guided tour through old Whanganui, giving your legs a workout as you pass historic buildings and sights. Tours depart from the i-SITE (p259); book tickets inside.

🎭 Festivals & Events

Artists Open Studios & Festival of Glass
ART

(☑ 06-348 0157, 027 3042 126; www.openstudios. co.nz; ☺ Mar) Classy glass fest. Plenty of open studios, demonstrations and workshops.

🛏 Sleeping

★ Anndion Lodge
HOSTEL $

(☑ 0800 343 056, 06-343 3593; www.anndion lodge.co.nz; 143 Anzac Pde; s/d/f/ste from $75/88/105/135; @🛜🏊) Formerly run by Ann and Dion (Anndion, get it?), this hostel continues to attract travellers with its stereo systems, huge communal kitchen, pool tables, big TVs, spa, sauna, swimming pool, barbecue area and restaurant.

Whanganui River Top 10 Holiday Park
HOLIDAY PARK $

(☑ 06-343 8402, 0800 272 664; www.wrivertop10. co.nz; 460 Somme Pde, Aramoho; unpowered/ powered sites $39/46, cabins/units from $76/130; 🛜🏊) This tidy Top 10 park sits on the Whanganui's west bank 6km north of Dublin Bridge. Facilities (pool, games room, jumping pillow) are prodigious. Kayak hire is also available: the owners shuttle you up river then you paddle back. Budget cabins by the river have big-dollar views, or opt for a glamping tent ($100) in summer. Local buses trundle past.

Tamara Backpackers Lodge
HOSTEL $

(☑ 06-347 6300; www.tamaralodge.com; 24 Somme Pde; dm/s/tr/q from $29/44/93/116, d & tw with/without bathroom from $86/62; @🛜) Tamara is a photogenic, mazelike, two-storey heritage house with a wide balcony, lofty ceilings, a kitchen, a TV lounge, free bikes, a leafy back garden and incredibly helpful staff who will tell you what to see and where to be seen. Ask for one of the doubles overlooking the river.

Braemar House YHA
HOSTEL $

(☑ 06-348 2301; www.braemarhouse.co.nz; 2 Plymouth St; dm/s/tw/d $35/50/70/75, guesthouse incl breakfast s & d $140; @🛜) Riverside Braemar brings together an 1895 Victorian B&B guesthouse and a reliable YHA backpackers (although there are separate lounge areas). Centrally heated guesthouse rooms are floral and fancy; airy dorms conjure up a bit more fun out the back. Chooks patrol the lawns out in the yard.

★ **Browns Boutique B&B** B&B $$
(☑ 0273 082 495; www.brownsboutiquebnb.co.nz; 34 College St, College Estate; d/s incl breakfast $190/175) Owned by the same family for more than 50 years, this 1910 house was coincidently built by an unrelated Brown. There are two rooms at the back with private entrances that look out onto the patio, and in addition to gorgeous decor and little touches (tiles made by a Moroccan-New Zealander, a typewriter for a guestbook), the free-range, gourmet breakfasts are divine.

151 on London MOTEL $$
(☑ 0800 151 566, 06-345 8668; www.151onlondon. co.nz; 151 London St; d $130-180, 2-bedroom apt from $200; ☎) This snappy-looking spaceship of a motel wins plenty of fans with its architectural angles, quality carpets and linen, natty lime/silver/black colour scheme and big TVs. At the top of the price tree are some excellent upstairs/downstairs apartment-style units sleeping six: about as ritzy as Whanganui accommodation gets. Cafe across the car park.

Aotea Motor Lodge MOTEL $$
(☑ 06-345 0303; www.aoteamotorlodge.co.nz; 390 Victoria Ave; d from $145, 1-bedroom ste from $215; ☎) On the upper reaches of Victoria Ave, this flashy, two-storey contemporary motel features roomy suites, lavish linen, leather chairs, dark timbers and plenty of marble and stone. Every room has a spa bath. Romance is never far away in Whanganui.

Siena Motor Lodge MOTEL $$
(☑ 06-345 9009, 0800 888 802; www.siena.co.nz; 335 Victoria Ave; d/1-bedroom from $135/155; ☎) Aiming for Tuscany but hitting Taranaki, the compact rooms here are four-star and spotless. Business travellers enjoy double glazing, a DVD library, gym passes, heated towel rails, coffee plungers and real coffee. One of Whanganui's steadiest performers. Look for the neon sign.

Kings Court Motel MOTEL $$
(☑ 0800 221 222, 06-345 8586; www.kingscourt motel.co.nz; 60 Plymouth St; d/1-bedroom from $110/140; ☎) This four-star motel boasts a lovely garden setting and is walking distance from the centre of town. There are eight studio units and four one-bedders, all basic but spotless and with pictures of Whanganui on the walls, 'rather than Paris or the Notre Dame', as the owner will tell you.

Riverview Motel MOTEL $$
(☑ 0800 102 001, 06-345 2888; www.wanganui motels.co.nz; 14 Somme Pde; d $98-145; ☎) Take your pick from one of 10 older-but-updated kitchenette units in the main block (rooms 6 and 7 have views of the river), or the five spa suites out the back. Tidy, affordable and central, with a charming host.

WHANGANUI OR WANGANUI?

Yeah, yeah, we know, it's confusing. Is there an 'h' or isn't there? Either way, the pronunciation is identical: 'wong-ga', not 'fong-ga' (as in the rest of the country when a 'w' and 'h' meet).

In the local dialect *whanga* (harbour) is pronounced 'wong-ga', which is how the original 'Wanganui' spelling came about. But in 1991 the New Zealand Geographic Board officially adopted the correct Māori spelling (with an 'h') for the Whanganui River and Whanganui National Park. This was a culturally deferential decision: the Pākehā-dominated town and region retained the old spelling, while the river area – Māori territory – adopted the new.

In 2009 the board assented that the town and region should also adopt the 'h'. This caused much community consternation; opinions on the decision split almost evenly (outspoken Mayor Michael Laws was particularly anti-'h'). Ultimately, NZ Minister for Land Information Maurice Williamson decreed that either spelling was acceptable, and that adopting the querulous 'h' is up to individual businesses or entities. A good old Kiwi compromise!

This middle-ground held shakily until 2014, when the Wanganui District Council voted to ask the New Zealand Geographic Board to formalise the change to Whanganui. A public consultation process began, culminating in an announcement in late 2015 by Land Information Minister Louise Upston that the district's name would be officially changed to Whanganui. Whanderful!

WORTH A TRIP

KAI IWI

A wild ocean frontier, **Kai Iwi Beach** (Mowhanau Dr, off Rapanui Rd; ⊘24hr; 🖭) is strewn with black sand, the ruin of a gun emplacement from WWII and masses of driftwood (you might see locals collecting it for their next 'piece'). There's also a big playground with a flying fox and plenty of paddle-friendly water for young kids.

Follow Great North Rd 4km north of town, then turn left onto Rapanui Rd and head seawards for 10km.

Set 11km from Whanganui centre (pair it with a trip to Kai Iwi Beach), **Bason Botanic Gardens** (www. basonbotanicgardens.org.nz; 552 Rapanui Rd, Rapanui; ⊘8am-dusk) spread over 25 hectares and feature orchids, tropical plants, sculpture and interesting architecture (swirly brick barbecues for your picnic). Check the website for what's on.

✖ Eating

★**Yellow House Cafe** CAFE **$**
(The Yellow House; 📞06-345 0083; www.yellow housecafe.co.nz; cnr Pitt & Dublin Sts; meals $11-19; ⊘8am-4pm Mon-Fri, 8.30am-4pm Sat & Sun; 🖉) Detour from the main drag for funky tunes, butterscotch pancakes, local art and courtyard tables beneath a chunky-trunk cherry blossom tree. Super-friendly staff bend over backwards to recommend what to do in town. Try a venison burger for lunch on the sunny terrace. If you want to give high tea a whirl, book in advance.

★**Mischief on Guyton** CAFE **$**
(📞06-347 1227; www.facebook.com/mischiefon guyton; 96 Guyton St; mains $10-23; ⊘7.30am-3pm Mon-Fri) With cheeky signage and a flip calendar of quotes not suitable to print but good for a laugh with your coffee, Mischief on Guyton is true to its name. Step inside (or through to the courtyard) for a combined brunch and lunch menu featuring interesting dishes like the wonderfully named rockamorocca: oven-baked eggs with dukkah on pita bread.

★**Citadel** BURGERS **$$**
(📞06-344 7076; www.facebook.com/the-citadel. castlecliff; 14a Rangiora St, Castlecliff; burgers $12-19; ⊘9am-8pm Thu & Sun-Mon, to 9pm Fri & Sat; 🖭) Looking for the best burgers on the North Island? Community-minded Citadel, 10 minutes' drive from Whanganui centre, is a contender. Alongside classics, the Eh Monster is a feat of endurance. Order it (alongside loaded fries) and watch heads turn. Graffiti that looks like a children's book illustration covers the outdoor deck wall. Breakfast menu, kids' menu and wooden playground, too.

Big Orange CAFE **$$**
(📞06-348 4449; www.facebook.com/bigorange cafe; 51 Victoria Ave; meals $14-24; ⊘7.30am-3pm Mon-Fri, 8am-3pm Sat & Sun; 🛜🖭) Inside a gorgeous old Whanganui red-brick building, Big Orange is a babbling espresso bar serving gourmet burgers, big breakfasts, muffins, cakes and sandwiches. The outdoor tables overlooking the roundabout are hot property, and from 5pm Ceramic Lounge (p258) in the same building takes over with dinner and drinks. Ask about 'pay it forward' coffee.

Ceramic Lounge MODERN NZ **$$**
(📞06-348 4449; www.facebook.com/ceramic loungebar; 51 Victoria Ave; mains $23-40; ⊘5pm-late Wed-Sat; 🛜) In a split-business arrangement with adjacent Big Orange (p258), Ceramic takes over for the dinner shift, serving upmarket food (including venison *carpaccio* and lamb rump with caramelised root veggies) in a low-lit, rust-coloured interior. Occasional DJs flow tunes across the tables to the cocktail-sipping crowd.

Mud Ducks CAFE **$$**
(📞06-348 7626; www.facebook.com/MudDucks; 31 Taupo Quay; dishes $13-24; ⊘8.30am-4pm; 🛜) Considering it's located within the i-SITE (p259), Mud Ducks is a pretty spiffy cafe. With an outdoor deck and lovely timber beams, it's a good spot to rest and take advantage of free wi-fi. Brunch could be a breakfast buttie on the go, while lunch ranges from fresh salads to a meatloaf burger.

🍷 Drinking & Entertainment

Frank Bar + Eatery COCKTAIL BAR
(📞027 441 9577, 027 4222 555, 06-348 4808; www.facebook.com/pg/frankwhanganui; 98 Victoria Ave; burgers $18.50, platters $25-45; ⊘5-9pm Tue & Wed, to 10pm Thu, to midnight Fri & Sat) With DJs and events lined up every weekend and a solid cocktail list, we'll be Frank when we tell you that this is the place for a night out. The lofty space is split into an industrial-chic dining area with a mezzanine up above. Burgers and big share platters for eats. Happy hour is 6pm to 9pm Thursday to Saturday.

Lucky Bar + Kitchen
BAR

(📱021 126 3936; www.facebook.com/luckybar whanganui; 53 Wilson St; mains $26-28; ⏱4pm-late Wed-Sat, kitchen closes 9pm) One of the few places for a night out in Whang, Lucky serves local fare worth eating, even if you're not into live music. With boxes stacked behind a small stage, round paper lanterns hanging from the ceiling and disco lighting, there's an endearing high-school vibe here, but all ages get up to dance when the tunes are right.

Article
COFFEE

(📱027 752 2472; www.facebook.com/pg/Article whanganui; cnr Rutland St & Drews Ave; drinks $3-5; ⏱9am-3pm Sat, 10am-2pm Sun) Article serves fair-trade organic Devil's Cup coffee, milkshakes (and sometimes doughnuts) in the old *Wanganui Chronicle* building. Inside is a collection of things you wish you'd found at secondhand stores, and a vintage-clothing shop. It also has local arts and crafts for sale and boardgames to play the afternoon away in the light from the big arched windows.

Savage Club
LIVE MUSIC

(📱021 256 7647; www.whanganuimusiciansclub. co.nz; 65 Drews Ave; ⏱7pm 1st Fri of the month) The first Friday of every month is club night here; that means a scheduled performance from local and international stars, and even open mic earlier on. This is where the musos go for gigs. Search Whanganui Musicians Club on Facebook to see what's on. Better yet, it's BYO before 9pm.

🛍 Shopping

River Traders Market & Whanganui Farmers Market
MARKET

(📱027 229 9616; www.therivertraders.co.nz; Moutoa Quay; ⏱9am-1pm Sat) Spend Saturday morning like a local at the River Traders Market, next to the Waimarie Centre, which is crammed with local arts and crafts. The Whanganui Farmers Market runs concurrently alongside, with loads of organic produce. Gather a picnic and enjoy under some trees by the river.

ℹ Information

MEDICAL SERVICES

Whanganui Hospital (📱06-348 1234; www. wdhb.org.nz; 100 Heads Rd; ⏱24hr) Accident and emergency.

TOURIST INFORMATION

DOC (Department of Conservation; 📱06-349 2100; www.doc.govt.nz; 34-36 Taupo Quay; ⏱8.30am-4.30pm Mon-Fri) For national park and regional camping info.

Whanganui i-SITE (📱0800 92 64 26, 06-349 0508; www.whanganuinz.com; 31 Taupo Quay; ⏱9am-5pm Mon-Sun Nov-Apr, 9am-5pm Mon-Fri, to 4pm Sat & Sun May-Oct; 🕿) Tourist and DOC information (if the DOC office across the street is closed) in an impressive renovated riverside building (check out the old floorboards!). **Sarjeant Gallery** (p254) exhibition space upstairs; internet access downstairs.

ℹ Getting There & Away

AIR

Whanganui Airport (📱06-349 0001; www. wanganuiairport.co.nz; Airport Rd) is 4km south of town, across the river towards the sea. Air New Zealand (www.airnewzealand.co.nz) has daily direct flights to/from Auckland, with onward connections.

BUS

InterCity (www.intercity.co.nz) buses operate from the **Whanganui Travel Centre** (📱06-345 7100; 156 Ridgway St; ⏱8.15am-5.15pm Mon-Fri).

DESTINATION	COST	TIME (HR)	FREQUENCY (DAILY)
Auckland	from $33	8	1
Hamilton	from $31	5½	1
New Plymouth	from $17	2½	1-2
Palmerston North	from $18	1½	3-4
Wellington	from $24	4	2-3

ℹ Getting Around

BICYCLE

Bike Shed (📱06-345 5500; www.bikeshed. co.nz; cnr Ridgway & St Hill Sts; ⏱8am-5.30pm Mon-Fri, 9am-2pm Sat) Hires out city bikes from $35 per day, including helmet and lock. Also a good spot for info on the **Mountains to Sea bike trail** (www.mountainstosea.co.nz) from Mt Ruapehu to Whanganui, which is part of the Nga Haerenga, New Zealand Cycle Trail (www.nzcycletrail.com).

BUS

Horizons (www.horizons.govt.nz; tickets adult/child $2.50/1.50) Operates four looped council-run bus routes departing Trafalgar Square shopping centre on Taupo Quay, including orange and purple routes past the Whanganui River Top 10 Holiday Park in Aramoho.

WHANGANUI NATIONAL PARK

The Whanganui River may not pay taxes or vote, but it has the same rights as a human being. That's because in early 2017 it became the first river to be legally recognised as a person, following a 140-year battle. The new legislation recognises the spiritual connection between Māori *iwi* and the river, considered an ancestor.

Curling 290km from Mt Tongariro to the Tasman Sea, it's the longest navigable river in New Zealand, and visitors traverse it by canoe, kayak, jetboat, and bike.

The native bush here is thick, podocarp, broad-leaved forest interspersed with ferns. Occasionally you'll see poplars and other introduced trees along the river, remnants of long-vanished settlements. There are also traces of Māori settlements, with old *pā* (fortified village) and *kainga* (village) sites, and Hauhau *niu* (war and peace) poles at the convergence of the Whanganui and Ohura Rivers at Maraekowhai.

History

In Māori legend the Whanganui River was formed when Mt Taranaki fled the central North Island for the sea after fighting with Mt Tongariro over the lovely Mt Pihanga, leaving a long gouge behind him. He turned west at the coast, finally stopping where he resides today. Mt Tongariro sent cool water to heal the gouge – and the Whanganui River was born.

Kupe, the great Polynesian explorer, is believed to have travelled 20km up the Whanganui around AD 800; Māori lived here by 1100. By the time Europeans put down roots in the late 1830s, Māori settlements lined the river valley. Missionaries sailed upstream and their settlements – at Hiruharama, Ranana, Koriniti and Atene – have survived to this day.

Steamers first tackled the river in the mid-1860s. In 1886 a Whanganui company established the first commercial steamer transport service. Others soon followed, utilising the river between Whanganui and Taumarunui.

New Zealand's contemporary tourism leviathan was seeded here. Internationally advertised trips on the 'Rhine of Māoriland' became so popular that by 1905, 12,000 tourists a year were making the trip upriver from Whanganui to Pipiriki or downriver from Taumarunui. The engineering feats and skippering ability required on the river became legendary.

From 1918 land upstream of Pipiriki was granted to returning WWI soldiers. Farming here was a major challenge, with many families struggling for years to make the rugged land productive. Only a few endured into the early 1940s.

The completion of the railway from Auckland to Wellington and improved roads ultimately signed river transport's death warrant; 1959 saw the last commercial riverboat voyage. Today, just one old-fleet vessel cruises the river – the PS Waimarie (p254).

◉ Sights

The scenery along the **Whanganui River Road** en route to Pipiriki from Whanganui is camera conducive – stark, wet mountain slopes plunge into lazy jade stretches of the Whanganui River.

About 7km north of Parikino as the river and road bend into an obvious U-shape, cars slow to admire the **Oyster Cliffs**, where fossilised oysters jut from rock that used to be submerged in the ocean. If you cross a bridge and see the Moukuku Scenic Reserve sign, you've gone too far.

The Māori villages of **Atene, Koriniti, Ranana** and **Hiruharama** crop up as you travel further upstream – ask a local before you go sniffing around. Along the road you'll spot some relics of earlier settlements, such as the 1854 **Kawana Flour Mill** (☏04-472 4341; www.nzhistory.net.nz/media/photo/kawana-flour-mill; 4075 Whanganui River Rd; ☉dawn-dusk) **FREE** near Matahiwi and *pā* sites.

Pipiriki is beside the river at the north end of Whanganui River Rd. It's a rainy river town without much going on (no shops or petrol), but was once a humming holiday hot spot serviced by river steamers and paddleboats. Pipiriki is the end point for canoe trips coming down the river and the launching pad for jetboat rides.

St Joseph's Church　　　　CHURCH
(☏06-342 8190; www.compassion.org.nz; Whanganui River Rd; ☉9am-5pm) **FREE** Around a corner in the Whanganui River Rd in Jerusalem, the picture-perfect, red-and-mustard spire of St Joseph's Church stands tall on a spur of land above a deep river bend. A French Catholic mission led by Suzanne Aubert established the Daughters of the Sisters of Compassion here in 1892. Slip off your shoes and explore the (slightly creepy) convent and Madeline-like dorms.

The sisters take in bedraggled travellers, offering 20 dorm-style beds (adults $20, children $5, linen $10 extra) and a simple kitchen – book ahead for the privilege. **Moutoa Island**, site of a historic 1864 battle, is just downriver.

Bridge to Nowhere   BRIDGE

(Whanganui River) **FREE** To say this bridge looks out of place is an understatement. With no roads on either side, you don't need to be a genius to figure out its name. Originally built so that horses could cross the river to Mangapurua Valley farm land that was provided to soldiers after WWI, they deserted the poor soil in 1942, and the forest regained its natural position. It's on the Mangapurua Track for trampers and mountain bikers, or it's a 40-minute walk from Mangapurua Landing, upstream from Pipiriki, accessible by jetboat or kayak.

🏃 Activities

One of NZ's 'Great Walks', the Whanganui Journey is actually a canoe or kayak trip down the Whanganui River in Whanganui National Park. There are also jetboat tours to be had on the river, plus cycling along the Whanganui River Rd.

Canoeing & Kayaking

The most popular stretch of river for canoeing and kayaking is the 145km downstream run from Taumarunui to Pipiriki. This has been added to the NZ Great Walks system as the **Whanganui Journey**. It's a Grade II river – easy enough for the inexperienced, with enough roiling rapids to keep things interesting. If you need a Great Walks Ticket, you must arrange one before you start paddling.

Taumarunui to Pipiriki is a five-day/four-night trip, **Ohinepane to Pipiriki** is a four-day/three-night trip, and **Whakahoro to Pipiriki** is a three-day/two-night trip. **Taumarunui to Whakahoro** is a popular overnight trip, especially for weekenders, or you can do a one-day trip from **Taumarunui to Ohinepane** or **Ohinepane to Whakahoro**. From Whakahoro to Pipiriki, 87km downstream, there's no road access so you're wed to the river for a few days. Most canoeists stop at Pipiriki.

The season for canoe trips is usually from October to Easter. Up to 5000 people make the river trip each year, mostly between Christmas and the end of January. During winter the river is almost deserted – cold currents run swift and deep as wet weather and short days deter potential paddlers.

To hire a two-person Canadian canoe for one/three/five days costs around $100/200/250 per person not including transport (around $50 per person). A single-person kayak costs about $70 per day. Operators provide you with everything you need, including life jackets and waterproof drums (essential if you go bottom-up).

You can also take guided canoe or kayak trips – prices start at around $350/850 per person for a two-/five-day guided trip.

Whanganui River Canoes   CANOEING, KAYAKING

(☑0800 408 888, 06-385 4176; www.whanganui rivercanoes.co.nz; Raetihi Holiday Park, 10 Parapara Rd, Raetihi; hire per person 3/4/5 days from $160/170/180, guided trips per person 3/4/5 days from $665/785/885) Kayak and canoe hire, plus all-inclusive guided trips. The one-day trip – jetboat to Bridge to Nowhere then canoe down to Pipiriki – is a good option if you're short on time.

Owhango Adventures   CANOEING, KAYAKING

(Map p292; ☑0800 222 663, 07-895 4854, 027 678 6461; www.canoewhanganuiriver.com; 2191 SH4, Owhango; trips 1/2/3/4/5 days per person from $100/150/170/170/170, river guides per day $225) Myriad multiday options down the big river, with or without a river guide to point out the sights. Book your own DOC accommodation. Two- to five-night trips with four or more people are eligible for a free night's accommodation before departure.

Jetboating

Hold onto your hats – jetboat trips give you the chance to see parts of the river that would otherwise take you days to paddle through. Jetboats depart from Pipiriki and Whanganui; four-hour tours start at around $125 to $150 per person. Most operators can also provide transport to the river ends of the Matemateāonga and Mangapurua Tracks.

Bridge to Nowhere Tours   OUTDOORS

(☑0800 480 308, 06-385 4622; www.bridgeto nowhere.co.nz; 11 Owairua Rd, Pipiriki; jetboating adult/child from $140/70, 2-day canoeing adult/child from $235/165) Jetboat tours, canoeing, mountain biking, tramping – the folks at **Bridge to Nowhere Lodge** (☑06-385 4622, 0800 480 308; www.bridgetonowhere. co.nz; Whanganui National Park; tent/cabins/dm $15/30/55) coordinate it all, with accommodation and accommodation plus meal packages in the middle of nowhere afterwards.

Whanganui National Park Area

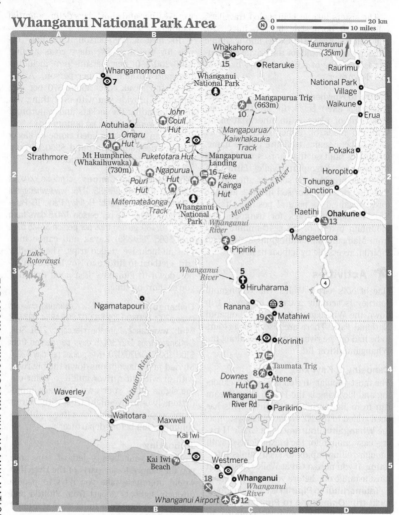

Following a six-hour ride, mountain bikers can get picked up from Mangapurua Landing and travel to their lodge accommodation via jetboat, or get shuttled one-way or return to Raetihi. Water sports are thrown in the mix with tours that include a jetboat from Pipiriki to Mangapurua Landing, a 40-minute walk to the Bridge to Nowhere and then a canoe trip back to the start.

**Whanganui Scenic
Experience Jet** BOATING, CANOEING
(☑ 06-342 5599, 0800 945 335; www.whanganui
scenicjet.com; 1195 Whanganui River Rd; 2-8hr trips

adult $80-200, child $60-160) Jetboat tours up-river from Whanganui, plus longer expeditions into the national park with tramping detours. Canoe and canoe/jetboat combo trips also available.

Mountain Biking

The Whanganui River Rd and Mangapurua/Kaiwhakauka Track have been incorporated into the 317km **Mountains to Sea** Mt Ruapehu–Whanganui bike track (www.mountainstosea.co.nz), itself part of the Nga Haerenga, New Zealand Cycle Trail project (www.nzcycletrail.com). As part of

Whanganui National Park Area

the experience, from Mangapurua Landing on the Whanganui River near the Bridge to Nowhere, you catch a (pre-booked) jetboat downstream to Pipiriki, then continue riding down the Whanganui River Rd. For repairs and info, try Bike Shed (p259) in Whanganui.

Hiking

The Matemateāonga and Mangapurua/Kaiwhakauka Tracks are brilliant longer tramps (downloadable from www.doc.govt.nz). Both are one-way tracks beginning (or ending) at remote spots on the river, so you have to organise jetboat transport to or from the river trailheads – ask any jetboat operator. Between Pipiriki and the Matemateāonga Track is around $50 per person; for the Mangapurua Track it's around $100.

Atene Viewpoint Walk &
Atene Skyline Track   TRAMPING
(☑06-349 2100; www.doc.govt.nz; Whanganui River Rd; ☉daylight hrs) **FREE** At Atene, on the Whanganui River Rd about 22km north of the SH4 junction, tackle the short Atene Viewpoint Walk – about a one-hour ascent. The track travels through native bush and farmland along a 1959 roadway built by the former Ministry of Works and Development during investigations for a Whanganui River hydroelectric scheme (a dam was proposed at Atene that would have flooded the river valley almost as far as Taumarunui). The track ends on a black beech ridge – expect great views across the national park.

From the viewpoint walk you can continue along the circular 18km Atene Skyline Track. The track takes six to eight hours, showcasing native forest, sandstone bluffs

and the **Taumata Trig** (523m), with its broad views as far as Mt Ruapehu, Mt Taranaki and the Tasman Sea. The track ends back on the Whanganui River Rd, 2km downstream from the starting point.

Matemateāonga Track   TRAMPING
(☑06-349 2100; www.doc.govt.nz; Whanganui National Park) **FREE** Three to four days from end to end, the 42km Matemateāonga Track gets kudos as one of NZ's best walks. Probably due to its remoteness, it doesn't attract the hordes of trampers that amass on NZ's more famous tracks. Penetrating deep into wild bush and hill country, it follows the crest of the Matemateāonga Range along the route of the Whakaihuwaka Rd. Work on the road began in 1911 to create a more direct link from Stratford to the railway at Raetihi. WWI interrupted progress and the road was never finished.

On a clear day, a 1½-hour side trip to the top of **Mt Humphries** (732m) rewards you with sigh-inducing views all the way to Mt Taranaki and the volcanoes of Tongariro. There's a steep section between the Whanganui River (75m above sea level) and the Puketotara Hut (427m above sea level), but mostly it's easy walking. There are four DOC backcountry huts along the way: Omaru (eight bunks), Pouri (12 bunks), Ngapurua (10 bunks) and Puketotara (eight bunks); hut tickets cost $15/7.50 per adult/child per night. There's road access at the track's western end.

Bridge to Nowhere Track   TRAMPING
(☑06-349 2100; www.doc.govt.nz; Whanganui National Park; ☉daylight hrs) **FREE** The most popular track in Whanganui National Park is the 40-minute walk from Mangapurua

TARANAKI & WHANGANUI WHANGANUI NATIONAL PARK

Landing (30km upstream from Pipiriki by jetboat) to the long-lost Bridge to Nowhere (p261). Contact jetboat operators for transport (around $100 per person one way).

Mangapurua/Kaiwhakauka Track TRAMPING
(☑ 06-349 2100; www.doc.govt.nz; Whanganui National Park) `FREE` The Mangapurua/Kaiwhakauka Track is a 40km trail between Whakahoro and the Mangapurua Landing, both on the Whanganui River. The track runs along the Mangapurua and Kaiwhakauka Streams (both Whanganui River tributaries). Between these valleys a side track leads to the 663m **Mangapurua Trig**, the area's highest point, from which cloudless views extend to the Tongariro and Egmont National Park volcanoes. The route also passes the amazing Bridge to Nowhere (p261). Walking the track takes 20 hours (three to four days).

🛏 Sleeping & Eating

Whanganui National Park has a sprinkling of huts, a lodge and numerous camping grounds (free to $15 per hut outside of the Great Walks season, which runs October to April). Along the Taumarunui–Pipiriki section are two huts classified as Great Walk Huts during summer ($32 per night) and Backcountry Huts in the off-season: John Coull Hut and Tieke Kainga Hut, which has been revived as a *marae* (you can stay here, but full *marae* protocol must be observed – eg no alcohol). The Whakahoro Bunkroom is also on this stretch of river. On the lower part of the river, Downes Hut is on the west bank, opposite Atene.

ℹ CAMPING & HUT PASSES

Great Walk Tickets are required in Whanganui National Park from 1 October to 30 April for the use of huts (adult/child $22 to $70/free) and campsites (adult/child $6 to $20/free) between Taumarunui and Pipiriki. Outside the main season you'll only need a **Backcountry Hut Pass** (adult/child for one year $122/61, for six months $92/46), or you can pay on a night-by-night basis (adult/child $5/2.50). Passes and tickets can be purchased online (www.greatwalks.co.nz); via email (greatwalks@doc. govt.nz); by phone (0800 694 732); or at DOC offices in Whakapapa, Taumarunui, Ohakune or Whanganui (p259).

Along the River Rd there are a couple of lodges for travellers to bunk down in. There's also a free informal campsite with toilets and cold water at Pipiriki, and another one (even less formal) just north of Atene. Also at Pipiriki are a campsite, some cabins and a cottage run by **Whanganui River Adventures** (☑ 0800 862 743, 06-385 3246; www. whanganuiriveradventures.co.nz; 2522 Pipiriki-Raetihi Rd, Pipiriki; trips from $80).

Flying Fox LODGE, B&B **$$**
(☑ 06-927 6809; www.theflyingfox.co.nz; Whanganui River Rd; campsites $15, summer glamping d $60, d $90-240; 🐾) 🚲 Accessible only by boat or eponymous flying fox (park on the side of Whanganui River Rd and launch yourself across the river), this eco-attuned getaway is on the riverbank across from Koriniti. You can self-cater in the Brewers Cottage, James K or Glory Cart; opt for B&B ($120 per person); or pitch a tent in a bush clearing.

Matahiwi Gallery Cafe CAFE **$**
(☑ 06-342 8112; www.facebook.com/Matahiwi gallery; 3925 Whanganui River Rd, Matahiwi; snacks $4-8; ⏰ 9am-4pm Wed-Sun Oct-May) This old schoolhouse with a model steamboat out the front has been reborn as a casual cafe, serving cakes, slices, scones and gluten-free muffins washed down with coffee. Local arts and crafts also on display. Call ahead if you want to be sure it's open.

ℹ Information

For national park information, try the affable **Whanganui** (p259) or **Taumarunui** (p232) i-SITEs, or check out www.doc.govt.nz and www. whanganuiriver.co.nz. Otherwise, a more tangible resource is the NZ Recreational Canoeing Association's *Guide to the Whanganui River* ($10; see http://rivers.org.nz/whanganui-guide).

DOC's **Pipiriki** (☑ 06-385 5022; www.doc. govt.nz; Owairua Rd, Pipiriki; ⏰ irregular) and **Taumarunui** (☑ 07-895 8201; www.doc.govt.nz; Cherry Grove Domain, Taumarunui; ⏰ irregular) centres are field bases rather than tourist offices, and aren't always staffed.

Mobile-phone coverage along the River Rd is patchy at best.

ℹ Getting There & Away

From the north, there's road access to the Whanganui River at Taumarunui, Ohinepane and Whakahoro, though the latter is a long, remote drive on mostly unsealed roads. Roads to Whakahoro lead off from Owhango and Raurimu, both on SH4. There isn't any further road access to the river until Pipiriki.

From the south, the Whanganui River Rd veers off SH4 14km north of Whanganui, rejoining it at Raetihi, 91km north of Whanganui. It takes about two hours to drive the 79km between Whanganui and Pipiriki. The full circle from Whanganui through Pipiriki and Raetihi and back along SH4 takes four hours minimum (longer if you want to stop, explore and take photos). Alternatively, take a River Rd tour from Whanganui.

There are no petrol stations or shops along the River Rd.

PALMERSTON NORTH

POP 80,080

The rich farming region of Manawatu embraces the districts of Rangitikei to the north and Horowhenua to the south. The hub of it all, on the banks of the Manawatu River, is Palmerston North. Massey University, New Zealand's largest, informs the town's cultural and social structures and as a result 'Palmy' has an open-minded, rurally bookish vibe.

However, none of this impressed a visiting John Cleese who reportedly said, 'If you wish to kill yourself but lack the courage to, I think a visit to Palmerston North will do the trick'. The city exacted revenge with an exemplary sense of humour by naming a rubbish dump after him. We think Cleese needs to return (it has been over a decade now) to explore excellent mountain biking and lush walking tracks beyond the city and great coffee, beer and friendly locals within.

Sights

Te Manawa   MUSEUM
(06-355 5000; www.temanawa.co.nz; 326 Main St; 10am-5pm, to 7.30pm Thu;) FREE Te Manawa merges a museum and art gallery into one experience, with vast collections joining the dots between art, science and history. The museum has a strong Māori focus and includes plenty of social history, information on native animals and wetlands, and an interactive science display on Manawatu River. The gallery's exhibits change frequently. Kids under eight will get a kick out of the interactive play area. The New Zealand Rugby Museum (p265) is in the same complex.

New Zealand Rugby Museum   MUSEUM
(06-358 6947; www.rugbymuseum.co.nz; Te Manawa Complex, 326 Main St; adult/child/family $12.50/5/30; 10am-5pm) Fans of the oval ball holler about the New Zealand Rugby Museum, an amazing space overflowing with rugby paraphernalia, from a 1905 All Blacks jumper to a scrum machine and the actual whistle used to start the first game of every Rugby World Cup. Of course, NZ won back-to-back Rugby World Cups in 2011 and 2015: quiz the staff about the All Blacks' 2019 prospects.

The Square   PARK
(06-356 8199; www.pncc.govt.nz; The Square; 24hr) FREE Taking the English village green concept to a whole new level, the Square is Palmy's heart and soul. The Square's Māori name, Te Marae o Hine, was chosen to symbolise all tribes and races living together peacefully, which they certainly do when the sun comes out and everyone gathers on the lawn to lunch. The 7 spacey hectares feature a clock tower, duck pond, giant chess set, Māori carvings, statues and trees of all seasonal dispositions and free wi-fi.

Activities & Tours

Swing into the i-SITE (p269) and pick up the *Discover City Walkways* booklet and print outs of suggested itineraries for shoppers, eaters, explorers and everything in between.

Timeless Horse Treks   HORSE RIDING
(027 446 8536, 06-376 6157; www.timeless horsetreks.co.nz; Gorge Rd, Ballance; 30/60/90min rides from $25/50/85;) Flee Palmerston North and visit Timeless Horse Treks. Gentle trail rides take in the Manawatu River and surrounding hills. Palmy pick-up/drop-off available.

Sleeping

@ the Hub   HOTEL $
(06-356 8880; www.atthehub.co.nz; 25 Rangitikei St; r $99-170;) There are two @ the Hubs, one WEST (short-term accommodation) and one EAST (long-term). The latter is geared to students, but travellers can book anything from a serviced en suite with kitchenette and simple student shoebox to a three-bedroom family apartment. Great location but fairly sterile. Ask for a window room overlooking the Square, or risk no windows at all.

Peppertree Hostel   HOSTEL $
(06-355 4054; www.peppertreehostel.co.nz; 121 Grey St; dm/s/d/f $31/65/78/124;) Inexplicably strewn with green-painted, succulent-filled boots, this endearing 100-year-old house is the best budget option in town. Mattresses are thick, the kitchen will never run out of spatulas and the piano and wood fire make things feel downright homey. Unisex bathrooms, but there is a gals-only dorm. Nine rooms and 35 beds.

Palmerston North

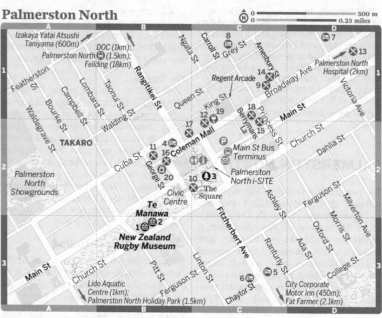

Palmerston North

Palmerston North
Holiday Park
HOLIDAY PARK $

(☏06-358 0349; www.palmerstonnorthholiday-park.co.nz; 133 Dittmer Dr; campsites/cabins from $35/50, d/f units $95/105; 🛜) About 2km from the Square, off Ruha St, this shady park with daisy-speckled lawns is quiet, affordable and right beside Victoria Esplanade gardens. Trees and gardens add calm, until the kids take over the playground!

Hacienda Motor Lodge
MOTEL $$

(☏06-357 3109; www.hacienda.co.nz; 27 Victoria Ave; d from $125, 1- & 2-bedroom from $155, 2-/3-bedroom apt $220/230) Clean, comfortable and with a feminine touch (pastel cushions, artwork and lush throw blankets) Hacienda's little touches make all the difference. Studio units range from basic travellers accommodation through to spa suites, and there are one- and two-bedroom units and apartments. Lovely beds, top toiletries and affable hosts.

AROUND PALMERSTON NORTH

Venture outside Palmerston North for landscapes and beaches in direct contrast with the faster, more corporate pace of the student city. About 12km east of town, SH2 dips into Manawatu Gorge. Māori named the gorge Te Apiti (the Narrow Passage), believing the big reddish rock near the centre of the gorge was its guardian spirit. It's an 11km, uphill slant to get to the viewpoints and takes around four hours one way. On the southwestern edge of the Gorge is the **Taratua Wind Farm**, allegedly the largest in the southern hemisphere. North of the Gorge is **Te Āpiti Wind Farm**, with 55 turbines creating enough power for around 39,000 New Zealand homes each year. It's on private land, but through the gate there is a public viewing platform with mesmerising views, just off Saddle Rd.

At the time of writing, the SH3 road through the Manawatu Gorge was closed due to landslips, but the walking tracks were open. Check before you go at the Palmerston North i-SITE (p269) or with the local Department of Conservation (call ☑ 06-350 9700).

South of Palmerston North is **Shannon** (population 1240) and **Foxton** (population 2650), quiet country towns en route to Wellington. **Foxton Beach** is one of a string of broad, shallow Tasman Sea beaches along this stretch of coast – other worthy beaches include **Himatangi**, **Hokio** and **Waikawa**. **Levin** (population 20,900) is more sizeable, but is too close to both Wellington and Palmerston North to warrant the through-traffic making an extended stop.

Park yourself in Palmy in the evening and treat the rest as day-trip terrain. Take your own car; otherwise InterCity (www.intercity.co.nz) and Naked Bus (www.nakedbus.com) services pass through Levin and Shannon (and sometimes Foxton) en route between Palmerston North and Wellington.

Destiny Motel　　　　　　　MOTEL $$
(☑ 06-355 0050; www.destinymotel.co.nz; 127 Fitzherbert Ave; d/ste/2-bedroom from $145/165/259; [P][🗢]) Destiny's studios and suites pop with colours and patterns, making it stand out from the safe-but-boring colour schemes of most motels. Stylish, contemporary and with all the mod cons, it's more like a boutique hotel.

City Corporate Motor Inn　　　MOTEL $$
(☑ 06-355 4522; www.citycorporate.co.nz; 209 Fitzherbert Ave; d $160-180, apt $240; [P][❋][🗢]) Not a motel person? This could be what turns you. These luxury rooms with oversized double spa baths beside the beds, roomy work stations and handsome leather and timber finishes are as good as it gets. Homemade baked goodies take it from corporate to comfort. Splurge on an apartment if you want to do your own cooking.

Fitzherbert Castle Motel　　　MOTEL $$
(☑ 0800 115 262, 06-358 3888; www.fitzcastle motel.co.nz; 124 Fitzherbert Ave; d $120-145, f from $145; [P][🗢]) It looks unapologetically like a Tudor castle from the outside, but inside it's more like an intimate hotel. Offers 14 immaculate rooms with cork-tiled bathroom floors and quality carpets, plenty of trees, friendly staff and small kitchens in some units. Free wi-fi and laundry.

✖ Eating & Drinking

★ **Saigon Corner**　　　　　VIETNAMESE $
(☑ 06-355 4988; www.facebook.com/saigon cornernz; 54 Princess St; mains $8.50-16; ⊙ 11am-3pm & 5-8.30pm Tue-Sat, 11am-3pm Mon; [☑]) The pick of Palmy cheap eats, this cheerful, casual Vietnamese restaurant nails all the classics: *pho, banh mi*, rice-paper rolls and noodle and rice dishes. Fresh and filled with locals, it's good to eat in or take away.

★ **Local**　　　　　　　　　　CAFE $
(☑ 06-280 4821; www.cafelocal.co.nz; 240 Broadway Ave; dishes $10-15; ⊙ 7am-3.30pm Mon-Wed, to 7pm Fri & Fri, 8am-4pm Sat; [🗢][♿]) Brilliant Local specialises in build-your-own meals. For breakfast, that means eggs with additions like potato herb hash and grilled salmon, and for lunch, wholesome bowls with your choice of protein on salad. Sharing the building with property brokers, Local scores top marks for the teal banquettes, tiled features and a roomy outdoor area. Try the curly fries.

Wholegrain Organics　　　HEALTH FOOD $
(☑ 06-328 5917; www.wholegrainorganics.co.nz; 135 The Square; mains $8-18; ⊙ 9am-6pm Mon & Tue, to 9pm Wed & Thu, 11.30am-4pm Sun; [☑]) 🍃 This bright cafe is also a registered charity that teaches 12 to 19-year-olds how to cook nutritious and sustainable food. One hundred per

cent vegan, the breakfast bowls, wholegrain pizza and tofu scramble are local favourites. Don't miss the raw desserts!

Fat Farmer
EUROPEAN $$

(📌06-358 4999; www.thefatfarmer.co.nz; 360 Albert St, Hokowhitu; $14-32; ☺4.30pm-late Tue & Wed, 3.30pm-late Thu-Sat) There's a definition of the noun 'farmer' on the wall at this restaurant and bar: 'someone who is outstanding in their field'. And while they may not take themselves seriously, dishes such as pan-fried goat's cheese and slow-roasted jerk chicken aren't mucking about. Best with Tuatara on tap. Book ahead if you want to sit in the dining room.

A few kilometres southeast of Palmy CBD and owned by the same team behind **Aberdeen** (📌06-952 5570; www.aberdeenonbroadway.co.nz; 161 Broadway Ave; mains $26-40; ☺11.30am-2.30pm & 5.30pm-late Fri, 5.30pm-late Sat-Thu; 🚲).

Arranged Marriage
SOUTH INDIAN $$

(📌06-351 6300; www.arrangedmarriage.co.nz; 32b The Square; $16-23; ☺noon-2pm & 5-9.30pm Tue-Sun; 🚲) A taste of Kerala right on The Square, this is the second restaurant from the Kathakali (p244) team in New Plymouth. The decor is fun and vibrant without being gaudy (love the coconut wall) and the food aromatic. You'll find butter chicken and vegetable korma here, but order the signature *dosa*. The $12 lunch deals are great, too.

HARU Japanese Restaurant
JAPANESE $$

(📌06-358 4278; www.facebook.com/harujapanese; 19 Broadway Ave; mains $19-28; ☺11.30am-2.30pm & 5pm-late Tue-Sun, 5pm-late Mon; 🚲) A wonderful option for Japanese in Palmy. The all-wooden interior gives the place a warm and rustic vibe, but the food is nothing but meticulous. The dinner set is great for the indecisive, but the traditional *kaiseki* ($45 per person) is an experience. Lunch sets are also great value.

Yeda
ASIAN $$

(📌06-358 3978; www.yeda.co.nz; 78 Broadway Ave; mains $16-19; ☺11am-9pm) Yeda feels a little like a beer or uni hall, probably because the long, minimalist room with concrete floors is packed with students. It covers all Asian bases, from Vietnamese *pho* to Thai chicken and dumplings. Sip sake or an Asahi while you wait. Ask about Saturday afternoon cooking classes ($40 per person).

Izakaya Yatai
JAPANESE $$

(📌06-356 1316; www.yatai.co.nz; 316 Featherston St; mains $19-27; ☺takeaway only noon-2pm Tue-Fri, 6-9pm Tue-Sat; 🚲) 🌿 Simple, fresh, authentic Japanese food cooked by Atsushi Taniyama in an unpretentious suburban house with empty sake bottles lining the window sills. All the chicken, pork, beef and eggs on the menu are NZ free-range. Great vegetarian and set-menu options available as well.

Café Cuba
CAFE $$

(📌06-356 5750; www.cafecuba.co.nz; cnr George & Cuba Sts; breakfast $10-20, dinner $12-29; ☺7am-5pm Mon, to 9pm Tue-Sun; 🚲🍴) This bustling cafe focuses on coffee in the morning and switches to booze at night. Breakfast classics, generous cabinet food, and everything from Thai chicken curry to a southern fried-chicken burger form lunch onwards. Save room for a decadent slice of cake. Kid-friendly, too.

★Nero Restaurant
INTERNATIONAL $$$

(📌06-354 0312; www.nerorestaurant.co.nz; 36 Amesbury St; mains $39-44; ☺11am-3pm & 5pm-late Mon-Fri, 5pm-late Sat) Set in a refreshed 1918 Victorian with a manicured alfresco, Nero is the peak of fine dining in Palmy. The chef and owner is an ambassador for Beef & Lamb New Zealand, but also serves dishes like sticky pork belly and cauliflower steak with flair. Don't forget to say 'hi' to Truffles, the cat.

Table 188 Kitchen and Bar
BISTRO $$$

(📌06-3530076; www.facebook.com/table188kitchenandbar; cnr The Square & Coleman Mall; mains $30-38; ☺noon-2pm & 5.30pm-late Tue-Sun) Formerly located at 188 Featherston St (hence the name), this classy bistro remains on the top branch of Palmy's dining tree. The seasonal menu is a bit French, a bit Italian and a lot NZ. Try the duck with kumara, coconut and tamarind purée for a posh dinner.

★Brew Union
MICROBREWERY

(📌06-280 3146; www.brewunion.co.nz; 41 Broadway Ave; ☺11am-10pm) 🌿 An impressive warehouse formerly housing a butcher, followed by a record store and sports shop, is now the best spot for a drink in Palmy. Reaching across an entire block, the microbrewery-bar and restaurant has 21 beers on tap and 45 gins on the shelf. Come for a drink, stay for wood-fired pizza. Live DJs and music Friday through Sunday.

🛍 Shopping

⭐ **Herb Farm**   COSMETICS
(📞06 326 8633; www.homeoftheherbfarm.co.nz;
Grove Rd, RD10; ⊙10am-4.30pm; 🚗) Demand
for Lynn Kirkland's homemade natural
remedies led to the Herb Farm opening
in 1993. Her daughter joined the business,
and together they sell beautiful, natural
skincare and health products on 1 hectare
of fairytale-like gardens. Less than 20 minutes from central Palmy, grab a free-range,
organic bite at the cafe ($13 to $22) and
enjoy the serenity.

Bruce McKenzie Booksellers   BOOKS
(📞06-356 9922; www.bmbooks.co.nz; 37 George St;
⊙9am-5.30pm Mon-Fri, to 5pm Sat, 10am-4pm Sun)
An excellent independent bookshop. Pick up
that guide to NZ craft beer you've been looking for and browse through novels by NZ
authors.

ℹ Information

MEDICAL SERVICES
Palmerston North Hospital (📞06-356 9169;
www.midcentraldhb.govt.nz; 50 Ruahine St;
⊙24hr) Accident and emergency assistance.

Palms Medical Centre (📞06-354 7737; www.
careforyou.co.nz/the-palms; 445 Ferguson St;
⊙8am-8pm daily, GP 9am-5pm Mon-Fri) Urgent
medical help, plus doctors by appointment and
a pharmacy.

TOURIST INFORMATION
DOC (Department of Conservation; 📞06-350
9700; www.doc.govt.nz; 28 North St; ⊙8am-
4.30pm Mon-Fri) Two kilometres north of the
Square.

Palmerston North i-SITE (📞0800 6262 9288,
06-350 1922; www.manawatunz.co.nz; The
Square; ⊙9am-5.30pm Mon-Thu, to 7pm Fri
& Sun, to 3pm Sat; 📶) A super-helpful source
of tourist information; free wi-fi throughout the
Square.

ℹ Getting There & Away

AIR
Palmerston North Airport (📞06-351 4415;
www.pnairport.co.nz; Airport Dr) is 4km north of
the town centre.

Air New Zealand (www.airnewzealand.
co.nz) runs daily direct flights to Auckland,
Christchurch and Wellington. Jetstar (www.
jetstar.com) has flights to/from Auckland and
Wellington. Originair (www.originair.nz) flies
between Palmy and Nelson, down south.

BUS
InterCity (www.intercity.co.nz) buses operate
from the **Main St bus terminus** on the east side
of the Square; destinations include the following:

DESTINATION	COST	TIME (HR)	FREQUENCY (DAILY)
Auckland	from $42	9½	3
Napier	from $24	3½	3
Taupo	from $24	4	3
Wellington	from $22	2¼	9
Whanganui	from $18	1½	4

Naked Bus (www.nakedbus.com) services also
depart the Main St bus terminus to most North
Island hubs:

DESTINATION	COST	TIME (HR)	FREQUENCY (DAILY)
Auckland	from $28	10	2-4
Napier	from $22	2½	2-4
Taupo	from $15	4	2-3
Wellington	from $13	2½	2-4

TRAIN
KiwiRail Scenic Journeys (📞0800 872 467,
04-495 0775; www.kiwirailscenic.co.nz) runs
long-distance trains between Wellington and
Auckland, stopping at the retro-derelict **Palmerston North Train Station** (Mathews Ave),
off Tremaine Ave about 2.5km north of the
Square. From Palmy to Wellington, take the
Northern Explorer ($69, 2½ hours) departing
at 4.20pm Monday, Thursday and Saturday;
or the Capital Connection ($35, two hours) de-
parting Palmy at 6.15am Monday to Friday. To
Auckland, the Northern Explorer ($179, nine
hours) departs at 10am on Tuesday, Friday
and Sunday. Buy tickets from KiwiRail Scenic
Journeys directly, or on the train and at the
i-Site for the Capital Connection (no ticket
sales at the station).

ℹ Getting Around

BICYCLE
Crank It Cycles (📞06-358 9810; www.crankit
cycles.co.nz; 244 Cuba St; half/full day $35/50;
⊙8am-5.30pm Mon-Fri, 9.30am-3pm Sat,
10am-2pm Sun) hires out city bikes, including
helmet and lock (deposit $50). You can also hire
electric bikes from the **i-SITE**.

BUS
Horizons (📞0508 800 800, 06 9522 800; www.
horizons.govt.nz; adult/child $1.50/2.50) runs
daytime buses departing from the **Main St bus
stop** on the east side of the Square.

Taupo & the Ruapehu Region

Best Places to Eat

➡ Cadillac Cafe (p290)

➡ Storehouse (p285)

➡ Southern Meat Kitchen (p285)

➡ Spoon & Paddle (p286)

➡ Blind Finch (p300)

Best Places to Stay

➡ Station Lodge (p299)

➡ Braxmere (p290)

➡ River Lodge (p299)

➡ Lake Motel (p283)

➡ Ruapehu Country Lodge (p299)

Why Go?

Welcome to the New Zealand you've been waiting for, a picturesque landscape characterised as much by volcanic mountains as it is by bodies of water and native forest. Much of it is thanks to the Taupo Volcanic Zone – a line of geothermal activity that stretches via Rotorua to Whakaari (White Island) in the Bay of Plenty. It's beautiful, but it's what's on the inside that counts: thermal activity bubbling beneath the surface that's responsible for some of the North Island's star attractions, including the country's largest lake and the three snowcapped peaks of Tongariro National Park.

Thrill seekers are in for a treat – the area rivals Queenstown for outdoor escapades. And when the action finally exhausts you (or if you had a relaxing holiday in mind), try some therapeutic fly-fishing or soak the day away in a thermal bath. There's truly something for everyone in Taupo and the Ruapehu region.

When to Go

➡ Equally popular in winter and summer, there's not really a bad time to visit the centre of New Zealand.

➡ The ski season runs roughly from July to October, but storms and freezing temperatures can occur at any time on the mountains, and above 2500m there is a permanent snowcap.

➡ Due to its altitude, the Ruapehu region has a generally cool climate, with average high temperatures ranging from 0°C in winter up to around 24°C in summer.

➡ Lake Taupo is swamped with Kiwi holidaymakers from Christmas to late January, so it pays to book ahead for accommodation during this time.

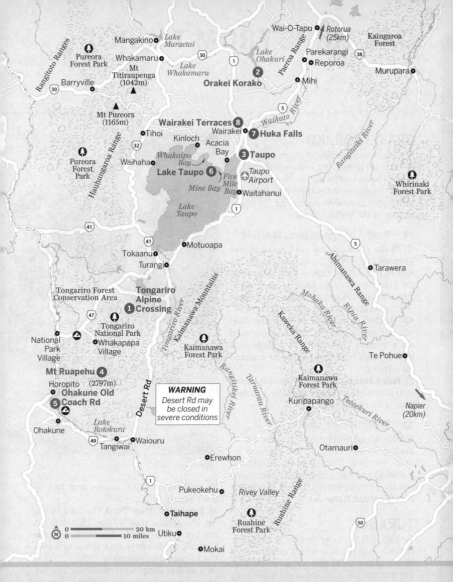

Taupo & the Ruapehu Region Highlights

1 Tongariro Alpine Crossing (p291) Seeing why this is considered the best one-day tramp in New Zealand.

2 Orakei Korako (p283) Rediscovering this volcanic 'lost valley'.

3 Taupo (p276) Bungy jumping with a view towards Waikato River.

4 Mt Ruapehu (p291) Skiing through fresh powder at Turoa or Whakapapa.

5 Ohakune Old Coach Road (p298) Mountain biking over the 284m Hapuawhenua Viaduct.

6 Lake Taupo (p277) Kayaking or cruising to the modern Māori rock carvings.

7 Huka Falls (p277) Jetboating up the Waikato River to the base of the falls.

8 Wairakei Terraces (p277) Soaking up the healing geothermal waters of these hot pools.

DAY TRIPS FROM TAUPO

ORAKEI KORAKO

Rotorua may have most of the country's geo-thermal attractions but it doesn't have all of them. This colourful site north of Taupo is one of the very best. Combine it on a day trip with sights around Wairakei and the upper reaches of the Waikato River.

☆ Best Things to See/Do/Eat

◉ **Huka Falls** As you head north on the Thermal Explorer Highway, look out for the sign to Huka Falls. Only a short walk from the road, the Waikato River crashes wildly into a basin of clear blue water at a volume of 220,000 litres per second. (p277)

◉ **Orakei Korako** Start with the boat trip across the river to the rainbow-hued silica terraces, then take a 90-minute walk past geysers, bubbling pools and a sacred cave. (p283)

🍯 **Huka Honey Hive** On your way home, stop at the Huka Honey Hive for a honey-and-fig ice cream. (p287)

☆ How to Get There

It takes about 30 minutes to get to Orakei Korako. Head north on the Thermal Explorer Highway, join SH1 in the direction of Auckland and follow the signs. Alternatively you can arrive in splashy, speedy style on the **New Zealand River Jet**.

TURANGI

Turangi isn't the most exciting town (unless you're a trout fisher, in which case there few places in the world that are more exciting) but this day trip is all about the drive along the lake, with a few low-key attractions to enjoy at the end.

☆ Best Things to See/Do/Eat

◉ **Tongariro National Trout Centre** Walk around the trout hatchery, check out the displays of historic fishing gear and learn a bit about river life in the freshwater aquariums. If you're lucky you might strike one of their public fishing days, where (for

Huka Falls (p277)

an additional fee) you can try your luck on the Tongariro River. (p287)

🚶 **Tongariro River Trail** The entire walking and cycling trail is 15km long, but you can cut it short with a 4km circuit on the Lookout Track. Afterwards, rest your legs in the Tokaanu Thermal Pools. (p288)

🍴 **Cadillac Cafe** Our favourite Turangi eatery is this 1950s-Americana-themed cafe in the town centre. (p290)

☆ How to Get There

Follow the lake south on SH1 and you can't miss it. The journey takes 45 minutes but expect to stop for photos along the way. InterCity and Mana Bus services stop here.

TONGARIRO NATIONAL PARK

It makes for a lengthy day trip from Taupo, but the smouldering volcanoes of Tongariro National Park are one of the must-see attractions of the North Island.

☆ Best Things to See/Do/Eat

☉ **Mt Ngauruhoe** Eyeball conical Mt Doom as you drive along SH47 to Whakapapa Village. Of course you won't miss his buddies, Mt Tongariro and Mt Ruapehu, sitting smoking beside him. (p293)

🥾 **Short Hikes** We don't suggest tackling the famous Tongariro Alpine Crossing on a day trip from Taupo, but there are plenty of short tracks departing from Whakapapa Village that will get you out among the alpine scenery. If you've got five to six hours to spare, the Tama Lakes Track is excellent. (p293)

🍴 **Chateau Tongariro High Tea** Swap your high-vis mountain gear for something a little more elegant and head to the grand lounge of the 1929 Chateau Tongariro Hotel for sandwiches, scones and cake. (p295)

☆ How to Get There

Follow SH1 and turn off at Turangi onto SH41. Past the town, turn left onto SH47; allow 90 minutes each way for the journey. If you'd like to loop around the mountains and return via the Desert Rd, add an additional hour to the journey.

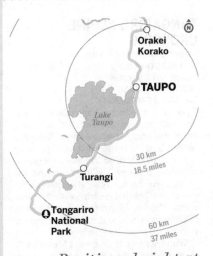

Positioned right at the very heart of the North Island, Taupo makes a great base for exploring the island's core. Highlights include geothermal areas, active volcanoes, NZ's longest river and, of course, the great lake itself.

HIKING IN TONGARIRO NATIONAL PARK

TONGARIRO ALPINE CROSSING

START MANGATEPOPO RD
END KETETAHI RD
DURATION 7-8 HOURS
DISTANCE 19.4KM
DIFFICULTY MODERATE

You don't get to be routinely called the best day walk in New Zealand without being something pretty special. And the Tongariro Alpine Crossing is indeed that. This tramp is like a mobile field guide to volcanoes, threading between Mt Tongariro and the perfectly conical Mt Ngauruhoe, passing neon-bright lakes that contrast with the black earth, while vents steam, hiss and fart in sulphurous clouds, and rocks spat from the volcanoes take on crazy shapes.

With big reputations come big crowds. In the early 1990s the Crossing would attract around 20,000 trampers a year; today that number is up to around 130,000. On the busiest days there can be more than 2000 people on the track. It's these sort of numbers that have led to recent changes on the Crossing. Parking restrictions at the trailhead now apply, making it all but compulsory to use the abundant shuttle services, while in late 2017 signs marking the side trails to Mts Tongariro and Ngauruhoe were taken down, with trampers requested not to climb them.

The crowds are the price of volcanic paradise, for the Alpine Crossing is truly something to behold. But don't let the big numbers fool you into thinking that the Alpine Crossing is a casual stroll. It's a long day – and fierce in bad weather – climbing 750m from its start to the top of Red Crater and then descending 700m to Ketetahi Rd.

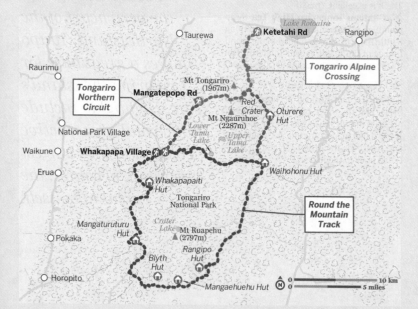

For trampers, Tongariro calls like a siren, drawing tens of thousands of people a year across the track that's almost universally acclaimed as the best day walk in the country.

TONGARIRO NORTHERN CIRCUIT

START/END WHAKAPAPA VILLAGE
DURATION 4 DAYS
DISTANCE 50KM
DIFFICULTY MODERATE

Circumnavigating Mt Ngauruhoe, this track is a Great Walk for a number of good reasons. The route can be easily walked in four days, and though there is some moderate climbing, the track is well marked and well maintained, putting it within the ability of people of medium fitness and tramping experience. But most of all, the Northern Circuit includes spectacular and colourful volcanic areas that have helped earn the park its status as a Unesco World Heritage Site.

The traditional place to start and finish the tramp is Whakapapa Village, the site of the park's visitor centre. However, many trampers begin at Mangatepopo Rd to ensure they have good weather for the tramp's most dramatic day – the Alpine Crossing section. This reduces it to a three-day tramp, with stays at Oturere and Waihohonu Huts, ending at Whakapapa Village. If doing this, note that you'll need to use one of the myriad shuttles that service the Alpine Crossing, with changes to parking regulations preventing trampers from parking for extended times at the Mangatepopo Rd car park.

ROUND THE MOUNTAIN TRACK

START/END WHAKAPAPA VILLAGE OR OHAKUNE MOUNTAIN RD
DURATION 4-6 DAYS
DISTANCE 66KM
DIFFICULTY DIFFICULT

This off-the-beaten-track hike is a quieter alternative to the busy Tongariro Northern Circuit, but it's particularly tough, has some potentially tricky river crossings, and is not recommended for beginners or the unprepared. Looping around Mt Ruapehu, the trail

FRERD/SHUTTERSTOCK ©

Mt Ngauruhoe (p293)

takes in diverse country from glacial rivers to tussocky moors to majestic mountain views.

Six days is a realistic estimate for this hike if you're including side trips to the Blyth Hut or Tama Lakes.

The track is safest from December to March when there is little or no snow, and less chance of avalanche. At other times of year, navigation is made difficult by snow covering the track, and full alpine gear (ice axe, crampons and specialised clothing) is a requirement. To attempt the track you should prepare thoroughly. Take sufficiently detailed maps, check on the latest conditions, and carry clothing for all climes and more-than-adequate food supplies. Be sure to leave your plans and intended return date with a responsible person, and check in when you get back.

This track is served by Waihohonu, Rangipo, Mangaehuehu, Mangaturuturu and Whakapapaiti Huts, and a side trip can be made to Blyth Hut.

LAKE TAUPO REGION

New Zealand's largest lake, Lake Taupo (also known as Taupo Moana), sits in the caldera of a volcano that began erupting about 300,000 years ago. It was formed by a collapse during the Oruanui super eruption about 26,500 years ago, which spurted 750 cu km of ash and pumice, making Krakatoa (8 cu km) look like a pimple.

The last major cataclysm was in AD 180, shooting enough ash into the atmosphere for ancient Romans and Chinese to record unusual skies. The area is still volcanically active and, like Rotorua, has fascinating thermal hot spots.

Today the 622-sq-km lake (about the size of Singapore) and its surrounding waterways attract fishing enthusiasts from around the world who visit to snag trophy trout. Positioned by the lake, both Taupo and Turangi are popular tourist centres. Taupo, in particular, has plenty of activities and facilities catering to families and independent travellers alike.

Taupo

POP 32,900

Travelling into Taupo on a clear day along the northeastern shores of the lake is breathtaking: beyond the lake you can see the snowcapped peaks of Tongariro National Park.

ESSENTIAL TAUPO & THE RUAPEHU REGION

Eat trout – but you'll have to catch it first! It's illegal for restaurants to serve it.

Drink Lakeman Brewing's Taupo Pale Ale.

Read *Awesome Forces* by Hamish Campbell and Geoff Hicks – the geological story of New Zealand in explosive detail.

Listen to the sonorous chirruping of tui along the Tongariro River Trail.

Watch *The Lord of the Rings* and *The Hobbit* movies, and spot Tongariro's movie-star mountains and rapids.

Pedal Taupo's Craters MTB Park.

Explore Tongariro National Park's alpine flora and geological oddities.

Online www.greatlaketaupo.com, www.visitruapehu.com, www.nationalpark.co.nz, www.visitohakune.co.nz

With an abundance of adrenaline-pumping activities, thermally heated waters, lakeside strolls and some wonderful places to eat, Taupo now rivals Rotorua as the North Island's premier resort town. It's also a magnet for outdoor athletes and is one of New Zealand's greatest cycling destinations, both on- and off-road.

The Waikato River, NZ's longest, starts at Lake Taupo, before crashing its way through the Huka Falls and Aratiatia Rapids and then settling down for a sedate ramble to the west coast, just south of Auckland.

History

Let's start at the start, back in AD 180 when the Taupo eruption became the largest and most violent in recorded history. Debris was deposited as far as 30,000 sq km and all of New Zealand was covered in ash, in some places up to 10m deep. Everything living was destroyed and there were reports from ancient Rome and China of unusual red sunsets. In the process, Lake Taupo formed in the volcanic caldera.

But Māori legend tells of Ngātoro-i-rangi, a priest who created the lake while searching for a place to settle. Climbing to the top of Mt Tauhara, he saw a vast dust bowl. He hurled a totara tree into it and water swelled to form the lake. One of the early Māori, Tia, was first to explore the region. After Tia discovered the lake and slept beside it draped in his cloak, it became known as Taupō Nui a Tia (Great Cloak of Tia). Descendants of the original Ngāti Tūwharetoa inhabitants remain today.

Europeans settled here in force during the East Coast Land War (1868–72), when Taupo was a strategic military base. A redoubt was built in 1869 and a garrison of mounted police remained until the defeat of Te Kooti later that year.

In the 20th century the mass ownership of the motorcar saw Taupo grow from a lakeside village of about 750 people to a large resort town, easily accessible from most points on the North Island. Today the population increases considerably at peak holiday times, when New Zealanders and international visitors alike flock to the 'Great Lake'.

◉ Sights

Many of Taupo's attractions are outside the town, with a high concentration around Wairakei to the north. The main attraction in the centre is the lake and everything you can do in, on and around it.

★**Taupo Museum**   MUSEUM
(Map p280; ☑07-376 0414; www.taupodc.govt.nz;
4 Story Pl; adult/child $5/free; ⏱10am-4.30pm)
With an excellent Māori gallery and quirky
displays, which include a 1960s caravan set
up as if the occupants have just popped down
to the lake, this little museum makes an interesting rainy-day diversion. The centrepiece is
an elaborately carved Māori meeting house,
Te Aroha o Rongoheikume. Historical displays cover local industries, volcanic activity
and a mock-up of a 19th-century shop.

There's also a gallery devoted to local
and visiting exhibitions. Horticulture lovers should check out the rose garden next
door, as well as the 'Ora Garden of Wellbe-
ing' in the courtyard, a recreation of NZ's
gold-medal-winning entry into the 2004
Chelsea Flower Show.

Māori Rock Carvings   HISTORIC SITE
Accessible only by boat, these 10m-high carvings were etched into the cliffs near Mine Bay
by master carver Matahi Whakataka-Bright-
well in the late 1970s. They depict Ngātoro-i-
rangi, the visionary Māori navigator who
guided the Tūwharetoa and Te Arawa tribes
to the Taupo area a thousand years ago. Go
bright and early or take a sunset cruise.

★**Huka Falls**   WATERFALL
(Map p278; www.greatlaketaupo.com; Huka Falls
Rd) Clearly signposted and with a car park
and kiosk, these falls mark where NZ's longest river, the Waikato, is slammed into a
narrow chasm, making a dramatic 11m drop
into a surging crystal-blue pool at 220,000
litres per second. From the footbridge you
can see the full force of this torrent that the
Māori called Hukanui (Great Body of Spray).

Take one of the short walks around the
area, or walk the Huka Falls Walkway back
to town or the Aratiatia Rapids Walking/
Cycling Track to the rapids. On sunny days
the water is crystal clear and you can take
great photographs from the **lookout** (Map
p278) on the other side of the footbridge.

★**Wairakei Terraces &**
Thermal Health Spa   HOT SPRINGS
(Map p278; ☑07-378 0913; www.wairakeiter
races.co.nz; Wairakei Rd; thermal walk adult/child
$15/7.50, pools $25, massage from $85; ⏱8.30am-
9pm Oct-Mar, to 8.30pm Apr-Sep, closes 7pm Thu)
🌿 Mineral-laden waters from the Wairakei
geothermal steamfield cascade over silica
terraces into pools (open to those 14 years
and older) nestled in native gardens. For the

price, we think there are better self-guided
tours than the **Terraces Walkway** featuring
a recreated Māori village, and artificially
made geysers and silica terraces, but spending a few hours soaking in the therapeutic
waters is well worthwhile.

Visit at dusk and watch the sunset over
the pools. The evening **Māori Cultural Experience** (adult/child $104/52) includes a
traditional challenge, welcome, concert, tour
and *hāngi* meal and gives an insight into
Māori life in the geothermal areas.

Wairakei Natural
Thermal Valley   NATURAL FEATURE
(Map p278; ☑07-374 8004; www.wairakeitouristpark.
co.nz; Wairakei Thermal Valley, off SH1; adult/child
$10/5; ⏱9am-1hr before sunset) This thermal
walk (around 1.8km) is on a secluded property and peaceful camping site, surrounded
by peacocks and other animals (sites $18 to
$21 per person, cabins $75-95, a cottage from
$125, summer teepee from November to early
April – depending on the weather – $65-85).
Tickets are purchased from the cafe to explore
mud pools, silica formations, the 'champagne
cauldron' and rare and endangered plant life.
Kids will get a kick out of pointing the loaned
thermal laser gun.

Craters of the Moon   NATURAL FEATURE
(Map p278; ☑027 6564 684; www.cratersof
themoon.co.nz; Karapiti Rd; adult/child/family
$8/4/20; ⏱8.30am-5pm) This geothermal
area sprang to life when hydroelectric tink-
ering around the power station caused water
levels to fall. The pressure shifted, creating
new steam vents and bubbling mud pools.
The 2.7km perimeter loop walk takes about
45 minutes and affords great views down to
the lake and mountains beyond. There's a
kiosk at the entrance, staffed by volunteers
who keep an eye on the car park.

More active from June through August when it's cold and wet (from December through February, summer can dry
everything out), it's signposted from SH1
about 5km north of Taupo.

Aratiatia Rapids   WATERFALL
(Map p278; www.greatlaketaupo.com) Two kilometres off SH5, this was a spectacular part
of the Waikato River until the government
plonked a hydroelectric dam across the water-
way, shutting off the flow. But the floodgates
still open from October to March at 10am,
noon, 2pm and 4pm and April to September
at 10am, noon and 2pm. You can see the water

Taupo & Wairakei

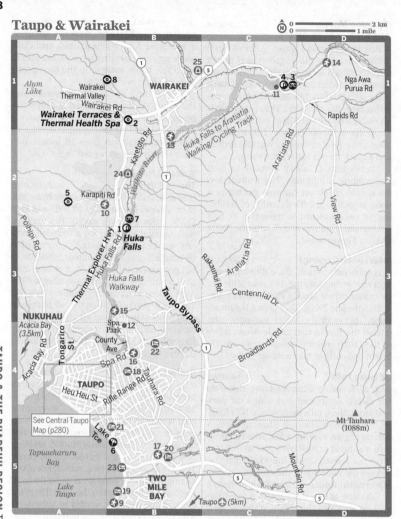

TAUPO & THE RUAPEHU REGION TAUPO

surge through the dam from two good **vantage points** (Map p278; off Aratiatia Rd).

Drive here or leisurely cycle along the river from town (four-hour return; 30km). You might recognise the rapids from the scene in *The Hobbit: The Desolation of Smaug*, when the dwarves escape from the elves in barrels.

🏃 Activities

Adrenaline addicts should look out for special deals that combine several activities for a reduced price. Some operators offer backpacker discounts.

For megadiscounts on rafting, sailing to the Māori Rock Carvings (p277), cultural experiences and more, try booking through www.bookme.co.nz or www.grabone.co.nz/rotorua-taupo.

Adventure & Adrenaline

More than 30,000 jumps a year are made over Taupo, which makes it the skydiving capital of the world. With the deep-blue lake and snow-capped volcanic peaks of Tongariro National Park as a backdrop, it's certainly a picturesque place to do it. Just remember to keep your eyes open. Companies provide free transport to Taupo Airport (p287).

Taupo & Wairakei

Skydive Taupo SKYDIVING
(☎07-378 4662, 0800 586 766; www.skydivetaupo.co.nz; Anzac Memorial Dr; 12,000ft/15,000ft jump from $279/359) Packages available (from $458), including a reduced-price second jump for altitude junkies.

Taupo Tandem Skydiving SKYDIVING
(☎0800 826 336; www.taupotandemskydiving.com; Anzac Memorial Dr; 12,000ft/15,000ft jump $279/359) Various packages that include DVDs, photos, T-shirts etc ($418 to $659); bungy combo available.

★**Taupo Bungy** BUNGEE JUMPING
(Map p278; ☎0800 888 408; www.taupobungy.co.nz; 202 Spa Rd; solo/tandem jump $169/338; ⊙9.30am-5pm) On a cliff high above the Waikato River, this picturesque bungy site is the North Island's most popular. The courageous throw themselves off the edge of a platform, jutting 34m out over the cliff, for a heart-stopping 47m plunge. The 11m Cliffhanger swing is just as terrifying (solo/tandem swing $145/290).

Rafting NZ
Adventure Centre ADVENTURE SPORTS
(Adventure Centre; Map p280; ☎0508 238 3688, 07-378 8482; www.theadventurecentre.co.nz; 47 Ruapehu St; ⊙9am-5pm Dec-May, 10am-5pm Jun-Nov) With a handy location in central Taupo, this well-run operation can hook you up with everything from rafting on the Tongariro River through to skydiving, jetboating and bungy jumping, and more leisurely pursuits such as lake cruises and fishing. Also home of the **Adventure 6D Cinema**, where

you can virtually go rafting and plunge off waterfalls (adult/child $15/9).

Rapids Jet ADVENTURE SPORTS
(Map p278; ☎07-374 8066, 0800 727 437, 0274 308 730; www.rapidsjet.com; Nga Awa Purua Rd; adult/child $115/65; ⊙9am-5pm Oct-Mar, 10am-4pm Apr-Sep) This sensational 35-minute ride shoots along the lower part of the Aratiatia Rapids – rivalling boat trips to Huka Falls for thrills (and price!). The boat departs from the end of the access road to the Aratiatia lookouts. Go down Rapids Rd and then turn into Nga Awa Purua Rd.

Hukafalls Jet ADVENTURE SPORTS
(Map p278; ☎07-374 8572, 0800 485 253; www.hukafallsjet.com; 200 Karetoto Rd; adult/child $129/89) This 30-minute thrill ride takes you up the river to the spray-filled foot of the Huka Falls and down to the Aratiatia Dam, all the while dodging daringly and doing acrobatic 360-degree turns. Trips run all day, weather dependent (prices include shuttle transport from Taupo).

New Zealand River Jet ADVENTURE SPORTS
(☎0800 748 375, 07-333 7111; www.riverjet.co.nz; Mihi Bridge, SH5; adult/child $179/99, incl entry to Orakei Korako) New Zealand River Jet will zip you to Orakei Korako (p283) in thrilling fashion along the Waikato River and through the 50m-high Tutukau Gorge. It also offers the Squeeze jetboat ride, where you disembark in warm water and edge your way through a crevice to a concealed natural thermal waterfall surrounded by native bush (adult/child $169/89).

Central Taupo

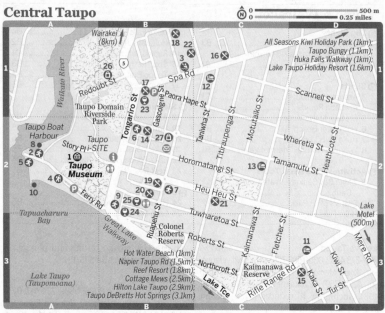

N 0 _____ 500 m
0 _____ 0.25 miles

Big Sky Parasail ADVENTURE SPORTS
(Map p280; ☏0800 724 4759; www.bigskypara
sail.co.nz; Taupo Boat Harbour, Redoubt St; tandem/
solo $95/115; ⏱9am-6pm mid-Oct–May) Lofty
parasailing flights from the lakefront.
Choose from 1000ft or 500ft, although according to one instructor, the latter is 'like

going halfway up a Ferris wheel'. Bookings
essential. Early bird special $85.

Walking & Cycling
Grab trail maps and hire bikes from **Pack
& Pedal** (Map p280; ☏07-377 4346; www.pack
andpedaltaupo.com; 5 Tamamutu St; 2hr/half-day/
full-day rental $30/40/60; ⏱8.30am-6pm Mon-Fri,

8.30am-5pm Sat, 9am-4pm Sun) or the i-SITE (p287), including the *10 Great Rides* map. You'll need to become a temporary member of **Bike Taupo** ($10 for one week) to ride on local tracks. The bike shops in town can sort out a temporary membership.

Great Lake Trail   WALKING, CYCLING
(www.greatlaketrail.com) A purpose-built 71km track from Whakaipo Bay to Waihaha in the remote northwestern reaches of the lake. The **W2K** section between Whakaipo and Kinloch has splendid views across the lake to Tongariro National Park.

A number of boat shuttle companies link different sections of the trail, providing pickups and drop-offs to different bays. Ask for more information at the i-SITE (p287) to see which best suits you.

Great Lake Walkway   WALKING, CYCLING
(Lion's Walk; Map p280; www.greatlaketaupo.com/things-to-do/biking/trails/lions-walk) This pleasant path follows the Taupo lakefront south from the Taupo Boat Harbour to Five Mile Bay (10km). It's flat, easy walking or cycling along public-access beaches, with plenty of opportunities for coffee stops along the way.

Huka Falls Walkway   WALKING, CYCLING
(Map p278; County Ave) Starting from the Spa Park car park at the end of County Ave (off Spa Rd), this scenic, easy walk is just over 3km one-way to reach Huka Falls, following the east bank of the Waikato River. Continuing on from the falls is the 7km **Huka Falls to Aratiatia Rapids Walking Track** (another two-plus hours). The Taupo–Huka Falls-Ariatiatia loop bike ride will take around four hours in total.

Craters MTB Park   MOUNTAIN BIKING
(Map p278; www.biketaupo.org.nz; Karapiti Rd; ⊘24hr) **FREE** For 50km of exciting off-road mountain-biking trails for all abilities, head to the Craters MTB Park, around 10 minutes' drive north of Taupo in the Wairakei Forest just before the Craters of the Moon (p277) entrance.

Don't forget to arrange a temporary membership with Bike Taupo before heading up there. Bike shops in town can sort out temporary memberships.

Watersports
Lake Taupo is famously chilly, but in several places – such as **Hot Water Beach** (Map p278; Lake Tce, Hilltop) **FREE**, immediately south of the town centre – there are thermal springs just below the surface. You can swim right in front of the town, but **Acacia Bay**, 5km west, is a particularly pleasant spot. Even better and quieter is **Whakaipo Bay**, another 7km further on, an undeveloped waterfront reserve perfect for a lazy day.

**2 Mile Bay Sailing &
Watersports Centre**   SAILING, KAYAKING
(Map p278; ☑027 588 6588; www.sailingcentre.co.nz; Lake Tce; ⊘9am-10pm Nov-Apr, 9am-7pm Mon-Thu, to 8pm Fri-Sun May-Oct) A lakeside cafe-bar that pumps mellow Ben Harper tunes and hires out paddle boards, kayaks, windsurfers and canoes (from $30), sailboats ($75) and catamarans (from $95); rates are per hour, or take an hour-long lesson for $50. **Pizza** available from 11am, or swing by from 4pm on a Sunday for local **music jam sessions** jutting over the lake.

Taupo Kayaking Adventures   KAYAKING
(☑0274 801 231; www.tka.co.nz; 2/876 Acacia Bay Rd, Acacia Bay; tours from $60) Runs guided kayaking trips from its base in Acacia Bay to the Māori rock carvings, with the return trip taking around four hours ($100, including refreshments). Longer trips and walk/bike combos also available.

Canoe & Kayak   CANOEING, KAYAKING
(Map p280; ☑07-378 1003; www.canoeandkayak.co.nz/taupo; 54 Spa Rd; ⊘9am-5pm Mon-Fri, to 3pm Sat & Sun Nov-Mar, 9am-5pm Mon-Fri, to 3pm Sat) Guided tours, including a two-hour trip on the Waikato River ($59) and a half-day to the Māori rock carvings for $99.

**★Spa Thermal Park
Hot Spring**   HOT SPRINGS
(Map p278; Country Ave; ⊘7am-8pm) **FREE** The hot thermal waters of the Otumuheke Stream meet the bracing Waikato River at this pleasant and well-worn spot under a bridge, creating a free spa bath with natural nooks. Take care: people have drowned trying to cool off in the fast-moving river. It's near the beginning of the Huka Falls Walkway, a couple of kilometres from the centre of town.

Turn off Spa Rd into Country Ave, park in the car park and follow the signs (and people with towels!).

Taupo DeBretts Hot Springs   HOT SPRINGS
(Map p278; ☑07-378 8559; www.taupodebretts.co.nz; 76 Napier–Taupo Rd; adult/child $22/11; ⊘8.30am-9.30pm; 🚼) 🎿 A variety of therapeutic mineral-rich indoor and outdoor thermal pools and freshwater chlorinated

pools. The kids will love the heated dragon slide, two curved racing hydroslides and the interactive 'Warm Water Playground', while adults can enjoy a great selection of treatments, such as relaxation massages.

Fishing & Boating

⭐ **Sail Barbary**   BOATING
(Map p280; ☑ 07-378 5879; www.sailbarbary.com; Taupo Boat Harbour, Redoubt St; adult/child $49-54/29-54; ◷ 10.30am & 2pm year-round, plus 5pm Dec-Feb) 🏊 A classic 1926 yacht offering 2½-hour cruises to the Māori rock carvings daily. The evening cruises includes buffet pizza and a drink. Being open to the elements, this is a more adventurous option, but custom-made waterproof, fleece-lined ponchos with hoods are handed out to anyone who's chilly.

Fish Cruise Taupo   FISHING, CRUISE
(Launch Office; Map p280; ☑ 07-378 3444; www.fishcruisetaupo.co.nz; Taupo Boat Harbour, 65 Redoubt St; ◷ 9am-5pm Oct-Mar, 9.30am-3pm Apr-Sep) Representing a collective of 13 local boats, this booking office can hook you up with private charters whether you're looking for fishing on a small runabout, or a leisurely cruise on a yacht.

Sail Fearless   BOATING
(Map p280; ☑ 022 189 1847; www.sailfearless.co.nz; Taupo Marina; adult/child $29-49/20-39; ◷ sailing times 9.30am, 12.30pm, 3.30pm & 6.30pm Oct-May) Yarr, me hearties! Welcome to Lake Taupo's only pirate-themed tour boat. Leisurely sailing trips taking around two to 2½ hours – including visiting the Māori rock carvings – on a ketch with striking brick-red sails. The two later tours include pizza and up to three drinks, and jumping overboard is not unheard of.

Ernest Kemp Cruises   BOATING
(Map p280; ☑ 07-378 3444, 021 669 139; www.ernestkemp.co.nz; Taupo Boat Harbour, Redoubt St; adult/child $35-44/10-22; ◷ 10.30am & 2pm year-round, 5pm departure Oct-Apr) Board the *Ernest Kemp* replica steamboat for a two-hour cruise to view the Māori rock carvings, Hot Water Beach, lakefront and Acacia Bay. Lively commentary and complimentary tea and coffee. Book at Fish Cruise Taupo. A special 90-minute cruise departs at 12.30pm during school holidays (adult/child $35/10). Check out the cocktail cruise, too.

Chris Jolly Outdoors   BOAT TOUR, FISHING
(Map p280; ☑ 07-378 0623, 0800 252 628; www.chrisjolly.co.nz; Taupo Boat Harbour, Ferry Rd;

◷ adult/child $46/18) Operates the *Cruise Cat*, a large, modern launch that offers fishing trips and daily cruises to the Māori rock carvings (10.30am and 1.30pm plus 5pm from December to April). Sunday brunch trips (add $18) are also worthwhile. Charters plus guided tramping and mountain-biking trips and pickups are also available.

Taupo Troutcatcher   FISHING
(Map p280; ☑ 0800 376 882; www.taupotroutcatcher.co.nz; Taupo Marina, Ferry Rd; per hour from $110; ◷ 9am-9pm, weather dependant) Two decades of fishing experience on Lake Taupo adds up to a good choice of operator if you're looking to catch your dinner. Boats accommodating up to five or 10 people are both available.

Huka Falls River Cruise   BOATING
(Map p278; ☑ 0800 278 336, 027 2490 204; www.hukafallscruise.co.nz; Aratiatia Dam; adult/child $39/15; ◷ 10.30am, 12.30pm & 2.30pm year-round, plus 4.30pm Dec-Feb) For a photo-friendly ride, this boat offers a relaxed jaunt (80 minutes) from Aratiatia Dam to Huka Falls.

Lake Fun Taupo   BOATING
(Map p280; ☑ 0800 876 882; www.lakefuntaupo.co.nz; Taupo Marina, Ferry Rd; ◷ 9am-9pm, weather dependent) Located at the marina about 500m from the i-SITE (p287), this outfit hires out single/double kayaks ($25/35 per hour), paddle boards ($30 per hour), self-drive motor boats (from $120 per hour) and jet skis ($150 per hour).

Taupo Rod & Tackle   FISHING
(Map p280; ☑ 07-378 5337; www.tauporodandtackle.co.nz; 7 Tongariro St; full-day gear rental $20-35; ◷ 8am-5pm Mon-Fri, to 4pm Sun, 7am-4pm Sat Dec-May, 8am-5pm Mon-Fri, to 4pm Sat & Sun Jun-Nov) Rental gear and a great point of contact for fishing guides and boat charters. Fishing and game licenses also available.

🢒 Tours

Taupo's Floatplane   SCENIC FLIGHTS
(Map p280; ☑ 07-378 7500; www.tauposfloatplane.co.nz; Taupo Boat Harbour, Ferry Rd; flights $109-955) Located near the marina, the floatplane offers a variety of trips, including quick flights over the lake and longer forays over Mt Ruapehu or Whakaari (White Island). The three-hour 'Taupo Trifecta' combines a scenic flight, visit to Orakei Korako and jetboat ride ($645).

🎊 Festivals & Events

Heralding itself as the events capital of NZ, Taupo hosts numerous shindigs throughout

GEOTHERMAL WONDERS AT ORAKEI KORAKO

A little off the beaten track, **Orakei Korako** (☑ 07-378 3131; www.orakeikorako.co.nz; 494 Orakei Korako Rd; adult/child $36/15; ☺8am-4.30pm) gets fewer visitors than other thermal areas. But since the destruction of the Pink and White Terraces, it's arguably the best thermal area left in NZ, with active geysers, stunning terraces, bubbling rainbow land and the country's only geothermal cave. Entry includes the boat ride across the lake from the **visitor centre and cafe** (free wi-fi). Visit the toilets, punningly named 'guysers' and 'galsers', before crossing over.

A walking track follows stairs and boardwalks around the colourful silica terraces for which the park is famous, and passes geysers and **Ruatapu Cave** (allow 1½ hours). This impressive natural cave has a jade-green pool, thought to have been used as a mirror by Māori women preparing for rituals (Orakei Korako means 'the Place of Adorning').

It's about 30 minutes to Orakei Korako from Taupo. Take SH1 towards Hamilton for 23km, and then travel for 14km from the signposted turn-off. From Rotorua the turn-off is on SH5, via Mihi. You can also arrive via the **New Zealand River Jet** (p279).

the year, including music festivals and international sporting events. See www.greatlaketaupo.com and www.eventpromotions.co.nz for more details.

Wanderlust MUSIC, CULTURAL
(www.wanderlust.com/festivals/great-lake-taupo; ☺Feb/Mar) A self-described 'all-out celebration of mindful living', four-day Wanderlust combines relaxing and recharging music with yoga, meditation and a focus on alternative therapies and natural health.

Graffiato Street Art Festival ART
(www.taupostreetart.co.nz; ☺Oct) FREE Watch local and international street artists create large-scale works in the streets of Taupo over three colourful days. Collect a Taupo Street Art map from the i-SITE (p287) or website and keep an eye out for art honouring Māori *iwi* (tribes).

Lake Taupo Cycle Challenge SPORTS
(www.cyclechallenge.com; ☺Nov) One of NZ's biggest annual cycling events, the 160km Lake Taupo Cycle Challenge sees some 10,000 people pedalling around the lake on the last Saturday in November.

🛏 Sleeping

🛏 Town Centre

Finlay Jacks HOSTEL $
(Map p280; ☑07-378 9292; www.finlayjacks.co.nz; 20 Taniwha St; dm/s/d/f from $23/35/80/120; ☎) Our pick of Taupo's hostels, Finlay Jacks has turned an ageing motel into a colourful hub for young people. The largest rooms are 12-bed dorms, but they feel smaller, with bunks separated into lots of eight and four.

Affordable private rooms with en suites have super-comfy beds. We love the pop-culture prints on the walls, patterned bed covers and grassy lawn.

Haka Lodge HOSTEL $
(Map p280; ☑07-377 0068; www.hakalodge.com; 56 Kaimanawa St; d $28-33, d $69, 1-bdrm apt $149; ☎) Haka Lodge has a fantastic, community feel from the moment you walk in. We love the custom, creak-proof wooden dorm bunks with built-in storage and the 2nd-storey barbecue deck beside the spotless, modern kitchen. Check out their recipe for pikelets (thin crumpets) on the wall of the kitchen. Comfortable lounge with beanbags inside, volleyball net, hammocks and spa pool outside.

All Seasons Kiwi Holiday Park HOLIDAY PARK $
(Map p278; ☑0800 777 272, 07-378 4272; www.taupoallseasons.co.nz; 16 Rangatira St; sites from $25, dm $46, units $72-165; ☎) 🐾 A pleasant holiday park with corrugated-iron native birds scattered between well-established trees and hedgerows between sites. Also has a playground, games room, thermal pool, bike hire and good kitchen facilities. Lots of accommodation options, from lodge rooms and cabins to self-contained motels. It's a 20-minute walk downhill to town. Energy-saving lighting and solar water heating a bonus.

⭐**Lake Motel** MOTEL $$
(Map p278; ☑07-378 4222, 021 951 808; www.thelakeonline.co.nz; 63 Mere Rd; studio $125-175, 1-bdrm units $145-185; @☎) A reminder that 1960s and '70s design wasn't all *Austin Powers*-style groovaliciousness, this boutique motel is crammed with furniture from the era's signature designers. The four one-bedroom

MĀORI TAUPO & THE RUAPEHU REGION

The North Island's central region is home to a group of mountains that feature in several Māori legends of lust and betrayal, which end with mountains fleeing to other parts of the island (just like in Mt Taranaki's sad tale (p436).

Long after that was over, the *tohunga* (priest) Ngātoro-i-rangi, fresh off the boat from Hawaiki, explored this region and named the mountains that remained. The most sacred was Tongariro because it had at least 12 volcanic cones and was seen as the leader of all the other mountains.

The major *iwi* (tribe) of the region is Ngāti Tūwharetoa (www.tuwharetoa.co.nz), one of the few *iwi* in New Zealand that has retained an undisputed *ariki* (high chief). The current *ariki* is Sir Tumu Te Heuheu Tukino VIII, whose great-great-grandfather, Te Heuheu Tukino IV (a descendant of Ngātoro-i-rangi), gifted the mountains of Tongariro to New Zealand in 1887.

To discover the stories of local Māori and their ancestors, visit **Taupō Museum** (p277), the carved cliff faces at **Mine Bay** (p277) or **Wairakei Terraces** (p277).

units sleep between two to four people and have kitchenettes and living areas, and, along with the two studios (maximum two people), use of the garden. Look out for paintings of well-known musos by the owners' son.

Beechtree Suites
MOTEL **$$**
(Map p280; ☑ 07-377 0181, 0800 233 248; www. beechtreemotel.co.nz; 56 Rifle Range Rd; apt $175-220; @ 🖥) The Beechtree offers classy rooms, fresh and modern in design with neutral-toned decor, large windows, ground-floor patios and upstairs balconies. Accommodation ranges from queen studios for two people to a three-bedroom spa suite that sleeps up to seven. Ask for a room with a spa bath.

🛏 Waipahihi & Two Mile Bay

Cottage Mews
MOTEL **$$**
(Map p278; ☑ 0800 555 586, 07-378 3004; www. cottagemews.co.nz; 311 Lake Tce, Two Mile Bay; d $125-150, q $170; 🖥) Few motels muster much charm, but this cute gable-roofed block, festooned with hanging flowers, manages to seem almost rustic. Some units have lake views, most have spa baths with a jug of lavender bath gel ready to go and all have a small private garden. Bikes and kayaks for hire. Direct beach access a plus.

Reef Resort
RESORT **$$**
(Map p278; ☑ 0800 733 378, 07-378 5115; www. reefresort.co.nz; 219 Lake Tce; d/1-bdrm from $166-217/200-242; 🖥🖳) Reef Resort stands out among Taupo's waterfront complexes for its classy, well-priced one- to three-bedroom apartments, centred on an appealing pool patio complete with thermal spa pool. It's worth paying a little extra for lake views. Cruiser bikes available to hire for $5 per hour.

Hilton Lake Taupo
HOTEL **$$$**
(Map p278; ☑ 07-378 7080; www.hilton.com/lake taupo; 80-100 Napier Rd; r from $219; 🖥🖳) Occupying the historic Terraces Hotel (1889) and a modern extension, this large complex offers the expected Hilton standard of luxury, from studios through to presidential suites, an outdoor heated pool, and Bistro Lago, the decent in-house restaurant. It's a little out of town but is handy for the De-Bretts thermal complex (p281).

🛏 Acacia Bay

Te Moenga Lodge
B&B **$$**
(☑ 021 680 863, 07-378 0894; www.temoenga. co.nz; 60 Te Moenga Park, Acacia Bay; r/6-bed apt incl breakfast $180/290-$380; 🖥🖳) As you drive to the very end of the street and park on top of the hill, two friendly border collie–golden retriever crosses will welcome you to Te Moenga. There are two studios, two separate chalets and an apartment for six. With Lake Taupo in front of you, it's possible you won't notice the stylish, homely decor. Best enjoy the view from the pool.

★ Acacia Cliffs Lodge
B&B **$$$**
(☑ 07-378 1551, 021 821 338; www.acaciacliffslodge. co.nz; 133 Mapara Rd, Acacia Bay; d $650-750; ⊘ closed May-Sep; @ 🖥) 🖉 This luxurious B&B, high above Acacia Bay, offers four contemporarily and artfully designed suites, three with grand lake views and one that compensates for the lack of them with a curvy bath and private garden. The chef-owner dishes up fine-dining fare at a heated table, with three-course dinners available (per person $95). Tariff includes breakfast, pre-dinner drinks, canapes and Taupo Airport transfer.

Serenity on Wakeman
B&B $$$

(☑ 027 454 6518; www.tauposerenity.co.nz; 57 Wakeman Rd, Acacia Bay; r $290-380; ☎) Views of the lake don't get much better than this, but with only two rooms (technically, the third is reserved for groups), you'll have to book ahead. It's all in the details here, from bathrobes to breakfast on the deck. The upstairs suite has a private balcony, king bed and double spa bath. Luxurious, peaceful and romantic.

🛏 Other Areas

★ Waitahanui Lodge
MOTEL $$

(☑ 07-378 7183, 0800 104 321; www.waitahanuilodge.co.nz; 116 SH1, Waitahanui; d $119-199; ☎) Ten kilometres south of Taupo, these five beachfront, beach-hut-style units are ideally positioned for swimming, fishing and superb sunsets. Pick of the bunch are the two absolute-lakefront units, numbers three and four, but all have lake access, sociable communal areas plus free use of rowboats and kayaks. The units are all self-contained with kitchenettes, or you can fire up the shared barbecue.

Lake Taupo Holiday Resort
HOLIDAY PARK $$

(Map p278; ☑ 0800 332 121, 07-378 6860; www.laketauporesort.co.nz; 41 Centennial Dr; sites/cabins/units from $36/103/138; @☎🏊) This slick 8-ha park about 2.5km from the i-SITE has all mod cons, including a huge heated swimming pool – we're talking a thermally heated lagoon with a movie screen and bar – a jumping pillow, *pétanque,* basketball, volleyball and tennis courts, and an on-site shop. Manicured grounds, swish accommodation options and spotless facilities help make it a contender for camp of the year.

🍴 Eating

Raw Balance
HEALTH FOOD $

(Map p280; ☑ 021 138 2066; www.facebook.com/rawbalancenz; 45 Oruanui St; smoothies $8, mains $8-12, raw sweets $2-7; ☉ 8am-5pm Mon-Fri, Sat 9am-3pm; ☑) 🍃 This is heaven for vegans, the gluten-free inclined, health conscious and environmentally aware. In winter, raw sweets and salads are complemented by a daily hot special (perhaps dhal and rice). Takeaway packaging is recyclable but discouraged, with containers available to buy and reuse, and some cushion-pimped wooden pallets to sit on and enjoy.

There's also a communal table in the mini-library, complete with more than 60 Lonely Planet guidebooks! Check Facebook for pop-up dinner parties.

Pauly's Diner
BURGERS $

(Map p280; ☑ 07-378 4315; www.paulysdiner.nz; 3 Paora Hape St; burgers $12-15; ☉ 11.30am-8.30pm Wed-Sun & alternating Mon) Two brothers from Auckland set up this popular burger joint in an old fish and chipper, and it seems they've got the formula just right (selling out isn't uncommon). The shop only seats about a dozen, plus a few more outside, and specials are posted on Instagram (Dorito chip-fried chicken is a thing). Shakes and deep-fried goodies also available.

Merchant
DELI $

(Map p280; ☑ 07-378 4626; www.themerchant.co.nz; 114 Spa Rd; ☉ 9am-6pm Mon & Sun, to 6.30pm Tue-Thu & Sat, to 7pm Fri) Championing NZ artisan producers and importing specialities from abroad, this grocery on the town fringe is a fruitful stop for those looking to stock up on supplies. **Scenic Cellars** is also located here, stocking craft beer and rare premium NZ wines, alongside single-malt whiskies and more. Ask for the incredibly knowledgeable Lea if you don't know what to buy.

★ Storehouse
CAFE $$

(Map p280; ☑ 07-378 8820; www.facebook.com/storehousenz; 14 Runanga St; mains $13-18; ☉ 7am-3.30pm Mon-Fri, 8am-3.30pm Sat, to 3pm Sun; ☎) If you're looking for Taupo's coolest cafe, you've just found it. Setting the scene since 2013, Storehouse is located in an old plumbing store over two levels. Downstairs, indoor plants drape over warehouse beams, and upstairs a bike is inexplicably fastened to the wall. The breakfast salad bowl often sells out – guess that means we're having fried-chicken waffles.

Festoon lights hang above a cosy kids' play nook, and there's a small store selling local goods, from honey to merino clothing.

★ Replete Cafe & Store
CAFE $$

(Map p280; ☑ 07-377 3011; www.replete.co.nz; 45 Heu Heu St; mains $13-18; ☉ 8am-5pm Mon-Fri, to 4pm Sat & Sun; ☎) "You don't come to Taupo without stopping for coffee here," a customer tells us, "It's an institution." He's not wrong. Established in 1993, Replete is split into a cafe and shop selling designer kitchenware, ceramics and souvenirs. The cafe cabinet is one of the best looking in town, while lunch has an Asian flair (Japanese bolognese or Sri Lankan curry, anyone?).

★ Southern Meat Kitchen
SOUTH AMERICAN $$

(SMK; Map p280; ☑ 07-378 3582; www.facebook.com/smktaupo; 40 Tuwharetoa St; mains $22-34;

🕐 noon-midnight Wed-Sun, 4-11pm Mon & Tue) Calling all carnivores! SMK slow-cooks beef brisket, pulled pork and shredded chicken on an American wood-fire smoker – and you can order it by the half-pound (upgrade to a pound for $8). Arrives with mac 'n' cheese, slaw and rice. Save room for jalapeño-and-cheddar cornbread, served in a skillet with addictive honey butter. Beer tasting paddles for $15.

Spoon & Paddle
CAFE $$

(Map p280; 📞07-378 9664; www.facebook.com/spoonandpaddle; 101 Heu Heu St; mains $15-20; 🕐8am-4pm; 🅿🛜👶) Filling a 1950s house with colourful decor, this cafe feels like popping into a friend's place for brunch with a whole lot of strangers. Breakfast runs all day, and from 11.30am you can order tasty international numbers, including pork-belly *bao*, local beef-brisket soft-shell tacos or a lamb-shoulder salad bowl. Great coffee and a playground for the kids.

A mini-fort in the garden will get the kids exploring, while Mum and Dad tuck into mid-afternoon treats such as macarons or lemon meringue pie.

Bistro
MODERN NZ $$

(Map p280; 📞07-377 3111; www.thebistro.co.nz; 17 Tamamutu St; mains $26-39; 🕐5pm-midnight) Popular with locals – bookings are recommended – the Bistro focuses on doing the basics very, very well. That means harnessing local and seasonal produce for dishes such as bacon-wrapped Wharekauhau lamb, washed down with your pick from the small but thoughtful beer-and-wine list. Even the kids' menu is tempting.

Brantry
MODERN NZ $$$

(Map p280; 📞07-378 0484; www.thebrantry.co.nz; 45 Rifle Range Rd; 3-course set menu $55-60; 🕐from 5.30pm Tue-Sat, daily from 5.30pm Dec-Jan) Operating out of an unobtrusive 1950s house, the Brantry continues its reign as one of the best in the region for well-executed, brilliant-value fine dining centred around a three-course menu. There's an impressive wine list with friendly staff to help with difficult decisions. Sit in the covered al fresco dining area (blankets provided) or dine in the cellar.

Drinking & Nightlife

Crafty Trout Brewing
BREWERY

(Map p280; 📞07-989 8570; www.craftytrout.co.nz; 131-135 Tongariro St; mains $18-28, pizzas $14-49; 🕐Bier Kafe noon-late Wed-Mon, shop & brewery 10am-4pm Wed-Mon; 🛜) Somewhere between an alpine and a fishing lodge, only the five cuckoo clocks at Crafty Trout interrupt the German music. Comfy leather sofas and the sunny verandah are great places to dig into robust meals, including tasty fish and chips and wood-fired pizza, washed down with any of the 10 beers and ciders. Grab a porter-filled chocolate truffle for dessert.

Take a brewery tour (1pm except Tuesdays, $15) or play a game (there's giant Jenga for the whole family, hammer toss for adults).

Lakehouse
CRAFT BEER

(Map p280; 📞07-377 1545; www.lakehousetaupo.co.nz; 10 Roberts St; breakfast $9-20, mains $20-30; 🕐8am-late (kitchen closes 9pm)) Welcome to craft beer central, with a fridge full of interesting bottles, and nine taps serving a rotating selection of NZ brews. Order a tasting box of four beers ($15), partner them with a pizza or stone-grilled steak, and sit outside for lake views – and, if the clouds lift, glimpses of the mountains. Check the blackboard wall for daily specials.

Vine Eatery & Bar
WINE BAR

(Map p280; 📞07-378 5704; www.vineeatery.co.nz; 37 Tuwharetoa St; tapas $8-14, mains $17-39; 🕐11am-midnight) Wine glass chandeliers hang from the industrial ceiling at this restaurant-cum-wine bar, where you can sit in comfy booths, at raised stools or by the fire. Bottles are available to take home, with a zap-chilling service that cools them in five minutes. Share traditional tapas with a glass (there's whisky and craft beer, too) or linger longer with larger mains.

Shopping

Torpedo7
SPORTS & OUTDOORS

(Map p280; 📞07-376 0051; www.torpedo7.co.nz; 41 Tamamutu St; 🕐9am-5.30pm Mon-Fri, to 4pm Sat, 10am-4pm Sun) Ginormous sporting and equipment store selling everything you need for cycling, motorbiking, snow sports, camping, tramping and more.

Lava Glass
ARTS & CRAFTS

(Map p278; 📞07-374 8400; www.lavaglass.co.nz; 165 SH5; glass-blowing display/garden entry/combo $5/7.50/10; 🕐10am-5pm) More than 600 unique glass sculptures fill the garden and surroundings of this gallery, around 10km north of Taupo on SH5. Glass-blowing displays and an excellent cafe (open 9am-4pm) provide great reasons to linger while you're considering what to purchase in the Lava Glass shop. All items can be carefully shipped anywhere in the world (free when you spend more than $200).

Look closely and you'll see the colours of Taupo in the glass sculptures: the crystal blue of Huka Falls, the earthy colours of Tongariro Alpine Crossing and the fiery lava reds of the volcanoes.

Taupo Market   FOOD, CRAFTS
(Map p280; ☑ 027 306 6167, 07-3782 980; www.taupomarket.kiwi.nz; Redoubt St; ⊙9am-1pm Sat) Plenty of food stalls and trucks, local souvenirs, arts and crafts and a scattering of produce are all good reasons to make your first coffee of the day an al fresco espresso at this popular weekend market.

On the first Saturday of the month there's an additional **trash and treasure fair**, plus keep an eye out for the **Gypsy Fair** that pops up a handful of times every year.

Kura Gallery   ART
(Map p280; ☑ 07-377 4068; www.kura.co.nz; 47a Heu Heu St; ⊙10am-5pm Mon-Fri, to 4pm Sat & Sun) This compact gallery represents more than 70 artists from around NZ. Works for sale include weaving, carving, painting and jewellery. Many items are imbued with a Māori or Pasifika influence.

Huka Honey Hive   FOOD & DRINKS
(Map p278; ☑ 07-374 8553; www.hukahoneyhive.com; 65 Karetoto Rd; ⊙10am-5pm) This sweet spot has a glass-enclosed viewing hive, honey tastings and a cafe, and sells all manner of bee products – edible, medicinal and cosmetic – as well as mead. The manuka-honey ice cream is popular at the cafe, but we recommend the honey-and-fig flavour. FYI, manuka honey with a grading above 5+ is for medicinal use.

ⓘ Information

Taupo i-SITE (Map p280; ☑ 07-376 0027, 0800 525 382; www.greatlaketaupo.com; 30 Tongariro St; ⊙9am-4.30pm May-Oct, 8.30am-5pm Nov-April) Handles bookings for accommodation, transport and activities; dispenses cheerful advice; and stocks Department of Conservation (DOC) maps and town maps.

ⓘ Getting There & Away

Taupo Airport (☑ 07-378 7771; www.taupoairport.co.nz; Anzac Memorial Dr) is 8km south of town. Expect to pay about $25 for a 12-minute cab from the airport to the centre of town.

Air New Zealand (☑ 09-357 3000, 0800 737 000; www.airnz.co.nz) flies from Auckland to Taupo two to three times daily (50 minutes), and **Sounds Air** flies between Wellington and Taupo at least once per day except Tuesday and Wednesday (one hour).

InterCity (☑ 07-348 0366; www.intercity-coach.co.nz), **Mana Bus** (www.manabus.com) and **Naked Bus** (www.nakedbus.com/nz) services stop outside the Taupo i-SITE, where bookings can be made.

ⓘ Getting Around

Local Connector buses are run by **Busit!** (☑ 0800 4287 5463; www.busit.co.nz), including the Taupo North service running as far as Huka Falls and Wairakei, twice daily Monday to Friday.

Great Lake Shuttles (☑ 021 0236 3439; www.greatlakeshuttles.co.nz) offers charter services around the area, and can hook you up with bike hire.

Taxi companies include **Blue Bubble Taxis** (☑ 07-378 5100; www.taupo.bluebubbletaxi.co.nz) and **Top Cabs** (☑ 07-378 9250).

There are plenty of shuttle services operating year-round to Turangi and Tongariro National Park. Ask at the Taupo i-SITE which will best suit your needs as services vary according to season (ski or hike).

Turangi

POP 3000

If you love trout, shout it out! Turangi is known as the 'Trout Fishing Capital of the World'. Perched on Lake Taupo's south and set on the Tongariro River, it's also a fantastic white-water rafting destination and is a short hop, ski and tramp from the ski fields and walking tracks of Tongariro National Park.

A small town, Turangi blossomed when the Tongariro Hydro Power Development was given the go-ahead in the 1960s. Over two years, the population quadrupled, peaking at 6,500 people in 1968.

◎ Sights

Tongariro National Trout Centre   AQUARIUM
(☑ 07-386 8085; www.troutcentre.com; SH1; adult/child $15/free; ⊙10am-4pm Dec-Apr, 10am-3pm May-Nov) Around 4km south of Turangi, this DOC-managed trout centre has a hatchery, an underwater viewing chamber, a museum with polished educational displays, a collection of rods and reels dating back to the 1880s, and freshwater aquariums displaying river life.

Meander along the Tongariro River and check the website to see if you're visiting during a public fishing day (adult/child $30/10 including the gear and your catch).

Turangi

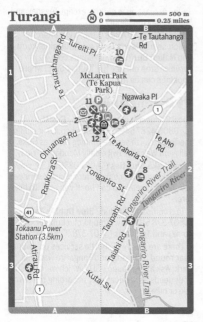

Volcanic Activity Centre MUSEUM
(www.volcanoes.co.nz; i-SITE, 1 Ngawaka Pl; adult/child $12/7; ☉9am-4pm) This interactive science museum moved from Taupo to Turangi and it now adjoins the local i-SITE (p291). Learn about the area's geothermal activity with this excellent, if text-heavy, display. A favourite exhibit with kids is the Earthquake Simulator. You can also configure your own tornado then watch it wreak havoc, or see a simulated geyser above and below ground.

⚡ Activities

Aside from **trout fishing**, the Tongariro River Trail offers enjoyable walks from the centre of town, or cut down time by cycling. Further afield, good leg-stretchers include **Hinemihi's Track**, near the top of Te Ponanga Saddle, 8km west of Turangi on SH47 (15 minutes return); **Maunganamu Track**, 4km west of Turangi on SH41 (40 minutes return); and **Tauranga–Taupo River Walk** (30 minutes), which starts at Te Rangiita, 12km north of Turangi on SH1.

The Tongariro River has some superb Grade III rapids for **river rafting**, as well as Grade I stretches suitable for beginners in the lower reaches during summer.

★**Tongariro River Trail** WALLKING, CYCLING
(www.greatlaketaupo.com) The Tongariro River Trail is a 15km dual-use walking and cycling track starting from town and taking in the National Trout Centre (p287) en route upriver to the Red Hut suspension bridge. Walk the loop (four hours) or bike (two hours) it on easy terrain. Go in the morning to see the trout fisherman knee-deep in the river.

Shorten your outing by crossing at Major Jones Bridge – a circuit known as the Tongariro River Lookout Track, which is a 3-4km riverside ramble passing lookout points to Mt Pihanga. Hire bikes from Central Plateau Cycles (p291) or Tongariro River Rafting and explore the trail.

Tongariro River Rafting RAFTING
(☎0800 101 024, 07-386 6409; www.trr.co.nz; 95 Atirau Rd; ☉9am-5pm) ◢ Test the white waters with a Grade II Gentle Family Float (adult/child $95/79) or splash straight into the Grade III white-water rapids ($139/125). Turangi's original rafting company also hires out mountain bikes (two hours free when you book a trip) and runs guided rides, including 42 Traverse, Tongariro River Trail, Tree Trunk Gorge and Fishers Track. Ask about multi-activity combos.

Raft fishing is available in summer (price on enquiry).

Rafting NZ   RAFTING

(☑ 0800 865 226, 07-386 0352; www.rafting newzealand.com; 41 Ngawaka Pl; ⊙ 8am to 4-7pm, tour dependent) The main trips offered by this slick outfit are a four-hour, Grade III trip on the Tongariro River with an optional waterfall jump (adult/child $179/149), and a family float over more relaxed rapids (Grade II, $139/119, three hours base to base). Groups of four or more can tackle a two-day trip overnighting at a riverside camp (Grade III+, $410 per person).

Tokaanu Thermal Pools   HOT SPRINGS

(☑ 07-386 8575; www.nzhotpools.co.nz; Mangaroa St, Tokaanu; adult/child $8/6, private pools per 20min $12/8; ⊙ 10am-9pm) Soak in thermally heated water at this unpretentious, family-oriented facility, 5km northwest of Turangi. Check out the private pools before committing, they can be a little grimy. A 500m stroll along the boardwalk (wheelchair accessible) showcases boiling mud pools, a trout-filled stream and thermal springs used by the Ngāti Tūwharetoa for bathing and cooking for more than 500 years.

🛏 Sleeping

Extreme Backpackers   HOSTEL $

(☑ 07-386 8949; www.extremebackpackers.co.nz; 26 Ngawaka Pl; dm $26-28, d $64-74, f $85; ☎) Crafted from native timber and corrugated iron, this modern backpackers' hostel has a sunny courtyard with tables and hammocks, a lounge with an open fire and a neat communal kitchen. Dorms range from four to eight beds and the pricier private rooms have en suites. Staff will happily help with arrangements for the Alpine Crossing and other activities.

Riverstone Backpackers   HOSTEL $

(☑ 07-386 7004; www.riverstonebackpackers. com; 222 Te Rangitautahanga Rd; dm $35, t $76, d without/with bathroom $76/82; ☎) This homey

---

ABOUT TROUT

Early European settlers who wanted to improve New Zealand's farming, hunting and fishing opportunities are responsible for the introduction of such ghastly wreckers as possums and rabbits. But one of their more benign introductions was that of trout – brown and rainbow – released into NZ rivers in the second half of the 19th century.

Today they are prized by sports anglers, who you'll find thigh-deep in limpid rivers and on the edge of deep green pools. Celebrities have also tried their luck in these North Island waters, including ex-American president Jimmy Carter, Michael Keaton, Harrison Ford and Liam Neeson – they all stay at the exclusive Tongariro Lodge (p290).

Tall tales boast of Taupo trout weighing more than a sack of spuds and measuring the length of a surfboard. Truth be told, more than 28,000 legal trout are bagged annually, by both domestic and international fishing enthusiasts.

Trout fishing is highly regulated, with plenty of rules regarding where and how they're to be fished. Licences are required and can be bought online at www.doc.govt.nz or www. fishandgame.org.nz. Our advice is to seek out a guide. Most offer flexible trips, with $300 for a half-day a ballpark figure.

Creel Tackle House & Cafe (p290) Fishing equipment for hire, tips and coffee.

Bryce Curle Fly Fishing (☑ 07-386 6813, 027 204 9401; www.brycecurleflyfishing.com; 59 Kahotea Dr, Motuoapa; ⊙ by appt) Turangi-based guide.

Flyfishtaupo (☑ 027 4450 223, 07-377 8054; www.flyfishtaupo.com) Guide Brent Pirie offers a range of fishing excursions, including seniors-focused 'Old Farts & Tarts' trips.

Greig's Sporting World (Barry Greig's Sporting World; ☑ 07-386 6911; www.greigsports.co.nz; 59 Town Centre; ⊙ 8.30am-5pm) Sells gear and handles bookings for guides and charters.

Sporting Life (☑ 07-386 8996; www.sportinglife-turangi.co.nz; The Mall, Town Centre; ⊙ 8.30am-5.30pm Mon-Sat, 9.30am-5pm Sun) Sports store laden with fishing paraphernalia, available to hire. Its website details the latest fishing conditions.

Ian & Andrew Jenkins (☑ 07-386 0840; www.tui-lodge.co.nz; Tui Lodge, 196 Taupahi Rd; ⊙ by appt) Father and son fly-fishing guides.

Central Plateau Fishing (☑ 027 681 4134, 07-378 8192; www.cpf.net.nz) Turangi-based guide Brett Cameron.

backpackers' hostel resides in a refitted house close to the town centre. Along with an enviable kitchen and comfortable lounge, it sports a stylish landscaped yard with a large wooden deck and pizza oven.

★ Braxmere
MOTEL $$

(☑ 07-386 6449; www.braxmere.co.nz; 88 Waihi Rd, Tokaanu; unit $180; ☜) Just 8km from Turangi on the southern fringes of Lake Taupo, Braxmere is a collection of 10 self-contained units with only a grassy lawn separating them from the lake. All are spacious one-bedroom numbers with decks and barbecues, the decor is maritime-chic and there's the added bonus of **Lakeland House restaurant** (☑ 07-386 6442; www.braxmere.co.nz; 88 Waihi Rd, Tokaanu; mains lunch $20-40, dinner $27-40; ☉ 10am-3pm & 6pm-late) on-site. When we visited, there were plans for a private thermal pool.

Troutbeck Fishing Lodge
B&B $$

(☑ 027 600 6344; www.troutbeckfishinglodge.co.nz; 35 Heuheu Pde; r incl breakfast $125-200; ☜) This peaceful fishing lodge is around 12km north of Turangi on SH1 and over the road from the Tauranga Taupo River. Two basic but cosy en-suite garden units share a lounge in the lodge, which boasts a king room with private deck and spa pool upstairs. Pay a little more and host Tracy will cook an excellent dinner, or book into a fly-fishing adventure with her husband, Jason.

Motuoapa Bay Holiday Park
HOLIDAY PARK $$

(☑ 07-386 7162; www.motuoapabayholidaypark. co.nz; 2 Motuoapa Esplanade, Motuoapa; sites $20, cabins & units $70-140; ☜) Around 8km north of Turangi, this adorable holiday park not only boasts lakeside location and assorted accommodation, but you can sleep in colourful VW Kombi vans and quirky wooden cabins shaped like boats (suitable for two to seven people). There are also self-contained motel units with one sleeping up to eight people.

Creel Lodge
MOTEL $$

(☑ 07-386 8081, 0800 273 355; www.creel.co.nz; 183 Taupahi Rd; 1-/2-bdrm ste $140/145-155; ☜) ⦿ Set in green and peaceful grounds, this heavenly hideaway backs onto a fine stretch of the Tongariro River. Nineteen spacious one- and two-bedroom suites sleeping two and four people respectively are named after fishing flies and local mountains. They have separate lounges, kitchens, soothing patios for sundowners and free use of barbecues. Creel Tackle House & Cafe is also on-site.

Tongariro Lodge
LODGE $$$

(☑ 07-386 7946; www.tongarirolodge.co.nz; 83 Grace Rd; 1-bdrm chalet $175, 2-/5-bdrm villas from $269-750; ☜) Three kilometres from Turangi on the Tongariro River, famed angler Tony Hayes established Tongariro Lodge in 1982. Across the 9-ha property are more affordable chalets with sunny decks and en suites, while larger, more luxurious options are ideal for groups and spoils.

Oreti Village
APARTMENT $$$

(☑ 0800 574 413, 07-386 7070; www.oretivillage. com; Mission House Dr, Pukawa; apt $220-310; ☜ ▣) This enclave of smart, self-contained apartments sleeping between four and nine people sits high over the lake, surrounded by bird-filled native bush and landscaped with colourful rhododendrons. Ask about the walking track to the private black-sand beach, and be sure to buy a bottle of NZ wine from the fantastic restaurant to enjoy on the balcony – best views this side of Lake Taupo.

✗ Eating

Creel Tackle House & Cafe
CAFE $

(☑ 07-386 7929; www.creeltackle.com; 183 Taupahi Rd; lunch $10-15; ☉ cafe 8am-4pm, tackle shop 7.30am-5pm) One of the best cafes in Turangi is a tiny room behind a fishing tackle shop. Beside native rimu-wood tables, homemade preserves perch on the windowsill. There's a cabinet loaded with pies and pastries, a selection of bagels and, come lunchtime, pray the chorizo burger is still on the menu. Local giftware also for sale.

★ Cadillac Cafe
CAFE $$

(☑ 07-386 0552; www.facebook.com/Thymefor foodcafe; 35 Turangi Town Centre; mains $9-20; ☉ 8.30am-3pm) Step back in time at Cadillac with its array of vintage chairs, posters and impressive toy collection from the '50s and '60s. Retro games are available while you wait for your massive burger, sticky ribs or fish and chips. Just try to resist the American cakes in the rotating cabinet. Kids' and gluten-free menus available. Lots of outdoor seating.

Hydro Eatery
CAFE $$

(☑ 07-386 6612; www.facebook.com/Hydroeatery; cnr Ohuanga Rd & Pihanga St; breakfast $9-19, lunch $16-19; ☉ 8am-3pm) Spacious, modern and clean – almost at the expense of character – this all-day cafe with geometric blue plastic chairs serves breakfast classics for breakfast and burgers, seafood and nachos for lunch. There's a kids' menu, and the best spot is on the outdoor deck.

ℹ Information

The **Turangi i-SITE** (☑ 07-386 8999, 0800 288 726; www.greatlaketaupo.com; 1 Ngawaka Pl; ⊘ 9am-4.30pm summer, 8.30am-4pm winter; ☎) is a good stop for information on Tongariro National Park, Kaimanawa Forest Park, trout fishing, and snow and road conditions. It issues DOC hut tickets, ski passes and fishing licences, and makes bookings for transport, accommodation and activities. Also home to the **Volcanic Activity Centre** (p288).

ℹ Getting There & Away

InterCity (p287), **Mana Bus** (www.manabus. com) and **Naked Bus** (www.nakedbus.com/nz) coaches **stop** (Ngawaka Pl) outside the **Turangi i-SITE** (p291). **Backyard Tours** (☑ 022 314 2656, 07-386 5322; www.backyardtours.com) and **Turangi Alpine Shuttles** (☑ 0272 322 135, 0508 427 677; www.alpineshuttles.co.nz) can both arrange transfers for the Tongariro Alpine Crossing.

ℹ Getting Around

Rent bikes from basic to boss at **Central Plateau Cycles** (☑ 07-386 0186; www.facebook. com/pg/Centralplateaucycles; 259/3 Te Rangitautahanga Rd; 2hr $20, half-/full-day hire $30/45; ⊘ 9am-5pm Mon-Fri, to 2pm Sat).

RUAPEHU REGION

One of New Zealand's premier destinations for adventure, one is never short of fresh air in the Ruapehu region. Tongariro National Park is a highlight, and aside from tramping in summer and snow sports in winter, the Tongariro Alpine Crossing is considered one of the best day-long hikes in the world. If mountain biking or kayaking sound more up your alley, you can take these down the mountain at National Park Village and Ohakune.

Tongariro National Park

Even before you arrive in Tongariro National Park its three mighty volcanoes – Ruapehu, Ngauruhoe (p293) and Tongariro (p293) – steal your breath from the horizon. It would be a wasted opportunity not to get closer, which is possible on the ski fields and during the other-worldly, day-long **Tongariro Alpine Crossing** (www.tongarirocrossing.org.nz), as well as other walks to natural features. You don't have to cover all 796 sq km of the National Park to be awed by nature.

The National Park – New Zealand's first – was gifted by local Tuwharetoa Māori more than a century ago. Long before it was granted dual Unesco World Heritage status for its volcanic landscape and deep cultural importance, the Māori believed that the mountains were strong warriors who fought among each other. In the process, they created the landscape that attracts more than 200,000 visitors each year. Visit once and you'll understand why it was worth fighting for.

History

Established in 1887, Tongariro was New Zealand's first national park. The previous year, during the aftermath of the New Zealand Wars, the Native Land Court met to determine the ownership of the land around Tongariro. Ngāti Tūwharetoa chief Horonuku Te Heuheu Tukino IV pleaded passionately for the area to be left intact, mindful of Pākehā (white people) eyeing it up for grazing. "If our mountains of Tongariro are included in the blocks passed through the court in the ordinary way," said the chief, "what will become of them? They will be cut up and sold, a piece going to one Pākehā and a piece to another."

In 1887 chief Horonuku ensured the land's everlasting preservation when he presented the area to the Crown for the purpose of a national park, the first in New Zealand and only the fourth in the world. With incredible vision for a man of his time, the chief realised that Tongariro's value lay in its priceless beauty and heritage, not as another sheep paddock.

Development of the national park was slow, and it was only after the main trunk railroad reached the region in 1909 that visitors arrived in significant numbers. Development mushroomed in the 1950s and 1960s as roads were sealed, tracks cut and more huts built.

◎ Sights

Located within the bounds of Tongariro National Park on the lower slopes of Mt Ruapehu, Whakapapa Village (pronounced 'faka-pa-pa'; altitude 1140m) is the gateway to the park, home of the park's visitor centre , and the starting point for numerous walking tracks.

Mt Ruapehu   VOLCANO
(www.mtruapehu.com) Mt Ruapehu (2797m) is the North Island's highest mountain and one of the world's most active volcanoes. One year-long eruption began in March 1945, spreading lava over Crater Lake and

Tongariro National Park & Around

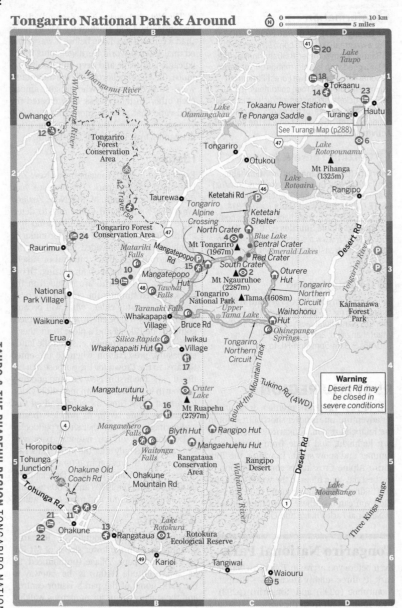

sending clouds of ash as far as Wellington. During the heavy ashfalls, hundreds of cases of 'Ruapehu throat' were reported. On Christmas Eve 1953, the crater-lake lip collapsed and an enormous lahar (volcanic mudflow) swept away everything in its path, including a railway bridge. A crowded train plunged into the river, killing 151 people, making it one of NZ's worst tragedies.

Tongariro National Park & Around

Ruapehu also rumbled in 1969 and 1973, and significant eruptions occur with suspicious frequency. In 2007 a primary school teacher almost died when a rock was propelled through the roof of a trampers' shelter, crushing his leg.

Mt Ngauruhoe VOLCANO
(☑07-892 3729; www.visitruapehu.com/explore/tongariro-national-park/volcanoes) Northeast of Ruapehu, Mt Ngauruhoe (2287m) is the national park's youngest volcano. Its first eruptions are thought to have occurred 2500 years ago. Until 1975 Ngauruhoe had erupted at least every nine years, including a 1954 eruption that lasted 11 months and disgorged 6 million cu m of lava. Its steam vents have temporarily cooled, suggesting that the main vent has become blocked.

Ngauruhoe is a conical, single-vent volcano with perfectly symmetrical slopes – which is the reason that it was chosen to star as Mt Doom in Peter Jackson's *The Lord of the Rings*.

Mt Tongariro VOLCANO
(www.visitruapehu.com/explore/tongariro-national-park) Ongoing rumbles are reminders that all the volcanoes in the area are very much in the land of the living. The last major event was in 2012 when Mt Tongariro – the northernmost and lowest peak in the park (1967m) – gave a couple of good blasts from its northern craters, causing a nine-month partial closure of the famous Alpine Crossing Track (p291). (To see video of recent eruptions, visit www.doc.govt.nz/eruption.)

⚶ Activities

Tramping
The DOC and i-SITE visitor centres at **Whakapapa** (Whakapapa Visitor Centre; ☑07-892 3729; www.doc.govt.nz/tongarirovisitorcentre; Bruce Rd; ⊙8am-5pm daily last weekend Oct-Apr, 8.30am-4.30pm daily May-last Fri Oct), Ohakune (p301) and Turangi (p291) have maps and information on walks in the park, as well as current track and weather conditions. Each January, DOC offers an excellent guided-walks program in and around the park; ask at DOC centres for information or book online.

The safest and most popular time to tramp in the national park is December to March, when the tracks have usually been cleared of snow and the weather is more settled. In winter many of the tracks become full alpine adventures, requiring mountaineering experience, an ice axe and crampons. Guided winter tramps are available with Adrift Outdoor Guided Adventures (p296).

The **Tongariro Northern Circuit** (www.doc.govt.nz/tongarironortherncircuit) is a favourite among more experienced trampers, but the park boasts more than 14,000km of track to choose from. These range from short ambles to excellent day walks such as the **Whakapapa Valley** and **Tama Lakes Tracks**, both of which begin from the **Tongariro National Park Visitor Centre** at Whakapapa. There are also a number of challenging routes that should only be attempted by the fit, experienced and well-equipped, such as the **Round the Mountain Track**, a remote 71km, four- to six-day tramp, circuiting Mt Ruapehu.

ⓘ MOUNTAIN SAFETY

Many visitors to New Zealand come unstuck in the mountains. Compared to some overseas competitors, they might seem small at face value, but the weather can change dramatically in minutes, and rescues (and fatalities) are not uncommon. When heading out, you must be properly equipped and take safety precautions, including leaving your itinerary with a responsible person and checking in with the nearest visitor centre. Appropriate clothing is paramount. Think wool, and several layers of it, topped with a waterproof jacket and even waterproof pants. Gloves and a hat are good too, even in summer. And don't even think about wearing anything other than sturdy boots. Take plenty of water, snacks and sunscreen, especially on hot days.

Scattered around the park's tramping tracks are 10 huts, most of which cost $15 per person. However, as the Tongariro Northern Circuit is a Great Walk, Mangatepopo, Oturere and Waihohonu huts are designated Great Walk huts ($36) during the Great Walk season (mid-October to April). Each hut has gas cookers, heating, cold running water and good old long-drop toilets, along with communal bunk rooms with mattresses. Campsites are located next to the huts; the $14 fee allows campers to use the hut facilities.

Great Walk hut tickets must be obtained in advance, either from the Tongariro National Park Visitor Centre, **Great Walks Bookings** (☑0800 694 732; www.greatwalks. co.nz) or DOC visitor centres nationwide. It pays to book early during the Great Walk season. In the low season, the huts become Standard huts ($5), the gas cookers are removed, and fees can be paid with Backcountry Hut Passes and tickets.

For more information about the Alpine Crossing, Northern Circuit and Round the Mountain Track, see Hiking in Tongariro National Park (p291). Shorter tracks include:

Tama Lakes Track
TRAMPING
(Ngauruhoe Pl) Part of the Tongariro Northern Circuit, starting at Whakapapa Village, this 17km-return track leads to the Tama Lakes, on the Tama Saddle between Ruapehu and Ngauruhoe (five to six hours return). The upper lake affords fine views of Ngauruhoe and Tongariro.

Silica Rapids Track
TRAMPING
(Bruce Rd) From Whakapapa Village this 2½-hour, 7km loop track takes trampers alongside a bubbling stream and through mountain beech forest before arriving at the terraces of Silica Rapids, named for the silica mineral deposits formed there by rapids on the Waikare Stream.

Whakapapa Nature Walk
WALKING
(Bruce Rd) Around 1km and suitable for wheelchairs, this loop track begins about 250m above the Tongariro National Park Visitor Centre, passing through beech forest and gardens typical of the park's vegetation zones.

Taranaki Falls Track
TRAMPING
(Ngauruhoe Pl) A two-hour, 6km loop track heads from the village to Taranaki Falls, which plunge 20m over a 15,000-year-old lava flow into a boulder-ringed pool.

Ridge Track
TRAMPING
(Bruce Rd) A 30-minute, 1.2km return walk from the village that climbs through beech forest to alpine-shrub areas for views of Ruapehu and Ngauruhoe.

Skiing
The linked **Whakapapa** (☑07-892 4000; www.mtruapehu.com/winter/whakapapa; Bruce Rd; daily lift pass adult/child $119/69) and **Turoa** (☑06-385 8456; www.mtruapehu.com/winter/Turoa; Okahune Mountain Rd; daily lift pass adult/child $119/69) resorts straddle Mt Ruapehu and are New Zealand's two largest ski areas. Each offers similar skiing at an analogous altitude (around 2300m), with areas to suit every level of experience – from beginners' slopes to black-diamond runs for the pros. The same lift passes cover both ski areas.

The only accommodation at the Whakapapa ski field is in private lodges (mainly owned by ski clubs), so most visitors stay at Whakapaka or National Park Village. Turoa is only 16km from Ohakune, which has the best après-ski scene.

⛵ Tours

Mountain Air
SCENIC FLIGHTS
(☑0800 922 812; www.mountainair.co.nz; SH47; flights 15/25/35min $120/195/245; ☺8am-7pm) Located just before the S48 turn-off, Mountain Air offers scenic flights from its base halfway between Whakapapa Village and National Park. Turangi and Taupo departures also available.

Walking Legends TRAMPING
(☑ 021 545 068, 0800 925 569, 07-312 5297; www.
walkinglegends.com) Guided tramps tackling
the Tongariro Alpine Crossing (3½ days,
$1590) and the Tongariro Northern Circuit
(three days, $970).

🛏 Sleeping & Eating

Whakapapa Holiday Park HOLIDAY PARK $
(☑ 07-892 3897; www.whakapapa.net.nz; SH48;
sites per person $23, dm $28, cabins $76-140,
self-contained units $130-140; 🛜) This popu-
lar park beside Whakapapanui Stream has
a wide range of accommodation options,
including campervan sites surrounded by
beautiful beech forest (site 21 has a mountain view), a five-room, 32-bed backpackers'
lodge and cabins sleeping up to six people
(linen required) and self-contained two-
bedroom units with en suites. The store
stocks basic groceries. The huge communal
kitchen was recently updated.

Chateau Tongariro Hotel HOTEL $$$
(☑ 07-892 3809, 0800 242 832; www.chateau.
co.nz; Bruce Rd; d $195-290, ste from $1000;
@🛜🏊) Despite its sublime setting, the
grandeur of this iconic 1929 hotel is a touch
faded, so it's worth checking out both the
Tongariro Wing and Heritage Wing before
deciding on a room. Still, the Chateau is un-
deniably romantic, complete with high tea
in the lounge overlooking Mt Ngauruhoe,
aperitifs in the foyer bar and dining in the
grand Ruapehu Room.

Ruapehu Room INTERNATIONAL $$$
(☑ 0800 242 832, 07-892 3809; www.chateau.
co.nz/ruapehu-restaurant; Bruce Rd; mains $30-
43; ☺6.30-10am, 6.30-9pm, noon-2pm Sun) The
Chateau Tongariro Hotel's elegant à la carte
option, think white tablecloths and chandeliers. Bookings are recommended and note
that gentlemen dining must wear a collared
shirt and long trousers. The Sunday carvery
lunch is very popular.

Chateau Tongariro High Tea CAFE $$
(☑ 0800 242 832; www.chateau.co.nz/chateau-
high-tea; Bruce Rd; high tea $32; ☺11am-5pm)
Wind back the years with a dainty selec-
tion of sandwiches, scones and other sweet
treats with high tea in the Chateau's elegant
lounge. Ask for a spot by the fireplace or in
front of the massive windows with direct
views of Mt Ngauruhoe. Bookings are rec-
ommended on weekends. Upgrade from tea
and coffee to sparkling wine for $13.

ℹ Information

Tongariro National Park Visitor Centre (p293)
has maps and info on all corners of the park,
including walks, huts and current skiing, track
and weather conditions. It's important to check
in with them before setting off to do the Ton-
gariro Alpine Crossing.

The *Walks in and around Tongariro National Park*
brochure provides a helpful overview of 30 walks
and tramps in the park ($3). Exhibits on the geo-
logical and human history of the area should keep
you busy for a couple of hours on a rainy day.

Further national park information is available
from the i-SITEs in **Ohakune** (p301), **Turangi**
(p291) and **Taupo** (p287).

ℹ Getting There & Away

CAR & MOTORCYCLE
Tongariro National Park is bounded by roads:
SH1 (called the Desert Rd) to the east, SH4 to
the west, SH46 and SH47 to the north and SH49
to the south. The main road up into the park is
SH48, which leads to Whakapapa Village and
continues further up the mountain as Bruce Rd
leading to the Whakapapa Ski Area.

Ohakune Mountain Rd leads up to the Turoa
Ski Area from Ohakune. The Desert Rd is regu-
larly closed when the weather is bad; detours will
be in operation. Likewise, Ohakune Mountain Rd
and Bruce Rd are subject to closures, and ac-
cess beyond certain points may be restricted to
4WDs or cars with snow chains. Ask your hotel or
call the **visitor centre** (p293) if you're uncertain.

SHUTTLE
Tongariro National Park is well serviced by shut-
tle operators, which travel between Whakapapa
Village, National Park Village, Ohakune, Taupo
and Turangi, as well as popular trailheads. In
summer tramping trips are their focus, but in
winter most offer ski-field shuttles. Book your
bus in advance to avoid unexpected strandings.

Many shuttle operators are offshoots or affiliates
of accommodation providers, so ask about trans-
port when you book your stay. **Roam** (☑ 021 588
734, 0800 762 612; www.roam.net.nz; Whakapa-
pa Holiday Park, Bruce Rd; adult/child $35/25) is
a local Whakapapa Village-based company

Otherwise, try Taupo-based **Tongariro Expe-
ditions** (☑ 0800 828 763, 07-377 0435; www.
tongariroexpeditions.com) or Turangi-based
Turangi Alpine Shuttles (p291).

National Park Village
POP 200
The small sprawl of National Park Village
is the most convenient place to stay when
tackling New Zealand's best one-day tramp

– the Tongariro Alpine Crossing (p291) – with more accommodation and eating options than nearby Whakapapa.

More than 100,000 people complete the 19.4km, mixed-terrain walk each year, which is as invigorating as it is challenging. Eerie rock formations and steaming craters look more like something from Mars than New Zealand soil, but the ultimate photo stop is the Emerald Lakes. Depending on the weather, you'll see people sitting in portable chairs enjoying the view or scrambling down the other side to escape bone-chilling winds.

National Park Village is busiest during the ski season, but in summer it makes a quieter base than Taupo for active travellers making the most of nearby outdoor activities. A lesser-known fact about the area is that it's a hot spot for train enthusiasts. Who knew?

🏃 Activities

There's little to do in the village itself, its major enticement being its proximity to national park tramps, mountain-bike trails, canoe trips on the Whanganui River and winter skiing. Most accommodation in town offers packages for shuttles to the Tongariro Alpine Crossing (p291) as well as lift passes and ski hire, sparing you the steeper prices further up the mountain. The best ski gear can be hired from **Eivins** (☑07-892 2843; www.facebook.com/EivinsRentals; cnr SH4 & Waimarino Tokaanu Rd; ski hire from $26/33 half-/full day, board hire from $32/40 half-/full day; ☺7am-6pm Thu-Mon Nov-Jun, daily Jul-Oct) and **Ski Biz** (☑07-892 2717; www.skibiz.co.nz; 10 Carroll St; ☺7.30-10.30pm & 4-7pm summer, 7.30am-7pm, to midnight Fri winter).

Daily shuttles leave from here to the Tongariro Alpine Crossing and Whakapapa Village in summer, and the ski area in winter.

When the conditions are favourable, experienced outdoor climbers with their own gear can find spots near Mangatepopo Valley and Whakapapa Gorge. Otherwise head to the indoor climbing wall at **National Park Backpackers** (☑07-892 2870; www.npbp.co.nz; 4 Findlay St; sites $15, dm $26-30, d $62-90; 🛜).

My Kiwi Adventure   MOUNTAIN BIKING
(☑0800 784 202, 021 784 202; www.mykiwi adventure.co.nz; 2 Findlay St; paddle boarding $50, mountain biking from $45; ☺8am-5.30pm) Offers the only-in-National-Park activity of stand-up paddle boarding on Lake Otamangakau (Nov-Apr, 2½hr). Trips include gear and shuttle transport. Plenty of mountain-biking adventures on standout local tracks, but we

recommend the Tongariro Adventure Package ($75), which combines the Tongariro Alpine Crossing and biking the Old Coach Rd over two days. Stand-alone bike rental (half-/full day $35/55) also available.

Adventure Outdoors   TRAMPING, KAYAKING
(☑0800 386 925, 027 242 7209; www.adventure outdoors.co.nz; 60 Carroll St; ☺by appt) Offers guided trips on the Tongariro Alpine Crossing – in winter ($185) and in time for the summer sunrise ($345) – and negotiating the Whanganui or Whakapapa Rivers on inflatable two-person kayaks ($235). Wetsuits and life-jackets are all provided so you're good to go.

42 Traverse   MOUNTAIN BIKING
(Kapoors Rd (off SH47)) This four- to six-hour, 46km mountain-bike trail through the Tongariro Forest is one of the most popular one-dayers on the North Island. The Traverse follows old logging tracks, making for relatively dependable going, although there are plenty of ups and downs – more downs as long as you start from Kapoors Rd (off SH47) and head down to Owhango.

Adrift Guided Outdoor Adventures   CANOEING, TRAMPING
(☑07-892 2751; www.adriftnz.co.nz; 53 Carroll St; ☺by appt) Runs guided canoe trips on the Whanganui River (one/three days $295/950), and lots of different guided tramps in Tongariro National Park (two hours to three days, $115 to $950) including the Tongariro Alpine Crossing (from $195) and tramps to Crater Lake on Mt Ruapehu ($225). Half-day mountain-bike excursions ($205) are also available.

Fishers Track   MOUNTAIN BIKING
(Fisher Rd) Starting from National Park railway station, this track is a 17km (mainly) downhill blast, and now forms part of the Ruapehu Whanganui Trails. Ideal for mountain bikers with little experience.

🛌 Sleeping

Pipers Lodge   HOSTEL $
(☑07-892 2777; www.piperslodge.co.nz; 18 Millar St; dm $55, tw/d $70-95, q $125, f $145; 🛜) Back when Pipers started in 1966 it was a ski lodge, but these days you'll find everyone from backpackers and adventurous couples to school groups and families staying here year-round. It's nothing flash, but it's got a **ski shop** on site, three spa pools, a games room, bar and dining area, Tongariro Crossing packages and, most importantly, history.

Plateau Lodge   LODGE, HOSTEL **$**
(☑ 07-892 2993, 0800 861 861; www.plateaulodge.
co.nz; 17 Carroll St; sites $40, dm $30, d $78-120, apt
from $165; 🖎) Family-friendly Plateau has cosy
rooms, some with en suite and TV, as well as
an attractive communal lounge and kitchen.
The dorms don't get bigger than two sets of
bunks, and there are also two- and three-bedroom apartments sleeping up to six. Campervan sites have the best access to the covered
spa pool. Local **shuttle services** available.

Howard's Lodge   LODGE **$**
(☑ 07-892 2827; www.howardslodge.co.nz; 43 Carroll
St; dm/tw/d/f from $19/75/75/90; 🖎) Howard
has moved on, but he's left his legacy in this
large, freshly decorated lodge with spa, two
comfortable lounges with supersized TVs,
and spotless, well-equipped kitchens. Dorms
are relatively roomy, and have between three
to eight beds. For outdoor action, there are
plenty of skis, snowboards, tramping gear
and mountain bikes for **hire**. Howard's also
runs **shuttle services** around the park. Book
InterCity buses and inter-island ferries here.

Tongariro Crossing Lodge   LODGE **$$**
(☑ 07-892 2688; www.tongarirocrossinglodge.
com; 27 Carroll St; d $189-209; 🖎) This pretty
white weatherboard cottage is decorated
with a baby-blue trim and rambling blooms
in summer. The new owners have refreshed
the six, spacious rooms – most of which
have a living area. The two studios share a
kitchen, another two are self-contained and
the remainder are great for families. Dotted
with period furniture, there's a sunny deck
and barbecue area, too.

Discovery Lodge   LODGE **$$**
(☑ 07-892 2744, 0800 122 122; www.discovery.net.
nz; SH47; sites $18, cabins $60, d from $100, 1-bdrm
from $160; 🖎) A fabulous base for the Ton-
gariro Alpine Crossing, this complex has a
range of rooms, from basic cabins and motel rooms through to upmarket chalets. An
on-site **restaurant** has views of Ruapehu
from the large deck, plus a **bar**, lounge and
shuttle transport. Owner and world-class
mountain runner Callum Harland holds
the unofficial Crossing record at a mind-
boggling 1 hour 25 minutes!

Wood Pigeon Lodge   LODGE **$$**
(☑ 07-892 2933; www.woodpigeonlodge.com; 130
Top Mill Rd, Raurimu; d $200-250; 🖎) Three sep-
arate options make up this very comforta-
ble accommodation overflowing with rural
charm in Raurimu, around 5km north of
National Park Village. Sleeping up to five,
the Tree House is self-sufficient for electric-
ity, harnessing wind and solar energy. More
cosy and compact is the Hut, with a wonder-
fully warm wooden interior and an outdoor
bathtub. Two-night minimum stay.

For groups of up to 11 people ($20 per
person extra after eight people), the Barn is
a spacious and rustic option. At this price,
you might expect better wi-fi, but given the
location it's the perfect opportunity to re-
connect with the outdoors.

Park Hotel   HOTEL **$$**
(☑ 07-892 2748, 0800 800 491; www.the-park.
co.nz; 2/6 Millar St; d/tw/f from $115/115/125; 🖎)
Positioned on SH4, this is our pick when
tackling Tongariro Crossing. Neat and super affordable, the twin, queen and family
mezzanine rooms are quiet and comfortable.
The B&B and two-night crossing packages
are great value and once you've conquered
the mountain, there are spa pools for soaking. **Spiral Restaurant & Bar** (mains $20 to
$34) is a decent place to eat.

Parkview Apartments   APARTMENT **$$$**
(☑ 021 252 4930; www.parkviewnationalpark.com;
24 Waimarino–Tokaanu Rd; d $290; 🖎) Stylish
and thoroughly modern accommodation
comes to National Park Village at these
apartments. Both with two bedrooms and
sleeping up to four people, or two adults and
three children, the expansive windows make
it easy to take in the beautiful alpine scenery,

RAILWAY COUNTRY

National Park Village is railway country.
About 20km south on SH4 at Horopito
is a monument to the **Last Spike**, the
spike that marked the 23-year comple-
tion of the Main Trunk Railway Line be-
tween Auckland and Wellington in 1908
(although Horopito is better known for
Smash Palace, New Zealand's most
famous car graveyard).

Five kilometres north from National
Park Village, at **Raurimu**, is evidence of
the engineering masterpiece that is the
'spiral' – a solution that enabled trains to
travel across the steep drop of the land
between Raurimu and National Park.
Trainspotters will marvel, while non-train-
spotters will probably wonder what the
hell they're looking at (there's not much
to see unless admired from the air).

although indoor distractions such as big-screen TVs, gas fireplaces and contemporary kitchens make staying inside a temptation.

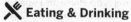

Eating & Drinking

There's adequate eating to be had at the **Station Cafe** (☑07-892 2881; www.stationcafe.co.nz; cnr Findlay St & Station Rd; lunch $15-28, dinner $29-35; ☺9am-9pm) and **Schnapps** (☑07-892 2788; www.schnappsbarruapehu.com; cnr SH4 & Findlay St; ☺noon-late) at the local pub, but if you're coming from bigger towns or cities, it's best to lower your expectations.

❶ Getting There & Away

The Village lies at the junction of SH4 and SH47 at 825m above sea level, 15km from the hub of Whakapapa Village.

InterCity (☑09-583 5780; www.intercity.co.nz) buses stop at National Park Station at the **Station Cafe** (p298), where the *Northern Explorer* train run by **KiwiRail Scenic** (☑04-495 0775, 0800 872 467; www.kiwirailscenic.co.nz) also pulls up.

Tongariro Crossing Shuttles (☑07-892 2993; www.tongarirocrossingshuttles.co.nz) offers a return shuttle from National Park Village to the Tongariro Alpine Crossing ($40) and Whakapapa for the Tongariro Northern Circuit ($35).

Ohakune

POP 1000

Outdoor adventurists look no further: Ohakune pumps with snow enthusiasts in winter and trampers and mountain bikers in summer. The vibe is best when snow drifts down on **Turoa Ski Area** and people defrost together over a drink back in town. Despite the chill outside, the après-ski culture comes in hot every season.

When the snow clears the town quietens – and accommodation prices drop. It's the perfect time to ride the fantastic Old Coach Road mountain-bike trail and provides easy access for exploring Whanganui National Park.

There are two distinct parts to Ohakune: the commercial hub is strung along the highway, but in winter the northern end around the train station, known as the Junction, is the epicentre of the action. The two are linked by the 2km **Mangawhero River Walkway**, a leafy amble along the riverbank.

🏃 Activities

⭐**Ohakune Old Coach Road**   MOUNTAIN BIKING
(www.ohakunecoachroad.co.nz; Marshalls Rd) One of NZ's best half-day (three to four hours) cycle rides, this gently graded route passes engineering features including the historic Hapuawhenua and Toanui viaducts – the only two remaining curved viaducts in the southern hemisphere. It also passes through ancient forests of giant rimu and totara that survived the Taupo blast of AD 180, being in the lee of Ruapehu. From the Ohakune railway station, ride down Old Coach Rd, turn right into Marshalls Rd and join the track.

Mountain Bike Station   MOUNTAIN BIKING
(☑06-385 9018, 0800 245 464; www.mountain bikestation.co.nz; Ohakune Shopping Centre, 27 Goldfinch St; ☺7.30am-6pm Mon-Fri, 7am-6pm Sat & Sun Jul-Oct, 9am-6pm Nov-Jun) Rents mountain bikes (half-/full day from $35/50) and provides cost-per-person transfers to biking routes, including to the Turoa Ski Field ($20), Horopito ($15) and Whanganui ($180). Longer bike and transport packages are also available. Often open longer during peak season, hours are subject to demand. Same building as **SLR** (☑06-385 9018; www.slr.co.nz).

Waitonga Falls Track   TRAMPING
(www.doc.govt.nz; Ohakune Mountain Rd) The path to Waitonga Falls (1½ hours return, 4km), Tongariro's highest waterfall (39m), offers magnificent views of Mt Ruapehu. The track starts from Ohakune Mountain Rd.

Yeti Tours   CANOEING, KAYAKING
(☑06-385 8197, 0800 322 388; www.yetitours.co.nz; 3 Burns St; guided tours 2-6 days $420-895, hire 2-8 days $175-250; ☺by appt) Leads guided canoeing safaris on the Whanganui and Mokau Rivers, and hires canoes and kayaks.

Ruapehu Homestead   HORSE RIDING
(☑027 267 7057; www.ruapehuhomestead.kiwi.nz; cnr Piwara St & SH49, Rangataua; 30min-3hr adult $30-180, child $25-150; ☺treks 10am, noon & 2pm) Four kilometres east of Ohakune (near Rangataua), Ruapehu Homestead offers guided treks around its paddocks, as well as longer rides along the river and on backcountry trails with views of the mountain.

Canoe Safaris   CANOEING, RAFTING
(☑0800 272 3353, 06-385 9237; www.canoe safaris.co.nz; 6 Tay St; 1-5 day tour $185-1195, canoe & kayak hire $185-210) Offers guided canoeing trips on the Whanganui and Rangitikei Rivers. Also offers canoe and kayak hire. The one-day **lavender farm tour** includes lunch on the riverbank and a drink at a lavender-farm cafe – perfect for the whole family.

Lake Surprise Track   TRAMPING
(Okahune Mountain Rd) A moderately challenging walk climbs to shallow Lake Surprise (five hours return, 9km). The track starts 15km up Ohakune Mountain Rd.

Mangawhero Forest Walk   WALKING
(Ohakune Mountain Rd) An easy stroll starting near the beginning of Ohakune Mountain Rd, 13km up from the rail bridge (one-hour loop, 3km), taking in native forest and the Mangawhero River. It is well graded and suitable for wheelchairs and pushchairs.

🛌 Sleeping

LKNZ Lodge   HOSTEL $
(🖉 06-385 9169; www.lknz.co.nz; 1 Rata St; campsites $30, dm $23-28, d $65-99, f $159; 🛜) From budget to flashpacker, LKNZ rooms are spread over four lodges. During the ski season at least one is rented out by instructors. Tidy doubles with wooden bed-frames are a bargain and there's a drying room, 500 DVDs, bikes for hire, pay-per-use spa pools and a sauna and a **cafe** (open from 7.30am; try the nachos).

Station Lodge   HOSTEL $
(🖉 06-385 8797; www.stationlodge.co.nz; 60 Thames St; dm $28, r $70, apt $130-220, chalets $220-250; @🛜) 🏄 Housed in a lovely old villa with wooden floors and high ceilings, this excellent YHA hostel has a well-equipped kitchen, comfortable lounge, spa pool, and a garden with a pizza oven. If you're after privacy, apartments sleeping between two to six people and separate chalets (some with two bedrooms, gas fireplaces and private spa pools) are available.

Peaks Motor Inn   MOTEL $$
(🖉 0508 843 732, 06-385 9144; www.thepeaks. co.nz; cnr Mangawhero Tce & Shannon St; d/1-bdrm unit from $149/169; 🛜) This well-kept motel offers spacious rooms with good bathrooms and full kitchens. Communal facilities include grassy lawns, a basic gym, large outdoor spa, and sauna. Check the website for good-value packages incorporating transport for the Tongariro Alpine Crossing.

★ River Lodge   B&B $$$
(🖉 021 292 2883, 06-385 4771; www.theriverlodge. co.nz; 206 Mangawhero River Rd; chalets incl breakfast $290, 1-/2-bdrm $260/290; 🛜) Just 8km from town, this charming property was designed with Mangawhero River in mind. Fish with direct access, laze in a hammock, borrow a picnic rug or walk along the barefoot-massage path. There are three double rooms in the house, one with a separate single bed, and two charismatic chalets for two with private spa pools and fireplaces.

★ Ruapehu Country Lodge   B&B $$$
(🖉 06-385 9594, 021 707 850; www.ruapehucountry lodge.co.nz; 630 Raetihi–Ohakune Rd; d $295; 🛜) Around 5km west of Ohakune on the road to Raetihi, Ruapehu Country Lodge is the perfect combination of country elegance and classy decor. You'll get a friendly welcome from Heather and Peter, as well as the alpacas beside the manicured driveway. Framed by expansive gardens on 2 hectares, the lodge is separated from the local golf course by a meandering river.

Manuka Lodge   B&B $$$
(🖉 06-385 8303; www.manukalodgenz.com; 18 Manuka St; 🕙 incl breakfast $205-225, extra person $65; 🛜) This four-bedroom B&B feels like home thanks to chatty hosts who offer a delicious cooked breakfast (Volcano coffee and homemade bread included) and organise **shuttles** for the Tongariro Crossing. All rooms have en suite and funky wallpaper. Love the reclaimed matai bed-heads and bed-side tables. Make the most of the pool spa at night – the stars are to die for.

Powderhorn Chateau   HOTEL $$$
(🖉 06-385 8888; www.powderhorn.co.nz; cnr Thames St & Mangawhero Tce; r from $260; @🛜🖵) At this Swiss-style chalet, guests stay in rooms where their favourite *Lord of the Rings* characters set up during filming. Peter Jackson booked out the eight-person apartment, but there are another 33 more affordable options. With woody interiors, possum-fur blankets and a spa-temperature indoor pool with an intercom to the bar, this is the place for mountain recovery and revelry.

> ### SEEING ORANGE
>
> If you're travelling northwest along the State Highway into Ohakune, the first thing you'll see is a **Big Carrot** (Rangataua Rd; 🚻). This tribute to the carrot capital of the country goes back to the 1920s, when Chinese settlers cleared the land to grow them. Sit anywhere long enough with a view of the road and you're likely to see a truck overflowing with soil and specks of orange. There's even an annual **Carrot Carnival** (www.carrotcarnival.org.nz; ⊙ early Jun).

TAUPO & THE RUAPEHU REGION OHAKUNE

✕ Eating

★ Eat Takeaway Diner
CAFE $

(☑ 020 4126 5520; www.facebook.com/eattakeaway diner; 49 Clyde St; snacks & mains $9-14; ⊗ 8am-3pm, closed public holidays & Oct 23-31; 🕾 🎤) 🍴 Bagels, innovative salads, and tasty American and Tex Mex-influenced dishes combine with the best coffee in town at this modern spot on Ohakune's main drag. All white tiles and pops of blue, there's a strong focus on organic ingredients, sustainable practices and dietary requirement-friendly options, like the vegan 'cheeseburger', salad bowl and burrito.

Chocolate Eclair Shop
BAKERY $

(Johnny Nation's Chocolate Eclair Shop; ☑ 06-385 8152; www.facebook.com/johnnynationschocolate eclairshop; 78 Clyde St; baked treats from $2; ⊗ 6.30am-6.30pm, closed for 6 months over ski season) At the time of writing, Allan Nation is 64 years old. He's been getting up at 2am to bake since he was 17. Allan learned from his late father, who also baked in the original ovens that used to feed soldiers at Waiouru Army Camp. The shop looks like a convenience store, but the world-famous homemade chocolate eclairs are why you're here.

★ Blind Finch
BURGERS, BREAKFAST $$

(☑ 06-385 8076; www.theblindfinch.co.nz; 29 Gold-finch St; burgers & breakfast $15.50; ⊗ 9am-10pm Jul-Oct; 4-10pm Mon-Fri, 9am-10pm Sat & Sun, Nov-Jun; 🕾) After tramping Mt Tongariro, skiing

OFF THE BEATEN TRACK

LINGER AT THE LAKES

Lake Rotokura (☑ 07-892 3729; www. doc.govt.nz) is 12km southeast of Ohakune at Karioi, just off SH49 (*karioi* means 'places to linger'). It's one of two lakes in the Lake Rotokura Ecological Reserve: the first is Dry Lake, actually quite wet and perfect for picnicking; the furthest is Rotokura, *tapu* (sacred) to Māori, so eating, fishing and swimming are prohibited. It's a one-way, 1km walk from the start of the track to Rotokura, with an optional loop track around the lake. Allow an hour to admire ancient beech trees and waterfowl if you decide to do the whole stroll.

To get here, drive 11km south east along SH49 from Ohakune, then 1km from the turn-off along Karioi Station Rd. Cross the railway line until you reach Rotokura car park.

Mt Ruapehu or mountain biking, there's nothing better than these beast-sized burgers cooked on a custom-made manuka wood-fire grill. Licensed until 2am, Blind Finch boasts a **bar** and regularly hosts impromptu jam sessions, burger bingo, trivia and events. More than half a dozen varieties of eggs Benedict for breakfast, available until 2am.

Cyprus Tree
ITALIAN $$

(☑ 06-385 8857; www.cyprustree.co.nz; cnr Clyde & Miro Sts; mains $24-34; ⊗ 4.30pm-late Mon-Fri, 9am-late Sat & Sun) Open year-round, this restaurant and bar serves up Italian and Kiwi-influenced dishes: think wild venison on potato-and-herb rosti to slow-cooked lamb papardelle. There's a special menu for little kids, and Ohakune's best range of NZ craft beers for big kids. Bar snacks from 3pm to 5pm. Couches next to fire in winter, the outdoor deck in summer.

Powderkeg
BISTRO, BAR $$

(☑ 06-385 8888; www.powderhorn.co.nz; cnr Thames St & Mangawhero Tce; mains $22-36; ⊗ 7.30am-2.30pm & 4pm-late) The Powderkeg is the party bar of the Powderhorn Chateau, with DJs in winter and occasional dancing on the tables. Food-wise, it's also no slouch year-round with top-notch burgers and pizza, meaty mains such as lamb rump, and another good selection of NZ craft beers that are just the thing after negotiating the Old Coach Road on two wheels.

OCR Eatery & Wine Bar
CAFE $$

(☑ 06-385 8322; www.ocrcafe.co.nz; 2 Tyne St; breakfast $16-27, lunch $16-27, dinner $17-32; ⊗ 9am-3pm Fri-Sun Nov-Feb, 8am-9pm Fri & Sat, to 3pm Sun Mar-Oct, daily Dec 27-Jan 7 & during ski season) Short for Old Coach Road, OCR has limited opening hours but remains a favourite among locals and visitors. Burgers, sandwiches, salads and breakfasts are made with care, as are the home-baked cakes and slices. A rootsy soundtrack and wood burner lend a rustic vibe. Ask if they have Scoria Red IPA craft beer from Ohakune-based Little Thief Brewing.

Osteria
ITALIAN $$

(☑ 06-385 9183; www.osteria.co.nz; 73 Clyde St; mains $20-36; ⊗ 4-10pm Mon-Fri, to 11pm Sat & Sun, closed Mon Jul-Oct) Warm up with a pizza or generous risotto in this contemporary Italian restaurant with rustic touches (wooden chairs, open fireplaces, old photos and the odd mounted deer head). There's a menu page dedicated to Australian and NZ wines, with another reserved for Italy. Share the dessert pizza at the end.

🍷 Drinking & Nightlife

Craft Haus
COFFEE

(☑06-385 8683, 022 3858 683; www.thecrafthaus.co.nz; 31 Thames St; drinks $3-5; ⊘10am-2pm Mon, Tue, Thu, Fri, 10am-5pm Sat & Sun) 'Local is the new black' says the sign on the brick wall at this coffee house-gallery-clothing store-brewery inside the heritage Ohakune train station, right on the platform. **Volcano Coffee** roasts out the back, **Ruapehu Brewing Co.** brews, **Opus Fresh** sells beautiful merino-wool pieces, and local arts and crafts.

Kitchen
CRAFT BEER

(☑06-385 8664; www.4thames.co.nz; 4 Thames St; mains $22-25; ⊘8am-6pm Mon-Fri, 7am-6pm Sat & Sun, to late during ski season) The friendly owner refers to the Kitchen as his 'bach (beach house) with a bar attached'. Serving only NZ craft beer from more than 20 breweries, it's packed during winter and on the first weekend of September during a spring party. Local musicians and a simple, tasty menu that swings between Mexican and Asian fare.

ℹ️ Information

Ruapehu i-SITE (☑0800 047 483, 06-385 8427; www.visitruapehu.com; 54 Clyde St; ⊘8am-5.30pm) can make bookings for activities, transport and accommodation; DOC officers are usually on hand from 10am to 4.30pm.

Visit Ohakune (www.visitohakune.co.nz) is a useful website for 'The Mountain Town' and around.

ℹ️ Getting There & Away

InterCity (p287) has a direct bus services from Taupo and Auckland and passes through on services between Palmerston North and Auckland and Wellington and Auckland, stopping on Clyde St near the i-SITE. The *Northern Explorer* train is run by **KiwiRail Scenic** (p298).

Dempsey Buses (☑06-385 4022; www.dempseybuses.co.nz) offer services around the Ruapehu region, including shuttles and buses servicing the Tongariro Alpine Crossing (leaving Ohakune at 7.15am during summer at $50 per person), a daily shuttle to the Ohakune Old Coach Rd, shuttles to the Turoa ski field car park to hit the slopes or take a downhill Ohakune Mt Rd bike ride, on-demand service to the 42nd Traverse bike ride and services to and from the Mangapurua Track and Bridge to Nowhere.

Waiouru

POP 740

Waiouru (altitude 792m) is primarily an army base and a refuelling stop for those

RIDING RAPIDS & STEADS

River Valley (☑06-388 1444; www.rivervalley.co.nz; Mangahoata Rd, Taihape; ⊘7.30am-5pm) is an adventure centre and lodge about 30km northeast of Taihape (follow the signs from Taihape's Gretna Hotel). Its popular half-day white-water rafting trip tackles the thrilling Grade V rapids of Rangitikei River ($175). Horse treks are also offered, (two hours/half-day $129/$175).

Lodge accommodation is also available (sites per person $18, dm $31, d $169-175, B&B $199). Meals in the on-site restaurant feature ingredients fresh from the lodge's gardens.

taking the 56km-long Desert Rd leading to Turangi. In winter, the road occasionally closes due to snow. A barren landscape of reddish sand with small clumps of tussock, the **Rangipo Desert** isn't actually a desert. This unique landscape is in fact the result of two million years of volcanic eruptions – especially the Taupo eruption about 2000 years ago that coated the land with thick deposits of pumice and destroyed all vegetation.

⊙ Sights

National Army Museum
MUSEUM

(☑06-387 6911; www.armymuseum.co.nz; cnr SH1 & Hassett Dr; adult/child $15/5; ⊘9am-4.30pm) 🌿 At the south end of the town in a large, concrete castle is the National Army Museum, which preserves the history of the NZ military and its various campaigns, from colonial times to the present. Its moving stories are well told through displays of arms, uniforms, memorabilia and other collections. The on-site **cafe** is open 9am to 4pm. For a truly memorable visit, attend the dawn service on Anzac Day (25 April).

ℹ️ Information

Waiouru i-SITE (☑06-387 5279; www.visitruapehu.com; National Army Museum, cnr SH1 & Hassett Dr; ⊘9am-4.30pm)

ℹ️ Getting There & Away

Waiouru is located at the junction of SH1 and SH49, 27km east of Ohakune. **InterCity** (p287) services Waiouru en route from Auckland to Wellington. Multiple direct services leave in the morning and evening from Auckland and throughout the day from Wellington, taking 6¾ hours and 4¾ hours respectively.

Rotorua & the Bay of Plenty

Best Places to Eat

➜ Macau (p330)
➜ Me & You (p330)
➜ Eightyeight (p335)
➜ Post Bank (p335)
➜ Grindz Café (p330)

Best Places to Stay

➜ Warm Earth Cottage (p325)
➜ Sport of Kings (p315)
➜ Asure Harbour View Motel (p329)
➜ Ohiwa Beach Holiday Park (p344)
➜ City Lights Boutique Lodge (p316)

Why Go?

Captain Cook named the Bay of Plenty when he cruised past in 1769, and plentiful it remains. Blessed with sunshine and sand, the bay stretches from Waihi Beach in the west to Opotiki in the east, with the holiday hubs of Tauranga, Mt Maunganui and Whakatane in between.

Offshore from Whakatane is New Zealand's most active volcano, Whakaari (White Island). Volcanic activity defines this region, and nowhere is this subterranean spectacle more obvious than in Rotorua. Here the daily business of life goes on among steaming hot springs, explosive geysers, bubbling mud pools and the billows of sulphurous gas responsible for the town's trademark eggy smell.

Rotorua and the Bay of Plenty are also strongholds of Māori tradition, presenting numerous opportunities to engage with NZ's rich indigenous culture: check out a power-packed concert performance, chow down at a *hāngi* (Māori feast) or skill up with some Māori arts-and-crafts techniques.

When to Go

➜ The Bay of Plenty is one of NZ's sunniest regions; Whakatane records a brilliant 2350 average hours of sunshine per year! In summer (December to February) maximums hover in the high 20s (Celsius). Everyone else is here, too, but the holiday vibe is heady and the beaches irresistible.

➜ Visit Rotorua any time: the geothermal activity never sleeps, and there are enough beds in any season.

➜ The mercury can slide below 5°C overnight here in winter, making the hot pools even more appealing. It's usually warmer on the coast, where you'll have the beaches all to yourself.

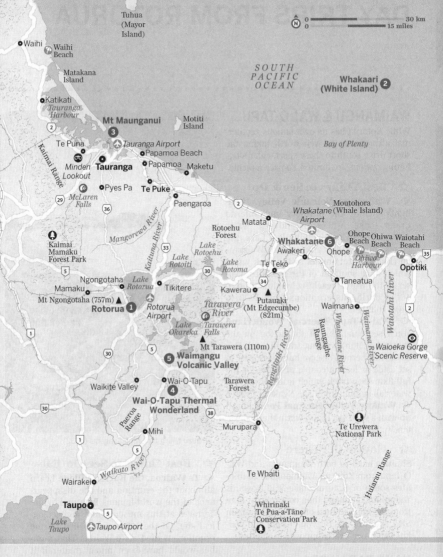

Rotorua & the Bay of Plenty Highlights

1 **Rotorua** (p306) Peering through the sulphurous steam at a unique town where geothermal activity, Māori culture and world-class mountain biking come together.

2 **Whakaari (White Island)** (p342) Stepping into the steaming crater of an active volcano on a tiny island.

3 **Mt Maunganui** (p332) Lazing at the beach, carving up the surf and hiking up the signature mountain, then relaxing in the thermal pools.

4 **Wai-O-Tapu Thermal Wonderland** (p321) Marvelling at the unearthly hues of the region's most colourful geothermal attraction.

5 **Waimangu Volcanic Valley** (p321) Walking down through a fizzing, spurting and sizzling valley to a blissfully peaceful lake.

6 **Whakatane** (p337) Soaking up the sunny small-town vibe in a place where Māori culture and beach culture go hand in hand.

DAY TRIPS FROM ROTORUA

WAIMANGU & WAI-O-TAPU

While Rotorua has its own famous geothermal attractions, it's well worth taking the short drive south to these spectacular sites. Eating options are limited, so pack a picnic.

☆ Best Things to See & Do

◉ **Waimangu Volcanic Valley** Highlights include the powdery blue Inferno Crater Lake, where overflowing water can reach 80°C, and Frying Pan Lake, the largest hot spring in the world. Waimangu (Black Water) refers to the dark water which once shot out of the mightiest geyser in the world, reaching heights of up to 400m during its eruptions from 1900 to 1904. (p321)

◉ **Wai-O-Tapu Thermal Wonderland** You'll see a fair bit of the action on the shortest (1.5km) walking trail through this colourful thermal reserve but you're best to set aside at least a couple of hours for the full 3km loop track which leads down to a waterfall spilling into Lake Ngakoro. (p321)

🏃 **Waikite Valley Thermal Pools** Finish up with a soothing dip in warm thermal waters. (p324)

☆ How to Get There

Shuttles head to both Waimangu and Wai-O-Tapu from Rotorua. Waimangu is 20 minutes south of Rotorua; take SH5 (towards Taupo) for 15km and then continue for 6km from the marked turn-off. Further south on SH5, the turn-offs for Wai-O-Tapu and Waikiti Valley are nearly opposite each other.

LAKE TARAWERA

Providing a mirror for Mt Tarawera (1110m), this pretty lake is a popular destination for swimming, fishing, boating and walks. It may look tranquil now, but it was a very different story on the night of 10 June 1886, when the volcano sprang into life, blanketing the surrounding countryside in ash and mud up to 20m thick.

ROWAN SIMS PHOTOGRAPHY/SHUTTERSTOCK©

Mauao hiking trail, Mt Maunganui (p332)

☆ Best Things to See/Do/Eat

◉ **Te Wairoa, the Buried Village** Learn all about the eruption and the disappearance of the world-famous Pink and White Terraces at this museum and archaeological site. Of the 153 people killed by the eruption, 17 died at Te Wairoa. That number would have been much greater if it weren't for the actions of famed tour guide Sophia Hinerangi, who sheltered 62 people in her small whare (traditional sloperoofed house). (p321)

🏃 **Tarawera Trail** Starting from Te Wairoa, this track heads down to the lake and wanders through forest to Hot Water Beach. Prebook a water taxi to ferry you back to the Landing. (p323)

✕ **Landing Cafe** Finish your day with a meal, coffee or cold beverage at this lakeside cafe. (p324)

☆ **How to Get There**

Lake Tarawera is 19km southeast of central Rotorua; take Tarawera Rd, which is well signposted from SH30 to the east of town. You'll need your own wheels to get here.

MT MAUNGANUI

If the temperature cranks up and you fancy an ocean dip, pack your sunblock and head to the Mount. It's one of New Zealand's most popular beach towns, with a lively dining and bar scene which leaves Rotorua in its shade.

☆ **Best Things to See/Do/Eat**

◉ **Mauao** No trip would be complete without a sweaty trek to the top of the Mount itself. The views from the summit of this extinct volcano are outstanding, completely justifying the 50-minute ascent. (p332)

🏊 **Main Beach** You can take a gentle dip on the harbour side but, unless you've got toddlers in tow, the rough-and-tumble surf of Main Beach is much more fun. (p332)

✕ **Eightyeight** There are plenty of good options along the main Maunganui Rd strip, but our favourite daytime escape is this excellent little cafe with a counter perpetually groaning under the weight of drool-inducing baked goods. (p335)

☆ **How to Get There**

Mount Maunganui is 74km due north of Rotorua. It takes about an hour if you head east of the lake via SH33 and SH2 (partly tolled), and about 10 minutes longer if you head west of the lake on SH36. Allow 90 minutes by bus.

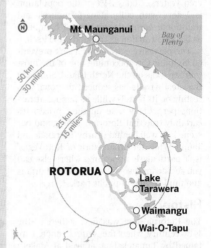

From Rotorua you can be in Tauranga, Mount Maunganui, Whakatane or even Taupo in little over an hour. Day-trip options include lakes, mountains, breathtaking ocean beaches and numerous geothermal areas.

ROTORUA

POP 65,300

Catch a whiff of Rotorua's sulphur-rich air and you've already had an introduction to NZ's most dynamic geothermal area. The Māori revered this place, naming one of the most spectacular springs Wai-O-Tapu (Sacred Waters). Today 34% of the population is Māori, with cultural performances and traditional *hāngi* (steam-cooked banquets) as big an attraction as the landscape itself.

The pervasive eggy odour hasn't prevented 'Sulphur City' becoming one of the most touristy spots on the North Island. Some say this steady trade has seduced the town into resting on its laurels while its famous attractions perpetually hike up their prices. It's certainly true that Rotorua's dining and bar scene lags well behind nearby Tauranga and Taupo. While the urban fabric of 'RotoVegas' isn't particularly appealing, where else can you see steam casually wafting out of drains and mud boiling in public parks?

History

The Rotorua area was first settled in the 14th century when the *Arawa* canoe, captained by Tamatekapua, arrived at Maketu in the central Bay of Plenty. Settlers took the tribal name Te Arawa to commemorate the vessel that had brought them here.

ESSENTIAL ROTORUA & BAY OF PLENTY

....

Eat a *hāngi* (earth-cooked) meal at one of the 'dinner and show' Māori cultural experiences in Rotorua.

Drink local craft beer from Rotorua's Croucher Brewing Co (p318).

Read *Tangata Whenua, An Illustrated History* – a hefty but beautiful summation of all things Māori.

Listen to *Kora,* the eponymous rootsy album from Whakatane's soulful sons.

Watch *Utu* (1983), a classic NZ movie including a memorable eyeball-eating scene inspired by the death of Rev Carl Völkner in Opotiki in 1865.

Go green by negotiating the verdant bush-clad experience of Rotorua's Redwoods Treewalk (p313).

Online www.rotoruanz.com, www.bayofplentynz.com

In the next few hundred years, subtribes spread and divided through the area (the main subtribe of Te Arawa who live in Rotorua today are known as Ngāti Whakaue). A flashpoint occurred in 1823 when the Arawa lands were attacked by Northland tribe Ngāpuhi, led by Hongi Hika, in the so-called Musket Wars. After Te Arawa were defeated at Mokoia Island, the warring parties made their peace.

During the Waikato War (1863–64), Te Arawa threw in its lot with the government against its traditional Waikato enemies, preventing East Coast reinforcements getting through to support the Kingitanga (King Movement).

With peace in the early 1870s, word spread of scenic wonders, miraculous landscapes and watery cures for all manner of diseases. Rotorua boomed. Its main attraction was the fabulous Pink and White Terraces, formed by volcanic silica deposits. Touted at the time as the eighth natural wonder of the world, they were destroyed in the 1886 Mt Tarawera eruption.

◉ Sights

◎ City Centre

Lake Rotorua   LAKE
(Map p308) Lake Rotorua is the largest of the district's 18 lakes and is – underneath all that water – a spent volcano. Near the centre of the lake is **Mokoia Island**, which has for centuries been occupied by various subtribes of the area. The lake can be explored by boat, with several operators situated at the lakefront.

Government Gardens   GARDENS
(Map p308; Hinemaru St) The manicured Government Gardens surrounding the Rotorua Museum are a wonderful example of the blending of English (rose gardens, croquet lawns and bowling greens) and Māori traditions (carvings at the entrance and subtly blended into the buildings). Being Rotorua, there are steaming thermal pools scattered about, and it's well worth taking a walk along the active geothermal area at the lake's edge.

Rotorua Museum   NOTABLE BUILDING
(Map p308; ☑07-350 1814; www.rotoruamuseum.co.nz; Oruawhata Dr; adult/child $20/8) Constructed in a striking faux-Tudor style, Rotorua's most magnificent building opened in 1908 as an elegant spa retreat called the Bath House.

HINEMOA & TŪTĀNEKAI – A LOVE STORY

Hinemoa was a young woman of a *hapū* (subtribe) that lived on the eastern shore of Lake Rotorua, while Tūtānekai was a young man of a Mokoia Island *hapū*. The pair met and fell in love during a regular tribal meeting. While both were of high birth, Tūtānekai was illegitimate, so marriage between the two was forbidden.

Home on Mokoia, the lovesick Tūtānekai played his flute for his love, the wind carrying the melody across the water. Hinemoa heard his declaration, but her people took to tying up the canoes at night to ensure she wouldn't go to him.

Finally, Tūtānekai's music won her over. Hinemoa undressed and swam the long distance from the shore to the island. When she arrived on Mokoia, Hinemoa found herself in a quandary. Having shed her clothing in order to swim, she could hardly walk into Tūtānekai's village naked. She hopped into a hot pool to think about her next move.

Eventually a man came to fetch water from a spring beside the hot pool. In a deep man's voice, Hinemoa called out, 'Who is it?' The man replied that he was Tūtānekai's slave on a water run. Hinemoa grabbed the slave's calabash (gourd) and smashed it to pieces. More slaves came, but she smashed their calabashes too, until finally Tūtānekai came to the pool and demanded that the interloper identify himself – imagine his surprise when it turned out to be Hinemoa. He secreted her into his hut.

Next morning, after a suspiciously long lie-in, a slave reported that someone was in Tūtānekai's bed. The two lovers were rumbled, and when Hinemoa's superhuman efforts to reach Tūtānekai had been revealed, their union was celebrated.

Descendants of Hinemoa and Tūtānekai still live around Rotorua today.

In 1969 it was converted into a museum, with an art gallery added later. Sadly it was closed in November 2016 after cracks were spotted following the major earthquake in Kaikoura, 650km away. Seismic strengthening was being planned at the time of research, but the work is expected to take years to complete.

Kuirau Park
PARK

(Map p308; Ranolf St) Want some affordable geothermal thrills? Just west of central Rotorua is Kuirau Park, a volcanic area you can explore for free. It's a wonderful juxtaposition of genteel gardening and nature at its most unpredictable. Steam hisses and mud boils from fenced-off sections, while parents push strollers past duck-filled ponds and through the wisteria arbour. Occasional eruptions cover the park in mud, thwarting the best plans of the council's gardeners.

◉ Whakarewarewa

Rotorua's main drawcard is Whakarewarewa (pronounced 'fah-kah-*reh*-wah-*reh*-wah'), a geothermal reserve 3km south of the city centre. This area's full name is Te Whakarewarewatanga o te Ope Taua a Wāhiao, meaning 'The War Dance of the War Party of Wāhiao'. The area is as famous for its Māori cultural significance as for its steam and bubbling mud. There are more than 500 springs here, including some famed geysers.

The active area is split between the still-lived-in Māori village of Whakarewarewa (p308) and the Te Puia complex, which are separated from each other by a fence. Both offer cultural performances and geothermal activity galore; the village is cheaper to visit but Te Puia has a kiwi house and important Māori art institutions.

Te Puia
CULTURAL CENTRE

(Map p320; ☑ 07-348 9047; www.tepuia.com; Hemo Rd, Whakarewarewa; adult/child $54/29, incl performance $69/35, Te Pō $125/63; ⊗ 8am-5pm) Te Puia dials up the heat on *Māoritanga* (things Māori) with explosive performances from both its cultural troupe and from **Pōhutu** (Big Splash), its famous geyser which erupts around 20 times a day, spurting hot water up to 30m skyward. You'll know when it's about to blow because the adjacent **Prince of Wales' Feathers** geyser will start up shortly before. Also here is the **National Carving School** and the **National Weaving School**, where you can watch the students at work.

Daytime visits (*Te Rā*) include an informative guided tour of the entire complex (departing on the hour), which also features a *wharenui* (carved meeting house), a recreated precolonial village, a nocturnal kiwi enclosure and a large chunk of the Whakarewarewa thermal zone, including three major geysers and a huge pool of boiling mud. After the tour you're welcome to wander

Rotorua

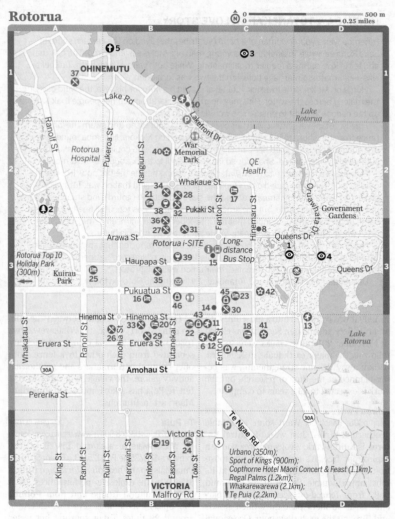

around at your leisure. It's well worth paying extra for the cultural performance (10.15am, 12.15pm and 3.15pm), incorporating a traditional welcome into the *wharenui* and a 45-minute *kapa haka* (traditional song and dance) concert.

The three-hour *Te Pō* (night) experience starts at 6pm and includes a cultural show and a *hāngi* meal, followed by a tour through the thermal zone on a people mover.

The exit is, inevitably, through the gift shop, which in this case gives you the opportunity to buy genuine Māori art and craft,

along with beauty products made from Te Puia's mineral-rich mud.

Whakarewarewa VILLAGE
(Map p320; ☑ 07-349 3463; www.whakarewa
rewa.com; 17 Tyron St; adult/child $40/18, incl
hāngi $70/40; ☺ 8.30am-5pm) Unlike made-
for-tourists experiences of Māori culture,
Whakarewarewa is a living village where the
local Tūhourangi/Ngāti Wāhiao people have
resided for centuries. Villagers lead the tours
(departing hourly from 9am to 4pm) and tell
stories of their way of life amid the steamy
bubbling pools, silica terraces and geysers.

Rotorua

◉ Sights
1 Government Gardens............................C3
2 Kuirau Park...A2
3 Lake Rotorua..C1
4 Rotorua Museum..................................D3
5 St Faith's Anglican Church..................B1

◉ Activities, Courses & Tours
6 Bike Barn...C4
7 Blue Baths..D3
8 Happy Ewe Tours.................................C3
9 Kawarau Jet..B1
10 Mana Adventures.................................B1
11 Mountain Bike Rotorua Adventure
    Hub..C4
12 O'Keefe's Anglers Depot C4
13 Polynesian Spa.....................................D4
14 Rotorua Duck Tours.............................C3
15 Thermal Land Shuttle...........................C3
   Volcanic Air .... (see 10)
   Wall ....(see 22)

◉ Sleeping
16 Astray...B3
17 Aura..C2
18 Crash Palace..C4
19 Funky Green Voyager...........................B5
20 Quest Rotorua Central B4
21 Regent of Rotorua...............................B2
22 Rock Solid Backpackers.......................B4
23 Rotorua Central Backpackers C3
24 Victoria Lodge......................................B5

25 YHA Rotorua...A3

◉ Eating
26 Abracadabra Cafe Bar B4
27 Artisan Cafe B3
28 Atticus Finch..B2
29 Capers Epicurean.................................B4
30 Coconut Cafe & Restaurant C3
31 Fat Dog...B3
32 Indian Star..B2
33 Le Café de Paris...................................B4
34 Leonardo's Pure Italian.......................B2
35 Sabroso..B3
36 Thai Restaurant....................................B3
37 Third Place..A1

◉ Drinking & Nightlife
38 Brew B2
39 Pig & Whistle..B3
   Ponsonby Rd...............................(see 34)

◉ Entertainment
   Basement Cinema.......................(see 22)
40 Matariki...B2
41 Millennium Hotel Feast & Revue C4
42 Tamaki Māori Village............................C3

◉ Shopping
43 Moko 101 ....B4
44 Mountain Jade C4
45 Rākai Jade...C3
46 Rotorua Night Market B3

While most of the geothermal zone is across the fence in Te Puia, the view of the Pōhutu geyser is just as good from here, and considerably cheaper.

The admission also includes a cultural performance (daily at 11.15am and 2pm, with an additional show at 12.30pm from November to March) and a self-guided nature trail. The village shops sell authentic arts and crafts, and you can learn more about Māori traditions such as flax weaving, carving and *tā moko* (tattooing). Nearby you can eat tasty, buttery sweetcorn ($2) pulled straight out of the hot mineral pool – the only genuine geothermal *hāngi* meal in town.

Redwoods Whakarewarewa Forest FOREST
(Map p320; ☑07-350 0110; www.redwoods.co.nz; Long Mile Rd, Whakarewarewa) This magical forest park is 3km southeast of town on Tarawera Rd. From 1899, 170 tree species were planted here to see which could be grown successfully for timber. Mighty Californian redwoods (up to 72m high) give the park its grandeur today. Walking tracks range from a half-hour wander through the Redwood Grove to a whole-day route to the Blue and Green Lakes. Several walks start from the **Redwoods i-SITE** (Map p320; ☑07-350 0110; www.redwoods.co.nz; Long Mile Rd, Whakarewarewa; ⊙8.30am-9.30pm), where you'll also find the spectacular Redwoods Treewalk (p313).

Aside from walking, the forest is great for picnics, and is acclaimed for its accessible mountain biking. There are close to 100km of tracks to keep bikers of all skill levels happy for days on end. Note that not all tracks in the forest are designated for bikers, so adhere to the signposts. Pick up a trail map at the i-SITE. Mountain Bike Rotorua (p311) and Planet Bike (p311) offer bike hire, across the park off Waipa State Mill Rd, where there are also toilets and a shower. At the time of research, a professional-standard BMX track was being constructed in this section of the park.

◉ Ohinemutu

Ohinemutu is a lakeside Māori village that is home to around 260 people. Highlights include the 1905 **Tama-te-Kapua Meeting House** (not open to visitors), many steaming volcanic vents, and the wonderful Māori-British mash-up that is St Faith's. Be respectful if you visit the village: the residents don't appreciate loud, nosy tourists wandering around taking photos of their private property.

St Faith's Anglican Church CHURCH
(Map p308; ☑ 07-348 2393; Korokai St, Ohinemutu; admission by donation; ⊙ 8am-6pm, services 9am Sun & 10am Wed) Consecrated in 1918, Ohinemutu's historic timber church is intricately decorated with Māori carvings, *tukutuku* (woven panels), painted scrollwork and stained-glass windows. One window features an etched image of Christ wearing a Māori cloak, appearing to walk on the waters of Lake Rotorua, visible through the glass. Behind the church is a military graveyard and memorial.

◉ Fairy Springs

Volcanic Hills Winery WINERY
(Map p320; ☑ 07-282 2018; www.volcanichills.co.nz; 176 Fairy Springs Rd, Fairy Springs; tastings 3/5 wines $9.50/15; ⊙ 11am-5.30pm) Perched at the top of the gondola, this winery-run bar gives you

the opportunity to sample its vintages while soaking up stupendous lake views. The wine is made at the bottom of the hill from grapes sourced from NZ's wine regions. You'll save a couple of dollars if you purchase your tasting as a combo with your gondola ticket.

Rainbow Springs NATURE CENTRE
(Map p320; ☑ 07-350 0440; www.rainbowsprings. co.nz; 192 Fairy Springs Rd, Fairy Springs; 24hr passes adult/child/family $40/20/99; ⊙ 8.30am-10pm) 🌿 The natural springs here are home to wild trout and eels, which you can peer at through an underwater viewer. There are interpretive walkways, a 'Big Splash' water ride and plenty of animals, including tuatara (a native reptile) and native birds. The **Kiwi Encounter** offers a rare peek into the lives of these endangered birds: excellent 30-minute tours (an extra $10 per person) have you tiptoeing through incubator and hatchery areas. There's also a free-flight exotic bird show at 11.30am. It's around 3km north of central Rotorua.

◉ Ngongotaha & Ngongotaha Valley

Wingspan BIRD SANCTUARY
(Map p320; ☑ 07-357 4469; www.wingspan.co.nz; 1164 Paradise Valley Rd, Ngongotaha Valley; adult/

ℹ️ ROTORUA ON THE CHEAP

In NZ's ever-expanding quest for high-value tourism (ie targeted to the very rich), it can sometimes feel like the urge to fleece has gravitated from the sheep farms to the tourist attractions. Sadly, this is particularly true in Rotorua. However, there are still ways for the budget-conscious traveller to get a good whiff of this geothermal and cultural wonder.

Thermal activity can be seen free of charge in **Kuirau Park** (p307), Ohinemutu village and along the lakeshore by the **Government Gardens** (p306). If it's warm water you're after, eschew the pricey spas and take a dip at the **Blue Baths** (p313) or, for a mineral soak, go to **Hell's Gate** (p322). Many of the local motels and holiday parks also have their own thermally heated pools, some with actual mineral water.

There are lots of nature walks in the district; enquire at the Rotorua i-SITE (p319). If the **Redwoods Treewalk** (p313) is outside your budget, park nearby and wander into the forest. Go at night for the magical sight of the lanterns illuminating the canopy.

If you can afford to visit just one of the ticketed geothermal areas, here's a guide for helping you choose:

➡ **Whakarewarewa** (p308) An authentic experience of Māori life amid the steam.

➡ **Te Puia** (p307) A slick combination of geothermal features and traditional Māori culture, but by far the most expensive.

➡ **Waimangu Volcanic Valley** (p321) The best for feeling like you're among nature at its wildest, without the crowds.

➡ **Wai-o-Tapu Thermal Wonderland** (p321) The most impressive and colourful geothermal features and also the cheapest, but usually the most crowded.

➡ **Hell's Gate** (p322) More of the same but with the added bonus of a muddy foot bath at the end.

child $25/10; ⊙9am-3pm) The Wingspan National Bird of Prey Centre is dedicated to conserving threatened NZ raptors, particularly the karearea (NZ falcon). Learn about the birds in the museum display, then take a sneaky peek into the incubation area before walking through the all-weather aviary. Make sure you're here by 1.30pm for the 2pm flying display.

Agrodome
AGRICULTURAL CENTRE

(Map p320; ☑07-357 1050; www.agrodome. co.nz; 141 Western Rd, Ngongotaha; adult/child shows $36/19, tours $49/25, wagon ride $20/15, 4WD tour $99/89; ⊙8.30am-5pm) Learn everything you need to know about sheep at this model Kiwi farm. Shows (9.30am, 11am and 2.30pm) include a parade of champion rams, lamb feeding, and shearing, milking and doggy displays. Yes, some of the jokes are corny, but it's still very entertaining. Farm tours on a tractor train depart at 10.40am, 12.10pm, 1.30pm and 3.40pm. You can also take a ride on a Clydesdale-drawn wagon or rev it up on a 4WD Back Country Adventure (10.45am, 12.15pm and 3.45pm).

Paradise Valley Springs
NATURE CENTRE

(☑07-348 9667; www.paradisevalleysprings.co.nz; 467 Paradise Valley Rd, Ngongotaha Valley; adult/child $30/15; ⊙8am-dusk, last entry 5pm) 🍃 At the foot of Mt Ngongotaha, 8km from Rotorua, this 6-hectare park has trout springs, big slippery eels, native birds and various land-dwelling animals such as deer, alpacas, possums and a pride of lions (fed at 2.30pm). There's also a coffee shop and an elevated treetop walkway.

🏃 Activities

Cycling

Between Redwoods Whakarewarewa Forest (p309) and the Skyline Rotorua MTB Gravity Park, Rotorua is well established as a mountain-biking and BMX destination. Additionally, the two-day, 48km **Te Ara Ahi (Thermal by Bike)** trail starts in Rotorua and heads south via various geothermal attractions to the Waikite Valley Thermal Pools (p323). This intermediate-level route is designated as one of the New Zealand Cycle Trail's 'Great Rides' (www.nzcycletrail. com). For more information, enquire at the Rotorua i-SITE or get online at www.ride rotorua.com.

★Skyline Rotorua
MTB Gravity Park
MOUNTAIN BIKING

(Map p320; ☑07-347 0027; www.skyline.co.nz; 178 Fairy Springs Rd, Fairy Springs; 1/15/40 gondola uplifts with bike $30/59/110; ⊙9am-5.30pm) More evidence of Rotorua's status as a world-class mountain-biking destination is the network of 11 MTB tracks coursing down Mt Ngongotaha. There are options for riders of all experience levels, and access to the top of the park is provided by the Skyline gondola (p312). Bike rental is available on-site from Mountain Bike Rotorua.

Planet Bike
CYCLING

(Map p320; ☑07-346 1717; www.planetbike.co.nz; 8 Waipa Bypass Rd, Whakarewarewa; hire per 2hr/day from $35/60) Bike hire (hardtail, full suspension, electric and kids' bikes) and guided mountain-bike rides (from $150) in the Redwoods Whakarewarewa Forest (p309).

Mountain Bike Rotorua
MOUNTAIN BIKING

(Map p320; ☑07-348 4295; www.mtbrotorua. co.nz; Waipa State Mill Rd, Whakarewarewa; hire per 2hr/day from $35/60, guided rides from $130; ⊙9am-5pm) This outfit hires out bikes at the Waipa Mill car park entrance to the Redwoods Whakarewarewa Forest (p309), the starting point for the bike trails. You can also stop by their central Rotorua **adventure hub** (Map p308; ☑07-348 4290; www.mtbrotorua.co.nz; 1128 Hinemoa St; ⊙9am-5pm) for rentals, mountain-biking information and a cool little cafe, and they can fit you out with a bike at the Skyline MTB Gravity Park, too.

Bike Barn
CYCLING

(Map p308; ☑07-347 1151; www.bikebarn.co.nz; 1109 Eruera St; bikes per half-/full day from $35/50; ⊙8.30am-5.30pm Mon-Fri, 10am-3pm Sat & Sun) Bike hire (hardtail and full suspension) and repairs in downtown Rotorua.

Action & Adventure
Rotorua Canopy Tours
ADVENTURE SPORTS

(Map p320; ☑07-343 1001; www.canopytours. co.nz; 147 Fairy Springs Rd, Fairy Springs; 3hr tours adult/child $149/119; ⊙8am-8pm Oct-Apr, to 6pm May-Sep) Explore a 1.2km web of bridges, flying foxes, zip-lines and platforms, 22m high in a lush native forest canopy 10 minutes out of town (they say that rimu tree is 1000 years old!), with plenty of native birds to keep you company. All trips depart from their office opposite the gondola.

DON'T MISS

HAKA & HĀNGI

Māori culture is a big-ticket item in Rotorua and, although the experiences are commercialised, they're still a great introduction to authentic Māori traditions. The two big activities are *kapa haka* (traditional performing arts) concerts and *hāngi* (earth-cooked) feasts, often packaged together in an evening's entertainment featuring a *pōwhiri* (welcoming ceremony), the famous *haka* (war dance), *waiata* (songs) and *poi* dances, where women showcase their dexterity by twirling balls of flax.

Tamaki Māori Village and family-run Mitai Māori Village are established favourites, with the experience heightened due to their recreated precolonial village settings. **Te Puia** (p307) and **Whakarewarewa** (p308) offer the added thrill of being situated within an active geothermal zone. Both stage daytime shows; Te Puia also has an evening *hāngi*-and-show package while Whakarewarewa serves *hāngi*-cooked lunches.

Many of the big hotels also offer packages; these may lack the magical settings but they're usually considerably cheaper.

Tamaki Māori Village (Map p308; ☑07-349 2999; www.tamakimaorivillage.co.nz; booking office 1220 Hinemaru St; adult/child $130/70) Tamaki offers a 3½-hour twilight Māori cultural experience starting with free transfers from Rotorua to its recreated precolonial village, 15km south of Rotorua. The encounter is very hands-on, taking you on an interactive journey through Māori history, arts, traditions and customs. The concert is followed by a *hāngi*.

Mitai Māori Village (Map p320; ☑07-343 9132; www.mitai.co.nz; 196 Fairy Springs Rd, Fairy Springs; adult $116, child $23-58; ⊙6.30pm) This family-run outfit offers a popular three-hour evening event with a concert, *hāngi* and glowworm bush walk. The experience starts with the arrival of a *waka taua* (war canoe) and can be combined with a night-time tour of Rainbow Springs next door, including a walk through the kiwi enclosure. Pick-ups and a concert-only option are available.

Matariki (Map p308; ☑07-346 3888; www.novotelrotorua.co.nz; 11 Tutanekai St; concerts adult/child $35/18, incl hāngi $69/35) The Novotel's Māori cultural experience includes a performance of traditional song and dance followed by a *hāngi*. It's held in a separate building adjacent to the hotel, facing the lakeside park.

Millennium Hotel Feast & Revue (Map p308; ☑07-347 1234; www.millenniumrotorua.co.nz; 1270 Hinemaru St; adult/child $70/35) Entertaining poolside shows include a live performance from local Māori performers and a *hāngi*.

Copthorne Hotel Māori Concert & Feast (Map p320; ☑07-348 0199; www.millenniumhotels.co.nz; 328 Fenton St, Glenholme; per person $47) One of Rotorua's less expensive Māori concert and *hāngi* options. It only operates when booked by a tour group; call ahead and see whether one is scheduled during your stay.

Skyline Rotorua CABLE CAR
(Map p320; ☑07-347 0027; www.skyline.co.nz; 178 Fairy Springs Rd, Fairy Springs; adult/child gondola $30/15; ⊙9am-10pm) The cable car ride up the side of Mt Ngongotaha is only a teaser for the thrills on offer at the top. Most popular is the **luge**, which shoots along three different tracks (one/three/five/seven rides $14/28/38/45). For even speedier antics, try the **Sky Swing** (adult/child $89/74), the **Zoom Zipline** ($95/85) or the mountain-bike Gravity Park. The summit also offers a restaurant, wine-tasting at the Volcanic Hills Winery (p310), a nature trail and stargazing sessions ($93/49).

Note that the Sky Swing and Zipline prices include the gondola and five luge rides. A baffling array of combination tickets is available.

Adventure Playground OUTDOORS
(Map p320; ☑0800 782 396; www.adventureplayground.co.nz; 451 Ngongotaha Rd, Ngongotaha; ⊙from 10am) Horse trekking (one/two hours $65/120), clay-bird shooting (from $75) and self-drive 4WD tours (half-/full day $85/140) are all on offer at this versatile activities centre. Kids can take a 10-minute hand-held horse ride for $20.

Kawarau Jet
BOATING

(Map p308; ☑07-343 7600; www.kjetrotorua. co.nz; Lakefront Dr; 30min adult/child $85/54; ☺9am-6pm) Speed things up on a jetboat ride with Kawarau Jet, which tears around the lake. Parasailing (30 minutes tandem/solo $85/115) is also available.

Agroventures
ADVENTURE SPORTS

(Map p320; ☑07-357 4747; www.agroventures. co.nz; 1335 Paradise Valley Rd, Ngongotaha; 1/2/4 rides $49/85/129, bungy $129; ☺9am-5pm) Agroventures is a hive of action, 9km north of Rotorua (free shuttles available). Start off with the 43m **bungy** and the **Swoop**, a 130km/h swing. The **Freefall Xtreme** simulates skydiving, and also here is the **Shweeb**, a monorail velodrome from which you hang in a clear capsule and pedal yourself along at speeds of up to 50km/h.

Alongside is the **Agrojet**, one of NZ's fastest jetboats, splashing and weaving around a very tight 1km course. Plus there's a **BMX** airbag and ramps for practising your jumps (two hours $30, BYO bike).

Wall
CLIMBING

(Map p308; ☑07-350 1400; www.basementcinema. co.nz; 1140 Hinemoa St; adult/child $16/13, shoe hire $5; ☺noon-10pm Mon-Fri, 10am-9pm Sat & Sun) Get limbered up at the Wall, a three-storey indoor climbing wall with overhangs aplenty.

Zorb
ADVENTURE SPORTS

(Map p320; ☑07-357 5100; www.zorb.com; 149 Western Rd, Ngongotaha; 1-/2-/3-person ride $45/70/90; ☺9am-5pm, to 7pm Jan) The Zorb is 9km north of Rotorua on SH5 – look for the grassy hillside with large, clear, people-filled spheres rolling down it. There are three courses: 150m straight, 180m zigzag or 250m 'Drop'. Do your zorb strapped in and dry, or freestyle with water thrown in. And you can even rattle around with up to two friends inside.

OGO
ADVENTURE SPORTS

(Map p320; ☑07-343 7676; www.ogo.co.nz; 525 Ngongotaha Rd, Fairy Springs; 1/2/3 rides $45/80/99; ☺9am-5pm) The OGO (about 5km north of town) involves careening down a grassy hillside in a big bubble, with water or without. Yes, it is very similar to the Zorb.

aMAZEme
OUTDOORS

(Map p320; ☑07-357 5759; www.amazeme.co.nz; 1335 Paradise Valley Rd, Ngongotaha; adult/child/family $16/10/50; ☺10am-4pm; ⊞) This amazing 1.4km maze is constructed from immaculately pruned, head-high escallonia hedge.

Lose yourself (or the kids) in the endless spirals. There's also a butterfly house and a small critter petting zoo.

Swimming & Soaking

Polynesian Spa
HOT SPRINGS

(Map p308; ☑07-348 1328; www.polynesianspa. co.nz; 1000 Hinemoa St; family pools adult/child $23/10, adult/deluxe pools $30/50, private pools per 30min from $20; ☺8am-11pm) A bathhouse opened at these Government Gardens springs in 1882, and people have been taking to the waters ever since. Choose between the heated freshwater family pool, or the series of small adults-only mineral pools (36°C to 42°C) by the lake's edge. The deluxe option offers even more picturesque rock-lined lakeside pools and includes a free locker ($5 otherwise) and towel.

Spa treatments are also available, including massage, mud and beauty treatments.

Blue Baths
SWIMMING

(Map p308; ☑07-350 2119; www.bluebaths.co.nz; Queens Dr; adult/child $11/6; ☺10am-6pm) The gorgeous Spanish Mission-style Blue Baths opened in 1933 (and, amazingly, were closed from 1982 to 1999) and they now regularly host special events (performances, weddings etc). If you feel like taking a dip, the pool is a fraction of the price of the nearby Polynesian Spa, but note that while it's geothermically heated, it's not mineral water.

Walking

There are plenty of opportunities to stretch your legs around Rotorua, including the popular lakefront stroll (20 minutes). There are also a couple of good walks at Mt Ngongotaha: the easy 2.5km **Ngongotaha Nature Loop** through native forest, and the steep 5km return **Jubilee Track** to the (viewless) summit.

There are also dozens of more challenging tracks in the broader Rotorua Lakes area (p323).

Redwoods Treewalk
WALKING

(Map p320; ☑07-350 0110; www.treewalk.co.nz; Long Mile Rd, Whakarewarewa; adult/child $25/15; ☺8.30am-9.30pm) ✎ More than 500m is traversed on this walkway combining 23 bouncy wooden bridges suspended between century-old redwood trees. Most of the pathway is around 6m off the forest floor, but it ascends to 20m in some parts. It's at its most impressive at night when it's lit by striking wooden lanterns, hung from the trees.

Fishing & Boating

There's always good trout fishing to be had somewhere around Rotorua. Hire a guide or go solo: either way a licence (per day $20) is essential, and available from **O'Keefe's Anglers Depot** (Map p308; ☑07-346 0178; www.okeefesfishing.co.nz; 1113 Eruera St; ⊙8.30am-5pm Mon-Fri, 9am-2pm Sat). Note that not all of the Rotorua Lakes can be fished year-round; check with O'Keefe's or the i-SITE (p319).

Trout Man   FISHING
(Map p320; ☑021 951 174; www.waiteti.com; 14 Okona Cres, Ngongotaha; 2hr/day trips from $55/175) Learn to fish with experienced angler Harvey Clark.

Mana Adventures   BOATING
(Map p308; ☑07-348 4186; www.manaadventures.co.nz; Lakefront Dr; ⊙9am-5pm) Down at the lake, Mana Adventures offers (weather permitting) rental pedal boats (adult/child $10/8 per 20 minutes), kayaks ($16/28 per half-hour/hour) and walking on water inside a giant inflatable ball ($11 per five minutes).

☞ Tours

Happy Ewe Tours   CYCLING
(Map p308; ☑022 622 9252; www.happyewetours.com; departs 1148 Hinemaru St; adult/child $60/30; ⊙10am & 2pm) Saddle up for a three-hour, small-group bike tour of Rotorua, wheeling past 27 sights around the city. It's all flat and slow-paced, so you don't need to be at your physical peak (you're on holiday after all).

Foris Eco Tours   ECOTOUR
(☑07-542 5080; www.foris.co.nz; from $295) ✔ Check out ancient rainforest and native bird life in Whirinaki Te Pua-a-Tāne Conservation Park, or take a rafting and trout-fishing trip along the easy-going Rangitaiki River.

Elite Adventures   TOURS
(☑07-347 8282; www.eliteadventures.co.nz; half-/full day from $155/290) Small-group tours covering a selection of Rotorua's major cultural and natural highlights.

Volcanic Air   TOURS
(Map p308; ☑07-348 9984; www.volcanicair.co.nz; Lakefront Dr; trips $95-1045) Offers a variety of float-plane and helicopter flights taking in Mt Tarawera and surrounding geothermal sites, including a 3½-hour flight over Whakaari.

Rotorua Duck Tours   TOURS
(Map p308; ☑07-345 6522; www.rotoruaduck tours.co.nz; 1241 Fenton St; adult/child $69/45; ⊙tours 11am, 1pm & 3.30pm Oct-Apr, 11am & 2.15pm May-Sep) Ninety-minute trips in an amphibious biofuelled vehicle take in the major sites around town and head out onto three lakes (Rotorua, Okareka and Tikitapu/Blue). Longer Lake Tarawera trips are also available.

Geyser Link Shuttle   TOURS
(☑03-477 9083; www.travelheadfirst.com; half-/full day $82/135) Tours some of the major sights around Rotorua, including a half-day in Wai-O-Tapu or Waimangu, or a full day visiting both. Trips incorporating Hobbiton, Whakarewarewa and Mitai Māori Village are also available.

Thermal Land Shuttle   TOURS
(Map p308; ☑0800 894 287; www.thermal shuttle.co.nz; departs 1167 Fenton St; adult/child from $65/33) Daily scheduled shuttles and tours around a selection of key sights, including Waimangu, Wai-O-Tapu, Waitomo Caves and stops on the Te Ara Ahi cycle trail. Transport-only or entry-inclusive options are available.

🛌 Sleeping

🏙 City Centre

Rotorua Central Backpackers   HOSTEL $
(Map p308; ☑07-349 3285; www.rotorua centralbackpackers.co.nz; 1076 Pukuatua St; dm/s/d without bathroom $28/62/66; 🛜) Built as flats in 1936, this heritage hostel retains original features including dark-wood skirting boards and door frames, deep bathtubs and geothermally powered radiators. Dorms have no more than six beds (and no bunks), plus there's a spa pool and barbecue. Perfect if you're not looking to party.

Crash Palace   HOSTEL $
(Map p308; ☑07-348 8842; www.crashpalace.co.nz; 1271 Hinemaru St; dm/s from $24/50, d with/without bathroom $78/70; @🛜) Crash occupies a big, blue 1930s hotel near Government Gardens. The atmosphere strikes a balance between party and pristine, without too much of either. There's lots of art on the walls, a pool table and DJ console in the lobby, and a beaut terrace and thermally heated hot tub out the back. Limited off-street parking.

YHA Rotorua
HOSTEL $

(Map p308; ✆07-349 4088; www.yha.co.nz; 1278 Haupapa St; dm $26-31, with/without bathroom s $85/75, d from $94/84; @ 🛜) 🗷 Bright and sparkling, this classy, purpose-built hostel is great for those wanting to get outdoors, with staff eager to assist with trip bookings, and bike storage and hire. Pricier rooms come with bathrooms, and there's a barbecue area and deck for hanging out on (though this ain't a party pad). Off-street parking is a bonus.

Rock Solid Backpackers
HOSTEL $

(Map p308; ✆07-282 2053; www.rocksolid rotorua.co.nz; 1140 Hinemoa St; dm/s from $27/60, d with/without bathroom $95/75; 🛜) Cavernous Rock Solid occupies a former shopping mall: you might be bunking down in a florist or a delicatessen. Dorms over the street are sunny, and there's a big, bright kitchen. Downstairs is the Wall (p313) rock-climbing facility, and the hostel's spacious lounge looks right out at the action. Free wi-fi, and table-tennis and pool tables seal the deal.

Astray
MOTEL, HOSTEL $

(Map p308; ✆07-348 1200; www.astray.co.nz; 1202 Pukuatua St; dm/s $25/45, d with/without bathroom from $95/70; 🛜) Even if you are 6ft 3in, Astray – a 'micro-motel' that would probably be more at home in Tokyo than Rotorua – is a decent budget bet. Clean, tidy, quiet, friendly and central: just don't expect acres of space.

Aura
MOTEL $$

(Map p308; ✆07-348 8134; www.aurarotorua.co.nz; 1078 Whakaue St; unit from $145; 🛜🏊) Plenty of Rotorua's motels have thermally heated freshwater spa pools but Aura differentiates itself with two natural mineral-water spas and a heated outdoor swimming pool. It's an older complex but it's been fully renovated, and the friendly owners can sort you out with a free Dutch-style bike for lakeside explorations.

Rotorua Top 10 Holiday Park
HOLIDAY PARK $$

(Map p320; ✆07-348 1886; www.rotoruatop10. co.nz; 1495 Pukuatua St; sites from $55, unit with/without bathroom from $175/150; 🏊@🛜🏊) Everything's kept spick and span at this small but perfectly formed holiday park. Facilities include a small outdoor pool, hot mineral spas and a super children's playground. Cabins are in good nick and have kettles, toasters and small fridges, or you can opt for a smart self-contained motel unit.

Regent of Rotorua
BOUTIQUE HOTEL $$$

(Map p308; ✆07-348 4079; www.regentrotorua. co.nz; 1191 Pukaki St; s/d from $210/280; 🏊🛜🏊) A renovated 1960s motel, the Regent delivers glitzy glam in spades, with hip black-and-white decor, statement mirrors and feature wallpaper. Both the small outdoor and indoor pools are heated. If you tire of the well-regarded restaurant, Tutanekai St (known as Eat Streat) is a brief amble away.

Quest Rotorua Central
APARTMENT $$$

(Map p308; ✆07-929 9808; www.questrotorua central.co.nz; 1192 Hinemoa St; apt from $210; 🏊🛜) Your quest for an upmarket, self-contained apartment ends at this modern four-storey block in the heart of the town centre. Double-glazing keeps the street noise at bay, although Rotorua isn't particularly noisy after dark anyway. Even the studio units are spacious and have full kitchen and laundry facilities.

🏠 Victoria, Glenholme & Fenton Park

Funky Green Voyager
HOSTEL $

(Map p308; ✆07-346 1754; www.funkygreen voyager.co.nz; 4 Union St, Victoria; dm $28-29, with/without bathroom s $70/47, d $78/66; 🛜) 🗷 Green on the outside and the inside – due to several cans of paint and a dedicated environmental policy – the shoe-free Funky GV features laid-back tunes and plenty of sociable chat among a spunky bunch of guests and worldly-wise owners. The best rooms have bathrooms; dorms are roomy with quality mattresses and solid timber bunks.

★ Sport of Kings
MOTEL $$

(Map p320; ✆07-348 2135; www.sportofkings motel.co.nz; 6 Peace St, Fenton Park; units from $159; 🛜🏊) Situated near the racecourse (if you hadn't already guessed), this friendly complex leads the motel pack with 16 spiffy, comfortable units. Some have their own thermal spas, while other guests can book one of the private tubs or splash about in the heated pool. Plus there's an electric-car charging station, a bike wash-down area and free daily newspapers.

Regal Palms
MOTEL $$

(Map p320; ✆07-350 3232; www.regalpalms. co.nz; 350 Fenton St, Glenholme; r from $185; 🏊@🛜🏊) A large upmarket motel with resort ambitions, Regal Palms has tree-shaded gardens, a swimming pool, a gym, a sauna and kids' playground facilities including a mini-golf course. The rooms and apartments – all with spa baths – are spacious and modern, and there's an on-site lounge bar.

Victoria Lodge MOTEL $$
(Map p308; ☎07-348 4039; www.victorialodge.co.nz; 10 Victoria St, Victoria; unit from $129;) The friendly Vic has seen a lot of competitors come and go, maintaining its foothold in the market with individual-feeling units with shallow thermally heated tubs. Fully equipped apartments can squeeze in seven, though four would be comfortable.

Ngongotaha

Waiteti Trout Stream Holiday Park HOLIDAY PARK $
(Map p320; ☎07-357 5255; www.waiteti.com; 14 Okona Cres, Ngongotaha; sites/s/tw from $21/35/55, unit with/without bathroom $105/60;) This keenly maintained campground is a great option if you don't mind the 8km drive into town. Set in gardens abutting a trout-filled stream, it's a cute classic with character-filled motel units, compact cabins, a tidy backpackers' lodge (private rooms only) and beaut campsites by the water. Kayaks and dinghies are free, and you can book a fly-fishing lesson.

Doolan's Country Retreat B&B $$$
(Map p320; ☎07-357 5994; www.doolanscountryretreat.co.nz; 165 Dalbeth Rd, Ngongotaha; r $230-322;) Plonked on a rural hilltop surrounded by lush gardens, this interesting brick house takes the shape of three interconnected octagons, one of which contains a large, open-plan communal lounge and dining area. Three of the four guest bedrooms have en suites, while the fourth has its own bathroom accessed from the corridor.

Mokoia Downs Estate B&B B&B $$$
(Map p320; ☎07-332 2930; www.mokoiadowns.com; 64 Mokoia Rd, Ngongotaha; r $285;) The B&B accommodation here is simple and comfortable, but the real appeal is the warm welcome from the English-Irish owners Mick and Teresa, plus the added attractions at this great semirural retreat. Say hi to the sheep, donkeys and miniature horses, kick back in the private cinema and library, or sample Mick's liqueurs made from organic fruit in his microdistillery.

Other Areas

All Seasons Holiday Park HOLIDAY PARK $$
(Map p320; ☎07-345 6240; www.allseasonsrotorua.co.nz; 50-58 Lee Rd, Hannahs Bay; sites from $23, unit with/without bathroom $129/95;) Jurassic Park meets holiday park at this dinosaur-themed campground, 8km northeast of the city centre. Kids will love the colourful concrete beasts, fanciful playground and covered heated pool. Their parents will appreciate the reasonable rates, the robes in the modern motel units, and the well-equipped campers' kitchen. It's near the airport but there aren't many flights, and none at night.

Sandi's Bed & Breakfast B&B $$
(Map p320; ☎07-348 0884; www.sandisbedandbreakfast.co.nz; 103 Fairy Springs Rd, Fairy Springs; s/d incl breakfast $85/130;) Major renovations were underway when we last visited this friendly B&B, run by the good-humoured Sandi, who offers continental breakfasts and local advice. It's on a busy road a couple of kilometres north of town, so the best bets are the two bohemian chalets out the back.

B&B @ the Redwoods B&B $$
(Map p320; ☎07-345 4499; www.theredwoods.co.nz; 3 Awatea St, Lynmore; r $180-229;) Like it says on the tin, this pleasant place offers three en-suite B&B rooms in a suburban house at the forest's edge. Two have views over the lake while the third faces the front garden. All have access to a large guest lounge where you can help yourself to a hot drink or share an evening glass of wine.

★**City Lights Boutique Lodge** B&B $$$
(Map p320; ☎07-349 1413; www.citylights.nz; 56c Mountain Rd, Western Heights; r/cottage/apt/ste $275/275/285/355;) Looking down on Rotorua from the slopes of Mt Ngongotaha, this upmarket lodge has three en-suite B&B rooms in the main house, a self-contained apartment attached to it and a separate garden cottage further down the drive. Plus there's a gym, a sauna and pet alpacas.

Koura Lodge B&B $$$
(Map p320; ☎07-348 5868; www.kouralodge.co.nz; 209 Kawaha Point Rd, Kawaha Point; r from $525;) Secluded on the lake's western shore, this upmarket lodge features spacious rooms and suites, and a two-bedroom apartment. Decks and balconies segue to lake views, and kayaking right from the property is possible.

Gourmet breakfasts around the huge wooden table are perfect for meeting other travellers. A hot tub and sauna are added diversions.

✖ Eating

The lake end of Tutanekai St – known as 'Eat Streat' – is a car-free strip of eateries beneath a canopy roof. There are plenty of other perfectly adequate options around town but few that are memorable.

Le Café de Paris   CAFE $

(Map p308; ☑ 07-348 1210; www.facebook.com/cafedeparisrotorua; 1206 Hinemoa St; mains $10-18; ⊙ 7.30am-4pm Tue-Sat; ☜) The greeting is *très français* but this little cafe walks a fine line between a traditional *crêperie* and the kind of cafe that Kiwi retirees gravitate to. *Galettes* (savoury crêpes) are cooked to order and served alongside toasted sandwiches and jam scones. The coffee's good too.

Coconut Cafe & Restaurant   SOUTH INDIAN $

(Map p308; ☑ 07-343 6556; www.coconutcafe.co.nz; 1240 Fenton St; mains $9-18; ⊙ 11am-3pm & 5-11pm; ☑⛨) Owned by a friendly southern Indian family from Kerala, this riot of yellow and lime-green decor also serves up authentic dishes from Sri Lanka. Try the fish *moilee* (a hearty Keralan-style curry laced with coconut milk), and wash it down with a Kingfisher beer or a refreshing mango lassi.

Artisan Cafe   CAFE $$

(Map p308; ☑ 07-348 0057; www.artisancafe rotorua.com; 1149 Tutanekai St; mains $11-24; ⊙ 7am-4pm; ☜) A spinning wheel and a Mary Poppins-type bicycle lend a folksy feel to Rotorua's best cafe. Yet there's nothing old-fashioned about the food, which includes cooked breakfasts, burgers, salads and a couple of vegan options. Even hardened blokes should consider ordering the Little Miss Bene, an eggs Benedict of agreeably modest proportions.

Sabroso   LATIN AMERICAN $$

(Map p308; ☑ 07-349 0591; www.sabroso.co.nz; 1184 Haupapa St; mains $21-25; ⊙ 5-9pm Wed-Sun) This modest Latin American *cantina* – adorned with sombreros, guitars and salt-and-pepper shakers made from Corona bottles – serves zingy south-of-the-border fare. The black-bean chilli and the seafood tacos are excellent, as are the zesty margaritas. Booking ahead is highly recommended as Sabroso is *muy popular*. Buy a bottle of the owners' hot sauce to enliven your next Kiwi barbecue.

Abracadabra Cafe Bar   MEDITERRANEAN, MEXICAN $$

(Map p308; ☑ 07-348 3883; www.abracadabra cafe.com; 1263 Amohia St; mains $26-32, tapas $11-15; ⊙ 10.30am-11pm Tue-Sat, to 3pm Sun; ☜⛨) Channelling Spain, Mexico and North Africa, Abracadabra is a magical cave of spicy delights, from beef-and-apricot tagine to chicken enchiladas. There's an attractive front deck and a great beer terrace out the back – perfect for sharing some tapas over a few local craft brews.

Leonardo's Pure Italian   ITALIAN $$

(Map p308; ☑ 07-347 7084; www.leonardospure.co.nz; Eat Streat, 1099 Tutanekai St; mains $22-36; ⊙ 5pm-late; ☑) Although it looks cavernous from the outside, Leonardo's is surprisingly pleasant inside, with dark wood, soft lighting and welcoming service. Sometimes the simple things are the best, and that's certainly the case with its traditional (ie creamless) *tagliatelle alla carbonara*. The desserts are more hit and miss.

Thai Restaurant   THAI $$

(Map p308; ☑ 07-348-6677; www.thethai restaurant.co.nz; 1141 Tutanekai St; mains $24-29; ⊙ noon-2.30pm & 5pm-late; ☑) Our pick of the global selection of ethnic eateries along Tutanekai St, the Thai overcomes an unimaginative name with excellent service and top-notch renditions of classics such as *pad thai* and green curry. The seafood dishes are particularly good.

Atticus Finch   INTERNATIONAL $$

(Map p308; ☑ 07-460 0400; www.atticusfinch.co.nz; Eat Streat, 1106 Tutanekai St; lunch $16-20, shared plates $7.50-34; ⊙ noon-2.30pm & 5pm-late; ☑) Named after the righteous lawyer in *To Kill a Mockingbird*, the hippest spot on Eat Streat follows through with a Harper Lee cocktail and a Scout Sangria. Beyond the literary references, the menu of shared plates channels Asia and the Mediterranean rather than the American South, and a concise menu of NZ beer and wine imparts a local flavour.

Third Place   CAFE $$

(Map p308; ☑ 07-349 4852; www.thirdplace cafe.co.nz; 35 Lake Rd, Ohinemutu; mains $15-20; ⊙ 7.30am-4pm; ☜) This super-friendly cafe is away from the hubbub and has awesome lake views. All-day breakfast/brunch sidesteps neatly between fish and chips, and a 'mumble jumble' of crushed kumara (sweet potato), green tomatoes and spicy chorizo topped with a poached egg and hollandaise sauce. Hangover? What hangover? Slide into a red-leather couch or score a window seat overlooking Ohinemutu.

Fat Dog
CAFE $$

(Map p308; ☑07-347 7586; www.fatdogcafe.co.nz; 1161 Arawa St; mains breakfast $13-19, lunch & dinner $19-26; ⊙7am-9pm; 🛜🐾) With paw prints and silly poems painted on the walls, this is the town's most child-friendly cafe. During the day it dishes up burgers, nachos, salads and massive sandwiches; in the evening it's candlelit lamb shanks and venison. Fine craft brews are also served.

Urbano
BISTRO $$

(Map p320; ☑07-349 3770; www.urbanobistro. co.nz; 289 Fenton St, Glenholme; mains brunch $15-25, dinner $26-44; ⊙9am-11pm Mon-Sat, to 3pm Sun) This hip suburban diner, with a darkened interior and streetside tables, offers casual cafe-style dining by day (cooked breakfasts, salads, burgers, curry of the day) and a more ritzy bistro vibe at night. Coffee comes in bucket-like proportions.

Capers Epicurean
CAFE $$

(Map p308; ☑07-348 8818; www.capers.co.nz; 1181 Eruera St; mains brunch $13-23, dinner $23-26; ⊙7am-9pm; 🐾) This slick, barn-like cafe is perennially busy, with diners choosing from gourmet sandwiches, salads and cakes, and a blackboard menu of breakfasts and other tasty hot dishes. The deli section is stocked with relishes, jams and chocolates.

Indian Star
INDIAN $$

(Map p308; ☑07-343 6222; www.indianstar.co.nz; Eat Street, 1118 Tutanekai St; mains $15-23; ⊙11am-2pm & 5-10pm; 🍴) This is one of many Indian eateries around town, elevating itself above the competition with immaculate service and reliable renditions of subcontinental classics. It has sizeable portions and good vegetarian selections (try the chickpea masala).

Drinking & Entertainment

Ponsonby Rd
COCKTAIL BAR

(Map p308; ☑021 151 2036; www.ponsonbyrd. co.nz; Eat Street, 1109 Tutanekai St; ⊙4pm-3am Tue-Sat; 🛜) Former TV weatherman turned Labour MP Tamati Coffey has introduced an approximation of flashy big-city style to Rotorua – the bar's name is a nod to an Auckland eating strip. Drenched in red light and trimmed with velvet, the decor is certainly vibrant, while the front terrace is perfect for cocktail-sipping and people-watching. Look forward to live music most weekends.

Brew
CRAFT BEER

(Map p308; ☑07-346 0976; www.brewpub.co.nz; Eat Streat, 1103 Tutanekai St; ⊙11am-1am) Run by the lads from Croucher Brewing Co, Rotorua's best microbrewers, Brew sits in a sunny spot on 'Eat Streat'. Thirteen taps showcase the best of Croucher's brews as well as guest beers from NZ and overseas. Try the hoppy Sulfur City Pilsner with pizza or a burger. There's regular live music, too.

Pig & Whistle
PUB

(Map p308; ☑07-347 3025; www.pigandwhistle. co.nz; 1182 Tutanekai St; ⊙11am-late; 🛜) Inside an art-deco former police station (look for the Māori motifs on the facade), this busy pub serves up frosty lager, big-screen TVs, a beer garden, live music and pub grub. The menu runs the gamut from harissa-spiced chicken salad to hearty burgers and fish and chips.

Basement Cinema
CINEMA

(Map p308; ☑07-350 1400; www.basement cinema.co.nz; 1140 Hinemoa St; adult/child $15/12; ⊙sessions vary) Oddly combined with a rock-climbing facility and a hostel, Basement offers offbeat, foreign-language and art-house flicks. Tickets are just $10 on Tuesdays.

🛍 Shopping

South of town, Te Puia and Whakarewarewa Village have excellent selections of genuine Māori-made arts.

Rotorua Night Market
MARKET

(Map p308; www.rotoruanightmarket.co.nz; Tutanekai St; ⊙5pm-late Thu) Tutanekai St is closed off on Thursday nights between Haupapa and Hinemoa Sts to allow this market to spread its wings. Expect local arts and crafts, souvenirs, cheesy buskers, coffee, wine and plenty of ethnically diverse food stalls for dinner.

Rākai Jade
ARTS & CRAFTS

(Map p308; ☑027 443 9295; www.rakaijade.co.nz; 1234 Fenton St; ⊙9am-5pm Mon-Sat) In addition to purchasing off-the-shelf *pounamu* (greenstone, jade) pieces, you can work with Rākai's on-site team of local Māori carvers to design and carve your own pendant or jewellery. A day's notice for 'Carve Your Own' experiences ($150) is preferred if possible; allow a full day.

Mountain Jade
ARTS & CRAFTS

(Map p308; ☑07-349 1828; www.mountainjade. co.nz; 1288 Fenton St; ⊙9am-6pm) Watch the carvers at work through the streetside window then call in to peruse the high-end handcrafted greenstone jewellery and other objects. There's a second store at 1189 Fenton St.

Moko 101
ART

(Map p308; ☑ 021 165 7624; www.facebook.com/
MOKO101; 1130a Hinemoa St; booking fee $50,
tattooing per hour $150; ☺ 10am-5pm Mon-Fri)
Traditional *tā moko* (Māori tattooing) is
offered here, albeit with modern tattooing equipment rather than stone chisels.
Works from local Māori artists are also displayed for sale.

ℹ Information

MEDICAL SERVICES

Lakes Primecare (☑ 07-348 1000; 1165 Tutanekai St; ☺ 8am-10pm) Urgent medical care
with a late-opening pharmacy next door.

Rotorua Hospital (☑ 07-348 1199; www.
lakesdhb.govt.nz; Pukeroa Rd; ☺ 24hr) Round-
the-clock emergency department.

TOURIST INFORMATION

Redwoods i-SITE (p309) Sells tickets for the
Redwoods Treewalk, and provides information
on Whakarewarewa Forest and all of Rotorua.

Rotorua i-SITE (Map p308; ☑ 07-348 5179;
www.rotoruanz.com; 1167 Fenton St; ☺ 7.30am-
6pm; ☎) The hub for travel information and
bookings, including DOC walks. Also has a
charging station, showers and lockers, and
plenty of information on Rotorua's world-class
mountain-biking scene.

ℹ Getting There & Away

AIR

Air New Zealand (☑ 0800 737 000; www.
airnewzealand.co.nz) flies to/from Auckland,
Wellington and Christchurch.

BUS

All of the **long-distance buses** (Map p308; Fenton St) stop outside the Rotorua i-SITE, where
you can arrange bookings.

InterCity (☑ 07-348 0366; www.intercity.
co.nz) destinations include Auckland (from
$21, four hours, six daily), Hamilton (from
$15, 1½ hours, five daily), Taupo (from $13,
one hour, four daily), Napier ($20, four hours,
daily) and Wellington (from $26, 7½ hours,
three daily).

Mana Bus (☑ 09-367 9140; www.manabus.
com) has coaches to/from Auckland (from $21,
four hours, five daily), Hamilton ($20, 1¾ hours,
daily), Taupo ($23, one hour, two daily), Napier
($23, 3¼ hours, daily) and Wellington (from
$25, 7¼ hours, two daily).

Baybus (☑ 0800 422 928; www.baybus.co.nz)
operates the twice-daily Twin City Express
service to/from Tauranga ($12.20, 1½ hours) and
Mt Maunganui ($11.60, 1¾ hours) via Okere Falls
($3.90, 25 minutes).

ℹ Getting Around

TO/FROM THE AIRPORT

Rotorua Airport (ROT; Map p320; ☑ 07-345
8800; www.rotorua-airport.co.nz; SH30) is located 9km northeast of town. **Super Shuttle**
(☑ 09-522 5100; www.supershuttle.co.nz; 1st
passenger/each additional passenger $21/5)
offers a door-to-door airport service. **Baybus**
(p319) route 10 stops at the airport hourly. A
taxi to/from the town centre costs about $30.

BUS

Baybus (p319) has buses operating on 11 local
routes from 6.30am to 6pm (cash fare $2.70,
day pass $8.60). The most useful are route 1 to
Ngongotaha (25 minutes, hourly) via Rainbow
Springs/Skyline Gondola, 3 to the Redwoods
(10 minutes, half-hourly), 10 to the airport (18
minutes, hourly) and 11 to Whakarewarewa (13
minutes, half-hourly).

Many local attractions offer free pick-up/drop-
off shuttle services.

CAR & MOTORCYCLE

The big-name car-hire companies vie for your attention at Rotorua Airport. Otherwise, try **Rent
a Dent** (☑ 07-349 3993; www.rentadent.co.nz;
39 Fairy Springs Rd, Fairy Springs; ☺ 8am-5pm
Mon-Fri, to noon Sat).

Rotorua Lakes

Lake Rotorua is the largest of 18 *roto* (lakes)
scattered like splashes from an upturned
wine glass to the north and east of the town
of Rotorua. The district's explosive volcanic
past and steamy present is on display at various interesting sites arrayed around the lakes
and the three main rivers that connect them.

◎ Sights

★ Waimangu
Volcanic Valley
NATURAL FEATURE

(Map p320; ☑ 07-366 6137; www.waimangu.co.nz;
587 Waimangu Rd; adult/child walk $39/12, cruise
$45/12; ☺ 8.30am-5pm, last admission 3pm) Cre-
ated during the eruption of Mt Tarawera
in 1886, the Waimangu geothermal area
spreads down a valley to **Lake Rotomaha-
na** (Warm Lake). The experience is quite
different from the other ticketed thermal
areas as it involves a stroll down the lush,
bush-lined valley, with a return by shuttle
bus from either the 1.5km, 2.8km or 3.6km
point. The last bus stop is by the lake, where
it's possible to take a 45-minute boat cruise
past steaming cliffs.

Rotorua Lakes

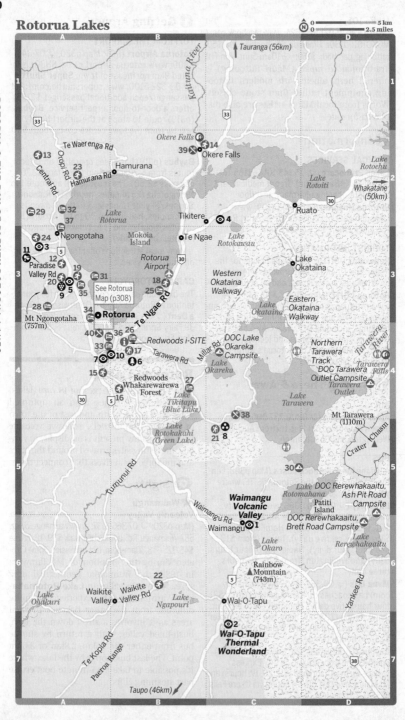

Rotorua Lakes

★ **Wai-O-Tapu Thermal Wonderland** NATURAL FEATURE
(Map p320; ☑ 07-366 6333; www.waiotapu. co.nz; 201 Waiotapu Loop Rd; adult/child $33/11; ⏰ 8.30am-5pm) The most colourful of the region's geothermal attractions, Wai-O-Tapu (Sacred Waters) has a variety of features packed into a relatively compact area, with the highlights being the orange-rimmed, 65m-wide **Champagne Pool** and the unearthly lemon-lime-hued **Devil's Bath**. Just outside the gate (but requiring a ticket) is the **Lady Knox Geyser**, which spouts off (with a little prompting from an organic soap) punctually at 10.15am and gushes up to 20m for about an hour (be here by 9.45am to see it).

Te Wairoa, the Buried Village ARCHAEOLOGICAL SITE
(Map p320; ☑ 07-362 8287; www.buriedvillage.co.nz; 1180 Tarawera Rd; adult/child $35/10; ⏰ 9am-5pm) The village of Te Wairoa was once the main staging post for Victorian-era tourists coming to visit the famous Pink and White Terraces on the shores of Lake Tarawera. When Mt

Tarawera erupted in 1886, the entire village was covered in mud up to 2m thick. Today a museum houses objects dug from the ruins, and guides in period costume escort groups through the excavated sites. There's also a bush walk to the 30m Te Wairoa Falls.

Hell's Gate NATURAL FEATURE
(Map p320; ☑ 07-345 3151; www.hellsgate.co.nz; SH30, Tikitere; adult/child $35/18, pools $20/10, combo incl mud bath $90/45; ⏰ 8.30am-8.30pm)
✐ Known as Tikitere to the Ngāti Rangiteaorere people, this highly active geothermal reserve lies 16km northeast of Rotorua on the Whakatane road (SH30). It's not the most colourful of the Rotorua thermal areas but, among all the bubbling pools and steaming vents, there are some unique features such as a 2.4m-high mud volcano and the largest natural hot waterfall in the southern hemisphere. There's also a small but well-priced set of therapeutic outdoor mineral pools attached to the complex.

The diabolic name originated from a 1934 visit by Irish playwright George Bernard

OFF THE BEATEN TRACK

WHIRINAKI TE PUA-A-TĀNE CONSERVATION PARK

This lush podocarp (conifer) forest park offers canyons, waterfalls, lookouts and streams, plus the **Oriuwaka Ecological Area** and **Arohaki Lagoon**. Walking tracks here vary in length and difficulty: the DOC booklet *Walks in Whirinaki Te Pua-a-Tāne Conservation Park* details walking and camping options. It's free online or you can pick one up at DOC's **Murupara office** (☑ 07-366 1080; www.doc.govt.nz; Main Rd, Murupara; ☺ 9am-5pm Mon-Fri).

A good shortish walk is the 9.3km **Whirinaki Waterfall Loop Track** (three hours), which follows the Whirinaki River. Longer walks include the **Whirinaki Track** (two days), which can be combined with **Te Hoe Track** (four days). There's also a rampaging 16km mountain-bike track.

The conservation park is 90km southeast of Rotorua off SH38, en route to Te Urewera National Park (take the turn-off at Te Whaiti to Minginui). There are several camping areas and 10 backcountry huts (free to $15) in the park; pay at the DOC office.

Shaw, who described it as the gateway to hell. However, Tikitere has long been known to local Māori as a place of healing. Warriors would ritually bathe in the hot waterfall to physically and spiritually cleanse themselves when returning from battle, and sulphur-infused water drawn from the pools was used as an insecticide and to heal septic wounds. After completing your loop of the complex, stop to soak your feet in the soothing warm mud in the designated place near the entrance.

There's also a cafe and a workshop where you can try your hand at woodcarving.

🏃 Activities

Rafting, Kayaking & Sledging

There's plenty of white-water action around Rotorua, with the chance to take on the Grade V **Kaituna River**, complete with a startling 7m drop at Tutea Falls – the highest commercially rafted waterfall in the world. Some companies head further out to the **Rangitaiki River** (Grade III–VI) and **Wairoa River** (Grade V), raftable only when the dam is opened every second Sunday. Sledging (in case you didn't know) is zooming downriver on a body board. Most operators can arrange transfers.

Rotorua Rafting   RAFTING
(Map p320; ☑ 0800 772 384; www.rotorua-rafting. co.nz; 761 SH33, Okere Falls; rafting $85-90) The minimum age for rafting the Grade V-rated Kaituna River is 13, but 10-year-olds are allowed on the Grade III-rated section of the river. Transfers from central Rotorua are included in the price.

Kaitiaki Adventures   RAFTING, HIKING
(☑ 07-357 2236; www.kaitiaki.co.nz) 🏃 Offers white-water rafting trips on the Kaituna ($109) and Wairoa ($138) rivers, plus sledging on a Grade III section of the Kaituna

($120). They also lead 4½-hour guided hikes up Mt Tarawera, including a walk around the crater's edge ($164). Prices include shuttles from central Rotorua; add-ons include a helicopter ride to the crater's edge.

Wet 'n' Wild   RAFTING
(Map p320; ☑ 07-348 3191; www.wetnwildrafting. co.nz; 58a Fryer Rd, Hamurana) Runs trips on the Kaituna ($99), Wairoa ($115) and Mokau ($160), as well as easy-going Rangitaiki trips (adult/child $140/120) and longer trips to remote parts of the Motu and Mohaka (two to five days, $650 to $1095).

Kaituna Cascades   RAFTING
(Map p320; ☑ 07-345 4199; www.kaitunacascades. co.nz; 18 Okere Falls Rd, Okere Falls) Rafting on the Kaituna ($95), Rangitaiki ($140) and Wairoa ($120) rivers, plus combos.

River Rats   RAFTING, KAYAKING
(Map p320; ☑ 07-345 6543; www.riverrats.co.nz; Hangar 14s, Rotorua Airport, 837 Te Ngae Rd) 🏃 White-water rafting trips take on the Kaituna ($105), Wairoa ($129) and Rangitaiki ($139), including a scenic trip on the lower Rangitaiki (Grade II) that is good for youngsters ($139). Kayaking options include freedom hire (two hours from $30) and guided paddles to hot pools on Lake Rotoiti ($119). There's also exciting river sledging on the Kaituna ($129).

Note, River Rats also markets the rafting trips under the more backpacker-focused Raftabout (www.raftabout.co.nz) brand.

Waimarino Kayak Tours   KAYAKING
(Map p320; ☑ 07-576 4233; www.glowworm kayaking.com; departs Okere Falls Store, 757a SH33, Okere Falls; adult/child $130/85) Take a guided paddle on Lake Rotoiti to natural thermal pools and a glowworm cave.

Kaituna Kayaks KAYAKING
(Map p320; ☑ 021 277 2855; www.kaitunakayaks.
co.nz; departs Rotorua Rafting, 761 SH33, Okere
Falls; tandem trip $150, lessons per half-/full day
from $100/220) Guided tandem white-water kayaking trips and lessons (cheaper for
groups) on the Kaituna River.

Rotorua Paddle Tours TOURS
(Map p320; ☑ 0800 787 768; www.rotoruapaddle
tours.co.nz; Rotorua Rafting, 761 SH33, Okere Falls;
tours $80; ☺ 9am, noon & 3pm) Keen to try
stand-up paddle boarding without any waves
to contend with? This outfit leads trips on
the Blue Lake (Tikitapu) and on the channel
between Lake Rotorua and Lake Rotoiti. Allow three hours for the round-trip, with one
hour on the water. No experience required.

Hiking

Numerous walks are outlined in DOC's
Walking and Hiking in Rotorua booklet,
which can be downloaded for free from its
website (www.doc.govt.nz).

A good starting point is the blissfully
beautiful 1½-hour (5.5km) **Blue Lake Track**,
which circles around Lake Tikitapu.

The 10.5km **Eastern Okataina Walkway** (three hours one-way) goes along the
eastern shoreline of Lake Okataina to Lake
Tarawera and passes the Soundshell, a natural amphitheatre that has *pā* (fortified village) remains and several swimming spots.
The 22.5km **Western Okataina Walkway**
(seven hours one-way) heads through the
forest west of Lake Okataina to Lake Rotoiti.

The 6km **Northern Tarawera Track**
(three hours one-way) connects to the Eastern Okataina Walkway, creating a two-day
walk from either Ruato or Lake Okataina to
Lake Tarawera with an overnight camp at either Humphries Bay (sites free) or **Tarawera
Outlet** (Map p320; ☑ 07-323 6300; www.doc.govt.
nz; adult/child $13/6.50). From Tarawera Outlet
you can walk on to the 65m **Tarawera Falls**
(two hours one-way, 5km). There's a forestry
road into Tarawera Outlet from Kawerau, a
timber town in the shadow of Putauaki (Mt
Edgecumbe), off the road to Whakatane;
access costs $5, with permits available from
the **Kawerau i-SITE** (☑ 07-323 6300; www.kaw-
eraunz.com; Plunkett St bus terminal; ☺ 9am-4pm).

The **Okere Falls** are about 21km northeast of Rotorua on SH33, with an easy 1.2km
track (30 minutes each way) past the 7m
falls (popular for rafting), through native

podocarp (conifer) forest and along the Kaituna River. Along the way is a lookout over
the river at Hinemoa's Steps.

Just north of Wai-O-Tapu on SH5, the
2.5km **Rainbow Mountain Summit Track**
(1½ hours one-way) is a strenuous walk up
the peak known to Māori as Maunga Kakaramea (Mountain of Coloured Earth). There
are spectacular views from the top towards
Lake Taupo and Tongariro National Park.

Tarawera Trail TRAMPING
(Map p320; www.doc.govt.nz) Starting at the
Te Wairoa car park on Tarawera Rd, this
five- to six-hour track meanders 15km along
Lake Tarawera and through forest to Hot
Water Beach where there is camping (p324)
available. From here water taxis from Totally Tarawera can be prebooked to ferry you
back to the Landing, where it's a 2km walk
back to the car park.

Other Activities

Totally Tarawera CRUISE
(Map p320; ☑ 07-362 8080; www.totallytarawera.
com; the Landing, 1375 Tarawera Rd; adult/child
tour $65/30, water taxi $25/15) ✦ Offers guided
cruises on Lake Tarawera taking in cultural
and geothermal sites (including Hot Water
Beach and a natural bush hot pool), as well
as a water taxi service between the Landing
and Hot Water Beach, which is the terminus
of the Tarawera Trail; bookings are essential.

Waikite Valley Thermal Pools HOT SPRINGS
(Map p320; ☑ 07-333 1861; www.hotpools.co.nz;
648 Waikite Valley Rd; adult/child $17/9, private pools
40min per person $20; ☺ 10am-9pm) ✦ Located
in a verdant valley around 30km south of Rotorua, these pools provide a more low-key (not
to mention cheaper) alternative to Rotorua's
thermal baths. The outdoor pools range from
a large family pool to small tubs, and private
spas are also available. There's also a cafe and
neighbouring campsite (sites per adult/child
from $22/11; pools free for campers).

To get here, turn off SH5 opposite the
Wai-O-Tapu turn-off, and continue 6km; the
gorgeous valley view as you come over the
hill is enough to justify the drive in itself.

Affordable Trout Fishing FISHING
(☑ 07-349 2555; www.rotoruatrout.co.nz; half-/full-
day charters $460/940) Pursue the trout in the
Rotorua Lakes with local fisherman Gordon
Randle.

Farmhouse   HORSE RIDING

(Map p320; ☑07-332 3771; www.thefarmhouse.
co.nz; 55 Sunnex Rd, Hamurana; 30min/1hr/2hr
$35/55/95; 🐎) New Zealand's biggest
horse-riding complex offers short beginners'
rides and longer treks through farmland
and native bush, 16km northwest of central
Rotorua. Small children can take a 15-min-
ute pony ride ($25).

🛏 Sleeping & Eating

Hot Water Beach Campsite   CAMPGROUND $

(Map p320; ☑07-349 3463; www.whakarewarewa.
com; adult/child $13/6.50) This simple camp-
site is located on the shores of Lake Tarawera and can only be reached by the Tarawera
Trail (p323) or by water taxi (p323) from the
Landing. Book through the Whakarewarewa Village (p308) office in Rotorua.

**Blue Lake Top 10
Holiday Park**   HOLIDAY PARK $$

(Map p320; ☑07-362 8120; www.bluelaketop10.
co.nz; 723 Tarawera Rd; sites from $45, unit with/
without bathroom from $130/80; @🐕🤖) 🍴 Set
alongside gorgeous Lake Tikitapu (aka the
Blue Lake), 6km before you get to Lake
Tarawera, this well-run holiday park has
spotless facilities and a handy range of cab-
ins and motel units.

Okere Falls Store   CAFE $

(Map p320; ☑07-362 4944; www.okerefalls
store.co.nz; 757a SH33, Okere Falls; snacks $7-15;
⊙7am-7pm, beer garden to 9pm Fri & Sat) 🍴
Around 20km from Rotorua, this cafe-store
is a handy refuelling stop near the top of
the lake. Cool down on the raffish balcony
with fruit smoothies and great views of Lake
Rotoiti, or kick back in the beer garden with
wine, local craft brews and home-baked sa-
voury pies. It also hosts regular live music
and a beer festival in October.

Landing Cafe   CAFE $$

(Map p320; ☑07-362 8502; The Landing, Tarawera
Rd; mains $15-24; ⊙10am-8pm) Friendly wait-
staff add extra sparkle to the lakeside setting
at this cafe-cum-bar-cum-bistro, serving
everything from bacon and eggs to pizza
and curries.

❶ Getting There & Away

The twice-daily **Baybus** (p319) *Twin City Express*
service stops in Okere Falls en route between
Rotorua ($3.90, 25 minutes) and Tauranga ($10,
one hour).

Some of the major attractions and activity operators provide transfers from Rotorua, or you
can try **Geyser Link Shuttle** (p314) or **Thermal
Land Shuttle** (p314).

BAY OF PLENTY

The Bay of Plenty stretches along the pohutukawa tree-studded coast from Waihi
Beach to Opotiki and inland as far as the
Kaimai Range. This is where New Zealanders have come on holiday for generations,
lapping up salt-tinged activities and lashings of sunshine.

Katikati

POP 4060

'Katikat' to the locals, this busy little stop
on the highway was the only planned Ulster
(Irish Scots) settlement in the world, and it
celebrates this history with a series of colourful murals. There are now more than
60 murals brightening up the town centre,
along with some wonderful street sculpture
(look for *Barry, a Kiwi Bloke* sitting reading
his newspaper on a park bench near the information centre).

◉ Sights & Activities

Western Bay Museum   MUSEUM

(☑07-549 0651; www.nzmuseum.com; 32 Main Rd;
adult/child $5/2; ⊙10am-4pm) Housed in a for-
mer fire station, this little regional museum
displays a selection of Māori artefacts from
the local tribe, Ngāi Te Rangi, along with
temporary exhibitions devoted to aspects of
the town's heritage. Don't miss the old Katikati Jail in the grounds, a compact hut with
room for only two prisoners at a time.

Haiku Pathway   PARK

(www.katikati.co.nz) Built as a millennium project, this unusual attraction consists of boulders inscribed with haiku verses wending
through a pretty park flanking the Uretara
River, just behind the main drag.

Katikati Bird Gardens   BIRD SANCTUARY

(☑07-549 0912; www.birdgardens.co.nz; 263
Walker Rd East, Aongatete; adult/child $10/8.50;
⊙10am-4.30pm daily Oct-May, Sat & Sun Jun-Sep;
🐎) About 7km south of town, this gorgeous
4-hectare private garden is all aflap with
native and exotic bird life (ever seen a ka-
waupaka?). Admission includes a packet of
grain, which will ensure your immediate

MĀORI BAY OF PLENTY

The Bay of Plenty's Māori name, *Te Moana a Toi* (The Sea of Toi), recalls an early Polynesian voyager whose descendants first settled in Whakatane. Later (probably around the 13th or 14th century) the Mātaatua *waka* (canoe) made landfall in Whakatane, and it's from this migration that most of the Bay's tribes trace their ancestry. These include **Te Whakatōhea** (www.whakatohea.co.nz) of Opotiki, **Ngāti Awa** (www.ngatiawa.iwi.nz) of Whakatane, and **Ngāi Te Rangi** (www.ngaiterangi.org.nz), **Ngāti Pūkenga** (www.ngatipukenga.com) and **Ngāti Ranginui** (www.ranginui.co.nz) of the Tauranga area. **Te Arawa** (www.tearawa.iwi.nz) of Rotorua take their name from a different ancestral *waka*.

Tribes in this region were involved on both sides of the New Zealand Wars of the late 19th century, with those fighting against the government suffering considerable land confiscations that have caused legal problems right up to the present day.

There's a significant Māori population in the region, and many ways for travellers to engage with Māori culture. Whakatane has a visitor-friendly main-street **marae** (p337) (traditional meeting place) and Toi's Pā (p339), perhaps New Zealand's oldest *pā* (fortified village) site. Rotorua has Māori villages, *hāngi* (Māori feasts) and cultural performances aplenty.

popularity upon arrival; have your camera handy for pigeon-on-head snaps. There's a cafe and gift shop here, too, plus boutiquey cottage accommodation (double B&B $175).

Leveret Estate WINERY
(📞 07-552 0795; www.wineportfolio.co.nz; 2389 SH2, Aongatete; ⏰ 9.30am-5pm) Transplanting Cape Dutch architecture from South Africa's wine country to SH2, 8km south of Katikati, this excellent winery is open for tastings and stock-ups. They make some particularly lovely (and well-priced) sauvignon blanc, chardonnay, pinot noir and late-harvest viognier.

Katikati Mural Tours CULTURAL
(📞 07-549 5250; www.muraltown.co.nz; depart 36 Main Rd; per person $10; ⏰ 11am Sat & Sun Oct-Mar) Guided tours depart from the information centre, taking in some of the 60-plus murals dotting the town. Bookings aren't necessary.

🛏 Sleeping

Kaimai View Motel MOTEL $$
(📞 07-549 0398; www.kaimaiview.co.nz; 84 Main Rd; unit from $135; 🛜🏊) This motel offers neat rooms (all named after NZ native trees) with CD players, kitchenettes and, in the larger rooms, spa baths. The namesake views extend over the back fence.

★ Warm Earth Cottage COTTAGE $$$
(📞 07-549 0962; www.warmearthcottage.co.nz; 202 Thompsons Track, Aongatete; r $290) Reignite your romance or simmer in simple pleasures at this rural idyll, 5km south of town then 2km west of SH2. Two pretty, electricity-less cottages sit by the swimmable Waitekohe River. Fire up the barbecue, melt into a wood-fired outdoor bath, or chew through a book in the lovely guest lounge-library. Big DIY breakfasts are included in the price.

🍴 Eating & Drinking

Ambria BISTRO $$
(📞 07-549 2272; www.ambria.co.nz; 5/62 Main Rd; mains lunch $17-20, dinner $26-37; ⏰ 5pm-late Tue & Wed, 11am-2pm & 5pm-late Thu-Sun) Surprisingly atmospheric, Ambria is a hip bar-eatery in a nondescript shopping strip on the eastern side of town. Grab a seat overlooking the river and order a glass of Kiwi wine to wash down your roasted confit duck with kumara mash. Gourmet pizzas straddle the lunch and dinner menus.

Talisman Hotel PUB
(📞 07-549 3218; www.talismanhotel.co.nz; 7 Main Rd; ⏰ 11am-late) The Talisman is better than your average small-town boozer, with an attractive garden bar and a bistro.

ℹ Information

Katikati Information Centre (📞 07-549 1658; www.katikati.org.nz; 36 Main Rd; ⏰ 8am-5pm Mon-Fri, 10am-2pm Sat & Sun; 🛜) Sells guides to the town's numerous murals (from $5); guided mural tours depart from here.

ℹ Getting There & Away

Three **InterCity** (p319) coaches a day stop here en route to Auckland (from $17, 3¼ hours), Thames (from $15, 1¼ hours), Waihi ($15, 29 minutes), Tauranga (from $15, 35 minutes) and Mt Maunganui ($15, 45 minutes).

OFF THE BEATEN TRACK

KAIMAI MAMAKU FOREST PARK

The backdrop to the western Bay of Plenty is the rugged 70km-long wilderness of **Kaimai Mamaku Forest Park** (www.doc.govt.nz). It lies 35km southwest of Tauranga, with tramps for the intrepid plus huts (free to $15 per person per night) and campsites ($8). For more info see DOC's pamphlet *Kaimai to Coast* (available online).

Mana Bus (p319) has a daily coach to/from Auckland ($18, 2¾ hours), Waihi ($26, 20 minutes), Tauranga ($26, 35 minutes), Mt Maunganui ($26, 1¼ hours) and Rotorua (from $10, 2¾ hours).

Baybus (p319) has two buses a day to Tauranga ($8.20, 50 minutes) and Thursday-only services to Waihi ($5, 30 minutes) and Waihi Beach ($5, 58 minutes).

Tauranga

POP 138,000

Tauranga (pronounced 'toe-run-gah') has been booming since the 1990s and in 2017 it leapfrogged Dunedin to become NZ's fifth-biggest city. It's especially popular with retirees cashing up from Auckland's hyperkinetic real-estate market, along with young families who can no longer afford to buy there.

Its rapid rise has left it with traffic snarls on its arterial routes to rival even Auckland's. It also has NZ's busiest port, with petrol refineries and mountains of coal and lumber spoiling what was once a lovely view from the city centre to Mt Maunganui.

However, this growth has also brought with it fancy hotels and a terrific crop of restaurants and bars enlivening its vamped-up waterfront. Tauranga's city centre is never going to rival its beachside 'burbs, Mt Maunganui and Papamoa, for visitor appeal but if you're staying at the Mount, it's well worth popping over for a bite and a look around.

👁 Sights

Tauranga Art Gallery GALLERY
(☑07-578 7933; www.artgallery.org.nz; cnr Wharf & Willow Sts; ⊙10am-4.30pm) FREE The city's pre-eminent gallery isn't afraid to ruffle feathers with challenging exhibitions of contemporary work. The building is a former bank, although you'd hardly know it – it's an altogether excellent space with no obvious compromise. The gift shop is also worth a look.

The Elms HISTORIC BUILDING
(☑07-577 9772; www.theelms.org.nz; 15 Mission St; adult/child $15/7.50; ⊙10am-4pm) Surrounded by mature trees and lovely gardens, Tauranga's original mission station incorporates the earliest buildings in the Bay of Plenty, along with one of the country's oldest oaks and first pianos. Fascinating guided tours tell the story of the mission, founded by Anglican priest Alfred Nesbit Brown in 1838, and its relations with local Māori. The property remained in the extended Brown family until 1997, retaining much of its original furniture, books and other chattels.

The oldest building is Nesbit Brown's free-standing office, built in 1838. The house wasn't completed until 1847, until which time the family lived in a *whare* (traditional house) built of bulrushes. There's also a reconstructed chapel (the original fell down) and various outbuildings.

Mission Cemetery CEMETERY
(Marsh St) Not far from The Elms mission house, this shady little cemetery has some interesting memorials relating to battles fought between local Māori and government forces in the 1860s. A prominent monument honours Rāwiri Puhirake, a Ngāi Te Rangi chief remembered for issuing a code of conduct for dealing mercifully with British civilians and wounded soldiers during the conflict.

Robbins Park GARDENS
(Cliff Rd) At its best in late spring and summer, this verdant pocket of roses sits behind an ivy-covered colonnade on a cliff overlooking the harbour. The neighbouring greenhouse is packed with bromeliads and palms.

Monmouth Redoubt ARCHAEOLOGICAL SITE
(Monmouth St; ⊙24hr) FREE Shaded by huge pohutukawa trees, spooky Monmouth Redoubt was originally a Māori *pā* (fortified village), which was taken over and adapted by British soldiers during the New Zealand Wars. At the foot of the Redoubt, on the end of the Strand, is **Te Awanui**, a ceremonial *waka* (canoe) carved in 1972, on display in an open-sided building.

Mills Reef Winery WINERY
(☑07-576 8800; www.millsreef.co.nz; 143 Moffat Rd, Bethlehem; ⊙10am-5pm) Stately Mills Reef, 7km from the town centre at Bethlehem, has tastings of its award-winning wines. This

Tauranga

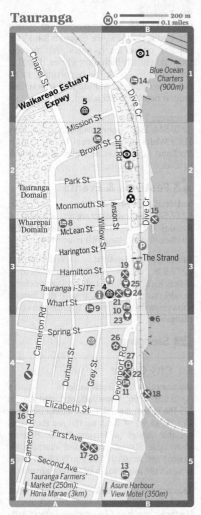

Tauranga

◉ Sights
1	Mission Cemetery	B1
2	Monmouth Redoubt	B2
3	Robbins Park	B2
4	Tauranga Art Gallery	B3
5	The Elms	A1

◈ Activities, Courses & Tours
6	Bay Explorer	B4
	Cycle Tauranga	(see 9)
7	Dive Zone	A4

⊟ Sleeping
8	City Suites	A3
9	Harbour City Motor Inn	A3
10	Harbourside City Backpackers	B3
11	Hotel on Devonport	B4
12	Roselands Motel	A2
13	Tauranga on the Waterfront	B5
14	Trinity Wharf	B1

⊗ Eating
15	Bobby's Fresh Fish Market	B3
16	Elizabeth Cafe & Larder	A4
17	Grindz Café	A5
18	Harbourside	B4
19	Macau	B3
20	Me & You	A5
21	Rye Bar & Grill	B3
22	The Med	B4

◎ Drinking & Nightlife
23	Brew	B4
24	Crown & Badger	B3
25	Phoenix	B3

◎ Entertainment
26	Rialto Cinemas	B4

⊞ Shopping
27	Vinyl Destination	B4

🏃 Activities

The free *Tauranga City Walkways* pamphlet (from the i-SITE) details walks around Tauranga and Mt Maunganui. History buffs should pick up the free *Historic Tauranga* brochure and stroll around the town's cache of historic sites.

★ Waimarino
Adventure Park
ADVENTURE SPORTS

(☑ 07-576 4233; www.waimarino.com; 36 Taniwha Pl, Bethlehem; park day pass adult/child $44/34; ☉ 10am-5pm) On the banks of the Wairoa River, 8km west of town, Waimarino offers kayaking (including a customised kayak slide!), rock-climbing, pedal boats, water trampolines, a rope course and a human catapult called 'The Blob'. You can also hire kayaks

isn't grape-growing country, so grapes are sourced from NZ's most acclaimed wine regions. There's also a refined restaurant that's open for brunch and lunch daily (mains $23 to $38).

Minden Lookout
VIEWPOINT

(Minden Rd, Wairoa) On clear days this wooden viewing platform, located about 13km west of the city centre, provides a panorama of nearly the entire Bay of Plenty; see if you can spot Whaakari steaming away in the distance. To get here, take SH2 to Te Puna and turn south on Minden Rd; the lookout is about 3km up the road.

MATAKANA ISLAND

About 24km long and forming the seaward side of Tauranga Harbour, privately owned Matakana is laced with secluded white-sand surf beaches on its eastern shore (experienced surfers only). The community lifestyle here is laid-back and beachy, but the only way you can visit it is on a private boat from Tauranga or Mt Maunganui.

here (per hour/day from $19/55) and take a paddle down the river to the harbour, or take a guided tour (p328).

Adrenalin Forest ADVENTURE SPORTS
(☑ 07-929 8724; www.adrenalin-forest.co.nz; TECT All Terrain Park, Whataroa Rd, Ngawaro; adult/child $43/28; ☺ 10am-2.30pm daily Oct-Mar, Wed-Sun Apr-Sep) About 30km from central Tauranga en route to Rotorua is this heart-starter: a series of high wires, flying foxes, platforms and rope bridges strung through a grove of tall conifers. There are six different routes of increasing difficulty to test your nerve.

Blue Ocean Charters FISHING
(☑ 07-544 3072; www.blueocean.co.nz; Tauranga Bridge Marina; trips from $100) Fishing, diving and sightseeing trips (including one to Tuhua Island) on the *Te Kuia* and the *Ratahi*.

Cycle Tauranga CYCLING
(☑ 07-571 1435; www.cycletauranga.co.nz; Harbour City Motor Inn, 50 Wharf St; 2hr/4hr/day $20/29/49) Has road-trail hybrid bikes for hire, including helmets, locks, saddlebags and maps. Tours are also available.

Dive Zone DIVING
(☑ 07-578 4050; www.divezonetauranga.co.nz; 213 Cameron Rd; trips from $150; ☺ 8am-6pm Mon-Fri, 7.30am-4pm Sat, 7.30am-2pm Sun) PADI courses and trips to local wrecks and reefs, plus gear rental.

☞ Tours

Waimarino Kayak Tours KAYAKING
(☑ 07-576 4233; www.glowwormkayaking.com; 36 Taniwha Pl, Bethlehem) Kayak tours don't get more magical than an evening paddle across Lake McLaren to a canyon filled with glowworms ($130). Daytime tour options include Lake McLaren ($105), the Wairoa River ($75) and Tauranga Harbour ($120). Trips either start from or include transfers from Waimarino Adventure Park (p327).

Bay Explorer CRUISE
(☑ 021 605 968; www.bayexplorer.co.nz; Strand Wharf; adult/child $150/65; ☺ departs 8am) This popular cruise incorporates wildlife-spotting – potentially including whales, dolphins and bird life – with the opportunity to go paddle boarding, kayaking and snorkelling around nearby Motiti Island.

Tauranga Tasting Tours TOURS
(☑ 07-544 1383; www.tastingtours.co.nz; tours $130) Whips around a local brewery, Mills Reef and Leveret Estate wineries, and back to town for cocktails.

★☆ Festivals & Events

National Jazz Festival MUSIC
(☑ 07-577 7460; www.jazz.org.nz; ☺ Easter) A five-day extravaganza of big blowers and scoobee-doobee-doo, with concerts galore.

Tauranga Arts Festival PERFORMING ARTS
(☑ 07-928 6213; www.taurangafestival.co.nz; ☺ Oct) Kicking off on Labour Day weekend in odd-numbered years, this 10-day festival showcases dance, comedy, theatre and other things arty.

🛏 Sleeping

🛏 City Centre

Harbourside City Backpackers HOSTEL $
(☑ 07-579 4066; www.backpacktauranga.co.nz; 105 The Strand; dm $31, r with/without bathroom $90/86; @🖧🛜) 🏄 Soak up the sea air at this sociable hostel (a former hotel), directly above the Strand's bars and restaurants. Rooms are smallish but you'll spend more time on the awesome roof terrace anyway.

Tauranga Tourist Park HOLIDAY PARK $
(☑ 07-578 3323; www.taurangatouristpark.co.nz; 9 Mayfair St; sites from $28, cabin with/without bathroom $88/58; 🛜) The layout at this harbourside holiday park feels a bit tight (don't expect rolling acres), but it's well maintained, clean and tidy. Aim for a site down by the bay under the pohutukawa trees.

★ Asure Harbour View Motel MOTEL $$
(☑ 07-578 8621; www.harbourviewmotel.co.nz; 7 Fifth Ave East; unit from $155; 🛜) A fresh sea breeze has blown through this older-style motel and imbued it with a palette of pale blues and greys along with the odd chandelier. Some of the upstairs rooms have gorgeous harbour views, and despite being on a quiet cul-de-sac it's only a short stroll to

the centre. The friendly owners even deliver free newspapers to your door.

Hotel on Devonport
HOTEL $$

(☑07-578 2668; www.hotelondevonport.net.nz; 72 Devonport Rd; r from $185; ❋@☎) City-centre Devonport is top of the town, with bay-view rooms, noise-reducing glass and slick interiors, all of which appeals to business travellers, air crew and upmarket weekenders. Guests have access to the gym at the venerable Tauranga Club, with whom they share the building.

City Suites
HOTEL $$

(☑07-577 1480; www.citysuites.co.nz; 32 Cameron Rd; units from $150; ☎❋) The spacious rooms here (all with either a terrace or a balcony) have king-sized beds and full kitchens. A swimming pool, free wi-fi and secure underground parking complete the list of essentials for wandering business bods.

Harbour City Motor Inn
MOTEL $$

(☑07-571 1435; www.taurangaharbourcity.co.nz; 50 Wharf St; unit from $155; ❋☎) With a winning location right in the middle of town (and with plenty of parking), this lemon-yellow motor inn has spa baths and kitchenettes in each room, and friendly staff who can offer sound advice on your itinerary.

Roselands Motel
MOTEL $$

(☑07-578 2294; www.roselands.co.nz; 21 Brown St; unit from $149; ☎) Spruced up with splashes of lime-green paint, slat-style beds and new TVs, this sweet, old-style motel is in a quiet but central location. Expect spacious units (all with kitchenettes) and friendly hosts.

Tauranga on the Waterfront
HOTEL $$

(☑07-578 7079; www.thetauranga.co.nz; 1 Second Ave; r from $180; ☎) A short stroll from central Tauranga, this well-established place has renovated studios with compact private courtyards, and brilliant harbour suites with huge picture windows and outstanding views. Sunlight streams in to brighten the chic and stylish decor, modern bathrooms are equipped with premium toiletries, and compact self-contained kitchenettes come with Nespresso machines for the first coffee of the day.

Trinity Wharf
HOTEL $$$

(☑07-577 8700; www.trinitywharf.co.nz; 51 Dive Cres; r from $210; ❋☎❋) This blocky three-storey number near the bridge has a slick, contemporary lobby – all white tiles and spiky pot plants – leading to the upmarket in-house Halo Lounge & Dining. Amenities include an underutilised gym, infinity-edge swimming pool and free wi-fi. It's Tauranga's flashiest offering by far.

🛏 Surrounds

850 Cameron
MOTEL $$

(☑07-577 1774; www.850motel.co.nz; 850 Cameron Rd, South Tauranga; units from $155; ☎) This slick two-storey brick block offers a selection of modern, self-contained apartments ranging from studios to two-bedroom units with spa baths. All have kitchens, and the top-floor apartments have shiny metal-and-glass balconies, although the view is hardly inspiring: across the car park to the back of a medical centre.

HOT FUZZ

The humble kiwifruit earns New Zealand more than a billion dollars every year, and with the Bay of Plenty in the thick of the growing action, it's no wonder the locals are fond of them.

The fruit's origins are in China, where it was called the monkey peach (they were considered ripe when the monkeys munched them). As they migrated to NZ, they were renamed the Chinese gooseberry. They were a lot smaller then, but canny Kiwis engineered them to more generous sizes and began exporting them in the 1950s.

In the 1960s NZ growers began to market them as kiwifruit (many countries dropped the 'fruit' bit, much to the consternation of New Zealanders, for at home a kiwi is either a bird or a fellow countryman), but the name was never copyrighted. Now NZ-exported kiwifruit have been sexily rebranded internationally as Zespri. Today the Zesprians grow two types of kiwifruit: the common fuzzy-skinned green fruit, and the golden fruit with its smooth complexion.

For visitors after a dollar or two, there's usually plenty of kiwifruit-picking work around the area, most of it during harvest (May and June); enquire at local i-SITEs and hostels, or check online at www.picknz.co.nz. Don't expect to make much more than the minimum wage ($15.75 an hour, at the time of writing).

Summit Motor Lodge
MOTEL **$$**

(☑07-578 1181; www.summitmotorlodge.co.nz; 213 Waihi Rd, Judea; unit from $140; ✳@🛜🏊) Gathered around a small kidney-shaped swimming pool and hot tub, this lovingly maintained motel has sparkling units with kitchens, trimmed with hanging flower baskets. It's located on a busy road, 3km west of the city centre.

🍴 Eating

★ Grindz Café
CAFE **$**

(☑07-579 0017; 50 First Ave; meals $10-19; ⊙8am-3.30pm; 🛜✏🖶) The chatter of well-caffeinated patrons on Grindz' outside tables brings a welcome burst of street life to otherwise scrappy First Ave. Inside it's a roomy, split-level affair, with funky wallpaper, antiques and retro relics. Cooked breakfasts, muffins, cakes, smoothies and salads are the order of the day, including vegetarian and vegan options and excellent coffee.

The Med
CAFE **$**

(☑07-577 0487; www.medcafe.co.nz; 62 Devonport Rd; mains $9-19; ⊙7am-4pm; 🛜✏🖶) Wonder Woman watches approvingly over the scrum of regulars enjoying terrific coffee and scrumptious all-day breakfasts. Order from the blackboard or from the cabinet crammed with sandwiches, salads, flans and cakes. Lunchtimes and weekends can be frantic but the on-to-it staff keep everything flowing.

Bobby's Fresh Fish Market
FISH & CHIPS **$**

(☑07-578 1789; 1 Dive Cres; fish & chips $6.20; ⊙8am-7pm) This local legend sells fresh fish as well as frying up arguably Tauranga's best fish and chips. Our pick, however, is the mussel fritters, fried up on a barbecue and served on white bread. Grab a seat among the expectant seagulls at the hexagonal outdoor tables on the water's edge.

Tauranga Farmers' Market
MARKET **$**

(☑07-552 5278; www.taurangafarmersmarket. co.nz; Tauranga Primary School, Arundel St; snacks $5-10; ⊙7.45am-noon Sat) Kick-start your Saturday morning with a brioche and an organic coffee, then explore this popular weekly market that usually features local dogs enjoying entertainment from an eclectic range of buskers.

★ Macau
ASIAN **$$**

(☑07-578 8717; www.dinemacau.co.nz; 59 The Strand; shared plates $10-33; ⊙11.30am-late) Zingy pan-Asian flavours take centre stage at Tauranga's top restaurant. Dishes – small

and large – are all designed to be shared. Menu highlights include lamb-rib *sang choy bow* (lettuce wraps), crispy Sichuan-spiced aubergine, and moreish steamed buns with roasted pork belly. Stylish decor, Asian-inspired cocktails and a good craft-beer list complete the picture.

★ Me & You
CAFE **$$**

(☑07-577 0567; 48 First Ave; mains $15-19; ⊙7am-3.30pm; 🛜✏) Our favourite Tauranga cafe combines retro decor with an appealing front deck, and the hip baristas really know their way around the coffee machine. A huge array of counter food – including drool-inducing baked goods and a forever-changing range of fresh salads – combines with a menu including eggy breakfasts and delicious fruit smoothies.

Elizabeth Cafe & Larder
CAFE **$$**

(☑07-579 0950; www.elizabethcafe.co.nz; 247 Cameron Rd; mains $10-25; ⊙8am-3pm; 🛜) 'Eat, drink, enjoy' at Elizabeth, a hip cafe-bar on the ground floor of a four-storey city-centre office block. Many of the customers drift down from upstairs, but you don't need a suit to enjoy a knock-out eggs Benedict on potato rösti or the fish taco with a zingy Mexican slaw. Interesting industrial aesthetics and Peroni on tap complete the picture.

Rye Bar & Grill
AMERICAN **$$**

(☑07-571 4138; www.ryekitchen.co.nz; 19 Wharf St; mains $23-40; ⊙4.30pm-late Tue-Thu, noon-late Fri-Sun) The cuisine of the USA's south is showcased at this rustic and relaxed spot on a pedestrian-friendly section of Wharf St. Grab an outdoor table and combine a burger, beef brisket or buttermilk fried chicken with a craft brew or whiskey.

Harbourside
MODERN NZ **$$**

(☑07-571 0520; www.harboursidetauranga.co.nz; 150 The Strand; mains $24-39; ⊙11.30am-2.30pm & 5.30pm-late) In a wonderfully atmospheric 100-year-old boathouse at the end of the Strand, Harbourside is the place for a romantic dinner, with lapping waves and the overhead railway bridge arching out over the harbour. The Asian-style roast duck is hard to beat, or you can just swing by for a moody pre-dinner drink.

Somerset Cottage
MODERN NZ **$$$**

(☑07-576 6889; www.somersetcottage.co.nz; 30 Bethlehem Rd, Bethlehem; mains $33-43; ⊙11.30am-2.30pm Wed-Fri, 6-9pm Mon-Sat) Locals head to this elegant venue, incongruously situated across from a suburban mall, for a special treat. The food is highly seasonal, made from the best NZ ingredients and impressively executed without being too fussy. Standout dishes include baked cheese soufflé, duck with coconut kumara, and its famous liquorice ice cream.

🍷 Drinking & Entertainment

Brew CRAFT BEER
(☑07-578 3543; www.brewpub.co.nz; 107 The Strand; 4-beer tasting rack $18; ⊘4pm-late Mon-Wed, 11am-late Thu-Sun) The long concrete bar here has room for plenty of elbows, and for plenty of glasses of Croucher's crafty seasonal ales and pilsners. The vibe is social, with communal tables, and good pizza and pub grub. Look forward to guest beers from around NZ, too.

Phoenix BAR
(☑07-578 8741; www.thephoenixtauranga.co.nz; 67 The Strand; ⊘10.30am-late Mon-Fri, 8.30am-late Sat & Sun) At the northern end of the Strand, this sprawling gastropub pours Monteiths beers (once niche, now mainstream) and serves pizza and meaty pub meals. On weekends earnest youngsters with guitars strum covers to the dressed-up drinkers on the terrace.

Crown & Badger PUB
(☑07-571 3038; www.crownandbadger.co.nz; 91 The Strand; ⊘9am-late) This particularly convincing black-painted Brit boozer does pukka pints and food along the lines of bangers and mash, and mini Yorkshire puds. Things get more lively on weekends with live bands.

Rialto Cinemas CINEMA
(☑07-577 0445; www.rialtotauranga.co.nz; Goddards Centre, 21 Devonport Rd; adult/child $17/11) Home to the Tauranga Film Society, the Rialto is the best spot in town to catch a flick – classic, offbeat, art-house or international. And you can sip a coffee or a glass of wine in the darkness. Tickets are discounted on Tuesdays.

🛍 Shopping

★ Vinyl Destination MUSIC
(☑027 412 7628; www.vinyldestination.co.nz; 52 Devonport Rd; ⊘9am-5pm) Not your ordinary record shop, this exceptionally hip establishment doubles as a cafe, a music venue and even a radio station (105.4FM). If there's anything interesting happening around town gig-wise, the clued-up staff here will certainly know about it.

ℹ Information

MEDICAL SERVICES

Tauranga Hospital (☑07-579 8000; www.bopdhb.govt.nz; 829 Cameron Rd, Tauranga South; ⊘24hr) Emergency and other services.

TOURIST INFORMATION

DOC Tauranga Office (☑07-578 7677; www.doc.govt.nz; 253 Chadwick Rd, Greerton; ⊘8am-4.30pm Mon-Fri) A field office rather than a visitor centre, but useful for information on walks and camping in the Kaimai Mamaku Forest Park.

Tauranga i-SITE (☑07-578 8103; www.bayofplentynz.com; 95 Willow St; ⊘8.30am-5pm; 🕾) Local tourist information, accommodation bookings, InterCity bus tickets and DOC maps.

ℹ Getting There & Away

AIR

Tauranga City Airport (TRG; ☑07-575 2456; www.taurangacityairport.co.nz; 73 Jean Batten Dr) is actually across the harbour in Mt Maunganui. **Air New Zealand** (p319) operates direct daily flights to Auckland, Wellington and Christchurch.

BUS

Coaches stop near the i-SITE on Wharf St.

InterCity (p319) destinations include Auckland ($22, 3¾ hours, three daily), Hamilton ($17, 1¾ hours, two daily), Taupo (from $22, three hours, two daily), Napier ($24, six hours, daily) and Wellington ($38, 9½ hours, daily).

Mana Bus (p319) has coaches to/from Auckland (from $15, 3½ hours, five daily), Hamilton ($13, two hours, daily), Katikati (from $15, 35 minutes, two daily) and Rotorua ($12, 1½ hours, daily).

Baybus (p319) has services to Mt Maunganui ($3.40, 28 minutes, every 15 minutes), Papamoa ($3.40, 30 minutes, hourly), Rotorua ($12.20, 1½ hours, two daily), Whakatane ($16, two hours, most days) and Katikati ($8.20, 50 minutes, two daily).

CAR & MOTORCYCLE

If you're heading to Cambridge on SH29, the Takitimu Dr toll road costs $1.80 per car. Heading east to Whakatane or south to Rotorua, there's also the option of the Tauranga Eastern Link ($2 per car), which begins near Papamoa. In both cases, free but slower alternative routes are possible. Tolls need to be paid online at www.nzta.govt.nz.

ℹ Getting Around

BICYCLE

Cycle Tauranga (p328) has road-trail hybrid bikes for hire, including helmets, locks, saddlebags and maps. Tours also available.

BUS

Tauranga's bright-yellow **Baybus** (p319) buses run on 14 different routes to most parts of the city.

CAR

Numerous car-rental agencies have offices in Tauranga, including cheapie **Rent a Dent** (☑ 07-578 1772; www.rentadent.co.nz; 19 Fifteenth Ave; ⊙ 8am-5pm Mon-Fri, to noon Sat).

Mt Maunganui

POP 19,100

Occupying a narrow peninsula punctuated by a volcanic cone, the Mount is an uptempo beach town with thermal hot pools, lively cafes and hip bars. Despite being swallowed by Tauranga in 1989, it still retains a distinct identity, shaped largely by its sun-soaked surfy vibe.

Maunganui means 'big mountain', so Mt Maunganui is a rather strange name (Mt Big Mountain?), especially considering that: a) it's not that big; and, b) its actual Māori name is Mauao, meaning 'caught by the dawn'.

Sunseekers flock to the Mount in summer, served by a cluster of high-rise apartment towers studding the spit. On the ocean side, long lovely Main Beach is popular with both surfers and swimmers, or you can cut across to the harbour side for a gentle dip at Pilot Bay Beach.

◉ Sights

★ Mauao   MOUNTAIN

Explore 232m-high Mt Maunganui itself on the walking trails winding around it and leading up to the summit of this extinct volcanic cone. The steep **summit walk** takes about 50 minutes (coming down is considerably quicker!). You can also clamber around the rocks on **Moturiki Island**, which adjoins the peninsula. The island and the base of Mauao comprise the **Mauao Base Track** (3.5km, 45 minutes), wandering through magical groves of pohutukawa trees that bloom between November and January.

Classic Flyers NZ   MUSEUM

(☑ 07-572 4000; www.classicflyersnz.com; 9 Jean Batten Dr; adult/child/family $15/7.50/30; ⊙ 9.30am-4pm; ⚒) Out near the airport, this interesting aviation museum showcases biplanes, retired US Air Force jets and the odd helicopter. Aside from the spitfires, kittyhawks, tiger moths and skyhawks, there's a buzzy on-site cafe and an excellent playground incorporating sections of fuselage. Plane freaks can take a nostalgic scenic flight on a DC3 (from $99) or a short blast in a biplane (from $355).

🏃 Activities

The Mount lays claim to being NZ's premier **surfing** town (they teach surfing at high school!). You can carve up the waves at **Main Beach**, which has beach breaks and a 100m artificial surf reef not far offshore.

Mount Hot Pools   HOT SPRINGS

(☑ 07-577 8551; www.mounthotpools.co.nz; 9 Adams Ave; adult/child $14/9; ⊙ 6am-10pm Mon-Sat, 8am-10pm Sun) If you've given your muscles a workout traipsing up and down Mauao, take a long relaxing soak at these thermally heated saltwater pools at the foot of the volcano. If the bustling family-friendly environment gets too much, private pools are available (from $32).

Aerius Helicopters   SCENIC FLIGHTS

(☑ 0800 864 354; www.aerius.co.nz; Tauranga Airport; flights from $115) Aerial excursions to as far away as Lake Tarawera, Rotorua and Whakaari (White Island).

Tauranga Tandem Skydiving   SKYDIVING

(☑ 07-574 8533; www.tandemskydive.co.nz; 2 Kittyhawk Way; jumps 10,000/12,000ft $325/375) Offers exhilarating jumps with views as far as Whakaari (White Island) and Mt Ruapehu on the way down.

Hibiscus   SURFING

(☑ 07-575 3792; www.surfschool.co.nz; Main Beach; 2hr/2-day lessons $75/165) Hires boards and offers a range of learn-to-surf lessons. Look for its van or red gazebo at Main Beach in summer.

Mount Surfshop   SURFING

(☑ 07-575 9133; www.mountsurfshop.co.nz; 98 Maunganui Rd; 4hr board hire $30; ⊙ 9am-5pm Mon-Sat, 10am-5pm Sun) Hires surfboards and sells them alongside beachy threads and skateboards.

Rocktopia   CLIMBING

(☑ 07-572 4920; www.rocktopia.co.nz; 9 Triton Ave; adult/child $17/13; ⊙ 9am-8pm; ⚒) This large climbing centre is split between Rock On, a large climbing wall painted like a bush-lined waterfall, and Clip n Climb, which is a little like a mini climbing theme park, featuring child-friendly challenges such as the 'Leap of Faith' and 'Vertical Drop Slide'.

Mt Maunganui

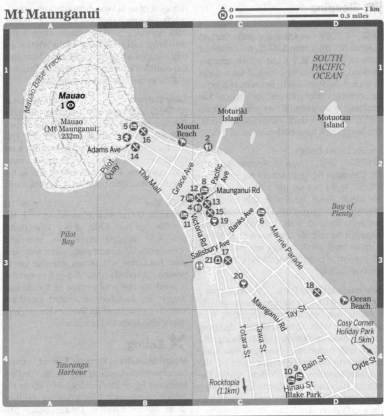

Mt Maunganui

Baywave   SWIMMING
(☏ 07-577 8550; www.bayvenues.co.nz; cnr Girven & Gloucester Rds; adult/child $7.50/5, hydroslide $4.90; ⊙ 6am-9pm Mon-Fri, 7am-7pm Sat & Sun)

This large aquatic centre has a 25m swimming pool, a wave pool, a hydroslide and aqua aerobics, along with a fitness centre and a sauna.

🛏 Sleeping

Seagulls Guesthouse
HOSTEL **$**

(☑ 07-574 2099; www.seagullsguesthouse.co.nz; 12 Hinau St; dm/s from $34/70, d with/without bathroom $99/78; @ 🛜) Can't face another crowded, alcohol-soaked hostel? On a quiet street not far from town, Seagulls is a gem: an upmarket backpackers' spot where the emphasis is on peaceful enjoyment of one's surrounds rather than wallowing in excess. The best rooms have bathrooms and TVs.

Pacific Coast Lodge
HOSTEL **$**

(☑ 07-574 9601; www.pacificcoastlodge.co.nz; 432 Maunganui Rd; dm/r without bathroom from $30/88; @ 🛜) Set on the main road but a few blocks from the centre, this efficiently run, sharp-looking hostel is sociable but not party-focused, with drinkers gently encouraged to migrate into town after 10pm. Purpose-built bunk rooms are roomy and adorned with beachy murals. Free bikes and surfboards, too!

Beachside Holiday Park
HOLIDAY PARK **$**

(☑ 07-575 4471; www.mountbeachside.co.nz; 1 Adams Ave; sites/on-site vans/cabins from $45/75/110) With three different camping areas nooked into the foot of Mt Maunganui itself, this community-run park has spectacularly positioned camping with all the requisite facilities. Plus it's right next to the Mount Hot Pools (discounts for campers) and a strip of eateries. Reception doubles as the local info centre.

Mount Backpackers
HOSTEL **$**

(☑ 07-575 0860; www.mountbackpackers.co.nz; 87 Maunganui Rd; dm $30-40; @ 🛜) If you're after a no-frills dorm room that's handy for the beach and the bars, this main-drag hostel could be for you (pack the earplugs though). Extras include cheap surfboard and bike hire.

Westhaven Motel
MOTEL **$$**

(☑ 07-575 4753; www.westhavenmotel.co.nz; 27a The Mall; units from $130; 🛜) If you can look past the tatty blinds, thin towels and unremarkable decor, Westhaven is a spacious and surprisingly affordable option, especially for those travelling with families or groups of friends. It's handy for both the shops and the beach, and only a short stroll from the hot pools.

Mission Belle Motel
MOTEL **$$**

(☑ 07-575 2578; www.missionbellemotel.co.nz; 1 Victoria Rd; unit from $170; 🛜) With a distinctly Spanish Mission look – resembling something out of an old spaghetti-western movie – this family-run motel goes all modern inside, with especially good two-storey family suites with large bathtubs. Some of the studios are tiny but they all have kitchenettes. Note that the complex backs on to Astrolabe Brewbar (p335), so the rear units can be noisy.

Cosy Corner
HOLIDAY PARK **$$**

(☑ 07-575 5899; www.cosycorner.co.nz; 40 Ocean Beach Rd; sites from $56, unit with/without bathroom $128/94; ⊙ Christmas-Easter; 🛜⛱) 🏄 This compact, spartan camping ground has a sociable feel, with barbecues, a playground and a games room. It's handy for the beach, too (access is via a little path just across the road).

Belle Mer
APARTMENT **$$$**

(☑ 07-575 0011; www.bellemer.co.nz; 53 Marine Pde; apt from $300; 🛜⛱) This flashy beachside complex offers one-, two- and three-bedroom apartments, some with seaview balconies and others opening on to private courtyards (though you'll more likely head for the pool terrace or the beach). Rooms are tastefully decorated and have everything you need for longer stays, including full kitchens and laundries.

🍴 Eating

Mount Mainstreet Farmers Market
MARKET **$**

(www.mountmaunganui.org.nz; Phoenix Car Park, Maunganui Rd; ⊙ 9am-1pm Sun) Roll up to the local farmers market for a Sunday-morning fix-me-up: fresh fruit and vegies, coffee, pastries, honey, cheese, juices... Arts and crafts are banned!

★ Eightyeight
CAFE **$$**

(☑ 07-574 0384; 88 Maunganui Rd; mains $14-20; ⊙ 7am-4.30pm) Don't come to this excellent little cafe if you're on a diet. Not that there aren't healthy options – it's just that the portions are so generous and the baked goods on the counter are completely irresistible. It's tiny inside so take a seat in the rear courtyard under the flower baskets.

★ Post Bank
BISTRO **$$**

(☑ 07-575 4782; www.postbank.co.nz; 82 Maunganui Rd; mains $28-38; ⊙ noon-2.30pm Tue-Fri, 5pm-late nightly) Bookcases crammed with an eclectic range of tomes give Post Bank the ambience of a gentlemen's club, but there's nothing stuffy about the food on offer. European influences pervade a menu playfully divided into Chapters 1, 2 and 3 and Epilogue. The smoothly professional team behind the bar concoct classy cocktails worthy of a 1920s speakeasy.

Fish Face
SEAFOOD $$

(☑07-575 2782; www.fish-face.co.nz; 107 Maunganui Rd; mains $22-29; ☺noon-9pm Wed-Mon, 4-9pm Tue; ⊞) White walls emblazoned with funky fish cartoons set the scene for this fresh, fun and informal 'seafood and wine bar'. The menu splashes its way through multiple cuisines; hence blue cod comes either Moroccan-style or as part of a Balinese curry, or you can try a classic spaghetti marinara or kingfish ceviche. You really can't go wrong.

Smart India
INDIAN $$

(☑07-574 9909; www.smartindia.co.nz; 245a Maunganui Rd; mains $17-23; ☺11.30am-2.30pm & 5-10pm; ☑) It may not look promising from the outside but this colourful little Indian restaurant serves curries that rival even the lime and orange walls for zing. A tender, still-pink lamb *saagwala* (with spinach) is a highlight, as is a flavour-filled mushroom *mutter korma* (with peas). The service is excellent too. Call in at lunchtime for a $10 curry special.

Pronto
BURGERS $$

(☑07-572 1109; www.prontoburgers.co.nz; 7/1 Marine Pde; burgers $15-18; ☺9.30am-3pm Mon, to 8pm Tue-Sun; ⊞) Pronto's menu of gourmet burgers reads like it belongs in a bistro: chicken parmigiana, pulled lamb shoulder, chicken schnitzel, Moroccan chicken, pork belly... The peri peri chicken with chunky avocado is pretty hard to beat. Service can be patchy, though. Grab a streetside seat for ocean and mount views.

Tay Street Beach Cafe
CAFE $$

(☑07-572 0691; www.taystreetbeachcafe.co.nz; cnr Tay St & Marine Pde; breakfast $10-21, mains $19-29; ☺7.30am-3pm Sun-Wed, to 9pm Thu-Sat) Around 2km south of Mauao, this beach-facing cafe is removed from the Mount's occasional bustle. Savvy locals crowd in for coffee in bright morning sunshine, linger over brunch classics, wolf down prawn tacos for lunch and return later in the week for an evening bistro meal. A good wine and craft-beer selection seals the deal.

Mount Bistro
BISTRO $$$

(☑07-575 3872; www.mountbistro.nz; 6 Adams Ave; mains $36-38; ☺5.30-10pm Tue-Sun) The buttermilk-coloured Mount Bistro is on to a good thing: quality local meats (lamb, beef, venison, chicken) and fish creatively worked into classic dishes (lamb shanks, seafood chowder) and served with flair. It makes for a classy night out.

▼ Drinking & Nightlife

★ Mount Social Club
BAR

(☑07-574 7773; www.mountsocialclub.co.nz; 305 Maunganui Rd; ☺8am-1am; 🛜⊞) ✔ A knowing blend of recycled materials, designer elements and lashings of utter kookiness, the Social is a visual feast. You can sit down to a proper meal inside but we prefer commandeering a bathtub couch in the courtyard, and we're certainly not ruling out dancing on the back of the day-glo truck when the band kicks in.

★ Hide
BAR

(☑07-572 0532; www.facebook.com/hide.thirst andhunger; 147b Maunganui Rd; ☺4-10pm Tue, noon-10pm Wed, Thu & Sun, noon-midnight Fri & Sat) Follow the sound of music and banter to this hip courtyard bar, tucked away behind the shops on the Mount's main street. It's the perfect place for a Moa beer and a burger on a balmy summer evening, and in the colder months they stoke up the open fire. We heartily endorse the chocolate rum Negroni.

★ Astrolabe Brewbar
PUB

(☑07-574 8155; www.astrolabe.co.nz; 82 Maunganui Rd; ☺9.30am-late; 🛜⊞) Astrolabe conjures up a funky retro bach (beach-hut) vibe, with floral carpets, bookshelves jammed with old novels, beach umbrellas and battered suitcases. If all that doesn't float your holiday boat, a Mac's Brewery beer might. Failing that, ask for a recommendation from the range of specialty gins and rums. There's even a playground for the kids, and stocks if they misbehave.

Rising Tide
PUB

(☑07-575 2739; www.therisingtidemt.com; 107 Newton St; ☺11am-late) Located in a light industrial area 4km from central Mt Maunganui, Rising Tide is home base for the Mount Brewing Co and Funk Estate microbreweries, who command nine of the 32 taps. Order snacks from the Johney's Dumpling House counter and settle in on the terrace with a tasting paddle. The adjacent Brewer's Field is used for gigs in summer.

🔒 Shopping

Little Big Markets
MARKET

(www.littlebigevents.co.nz; Coronation Park; ☺9am-2pm 1st Sat of the month Oct-Mar) Arts, crafts and tasty food all feature at this monthly morning market.

ℹ️ Information

The reception desk at **Beachside Holiday Park** (p334) doubles as an informal info centre; it's open from 8.30am to 8pm.

ℹ️ Getting There & Away

AIR

Tauranga City Airport (p331) is actually in Mt Maunganui, 4km from central Tauranga.

BUS

The Mount's main bus stop is on Salisbury Ave, just off Maunganui Rd.

Baybus (p319) has daytime services to Tauranga ($3.40, 28 minutes, every 15 minutes), Papamoa ($3.40, 34 minutes, hourly) and Rotorua ($11.60, 1¾ hours, twice daily).

InterCity (p319) destinations include Auckland ($22, four hours, two daily), Hamilton ($17, 2¾ hours, daily), Rotorua ($10, 1½ hours, daily), Taupo ($16, three hours, daily) and Napier ($19, six hours, daily).

Mana Bus (p319) has daily coaches to/from Auckland ($24, 4¾ hours), Hamilton ($17, 2½ hours), Katikati ($26, 1¼ hours) and Rotorua ($6, 1¼ hours).

CAR & MOTORCYCLE

Mt Maunganui is connected to Tauranga by bridge, or accessible from the south via SH2. For car hire, try **Rite Price Rentals** (☑ 07-575 2726; www.ritepricerentals.co.nz; 63 Totara St; ⊙ 8am-5pm Mon-Sat, to noon Sun).

Papamoa

POP 20,100

Papamoa is a burgeoning 'burb next to Mt Maunganui, separated by just an empty paddock or two, destined for subdivision. With big new houses on pristine streets, parts of Papamoa have the air of a gated community, but the beach beyond the sheltering dunes is awesome – you can't blame folks for moving in.

🏃 Activities

Blokart Recreation Park   ADVENTURE SPORTS
(☑ 07-572 4256; www.blokartrecreationpark.co.nz; 176 Parton Rd; blokarts 30min/1hr $30/50, drift karts 15min $25; ⊙ 10am-4.30pm Sat & Sun) Forget all that pesky water, this custom-built speedway is the place to attempt land-sailing (blokarts are like seated windsurfers on wheels). There are also electric-powered drift karts, so action is possible even when there's no wind. Both activities are loads of fun, easily mastered and highly recommended.

🛏️ Sleeping & Eating

Papamoa Beach Resort   HOLIDAY PARK $$
(☑ 07-572 0816; www.papamoabeach.co.nz; 535 Papamoa Beach Rd; sites from $24, unit with/without bathroom $153/93; @ 🖥️) 🏊 This sprawling resort is a spotless, modern complex, primed and priced beyond its caravan-park origins, with luxurious self-contained villas tucked directly behind the dunes. Small children will love the playground, the jumping pillow and the summertime kids' club.

Beach House Motel   MOTEL $$
(☑ 07-572 1424, 0800 429 999; www.beachhousemotel.co.nz; 224 Papamoa Beach Rd; unit from $155; 🖥️🌊) With its angular corrugated-iron exterior and tasteful cane furnishings, this upmarket motel offers an immaculate version of the Kiwi bach (beach house) holiday, relaxed and close to the water. Outside there's a small pool for when the beach is too windy, and flowers poking up from an old dinghy.

Bluebiyou   CAFE $$
(☑ 07-572 2099; www.bluebiyou.co.nz; 559 Papamoa Beach Rd; mains breakfast $16-20, lunch $19-26, dinner $22-37; ⊙ 10am-late) Bluebiyou is a casual, breezy bistro riding high on the dunes, serving big brunches, a whole heap of Italian-influenced dishes (bruschetta, pizza, pasta), seafood specialities and tapas. The delicately battered oysters are excellent. Drop by on Sunday afternoons for live music, happy-hour drinks and food specials.

ℹ️ Getting There & Away

Baybus (p319) has services to Mt Maunganui ($3.40, 50 minutes) and Tauranga ($3.40, 30 minutes) at least hourly, along with a bus to Whakatane ($14, 1½ hours) most days.

Whakatane

POP 18,800

A true pohutukawa paradise, Whakatane (pronounced 'fah-kah-*tah*-neh') sits on a natural harbour at the mouth of the river of the same name. It's the hub of a productive agricultural district, but there's much more to Whakatane than farming – blissful beaches, a sunny main-street vibe and volcanic Whakaari offshore for starters. And it's consistently one of the sunniest spots in the country – although in 2016 it narrowly forfeited its long-held title of 'NZ's sunniest town' to Blenheim.

◉ Sights

Pōhaturoa LANDMARK
(cnr The Strand & Commerce St) Beside a round-about on The Strand is Pōhaturoa, a large *tapu* (sacred) rock outcrop, where birth, death, war and *moko* (tattoo) rites were performed. The Treaty of Waitangi was signed here by Ngāti Awa chiefs in 1840. There's also a monument to respected Ngāti Awa chief Te Hurinui Apanui (1855–1924).

Te Kōputu a te whanga a Toi MUSEUM
(Whakatane Library & Exhibition Centre; ☑ 07-306 0509; www.whakatanemuseum.org.nz; 49 Kakaho-roa Dr; ⊙ 9am-5pm Mon-Fri, 10am-2pm Sat & Sun) FREE Attached to the library, this impressive museum and gallery has artfully presented displays on early Māori and European settlement in the area. Some of the Māori *taonga* (treasures) travelled from a distant Pacific island on the *Mātaatua* canoe more than 700 years ago. Other displays focus on Wha-kaari (White Island) and Moutohora (Whale Island). The gallery presents a varied series of NZ and international exhibitions.

Wairere Falls WATERFALL
(Toroa St) Tumbling down the cliffs behind town, picture-perfect Te Wairere occupies a deliciously damp nook, and once powered flax and flour mills and supplied Whakatane's drinking water. It's a gorgeous spot, and goes almost completely unheralded: in any other country there'd be a ticket booth, interpretive audiovisual displays and a hot-dog van!

Mataatua HISTORIC BUILDING
(☑ 07-308 4271; www.mataatua.com; 105 Muriwai Dr; adult/child 1hr tour $49/15, incl walk $98/30; ⊙ 10am-4pm Dec-Feb, to 2pm Mar-Nov) FREE Mataatua is a large, fantastically carved 1875 *wharenui* (meeting house) that is the centrepiece of Te Mānuka Tūtahi *marae* (traditional meeting place). The remarkable story of 'the house that came home' is told in the neighbouring visitor centre through displays and a fascinating eight-minute movie. To visit the *wharenui* you'll need to take an hour-long guided tour (usually at noon and 2pm; call ahead), which starts with a *powhiri* (traditional welcoming ceremony).

In 1879 Mataatua was dismantled and sent to Sydney, much to the consternation of the local Ngāti Awa people whose ancestors it embodied. Adding insult to injury, it was re-erected inside out, exposing its precious interior carvings to the harsh Australian elements. After a stint in Melbourne it was sent

to London and ended up spending 40 years in the Victoria & Albert Museum cellars. After 71 years in the Otago Museum, where it was cut down to fit the space, it finally came home in 2011.

Visits can be combined with the 90-minute 'Footsteps of Our Ancestors' walking tour, taking in nearby sites of cultural significance.

Muriwai's Cave CAVE
(Te Ana o Muriwai; 35 Muriwai Dr) This partially collapsed cave once extended 122m into the hillside and was the home of Muriwai, a famous seer and brother of Toroa, captain of the Mātaatua *waka* (canoe). Along with Wairere Falls and a rock in the harbour-mouth, the cave was one of three landmarks Toroa was told to look for by his father Irakewa before setting out from their Polynesian homeland. Carvings of the siblings flank the entry.

Just across the road, near the water's edge, is a carved shelter containing a ceremonial *waka*.

Te Pāpaka & Puketapu VIEWPOINT
(Hillcrest & Seaview Rds) On the cliff tops behind the town are a pair of ancient Ngāti Awa *pā* (fortified village) sites – Te Pāpaka (The Crab) and Puketapu (Sacred Hill) – both of which offer sensational (and very defensible) outlooks over Whakatane. Look for the track leading up from the car park at the top of Seaview Rd to the first, then cross Hillcrest Rd for the track to the second.

Whakatane Observatory OBSERVATORY
(☑ 07-308 6495; www.whakatane.info/business/whakatane-astronomical-society; 17 Hurinui Ave; adult/child $15/5; ⊙ 7.30pm Tue & Fri) Up on a hill top behind the town, this observatory offers abundant Bay of Plenty star-spotting when the sky is clear.

Awakeri Hot Springs HOT SPRINGS
(Awakeri; ☑ 07-304 9117; www.awakerisprings.co.nz; SH30; adult/child $7.50/5, private spa per 30min from $12; ⊙ 8am-9.30pm) About 16km from Whakatane on the road to Rotorua (SH30), this old-fashioned holiday park has a large thermal mineral pool, two smaller children's pools and six private spas.

🏃 Activities

The *Whakatāne Walkways Guide*, available from the i-SITE, details some highly scenic walks easily accessible from the town centre. The mother of them all is the **Ngā Tapuwae o Toi (Footsteps of Toi) Walkway**, a 16km

Whakatane

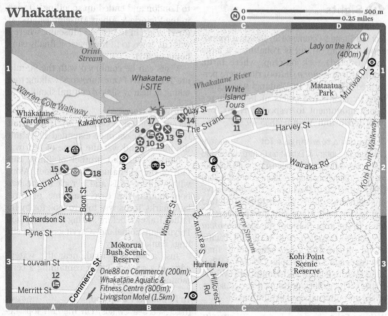

Whakatane

loop that takes between five and seven hours to complete. Starting in town it quickly joins the spectacular **Kōhī Point Walkway**: a bushy track with panoramic cliff-top views and a genuine 'gasp' moment when you first set eyes on **Otarawairere Bay**. A short detour rewards you with amazing views from **Toi's Pā** (Kapua-te-rangi), reputedly the oldest *pā* (fortified village) site in NZ. After 7km (about three hours) you'll reach Ohope, where you can catch the bus back to Whakatane if there aren't any more kilometres left in your legs.

A flatter option is the **Warren Cole Walkway** (one hour return), starting from the Landing Rd bridge and following the Whakatane River past Whakatane Gardens and Muriwai's Cave.

Onepū Mountain Bike Park MOUNTAIN BIKING
(SH30, Te Teko) FREE Bump and grind your way around 15km of trails in this patch of forest, 30km southwest of Whakatane on the way to Rotorua. There are even some BMX-type jumps to try. For information on this and other cycling tracks, pick up a copy of the *Whakatāne Cycling Guide* from the i-SITE.

Diveworks DIVING

(📞0800 354 7737, 07-308 2001; www.whaleisland tours.com; 96 The Strand; diving incl gear from $215) As well as guided eco tours to Moutohora (p340), Diveworks delves into the waters around it, including the wreck of the 44m *Seafire*. Other trips head to the Rurima Islands for crayfish and as far out as Whakaari.

White Island Flights SCENIC FLIGHTS

(📞07-308 7760; www.whiteislandflights.co.nz; Whakatane Airport; flights $249) Fixed-wing scenic flights over Whakaari, with lots of photo opportunities. A Whakaari/Mt Tarawera combo flight costs $339.

Whakatāne Aquatic & Fitness Centre SWIMMING

(📞07-308 4192; www.whakatane.govt.nz/aquatic; 28 Short St; adult/child $4.50/2.50; ⊙6am-8pm Mon-Fri, 7am-6pm Sat & Sun) Indoor and outdoor pools, spa pools and a tubular yellow worm of a waterslide ($4.50).

🛏 Sleeping

Windsor Lodge Backpackers HOSTEL $

(📞07-308 8040; www.windsorlodge-backpackers. co.nz; 10 Merritt St; dm $25, with/without bathroom s $84/49, d $88/68; @🛜) This hostel occupies a converted funeral parlour, so a restful sleep is on the cards. Rooms range from serviceable dorms to a couple of private en-suite rooms out the front. The large internal courtyard is great for summertime socialising.

Whakatane Hotel PUB $

(📞07-307 1670; www.whakatanehotel.co.nz; 79 The Strand; s $75, d with/without bathroom $85/75; 🛜) This lovely old art-deco pub has basic but decent rooms upstairs. It's what you'd expect from pub accommodation of its era: rooms have high ceilings, many share bathrooms and there's a communal kitchen. Expect noise from the bar downstairs.

One88 on Commerce MOTEL $$

(📞07-307 0915; www.one88oncommerce.co.nz; 188 Commerce St; unit from $149; 🛜) Located a 10-minute walk from the town centre, this modern motel has sparkling, spacious units and extra-large super-king suites. Most options feature spa baths and private courtyards along with kitchenettes and huge flatscreen TVs.

White Island Rendezvous MOTEL $$

(📞07-308 9500; www.whiteislandrendezvous. co.nz; 15 The Strand E; s/d from $99/140; 🛜) 🍃 Run by the on-the-ball White Island Tour

people (cheaper rates for guests), this immaculate complex includes a vaguely Tuscan-looking main block, a 'micro-village' of stylish corrugated-iron cabins, and B&B rooms in a charming villa next door. There are lots of balconies and decks for inhaling the sea air, and some units have spa baths.

Tuscany Villas MOTEL $$

(📞07-308 2244; www.tuscanyvillas.co.nz; 57 The Strand E; unit from $159; ❄🛜) This motel may be a long way from Florence, but it still offers a few rays of Italian sunshine with wrought-iron balconies, an outdoor pizza oven and a summertime wine bar. Rooms are luxurious and comfy, with super-king beds and spa pools.

Livingston Motel MOTEL $$

(📞07-308 6400; www.livingston.co.nz; 42 Landing Rd; unit from $130; 🛜) It's a bit of a hike into town, but this spotless, ranch-style motel is the pick of the half-dozen dotted along Landing Rd. Expect spacious, well-kept units, comfy beds and large spas in executive suites.

🍴 Eating & Drinking

Peejay's Cafe CAFE $

(📞07-308 9588; www.whiteisland.co.nz; 15 The Strand E; mains $10-19; ⊙6.30am-4pm) Part of the White Island Rendezvous complex, our favourite Whakatane cafe serves a mean kedgeree and tasty baked goods, including a delicious ginger slice. Ginger features prominently in many of the dishes, no doubt

---

THE NAMING OF WHAKATANE

Whakatane's name originated some six centuries ago, 200 years after the original Māori settlers arrived here. The warrior Toroa and his family sailed into the estuary in a huge ocean-going *waka* (canoe), the *Mātaatua*. As the men went ashore to greet local leaders, the tide turned, and the *waka* – with all the women on board – drifted out to sea. Toroa's daughter, Wairaka, cried out *'E! Kia whakatāne au i ahau!'* (Let me act as a man!) and, breaking the traditional *tapu* (taboo) on women steering a *waka*, she took up the paddle and brought the boat safely ashore. A whimsical statue of Wairaka, the **Lady on the Rock**, stands proudly at the mouth of Whakatane's harbour in commemoration of her brave deed.

WORTH A TRIP

MOUTOHORA (WHALE ISLAND)

It's quite unusual for the English version of a Māori place name to be an exact translation but this volcanic island, 9km off the coast near Whakatane, really does look like a cartoon whale from certain angles. It's one of the less active members of the Taupo Volcanic Zone, although there are hot springs along its shore. The summit is 353m high and the island has several historic sites, including an ancient *pā* (fortified village) site, a quarry and a camp.

Moutohora was once the site of a Ngāti Awa village but in 1867 it passed into European ownership. Since 1965 it has been a DOC-protected wildlife refuge for seabirds and shorebirds, and it's now completely predator free. In 1999, 40 tieke (the once-endangered North Island saddleback) were released; they now number around 1500. Fur seals are also frequently spotted.

The island's protected status means landing is restricted to a handful of licensed operators, departing from Whakatane.

White Island Tours (☑0800 733 529; www.whiteisland.co.nz; 15 The Strand; 5½hr trips adult/child $219/130) ⚓ runs half-day tours to the island (adult/child $99/59), incorporating a visit to a NZ fur seal colony and bird-watching.

Diveworks (p339) offers a two-hour circumnavigation of the island (adult/child $90/70) or a four-hour trip including a guided tour of the island ($120/75).

KG Kayaks (p341) heads to the island by catamaran and then unloads the kayaks for a wildlife-spotting paddle around the shoreline, entering sea caves when the conditions are right (per person $195).

---

aiming to settle the stomachs of those about to catch the boat to Whakaari. It gets frantic around tour-check-in time but it's a pleasantly laid-back spot otherwise.

Julian's Berry Farm CAFE $
(☑07-308 4253; www.juliansberryfarm.co.nz; 12 Huna Rd, Coastlands; mains $5-20; ⊗8.30am-5.30pm Nov-Feb; ⊕) Pick-your-own berry farms are a Kiwi summer tradition. Kids love it, but if you'd prefer to leave the back-breaking work to someone else, order from the cafe and grab a seat on the large sunny terrace. Berries make their way into most things, including muffins, hot cakes, smoothies and ice cream. There's also mini-golf and a petting farm.

Scilla Chocolates SWEETS $
(☑07-308 7261; www.bouquetfloral.co.nz; 230 The Strand; chocolates from $1.20; ⊗8.30am-5pm Mon-Fri, 9am-noon Sat) Pop into the Bouquet Floral Studio for delicious Belgian-style Scilla chocolates, handmade in nearby Ohope Beach. Gift boxes are a good present for the folks back home, if you can resist devouring them yourself.

L'Epicerie CAFE $$
(☑07-308 5981; www.lepicerie.co.nz; 73 The Strand; mains $10-20; ⊗7.30am-4pm; ⊕) *Sacré bleu!* This classic French cafe in central Whakatane is a real surprise, serving terrific omelettes,

croissants and crepes at communal tables. Fabulous coffee and deli shelves crammed with preserves, breads, mustards and deliciously stinky French cheeses complete a very Gallic scene. Try an excellent *galette* (savoury pancake) for a leisurely breakfast.

Roquette MEDITERRANEAN $$
(☑07-307 0722; www.roquette-restaurant.co.nz; 23 Quay St; mains lunch $22-37, dinner $30-37; ⊗10am-late Mon-Sat) Ritzy Roquette serves up refreshing Mediterranean-influenced fare with lots of summery salads, risotto and fish dishes. It's a modern waterside restaurant with lots of glass, good coffee and efficient staff to boot. Try the chargrilled lamb salad or the prawn-and-chorizo *arancini*. Call in before 6pm for a good-value early-bird menu (main plus wine $23).

Soulsa MODERN NZ $$
(☑07-307 8689; www.soulsa.co.nz; 14 Richardson St; mains $33; ⊗5.30-9pm Mon-Sat) Seasonal produce is creatively transformed into tasty dishes at this modern restaurant, serving everything from Asian-style broths to gamey Kiwi classics such as venison with kumara. There's also a good wine list.

Straight Up Espresso CAFE
(☑021 069 9637; 5 Boon St; ⊗7.30am-4pm Mon-Fri, 9.30am-12.30pm Sat; ☎) It does exactly what it is says on the tin, with the best, not

to mention strongest, coffee in town. Colourful wall art, cool tunes and tasty snacks are all valid reasons to linger.

Craic IRISH PUB
(☑07-282 3058; www.whakatanehotel.co.nz; Whakatane Hotel, 79 The Strand; ☺11am-late) The Craic is a busy locals' boozer of the Irish ilk; good for a pint or two, or a mug of hot chocolate if you're feeling subpar. Inside there are lots of cosy nooks, but when the sun's shining, the street tables are the place to be.

☆ Entertainment

Boiler Room LIVE MUSIC
(☑07-282 3058; www.facebook.com/BoilerRoom Whakatane; George St) Open for events only, the large gritty band room at the Whakatane Hotel hosts DJs, live bands and the occasional Kiwi stand-up comic.

WhakaMax Movies CINEMA
(☑07-308 7623; www.whakamax.co.nz; 99 The Strand; adult/child $14/9) Right in the middle of The Strand, WhakaMax screens new-release movies. Cheaper tickets before 5pm and on Tuesdays.

❶ Information

Whakatane Hospital (☑07-306 0999; www.bopdhb.govt.nz; cnr Stewart & Garaway Sts; ☺24hr) Emergency medical treatment.

Whakatane i-SITE (☑07-306 2030; www.whakatane.com; cnr Quay St & Kakahoroa Dr; ☺8.30am-5.30pm Mon-Fri, 9am-4pm Sat & Sun; ☎) Free wi-fi (including on the terrace outside the building after hours), tour bookings, accommodation and general DOC enquiries. Also bike hire (two hours, $10) for exploring nearby coastal paths.

❶ Getting There & Away

AIR

Whakatane Airport (WHK; 216 Aerodrome Rd, Thornton) is in Thornton, 9km west of town. **Air Chathams** (☑0800 580 127; www.airchathams.co.nz) has two to three flights a day between Whakatane and Auckland.

BUS

Baybus (p319) has services to Ohope ($3.40, 30 minutes, seven daily except Sunday), Opotiki ($9.50, 45 minutes, two per week), Papamoa ($14, 1½ hours, most days) and Tauranga ($16, two hours, most days).

On most days **InterCity** (p319) has a coach to Auckland ($38, six hours), Hamilton ($34, 3½ hours), Rotorua ($23, 1½ hours), Opotiki ($15, 35 minutes) and Gisborne ($16, three hours), stopping outside the i-SITE.

Ohope

POP 2760

Just 6km over the hill from Whakatane, Ohope has an extraordinarily gorgeous, just-short-of-endless beach, perfect for lazing or surfing. It's backed by sleepy Ohiwa Harbour, a top spot for kayaking and fishing.

🏃 Activities & Tours

KG Kayaks KAYAKING
(☑027 272 4073; www.kgkayaks.co.nz; 93 Kutarere Wharf Rd, Kutarere; tour from $85, 1/2/3hr hire from $25/45/65) Although it's based on the southern shores of the Ohiwa Harbour between Ohope and Opotiki, KG rents kayaks from a shed at Port Ohope in summer. Its 2½-hour guided Coastal Adventure departs Ohope Beach for a paddle around secluded bays. It also offers daytime and moonlight excursions on Ohiwa Harbour, and longer trips to Moutohora (p340).

Salt Spray Surf School SURFING
(☑021 149 1972; www.saltspraysurfschool.co.nz; West End Rd; 2hr lessons from $70) Rents boards and wet suits, and offers lessons for beginners, including targeted classes for kids and women.

Moanarua Tours BOATING
(☑07-312 5924; www.moanarua.co.nz; 2 Hoterini St; 3hr boat tours per person $85, 1hr bike/kayak rental $10/15) Offers boat trips with a Māori cultural and historical focus, plus sunset tours and fishing trips. Also bike and kayak hire for those who wish to go exploring.

🛏 Sleeping

Ohope Beach Top 10 Holiday Park HOLIDAY PARK **$$**
(☑07-312 4460; www.ohopebeach.co.nz; 367 Harbour Rd; sites from $21, unit with/without bathroom from $163/78; ☎☀) ✦ This vast complex is the very model of a modern holiday park, with a raft of family-friendly facilities: sports courts, mini-golf, jumping pillow, pool with hydroslides... Plus shady sites and some great apartments peeking over the dunes. It's busy as a woodpecker in summer (with prices to match).

Aquarius Motel MOTEL **$$**
(☑07-312 4550; www.aquariusmotel.co.nz; 103 Harbour Rd; unit from $135; ☎) Aquarius consists of a series of small blocks of units spreading back from the main road towards the beach (no need for a swimming pool). Rooms are simple but they all have kitchens.

DON'T MISS

WHAKAARI (WHITE ISLAND)

New Zealand's most active volcano lies 49km off the Whakatane coast, easily identified on clear days by its constant white plume of steam. This small island is estimated to be between 150,000 to 200,000 years old and was originally formed from three separate volcanic cones. The two oldest have been eroded, while the younger cone has risen up between them. Mt Gisborne is the highest point on the island, at 321m, but beneath the waterline the mountain descends a further 440m to the seabed.

Visiting Whakaari is an absolutely unforgettable once-in-a-lifetime experience. Licensed tours land directly in the crater and steer gingerly between chimneys of bright-yellow sulphur and steaming vents (temperatures of 600°C to 800°C have been recorded). You won't see any lava (it's not that kind of volcano) but you will get to touch and taste pure sulphur, and clean your 10c coins in an acidic thermal stream.

Tours also visit the ruins of a sulphur factory that operated on the island from 1923 to 1933. The volcanic atmosphere has corroded the metal but preserved the wood, leaving a photogenic tumble of remains. A previous attempt at mining on the island ended in tragedy; in 1914 all 10 men stationed here disappeared without a trace, the only survivor being Pete the camp cat (subsequently dubbed 'Peter the Great').

Visits to the island aren't without risk, but nobody has died here since then. Significant events happen every two to 10 years, usually taking the form of an ash eruption. Hard hats must be worn at all times and gas masks are provided; the fumes aren't dangerous but can irritate the throat.

Despite the harsh conditions, the island is home to a thriving gannet colony and the waters around it abound with marine life.

All tours depart from Whakatane and are subject to the weather and volcanic activity. Bookings are essential but trips can't be confirmed until the night before.

White Island Tours (p340) has the only boats permitted to land on the island and an enthusiastic crew of highly informative guides. The entire trip takes five to six hours, including upwards of an hour on the island and a picnic lunch while docked offshore. The tour keeps a watchful eye for marine wildlife on the 90-minute (each-way) boat journey.

Frontier Helicopters (☑ 0800 804 354; www.whiteislandvolcano.co.nz; Whakatane Airport; tour $695) offers a two-hour tour from Whakatane, circling the volcano for a bird's-eye view before landing in the crater for a tour.

Aerius Helicopters (p333) offers a similar experience, departing from Mt Maunganui ($870 per person).

Moanarua Beach Cottage
B&B $$

(☑ 07-312 5924; www.moanarua.co.nz; 2 Hoterini St; d $180) Well-travelled owners Miria and Taroi combine their warm welcome with information on local Māori heritage, art and culture. Accommodation is in a self-contained garden cottage trimmed with Māori design. Taroi can hook visitors up with bike and kayak rental, and arrange fishing and boating trips.

✗ Eating

Ohiwa Oyster Farm
FISH & CHIPS $

(☑ 07 312 4565; www.whakatane.info/business/ohiwa-oyster-farm; 111 Wainui Rd; meals $7.30-12; ⊙10am-6.30pm) Perched over a swampy back-reach of Ohiwa Harbour (serious oyster territory), this classic roadside fish shack is perfect for a fish-and-chip picnic

or to stock up on pots of oysters. Keep an eye out for stingrays hanging around the water's edge.

Moxi
CAFE $$

(☑ 021 283 1330; www.moxicafe.co.nz; 23 Pohutukawa Ave; mains breakfast $12-18, lunch $18-24; ⊙7am-3.30pm) Cobbled together out of shipping containers but with a very flash louvred roof, this mainly open-air cafe is Ohope's best. Portions aren't large and the service is so-so but the food is delicious and the coffee is first-rate. There's also craft beer and wine on offer, making it a great spot for a post-beach tipple.

Cadera
MEXICAN $$

(☑ 07-312 6122; www.facebook.com/Cadera.ohope; 19 Pohutukawa Ave; mains $18-25; ⊙4-10pm Tue & Wed, 4pm-midnight Thu, 11am-midnight Fri-Sun) Perfectly suited to its beachy setting, this relaxed restaurant-bar has the obligatory Frida Kahlo print on the wall and a menu of Mexican favourites (nachos, burritos, quesadillas). The tacos are particularly yummy.

ⓘ Getting There & Away

Baybus (p319) route 122 makes the short hop across the hill from Whakatane to Ohope ($3.40, 30 minutes, seven per day, no Sunday services), while 147 continues on to Opotiki ($9.50, 45 minutes) on Mondays and Wednesdays.

InterCity (p319) has a coach most days to Auckland ($39, 6½ hours), Hamilton ($34, four hours), Rotorua ($23, two hours), Opotiki ($15, 25 minutes) and Gisborne ($16, three hours).

Opotiki
POP 4180

Set out in a tidy grid pattern within the embrace of two rivers, Opotiki is a worn-around-the-edges kind of town with a scattering of historic buildings and a couple of exceptional beaches nearby (Ohiwa and Waiotahi). Aside from the beaches, its main appeal is as a gateway to both the East Coast and a series of mountain-biking trails in the hinterland. Māori traditions are alive and well here, with more than half of the population claiming Māori descent.

◎ Sights & Activities

Pick up the *Historic Opotiki* brochure from the i-SITE (p344) (or download it from www.opotikinz.com) for the lowdown on the town's heritage buildings.

Opotiki Museum   MUSEUM
(☏07-315 5193; www.opotikimuseum.org.nz; 123 Church St; adult/child $10/5; ◷10am-4pm Mon-Fri, to 2pm Sat) Run by volunteers, Opotiki's museum has heritage displays including Māori artefacts, militaria, recreated shopfronts (barber, carpenter, printer...), and agricultural items including tractors and a horse-drawn wagon. The admission charge includes entry to the Shalfoon & Francis general store a few doors down (you may have to ask for it to be opened for you).

Founded in the 1860s, the store closed its doors in 2000 and the shelves are still piled high with old grocery and hardware products. Handbags, sticky-tape dispensers, sets of scales, books – you name it, they had it. An amazing collection.

Hiona St Stephen's Church   CHURCH
(☏07-315 8319; www.hiona.org.nz; 124 Church St) White wooden St Stephen's (1862) is an Anglican church with a timber-lined interior and *tukutuku* (woven flax) panels in the sanctuary. Reverend Carl Völkner, known by the local Whakatōhea tribe to have acted as a government spy during the New Zealand Wars, was executed by Māori here in 1865. In 1992 the governor-general granted Mokomoko, the man the government in turn hanged for his 'murder', a full pardon, which is displayed in the lobby.

Hours vary but the church is usually open in the morning and until around 2pm.

Motu Trails   MOUNTAIN BIKING
(www.motutrails.co.nz) One of the New Zealand Cycle Trail's 'Great Rides', Motu Trails comprises three trails around Opotiki – the easy **Dunes Trail** (10km), the intermediate **Motu Road Trail** (67km) and the advanced **Pakihi Track** (44km). All of these distances are one way, necessitating shuttles, but parts of the trails can be combined to form the **Motu Trails Loop** (91km).

For bike hire, camping and lodge accommodation, and shuttle services see www.motucycletrails.com or www.hireandshuttle.co.nz.

Travel Shop   OUTDOORS
(☏07-315 8881; www.travelshop.co.nz; 104 Church St; hire 4/8hr $30/40; ◷9am-5pm Mon-Fri) This main-street travel agency rents bikes, kayaks and surfboards.

🛏 Sleeping & Eating

★**Ohiwa Beach Holiday Park** HOLIDAY PARK $
(☏07-315 4741; www.ohiwaholidays.co.nz; Ohiwa Harbour Rd; sites from $21, unit with/without bathroom from $95/65; 🐕🐾) Blissfully squeezed into a remote corner between Ohiwa Harbour and a gorgeous ocean beach, 14km west of Opotiki, this large holiday park distils the essence of the Kiwi summer: pohutukawa trees, phoenix palms, manicured lawns, rolling waves and endless sands. There are only a handful of units but there's ample space to pitch a tent. Bring coins for the showers.

Opotiki Beach House   HOSTEL $
(☏07-315 5117; www.opotikibeachhouse.co.nz; 7 Appleton Rd, Waiotahi Beach; dm/s/d from $30/49/68; 🐾) This cruisy, shoe-free beachside pad has a sunny, hammock-hung deck, sea views and a *very* wide sandy backyard. Beyond the dorms and breezy lounge are

WORTH A TRIP

HUKUTAIA DOMAIN

Around 8km south of town, this small but verdant patch of **forest** (501 Woodlands Rd; ☉ daylight hours) is home to around 1500 varieties of native plants, which can be seen on a 20-minute circuit. The most important specimen is Taketakerau, a sacred 23m puriri tree estimated to be more than 2000 years old. It was once used as a burial place for the distinguished dead of the Upokorehe *hapū* (subtribe) of Whakatōhea; the remains have since been reinterred elsewhere.

decent doubles and a quirky caravan (sleeps two) for those who want a real taste of the Kiwi summer holiday. It's right by Waiotahi Beach, about 5km west of town.

Central Oasis Backpackers HOSTEL $
(☎ 07-315 5165; centraloasis@hotmail.com; 30 King St; dm/s/d $25/35/56; ☏) Occupying a 19th-century wooden house, this central hostel is a snug spot with spacious rooms, a crackling fire and a lush garden to hang out in. There's also a handy coffee caravan – open to the public – serving organic coffee, tea and fresh juices.

Island View Holiday Park HOLIDAY PARK $$
(☎ 07-315 7519; www.islandviewholiday.co.nz; 6 Appleton Rd, Waiotahi Beach; dm & sites $25, unit with/without bathroom from $140/80; ☏☒) A rustic driftwood fence sets a Robinson Crusoe vibe at this chilled-out holiday park. Cabins open onto shared decks with barbecues and their own toilet blocks, meaning that what you sacrifice in privacy you stand to gain in sociability. Plus there are free kayaks, hammocks slung between trees, a volleyball court and a swimming pool.

Eastland Pacific Motor Lodge MOTEL $$
(☎ 07-315 5524; www.eastlandpacific.co.nz; 44 St John St; unit from $125; ☏) Bright, clean Eastland is a well-kept motel with units that are simple but pleasantly kitted out. Some have spa baths and, at $160, the two-bedroom units are top value.

Two Fish CAFE $
(☎ 07-315 5448; 102 Church St; mains $7-21; ☉ 8am-2.50pm Mon-Fri, to 1.50pm Sat) Decent eating options are thin on the ground in Opotiki, but this happy cafe serves up robust homemade burgers, chowder, toasties, steak sandwiches, salads and a jumbo selection in the cabinet. The coffee's excellent too. Grab a seat in the retro-groovy interior or in the courtyard.

☆ Entertainment

DeLuxe Theatre CINEMA
(☎ 07-315 6110; www.deluxetheatre.co.nz; 127 Church St; adult/child $14/7) Dating from 1926, this beguiling community-run cinema shows recent movies and hosts the odd concert.

❶ Information

The **Opotiki i-SITE** (☎ 07-315 3031; www.opotikinz.com; 70 Bridge St; ☉ 9am-4.30pm Mon-Fri, to 1pm Sat & Sun; ☏) and **DOC** (☎ 07-315 1001; www.doc.govt.nz; 70 Bridge St; ☉ 9am-4.30pm Fri) are in the same building. The i-SITE takes bookings for activities and transport, and stocks the indispensable free East Coast booklet *Pacific Coast Highway*. Showers are available, too ($3).

❶ Getting There & Away

BUS

Baybus (p319) route 147 ($9.50) heads to Whakatane (55 minutes) and Ohope (45 minutes) twice daily on Mondays and Wednesdays. Route 150 heads east along the coast as far as Potaka on Tuesdays and Thursdays.

InterCity (p319) has a coach most days to Auckland ($42, 6¾ hours), Hamilton ($34, 4¼ hours), Rotorua ($23, 2¼ hours), Whakatane ($15, 44 minutes) and Gisborne ($16, two hours).

CAR & MOTORCYCLE

Travelling east from Opotiki there are two routes: SH2, crossing the spectacular Waioeka Gorge, or SH35 around East Cape. The SH2 route offers some day walks in the Waioeka Gorge Scenic Reserve, with the gorge getting steeper and narrower as you travel inland, before the route crosses typically green, rolling hills, dotted with sheep, on the descent to Gisborne.

The East Coast

Best Places to Eat

➡ Mister D (p370)

➡ Bistronomy (p371)

➡ Crawford Road Kitchen (p359)

➡ Maina (p376)

➡ Elephant Hill (p376)

Best Places to Stay

➡ Stranded in Paradise (p352)

➡ St Andrews Escape (p375)

➡ Millar Road (p375)

➡ Ahi Kaa Motel (p358)

➡ Kiwiesque (p369)

Why Go?

New Zealand is known for its mix of wildly divergent landscapes, but on the East Coast it's the sociological contours that are most pronounced. There's a full spectrum of NZ life here, from the earthy settlements on the East Cape to Havelock North's moneyed, wine-soaked streets.

Māori culture is never more visible than it is on the East Coast. Exquisitely carved *marae* (meeting house) complexes dot the landscape, and *te reo* and *tikanga* (the language and customs) are alive and well.

Intrepid types will have no trouble losing the tourist crowds – along the Pacific Coast Hwy, through rural back roads, on remote beaches or in the mystical wilds of Te Urewera. And when the call of the wild gives way to caffeine withdrawal, you can get a quick fix in Gisborne or Napier. You'll also find plenty of wine here: the Hawke's Bay region is striped with vine rows.

When to Go

➡ The East Coast basks in a warm, mainly dry climate. Temperatures in summer (from roughly December to March) around balmy Napier and sunny Gisborne nudge 25°C; in winter (around June to August) they rarely dip below 8°C.

➡ The Hawke's Bay region enjoys mild, dry, grape-growing conditions year-round, with an average annual rainfall of just 800mm. Harvest time is autumn (March to May).

➡ In winter, heavy downpours sometimes wash out sections of the Pacific Coast Hwy (SH35) around the East Cape: check road conditions at either end (Opotiki or Gisborne) before you hit the highway.

The East Coast Highlights

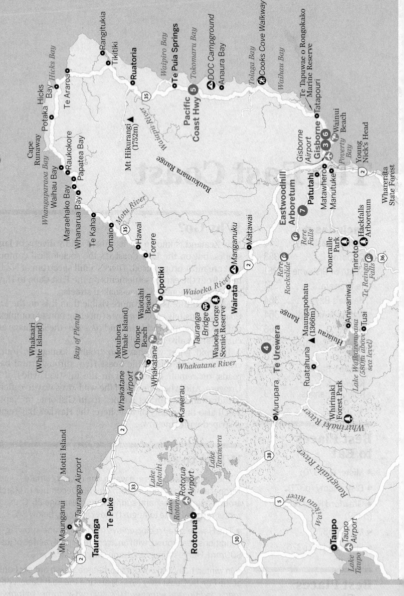

1 Napier (p366)
Time-warping back to the 1930s, surrounded by art deco, in this mighty charming town.

2 Hawke's Bay Wine Region (p377)
Sniffing and sipping your way around the local wineries.

3 Gisborne Wineries (p359)
Finding more fab NZ wine around Gisborne.

4 Te Urewera (p361)
Losing yourself in this area's mighty forests, rich in Māori culture.

5 Pacific Coast Hwy (p350) Counting off landmarks as you cruise around the East Cape: Cape Kidnappers, Tolaga Bay, Tokomaru Bay and the East Cape Lighthouse.

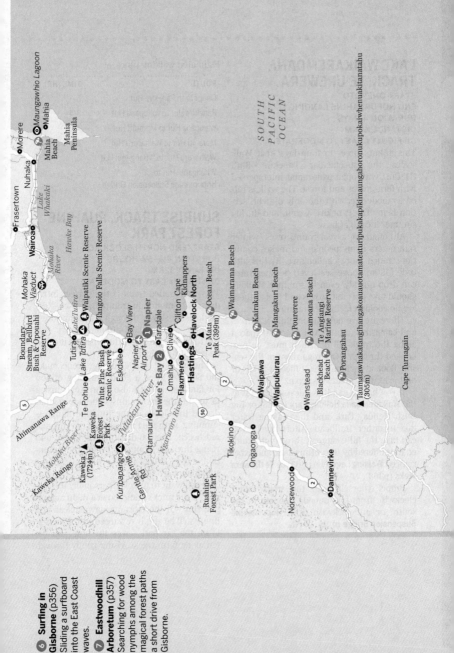

6 Surfing in Gisborne (p356) Sliding a surfboard into the East Coast waves.

7 Eastwoodhill Arboretum (p357) Searching for wood nymphs among the magical forest paths a short drive from Gisborne.

HIKING ON THE EAST COAST

LAKE WAIKAREMOANA TRACK, TE UREWERA

START ONEPOTO
END HOPURUAHINE LANDING
DURATION 4 DAYS
DISTANCE 46KM
DIFFICULTY EASY TO MODERATE

This 46km, three- to four-day Great Walk scales the spectacular Panekire Bluff (1180m), with open panoramas interspersed with fern groves and forest. The walk is rated as moderate, with the only difficult section being the Panekire ascent, and during summer it can get busy.

Although it's a year-round track, winter rain deters many people and makes conditions much more challenging. At this altitude (580m above sea level), temperatures can drop quickly, even in summer. Walkers should take portable stoves and fuel as there are no cooking facilities en route.

There are five **huts** (adult/child $32/free) and **campsites** (adult/child $14/free) spaced along the track, all of which must be pre-booked through DOC, regardless of the season. Book at regional DOC offices, i-SITEs or online at www.greatwalks.co.nz.

If you have a car, it is safest to leave it at the **Waikaremoana Holiday Park** (p363) or Big Bush Holiday Park, and then take a water taxi to either trailhead. Alternatively, you can take the fully catered, three-night guided tour offered by the enthusiastic and experienced **Walking Legends** (p363) or **Te Urewera Treks** (p363).

Propel yourself onto the track either clockwise from just outside **Onepoto** in the south, or anticlockwise from **Hopuruahine Suspension Bridge** in the north.

Estimated walking times:

ROUTE	TIME (HR)
Onepoto to Panekire Hut	5
Panekire Hut to Waiopaoa Hut	3-4
Waiopaoa Hut to Marauiti Hut	4-5
Marauiti Hut to Waiharuru Hut	1½
Waiharuru Hut to Whanganui Hut	2
Whanganui Hut to Hopuruahine Suspension Bridge	2

SUNRISE TRACK, RUAHINE FOREST PARK

START/END NORTH BLOCK RD
DURATION 4½–5½ HOURS
DISTANCE 12KM
DIFFICULTY EASY TO MODERATE

This well-graded track is the perfect introduction to mountain tramping in New Zealand, rising slowly through changing forest to offer a glimpse of alpine country – if you're new to life above the bushline it could be love at first sight.

The gradient and changing scene make the Sunrise Track a good tramping option for families, but it's also more than just a taster of the mountains. The forest that drapes the slopes of the Ruahine Range is stunning, with the track setting out through red beech, rimu and kahikatea forest, and rising through mountain beech and mountain cedar (kaikawaka) to top out among subalpine herb fields.

If you want to discover personally the reason for the track's name, book a night at Sunrise Hut – if the morning dawns clear and fine, you'll be amply rewarded by the views. From the car park, cross the stile and begin along farm tracks, rising gently through

In this region, the best hiking can be found inland, in the lush forest-draped mountains of Te Urewera and the Ruahine Forest Park.

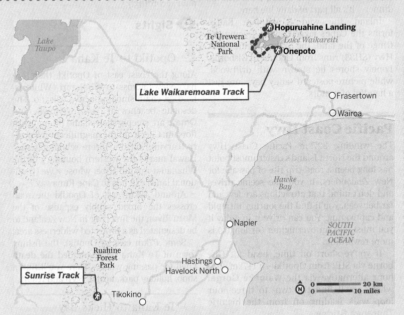

farmland to enter Ruahine Forest Park in just a few minutes. About 100m on, turn left at the second junction, descending at first through a beautiful section of mossy red-beech forest to cross a wooden bridge over a stream. Just beyond the bridge, take the left fork (signed to Sunrise Hut), beginning the climb.

A series of switchbacks among tall kahikatea and rimu makes the going easy to begin, before the track contours across the slopes to a junction with the track to Waipawa Forks Hut (one hour from the car park). Continue straight ahead. Around the top of the first set of switchbacks past the junction, the forest begins to thin. For the next hour you'll climb through a gradually shrinking forest – the final layer of stunted beech, padded with moss, is particularly enchanting.

When you step out of the bushline you're immediately greeted by **Sunrise Hut** (spoiler alert: you're actually greeted first by its

toilets). Sitting among tussocks at 1280m, the 20-bunk hut stares east over Hawke's Bay. The mezzanine bunks get the million-dollar views.

The track to Armstrong Saddle leaves from the right side of the hut and turns immediately right along a narrow ridge. The route simply follows this ridge north for 1km (20 to 30 minutes) to the saddle. Nearing the saddle – at about the point where the massive landslips fall away to the left – it becomes a poled route to assist in low visibility. From **Armstrong Saddle** (1369m), with its beautiful subalpine herb fields, there are views to Mt Ruapehu on a clear day. The saddle is named after a pilot, Hamish Armstrong, who crashed his Gypsy Moth plane here in 1935. Armstrong was never found.

Return to Sunrise Hut and retrace your steps back down the slopes to the North Block Rd car park.

EAST CAPE

The slow-paced East Cape is a unique and special corner of New Zealand. It's a quiet place, where everyone knows everyone, and community ties are built on rural enterprise and a shared passion for the ocean. Horse riding, tractors on the beach, fresh fish for dinner – it's all part of daily life here.

Inland, the wild Raukumara Range forms the Cape's jagged spine. Tracing the fringe of the land, the 327km Pacific Coast Hwy (SH35) runs from Opotiki to Gisborne. Lonely shores lie strewn with driftwood, while picture-postcard sandy bays lure just a handful of visitors.

Pacific Coast Hwy

The winding 327km Pacific Coast Hwy around the North Island's easternmost point has long been a road-trip rite of passage for New Zealanders. If you like scenic drives and don't mind that attractions are few and far between, you'll find the journey intrepid and captivating. You can drive it in a day if you must, but an overnighter (or longer) is more rewarding.

If you're short on time, head for Gisborne via SH2 from Opotiki – a 147km, 2½-hour alternative via the **Waioeka Gorge**, where you'll find the two- to three-hour loop walk leading off from the historic **Tauranga Bridge**.

ESSENTIAL EAST COAST
....

Eat delicious fresh produce from the Hastings Farmers Market (p373).

Drink Young Nick's Pale Ale at the Sunshine Brewery (p360).

Read Witi Ihimaera's 1987 novel *Whale Rider*; then watch the powerful 2002 movie adaptation.

Listen to international and NZ DJs at Gisborne's Rhythm & Vines (p357).

Watch *Boy* (2010), Taika Waititi's hilarious film, shot at Waihau Bay.

Go Green at Millton (p359) vineyard – organic, biodynamic and delicious to boot.

Online www.hawkesbaynz.com, www.gisbornenz.com, www.lonelyplanet.com/new-zealand/the-east-coast

---

Both routes are covered in the excellent *Pacific Coast Highway Guide,* available at Gisborne (p360) and Opotiki (p344) i-SITEs. Set off with a full petrol tank, and stock up on snacks and groceries – shops and petrol stations are in short supply. Sleeping and eating options are also pretty spread out: plan accordingly.

◉ Sights

◉ Opotiki to Te Kaha

Along the coast east of Opotiki, there are hazy views across to **Whakaari** (White Island), a chain-smoking active volcano. The desolate beaches at **Torere**, **Hawai** and **Omaio** are steeply shelved and littered with flotsam. Check out the magnificent *whakairo* (carving) on the Torere school gateway. Hawai marks the western boundary of the Whanau-a-Apanui tribe, whose *rohe* (traditional land) extends to Cape Runaway.

Around 42km east of Opotiki the road crosses the broad pebbly expanse of the **Motu River**, the first river in New Zealand to be designated as a protected wilderness area.

Some 67km east of Opotiki, the fishing town of **Te Kaha** once sounded the death knell for passing whales. Here you'll find a shop, holiday park, hostel, B&B and resort.

◉ Te Kaha to Hicks Bay

Around 24km east of Te Kaha, stop at **Papatea Bay** to see the gateway of **Hinemahuru Marae**, intricately carved with images of WWI Māori soldiers. At blink-and-you'll-miss-it **Raukokore**, the 1894 Anglican **Christ Church** (☑07-352 3979; ruakokore.church@gmail.com; SH35, Raukokore; ⊙8am-8pm Oct-Apr, 9am-5pm May-Sep) is a sweet beacon of belief on a lonely promontory. The simple white-and-grey interior is suitably demure (look for the mouse on high). There are services at 11am on Sundays.

Some 17km east of **Waihau Bay**, where there's a petrol pump, pub and accommodation, **Whangaparaoa** (Cape Runaway) was where kumara (sweet potato) was first introduced to NZ. It can only be reached on foot.

East of Whangaparaoa, the road tracks inland, crossing into hilly Ngāti Porou territory before hitting the coast at **Hicks Bay**, a real middle-of-nowhere settlement with a grand beach. There's safe sandy swimming at **Onepoto Bay** nearby.

MĀORI EAST COAST

The main *iwi* (tribes) in the region are Te Whānau-ā-Apanui (www.apanui.co.nz; west side of East Cape), Ngāti Porou (www.ngatiporou.com; east side of East Cape), Ngāti Kahungunu (www.kahungunu.iwi.nz; the coast from Hawke's Bay down) and Ngāi Tūhoe (www.ngaituhoe.iwi.nz; inland in Te Urewera).

Ngāti Porou and Ngāti Kahungunu are the country's second- and third-biggest *iwi*, respectively. In the late 19th century they produced the great leaders James Carroll (the first Māori cabinet minister) and Apirana Ngata (who was briefly acting prime minister). Ngata, whose face adorns New Zealand's $50 note, worked tirelessly in parliament to orchestrate a cultural revival within Māoridom. The region's magnificent carved *marae* (meeting houses) are part of his legacy.

Māori life is at the forefront around the East Cape, in sleepy villages centred upon the many *marae* that dot the landscape. Living in close communities, drawing much of their livelihoods from the sea and the land, the *tangata whenua* (local people) of the Cape offer a fascinating insight into what life might have been, had they not been so vigorously divested of their land in the 19th century.

You will meet Māori wherever you go. For accommodation with Māori flavour, consider **Hikihiki's Inn** (p363). For an intimate introduction to *Māoritanga* (things Māori), take a guided tour with **Long Island Guides** (☑ 06-874 7877; www.longislandtoursnz.com; half-day tours per person from $248) or **Waimarama Tours** (☑ 021 057 0935; www.waimaramamaori.co.nz; 2-4hr tours per person from $95, transport from $40).

For a more passive brush with the culture, visit Gisborne's **Tairawhiti Museum** (p355) and **C Company Memorial House** (p355), **Otatara Pā** (p372) in Napier and Tikitiki's **St Mary's Church** (p351).

◉ Hicks Bay to East Cape

Around 10km east of Hicks Bay is **Te Araroa**, a lone-dog village with shops, a petrol pump, a takeaway and a beautifully carved *marae* (meeting house). The geology changes here from igneous outcrops to sandstone cliffs: the dense bush backdrop doesn't seem to mind which it grows on. More than 350 years old, 20m high and 40m wide, **Te-Waha-O-Rerekohu**, allegedly NZ's largest pohutukawa tree, stands in the Te Araroa schoolyard.

From Te Araroa, drive out to see the **East Cape Lighthouse**, the easterly tip of mainland NZ. It's 21km (30 minutes) east of town along a mainly unsealed road, with a 25-minute climb (750 steps!) to the lighthouse. Set your alarm and get up there for sunrise.

◉ East Cape to Tokomaru Bay

Heading through farmland south of Te Araroa, the first town you come to is **Tikitiki**. If you haven't yet made it into a *marae*, you'll get a fair idea of what you're missing out on by visiting the extraordinary **St Mary's Church** (1889 SH35, Tikitiki; by donation; ⊙ 9am-5pm), built in 1924.

Beyond Tikitiki, **Mt Hikurangi** (1752m) juts out of the Raukumara Range – it's the highest nonvolcanic peak on the North Island and the first spot on Earth to see the sun each day. According to local tradition it was the first piece of land dragged up when Maui snagged the North Island. The Ngāti Porou version of the Maui story has his canoe and earthly remains resting here on their sacred mountain. Pick up the Ngāti Porou-produced *Mt Hikurangi* brochure from regional visitor-information centres for more info.

Continuing south, the road passes **Ruatoria** (shop, petrol and general desolation) and **Te Puia Springs** (ditto). Along this stretch a 14km loop road offers a rewarding detour to **Waipiro Bay.**

Eleven kilometres south of Te Puia Springs is **Tokomaru Bay,** perhaps the most interesting spot on the entire route, its broad beach framed by sweeping cliffs. The town has weathered hard times since the freezing works closed in the 1950s, but it still sports several attractions including good beginner surfing, swimming and a good pub (p353). You'll also find a supermarket, takeaway and post office in the town (and a B&B in the former post office), plus some crumbling surprises at the far end of the bay.

◎ Tokomaru Bay to Tolaga Bay

Heading south from Tokomaru Bay is a bucolic 22km stretch of highway to the turn-off to **Anaura Bay**, 6km away. It's a definite 'wow' moment when the bay springs into view far below. Captain Cook arrived here in 1769 and commented on the 'profound peace' in which the people were living and their 'truly astonishing' cultivations.

Back on the highway it's 14km south to **Tolaga Bay**, East Cape's largest community (population 830). Just off the main street, **Tolaga Bay Cashmere Company** (☑ 06-862 6746; www.cashmere.co.nz; 31 Solander St, Tolaga Bay; ☺ 10am-4pm Mon-Fri) inhabits the art-deco former council building.

Tolaga is defined by its amazing historic wharf. Built in 1929 and commercially functional until 1968, it's the longest in the southern hemisphere (660m), and is now largely restored after dedicated (and expensive!) preservation efforts.

🏃 Activities

Motu River Jet   BOATING
(☑ 027 470 7315, 07-315 5028; www.moturiverjet.com; SH35; adult/child from $95/65) Operates as many as six one-hour trips on the Motu River (which runs through the Raukumara Range near Opotiki) every day from December to March. Booking ahead is highly recommended; trips during other months by arrangement.

Wet 'n' Wild Rafting   RAFTING
(☑ 0800 462 7238, 07-348 3191; www.wetnwild rafting.co.nz; 2- to 5-day tours $995-1095) Based on the outskirts of Rotorua, Wet 'n' Wild Rafting also offers multiday excursions on the Motu River, with the longest taking you 100km down the river. The two-day tour requires you to be helicoptered in, and therefore costs nearly as much as the five-day trip.

Anaura Bay Walkway   TRAMPING
(www.doc.govt.nz; off Anaura Bay Rd, Anaura Bay) **FREE** At Aranura Bay, a 22km detour off the Pacific Coast Hwy south of Tokomaru Bay, the Anaura Bay Walkway is a two-hour, 3.5km ramble through steep bush and grassland, starting at the northern end of the bay.

Cooks Cove Walkway   TRAMPING
(www.doc.govt.nz; Wharf Rd, Tolaga Bay; ☺ closed Aug-Oct) Near the amazing old wharf at Tolaga Bay is Cooks Cove Walkway, an easy 5.8km, 2½-hour loop through farmland and native bush to a cove where the captain landed. At the northern end of the beach is the Tatarahake Cliffs Lookout, a sharp 10-minute walk to an excellent vantage point.

🛏 Sleeping

★ Stranded in Paradise   HOSTEL $
(☑ 06-864 5870; www.stranded-in-paradise.net; 21 Potae St, Tokomaru Bay; campsites per person $18, dm/s/d/f $32/48/75/96; �</a>) Up on the hill behind town, the 12-bed Stranded in Paradise scores points for views, eco-loos and free wifi. There are two tricky loft dorm rooms, a double downstairs and three wave-shaped cabins. Tenters have a panoramic knoll (astonishing bay views!) on which to pitch.

Anaura Bay Motor Camp   CAMPGROUND $
(☑ 06-862 6380; www.tairawhitigisborne.co.nz; Anaura Bay Rd, Anaura Bay; sites per adult/child from $20/11; ☎) Friendly Anaura Bay Motor Camp is all about the location – right on the beachfront by the little stream where Captain Cook once stocked up with water. There's a decent kitchen, showers and toilets.

Nga Puriri   COTTAGE $$
(☑ 06-864 4035; www.thepuriris.co.nz; 5138 Te Araroa Rd, Hicks Bay; d incl breakfast $160; ☎) Overlooking Hicks Bay, this wee self-contained weatherboard cottage is a delight, with room for two and breakfast eggs from the chooks (chickens) next door. There's safe sandy swimming at Onepoto Bay nearby.

Tui Lodge   B&B $$
(☑ 07-325 2922; tuilodge@yahoo.co.nz; 200 Copenhagen Rd, Te Kaha; s/d incl breakfast $155/175) Tui Lodge is a capacious, modern guesthouse that sits in groomed 3-acre gardens, irresistible to tui and many other birds. Delicious meals are available by arrangement, as are horse trekking, fishing and diving trips.

Oceanside Apartments   APARTMENT $$
(☑ 07-325 3699; www.waihaubay.co.nz; 10932 SH35, Waihau Bay; d from $120) Oceanside Apartments offers two nicely kept apartments with blue-and-white colour schemes, one below the owners' house, the other behind. Meals and picnic lunches by arrangement; kayaks for hire. Fishing advice is free!

🍴 Eating

Pacific Coast Macadamias   ICE CREAM $
(☑ 07-325 2960; www.macanuts.co.nz; 8462 SH35, Whanarua Bay; snacks $5-12; ☺ 10am-3pm daily 26 Dec-March, Sat & Sun only 1-24 Dec; 🚗) Heaven is

a tub of homemade macadamia-and-honey ice cream at Pacific Coast Macadamias, accompanied by views along one of the most spectacular parts of the coast. Toasted sandwiches and nutty sweet treats make this a great lunch stop. Call ahead to check it's open – hours can be very sketchy outside of summer (from roughly December to March).

Cottle's Cafe & Bakery BAKERY $
(☑ 06-862 6484; cnr Cook & Monkhouse Sts, Tologa Bay; pies $4-5; ☺ 7am-4pm) Decent coffee and excellent savoury pies make Cottle's an essential stop on Tologa Bay's main drag. The bacon-and-egg pie is deservedly popular all around East Cape, but we reckon the fish one is just as good. Grab a pie to go and devour it while taking in views of the Tologa Bay Wharf.

Te Puka Tavern PUB FOOD $$
(☑ 06-864 5465; www.tepukatavern.co.nz; 135 Beach Rd, Tokomaru Bay; mains $15-28; ☺ 11am-late; ☎) The well-run pub with cracker ocean views is a cornerstone of the community, keeping everyone fed and watered, and offering visitors a place to stay.

Four natty split-level, self-contained units sleep up to six (doubles $160, extra person $30) and there's room for four campervans (powered sites $15, unpowered sites free).

Waihau Bay Lodge PUB FOOD $$
(☑ 07-325 3805; www.thewaihaubaylodge.co.nz; Orete Point Rd, Waihau Bay; mains $25-35; ☺ 4pm-late Sun-Wed, from 2pm Thu-Sat) A two-storey timber pub by the pier, serving hefty meals and offering accommodation ranging from campsites ($15) to four-bed dorms (from $35 per person), en suite doubles ($140) and roomy en suite units sleeping eight (double $195, extra person $30).

🔒 Shopping

East Cape Manuka Company FOOD
(☑ 06-864 4824; www.eastcapemanuka.co.nz; 4464 Te Araroa Rd, Te Araroa; ☺ 9am-3pm daily Oct-Apr, Mon-Fri only May-Sep) The progressive East Cape Manuka Company sells soaps, oils, creams and honey made from potent East Cape manuka. It's a good stop for a coffee, a slice of cheesecake or a delicious manuka honey smoothie (meals and snacks $6 to $15). Check out the busy bees at work in the wall display.

❶ Getting There & Away

By far the most fun way to experience the Pacific Coast Hwy is with your own wheels (motorised or pedal-powered). Otherwise, Bay Hopper

---

> **OFF THE BEATEN TRACK**
>
> ### WILDLIFE-WATCHING
>
> Around 16km north of Gisborne, the DOC-managed **Te Tapuwae o Rongokako Marine Reserve** is a 2450-hectare haven for many species of marine life including fur seals, dolphins and whales. Get out amongst it with **Dive Tatapouri** (☑ 06-868 5153; www.divetatapouri.com; 532 SH35, Tatapouri).

(www.baybus.co.nz) runs between Opotiki and Potaka/Cape Runaway on Tuesday and Thursday afternoon. **Cooks Couriers** (☑ 021 371 364, 06-864 4711) runs between Te Araroa and Opotiki on Tuesday and Thursday, and between Gisborne and Hicks Bay daily Monday to Saturday.

Gisborne
POP 47,734

'Gizzy' to her friends, Gisborne (pronounced *Gis*-born, not Gis-bun) is a pretty place, squeezed between surf beaches and a sea of chardonnay, and it proudly claims to be the first city on Earth to see the sun each day. It's a good place to put your feet up for a few days, hit the beach and sip some wine.

If you're into festivals, make a dance-music-and-DJ date for late December, or experience the best of the local food, wine and beer scene in October. Across other times of the year, walking in an arboreal wonderland or exploring New Zealand's best regional museum are fine reasons to visit the country's most remote city.

History

The Gisborne region has been settled for more than 700 years. A pact between two migratory *waka* (canoe) skippers, Paoa of the *Horouta* and Kiwa of the *Takitimu*, led to the founding of Turanganui a Kiwa (now Gisborne). Kumara (sweet potatoes) flourished in the fertile soil and the settlement blossomed.

In 1769 this was the first part of NZ sighted by Captain Cook's expedition on the *Endeavour*. Eager to replenish supplies and explore, they set ashore, much to the amazement of the locals. Setting an unfortunate benchmark for intercultural relations, the crew opened fire when the Māori men performed their traditional blood-curdling challenge, killing six of them.

The *Endeavour* set sail without provisions. Cook, perhaps in a fit of petulance,

Gisborne

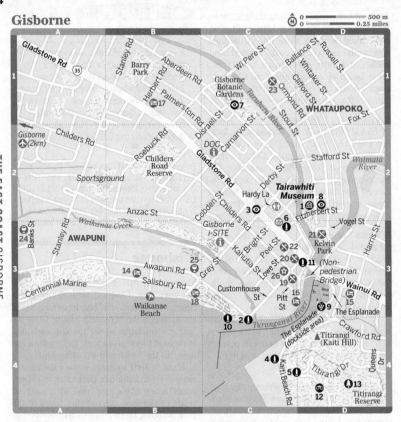

Gisborne

◉ Top Sights
1 Tairawhiti Museum	D2

◉ Sights
C Company Memorial House	(see 1)
2 Captain Cook Statue	C4
3 Clock Tower	C2
4 Cook Monument	C4
5 Cook's Plaza	C4
6 Footrot Flats Statue	C3
7 Gisborne Botanic Gardens	C1
8 Gisborne Farmers Market	D2
9 Gisborne Wine Centre	D3
10 Statue of Young Nick	C4
11 Te Tauihu Turanga Whakamana	D3
12 Titirangi Lookout	D4
13 Titirangi Reserve	D4

🛏 Sleeping
14 Ahi Kaa Motel	B3
15 Gisborne YHA	D3
16 Portside Hotel	C3
17 Teal Motor Lodge	B1
18 Waikanae Beach Top 10 Holiday Park	B3

✕ Eating
Crawford Road Kitchen	(see 9)
19 Flagship Eatery	C3
20 Frank & Albie's	C3
21 Marina Restaurant	D3
22 Muirs Bookshop & Cafe	C3
23 Neighbourhood Pizzeria	C1
PBC Cafe	(see 26)
USSCO Bar & Bistro	(see 19)

🍷 Drinking & Nightlife
24 Smash Palace	A3
25 Sunshine Brewery	B3

✦ Entertainment
26 Dome Cinema	C3

named the area Poverty Bay as 'it did not afford a single item we wanted'.

European settlement began in 1831 with whaling and farming; missionaries followed. In the 1860s battles between settlers and Māori erupted. Beginning in Taranaki, the Hauhau insurrection spread to the East Coast, culminating in the battle of Waerenga a Hika in 1865.

To discover Gisborne's historical spots, pick up the *Historic Walk* pamphlet from Gisborne i-SITE (p360).

⊙ Sights

⊙ City Centre

Gisborne Botanic Gardens GARDENS
(☑06-867 2049; www.gdc.govt.nz/botanical-gardens; Aberdeen Rd; ⊘24hr; 🖝) The town gardens are sitting pretty beside the Taruheru River – a beautiful spot for a picnic and a romp around the big **playground**. Wiggle through the NZ-native **Bushland Walkway**.

Clock Tower LANDMARK
(Gladstone Rd) Built in 1934, this art-deco clock tower is the undisputed highlight of Gisborne's main street.

Footrot Flats Statue STATUE
(Peel St, outside HB Williams Memorial Library) Gisborne is already well endowed with statues, but this one commemorating the hugely popular Footrot Flats cartoons (p358) by Gisborne local, the late Murray Ball, is our new favourite. Wal, the series' archetypal Kiwi farmer, stands with his devoted canine companion, 'The Dog', looking on. For more on *Footrot Flats*, see www.footrotflats.com, or check out the movie *Footrot Flats: The Dog's Tale.*

Te Tauihu Turanga Whakamana MONUMENT
(The Canoe Prow; cnr Gladstone Rd & Customhouse St) FREE Like a giant sundial, Te Tauihu Turanga Whakamana is a large modern sculpture in the shape of a *tauihu* (canoe prow) that celebrates early Māori explorers.

Statue of Young Nick MONUMENT
(Customhouse St) There's no let-up in Gisborne's *Endeavour* endeavours: in the riverside park is a dynamic statue of Nicholas Young, Captain Cook's cabin boy, whose eagle eyes were the first to spot NZ (the white cliffs at Young Nick's Head). There's another **Cook statue** (Customhouse St) nearby, erected on a globe etched with his roaming routes.

⊙ Kaiti

Gisborne Wine Centre WINERY
(☑06-867 4085; www.gisbornewinecentre.co.nz; Shed 3, 50 The Esplanade; ⊘11am-9pm Tue-Sat, to 5pm Sun) This harbourside spot has a wide selection of the region's vino to sample, though the pervasive sea scent may be hard to reconcile with the chardonnay on your palate. On the same premises is the international bistro Crawford Road Kitchen (p359).

Titirangi Reserve PARK
(www.gdc.govt.nz; Titirangi Dr, off Queens Dr; 🖝) High on a hill overlooking Gisborne, Titirangi was once a *pā* (fortified village). Reach it via Queens Dr, or on the track from the **Cook Monument** (Kaiti Beach Rd). Near the **lookout** (Titirangi Dr) at the top is yet another Cook edifice, at Cook's Plaza. Adjacent is a modest pohutukawa tree planted by Princess Diana in 1983.

Cook's Plaza MONUMENT
(Titirangi Dr) Near the summit of Kaiti Hill in Titirangi Reserve is Cook's Plaza. Due to a cock-up of historic proportions, the Cook statue here isn't garbed in British naval uniform, nor does it bear any facial resemblance to Captain Jim. A plaque proclaims, 'Who was he? We have no idea!'.

⊙ Whataupoko

★**Tairawhiti Museum** MUSEUM
(☑06-867 3832; www.tairawhitimuseum.org.nz; Kelvin Rise, Stout St; adult/child $5/free; ⊘10am-4pm Mon-Sat, from 1.30pm Sun) The Tairawhiti Museum, with its fab gallery extension, focuses on East Coast Māori and colonial history. It is Gisborne's arts hub, with rotating exhibits and excellent historic photographic displays. There's also a maritime wing, with displays on *waka* (canoes), whaling and Cook's Poverty Bay, although these pale in comparison to the vintage surfboard collection. There's also a shop, and a cafe overlooking Kelvin Park. Outside is the reconstructed **Wyllie Cottage** (1872), Gisborne's oldest house.

C Company Memorial House CULTURAL CENTRE
(www.ngatamatoa.co.nz; 10 Stout St; ⊘noon-3pm Tue-Fri & Sun, from 10am Sat) This cultural centre commemorates the dedication and commitment of the famed 28th (Māori) Battalion of the New Zealand Army that fought bravely in the European and North African

theatres in WWII. In particular the role of Māori men from the East Coast who made up the battalion's C Company is brought to life with poignant photos and stories.

Gisborne Farmers Market MARKET
(☑027 251 8608; www.gisbornefarmersmarket. co.nz; cnr Stout & Fitzherbert Sts; ⊙9.30am-12.30pm Sat) Stock up on fresh fruit, macadamia nuts (and macadamia nut paste!), smallgoods (cooked meats and meat products), honey, herbs, coffee, wine, bread, pastries, fish, cheese and Gisborne oranges…all of it locally grown or procured.

◉ Makaraka & Matawhero

East Coast

Museum of Technology MUSEUM
(ECMOT; ☑027 221 5703; www.ecmot.org.nz; SH2, Makaraka; adult/child $5/1; ⊙10am-4pm Sun-Fri, from 1pm Sat) Think analogue rather than digital; old-age rather than space-age. About 5km west of the town centre, this improbable medley of farm equipment, fire engines and sundry appliances has found an appropriate home in a motley old milking barn and surrounding outhouses. Dig the millennium welcome sign!

Matawhero Church CHURCH
(☑06-868 5513; www.standrewsgis.org.nz/faith. html; Church Ln, off Saleyard Rd, Matawhero; ⊙9am-5pm) FREE Some 7km west of the town centre in the suburb of Matawhero, this historic Presbyterian church is the only building in the village to have survived the 1868 raid by the rebellious Te Kooti (p356). It's a sweet, timber affair with a bell turret and lovingly tended gardens.

🏃 Activities

Water Sports
Surfing is de rigueur in Gisborne, with the teenage population looking appropriately shaggy. **Waikanae Beach** and **Roberts Road** are good for learners; experienced surfers get tubed south of town at the **Pipe**, or east at **Sponge Bay** and **Tuamotu Island**. Further east along SH35, **Wainui** and **Makorori** also have quality breaks.

There's safe swimming between the flags at Waikanae and **Midway Beach**.

Rere Rockslide SWIMMING
(Wharekopae Rd; ⊙daylight hours) This natural phenomenon occurs in a section of the Rere River 50km northwest of Gisborne along Wharekopae Rd. Grab a tyre tube or boogie

---

TE KOOTI, MYSTICAL WARRIOR

Māori history is littered with mystics, prophets and warriors, one of whom is the celebrated Te Kooti (rhymes with naughty, not booty).

In 1865 he fought with the government against the Hauhau (adherents of the Pai Marire faith, founded by another warrior-prophet) but was accused of being a spy and imprisoned on the Chatham Islands without trial.

While there, Te Kooti studied the Bible and claimed to receive visions from the archangel Michael. His charismatic preaching and 'miracles' – including producing flames from his hands (his captors claimed he used phosphorus from the head of matches) – helped win over the Pai Marire to his distinctly Māori take on Christianity.

In 1867 Te Kooti led an astounding escape from the Chathams, hijacking a supply ship and sailing to Poverty Bay with 200 followers. En route he threw a doubter overboard as a sacrifice. Upon their safe arrival, Te Kooti's disciples raised their right hands in homage to God rather than bowing submissively; *ringa tu* (upraised hand) became the name of his church.

Te Kooti requested a dialogue with the colonial government but was once again rebuffed, with magistrate Reginald Biggs demanding his immediate surrender. Unimpressed by Pākehā (white person) justice, Te Kooti commenced a particularly effective guerrilla campaign – starting with killing Biggs and around 50 others (including women and children, both Māori and Pākehā) at Matawhero near Gisborne.

A four-year chase ensued. Eventually Te Kooti took refuge in the King Country, the Māori king's vast dominion where government troops feared to tread.

Proving the pointlessness of the government's approach to the whole affair, Te Kooti was officially pardoned in 1883. By this time his reputation as a prophet and healer had spread and his Ringatu Church was firmly established. Today it claims more than 16,000 adherents.

NGATAPA

An arboreal nirvana, **Eastwoodhill Arboretum** (☑ 06-863 9003; www.eastwoodhill.org. nz; 2392 Wharekopae Rd, Ngatapa; adult/child/family $15/2/28; ⊙ 9am-5pm; ⍟) is the largest collection of northern-hemisphere trees and shrubs in the southern hemisphere. It's staggeringly beautiful, and you could easily lose a day wandering around the 25km of themed tracks in this pine-scented paradise. It's well signposted, 35km northwest of Gisborne.

There's basic accommodation in bunks and private rooms (dorm bed $35, double room $120 and twin room $70, all including garden admission). Meals are available by arrangement, or you can use the fully equipped kitchen (BYO food as there aren't any shops nearby).

board to cushion the bumps and slide down the 60m-long rocky run into the pool at the bottom. Three kilometres downriver, the **Rere Falls** send a 20m-wide curtain of water over a 5m drop; you can walk behind it if you don't mind getting wet.

Walking On Water Surf School SURFING
(WOW; ☑ 06-863 2969, 022 313 0213; www.wow surfschool.com; 2hr/3-day/4-day lessons per person from $60/140/185; ⍟) Surfing is just like walking on water, right? Wrong. It's even harder than that – but these guys know how to turn the most naive novice into an upstanding surfer in no time. Kids' lessons and gear hire, too.

Surfing With Frank SURFING
(☑ 06-867 0823, 021 119 0971; www.surfingwith frank.com; lessons $65-95) Frank offers lessons at Wainui, as well as tours of the best East Coast and Taranaki breaks. Three-hour board and wetsuit hire $30.

Walking

There are many miles of walks to tackle around Gisborne, starting with a gentle stroll along the river. The Gisborne i-SITE (p360) can provide you with brochures for the *Historic Walk* and the *Walking Trails of Gisborne City*.

Winding its way through farmland and forest with commanding views, the **Te Kuri Walkway** (two hours, 5.6km, closed August to October) starts 4km north of town at the end of Shelley Rd.

⌲ Tours

Haurata High Country Walks TRAMPING
(☑ 06-867 8452; www.haurata.co.nz; walks unguided/guided per person from $15/25) Take a tramp in the hills with Haurata, which offers guided or unguided short and long day walks through the gorgeous high country behind Gisborne. Meals, farmhouse accommodation and hot-

tub soaks also available. Haurata's 'Aerial Station' property is around 65km northwest of Gisborne. Allow 70 minutes for the drive.

Tairāwhiti Tours CULTURAL
(☑ 021 276 5484; www.tairawhititours.co.nz; tours per person from $225) Excellent 5½-hour guided tours around Gisborne, digging into history, wine, food and culture (all the interesting stuff). Discounts are available for groups.

✯✯ Festivals & Events

Rhythm & Vines MUSIC, WINE
(R&V; www.rhythmandvines.co.nz; ⊙ Dec) A huge event on Gizzy's music calendar, R&V is a three-day festival leading up to New Year's Eve, featuring big-time local and international bands and DJs. Local accommodation feels the squeeze.

First Light Wine & Food Festival WINE, FOOD
(www.firstlightwineandfood.co.nz; ⊙ Oct) Cellar-door spectacular, with local winemakers and foodies pooling talents. Buses leave from the Gisborne i-SITE (p360), and transport revellers between the venues.

🛏 Sleeping

Gisborne YHA HOSTEL $
(☑ 06-867 3269; www.yha.co.nz; 32 Harris St; dm/ s/d/f $29/52/68/130; @ ⍨) A short wander across the river from town, this rambling, mustard-coloured 1925 charmer houses a well-kept hostel. The rooms are large and comfy (even the 10-bed dorm in the attic), while a shared outdoor deck and lawns kindle conversation. There's a family en suite unit, and surfboard and bike hire are also available.

Waikanae Beach
Top 10 Holiday Park HOLIDAY PARK $
(☑ 0800 867 563, 06-867 5634; www.gisborne holidaypark.co.nz; 280 Grey St; sites per person from $27, cabins & units d $95-150; ⍨ ⍩) Right

by the beach and an easy 10-minute walk to town, this grassy holiday park offers basic cabins, better units and grassy lanes for pitching tents and parking vans. Surfboards and bikes are for hire, and a swimming pool was added in late 2017.

Ahi Kaa Motel
MOTEL $$

(☑06-867 7107; www.ahikaa.co.nz; 61 Salisbury Rd; d $140-170; @ 🛜) 🅿 An uptown motel offering on a quiet backstreet, a short sandy-footed stroll across the road from Waikanae Beach. Fancy linen, tasteful bathrooms, double glazing, outdoor showers, recycled timbers, solar power and recycling savvy – nice one!

Portside Hotel
HOTEL, APARTMENT $$

(☑0800 767 874, 06-869 1000; www.portside gisborne.co.nz; 2 Reads Quay; d/apt from $165/235; @ 🛜 ▣) The wandering business traveller's hotel of choice in Gisborne, Portside offers three levels of sassy two-bedroom apartments, right by the river mouth where the big ships come and go. Charcoal-and-cream colour scheme, with little glass-fronted balconies.

Teal Motor Lodge
MOTEL $$

(☑0800 838 325, 06-868 4019; www.teal.co.nz; 479 Gladstone Rd; d/f from $150/205; 🛜 ▣) With super street appeal on the main drag (500m into town), the vaguely alpine (and just a bit *Mad Men*) Teal boasts a solid offering of tidy, family-friendly units plus a saltwater swimming pool and immaculate lawns to run around on.

Knapdale Eco Lodge
LODGE $$$

(☑06-862 5444; www.knapdale.co.nz; 114 Snowsill Rd, Waihirere; d incl breakfast from $420; 🛜) 🅿 Indulge yourself at this rural idyll, complete with lake, farm animals and home-grown produce. The modern lodge is filled with international artwork, its glassy frontage flowing out to an expansive patio with brazier, barbecue and pizza oven. Five-course dinners by arrangement ($95). To get here head 10km northwest of Gisborne, via Back Ormond Rd.

✖ Eating

Neighbourhood Pizzeria
PIZZA $

(☑06-868 7174; www.neighbourhoodpizzeria. co.nz; 9 Ballance St; pizzas $10-18; ⊗ 4.30-8.30pm) Serving pies out of a hip caravan, Neighbourhood Pizzeria draws loyal locals most nights for what we reckon are among the country's best pizzas. Traditional flavours like margherita segue to pork and jalapeno or chicken and chorizo. Mozzarella comes from nearby Waimata, and the adjacent area includes an excellent weekday cafe and a cool store selling vintage and retro collectables.

Definitely worth the short detour north of the river.

THE STORY OF FOOTROT FLATS

From 1976 to 1994, the *Footrot Flats* cartoon strip by long-time Gisborne resident Murray Ball (1939–2017) ran in newspapers across New Zealand, and compilation books of the series sold millions throughout NZ and Australia. Oddly, it was also a big hit in Denmark.

At its heart, *Footrot Flats* is the story of the relationship between Wallace 'Wal' Footrot and his loyal border collie, nicknamed 'The Dog' in a fine example of Kiwi understatement. A revolving cast of characters includes Darlene 'Cheeky' Hobson, Wal's hairdresser girlfriend; Horse, an irascible and fierce tomcat based on an actual feline that lived at Ball's farm; and Prince Charles, a very spoilt Welsh corgi owned by Wal's Aunt Dolly. Not the most farm-savvy of canines, Prince Charles often needs to be taught the finer points of rural life by The Dog.

Life in the country is the ongoing background of the cartoon strip – along with quintessential NZ locations like the local rugby club in the fictional town of Raupo – and this proudly rural sensibility is a big reason why *Footrot Flats* was such a big hit with city dwellers and countryfolk alike. New Zealand is still a young country, and many late-20th-century Kiwis could easily identify with a country lifestyle in their family history from just a couple of generations earlier.

Beyond the gentle humour, cartoonist Ball was a fierce opponent of inequality, and over its lifespan, *Footrot Flats* also incorporated subtle commentary on environmentalism. The series was at its peak in the mid-1980s, spawning a feature-length cartoon in 1986, and an Auckland theme park which was open from 1986 to 1991. Charles M Schulz, creator of the *Peanuts* comic strip, and Ball were mutual admirers, and Schulz penned an introduction to the only *Footrot Flats* compilation to be published in the United States.

GISBORNE WINERIES

With hot summers and fertile loam soils, the Waipaoa River valley to the northwest of Gisborne is one of New Zealand's foremost grape-growing areas. The region is traditionally famous for its chardonnay, and is increasingly noted for gewürztraminer and pinot gris. See www.gisbornewine.co.nz for a cellar-door map. Opening hours scale back out of peak season. Four of the best:

Millton (☑06-862 8680; www.millton.co.nz; 119 Papatu Rd, Manutuke; ☺10am-5pm, reduced winter hours) Sustainable, organic and biodynamic to boot. Bring a picnic and kick back surrounded by sturdy-trunked vines. Cheese and charcuterie platters are also served in the lovely gardens over summer – perfect with Millton's Opou Vineyard chardonnay.

Matawhero (☑06-867 6140; www.matawhero.co.nz; Riverpoint Rd, Matawhero; ☺noon-4pm Sat & Sun) Enjoy a picnic in bucolic splendour, accompanied by a flight of fine wines. Matawhero is home to a particularly buttery chardy.

Kirkpatrick Estate (☑06-862 7722; www.kew.co.nz; 569 Wharekopae Rd, Patutahi; ☺open by appointment) Sustainable winery with lovely wines across the board, including a delicious malbec. Look forward to vineyard and valley views.

Bushmere Estate (☑06-868 9317; www.bushmere.com; 166 Main Rd, Matawhero; ☺11am-3pm Wed-Sun Sep-May) Great chardonnay, gewürztraminer and cafe lunches at the sassy restaurant Vines (lunch mains $26 to $30), and live music on summer Sundays. Longer hours in summer (from roughly December to March) and by appointment only from April to August.

Frank & Albie's CAFE $
(☑06-867 7847; www.frankandalbie.co.nz; 24 Gladstone Rd; mains $6-10; ☺7am-2.30pm Mon-Fri) 'We cut lunch, not corners' is the motto at Frank & Albie's, a neat little hipster nook on Gisborne's main drag (check out the old art-deco leadlighting above the door). Nifty plywood benches, recycled timber tables and dinky white stools set the scene for super sandwiches, coffee, teas and smoothies.

Muirs Bookshop & Cafe CAFE $
(☑06-867 9741; www.muirsbookshop.co.nz; 62 Gladstone Rd; meals $5-14; ☺8.30am-3.30pm Mon-Fri, 9am to 3pm Sat) Situated above a beloved, age-old independent bookseller in a lovely heritage building, this simple cafe offers a small but sweet selection of counter food and cakes. Fans of fine espresso and literature may need to be forcibly removed. Over-street balcony for balmy days. Show up around 9.30am for the best chance of a freshly baked chocolate brioche.

★**Crawford Road Kitchen** BISTRO $$
(☑06-867 4085; www.crawfordroadkitchen.co.nz; Shed 3, 50 The Esplanade; shared plates $11-25; ☺11am-9pm Tue-Thu, to 10pm Fri & Sat, to 5pm Sun) Attached to the Gisborne Wine Centre (p355), this bistro combines culinary smarts and international flavours with an interesting location beside Gisborne's inner harbour. Good-value shared plates could include feta-crusted lamb with beetroot puree or baked snapper with harissa and quinoa, and the excellent wine list features around 15 local wines by the glass. Craft beers are also proudly Gisborne-brewed.

Flagship Eatery CAFE $$
(☑06-281 0372; www.flagshipeatery.co.nz; 14 Childers Rd; mains $15-23; ☺7am-2.30pm Mon-Fri, from 8am Sat) East Coast sunshine often floods Flagship's heritage space, a relaxed location for breakfast or lunch. The rancheros eggs with chorizo and chilli is a spicy way to begin the day, while on-trend lunch plates include steamed bao buns crammed with pork belly, or pork and prawn dumplings with pickled cucumber. Gisborne wines and local craft beer are reasons to linger.

PBC Cafe CAFE $$
(☑06-863 3165; 38 Childers Rd; mains breakfast $15-25, lunch $20-32; ☺7am-3pm Mon-Fri, from 8am Sat & Sun; ☑) The creaky old grandeur of the Poverty Bay Club for gentlemen (1874) is reason enough to visit, and this cafe inside certainly adds impetus with appealing counter food, all-day brunch, pizza, blackboard specials and reasonable prices. Love the big pew along the outside wall. There's the Dome Cinema and a sweet little gift shop here, too.

Marina Restaurant FRENCH $$$
(☑06-868 5919; www.marinarestaurant.co.nz; 2 Vogel St; mains lunch $22.50, dinner $32-43; ☺lunch

noon-2pm Thu-Sat, dinner 6-9pm Tue-Sat) One of Gisborne's best restaurants, the Marina offers casual bistro-style lunches and formal fine-dining dinners, all with a Gallic accent. The building itself is lovely – an old white weatherboard boathouse by the river, with lofty ceilings, white linens and balloon-like wine glasses. You'll also find Marina at the weekly Gisborne Farmers Market (p356) serving up take-home treats on a Saturday morning.

The two- or three-course lunches ($28/35) are good value.

USSCO Bar & Bistro MODERN NZ $$$
(☑06-868 3246; www.ussco.co.nz; 16 Childers Rd; mains $36-45; ☺4.30pm-late Mon-Sat) Housed in the restored Union Steam Ship Company building (hence USSCO), this place is all class. Kitchen skills shine on a highly seasonal menu featuring the likes of roast duck with kumara (sweet potato) fondant, and the devilishly good desserts are always a highlight. Look forward to local wines, NZ craft beers, generous portions and multi-course deals.

🍷 Drinking & Entertainment

★**Smash Palace** BAR
(☑06-867 7769; www.smashpalacebar.com; 24 Banks St; ☺3-8pm Tue, Thu & Sun, to 11pm Wed & Fri, noon-11pm Sat) Get juiced at the junkyard: an iconic drinking den in Gisborne's industrial wastelands (make as much noise as you like!), full to the gunwales with ephemera and its very own DC3 crash-landed in the beer garden. Occasional live music; vinyl sessions Sunday afternoons.

★**Sunshine Brewery** MICROBREWERY
(☑06-867 7777; www.sunshinebrewery.co.nz; 49 Awapuni Rd; ☺noon-8pm Mon-Sat) Bottling up a clutch of quality beers including the excellent Electron IPA, Gisborne's own craft brewery has a fab tasting room near Waikanae Beach. Pizza from Neighbourhood Pizzeria (p358) is also served. Try one with the hoppy Offshore Indian Pale Lager. Sunshine's more interesting brews fall under its Sunrise Project banner. Tasting paddles (five beers) are $15.

★**Dome Cinema** CINEMA, BAR
(☑08-324 3005; www.domecinema.co.nz; 38 Childers Rd; tickets $14; ☺from 5pm Wed-Sun) The excellent Dome is located inside the charming old Poverty Bay Club building (1874): beanbags and art-house flicks now occupy the glass-domed ballroom. There's

a cool bar next door serving beer, wine and pizza amid black-painted floorboards. The PBC Cafe is also here.

ℹ️ Information

MEDICAL SERVICES
Gisborne Hospital (☑06-869 0500; www.tdh.org.nz; 421 Ormond Rd, Riverdale; ☺24hr)
Three Rivers Medical (☑06-867 7411; www.3rivers.co.nz; 75 Customhouse St; ☺8am-8pm Mon-Fri, 9am-6pm Sat & Sun) Doctors and dentists available by appointment.

TOURIST INFORMATION
DOC (Department of Conservation; ☑06-869 0460; www.doc.govt.nz; 63 Carnarvon St; ☺8am-4.30pm Mon-Fri) The local Department of Conservation office.
Gisborne i-SITE (☑06-868 6139; www.gisbornenz.com; 209 Grey St; ☺8.30am-5.30pm Mon-Fri, 9am-5pm Sat, 10am-4pm Sun; 🛜) Beside a doozy of a Canadian totem pole, this information centre has everything you need including a travel desk, internet access and toilets.

ℹ️ Getting There & Away

The **Gisborne i-SITE** (p360) handles bookings for local and national transport services.

AIR
Gisborne Airport (www.eastland.co.nz/gisborne-airport; Aerodrome Rd, Awapuni) is 3km west of the city. Air New Zealand (www.airnewzealand.co.nz) flies to/from Auckland and Wellington.

BUS
InterCity and Naked Bus services depart from Gisborne i-SITE, with daily buses to the following destinations.

DESTINATION	COMPANY	PRICE ($)	DURATION (HR)
Auckland	InterCity	85	9
Napier	InterCity	45	4
Opotiki	InterCity	31	2
Opotiki	Naked Bus	22	2
Rotorua	InterCity	60	5
Rotorua	Naked Bus	28	4½
Taupo	Naked Bus	25	6
Wairoa	InterCity	29	1½

ℹ️ Getting Around

A city–airport taxi fare costs about $20 to $22. Try **Gisborne Taxis** (☑0800 505 555, 06-867 2222; www.gisbornetaxis.co.nz).

MAHIA PENINSULA

Between Gisborne and Napier, the Mahia Peninsula's eroded hills, sandy beaches and vivid blue sea resemble the Coromandel, but without the tourist crowds and with the bonus of dramatic cliffs.

It's an enduring holiday spot for East Coasters, who come for boaty, beachy stuff, and you can get in on the action if you have your own transport. A day or two could be spent exploring the scenic reserve and the bird-filled Maungawhio Lagoon, hanging out at the beach (Mahia Beach at sunset can be spectacular), or even playing a round of golf. Mahia has several small settlements offering between them a few guesthouses, a holiday park, a bar-bistro and a couple of stores.

In recent years, the peninsula's eastern edge has become the launch location for New Zealand's very own rocket company. Check Rocket Lab's website (www.rocketlabusa. com) for information on this innovative and surprising Kiwi startup.

Gisborne Airport Car Rental (☑0800 144 129; www.gisborneairportcarhire.co.nz) is an agent for nine car-hire companies including big brands and local outfits.

South of Gisborne

From Gisborne heading south towards Napier, you can take the coast road or the inland road. The coastal route is a marginally better choice, being quicker and offering occasional views out to sea. However, SH36 (Tiniroto Rd) is also an interesting drive (or bike route) with several good stopping points along the way.

◉ Sights

Doneraille Park, 49km from Gisborne, is a peaceful bush riverside reserve with freedom camping for self-contained vehicles. **Hackfalls Arboretum** (☑06-863 7083; www. hackfalls.org.nz; 187 Berry Rd, Tiniroto; adult/child $10/free; ⊙9am-5pm) is a 3km detour from the turn-off at the Tiniroto Tavern. The snow-white cascades of **Te Reinga Falls**, 12km further south, are well worth a stop.

The busier SH2 route heads inland and soon enters the **Wharerata State Forest** (beware of logging trucks). Just out of the woods, 55km from Gisborne, **Morere Hot Springs** (☑06-837 8856; www.morerehotsprings. co.nz; SH2, Morere; adult/child $12/6, private pools $15/10, nonswimmers $3; ⊙10am-5pm, extended hours Dec-Feb) burble up from a fault line in the **Morere Springs Scenic Reserve**.

From Gisborne on SH2, keep an eye out for the brightly painted **Taane-nui-a-Rangi Marae** on the left. You can get a decent view from the road; don't enter unless invited.

Continuing south, SH2 leads to Nuhaka at the northern end of Hawke's Bay. From here it's west to Wairoa or east to the sea-

salty Mahia Peninsula. Not far from the Nuhaka roundabout is **Kahungunu Marae** (www.kahungunu.iwi.nz/our-marae; cnr Ihaka & Mataira Sts, Nuhaka).

🛏 Sleeping

Morere Hot Springs Lodge & Cabins BUNGALOW **$**
(☑06-837 8824; www.morerelodge.co.nz; SH2, Morere; d $100-120, extra person $30; ☎) A farmy enclave where the lambs gambol and the dog wags her tail at you nonstop. Sleeping options include a classic 1917 farmhouse (sleeps 12) with kitchen and sweet sleep-out, another two-bedroom farmhouse (sleeps four) and two photogenic cabins. Great value. Pizzas and other evening meals are available by arrangement.

ⓘ Getting There & Away

Drive the SH2 south of Gisborne, running close to the coast, or take SH36 inland via Tiniroto. Either way you'll end up in Wairoa.

InterCity (www.intercity.co.nz) buses take the SH2, departing daily from **Gisborne i-SITE** (p360) for Napier (from $14, four hours) via Wairoa (from $10, 1½ hours).

Te Urewera

Shrouded in mist and mysticism, Te Urewera encompasses 2127 sq km of virgin forest cut with lakes and rivers. The highlight is Lake Waikaremoana (Sea of Rippling Waters), a deep crucible of water encircled by the Lake Waikaremoana Track (p348), one of New Zealand's Great Walks. Rugged bluffs drop away to reedy inlets, the lake's mirror surface disturbed only by mountain zephyrs and the occasional waterbird taking to the skies.

History

The name Te Urewera still has the capacity to make Pākehā (white) New Zealanders feel slightly uneasy – and not just because it translates as 'The Burnt Penis'. There's something primal and untamed about this wild woodland, with its rich history of Māori resistance.

The local Ngāi Tūhoe people – prosaically known as the 'Children of the Mist' – never signed the Treaty of Waitangi and fought with Rewi Maniapoto at Orakau during the Waikato Wars. The army of Te Kooti took refuge here during running battles with government troops. The claimant of Te Kooti's spiritual mantle, Rua Kenana, led a thriving community beneath the sacred mountain Maungapohatu (1366m) from 1905 until his politically motivated 1916 arrest. This effectively erased the last bastion of Māori independence in the country. Maungapohatu never recovered, and only a small settlement remains today. Nearby, Ruatahuna's extraordinary Mataatua Marae celebrates Te Kooti's exploits.

Tūhoe remain proud of their identity and traditions, with around 40% still speaking *te reo* (the language) on a regular basis.

In 2014, following a settlement under the Treaty of Waitangi, administration of Te Urewera was passed to the Te Urewera

Lake Waikaremoana Track

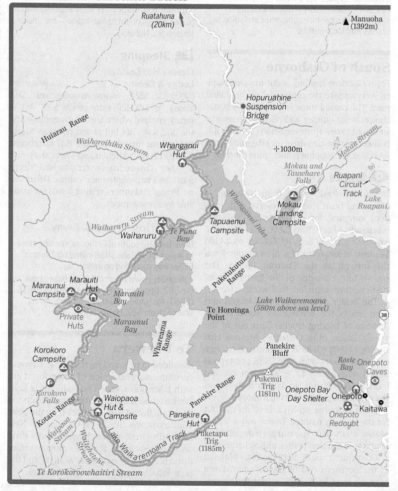

Board comprising both Tūhoe and the NZ government. Tūhoe and this board lead the formulation of annual plans for Te Urewera, and work with the Department of Conservation (DOC) to maintain tracks and visitor facilities in the area.

🏃 Activities

There are dozens of walks within Te Urewera's vast boundaries, most of which are outlined in DOC's *Lake Waikaremoana Walks* pamphlet ($2). Plenty of short walks kick off from near the eastern end of the lake or the Waikaremoana Holiday Park, or tackle the longer Lake Waikaremoana Track.

LAKE WAIKAREITI

With its untouched islands, **Lake Waikareiti** is an enchanting place. Starting near the far eastern end of Lake Waikaremoana, it's an hour's walk to its shore.

Accessed from the track to Lake Waikareiti, the more challenging **Ruapani Circuit Track** (a six-hour loop) passes through wetlands and dense, virgin forest. Also from Lake Waikareiti it's a three-hour walk to the **Sandy Bay Hut** at the northern end of the lake.

Walking Legends   TRAMPING
(📞 0800 925 569, 07-312 5297; www.walkinglegends.com; per person $1490-1590) This enthusiastic and experienced company offers fully catered, four-day guided tours around Lake Waikaremoana. Trips depart from Rotorua.

Te Urewera Treks   TRAMPING
(📞 07-929 9669; www.teureweratreks.co.nz/home; per person $1500) 🍃 Small-group, guided four-day tramps along the Lake Waikaremoana Great Walk. One- and three-day Te Urewera walks are also available, sometimes with tree-planting activities as part of the experience. Trips depart from Rotorua.

🛏 Sleeping

Waikaremoana Holiday Park   HOLIDAY PARK **$**
(📞 06-837 3826; www.doc.govt.nz/waikaremoana-holiday-park; 6249 Lake Rd/SH38; unpowered/powered campsites from $36/42, cabins/chalets d from $65/130) Right on the shore, this place has Swiss-looking chalets, fisher's cabins and campsites, most with watery views, plus an on-site shop. New chalets opened in late 2017 are tucked into the native forest.

Hikihiki's Inn   B&B **$$$**
(📞 06-8373 701; www.hikihiki.co.nz; 9 Rotten Row, Tuai; s/d $140/255) In the sweet lakeside settlement of Tuai, 6km from Onepoto, this little weatherboard gem serves as a B&B run by a charming and friendly '100% Kiwi' host.

ℹ Information

The **Te Urewera Visitor Centre** (Te Kura Whenua Paradise; 📞 06-837 3803; www.ngaituhoe.iwi.nz; 6249 Lake Rd; ⊗ 8.30am-4pm) offers weather forecasts, accommodation information and hut/campsite passes for the Lake Waikaremoana Track.

ⓘ Getting There & Away

Lake Waikaremoana is about an hour (64km) from Wairoa on SH38, which continues through to Rotorua – the entire SH38 route is named the **Te Urewera Rainforest Route**. Around 95km of the entire 195km Wairoa–Rotorua route is unsealed: it's a four-hour, bone-rattling drive (but a great adventure!).

Big Bush Water Taxi (☏ 0800 525 392, 06-837 3777; www.lakewaikaremoana.co.nz/water-taxi; per person one way $50-60) will boat you to either Onepoto or Hopuruahine trailhead, with hut-to-hut backpack transfers for the less gung-ho. It also runs minibus shuttles to and from Wairoa (from $50 per person one-way).

HAWKE'S BAY

Hawke Bay, the name given to the body of water that stretches from the Mahia Peninsula to Cape Kidnappers, looks like it's been bitten out of the North Island's eastern flank. Add an apostrophe and an 's' and you've got a region that stretches south and inland to include fertile farmland, surf beaches, mountainous ranges and forests. With food, wine and architecture the prevailing obsessions, it's smugly comfortable but thoroughly appealing, and is best viewed through a rosé-tinted wine glass.

Wairoa & Around

The small river town of Wairoa (population 4260) is trying hard to shake its rough-edged rep. Not scintillating enough to warrant an extended stay, the town does have a couple of points of interest, including an exceptional (and exceptionally early-opening) pie shop called **Oslers** (☏ 06-838 8299; 116 Marine Pde, Wairoa; pies $4-5, meals $7-15; ⊗ 8am-4pm Mon-Fri, to 2.30pm Sat & Sun). The arty **Eastend Cafe** (☏ 06-838 6070; eastendcafe@xtra.co.nz; 250 Marine Pde, Wairoa; meals $7-20; ⊗ 7am-3pm Mon-Fri, 8am-4pm Sat & Sun) is part of the revamped **Gaiety Cinema & Theatre** (☏ 06-838 3104; www.gaietytheatre.co.nz; 252 Marine Pde, Wairoa;

Hawke's Bay

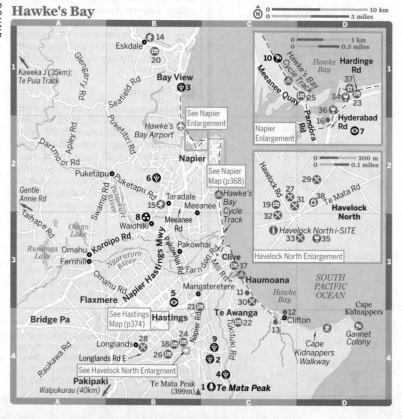

tickets from $10; ⊙10am-10pm Thu-Sun) complex – the town's cultural hub. Other diversions include the plaque-studded **River Walkway**, and the **Wairoa Museum** (☑06-838 3108; www.facebook.com/pg/WairoaMuseum; 142 Marine Pde, Wairoa; ⊙10am-4pm Mon-Fri, to noon Sat) FREE inside an old bank.

◉ Sights

The stretch of highway between Wairoa and Napier traipses through unphotogenic farmland and forestry blocks for much of its 117km. Most of it follows a railway line, currently only used for freight – you'll realise what a travesty this is when you pass under the **Mohaka Viaduct** (1937), the highest rail viaduct (97m) in Australasia.

Occupied by early Māori, **Lake Tutira** has walkways and a bird sanctuary. At Tutira village, just north of the lake, Pohokura Rd leads to the wonderful **Boundary Stream Scenic Reserve**, a major conservation area. Three loop tracks start from the road, ranging in length from 40 minutes to three hours. Also along this road you'll find the **Opouahi** and **Bellbird Bush Scenic Reserves**, which both offer rewarding walks. See www.doc. govt.nz for info on all of these reserves.

Off Waipatiki Rd, 34km outside Napier, Waipatiki Beach is a beaut spot boasting a low-key campsite and the 64-hectare **Waipatiki Scenic Reserve**. Further down the line, **White Pine Bush Scenic Reserve**, 29km from Napier on SH2, bristles with kahikatea and nikau palms. **Tangoio Falls Scenic Reserve**, 27km north of Napier, has Te Ana Falls, stands of wheki-ponga (tree ferns) and native orchids. Again, www.doc.govt.nz has the low-down on these reserves. Between White Pine and Tangoio Reserves the **Tangoio Walkway** (three hours return) follows Kareaara Stream.

The highway surfs the coast for the last 20km, with impressive views towards Napier. Hawke's Bay wine country starts in earnest at the mouth of the Esk River.

❶ Information

Wairoa i-SITE (☑06-838 7440; www.visitwairoa.co.nz; cnr SH2 & Queen St; ⊙8.30am-5pm Mon-Fri, 10am-4pm Sat & Sun) The spot for local info, including advice on Lake Waikaremoana and accommodation around town.

❶ Getting There & Away

The closest sizeable town to Te Urewera (p361), Wairoa is 98km southwest of Gisborne and 117km northeast of Napier. InterCity (www.intercity.co.nz) buses trundle in from Gisborne (1½ hours, from $10) and Napier (2¼ hours, from $14).

Hawke's Bay

Napier

POP 63,100

The Napier of today – a charismatic, sunny, composed city with the air of an affluent English seaside resort – is the silver lining of the dark cloud that was the deadly 1931 earthquake. Rebuilt in the popular architectural styles of the time, the city retains a unique concentration of art-deco buildings. Don't expect the Chrysler Building – Napier is resolutely low-rise – but you will find amazingly intact 1930s facades and streetscapes, which can provoke a *Great Gatsby*-esque swagger in the least romantic soul. Linger a while to discover some of regional New Zealand's best restaurants and also a few excellent wineries less visited than the bigger names around nearby Hastings and Havelock North.

History

The Napier area has been settled since around the 12th century and was known to Māori as Ahuriri (now the name of a suburb of Napier). By the time James Cook eyeballed the scene in October 1769, Ngāti Kahungunu was the dominant tribe, controlling the whole coast down to Wellington.

In the 1830s whalers hung around Ahuriri, establishing a trading base in 1839. By the 1850s the Crown had purchased – often by dubious means – 1.4 million acres of Hawke's Bay land, leaving Ngāti Kahungunu with less than 4000 acres. The town of Napier was planned in 1854 and obsequiously named after the British general and colonial administrator Charles Napier.

At 10.46am on 3 February 1931, the city was levelled by a catastrophic earthquake (7.9 on the Richter scale). Fatalities in Napier and nearby Hastings numbered 258. Napier suddenly found itself 40 sq km larger, as the earthquake heaved sections of what was once a lagoon 2m above sea level (Napier airport was once more 'port', less 'air'). A fevered rebuilding program ensued, resulting in one of the world's most uniformly art-deco cities.

◉ Sights

Napier's claim to fame is undoubtedly its architecture, and a close study of these treasures could take several days (especially if you're stopping to eat). Beyond the edge of town, the Hawke's Bay wineries are a treat.

◉ City Centre

Marine Parade STREET

Napier's elegant seaside avenue is lined with huge Norfolk Island pines, and dotted with motels and charming timber villas. Along its length are parks, quirky **sunken gardens** (Marine Pde; ◉24hr) FREE, a mini-golf course, a skate park, a sound shell, a swim centre and an aquarium. Near the north end of the parade is the **Tom Parker Fountain** (Marine Pde) FREE, best viewed at night when it's lavishly lit. Next to it is the **Pania of the Reef** (Marine Pde) FREE sculpture.

★**MTG Hawke's Bay** MUSEUM, THEATRE

(Museum Theatre Gallery; ☑06-835 7781; www.mtghawkesbay.com; 1 Tennyson St; ◉10am-5pm) FREE The beating cultural heart of Napier is the smart-looking MTG. It's a gleaming-white museum-theatre-gallery space by the water, and it brings live performances, film screenings and regularly changing gallery and museum displays together with touring and local exhibitions. Napier's public library – which has free wi-fi access – was set to be relocated to the building in early 2018.

★**Daily Telegraph Building** ARCHITECTURE

(☑06-834 1911; www.heritage.org.nz/the-list/details/1129; 49 Tennyson St; ◉9am-5pm Mon-Fri) The Daily Telegraph is one of the stars of Napier's art-deco show, with superb zigzags, fountain shapes and a symmetrically patterned facade. If the front doors are open, nip inside and ogle the painstakingly restored foyer (it's a real-estate office these days).

Napier Urban Farmers Market MARKET

(☑027 697 3737; www.hawkesbayfarmersmarket.co.nz; Clive Sq, Lower Emerson St; ◉9am-1pm Sat) Score some super-fresh local produce: fruit, vegies, bread, coffee, dairy products, honey, wine... Who needs supermarkets?

National Aquarium of New Zealand AQUARIUM

(☑06-834 1404; www.nationalaquarium.co.nz; 546 Marine Pde; adult/child/family $20/10.50/57; ◉9am-5pm, feedings 10am & 2pm, last entry 4.30pm) Inside this modern complex with its stingray-inspired roof are piranhas, terrapins, eels, kiwi, tuatara and a whole lotta fish. Snorkellers can swim with sharks ($100), or sign up for a 'Little Penguin Close Encounter' ($70).

◉ Bluff Hill & Ahuriri

Centennial Gardens   GARDENS
(www.napier.govt.nz; Coote Rd; ⊘24hr) Whoa! A massive waterfall right in the middle of Napier! There may be an artificial pump system in play, but we don't mind – it's still an impressive sight. Ducks, rockeries and flower beds revolve around the ponds below.

Napier Prison   HISTORIC BUILDING
(✆06-835 9933; www.napierprison.com; 55 Coote Rd; adult/child/family $20/10/50; ⊘9am-5pm) On the run from the law? Assuage your guilt with a tour of the grim 1906 Napier Prison on the hill behind the town. There's a self-guided audio set-up, available in 16 languages.

Bluff Hill Lookout   VIEWPOINT
(Lighthouse Rd) The convoluted route to the top of Bluff Hill (102m) goes up and down like an elevator on speed (best to drive), but rewards with expansive views across the port. Bring a picnic or some fish and chips.

National Tobacco
Company Building   ARCHITECTURE
(✆06-834 1911; www.heritage.org.nz/the-list/details/1170; cnr Bridge & Ossian Sts, Ahuriri; ⊘lobby 9am-5pm Mon-Fri) Around the shore at Ahuriri, the National Tobacco Company Building (1932) is arguably the region's deco masterpiece, combining art-deco forms with the natural motifs of art nouveau. Roses, raupo (bulrushes) and grapevines frame the elegantly curved entrance. During business hours, pull on the leaf-shaped brass door handles and enter the first two rooms.

🏃 Activities

Napier's pebbly ocean beach isn't safe for swimming. Instead, to cool off, locals head north of the city to **Westshore Beach** (off Ferguson Ave, Westshore), or to the surf beaches south of Cape Kidnappers.

Mountain Valley   ADVENTURE SPORTS
(✆06-834 9756; www.mountainvalley.co.nz; 408 McVicar Rd, Te Pohue; horse treks/rafting/fishing per person from $70/109/250) About 60km north of Napier on SH5, Mountain Valley is a hub of outdoorsy action: horse trekking, white-water rafting, kayaking and fly-fishing. There's also simple accommodation on-site (campsites/dorms/doubles from $16/22/100).

Ocean Spa   SWIMMING
(✆06-835 8553; www.oceanspanapier.co.nz; 42 Marine Pde; adult/child $11/8, private pools 30min $13/10; ⊘6am-10pm Mon-Sat, from 8am Sun) A spiffy waterfront complex that features a lane pool, hot pools, a beauty spa and a gym. Exhausting...

👉 Tours

Deco Centre   CULTURAL
(✆06-835 0022; www.artdeconapier.com; 7 Tennyson St; ⊘9am-5pm; 🚻) Start your explorations at the Deco Centre, which runs daily one-hour guided deco walks ($19) departing the Napier i-SITE (p372) at 10am; and daily two-hour tours ($21) leaving the Deco Centre at 2pm. There's also a little shop here, plus brochures for the self-guided *Art Deco Walk* ($10), *Art Deco Scenic Drive* ($3) and *Marewa Meander* ($3).

Other options include a minibus tour ($5, 1¼ hours), vintage car tour ($110, 1¼ hours) and the kids' *Art Deco Explorer* treasure hunt ($5).

Hawke's Bay Scenic Tours   TOURS
(✆06-844 5693, 027 497 9231; www.hbscenictours.co.nz; tours from $55) A grape-coloured bunch of tour options including the 2½-hour 'Napier Whirlwind' ($55), full-day Hawke's Bay scenic tour ($140), and a 4½-hour wine and brewery jaunt ($100).

Absolute de Tours   BUS
(✆06-844 8699; www.absolutedetours.co.nz; tours 90min/half-day from $50/70) Runs quick-fire bus tours of the city, Marewa and Bluff Hill in conjunction with the Deco Centre, as well as half-day tours of Napier and Hastings.

Waka Experience   BOATING
(✆021 168 7051, 06-390 6886; www.wakaexperience.co.nz; West Quay, Ahuriri; 2hr sailing per person from $105) Set sail around the calm Ahuriri waters aboard a traditional Māori ocean-going *waka* (canoe) – the impressive *Te Matau a Māui*. Learn about local Māori history and celestial navigation, and get a good look at Ahuriri from the water. Day and twilight sailings; minimum numbers apply.

⭐ Festivals & Events

Art Deco Weekend   CULTURAL
(www.artdeconapier.com; ⊘Feb) In the third week of February, Napier and Hastings co-host the sensational Art Deco Weekend. Around 125 events fill the week (dinners, picnics, dances, balls, bands, Gatsby-esque fancy dress), many of which are free. Expect around 40,000 art-deco fans!

Napier

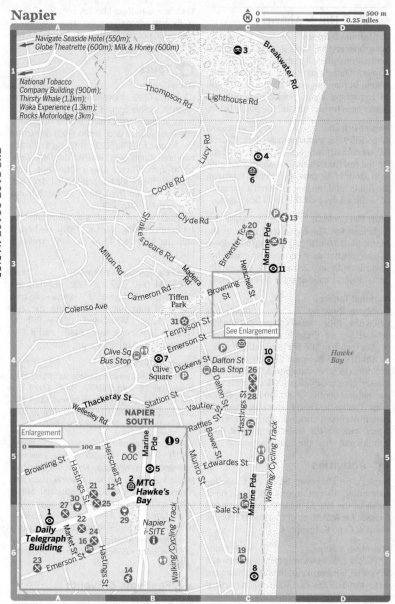

0   500 m
0   0.25 miles

Navigate Seaside Hotel (550m);
Globe Theatrette (600m); Milk & Honey (600m)

National Tobacco
Company Building (900m);
Thirsty Whale (1.1km);
Waka Experience (1.3km);
Rocks Motorlodge (3km)

Thompson Rd
Lighthouse Rd
Breakwater Rd
Lucy Rd
Coote Rd
Clyde Rd
Shakespeare Rd
Madeira Rd
Milton Rd
Cameron Rd
Colenso Ave
Brewster Tce
Marine Pde
Herschell St
Browning St
Tiffen Park
Tennyson St
Emerson St
Clive Sq Bus Stop
Clive Square
Dickens St
Dalton St
Dalton St Bus Stop
Hastings St
Thackeray St
Station St
Wellesley Rd
NAPIER SOUTH
Vautier St
Raffles St
Bower St
Munro St
Marine Pde
Edwardes St
Sale St
Walking/Cycling Track
Hawke Bay

See Enlargement

Enlargement
0   100 m

Browning St
Hastings St
Herschell St
Marine Pde
DOC
MTG Hawke's Bay
Napier i-SITE
Daily Telegraph Building
Market St
Emerson St
Hastings St
Walking/Cycling Track

🛏 Sleeping

Napier YHA   HOSTEL $
(☎06-835 7039; www.yha.co.nz; 277 Marine Pde;
dm/s/d from $30/45/69; ☜) Napier's friendly
YHA is housed in a lovely old timber beachfront villa with a seemingly endless ramble
of rooms. There's a fabulous reading nook
and a sunny rear courtyard. Staff can help
with bookings and local info. It's the best of
several hostels along Marine Pde. Bike hire
$20 per day.

Napier

Criterion Art Deco Backpackers HOSTEL **$**
(☑ 06-835 2059; www.criterionartdeco.co.nz; 48 Emerson St; dm/s/d/f without bathroom from $29/53/66/112, d with bathroom from $85; 🛜) The owners have spent a lot of money sprucing up this 1st-floor, ruby-red city-centre hostel – Napier's best Spanish Mission specimen – which has a beaut little balcony over Emerson St and an amazing old fireplace in the lounge area. A super-charming hostel in a top spot.

Seaview Lodge B&B B&B **$$**
(☑ 027 235 0202, 06-835 0202; www.aseaview lodge.co.nz; 5 Seaview Tce; r $150-190; 🅿 🛜) This

grand Victorian villa (1890) is queen of all she surveys – which is most of the town and a fair bit of ocean. The elegant rooms have tasteful period elements and feature either a separate or en suite bathroom. It's hard to resist a sunset tipple on the verandah, which opens off the relaxing guest lounge. Free wi-fi and off-street parking are a bonus.

Sea Breeze B&B B&B **$$**
(☑ 06-835 8067; www.seabreezebnb.co.nz; 281 Marine Pde; r incl breakfast $135-145; 🛜) Inside this Victorian seafront earthquake survivor (1906) are three richly coloured themed rooms (Chinese, Indian and Turkish), decorated with a cornucopia of artefacts. It's all tastefully done, avoiding the risk of being over the top. The price and location are right. Self-serve continental breakfast and free wi-fi included.

Nautilus HOTEL **$$**
(☑ 0508 628 845, 06-974 6550; www.nautilusnapier. co.nz; 387 Marine Pde; d/apt from $194/269; 🛜) A two-storey waterfront number with views from every room, kitchenettes, mod-deco decor, spa baths, private balconies and an in-house restaurant (not that you'll need it in Napier). Apartments sleep up to six. Outdoor furniture is starting to look a tad weary.

Rocks Motorlodge MOTEL **$$**
(☑ 0800 835 9626, 06-835 9626; www.therocks motel.co.nz; 27 Meeanee Quay, Westshore; units $135-200; 🛜) Just 80m from Westshore Beach, the Rocks has corrugated and mosaic stylings that have raised the bar on motel row. Interiors are plush and roomy with splashes of colour; some have spa baths, others claw-foot baths. Free (and fast) wi-fi, free gym and a laundry for grubby road warriors.

★ **Kiwiesque** B&B **$$$**
(☑ 06-836 7216; www.kiwiesque.com; 347 SH 5, Eskdale; d $295-345; 🛜) ∅ Located in rural Eskdale, around 18km north of Napier, Kiwiesque offers accommodation right beside expansive vineyards. For independent travellers, the best options are the four suites in the property's modern woolshed-influenced building. Breakfast packed with seasonal produce is included, bathrooms are elegant, and outdoor decks offer vineyard views. Eco-aware design includes double glazing and sheep-wool insulation in the walls.

Pebble Beach Motor Inn MOTEL **$$$**
(☑ 0800 723 224, 06-835 7496; www.pebblebeach. co.nz; 445 Marine Pde; r $219-315; 🛜) Unlike the majority of NZ motels, this one is truly

DON'T MISS

SEA WALLS
···

Painted as part of street-art festivals held in 2016 and 2017, the **Sea Walls** (Artists for Oceans) are almost 50 colourful and thought-provoking murals scattered across Napier. Pick up the *Sea Walls: Artists for Oceans* map from the Napier i-SITE (p372) or the **National Aquarium of New Zealand** (p366) to begin your own discovery of various works reinforcing and celebrating the well-being of our oceans' ecosystems.

owner-operated – the motel operators actually own the building – so maintenance and service top the list of staff priorities. There are 25 immaculate rooms over three levels, all with kitchens, spas, balconies and ocean views. Full to capacity most nights. Ask the friendly owners about the 'hole in one' golf story.

Navigate Seaside Hotel　HOTEL, APARTMENT **$$$**
(☑ 06-831 0077; www.navigatenapier.co.nz; 18 Hardinge Rd, Ahuriri; d/f/2-bedroom apt from $199/255/315; ☏) Navigate yourself towards Navigate for 26 snazzy apartment-style units over three levels, with funky furnishings, nifty perforated-metal balconies and sea views from the best rooms. There's a big kids' playground across the street for the offspring. The hotel opened in 2013, so everything is in good nick.

✗ Eating

Hapī　VEGAN **$**
(☑ 06-561 0142; www.hapi.nz; 89 Hastings St; mains $12-14; ☉ 7am-4pm; ☑) ✔ Welcome to Hapī, where virtuous and vital vegan flavours are also damn tasty. Breakfast bowls packed with acai, chia and quinoa team up with superior snacks like polenta fries or chipotle tofu tacos, and the drinks list of cold-pressed organic elixirs and plant-based smoothies is equally beneficial and bargain-priced.

Cafe Ujazi　CAFE **$**
(☑ 06-835 1490; www.facebook.com/ujazicafe; 28 Tennyson St; mains $10-22; ☉ 8am-5pm; ☑) The most bohemian of Napier's cafes, Ujazi folds back its windows and lets the alternative vibes spill out onto the pavement. It's a long-established, consistent performer offering blackboard meals and hearty counter food (vegetarian and vegan a speciality). Try

the classic *rewana* special – a big breakfast on traditional Māori bread. Oooh – homemade limeade!

★ Mister D　MODERN NZ **$$**
(☑ 06-835 5022; www.misterd.co.nz; 47 Tennyson St; mains $25-36; ☉ 7.30am-4pm Sun-Wed, to late Thu-Sat) This long, floorboarded room with its green-tiled bar is the pride of the Napier foodie scene. Hip and slick but not unaffordable, with quick-fire service delivering the likes of pulled pork with white polenta or roast-duck risotto. Addictive doughnuts are served with syringes full of chocolate, jam or custard (DIY injecting). Bookings essential.

Indigo　INDIAN **$$**
(☑ 06-834 4085; www.indigonapier.co.nz; 24a Hastings St; mains $16-26; ☉ 5pm-late daily, plus noon-2pm Thu-Sun; ☑) This stellar subcontinental outfit should really be charging more for its dishes than it does. Factor in one of the city's best selections of local Hawke's Bay craft beer, a huge array of gins and whiskies, and you're set for a good night. Amid the Indian culinary classics, seasonal chef's specials with an NZ twist could include lamb chop masala.

Milk & Honey　CAFE **$$**
(☑ 06-833 6099; www.themilkandhoney.co.nz; 19 Hardinge Rd, Ahuriri; mains & shared plates $15-34; ☉ 7am-9pm) One of the best options in the good eating and drinking hub around seaside Ahuriri village, Milk & Honey combines ocean and boardwalk views with a versatile all-day menu. Hawke's Bay beers and wines feature along with delicate seafood ceviche or a Japanese-influenced chicken salad. After dark the emphasis turns to shared plates like crispy prawns and fish sliders.

Throughout afternoons and evenings from November to March, pizza and Asian dumplings are available next door from Milk & Honey's Pizza/Pazzi and The Hatch.

Greek National Cafe　GREEK **$$**
(☑ 06-833 6069; www.greeknationalcafe.nz; 112 Emerson St; mains $20-29; ☉ 5-9pm Tue-Thu, 4-10pm Fri, 5-10pm Sat; ☑) Operated as a Kiwi diner serving steak and seafood for many decades, the National Cafe was reopened in 2017 by descendants of the original Greek owners. A few dishes from its heritage heyday linger, but now the emphasis is firmly on authentic flavours. Settle into the retro 1960s decor and partner meze and chargrilled octopus with ouzo, wine and retsina.

Be sure to order the *kessaria* pies with gooey cheese and pine nuts.

★ **Bistronomy** MODERN NZ $$$

(☑06-834 4309; www.bistronomy.co.nz; 40 Hastings St; mains lunch $22-28, dinner six/nine courses $75/100; ⊙noon-late Fri-Sun, from 5pm Wed & Thu; ♪) ✿ Bistronomy is proof that some of NZ's best food can be enjoyed outside the country's biggest cities. The finely judged seasonal tasting menus, which could include sumac-cured kingfish or chicken poached in kawakawa (a NZ forest herb), are highly recommended; they're great-value experiences you'll definitely talk about when you get back home. Lunch is slightly less formal, but equally excellent.

Pacifica MODERN NZ $$$

(☑06-833-6335; www.pacificarestaurant.co.nz; 209 Marine Pde; five courses without/with wine pairings $65/115; ⊙6-10pm Tue-Sat) ✿ Judged NZ'S top restaurant in 2017 by *Cuisine* magazine, Pacifica is a showcase for chef Jeremy Rameka's affinity with *kai moana* (seafood). The decor is surprisingly relaxed, and the good-value $65 five-course menu could include a mousse of mussels and scallops, or lemonfish marinated in coconut cream. A second menu including other proteins is available, as are recommended wine pairings.

MINT Restaurant MODERN NZ $$$

(☑06-835 4050; www.mintrestaurant.co.nz; 189 Marine Pde; mains $30-32; ⊙6-10pm Mon-Sat) Fine dining on Marine Pde: a concise and tightly edited menu features the likes of confit duck leg with duck and blue cheese risotto. Sensuously shaped glassware and snappy staff.

🍷 Drinking & Nightlife

Monica Loves BAR

(☑06-650 0240; www.monicaloves.co.nz; 39 Tennyson St; ⊙3-11pm Wed-Thu, to midnight Fri & Sat) Big-city laneway style comes to Napier at this bar tucked away off Tennyson St. Look for the big neon sign proclaiming 'Who shot the barman?' and you're in the right place for top cocktails, a beer list with regular surprises on the taps, and a knowingly Hawke's Bay-centric wine list. A compact open kitchen turns out interesting bar snacks ($8 to $18).

4th Door Lounge Bar COCKTAIL BAR

(☑06-834 0835; www.threedoorsup.co.nz/the-4th-door; 3 Waghorne St, Ahuriri; ⊙5pm-late Wed-Sat) The 4th Door offers an alternative to Ahuriri's waterfront bars. It's a classy, moody

---

CYCLE THE BAY

The 200km network of Hawke's Bay Trails (www.nzcycletrail.com/hawkes-bay-trails) – part of the national Nga Haerenga, New Zealand Cycle Trails project – offers cycling opportunities from short, city scoots to hilly, single-track shenanigans. Dedicated cycle tracks encircle Napier, Hastings and the coastline, with landscape, water and wine themes. Pick up the *Hawke's Bay Trails* brochure from the **Napier i-SITE** (p372) or online.

Napier itself is very cycle-friendly, particularly along Marine Pde, where you'll find **Fishbike** (☑0800 131 600, 06-833 6979; www.fishbike.nz; 22 Marine Pde, Pacific Surf Club; bike hire per half/full day $30/40, tandems per hr $35; ⊙9am-5pm) renting comfortable bikes – including tandems for those willing to risk divorce. **Napier City Bike Hire** (☑021 959 595, 0800 245 344; www.bikehirenapier.co.nz; 117 Marine Pde; half-day kids/city/mountain-bike hire from $20/25/30, full day from $25/35/40; ⊙9am-5pm) is another option.

Mountain bikers head to **Pan Pac Eskdale MTB Park** (☑06-873 8793; www.hawkes-baymtb.co.nz; off SH5; 3-week permits $10) for a whole lot of fun in the forest: see the website or call for directions. You can hire mountain bikes from **Pedal Power** (☑06-844 9771; www.avantiplus.co.nz/pedalpower; 340 Gloucester St, Taradale; half-/full day from $30/50; ⊙8am-5.30pm Mon-Fri, 9am-3pm Sat, 10am-3pm Sun), just out of the city centre, or from Napier City Bike Hire.

Given the conducive climate, terrain and multitudinous tracks, it's no surprise that numerous cycle companies pedal fully geared-up tours around the bay, with winery visits near-mandatory. Operators include the following:

Bike About Tours (☑06-845 4836, 027 232 4355; www.bikeabouttours.co.nz; tours half/full day from $25/30)

Coastal Wine Cycles (☑06-875 0302; www.winecycles.co.nz; 41 East Rd, Te Awanga; tours per day $40; 🚲)

On Yer Bike Winery Tours (☑06-650 4627; www.onyerbikehb.co.nz; full-day tours $55)

Tākaro Trails (☑06-835 9030; www.takarotrails.co.nz; day rides from $40)

OTATARA PĀ HISTORIC RESERVE

Wooden palisades, carved *pou* (memorial posts) and a carved gate help bring **Otatara Pā Historic Reserve** (📞06-834 3111; www.doc.govt.nz; off Springfield Rd; ⊙24hr) to life. An hour-long loop walk across grassy hills passes barely discernible archaeological remains but affords terrific views of the surrounding countryside. From the city head southwest on Taradale Rd and Gloucester St, then turn right into Springfield Rd just before the river.

the world's few working art-deco theatres. Worth going to for the original foyer lighting alone! Box office on-site.

ℹ Information

City Medical Napier (📞06-878 8109; www.hawkesbay.health.nz; 76 Wellesley Rd; ⊙24hr) Round-the-clock medical assistance.

DOC (Department of Conservation; 📞06-834 3111; www.doc.govt.nz; 59 Marine Pde; ⊙9am-4.15pm Mon-Fri) Maps, advice and passes.

Napier i-SITE (📞06-834 1911; www.napiernz.com; 100 Marine Pde; ⊙9am-5pm, extended hours Dec-Feb; 🛜) Central, helpful and right by the bay.

little nook, perfect for a pre-dinner drink, or a nightcap. Occasional live jazz and piano tunes on weekends.

Emporium   BAR
(📞06-835 0013; www.emporiumbar.co.nz; Masonic Hotel, cnr Tennyson St & Marine Pde; ⊙7am-late; 🛜) Napier's most civilised bar, Emporium is super atmospheric, with its marble-topped bar, fab art-deco details and old-fashioned relics strewn about. Brisk staff, creative cocktails, good coffee, NZ wines, bistro fare (plates $17 to $36) and a prime location seal the deal.

Thirsty Whale   BAR
(📞06-835 8815; www.thethirstywhale.co.nz; 62 West Quay, Ahuriri; ⊙11am-late Mon-Fri, from 9am Sat & Sun; 🛜) Does a whale drink? Or just filter krill? Either way, this big dockside bar is a sporty spot to join some fellow mammals for a brew or a bite (mains $12 to $39). Beneath 'Hawke's Bay's biggest screen' is the place to watch the All Blacks.

☆ Entertainment

Globe Theatrette   CINEMA
(📞06-833 6011; www.globenapier.co.nz; 15 Hardinge Rd, Ahuriri; tickets adult/child $16/14; ⊙1pm-late Tue-Sun) A vision in purple, this boutique 45-seat cinema screens art-house flicks in a sumptuous lounge with ready access to upmarket snacks and drinks.

Napier Municipal Theatre   THEATRE
(📞06-835 1059; www.napiermunicipaltheatre.co.nz; 119 Tennyson St; ⊙box office 9am-5pm Mon-Fri, to 12.30pm Sat) Not only the city's largest venue for the likes of rock concerts, dance and drama (1000 seats), but also one of

ℹ Getting There & Away

AIR

Hawke's Bay Airport (www.hawkesbay-airport.co.nz; SH2) is 8km north of the city.

Air New Zealand (📞0800 737 000; www.airnewzealand.co.nz) flies direct to/from Auckland, Wellington and Christchurch. Jetstar links Napier with Auckland, and Sounds Air has direct flights to Blenheim three times a week.

BUS

InterCity (www.intercity.co.nz) buses can be booked online or at the i-SITE. Naked Bus (https://nakedbus.com) tickets are best booked online. Some Naked Bus services are operated by ManaBus.

Both companies depart from **Clive Sq bus stop** (Clive Sq), with daily services (several daily for Hastings) to the following:

DESTINATION	COMPANY	PRICE ($)	DURATION (HR)
Auckland	InterCity	50	7½
Auckland	Naked Bus	26	9
Gisborne	InterCity	43	4
Hastings	InterCity	15	½
Palmerston North	InterCity	18	3
Taupo	InterCity	18	2
Taupo	Naked Bus	15	2
Wairoa	InterCity	14	2¼
Wellington	InterCity	33	5½
Wellington	Naked Bus	23	5

ℹ Getting Around

Most key sights around the city are reachable on foot, or you can speed things up by hiring a bicycle.

FROM GENESIS TO FERMENTATION

Although the first grapevines were planted near Kerikeri in the Bay of Islands in 1819, Hawke's Bay is regarded as the birthplace of the wine industry in New Zealand.

Planning to set up a French Catholic mission in Hawke's Bay in the mid-19th century, members of the Marist Brothers order overshot the region by around 240km, and actually alighted to the north near Gisborne. The better-organised Catholic Church soon caught up with them, and they were immediately instructed to decamp south to their original destination.

By 1851, a small Catholic winery producing sacramental wine had been established in what is now the Greenmeadows district near Taradale, and more than 165 years later, **Mission Estate Winery** (p377) is the oldest continuous winemaking enterprise in the country.

Another iconic Hawke's Bay winery to enjoy a long association with Greenmeadows is Church Road – the vineyard's earliest incarnations date back to 1927 – and the legendary founder Tom McDonald (1907–87) was one of the first people to recognise the potential of the area as a winemaking region. Only produced in truly exceptional vintages, Church Road's TOM series of wines commemorates one of the New Zealand wine industry's pioneering greats.

TO/FROM THE AIRPORT

A city–airport taxi or pre-booked airport shuttle costs around $20 to $25. Try **Blue Bubble Taxis** (☑ 06-835 7777, 0800 228 294; www.hawkesbay.bluebubbletaxi.co.nz) or the door-to-door **Super Shuttle** (☑ 0800 748 885; www.supershuttle.co.nz; one-way $20, extra person $5).

BUS

GoBay (www.hbrc.govt.nz) local buses (fitted with bike racks) run many times daily between Napier, Hastings and Havelock North. Napier to Hastings (adult/child $4.20/2) takes 30 minutes (express) or 55 minutes (all stops). Buses depart **Dalton St bus stop**.

CAR

See www.rentalcars.com for car-hire deals with companies at Hawke's Bay Airport, including the big brands and local outfits. **RAD Car Hire** (☑ 06-834 0688, 0800 736 823; www.radcarhire.co.nz; Hawke's Bay Airport, SH2; ◷7am-5pm Mon-Fri, to 1pm Sat, 9am-noon Sun) is also at the airport.

Hastings & Around

POP 77,900

Positioned at the centre of the Hawke's Bay fruit bowl, busy Hastings is the commercial hub of the region, 20km south of Napier. A few kilometres of orchards still separate it from Havelock North, with its prosperous village atmosphere and the towering backdrop of Te Mata Peak.

Imbibing and dining around the area's restaurants, breweries and vineyards, and trawling good farmers markets and seasonal fruit stands are fine foodie-focused reasons to explore, and balance can be provided by biking or tramping around Te Mata's spectacular natural profile.

◉ Sights

Like Napier, Hastings was devastated by the 1931 earthquake and also boasts some fine art-deco and Spanish Mission buildings, built in the aftermath. Main-street highlights include the **Westerman's Building** (cnr Russell St & Heretaunga St E), arguably the bay's best example of the Spanish Mission style, although there are myriad architectural gems here. The i-SITE (p378) stocks the *Art Deco Hastings* brochure ($1), detailing two self-guided walks.

Hastings City Art Gallery   GALLERY
(HCAG; ☑06-871 5095; www.hastingscityartgallery.co.nz; 201 Eastbourne St E; ◷10am-4.30pm) FREE The city's neat little gallery presents contemporary NZ (including Māori) and international art in a bright, purpose-built space. Expect some wacky stuff (much wackier than Hastings itself...).

Hastings Farmers Market   MARKET
(☑027 697 3737; www.hawkesbayfarmersmarket.co.nz; Showgrounds, Kenilworth Rd; ◷8.30am-12.30pm Sun) If you're around on Sunday, the Hastings market is mandatory. Bring an empty stomach, some cash and a roomy shopping bag.

★ **Te Mata Peak**   PARK
(☑06-873 0080; www.tematapark.co.nz; off Te Mata Rd, Havelock North; ◷5am-10pm) Rising dramatically from the Heretaunga Plains

Hastings

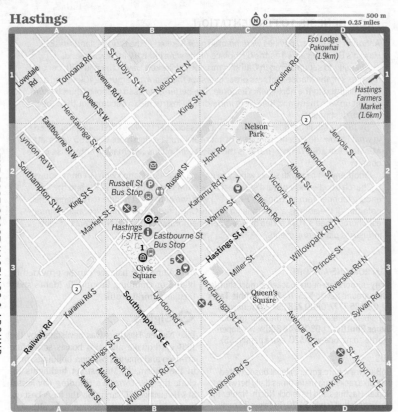

Hastings

16km south of Havelock North, Te Mata Peak (399m) is part of the 1-sq-km **Te Mata Trust Park**. The summit road passes sheep tracks, rickety fences and vertigo-inducing stone escarpments, cowled in a bleak, lunar-meets-Scottish-Highlands atmosphere.

On a clear day, views from the **lookout** fall away to Hawke Bay, the Mahia Peninsula and distant Mt Ruapehu.

The park's 30km of tracks offer walks ranging from 30 minutes to two hours: pick up the *Te Mata Park's Top 5 Walking Tracks* brochure from local i-SITEs. Mountain biking is also popular.

🛏 Sleeping

Cottages on St Andrews COTTAGES **$$**
(☑06-877 1644; www.cottagesonstandrews.nz; 14 St Andrews Rd, Havelock North; units $160, cottages $320; 🐾🏊) Modern self-contained two-bedroom cottages feature at this versatile spot in a quiet rural location around 1km from Havelock North. A heated pool, tennis court and a kids' adventure playground all maximise the appeal to travelling families, and there are also lambs, llamas and other farmyard critters to say g'day. A cheaper studio unit is also available.

Off The Track
COTTAGE $$

(☑ 06-877 0008; www.offthetrack.co.nz; 114 Havelock Rd, Havelock North; 1/2/3-bedroom cottages from $160/180/230; ☎) Not so much off the beaten track as just beside it, these three woody self-contained cottages are handy to Havelock North and a good option if you're trucking around with the family in tow. There's a busy cafe-restaurant here, too, but the cottages are privately positioned away from the hubbub.

Clive Colonial Cottages
COTTAGE $$

(☑ 06-870 1018; www.clivecolonialcottages.co.nz; 198 School Rd, Clive; d from $175; ☎) A two-minute walk to the beach and almost equidistant from Hastings, Napier and Havelock, these three tasteful kitchen cottages encircle a courtyard garden on a 2-acre spread. Communal areas include a barbecue, a giant chess set and a snooker room. Bikes on-site; track at your doorstep.

Havelock North Motor Lodge
MOTEL $$

(☑ 06-877 8627; www.havelocknorthmotorlodge. co.nz; 7 Havelock Rd, Havelock North; units $180-195; ☎) Smack-bang in the middle of Havelock North, this modern motel does the job well. Tidy, clean and simple one- and two-bedroom units feature spa baths, nice art and kitchenettes. Hungry? Across the street there's Mexican, Italian, Chinese, Indian, burgers...

★ St Andrews Escape
B&B $$$

(☑ 06-877 1525; www.standrewsescape.co.nz; 172 St Andrews Rd, Havelock North; d $210-250, cottages $250; ☎) Four lodge rooms with unique decor combine with a stand-alone cottage at this property near orchards and a compact lake around 3km from Havelock North. Our favourite accommodation in the main house is the 'Retro' room with a 1960s vibe, while the self-contained Te Whare (sleeps up to three) has Kiwiana design accents. Two-night minimum stay from Thursday to Saturday.

★ Millar Road
VILLA $$$

(☑ 06-875 1977; www.millarroad.co.nz; 83 Millar Rd, Hastings; villas/houses from $500/800; ☎☀) Set in the Tuki Tuki Hills with vineyard and bay views, Millar Road is architecturally heaven-sent. Two plush villas (each sleep four) and a super-stylish house (sleeps eight) are filled with NZ-made furniture and local artworks. Explore the 20-hectare grounds or look cool by the pool.

Mangapapa Petit Hotel
BOUTIQUE HOTEL $$$

(☑ 06-878 3234; www.mangapapa.co.nz; 466 Napier Rd, Havelock North; d incl breakfast $475-1100; ☎☀) A five-minute drive from Hastings, this heritage home (1885) – surrounded by leafy gardens, a tennis court, a swimming pool and a short golf course – has been sympathetically adapted into a boutique hotel. Twelve suites offer period-style luxury; a restaurant and day spa up the indulgence stakes. "Good afternoon Sir..", says the dapper doorman.

✖ Eating

✖ Hastings

Little Blackbird
CAFE $

(☑ 06-870 7462; www.littleblackbird.co.nz; 108 Market St S, Hastings; mains $8-18; ⊗ 7.30am-3.30pm Mon-Fri, 8am-2.30pm Sat) At the bottom of an old art-deco office building, mostly full of lawyers, is this tidy little eatery with retro interior design, funky lighting, Nicaraguan beans (!) and smiling staff (always a good sign). Head for the row of little tables by the street for some savoury scones or a beaut salad bowl.

Taste Cornucopia
CAFE $

(☑ 06-878 8730; www.tastecornucopia.co.nz; 219 Heretaunga St E, Hastings; meals $10-21; ⊗ 7.30am-4pm Mon-Fri, 8am-2pm Sat; ☑) ◢ A high-ceilinged organic cafe in central Hastings, Taste Cornucopia serves filling breakfasts, organic coffee, smoked fish pies, curries, vegetarian lasagne and buckwheat-and-corn pancakes. Hippie and wholesome.

★ Opera Kitchen
CAFE $$

(☑ 06-870 6020; www.eatdrinksharehb.co.nz; 306 Eastbourne St E, Hastings; mains $13-30; ⊗ 7.30am-4pm Mon-Fri, 9am-3pm Sat & Sun; ☑) Located in a high-ceilinged heritage building – formerly the HB Electric Power Board – our favourite Hastings cafe serves up sophisticated breakfast and lunch dishes with international accents. Spend a few hours browsing the design magazines and feasting on smoked fishcakes with a toasted nori sauce or Korean fried chicken with miso caramel. Heavenly pastries, great coffee and snappy staff.

Vidal
MODERN NZ $$$

(☑ 06-872 7440; www.vidal.co.nz; 913 St Aubyn St E, Hastings; lunch & dinner mains $30-39, 2-/3-course lunch $28/32; ⊗ 11.30am-3pm & 6pm-late Mon-Sat, 11.30am-3pm Sun) There's nothing suburban about this winery restaurant on the suburban backstreets of Hastings. The warm, wood-lined dining room is a worthy setting for such elegant food: order the eye fillet steak or the duo of duck, sip some syrah and feel your holiday come to fruition. Classy stuff.

✕ Havelock North

★ Maina
CAFE $$

(☑06-877 1714; www.maina.co.nz; 11 Havelock Rd, Havelock North; mains $12-24; ⊙7am-11pm Mon-Fri, from 8am Sat, 9am-3pm Sun; ☑) ✔ Blur the line between breakfast and lunch at the best new cafe in Hawke's Bay. This former post office is infused with stylish retro Kiwiana decor, and highlights include Te Mata mushrooms on organic sourdough or creamy pulled pork croquettes. Pizza and an ever-evolving selection of salads are also good, and superior homestyle baking includes perfect mid-morning coffee and doughnuts.

Alessandro's
PIZZA $$

(☑06-877 8844; www.alessandrospizzeria.co.nz; 24 Havelock Rd, Havelock North; mains $20-27; ⊙4.30-9pm Tue-Sun) Excellent Alessandro's does handmade wood-fired pizzas, thin and flavoursome, just like back in Napoli. Order the *noci e pere* (pear, Gorgonzola, mozzarella, walnuts and truffle honey) with a mean affogato for dessert. Snappy interior design; Peroni beer on tap.

Wright & Co
CAFE $$

(☑06-650 3664; www.wrightandco.nz; 10 Joll Rd, Havelock North; mains breakfast & lunch $13-27, dinner $24-34; ⊙7am-2.30pm Mon-Sun, plus 6pm-late Thu-Sat; ☑) ✔ This all-day cafe enlivened by blue butchers' tiles segues to a hip bistro from Thursday to Saturday night. Try the Thai-influenced breakfast curry bowl to start the day, or the wild mushroom risotto for lunch. House-made sodas and smoothies feature, and beers from the local Giant brewery and HB wines team well with dinner options like crayfish dumplings or venison.

Deliciosa
TAPAS $$

(☑06-877 6031; www.deliciosa.co.nz; 21 Napier Rd, Havelock North; tapas $10-22; ⊙11am-late Wed-Sat, from 4pm Mon & Tue) Great things come in small packages at this rosy little tapas bar. The kitchen delivers sassy, locally sourced edibles such as pork belly with pomegranate jus, and salt-and-pepper squid with orange and parsley. The wine list roams from Spain to Italy and back. Terrific beer list and breezy front terrace, too.

Malo
MODERN NZ $$$

(☑06-877 2009; www.malo.co.nz; 4 Te Aute Rd, Havelock North; mains $36-38; ⊙7am-11am & 4pm-late) ✔ Hotel restaurants can be hit-and-miss, but Malo at the Porters Boutique Hotel in Havelock North hits the right notes. Harnessing truckloads of regional and seasonal Hawke's Bay produce, the open kitchen turns out dishes with local lamb and venison, fresh oysters, tuna and kingfish from the raw bar, and beer snacks like Vietnamese rolls, sashimi and dumplings nightly from 4pm.

✕ Other Areas

Bareknuckle BBQ
BARBECUE $$

(☑021 773 303; www.bareknucklebbq.co.nz; 1091 Riverslea Rd South, Longlands; snacks & mains $13-28; ⊙11am-10pm Fri, to 5pm Sat) This authentic American barbecue place around 4km southwest of Hastings is hugely popular with locals. Pitmaster Jimmy Macken knows his stuff – Bareknuckle's barbecue was hand-built near the Texas-Mexico border – and he turns out fine brisket, ribs and pulled pork. Other dishes enjoyed in the raffish and ramshackle garden include tacos, and local craft beers are always on tap.

★ Elephant Hill
MODERN NZ $$$

(☑06-872 6060; www.elephanthill.co.nz; 86 Clifton Rd, Te Awanga; mains $36-42; ⊙cellar door 11am-5pm Nov-Mar, to 4pm Apr-Oct, restaurant noon-3pm & 6-9pm daily Nov-Mar, Thu-Sat only Apr-Oct) ✔ There's plenty of great vineyard dining around Hawke's Bay, but Elephant Hill in the beachy surroundings of Te Awanga is something special. Huge picture windows provide unencumbered views of Cape Kidnappers and vineyards, and Elephant Hill's award-winning wines partner supremely with seasonal dishes like Thai-style grilled gamefish with squid, or beef tartare with mustard ice-cream and truffle mayonnaise. Exquisite.

🍷 Drinking & Nightlife

★ GodsOwn Brewery
CRAFT BEER

(☑027 931 1042; www.godsownbrewery.co.nz; 3672 SH 50, Maraekakaho; ⊙3-10pm Thu & Fri, from noon Sat & Sun) ✔ This super microbrewery 22km east of Hastings is run from a safari tent, a caravan and a few outdoor tables. On a compact brewing set-up, traditional European beer styles like *biere de gardes* and *saisons* are crafted; the sheltered valley includes its own hop vines. Spent grain from the brewing process is used for tasty wood-fired flatbreads ($10 to $20).

Common Room
BAR

(☑027 656 8959; www.commonroombar.com; 227 Heretaunga St E, Hastings; ⊙3pm-late Wed-Sat) There's pretty much nothing wrong with this hip little bar in central Hastings: cheery staff, bar snacks, craft beer, local wines, a creative retro interior, a garden bar, Persian rugs, live

HAWKE'S BAY WINERIES

Once upon a time, this district was most famous for its orchards. Today it's vines that have top billing, with Hawke's Bay now New Zealand's second-largest wine-producing region (behind Marlborough). Expect excellent Bordeaux-style reds, syrah and chardonnay. Pick up the *Hawke's Bay Winery Guide* map or the *Hawke's Bay Trails* cycling map from **Hastings** (p378) or **Napier** (p372) i-SITEs, or download them from www.wine-hawkesbay.co.nz. A few of our faves:

Black Barn Vineyards (☑06-877 7985; www.blackbarn.com; Black Barn Rd, Havelock North; ⊙cellar door 10am-4pm, restaurant 10am-5pm Sun-Wed & to 9pm Thu-Sat (reduced hours Apr-Oct)) This hip, inventive winery has a bistro, a gallery, a popular summer Saturday morning farmers market (one of the first in NZ) and an amphitheatre for regular concerts and movie screenings. Tasting the flagship chardonnay is like kissing someone pretty on a summer afternoon. Excellent vineyard accommodation too (from $465).

Mission Estate Winery (☑06-845 9354; www.missionestate.co.nz; 198 Church Rd, Taradale; ⊙9am-5pm Mon-Sat, 10am-4.30pm Sun) New Zealand's oldest winery was established in 1851. Follow the *looong* tree-lined driveway up the hill to the restaurant (serving lunch and dinner, mains $28 to $38) and cellar door, inside a magnificently restored seminary. Call to book a guided tour.

Crab Farm Winery (☑06-836 6678; www.crabfarmwinery.co.nz; 511 Main North Rd, Bay View; ⊙10am-5pm daily, plus 6pm-late Fri) Decent, reasonably priced wines, and a great cafe with regular live troubadours and relaxed, rustic vibes. A good stop for lunch or a glass of rosé (preferably both).

Te Mata Estate (☑06-877 4399; www.temata.co.nz; 349 Te Mata Rd, Havelock North; ⊙9am-5pm Mon-Fri, from 10am Sat) The legendary Coleraine red at this unpretentious, old-school, family-run winery is worth the trip all on its own.

Craggy Range (☑06-873 0141; www.craggyrange.com; 253 Waimarama Rd, Havelock North; ⊙10am-6pm, closed Mon & Tue Apr-Oct) Definitely one of Hawke's Bay's flashiest wineries – wonderful wines, excellent restaurant and accommodation.

music and a tune-scape ranging from jazz to alt-country to indie. All the right stuff! Open Sundays as well from December to March.

Brave Brewing Co   CRAFT BEER
(☑027 460 8414; www.facebook.com/bravebeer; 408 Warren St; ⊙4-9pm Thu, from noon Fri-Sun) Brave's cool and compact tasting room on the edge of central Hastings showcases its own brews – ask if the Tigermilk IPA is available – and regular guest beers from brewing mates around the country. Curious beer fans should order a four-beer tasting paddle, and partner the different brews with delicious gourmet burgers ($15) from the on-site Carr's Kitchen.

Hugo Chang   COCKTAIL BAR
(☑06-877 3310; www.hugochang.com; 15b Joll Rd, Havelock North; ⊙4pm-late Tue-Sat) When the lights go down over Havelock North and a hush falls over the vine rows, over-25s with a yearning for some urban savvy head for Hugo Chang – a tucked-away, Asian-themed bar serving up cocktails, local wines and smooth beats. Dumplings are on tap, and on Wednesday nights they're just $8.

Shopping

Bellatino's   FOOD & DRINKS
(☑06-875-8103; www.bellatinos.myshopify.com; 9 Napier Rd, Havelock North; ⊙8am-6.30pm Mon-Fri, to 5pm Sat & Sun) Stock up at this excellent village deli with a separate corner dedicated to Hawke's Bay products including chocolate, olive oil and fruit preserves. Also good salads to take out if you're planning a vineyard or beachside picnic.

Strawberry Patch   FOOD
(☑06-877 1350; www.strawberrypatch.co.nz; 76 Havelock Rd, Havelock North; ⊙9am-5.30pm) Pick your own berries in season (late November to April), or visit year-round for fresh produce, picnic supplies, coffee and real fruit ice cream ($4).

ⓘ Information

MEDICAL SERVICES
Hastings Memorial Hospital (☑06-878 8109; www.hawkesbay.health.nz; Omahu Rd, Camberley; ⊙24hr)

TOURIST INFORMATION

Hastings i-SITE ([📱] 06-873 0080; www.hawkesbaynz.com; Westermans Bldg, cnr Russell St & Heretaunga St E; ⊙ 9am-5pm Mon-Fri, to 3pm Sat, 10am-2pm Sun) offers maps, brochures and bookings.

Havelock North i-SITE ([📱] 06-877 9600; www.havelocknorthnz.com; 1 Te Aute Rd; ⊙ 10am-5pm Mon-Fri, to 3pm Sat, to 2pm Sun; 🛜) provides local info in a cute little booth.

ℹ️ Getting There & Away

Napier's **Hawke's Bay Airport** (p372) is a 20-minute drive from Hastings. **Air New Zealand** ([📱] 06-873 2200; www.airnewzealand.co.nz; 117 Heretaunga St W, Hastings; ⊙ 9am-5pm Mon-Fri) flies from Napier to Auckland, Wellington and Christchurch.

InterCity buses stop at the **Russell St bus stop**. Book InterCity (www.intercity.co.nz) and Naked Bus (https://nakedbus.com) buses online or at the i-SITE.

ℹ️ Getting Around

GoBay (www.hbrc.govt.nz) local buses (with bike racks) run between Hastings, Havelock North and Napier. Daily Hastings to Napier buses (adult/child $4.20/2) take 30 minutes (express) or 55 minutes (all stops). Hastings to Havelock North buses run Monday to Saturday (adult/child $2.90/1.50, 35 minutes). Buses depart from the **Eastbourne St bus stop**.

Hastings Taxis ([📱] 0800 875 055, 06-878 5055; www.hastingstaxis.co.nz) is the local cab outfit.

Cape Kidnappers

From mid-September to late April, Cape Kidnappers (named when local Māori tried to kidnap Captain Cook's Tahitian servant boy) erupts with squawking gannets. These big ocean birds usually nest on remote islands but here they settle for the mainland, completely unfazed by human spectators.

The birds nest as soon as they arrive, and eggs take about six weeks to hatch, with chicks arriving in early November. In March the gannets start their migration; by May they're gone.

Early November to late February is the best time to visit. Take a tour or the walkway to the colony: it's about five hours return from Clifton. En route are interesting cliff formations, rock pools, a sheltered picnic spot and the gaggling gannets themselves. The walk is tide-dependent: leave no earlier than three hours after high tide; start back no later than 1½ hours after low tide.

👉 Tours

Gannet Beach Adventures   ECOTOUR
([📱] 06-875 0898, 0800 426 638; www.gannets.com; 475 Clifton Rd, Clifton; adult/child/family $44/24/106; 🛗) Ride along the beach on a tractor-pulled trailer before wandering out on the cape for 90 minutes. This four-hour, guided return trip departs from the Clifton waterfront, and is both good fun and great value.

Gannet Safaris   ECOTOUR
([📱] 06-875 0888; www.gannetsafaris.co.nz; 396 Clifton Rd, Te Awanga; adult/child $80/40; 🛗) Overland 4WD trips across farmland into the **gannet colony** ([📱] 06-834 3111; www.doc.govt.nz; off Clifton Rd, Clifton; ⊙ Nov-Jun) FREE. Three-hour tours depart at 9.30am and 1.30pm. Pickups from Napier and Hastings cost extra (adult/child additional $32/16).

ℹ️ Getting There & Away

No regular buses go to Clifton, but it's just a short drive from Hastings (20km). Alternatively tour operators will transport you for an additional fee, or you could bike it.

Central Hawke's Bay

Grassy farmland stretches south from Hastings, dotted with the grand homesteads of Victorian pastoralists. It's a untouristy area (aka 'Lamb Country'), rich in history and deserted beaches. The main regional town is **Waipukurau** (aka 'Wai-puk'; population 3750) – not exactly thrilling but a functional hub for petrol, motels, a supermarket and the Central Hawke's Bay Information Centre with adjunct coffee booth. Look for the handy *Limestone Route* driving map at the Napier and Hastings i-SITEs before you set off.

◉ Sights

There are no fewer than six windswept beaches along the coast here: **Kairakau, Mangakuri, Pourerere, Aramoana, Blackhead** and **Porangahau**. The first five are good for swimming, and between the lot they offer a range of sandy, salty activities including surfing, fishing and driftwoody, rock-pooly adventures. Between Aramoana and Blackhead Beach lies the DOC-managed **Te Angiangi Marine Reserve** – bring your snorkel.

It's a nondescript hill in the middle of nowhere, but the place with the world's longest name is good for a photo op. Believe it or not, **Taumatawhakatangihangakoauauotamateaturipukakapikimaungahoronukupokaiwhenuakitanatahu** is the abbreviated form of 'The Brow of a Hill Where Tamatea, the Man with the Big Knees, Who Slid, Climbed and Swallowed Mountains, Known as Land Eater, Played his Flute to his Brother'. To get there, fuel up in Waipukurau and drive 40km to the Mangaorapa junction on Rte 52. Turn left and go 4km towards Porangahau. At the intersection with the signposts, turn right and continue 4.3km to the sign.

Onga Onga, a historic village 16km west of Waipawa, has interesting Victorian and Edwardian buildings. Pick up a pamphlet for a self-guided walking tour from the info centre in Waipukurau.

**Central Hawke's
Settlers Museum** MUSEUM
(📞 06-857 7288; www.chbsettlersmuseum.co.nz; 23 High St, Waipawa; adult/child $5/1; ⏱ 10am-4pm) The Central Hawke's Bay Settlers Museum in Waipawa has pioneer artefacts, informative 'homestead' displays and a good specimen of a river *waka* (canoe). Look for the anchor of the ill-fated schooner *Maroro* out the front.

🍴 Eating

⭐**Paper Mulberry Café** CAFE $
(📞 06-856 8688; www.papermulberrycafe.co.nz; 89 SH2, Pukehou; snacks $4-10, lunch mains $10-17; ⏱ 7am-4pm) Halfway between Waipawa and Hastings, this retro cafe-gallery in a 100-year-old, aquamarine-coloured church serves excellent coffee, smoothies and homespun food (unbeatable fudge). Well worth a stop for a chomp, a browse through the local crafts on the side tables and to warm your buns by the wood heater in winter.

De La Mama BURGERS $
(📞 021 261 0180; www.facebook.com/DeLaMamaWaipawa; 85 High St, Waipawa; burgers $10-15; ⏱ noon-8pm Wed-Sun, from 5pm Tue) Look for the wall-covering Latin-themed mural and you've found this surprising place serving up some of the best burgers in the land. The New York and Cuban ones are our favourites, and it's pretty well mandatory to combine a few churros (Spanish fried-dough sweets) and a coffee before you continue north or south.

ℹ️ Information

The **Central Hawke's Bay Information Centre** (📞 06-858 6488; www.lambcountry.co.nz; Railway Esplanade, Waipukurau; ⏱ 9am-4pm Mon-Fri, to 1pm Sat) is in the old Waipukurau railway station. There's also a decent hole-in-the-wall coffee place here.

ℹ️ Getting There & Away

InterCity (www.intercity.co.nz) and Naked Bus (https://nakedbus.com) pass through Waipawa and Waipukurau on their Wellington–Napier routes.

Kaweka & Ruahine Ranges

The remote Kaweka and Ruahine Ranges separate Hawke's Bay from the Central Plateau. These forested wildernesses offer some of the North Island's best tramping. See www.doc.govt.nz for track, hut and campsite info on Ruahine Forest Park and the downloadable pamphlet *Kaweka Forest Park & Puketitiri Reserves*.

🏃 Activities

An ancient 136km Māori track, now known as the **Gentle Annie Road**, runs inland from Omahu near Hastings to Taihape, via Otamauri and Kuripapango (where there's a basic but charming DOC campsite, adult/child $6/3). This isolated route takes around three hours (or a couple of days by bike).

Hiking

Kaweka J, the highest point of the Kaweka Range (1724m), can be reached by a three- to five-hour tramp from the end of Kaweka Rd; from Napier take Puketitiri Rd then Whittle Rd. The drive is worthwhile in itself; it's partly unsealed and takes three hours return.

Enjoy a soak in **natural hot pools** (📞 06-834 3111; www.doc.govt.nz; off Makahu Rd; ⏱ daylight hours) FREE before or after the three-hour walk on **Te Puia Track**, which follows the picturesque **Mohaka River**. From Napier, take Puketitiri Rd, then Pakaututu Rd, then Makahu Rd. Parts of the road can be dicey – bring a 4WD if you can. For a longer walk, try the Sunset Track (p348).

Rafting

Mohaka Rafting RAFTING
(📞 027 825 8539, 06-839 1808; www.mohakarafting.com; day trips $115-210, 3 days per 2 people $3850) The mighty Mohaka can be rafted with Mohaka Rafting, either on efficient day trips (from scenic splash-abouts to serious rapids) or longer trips (helicopter in, raft out).

ℹ️ Getting There & Away

This is a remote part of New Zealand. Make sure your vehicle (there are no buses) is in good shape before you head on down the dirt road.

Wellington Region

Best Places to Eat

➡ Noble Rot (p401)

➡ Shepherd (p401)

➡ Logan Brown (p402)

➡ Clareville Bakery (p412)

➡ Whitebait (p402)

Best Places to Stay

➡ QT Museum Wellington (p399)

➡ Ohtel (p399)

➡ City Cottages (p399)

➡ Moana Lodge (p400)

➡ Dwellington (p398)

Why Go?

If your New Zealand travels thus far have been all about the great outdoors and sleepy rural towns, Wellington will make for a lively change of pace. Art-house cinemas, hip bars, live bands and endless cafes all await you in NZ's cultural capital.

Wellington is the crossing point between the North and South Islands, so travellers have long been passing through these parts. The likes of Te Papa and Zealandia now stop visitors in their tracks, while myriad other urban attractions reveal themselves over the course of a longer sojourn.

Less than an hour away to the north, the Kapiti Coast has a slower, beachy vibe, with Kapiti Island nature reserve a highlight. An hour away to the northeast over the Rimutaka Range, the Wairarapa plains are dotted with quaint towns and wineries, hemmed in by a rugged, wild coastline.

When to Go

➡ Wellington has a bad rep for blustery, cold, grey weather, but this isn't the whole story: 'Windy Welly' breaks out into blue skies and T-shirt temperatures at least several days a year, when you'll hear locals exclaim, 'You can't beat Wellington on a good day'.

➡ November to April are the warmer months here, with average maximums hovering around 20°C. From May to August it's colder and wetter – daily temperatures lurk around 12°C.

➡ The Kapiti Coast and Wairarapa are a different story – both warmer and less windy, with more blue-sky days to bask in.

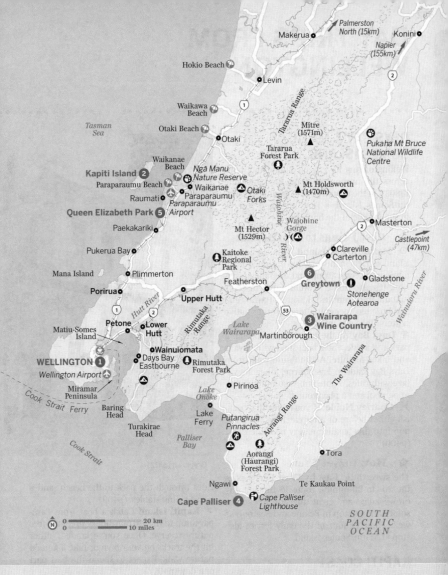

Wellington Region Highlights

1 Wellington (p386) Drowning in a sea of craft beer and top-notch coffee in New Zealand's most artsy, bohemian and political city.

2 Kapiti Island (p409) Hiking through native bush filled with some of the country's rarest bird species and perhaps even chancing upon a real live kiwi on a nocturnal walk.

3 Wairarapa Wine Country (p415) Struggling to maintain a straight line on your bicycle as you tour the wineries around Martinborough.

4 Cape Palliser (p416) Scaling the lighthouse steps on this wild and remote headland.

5 Queen Elizabeth Park (p409) Rambling through the dunes near beachy Paekakariki.

6 Greytown (p412) Soaking up the genteel, heritage ambience of the Wairarapa's prettiest town.

DAY TRIPS FROM WELLINGTON

DAYS BAY & MATIU/ SOMES ISLAND

Wellingtonians have been taking day trips across the harbour to Days Bay since the 1880s. On the way stop off at fascinating Matiu/Somes Island, a DOC-managed reserve in the middle of the harbour.

☆ Best Things to See/Do/Eat

◉ **Matiu/Somes Island** This 25-hectare island is rich in history, having once been a prisoner-of-war camp and quarantine station. It's also home to weta (large insects), tuatara (rare reptiles), kakariki (parakeets) and little blue penguins, among other native critters. Take a picnic lunch.

🌿 **Days Bay** At the bay there's a beach, a park and a cafe, and a boat shed with kayaks and bikes for hire. A 10-minute walk from Days Bay leads to Eastbourne, a beachy village with cafes, a cute pub, a summer swimming pool and a playground.

✕ **Charley Noble** If you're feeling peckish either before or after catching the ferry, pop into this bustling eatery near the dock. (p400)

☆ How to Get There

The sweet little **East by West Ferry** plies the 20- to 30-minute route 16 times a day on weekdays and eight times on weekends; some sailings stop in Petone and Seatoun as well. Three or four of the daily ferries also stop at Matiu/Somes Island.

KAPITI COAST

When the temperature heats up (it does happen from time to time, honest), head north to this beautiful sandy stretch of coast for a cooling dip in the surf.

☆ Best Things to See/Do/Eat

◉ **Queen Elizabeth Park** Take a picnic and find a secluded spot near the beach to base yourself for a few blissful hours of body-surfing and sunbathing. If you get bored there are walking and cycling trails, a tram museum (offering 2km heritage-tram

Greytown (p412)

rides through the park to the beach) and a horse-riding stables. (p409)

🌿 **Kapiti Island** Catch a boat from Paraparaumu to this extraordinary predator-free nature reserve. Once you've landed, either hit the tracks on your own or take a guided nature walk. Expect to spend the best part of a day. (p409)

✕ **Marine Parade Eatery** Gaze out over Kapiti Island from this excellent modern cafe on the Paraparaumu waterfront. (p410)

☆ How to Get There

Access to the Kapiti Coast is a snap: it's just a short drive away from Wellington, and there are good train connections to Paekakariki, Paraparaumu and Waikanae. From the latter two stations, buses head backwards and forwards to the beach.

THE WAIRARAPA

Take a drive along the Hutt Valley and then up and over the Rimutaka Range to visit the historic towns and acclaimed wineries of the Wairarapa. If you've got time, continue on to the wild coast at Cape Palliser or Castlepoint.

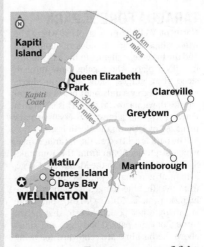

☆ Best Things to See/Do/Eat

◉ **Greytown's main street** The cutest of the Wairarapa towns is crammed full of historic buildings, many of them housing cafes and interesting independent shops. (p412)

☆ **Martinborough wine tasting** The region's best wineries are conveniently located in a circuit around the fringes of this attractive little town. Hire a bike and wobble your way from cellar door to cellar door. Just make sure you've got a sober driver at hand for the journey back to Wellington. (p414)

✗ **Clareville Bakery** There are plenty of fancier places, but our favourite spot for a bite is this bakery-cafe located along the main road between Carterton and Masterton. (p412)

☆ How to Get There

The Wairarapa is most easily explored by car; allow just over an hour to reach Greytown via SH1 and SH2. Trains head from Wellington to Masterton but you'll need to transfer to a bus to reach Greytown or Martinborough.

Base yourself in Wellington to explore the bottom end of the North Island. Within striking distance of the nation's capital are beaches and wineries galore.

HIKING IN THE WAIRARAPA

TARARUA FOREST PARK

North of Wellington is a place where the wind whips along the sides of mountains and the fog creeps silently in the early morning. It's a place where gales blow through steep river gorges, snow falls on sharp, greywacke (grey sandstone) peaks and rain trickles down narrow ridges. This is Tararua Forest Park, the largest conservation park managed by DOC on the North Island.

The park is centred on the Tararua Range, which stretches 80km from the Rimutaka Saddle in the south to the Manawatu Gorge, a natural gap that separates the Tararuas from the Ruahine Range, in the north. The highest peak is Mitre (1571m), but there are many other peaks close to that height throughout the park. The ridges and spurs above the bushline are renowned for being narrow, steep and exposed.

Only 50km from Wellington, the park used to be popular largely with weekend trampers from the windy city. Today trampers from around the country are attracted to the Tararuas' broken terrain and sheer features, which present a challenge to even the most experienced hikers.

The park has an extensive network of tracks, routes and huts, most accessible from the main gateways of Otaki Forks in the west (off SH1), and Holdsworth and Waiohine Gorge on the eastern, Wairarapa side.

These tracks are not as well formed as those in most national parks, so it's easy to lose them. On the open ridge-tops there are rarely signposts or poles marking the routes, only the occasional cairn. The Mt Holdsworth–Jumbo Circuit is less demanding than most routes through the Tararuas, and is therefore undertaken by a greater number of trampers.

The Wellington region's most satisfying hikes can be found across the ranges in the wilds of the Wairarapa.

☆ Mt Holdsworth–Jumbo Circuit

START/END HOLDSWORTH LODGE
DURATION 3 DAYS
DISTANCE 24KM
DIFFICULTY MODERATE TO DEMANDING

This classic Tararua tramp climbs through beech forest to quickly ascend to the alpine tops of the range. Mt Holdsworth brings wraparound views, while the huts along the route also provide expansive panoramas, bringing a serene sense of removal as you look out to the lights of Masterton in the evening.

Although you can cover this tramp in two days, it's a better idea to schedule three in order to savour the alpine walking and to build in the possibility of losing a day to the bad weather that can easily force you to sit out a day in one of the alpine huts.

CAPE PALLISER

Cape Palliser is best known for its landmark lighthouse and the North Island's largest breeding area for seals, but it also offers a standout half-day tramp to a geological oddity that's had more than its 15 minutes of cinematic fame.

JOHAN LARSON/SHUTTERSTOCK ©

Cape Palliser Lighthouse (p416)

☆ Putangirua Pinnacles

START/END PUTANGIRUA PINNACLES CAMPSITE
DURATION 3 HOURS
DISTANCE 6.5KM
DIFFICULTY EASY TO MODERATE

With their otherworldly appearance, the fragile and fluted cliffs and hoodoos of the Putangirua Pinnacles could easily inspire a sense of Middle-earth, which is exactly what they did for Sir Peter Jackson, who cast them as the Dimholt Road in *The Lord of the Rings* (he also used them as a location for the opening sequence of his 1992 splatter horror flick, *Braindead*).

The Pinnacles, as they're simply known locally, are cut into a wild section of coast near Cape Palliser. They've been formed due to the erosion of the soft earth by rain, creating a series of deep gullies. When boulders are exposed, they shed the rainwater, protecting the ground beneath from erosion and thus creating stone-capped hoodoos.

The Pinnacles present a raft of tramping options, none taking more than half a day (leaving time for a rehydrating pinot noir back in Martinborough, the centrepiece of the Wairarapa wine region, less than 45 minutes' drive away): you can walk to the Pinnacles' base along the stream bed, climb to a high lookout point along a ridge track, combine the two, or make a larger loop that also casts a wide eye along the entire Palliser Bay coast.

This tramp can be undertaken at any time of year, but the stream route should be avoided after heavy rain or in high wind when rockfall is common from the loose and fragile gravel cliffs. The stream, which needs to be crossed on the low route, can also rise quickly after rain.

WELLINGTON

🎵 04 / POP 208,000

On a sunny, windless day, Wellington is up there with the best of them. For starters it's lovely to look at, sitting on a hook-shaped harbour ringed with ranges that wear a cloak of snow in winter. Victorian timber architecture laces the bushy hillsides above the harbour, which resonate with native birdsong.

As cities go, it's really rather small but the compact nature of the downtown area gives it a bigger-city buzz and, being the capital, it's endowed with museums, theatres, galleries and arts organisations completely disproportionate to its size. Wellingtonians are rightly proud of their kickin' caffeine and craft-beer scene, and there's no shortage of beard-wearing, skateboard-lugging, artsy types doing interesting things in old warehouses across town.

Sadly, windless days are not the norm for Wellington. In New Zealand the city is infamous for two things: its frequent tremors and its umbrella-shredding, hairstyle-destroying gales that barrel through regularly.

History

Māori tradition has it that the explorer Kupe was first to discover Wellington Harbour. Wellington's original Māori name was Te Whanganui-a-Tara (great harbour of Tara),

ESSENTIAL WELLINGTON

Eat yourself silly: Wellington has a gut-busting number of great cafes and restaurants.

Drink coffee; Wellington is wide awake around the clock.

Read *The Collected Stories of Katherine Mansfield*.

Listen to The Mutton Birds' *Wellington* (1994) or The Mockers' *Murder in Manners St* (1980).

Watch *What We Do in the Shadows* (2014), where Wellington's vampires get their moment in the sun.

Go green at Zealandia (p395), a ground-breaking ecosanctuary within the city's confines.

Online www.wellingtonnz.com, www.wairarapanz.com, www.kapiticoast.govt.nz, www.lonelyplanet.com/new-zealand/wellington.

named after the son of a chief named Whatonga who had settled on the Hawke's Bay coast. Whatonga sent Tara and his half-brother to explore the southern part of the North Island. When they returned more than a year later, their reports were so favourable that Whatonga's followers moved there, founding the Ngāi Tara tribe (now known as Muaūpoko) and based around the Kapiti Coast.

By the time that Colonel William Wakefield arrived in 1839 to purchase land on behalf of the New Zealand Company, the Wellington area was split between three *iwi* (tribes), Ngāti Toa, Ngāti Raukawa and Te Āti Awa. On 22 January 1840 the first European settlers arrived in the New Zealand Company's ship *Aurora,* expecting to take possession of land that the local Māori denied selling. The Treaty of Waitangi was signed a few weeks later, and in the years that followed the Land Claims Commission was established to sort out the mess. Initially it attempted to act fairly to both sides but as the decades went on, the balance shifted in favour of the new arrivals.

By 1850 Wellington was a thriving settlement of around 5500 people, despite a shortage of flat land. Originally the waterfront was along Lambton Quay, but reclamation of parts of the harbour began in 1852. In 1855 a significant earthquake raised many parts of Wellington, including the lower Hutt Valley and the land on which the modern Hutt Rd now runs.

In 1865 the seat of government was moved from Auckland to Wellington, although it took until the turn of the century for the city to really flourish. In the early 1900s the port prospered, with export boards and banks springing up in its surrounds. Other industries developed, pushing urban sprawl further afield into the Hutt Valley, Porirua and the Kapiti Coast.

In modern times, the capital remains a stronghold of the public service, despite ongoing trims. It also boasts a good quotient of technological and creative industries.

⊙ Sights

Wellington is an arty kinda town – expect quality gallery experiences and some fab museums. There are also some great wilderness-in-the-city experiences to be had here, some interesting old buildings and a couple of awesome lookouts.

If you've got your own wheels, take a trip around the wild, rugged bays of the south coast and Miramar Peninsula.

MĀORI WELLINGTON

Referred to in legends as the 'mouth of Maui's fish' and traditionally called Te Whanganui-a-Tara, the Wellington area became known to Māori in the mid-19th century as 'Pōneke' (a transliteration of Port Nick, short for Port Nicholas, its English name at the time).

The major *iwi* (tribes) of the region were Te Āti Awa and Ngāti Toa. Ngāti Toa was the *iwi* of Te Rauparaha, who composed the now famous *Ka Mate haka*. Like most urban areas the city is now home to Māori from many *iwi*, sometimes collectively known as Ngāti Pōneke.

New Zealand's national museum, **Te Papa** (p393), presents excellent displays on Māori culture, traditional and modern, as well as a colourful *marae* (traditional meeting place). In its gift shop you can see excellent carving and other crafts, as you can in both **Kura** (p406) and **Ora** (Map p392; ☑04-384 4157; www.oragallery.co.nz; 23 Allen St; ⊙9am-6pm Mon-Sat, 10am-4pm Sun) galleries nearby.

Te Wharewaka o Pōneke (p397), **Kapiti Island Nature Tours** (p409) and **Kiwi Coastal Tours** (p397) offer intimate insights into the Māori culture of the rugged coast around Wellington.

◉ City Centre

St Mary of the Angels
CHURCH

(Map p392; ☑04-473 8074; www.smoa.org.nz; 17 Boulcott St; ⊙7am-6pm) Closed for seismic strengthening and restoration from 2013 to 2017, this pretty Catholic parish church is looking downright heavenly. Built in 1922, it was the first Gothic-style church in the world to have been constructed using reinforced concrete. The motto of the Marist order, *Sub Mariæ Nomine* ('under the name of Mary'), adorns the impressive Gothic facade, while colourful stained glass imported from Munich imbues the interior with warmth.

City Gallery Wellington
GALLERY

(Map p392; ☑04-913 9032; www.citygallery.org. nz; Civic Sq; ⊙10am-5pm) **FREE** Housed in the monumental old library in Civic Sq, Wellington's much-loved City Gallery does a cracking job of securing acclaimed contemporary international exhibitions, as well as unearthing up-and-comers and supporting those at the forefront of the NZ scene. Charges may apply for major exhibits.

★ Wellington Museum
MUSEUM

(Map p388; ☑04-472 8904; www.museums wellington.org.nz; 3 Jervois Quay, Queens Wharf; ⊙10am-5pm; 🖪) **FREE** For an imaginative, interactive experience of Wellington's social and maritime history, head to this beguiling little museum, housed in an 1892 bond store on the wharf. Highlights include a moving documentary on the *Wahine,* the inter-island ferry that sank in the harbour in 1968 with the loss of 51 lives. Māori legends are dramatically told using tiny holographic actors and special effects.

The 'Attic' has an eclectic set of exhibits including a whizz-bang time machine and a suitably kooky display on Wellington vampire flick *What We Do In The Shadows.*

Academy Galleries
GALLERY

(Map p388; ☑04-499 8807; www.nzafa.com; 1 Queens Wharf; ⊙10am-5pm) **FREE** The showcase of the esteemed New Zealand Academy of Fine Arts (founded 1882), the Academy Galleries presents frequently changing exhibitions by NZ artists, from canvases to ceramics to photography.

New Zealand Portrait Gallery
GALLERY

(Map p388; ☑04-472 2298; www.nzportraitgallery. org.nz; Shed 11, Customhouse Quay; ⊙10.30am-4.30pm) **FREE** Housed in a heritage red-brick warehouse on the waterfront, this excellent gallery presents a diverse range of NZ portraiture and caricature from its own collection and frequently changing guest exhibitions.

Wellington Cable Car
CABLE CAR

(Map p388; ☑04-472 2199; www.wellingtoncable car.co.nz; Cable Car Lane, rear 280 Lambton Quay; adult/child one way $4/2, return $7.50/3.50; ⊙departs every 10min, 7am-10pm Mon-Fri, 8.30am-9pm Sat & Sun; 🖪) One of Wellington's big-ticket attractions is the little red cable car that clanks up the steep slope from Lambton Quay to Kelburn. At the top are the Wellington Botanic Gardens (p393), Space Place (p393) and the small but nifty Cable Car Museum (Map p388; ☑04-475 3578; www.museumswelling ton.org.nz; 1A Upland Rd, Kelburn; ⊙9.30am-5pm) **FREE**. The latter evocatively depicts the cable car's story since it was built in 1902 to open up hilly Kelburn for settlement. Ride the cable car back down the hill, or wander down through the gardens.

Wellington

500 m
0.25 miles

Wellington Harbour

Wellington-Picton Ferry (Interislander Services)

Interislander

Port of Wellington Container Terminal

Aotea Quay

Westpac Stadium

Waterloo Quay

Thorndon Quay

InterCity

Wellington Railway Station

Bluebridge Ferries

Hutt Rd

Wellington Urban Mwy

Lennel Rd

Hobson St

28

Pipitea St

14

Bus Terminal

Murphy St

Molesworth St

Aitken St

Kate Sheppard Pl

Bunny St

30

Mana Bus

13

Thorndon Quay

WADESTOWN

Wadestown Rd

Park St

Tinakori Rd

Hawkestone St

10

19

THORNDON

New Zealand Parliament

Hill St

2

Lambton Quay

25

Bowen St

Grant Rd

Te Ahumairangi Hill

Sydney St W

Bolton St

32

Town Belt

Northern Walkway

WILTON

Churchill Rd

Wilton Rd

Mairangi Rd

Cecil Rd

Pembroke Rd

15

Bedford St

Pembroke Rd

Abermarle Rd

Wilton Rd

Randwick Rd

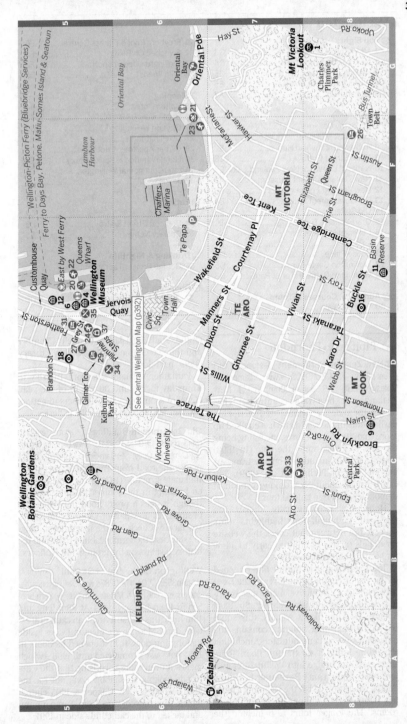

WELLINGTON REGION

Mt Victoria Lookout 1

Charles Plimmer Park

Upoko Rd

Hay St

Bus Tunnel

Town Belt

26

Austin St

Oriental Pde

Oriental Bay
Oriental Bay

McTanies St

21
23

Hawker St

MT VICTORIA

Elizabeth St

Queen St

Pirie St

Brougham St

Kent Tce

Cambridge Tce

Chaffers Marina

Te Papa

P

Wakefield St

Courtenay Pl

Tory St

Buckle St

Basin Reserve

11

16

E

Lambton Harbour

Customhouse Quay

East by West Ferry

Queens Wharf

Wellington–Picton Ferry (Bluebridge Services)
Ferry to Days Bay, Petone, Matiu-Somes Island & Seatoun

12
6
20 22
4

Wellington Museum

Jervois Quay

35

Civic Sq

Town Hall

Manners St

Dixon St

Ghuznee St

TE ARO

Vivian St

Taranaki St

Karo Dr

Webb St

Thompson St

MT COOK

Nairn St
6

See Central Wellington Map (p392)

Willis St

The Terrace

Featherston St

31

27 Grey St

24

37

29 34

18

Brandon St

Kelburn Park

Gilmer Tce

Plimmer Steps

Wellington Botanic Gardens
3

17

7

Upland Rd

Victoria University

Kelburn Pde

Central Tce

Grove Rd

Glen Rd

ARO VALLEY

33

36

Aro St

Epuni St

Central Park

Brooklyn Rd

Ohiro Rd

KELBURN

Glenmore St

Upland Rd

Raroa Rd

Raroa Rd

Holloway Rd

Moana Rd

Waiapu Rd

Zealandia
5

Wellington

◎ Pipitea & Thorndon

★ **New Zealand Parliament** HISTORIC BUILDING
(Map p388; ☎04-817 9503; www.parliament.nz;
Molesworth St; ⊙9.30am-4.30pm) FREE New
Zealand might be a young country but it has
one of the oldest continuously functioning
parliaments in the world and has chalked up
more than its share of firsts, including being
the first to give women the vote (in 1893)
and the first to include an openly transsexual Member of Parliament (in 1999). You
can learn all about NZ's unique version of
democracy on a free guided tour.

Hour-long tours usually depart on
the hour, with half-hour highlights tours
squeezed in between, but check the website
for details (arrive 15 minutes early to allow
for security and coat check).

Tours start with a 12-minute film screened
in the visitor centre in the foyer of the **Beehive** (1980), a distinctive modernist building designed by British architect Sir Basil
Spence. Looking like it sounds, this squat
but oddly charming building contains the
offices of government ministers, including
the Prime Minister on the 9th floor. Tours
then cross the bridge into Wellington's aus-
tere grey-and-cream **Parliament House**
(1922), where you'll visit the Debating Chamber, Banquet Hall and one of the committee
rooms. The longer tours also include the

Grand Hall, Legislative Council Chamber
and the neo-Gothic **Parliamentary Library**
(1899) next door.

Parliament usually sits from Tuesday to
Thursday for around 30 weeks of the year.
If you're keen to see the Members in action,
you can watch from the public galleries.

Old Government Buildings HISTORIC BUILDING
(Map p388; ☎04-472 4341; www.heritage.org.nz;
55 Lambton Quay; ⊙9am-5pm Mon-Fri) FREE
Across the road from Parliament, this grand
Italianate structure (1876) is the largest wood-
en building in the southern hemisphere, although it does a pretty good impersonation
of stone. It's now part of Victoria University's
law faculty. Check out the magnificent hanging staircase, the former cabinet room and the
history displays on the ground and 1st floors.

Wellington Cathedral of St Paul CATHEDRAL
(Map p388; ☎04-472 0286; www.wellingtoncathe-
dral.org.nz; cnr Hill & Molesworth Sts; ⊙8am-5pm
Sun-Fri, 10am-4pm Sat) FREE At 88m long and
18m high, this modern Anglican cathedral exudes quasi-Moorish architectural vibes inside
its lofty interiors. It first opened its doors in
1964 but wasn't completed until 1998 – which
makes it even more surprising that the exterior is looking so shabby. Look out for the
lovely wooden Lady Chapel, a 1905 church
which was moved here from Paraparaumu
and tacked to the cathedral's side in 1991.

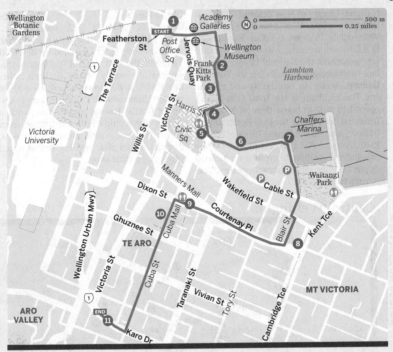

🏃 City Walk
City Sculpture

START POST OFFICE SQ
END KARO DR
LENGTH 2.8KM; ONE HOUR

Get started in windswept Post Office Sq, where Bill Culbert's ① **SkyBlues** twirls into the air. Cross Jervois Quay and pass between the Academy Galleries and Wellington Museum. At the Queens Wharf waterfront, turn right, past the big shed to the ② **Water Whirler**, the largely lifeless needle of kooky kineticist Len Lye that whirrs crazily into life on the hour several times a day.

Continue along the promenade below the ③ **mast of the Wahine**, which tragically sank in Wellington Harbour in 1968. Around the corner are the white, rather whale-like forms of the ④ **Albatross Fountain**. Detour up onto the flotsamy ⑤ **City to Sea Bridge** and check out the collection of weathered wooden sculptures here.

Back on the waterfront, continue past the *whare waka* (canoe house), to the mooring of the ⑥ **Hikitia**, the world's oldest working crane ship – something of a sculpture in itself.

Strip off and jump off the diving platform, or perhaps just keep going along the wharf, past the naked bronze form of ⑦ **Solace in the Wind** leaning over the harbour fringe.

Turn right and wander through the landscaped wetlands of Waitangi Park before crossing Cable St and cutting along Chaffers St, and then Blair St with its century-old warehouses.

At Courtenay Pl look to your left, to check out the leggy form of the industrial-cinematic ⑧ **Tripod**, before turning right. Continue along to wedge-shaped ⑨ **Te Aro Park** with its canoe prow and trip hazards.

Turn left when you hit Cuba St, heading up the pedestrian mall. Watch out for the sly, sloshy ⑩ **Bucket Fountain**; it exists solely to splash your legs.

Change down a gear and window-shop all the way to the top of Cuba St, where a remnant heritage precinct is bisected by the controversial inner-city bypass. Bookend your sculpture walk with Regan Gentry's brilliant but ghostly outline of a demolished house, ⑪ **Subject to Change**. Alongside is the curious 7.5m-deep Tonks' Well, dating from the 1860s.

National Library of New Zealand MUSEUM
(Map p388; 0800 474 300; www.natlib.govt.nz; 70 Molesworth St, Thorndon; 8.30am-5pm Mon-Sat) **FREE** As well as being a wonderful resource for researchers, the National Library has various exhibition spaces including the **Turnbull Gallery**, displaying rare books and ephemera. The highlight is **He Tohu** (The Signs), opened in 2017 to house three of NZ's most treasured documents: the 1835 Declaration of Independence of the United Tribes of NZ, the 1840 Treaty of Waitangi and the 1893 Women's Suffrage Petition. Interesting multimedia displays outline the significance of these documents to the nation.

Old St Paul's CHURCH
(Map p388; 04-473 6722; www.oldstpauls. co.nz; 34 Mulgrave St, Thorndon; tours $5-7.50; 9.30am-5pm) **FREE** Designed by Rev Fred Thatcher, the first vicar of Wellington, this wonderfully woody former Anglican cathedral (1866) is well worth a look. Despite its modest dimensions it's an exemplary example of Gothic Revival architecture, with a ceiling like a ship's hull constructed from native timbers. Inside are claret carpets, drawers of old altar textiles, brassy organ pipes and a little shop.

Central Wellington

Katherine Mansfield House HISTORIC BUILDING
(Map p388; 📞04-473 7268; www.katherinemans
field.com; 25 Tinakori Rd, Thorndon; adult/child $8/
free, guided tours $10; ⏰10am-4pm Tue-Sun) Often compared to Chekhov and Maupassant, Katherine Mansfield is one of NZ's most distinguished authors. Born in 1888, she died of tuberculosis in 1923 aged 34. This Tinakori Rd house is where she spent five years of her childhood. It now contains exhibits in her honour, including a biographical film.

★**Wellington Botanic Gardens** GARDENS
(Map p388; 📞04-499 4444; www.wellington.govt.
nz; 101 Glenmore St, Thorndon; ⏰daylight hours)

<FREE> These hilly, 25-hectare botanic gardens can be *almost* effortlessly visited via the Wellington Cable Car (p387) (nice bit of planning, eh?), although there are several other entrances hidden in the hillsides. The gardens boast a tract of original native forest, the beaut Lady Norwood Rose Garden, 25,000 spring tulips and various international plant collections. Add in fountains, a playground, sculptures, a duck pond, a cafe and city skyline views, and you've got a grand day out indeed.

Space Place OBSERVATORY
(Map p388; 📞04-910 3140; www.museums
wellington.org.nz; 40 Salamanca Rd, Kelburn; adult/
child/family $13/8/39; ⏰4-11pm Tue & Fri, 10am-
11pm Sat, 10am-5.30pm Sun) Located in the Carter Observatory at the top of the Botanic Gardens, this full-dome planetarium offers regular space-themed multimedia shows (eg *We Are Aliens, Dynamic Earth, Matariki Dawn*) and stargazing sessions. Check the website for show times.

◎ Te Aro

Te Papa MUSEUM
(Map p392; 📞04-381 7000; www.tepapa.govt.nz; 55 Cable St; tours adult/child $20/10; ⏰10am-6pm;
🚻) <FREE> New Zealand's national museum is hard to miss, taking up a sizeable chunk of the Wellington waterfront. 'Te Papa Tongarewa' loosely translates as 'treasure box' and the riches inside include an amazing collection of Māori artefacts and the museum's own colourful *marae* (meeting place); natural history and environment exhibitions; Pacific and NZ history galleries; themed hands-on 'discovery centres' for children; and Toi Art, a revitalised home for the National Art Collection, which opened in 2018. Big-name temporary exhibitions incur an admission fee, although general admission is free.

Introductory and Māori Highlights tours depart from the information desk on level two; it pays to book ahead.

Ngā Taonga Sound & Vision ARCHIVES
(Map p392; 📞04-384 7647; www.ngataonga.org.nz; 84 Taranaki St; screenings adult/child $10/8; ⏰library noon-4pm Mon-Fri) <FREE> Ngā Taonga is a vortex of NZ moving images into which you could get sucked for days. Its library holds tens of thousands of titles: feature films, documentaries, short films, home movies, newsreels, TV programs, advertisements... There are regular screenings in the cinema (check

Central Wellington

the website for the schedule), and a viewing library (free) where you can watch films until you're square-eyed. If the library is closed, there's a media player in the on-site cafe.

◎ Mt Cook & Newtown

Nairn Street Cottage   MUSEUM
(Map p388; ☏ 04-384 9122; www.museums wellington.org.nz; 68 Nairn St, Mt Cook; adult/child $8/4; ☺ 12-4pm Sat & Sun) Just a five-minute amble from the top of Cuba St, Wellington's oldest cottage (1857) has been carefully restored, complete with an organic garden and chooks (chickens). Admission is by tour only (on the hour noon to 3pm), retelling stories of early settlers and life in the mid-1800s.

Pukeahu National War Memorial Park   MEMORIAL
(Map p388; ☏ 04-385 2496; www.mch.govt.nz; Buckle St, Mt Cook; ☺ hall 10am-5pm) It seems strangely fitting that NZ's National War Memorial should be a musical instrument and contain as its centrepiece not a statue of a soldier, but of a grieving mother and her children. The statue is contained within the **Hall of Memories** at the base of the 51m-high, 49-bell, art-deco **Carillon** (1932).

PETONE & LOWER HUTT

These two attractions at the north end of Wellington Harbour can easily be combined in one trip.

Petone Settlers Museum (☑04-568 8373; www.petonesettlers.org.nz; The Esplanade, Petone; ⊙10am-4pm Wed-Sun Apr-Nov, daily Dec-Mar) Built for the centenary of the Treaty of Waitangi in 1940, this gorgeous little art-deco building on the shell-strewn Petone foreshore contains a fun and fascinating wee museum focusing on local history and industry. It's a 15-minute drive from downtown Wellington, or a 23-minute ride on the 83 bus.

Dowse Art Museum (☑04-570 6500; www.dowse.org.nz; 45 Laings Rd, Lower Hutt; ⊙10am-5pm; ♿) A beacon of culture and delight, the excellent Dowse is worth visiting for its jaunty architecture alone. It's a family-friendly, accessible art museum showcasing NZ art, craft and design, with a nice cafe to boot. The only permanent showcase is a carved *pataka* (traditional raised storehouse). It's a 20-minute drive, 30-minute ride on bus 83 or short train trip from central Wellington.

It's flanked by a sobering and oddly tranquil park with a prominent **Australian Memorial** consisting of 15 red sandstone columns.

New Zealand Cricket Museum   MUSEUM
(Map p388; ☑04-385 6602; www.nzcricket museum.co.nz; Museum Stand, Basin Reserve, Mt Cook; admission by donation; ⊙during cricket matches) Tucked under a stand at the Basin Reserve, the NZ Cricket Museum is a must-see for fans of the old game. It's only open during cricket matches or by special appointment; check the website for details.

Wellington Zoo   ZOO
(☑04-381 6755; www.wellingtonzoo.com; 200 Daniell St, Newtown; adult/child $24/12; ⊙9.30am-5pm; ♿) ✔ Committed to conservation, research and captive breeding, Wellington Zoo is home to a menagerie of native and exotic wildlife, including lions and tamarins. The nocturnal house has kiwi and tuatara. 'Close encounters' allow you to meet the big cats, red pandas, giraffes and mischievous meerkats (for a fee). The zoo is 4km south of the centre; catch bus 10 or 23.

⊙ Other Areas

★**Mt Victoria Lookout**   VIEWPOINT
(Map p388; Lookout Rd) The city's most impressive viewpoint is atop 196m-high Mt Victoria (Matairangi), east of the city centre. You can take the No 20 bus most of the way up, but the rite of passage is to sweat it out on the walk (ask a local for directions or just follow your nose). If you've got wheels, take Oriental Pde along the waterfront and then scoot up Carlton Gore Rd. Aside from the views there are some rather interesting info panels.

★**Zealandia**   WILDLIFE RESERVE
(Map p388; ☑04-920 9213; www.visitzealandia. com; 53 Waiapu Rd, Karori; adult/child/family exhibition only $9/5/21, full admission $20/10/46; ⊙9am-5pm; ♿) ✔ This ground-breaking ecosanctuary is hidden in the hills about 2km west of town: buses 3 and 20 stop nearby, or see the Zealandia website for info on the free shuttle. Living wild within the fenced valley are more than 30 native bird species, including rare little spotted kiwi, takahe, saddleback, hihi and kaka, as well as NZ's little dinosaur, the tuatara. An excellent exhibition relays NZ's natural history and world-renowned conservation story.

More than 30km of tracks can be explored independently, or on regular guided tours. The night tour provides an opportunity to spot nocturnal creatures including kiwi, frogs and glowworms (adult/child $85/40).

Weta Cave   WORKSHOP
(☑04-909 4100; www.wetanz.com; 1 Weka St, Miramar; single tour adult/child $25/12, both tours $45/20; ⊙9am-5.30pm) Academy Award-winning special-effects and props company Weta Workshop has been responsible for bringing the likes of *The Lord of the Rings, The Hobbit, King Kong, District 9* and *Thor: Ragnarok* to life. Learn how they do it on entertaining 45-minute guided tours, starting every half-hour; bookings recommended. Weta Cave is 8km east of the city centre: drive, catch bus 31 or book transport ($40 return) with your admission.

The main tour is a curiously laid-back Kiwi kind of affair starting with a lengthy stroll along a suburban road to a secondary building where you get to handle actual props, prosthetics and costumes. A second tour takes you to the *Thunderbirds Are Go* miniatures stage.

Otari-Wilton's Bush
GARDENS

(Map p388; ☎ 04-499 4444; www.wellington.govt.nz; 160 Wilton Rd, Wilton; ☯ daylight hours) FREE The only botanic gardens in NZ specialising in native flora, Otari features more than 1200 plant species including an extant section of native bush containing the city's oldest trees (such as an 800-year-old rimu). There's also an information centre, an 18m-high canopy walkway, 11km of walking trails and some beaut picnic areas. It's located about 5km northwest of the centre and well signposted; bus 14 passes the gates.

🏃 Activities

Wellington's harbour offers plenty of opportunities to get active: kayaking, paddle boarding, sailing, windsurfing... (Wellington is windy: might as well make the most of it!). Back on dry land there's rock climbing, cycling and high-wire walking to keep you entertained. Pick up the *Wellington City Cycle Map* for bike-trail info.

Switched On Bikes
CYCLING

(Map p388; ☎ 022 075 8754; www.switchedonbikes.co.nz; Queens Wharf; city & mountain bike hire 1hr/4hr/day $15/40/60, electric $20/45/75, guided tours from $95; ☯ 9am-5pm) If you're short on puff on those notorious Wellington hills, these guys rent out electric bikes for cruising the city or taking on guided tours around the harbour. Look for their shipping-container base near the end of the wharf.

Wellington Ocean Sports
WATER SPORTS

(Map p388; ☎ 04-939 6702; www.oceansports.org.nz; 115 Oriental Pde; harbour sails per person

$40; ☯ booking office 9am-5pm) Harness Wellington's infamous wind on a one-hour harbour sailing trip, departing most weekends (weather dependent) – no experience required! Ask about stand-up paddle boarding, windsurfing, *waka ama* (outrigger canoeing) and kayaking sessions.

Ferg's Kayaks
KAYAKING, CLIMBING

(Map p388; ☎ 04-499 8898; www.fergskayaks.co.nz; Shed 6, Queens Wharf; ☯ 10am-8pm Mon-Fri, 9am-6pm Sat & Sun) Stretch your tendons with indoor rock-climbing (adult/child $21/17), cruise the waterfront wearing in-line skates (one/two hours $20/25) or go for a paddle in a kayak (one/two hours $25/35) or on a stand-up paddle board (one/two hours $30/40). There's also bike hire (hour/day from $20/80) and guided kayaking trips.

Makara Peak Mountain Bike Park
MOUNTAIN BIKING

(www.makarapeak.org; 116 South Karori Rd, Karori; ☯ daylight hours) In hilly Karori, 7km west of the city centre, this excellent 230-hectare park is laced with 45km of single-track, ranging from beginner to extreme. The nearby **Mud Cycles** (☎ 04-476 4961; www.mudcycles.co.nz; 424 Karori Rd, Karori; half-day/full-day/weekend bike hire from $35/60/100; ☯ 9.30am-6.30pm Mon-Fri, 10am-5pm Sat & Sun) has mountain bikes for hire. To get here by public transport, catch bus 3.

Freyberg Pool & Fitness Centre
SWIMMING

(Map p388; ☎ 04-801 4530; www.wellington.govt.nz; 139 Oriental Pde; pool adult/child $6/3.70; ☯ 6am-9pm; 🚼) Built in 1963, modernist Freyberg Pool is the most striking piece of architecture on Oriental Bay. As well as a big indoor pool there's a gym, spa, and aerobics, yoga and pilates classes.

WELLINGTON FOR CHILDREN

Let's cut to the chase: Welly's biggest hit for kids is **Te Papa** (p393), with the whole caboodle looking like it's curated by a team of five-year-old geniuses. It has interactive activities galore, more creepy, weird and wonderful things than you can shake a squid at, and heaps of special events for all ages. See the dedicated Kids & Families page on the website for proof of Te Papa's prowess in this department.

Conveniently located either side of Te Papa are **Frank Kitts Park** and **Waitangi Park**, both with playgrounds and in close proximity to roller skates, ice creams, and life-saving espresso for the grown-ups.

A ride up the **cable car** (p387) and a lap around the **Wellington Botanic Gardens** (p393) will get the wee ones pumped up. When darkness descends head to **Space Place** (p393) to gaze at galaxies far, far away. On a more terrestrial plane, kids can check out some crazy New Zealand critters at the **Wellington Zoo** (p395) or **Zealandia** (p395).

Wild Winds WATER SPORTS
(Map p388; ☑ 04-473 3458; www.wildwinds.co.nz;
2 Hunter St; 2hr lesson $110; ⊙10am-5.30pm Mon-
Fri, to 3pm Sat) With all this wind and water,
Wellington was made for windsurfing and
kiteboarding. Tackle one or both with an introductory lesson.

On Yer Bike CYCLING
(Map p392; ☑ 04-384 8480; www.avantiplus.co.nz/
wellington; 181 Vivian St; city/mountain/electric
bike per day $30/40/60; ⊙8.30am-5.30pm Mon-
Sat) Quality bike hire in the city centre.

☞ Tours

Kiwi Coastal Tours DRIVING
(☑ 021 464 957; www.kiwicoastaltours.co.nz; 3/5hr
tours $150/250) Excellent 4WD exploration of
the rugged south coast in the company of a
local Māori guide with plenty of stories to tell.

Walk Wellington WALKING
(Map p392; ☑ 04-473 3145; www.walkwellington.org.
nz; departs Wellington iSITE, 111 Wakefield St; tour
$20; ⊙10am daily year-round, plus 5pm Mon, Wed
& Fri Dec-Mar) Great-value two-hour walking
tours focusing on the city and waterfront, departing from the i-SITE (p406). Book online,
by phone or just turn up.

Flat Earth DRIVING
(☑ 04-472 9635; www.flatearth.co.nz; half-/full-day
tours from $95/385) An array of themed small-
group guided tours: city highlights, Māori
treasures, arts, wilderness and Middle Earth
filming locations. Martinborough wine tours
also available.

Zest Food Tours FOOD & DRINK
(Map p392; ☑ 04-801 9198; www.zestfoodtours.
co.nz; departs Wellington iSITE, 111 Wakefield St; tours
from $185) Runs 3½- to five-hour small-group
foodie tours around the city, plus day tours
over the hills into the Wairarapa wine region.

Te Wharewaka o Pōneke CULTURAL
(Map p392; ☑ 04-901 3333; www.wharewakao
poneke.co.nz; Taranaki Wharf, 2 Taranaki St; tours
walking $30-40, 2hr waka $100, 3hr waka & walk
$125) Get set for (and maybe a little bit wet
on) a two-hour paddle tour in a Māori *waka*
(canoe) around Wellington's waterfront,
with lots of cultural insights along the way.
Call for the latest tour times and bookings –
minimum numbers apply.

✵ Festivals & Events

Check at the Wellington i-SITE (p406) for
comprehensive events listings.

New Zealand Festival CULTURAL
(www.festival.co.nz; ⊙Feb-Mar) A month-long
biennial (even years; around mid-February
to mid-March) spectacular of theatre, dance,
music, visual arts and literature. International acts aplenty. A real 'kick up the arts'!

Fringe CULTURAL
(https://fringe.co.nz/; ⊙Feb-Mar) Three weeks
of way-out-there experimental visual arts,
music, dance and theatre. Although it's held
around the same time as the biennial New
Zealand Festival, Fringe is held every year.

NZ International Comedy Festival COMEDY
(www.comedyfestival.co.nz; ⊙Apr-May) Three
weeks of hysterics. World-famous-in-NZ
comedians, and some truly world-famous
ones, too.

Matariki CULTURAL
(www.tepapa.govt.nz; ⊙mid-Jun–mid-Jul) Celebrates the Māori New Year, with a free festival of dance, music and other events at Te
Papa (p393).

**New Zealand International
Film Festival** FILM
(www.nzff.co.nz; ⊙Jul-Aug) Roving two-week
indie film fest screening the best of NZ and
international cinema.

Beervana BEER
(www.beervana.co.nz; Westpac Stadium; ⊙Aug)
A barrel-load of craft-beer aficionados roll
into town for a weekend of supping and
beard-stroking.

★ World of WearableArt FASHION
(WOW; www.worldofwearableart.com; TSB Bank
Arena; ⊙Sep-Oct) A two-week run of spectacular garments (dresses or sculptures –
it's a fine line) displayed in a spectacular
show. Tickets are hot property; hotel beds
anywhere near the city sell out weeks in
advance.

🛏 Sleeping

Accommodation in Wellington is more expensive than in regional areas, but there
are plenty of options close to the city centre. Free parking spots are a rarity – ask in
advance about options. Wellington's budget
accommodation largely takes the form of
multistorey hostel megaliths. Motels dot the
city fringes. Self-contained apartments are
popular, and often offer bargain weekend
rates. Book well in advance in summer and
during major events.

City Centre

Gilmer Apartment Hotel
HOTEL $$

(Map p388; ☑04-978 1400; www.10gilmer.co.nz; 10 Gilmer Terrace; apt from $118; P 🞖) There's a hip, artsy vibe to this 62-unit inner-city apartment hotel. Sizes range from studios to two-bedroom apartments, and they all have their own kitchens and laundries. The nonrefundable advance-purchase rates are a steal for this part of town.

CityLife Wellington
HOTEL $$

(Map p388; ☑04-922 2800; www.heritagehotels. co.nz; 300 Lambton Quay; apt from $162; 🞖) 🖉 It's big and more than a little corporate but this apartment-style hotel, right in the commercial heart of the city, has a range of plush studio, one- and two-bedroom apartments. Some have full kitchen and in-room laundry facilities, and some offer harbour glimpses.

Bolton Hotel
HOTEL $$$

(Map p388; ☑04-472 9966; www.boltonhotel. co.nz; 12 Bolton St; r from $297; 🞖🞖) Visiting diplomats and corporate types flock to the Bolton, filling 139 rooms spread over 19 floors. Rooms come in all shapes and sizes, but share a common theme of muted tones, fine linens and colourful artwork. Most have full kitchens; some come with park or city views. It's independent and just a bit arty.

Joyce's B&B
B&B $$$

(Map p388; ☑04-499 7338; www.joycesbnb.nz; 46 Aurora Tce, Kelburn; r $215; P 🞖) Perched above the motorway on *steeep* Aurora Tce, Joyce's is but a short stumble from the city. The two rooms have private bathrooms and one of them is like a little flat, with its own separate kitchen, laundry and an adjoining second bedroom. The free parking is a rare treat this close to the centre.

InterContinental Wellington
HOTEL $$$

(Map p388; ☑04-472 2722; www.intercontinental. com; 2 Grey St; r from $293; 🞖🞖) Occupying a big 1980s-style marble-clad tower in the city centre, the InterContinental offers all the usual five-star trimmings you'd expect from the international brand – including a gym, pool and an excellent restaurant.

Thorndon & Pipitea

★ Dwellington
HOSTEL $

(Map p388; ☑04-550 9373; www.thedwellington. co.nz; 8 Halswell St, Thorndon; dm/r from $29/85; P 🞖) Two conjoined heritage houses have been reinvented to create this terrific modern hostel, sandwiched between the US and Chinese embassies. There are no en suites, but the rooms are clean, bright and comfortable, and there's free wi-fi and breakfast. The location is handy for the ferries, trains and intercity buses, but a fair hike from the after-dark fun around Cuba St.

Hotel Waterloo & Backpackers
HOSTEL $

(Map p388; ☑04-473 8482; www.hotelwaterloo. co.nz; 1 Bunny St; dm $25-35, s with/without bathroom from $99/72, d $119/89; @ 🞖) 🖉 Housed in an art-deco hotel (1937) at the railway end of town, this budget hotel and hostel has tidy rooms and plenty of capacious, character-filled communal areas (be sure to check out the bar).

Te Aro

★ YHA Wellington City
HOSTEL $

(Map p392; ☑04-801 7280; www.yha.co.nz; 292 Wakefield St; dm/s from $36/87, d with/without bathroom $134/99; @ 🞖) 🖉 The trusty YHA wins points for fantastic communal areas including two big kitchens and dining areas, and separate rooms for games, reading and watching movies. Sustainable initiatives (recycling, composting and energy-efficient hot water) abound, and there's a comprehensive booking service and espresso machine at reception.

Trek Global
HOSTEL $

(Map p392; ☑04-471 3480; www.trekglobal.net; 9 O'Reilly Ave; dm/s from $23/59, d with/without bathroom $89/79; P @ 🞖) 🖉 A highlight of this back-lane hostel is the funky and welcoming foyer hang-out and snug TV lounge. The sleeping quarters and kitchens are squeezed between rabbit-warren corridors. It's relatively quiet with clean rooms and laudable extras such as bike hire, parking ($20 per day) and a women-only dorm with a suntrap terrace.

Cambridge Hotel
HOSTEL, HOTEL $

(Map p392; ☑04-385 8829; www.cambridge hotel.co.nz; 28 Cambridge Tce; dm $26-40, s with/without bathroom from $99/69, d $119/89; 🞖) Built in 1883, the Cambridge is the consummate corner pub, with old-fashioned budget rooms above; it's hard to believe that the queen stayed here in the 1960s. All of the hotel rooms have fridges and kettles, and some have tiny bathrooms. The backpacker wing has a snug kitchen-lounge and dorms with little natural light but sky-high ceilings.

Nomads Capital
HOSTEL $

(Map p392; 04-978 7800; www.nomadsworld. com; 118 Wakefield St; dm/r from $32/120;) Smack bang in the middle of town, Nomads has good security, spick-and-span rooms with en suites and an on-site cafe-bar. Kitchen and lounge spaces are short on elbow room, but slick service, heritage features and the hot location stop you from dwelling on the negatives. Plus they offer free breakfasts and light dinners.

★ City Cottages
RENTAL HOUSE $$

(Map p392; 021 073 9232; www.wellington cityaccommodation.co.nz; 5 & 7 Tonks Gr; cottage $170-200; P) These two tiny 1880 cottages squat amid a precious precinct of historic buildings. Clever conversion has transformed them into self-contained one-bedroom pads, comfortable for two but sleeping up to four (thanks to a sofa bed). It's not the quietest location but it's hip and exceedingly convenient. They also rent a modern two-bedroom studio and a historic townhouse (sleeping 10) nearby.

Gourmet Stay
HOTEL $$

(Map p392; 04-801 6800; www.gourmetstay. co.nz; 25 Frederick St; r with/without bathroom from $189/159; P) A bit like a dorm-less hostel for grown-ups, this backstreet hotel has 13 rooms, all with different configurations, spread between two neighbouring buildings. Most have en suites and all of them are tastefully designed, with nice linen and natty art. A free continental breakfast is provided and a blackboard lists foodie tips around town.

Victoria Court Motor Lodge
MOTEL $$

(Map p392; 04-385 7102; www.victoriacourt.co.nz; 201 Victoria St; unit from $165; P) Three-tier, lemon-yellow Victoria Court continues to deliver satisfaction in the city, with spacious studios and apartments with kitchenettes. There are two disabled-access units, and larger units sleep up to five. It's just a short stumble to Cuba St. Free on-site parking.

Quality Hotel
HOTEL $$

(Map p392; 04-385 2156; www.cqwellington. com; 223 Cuba St; ste from $183; P) A lopsided proposition, the high-rise Quality is joined to its lesser-quality sibling, the heritage Comfort Hotel, by way of a shared reception and facilities including an in-house bar, restaurant, pool and parking ($30 per night). Expect snazzy, spacious suites but be prepared for hit-and-miss service.

★ QT Museum Wellington
HOTEL $$$

(Map p392; 04-802 8900; www.qtwellington. com; 90 Cable St; r/apt from $215/296;) That there's a hippopotamus theme to the decor says a lot about the quirkiness of this art-filled hotel. In the hotel wing, black lifts open on to darkened corridors leading to flamboyantly decorated rooms. The apartment wing is marginally more restrained but equally luxurious, and the units have kitchenettes and laundry facilities.

At Home
APARTMENT $$$

(Map p392; 04-802 0858; www.athome wellington.com; L4, 181 Wakefield St; apt from $229;) You'd be forgiven for thinking the worst, entering this commercial building, ascending in the lift and walking along the featureless corridor to the cluttered reception. After the unpromising lead-up, the bright and spacious apartments come as a welcome surprise. All have kitchens, laundries and a writing desk, and the location couldn't be more central.

Mt Victoria & Oriental Bay

Booklovers B&B
B&B $$

(Map p388; 04-384 2714; www.booklovers.co.nz; 123 Pirie St, Mt Victoria; s/d from $180/220;) Author Jane Tolerton's elegant, book-filled B&B has three queen guest rooms (one with an extra single bed). A bus service runs past the front gate to Courtenay Pl and the train station, and the city's 'green belt' begins right next door. Free wi-fi and street parking.

Apollo Lodge
MOTEL $$

(Map p392; 04-385 1849; www.apollolodge. co.nz; 49 Majoribanks St, Mt Victoria; unit from $150; P) Within staggering distance of Courtenay Pl, Apollo Lodge is a loose collation of a couple of dozen varied units, ranging from studios to family-friendly two-bedroom units with full kitchens to long-stay apartments. It's good value for a location this close to the city.

★ Ohtel
BOUTIQUE HOTEL $$$

(Map p392; 04-803 0600; www.ohtel.nz; 66 Oriental Pde, Oriental Bay; r from $229;) Ever feel like you've walked into a design magazine? This bijou hotel has 10 individually decorated rooms with immersive NZ scenes plastered above the bathtubs and original, mid-century, Scandi-style furniture and ceramics, avidly collected by the architect-owner. The best rooms have decks and harbour views.

WORTH A TRIP

PLIMMERTON

In Plimmerton, 25km north of central Wellington (30 minutes by train), the exceptional **Moana Lodge** (☑04-233 2010; www.moanalodge.co.nz; 49 Moana Rd, Plimmerton; dm/s/d from $38/70/96; P ☎) justifies the schlep with sea views and a little sandy beach just across the road. The lovely old house is immaculate and inviting, with an affable host who will happily steer you towards the local sights.

Copthorne Hotel   HOTEL $$$
(Map p392; ☑04-385 0279; www.millenniumhotels.com; 100 Oriental Pde, Oriental Bay; d from $219; ☎⛱) This multistorey gleamer has a terrific location facing off with the harbour. Business bods surf through the lobby on a pervasive wave of slickness, while active types head for the heated indoor pool or free workouts at the Freyberg fitness centre across the road.

🛏 Other Areas

Wellington Top
10 Holiday Park   HOLIDAY PARK $
(☑04-568 5913; www.wellingtontop10.co.nz; 95 Hutt Park Rd, Seaview; sites from $35, units with/without bathroom $120/70; P ☎) Located 16km northeast of central Wellington, the Top 10 offers the closest camping to the city. Family-friendly facilities include communal kitchens, a games room and a playground, but the industrial-park block-location detracts. Follow the signs off SH2 for Petone and Seaview, or catch bus 83.

Capital View Motor Inn   MOTEL $$
(Map p392; ☑04-385 0515; www.capitalview.co.nz; 12 Thompson St, Mt Cook; unit from $140; P ☎) Many of the 21 rooms in this neat, well-maintained mini-tower building near the top of Cuba St do indeed enjoy capital views – especially the large, good-value penthouse (sleeps five). All are self-contained and spruce, and there's free parking.

Edgewater Lodge   B&B $$$
(☑04-388 4446; www.edgewaterwellington.co.nz; 423 Karaka Bay Rd, Karaka Bay; r from $290; P ☎) True to its name, the Edgewater is a big modern house set just across the road from a little beach. It's a 15-minute drive from the city but handy for the movie-making enclave

of Miramar – which might explain the Hobbity paraphernalia scattered about. One of the three rooms has a large sea-gazing deck, while another has its own external entrance.

✖ Eating

🍴 City Centre

Gelissimo Gelato   ICE CREAM $
(Map p392; ☑04-385 9313; www.gelissimo.co.nz; Taranaki Wharf, 11 Cable St; single scoop $5; ◔8am-5.30pm Mon-Fri, 10.30am-5.30pm Sat & Sun) The hottest thing in coldness is the gelato and sorbet made by Graham, who grew up in a fruiterer's shop and sure knows his apples (and raspberries, and chocolate...). It's a bit hard to find, nooked in behind the huge Mac's brew bar.

Nikau Cafe   CAFE $$
(Map p392; ☑04-801 4168; www.nikaucafe.co.nz; City Gallery, Civic Sq; mains $15-27; ◔7am-4pm Mon-Sat) 🍃 An airy affair at the sophisticated end of Wellington's cafe spectrum, Nikau consistently dishes up simple but sublime stuff (pan-fried halloumi, legendary kedgeree). Refreshing aperitifs, divine sweets, charming staff and a sunny courtyard complete the package. The organic, seasonal menu changes daily.

Charley Noble   MEDITERRANEAN $$$
(Map p388; ☑04-282 0205; www.charleynoble.co.nz; 1 Post Office Sq; mains $26-52; ◔7am-late Mon-Fri, 5pm-late Sat & Sun) Bustling to the point of mild chaos once the after-work crowd descends, this cavernous establishment occupies the gloriously renovated Huddart Parker building. Solo diners should opt for a seat by the large open kitchen for a first-row view of the culinary action. Highlights include shucked-to-order oysters and wood-fired meats.

Boulcott Street Bistro   BISTRO $$$
(Map p388; ☑04-499 4199; www.boulcottstreetbistro.co.nz; 99 Boulcott St; mains lunch $29-33, dinner $32-39; ◔noon-3pm Sun-Fri, 5.30-9pm daily) For more than 25 years the inimitable Rex Morgan has been serving classic bistro fare in this precious little heritage cottage, hidden away in high-rise surrounds. With no evening bookings, you may be forced to wait with a flute of fizz or glass of craft beer in the convivial bar. Look out for the lunchtime specials ($20) and two-course Sunday roasts ($45).

✕ Te Aro

Little Penang MALAYSIAN $
(Map p392; ☑ 04-382 9818; www.facebook.com/
littlepenang; 40 Dixon St; mains $12-17; ⊗ 11am-
3pm & 5-9pm Mon-Fri, 11am-9pm Sat; ✎) Among
a bunch of great Malaysian diners, Little
Penang steals the show with its fresh-fla-
voured, fiery street food. Order a *nasi lemak*
with the good eggy, nutty, saucy stuff; or go
for the bargain $9 roti bread with curry. And
don't bypass the curry puffs. The lunchtime
rush can border on the absurd.

Havana Coffee Works CAFE $
(Map p392; ☑ 04-384 7041; www.havana.co.nz;
163 Tory St; snacks $4-8; ⊗ 7am-5pm Mon-Fri)
Continuing Wellington's unwavering ob-
session with all things Cuba, this fantastic roastery and 'First Class' coffee lounge
offers heart-jolting coffee and smiles all
round. Nibbles are limited to the likes of
scones, bagels, cakes and pies from the
warmer. There's also a takeaway counter in
the roastery.

Midnight Espresso CAFE $
(Map p392; ☑ 04-384 7014; www.facebook.com/
midnightespresso; 178 Cuba St; mains $8-17;
⊗ 7.30am-3am; ✎) Let it all hang out after
midnight at this devilishly good late opener.
Munch on some cheesy lasagne, sticky date
pudding or spinach-and-basil muffins if you
must, but caffeine is really where it's at. Dig
the little brass repair plates in the old floorboards and the pinball machine.

KK Malaysian Restaurant MALAYSIAN $
(Map p392; ☑ 04-385 6698; www.kkmalaysian.
co.nz; 54 Ghuznee St; mains $13-16; ⊗ 11.30am-
9.30pm Mon-Sat, 5-9.30pm Sun; ✎) The still-life
vegetables and distressed Tuscan wall finishes here are a bit odd, but ignore the decor and focus on the food – some of the best
Malaysian in the capital. Couples meet after
work for a *roti chanai* (curry and bread)
and students slurp laksa lunches, all just a
few metres from Cuba St. Good vegetarian
options, too.

Martha's Pantry TEAHOUSE $
(Map p392; ☑ 04-385 7228; www.marthaspantry.
co.nz; 276 Cuba St; items $3.50-10; ⊗ 9am-5pm
Tue-Sun) Time for tea? This quaint little tea
room offers club sandwiches, cakes, freshly
baked scones with raspberry jam and cream,
and tea in fine bone china. With flower pots
and broad-rimmed sun hats strewn about,
it's charmingly old-fashioned.

★ Noble Rot FRENCH $$
(Map p392; ☑ 04-385 6671; www.noblerot.co.nz;
6 Swan Lane; mains $29-34; ⊗ 4pm-late) Noble
Rot thinks of itself as a wine bar, but this
cosy nook serves some of Wellington's best
food too. A French influence pervades the
menu (charcuterie, duck parfait, smoked-
cheese souffle, slow-cooked lamb), alongside
a few distinctly Kiwi touches such as spa-
ghetti with *puha* (a native green vegetable).
Needless to say, the wine list is exceptional.

★ Shepherd CONTEMPORARY $$
(Map p392; ☑ 04-385 7274; www.shepherd
restaurant.co.nz; 1/5 Eva St; mains $26-30;
⊗ 5.30pm-late Wed-Sun) This good Shepherd
leads the way with on-trend contemporary
cuisine, guiding its eager flock through fusion flavours, unusual produce and pickled
accompaniments. A long bar on one side
and an open kitchen on the other, with an
assortment of brightly painted stools and
high tables in between. The vibe is young
and edgy, and the food is thrilling.

★ Loretta CAFE $$
(Map p392; ☑ 04-384 2213; www.loretta.net.nz;
181 Cuba St; mains $13-28; ⊗ 9am-10pm Tue-Sun;
✎) From breakfast (waffles, crumpets, ce-
real) through lunch (sandwiches, fritters,
soup) and into dinner (pizzas, roast chicken,
schnitzel), Loretta has won leagues of fans
with her classy, well-proportioned offerings
served in bright, airy surrounds. We recom-
mend splitting a pizza and grain-filled salad
between two. Bookings for lunch only.

Field & Green BRITISH $$
(Map p392; ☑ 04-384 4992; www.fieldandgreen.
co.nz; 262 Wakefield St; mains $14-33; ⊗ 8am-
10pm Wed-Sat, to 3pm Sun) 'European soul
food' is their slogan, but it's the best of British which dominates here, including Red
Leicester scones, Welsh rarebit, kedgeree,
fish-finger sarnies, bacon butties with HP
sauce and pan-fried pork chops. It's actually
way more sophisticated than it sounds, with
a Scandi-chic sensibility to the decor and ac-
complished London-born chef Laura Green-
field at the helm.

WBC FUSION $$
(Map p392; ☑ 04-499 9379; www.wbcrestaurant.
co.nz; Level 1, 107 Victoria St; small plates $14-18, large
$25-28; ⊗ 10.30am-late Tue-Sat) At the Whole-
sale Boot Company (wonder why they use
the acronym?), flavours from Thailand, China
and Japan punctuate a menu filled with the
best of NZ produce, including freshly shucked

WORTH A TRIP

ARO VALLEY

For a local vibe and an interesting selection of cafes and bars, head to this studenty, city-fringe neighbourhood.

Aro Cafe (Map p388; ☑04-384 4970; www.arocoffee.co.nz; 90 Aro St, Aro Valley; mains brunch $9-23, dinner $23-28; ⊙7.30am-4pm Mon & Tue, 7.30am-4pm & 5.30-10pm Wed-Fri, 9am-4pm & 5.30-10pm Sat, 9am-5pm Sun) If this stretch of Aro St – and this long-running licensed cafe in particular – were any more photogenic it'd be a crime. Order from the cabinet or take a seat and someone will bring you a menu. The coffee's great too. In the evening it transitions into a neighbourhood bistro.

Garage Project Taproom (Map p388; ☑04-802 5324; www.garageproject.co.nz; 91 Aro St, Aro Valley; ⊙3-10pm Tue-Thu, noon-10pm Fri-Sun) The actual microbrewery occupies a former petrol station just down the road (68 Aro St) where they serve craft beer by the litre, petrol-pump style. If you'd rather consume your brew on premises in less industrial quantities, head to this narrow graffiti-lined bar. Order a tasting flight or chance your arm on the Pernicious Weed or Venusian Pale Ale.

oysters and clams (served raw, steamed or tempura-battered) and game meats (tahr tacos, kung po venison). Everything is packed with flavour and designed to be shared.

Prefab
CAFE $$

(Map p392; ☑04-385 2263; www.pre-fab.co.nz; 14 Jessie St; mains $11-26; ⊙7am-4pm Mon-Sat; 🛜🐾) A big industrial-minimalist space houses the city's slickest espresso bar and roastery, owned by long-time Wellington caffeine fiends. Beautiful house-baked bread features on a menu of flavourful, well-executed offerings. Dogs doze on the sunny terrace while the staff efficiently handle the bustle inside.

Fidel's
CAFE $$

(Map p392; ☑04-801 6868; www.fidelscafe.com; 234 Cuba St; mains brunch $9-22, dinner $13-26; ⊙8am-10pm; 🐾) A Cuba St institution for caffeine-craving alternative types, Fidel's cranks out eggs any which way, pizza and super salads from its itsy kitchen, along with Welly's best milkshakes. Revolutionary memorabilia adorns the walls of the low-lit interior, and there's a small outdoor area and a street-facing booth for takeaway coffees. The ever-busy crew copes with the chaos admirably.

★Whitebait
SEAFOOD $$$

(Map p392; ☑04-385 8555; www.white-bait.nz; 1 Clyde Quay Wharf; mains $38; ⊙5.30pm-late year-round, plus noon-3pm Wed-Fri Nov-Mar) Neutral colours and gauzy screens set an upmarket tone for this top-rated seafood restaurant. All the fish is sustainably sourced and deftly prepared, with a scattering of quality non-

fishy options rounding out the contemporary menu. Early diners (seatings before 6.30pm) can take advantage of a good-value set 'bistro' menu ($55 for an oyster, entree, main and petit four).

★Logan Brown
CONTEMPORARY $$$

(Map p392; ☑04-801 5114; www.loganbrown.co.nz; 192 Cuba St; mains $39-45; ⊙noon-2pm Wed-Sat & 5pm-late Tue-Sun; 🛜) 🍴 Deservedly ranked among Wellington's best restaurants, Logan Brown oozes class without being overly formal. Its 1920s banking-chamber dining room is a neoclassical stunner – a fitting complement to the produce-driven modern NZ cuisine. The three-course bistro menu ($45) won't hurt your wallet too badly (but the epic wine list might force a blowout). There's also a great-value $25 main-plus-wine lunch deal.

Jano Bistro
FRENCH $$$

(Map p392; ☑04-382 9892; www.janobistro.co.nz; 270 Willis St; mains $38; ⊙5.30pm-late Wed-Sun) Unexpected little Jano crops up on a bleak, windy stretch of Willis St – a small, yellow 1880s cottage with a herb garden out the front and buckets of charm inside. Shuffle past the fireplace and up the stairs to the loft dining room for a contemporary take on French cuisine.

🍴 Mt Victoria & Oriental Bay

Capitol
ITALIAN $$

(Map p392; ☑04-384 2855; www.capitolrestaurant.co.nz; 10 Kent Tce, Mt Victoria; mains brunch $10-27, lunch $18-27, dinner $28-38; ⊙noon-3pm & 5.30-9.30pm Mon-Fri, 9.30am-3pm & 5.30-9.30pm Sat

& Sun) This consistent culinary star serves simple, seasonal fare using premium local ingredients, with a nod to classic Italian cuisine (try the homemade tagliolini or the Parmesan-crusted lamb's liver). The dining room is a bit cramped and noisy, but elegant nonetheless.

Mt Vic Chippery FISH & CHIPS **$$**
(Map p392; ☑04-382 8713; www.thechippery.co.nz; 5 Majoribanks St, Mt Victoria; meals $12-20; ☺noon-8.30pm; ⛔) At this backwater fish shack it's fish and chips by numbers: 1. Choose your fish (from at least three varieties). 2. Choose your coating (beer batter, panko crumb, tempura...). 3. Choose your chips (five varieties!). 4. Add aioli, coleslaw, salad or sauce, and a quality soft drink. 5. Chow down inside or take away. There are burgers and battered sausages too.

Ortega Fish Shack SEAFOOD **$$$**
(Map p392; ☑04-382 9559; www.ortega.co.nz; 16 Majoribanks St, Mt Victoria; mains $34-39; ☺5.30pm-late Tue-Sat) Mounted trout, salty portraits, marine-blue walls and Egyptian floor tiles cast a Mediterranean spell over Ortega – a magical spot for a seafood dinner. Fish comes many ways (including as zingy sashimi), while desserts continue the Mediterranean vibes with Catalan orange crêpes and one of Welly's best cheeseboards.

🍷 Drinking & Nightlife

Wellingtonians love a late night. The inner city is riddled with bars, with high concentrations around raucous Courtenay Pl, bohemian Cuba St and along the waterfront. A creative live-music scene keeps things thrumming, along with great NZ wines and even better craft beer. See www.craftbeercapital.com for beery propaganda. For gig listings see www.undertheradar.co.nz and www.eventfinder.co.nz.

★Golding's Free Dive CRAFT BEER
(Map p392; ☑04-381 3616; www.goldingsfreedive.co.nz; 14 Leeds St; ☺noon-11pm; 🖥) Hidden down a busy little back alley near Cuba St, gloriously garish Golding's is a bijoux craft-beer bar with far too many merits to mention. We'll single out ex-casino swivel chairs, a nice wine list, a ravishing Reuben sandwich, and pizza from **Pomodoro** (Map p392; ☑04-381 2929; www.pizzapomodoro.co.nz; 13 Leeds St; pizza $16-26; ☺noon-2pm Wed-Fri & 5-9pm daily; 🖋) next door. Blues, Zappa and Bowie conspire across the airways.

★Hawthorn Lounge COCKTAIL BAR
(Map p392; ☑04-890 3724; www.hawthornlounge.co.nz; Level 1, 82 Tory St; ☺5pm-3am) This classy cocktail bar has a 1920s speakeasy feel, suited-up in waistcoats and wide-brimmed fedoras. Sip a whisky sour and play poker, or watch the behind-the-bar theatrics from the Hawthorn's mixologists, twisting and turning classics into modern-day masterpieces. Open 'til the wee small hours.

★Dirty Little Secret ROOFTOP BAR
(Map p392; ☑021 0824 0298; www.dirtylittlesecret.co.nz; Level 8, 7-8 Dixon St; ☺4pm-late Mon-Thu, noon-late Fri-Sun; 🖥) While it's not strictly a secret (it's packed to the gills on balmy evenings) this hip bar atop the historic Hope Gibbons Ltd building plays hard to get, with a nondescript entrance on Taranaki St next to Jack Hackett's Irish Pub. Expect craft beer, slugged-together cocktails, loud indie music and plastic awnings straining to keep the elements at bay.

★Library BAR
(Map p392; ☑04-382 8593; www.thelibrary.co.nz; Level 1, 53 Courtenay Pl; ☺5pm-late) You'll find yourself in the right kind of bind at moody, bookish Library, with its velveteen booths, board games and swish cocktails. An excellent all-round drink selection is complemented by a highly shareable menu of sweet and savoury treats. There's live music on occasion.

Laundry BAR
(Map p392; ☑04-384 4280; www.laundry.net.nz; 240 Cuba St; ☺4pm-2am) Tumble into this lurid-green, junk-shop juke joint any time of the day or night for a tipple and a plate of jerk chicken. Regular live music and DJs offset Southern-style bar food and carnival-esque decor pasted up with a very rough brush. There's also a backyard complete with a caravan.

Motel COCKTAIL BAR
(Map p392; ☑04-384 9084; www.motelbar.co.nz; Forresters Lane; ☺5pm-late Mon-Sat) The backlane location, retro neon sign and unpromising staircase generate a suitably seedy NYC-in-the-70s first impression but inside is a louche, low-lit tiki bar, where the barstaff shake up fruity cocktails before a backdrop of giant clams, Polynesian-style statues and pineapple lights. Campy, fun and a great place for a sneaky rendezvous.

Fortune Favours
CRAFT BEER

(Map p392; ☑ 04-595 4092; www.fortunefavours. beer; 7 Leeds St; ⊙ 11am-11pm) The bold and the beautiful head to the rooftop of this old warehouse to sup on beer brewed in the shiny vats downstairs. Along with seven of their own concoctions, they serve guest brews, wine and cocktails.

S&M's
GAY

(Map p392; ☑ 04-802 5335; www.scottyandmals. co.nz; 176 Cuba St) Don't get excited, there's nothing fetishistic about Scotty and Mal's upmarket bar, unless your fetish happens to be dark wood, chandeliers and fabulous cocktails. It's a great place for a quiet drink; don't come expecting a crowd.

Counterculture
BAR

(Map p392; ☑ 04-891 2345; www.counterculture. co.nz; 211 Victoria St; unlimited games $5; ⊙ noon-10pm Mon-Fri, 10am-10pm Sat & Sun; ☜⛲) Who doesn't secretly love a board game? Assume an ironic stance if you must, but here's the chance to embrace your inner games nerd in public. There are almost 400 games to choose from, staff to advise on rules, and craft beers and cocktails to take the edge off your ugly competitive streak.

Fork & Brewer
CRAFT BEER

(Map p392; ☑ 04-472 0033; www.forkandbrewer. co.nz; 20a Bond St; ⊙ 11.30am-late Mon-Sat) Aiming to improve on the 'kebab at 2am' experience, F&B offers excellent burgers, pizzas, pies, share plates and meaty mains to go along with its crafty brews (of which there are dozens – the Low Blow IPA comes highly recommended). Oh, and dark-beer doughnuts for dessert!

Little Beer Quarter
CRAFT BEER

(Map p392; ☑ 04-803 3304; www.littlebeerquarter. co.nz; 6 Edward St; ⊙ 3.30pm-late Sun & Mon, noon-late Tue-Sat) Buried in a back lane, lovely LBQ is warm, inviting and moodily lit in all the right places. Well-curated taps and a broad selection of bottled beer pack a hoppy punch. There are good cocktails, wines, and whiskies, too, plus zesty bar food. Call in for a $20 pizza and pint on Monday nights.

Rogue & Vagabond
CRAFT BEER

(Map p392; ☑ 04-381 2321; www.rogueandvagabond.co.nz; 18 Garrett St; ⊙ 11am-late) Fronting on to a precious pocket park, the Rogue is a lovably scruffy, colourful, kaleidoscopic craft-beer bar with heaps going on – via 18 taps including two hand-pulls. Voluminous,

chewy-crust pizza, burgers, po' boys, alcoholic milkshakes and regular, rockin' gigs add further appeal. Swill around on the patio or slouch on the lawn.

Havana
BAR

(Map p392; ☑ 04-384 7039; www.havanabar.co.nz; 32a-34 Wigan St; mains $25-28; ⊙ 11.30am-late) Go out of your way to find Havana, a mighty fine needle in Welly's hospitality haystack, hidden down a side street in two weathered old cottages sharing a groovy backyard. Fortify yourself with tapas and top-shelf booze, then have a chinwag, smoke a cigar, carouse or all of the above. Dinner is a treat.

Hashigo Zake
CRAFT BEER

(Map p392; ☑ 04-384 7300; www.hashigozake. co.nz; 25 Taranaki St; ⊙ noon-late; ☜) This bricky bunker is the HQ for a zealous beer-import business, splicing big-flavoured international brews into a smartly selected NZ range. Hop-heads stand elbow to elbow around the bar, ogling the oft-changing taps and brimming fridges, and squeeze into the sweet little side-lounge on live-music nights.

Southern Cross
PUB

(Map p392; ☑ 04-384 9085; www.thecross.co.nz; 39 Abel Smith St; ⊙ 8am-late; ⛲) Welcoming to all – from frenetic five-year-olds to knitting nanas – the democratic Cross rambles through a series of colourful rooms, combining a lively bar, a dance floor, a pool table and the best garden bar in town. There's good beer on tap, food for all budgets and regular events (gigs, quiz nights, karaoke, coffee groups).

☆ Entertainment

Wellington has a lively theatre scene and is the home of large national companies such as the Royal NZ Ballet and the NZ Symphony Orchestra. Most shows can be booked via **Ticketek** (www.ticketek.co.nz), **Ticketmaster** (www.ticketmaster.co.nz) and **TicketDirect** (www.ticketdirect.co.nz). Discounted same-day tickets for productions are sometimes available at the i-SITE (p406).

★ Embassy Theatre
CINEMA

(Map p392; ☑ 04-384 7657; www.embassytheatre. co.nz; 10 Kent Tce; ⊙ 10am-late) Wellywood's cinema mother ship is an art-deco darling, built in the 1920s. Today she screens mainly mainstream films with state-of-the-art sound and vision. Be sure to check out the glamorous Black Sparrow cocktail bar at the rear.

WELCOME TO WELLYWOOD

In recent years Wellington has stamped its name firmly on the world map as the home of New Zealand's dynamic film industry, earning itself the nickname 'Wellywood'. Acclaimed director Sir Peter Jackson still calls Wellington home; the success of his *The Lord of the Rings* films and subsequent productions such as *King Kong, The Adventures of Tintin* and *The Hobbit* have made him a powerful Hollywood player, and have bolstered Wellington's reputation.

Canadian director James Cameron is also in on the action; shooting has commenced for his four *Avatar* sequels, the first of which is due for a 2020 release. Cameron and his family are NZ residents, with landholding in rural Wairarapa. They have that in common with Jackson, who also has a property there.

Movie buffs can experience some local movie magic by visiting the **Weta Cave** (p395) or one of many film locations around the region – a speciality of local guided-tour companies.

Light House Cinema   CINEMA
(Map p392; ☑04-385 3337; www.lighthousecinema.
co.nz; 29 Wigan St; adult/child $18/13; ⊙10am-late;
🛜) Tucked away near the top end of Cuba
St, this small, stylish cinema throws a range
of mainstream, art-house and foreign films
up onto the screens in three small theatres.
High-quality snacks. Tuesday tickets $11.50.

San Fran   LIVE MUSIC
(Map p392; ☑04-801 6797; www.sanfran.co.nz; 171
Cuba St; ⊙3pm-late Tue-Sat) This much-loved,
midsize music venue is moving to a new beat;
it has boarded the craft-beer bandwagon and
rocks out smoky, meaty food along the way.
Gigs still rule, dancing is de rigueur, and the
balcony gets good afternoon sun.

Michael Fowler Centre   CONCERT VENUE
(Map p392; ☑04-801 4231; www.venues
wellington.com; 111 Wakefield St) The city's major
concert hall stages regular performances by
the **NZ Symphony Orchestra** (www.nzso.
co.nz), **Orchestra Wellington** (www.orches-
trawellington.co.nz) and assorted pop stars
and contemporary musicians. The i-SITE
(p406), near the entrance, acts as an outlet
for Ticketek and Ticketmaster.

St James Theatre   THEATRE
(Map p392; ☑04-801 4231; www.venueswellington.
com; 77 Courtenay Pl) This grand old heritage
theatre hosts big-ticket productions such as
the **Royal NZ Ballet** (www.rnzb.org.nz) and
NZ Opera (www.nzopera.com), plus the odd
rocker and comedian.

Circa Theatre   THEATRE
(Map p392; ☑04-801 7992; www.circa.co.nz; 1
Taranaki St) This attractive waterfront thea-
tre has two auditoriums in which it shows

everything from edgy new works to Christmas panto.

🔒 Shopping

★Unity Books   BOOKS
(Map p392; ☑04-499 4245; www.unitybooks.co.nz;
57 Willis St; ⊙9am-6pm Mon-Sat, 11am-5pm Sun)
Sets the standard for every bookshop in the
land, with dedicated NZ tables piled high.

Underground Market   MARKET
(Map p392; www.undergroundmarket.co.nz; under
Frank Kitts Park, Jervois Quay; ⊙10am-4pm Sat)
On Saturday mornings (and the occasional Sunday) the car park under Frank Kitts
Park is filled with stalls selling interesting
craft, artsy gifts, clothes by up-and-coming
designers, and nibbles – plus the inevitable
dreamcatchers and tie-dye that's de rigueur
in such settings.

Bello   GIFTS & SOUVENIRS
(Map p392; ☑04-385 0058; www.bello.co.nz; 140
Willis St; ⊙10am-6pm Mon-Fri, to 4pm Sat & Sun) A
sweet little boutique full of gorgeous things
– not the least of which are the charming
staff, who will point you in the direction
of designer glassware, refined fragrances,
floaty scarves and luxurious homewares.

Brown & Co   GIFTS & SOUVENIRS
(Map p392; ☑04-385 0102; www.brownandco.
co.nz; 253 Wakefield St; ⊙10am-5pm) Your one-
stop-shop for stuffed bats, Jesus terrariums,
monkey skulls, rabbit feet, art books and
kooky gifts for 'house and homme'.

Slow Boat Records   MUSIC
(Map p392; ☑04-385 1330; www.slowboat
records.co.nz; 183 Cuba St; ⊙9.30am-5.30pm Sat-
Thu, to 7.30pm Fri) Country, folk, pop, indie,

metal, blues, soul, rock, Hawaiian nose-flute music – it's all here at Slow Boat, Wellington's long-running music shop and Cuba St mainstay.

Moore Wilson's
FOOD & DRINKS

(Map p392; ☑04-384 9906; www.moorewilsons. co.nz; 93 Tory St; ☺7.30am-7pm) A call-out to self-caterers: this positively swoon-inducing grocer is one of NZ's most committed supporters of independently produced and artisanal produce. If you want to chew on the best of Wellington and NZ, here's your chance. Head upstairs for dry goods, wine, beer and kitchenware.

Mandatory
CLOTHING

(Map p392; ☑04-384 6107; www.mandatory.co.nz; 108 Cuba St; ☺10am-6pm Mon-Fri, to 4.30pm Sat, noon-4pm Sun) Fancy duds for dudes: great service and sharp tailoring for the capital's cool cats.

Harbourside Market
MARKET

(Map p392; ☑04-495 7895; www.harbourside market.co.nz; cnr Cable & Barnett Sts; ☺7.30am-1pm Sun) Around 25,000 locals visit this market every Sunday. Why? Well, it's in a scenic spot next to Te Papa, and you can find everything here from a jar of raspberry jam to an heirloom carrot to a cinnamon roll. There's lots of cooked meals for lunch, too.

Old Bank
SHOPPING CENTRE

(Map p388; ☑04-922 0600; www.oldbank.co.nz; 233-237 Lambton Quay; ☺9am-6pm Mon-Fri, 11am-3pm Sat & Sun) This dear old building on a wedge-shaped city site is home to an arcade of indulgent, high-end shops, predominantly jewellers and boutiques. Check out the fab tiled floors and Corinthian columns.

Kura
ART

(Map p392; ☑04-802 4934; www.kuragallery. co.nz; 19 Allen St; ☺10am-6pm Mon-Fri, 11am-4pm Sat & Sun) Contemporary Māori and NZ art: painting, ceramics, jewellery and sculpture. A gorgeous gallery – come for a look even if you're not buying.

🛈 Information

INTERNET ACCESS
Free wi-fi is available throughout most of Wellington's Central Business District (CBD; www. cbdfree.co.nz).

MEDICAL SERVICES
Wellington Accident & Urgent Medical Centre (☑04-384 4944; www.wamc.co.nz; 17 Adelaide Rd, Mt Cook; ☺8am-11pm) No appointment necessary; also home to an after-hours pharmacy.

Wellington Regional Hospital (☑04-385 5999; www.ccdhb.org.nz; Riddiford St, Newtown; ☺24hr) Has a 24-hour emergency department; 1km south of the city centre.

UFS Pharmacy (☑04-384 9499; www.ufs. co.nz; 45 Courtenay Pl; ☺8am-6pm Mon-Fri, 10am-2pm Sat) Handy city-centre pharmacy.

TOURIST INFORMATION
DOC Wellington Visitor Centre (p409) Maps, bookings, passes and information for local and national walks (including Great Walks), parks, huts and camping.

Wellington i-SITE (Map p392; ☑04-802 4860; www.wellingtonnz.com; 111 Wakefield St; ☺8.30am-5pm; 🛜) After an earthquake chased it out of its regular digs, the i-SITE has taken over the Michael Fowler Centre's old booking office. It looks like it will be here for the foreseeable future, but check its website for the latest. Staff book almost everything here, and cheerfully distribute Wellington's *Official Visitor Guide*, along with other maps and helpful pamphlets.

🛈 Getting There & Away

AIR
Wellington is an international gateway to NZ. **Wellington Airport** (WLG; ☑04-385 5100; www.wellingtonairport.co.nz; Stewart Duff Dr, Rongotai) has the usual slew of airport accoutrements: info kiosks, currency exchange, ATMs, car-rental desks, shops, espresso... If you're in transit or have an early flight, note that you can't linger overnight inside the terminal.

Domestic services include:

➜ **Air New Zealand** (☑0800 737 000; www. airnewzealand.co.nz) Flies to/from Auckland, Hamilton, Tauranga, Rotorua, Gisborne, Napier, New Plymouth, Palmerston North, Kapiti Coast, Nelson, Blenheim, Christchurch, Timaru, Queenstown, Dunedin and Invercargill.

➜ **Golden Bay Air** (www.goldenbayair.co.nz) Takaka

➜ **Jetstar** (www.jetstar.com) Auckland, Nelson, Christchurch and Dunedin.

➜ **Sounds Air** (☑0800 505 005; www.sound-sair.com) Taupo, Blenheim, Picton, Nelson and Westport.

BOAT
On a clear day, sailing into Wellington Harbour or into Picton in the Marlborough Sounds is magical. Cook Strait can cut up rough, but the big ferries handle it well, and offer the distractions of sport lounges, cafes, bars, information desks and cinemas.

Car-hire companies allow you to pick up and drop off vehicles at ferry terminals. If you arrive outside business hours, arrangements can be made to collect your vehicle from the terminal car park.

There are two ferry options:

Bluebridge Ferries (Map p388; ☑ 04-471 6188; www.bluebridge.co.nz; 50 Waterloo Quay; adult/child/car/campervan/motorbike from $53/27/120/155/51; ☎) Up to four sailings between Wellington and Picton daily (3½ hours).

Interislander (Map p388; ☑ 04-498 3302; www.interislander.co.nz; Aotea Quay; adult/child/car/campervan/motorbike from $56/28/149/181/84) Up to five sailings between Wellington and Picton daily; crossings take 3¼ to 3½ hours. A free shuttle bus heads from platform 9 at Wellington Railway Station to Aotea Quay, 50 minutes before every daytime sailing and returns 20 minutes after every arrival.

BUS

Wellington is a major terminus for North Island bus serves.

InterCity (Map p388; ☑ 04-385 0520; www.intercity.co.nz) coaches depart from platform 9 at Wellington Railway Station. Destinations include Auckland (from $28, 11¼ hours, three daily), Rotorua (from $26, 7½ hours, three daily), Taupo (from $26, six, hours, four daily), Napier (from $19, 5¼ hours, two daily) and Palmerston North (from $15, 2¼ hours, six daily).

Mana Bus (Map p388; ☑ 09-367 9140; www.manabus.com) departs from Bunny St, opposite the railway station. They have two daily services to Auckland (from $25, 11½ hours), Hamilton (from $30, nine hours), Rotorua (from $25, 7¼ hours), Taupo (from $23, 6¼ hours) and Palmerston North (from $15, two hours), one of which is an overnight sleeper service where you can pay extra for a bed.

TRAIN

Metlink (p407) commuter trains head as far as Paekakariki ($10.50, 46 minutes, every 30 minutes), Paraparaumu ($12, 55 minutes, every 30 minutes), Waikanae ($13, one hour, every 30 minutes) and Masterton ($18, 1¾ hours, six on weekdays, two on weekends).

Three days a week the **Northern Explorer** (www.greatjourneysofnz.co.nz) heads to/from Palmerston North (from $59, two hours), Ohakune (from $79, five hours), National Park (from $79, 5¼ hours), Hamilton (from $139, 8½ hours) and Auckland (from $139, 11 hours).

The daily **Capital Connection** heads from Palmerston North ($35, two hours), Waikanae ($15, 55 minutes) and Paraparaumu ($10, 48 minutes) to Wellington on weekday mornings, returning in the evening.

ⓘ Getting Around

TO/FROM THE AIRPORT

Wellington Airport is 6km southeast of the city.
Wellington Combined Shuttles (☑ 04-387

8787; www.co-opshuttles.co.nz; 1/2/3 passengers $20/26/32) provides a door-to-door minibus service (15 minutes) between the city and airport. It's cheaper if two or more passengers are travelling to the same destination. Shuttles meet all arriving flights.

The **Airport Flyer** (☑ 0800 801 700; www.airportflyer.co.nz; cash fare to city $9; ☎) bus runs between the airport, Wellington Railway Station and Lower Hutt every 20 minutes (every 10 minutes in peak hours) from around 7am to 9pm.

A taxi between the city centre and the airport takes around 15 minutes and costs about $30.

BICYCLE

If you're fit or keep to the flat, cycling is a viable option. If you'd like some extra help on the hills, consider an electric bike. They're available from **Switched On Bikes** (p396) and **On Yer Bike** (p397), while **Ferg's Kayaks** (p396) only hires the pedal-powered version.

CAR & MOTORCYCLE

There are a lot of one-way streets in Wellington, and parking gets tight (and pricey) during the day. If you've got a car or a caravan, park on the outskirts and walk or take public transport into the city centre. Freedom camping is permitted for self-contained vehicles at Evans Bay marina, 3km southeast of the city centre.

Along with the major international rental companies, Wellington has various lower-cost operators including **Apex Car Rental** (☑ 04-385 2163; www.apexrentals.co.nz; 186 Victoria St; ☺8am-5pm), **Jucy Rentals** (☑ 0800 399 736; www.jucy.co.nz; 13 Jean Batten St, Rongotai; ☺8am-6pm) and **Omega Rental Cars** (☑ 04-472 8465; www.omegarentalcars.com; 77 Hutt Rd; ☺8am-5pm). Most agencies have offices both at the airport and in the city centre. If you plan on exploring both the North and South Islands, most companies suggest you leave your car in Wellington and pick up another one in Picton after crossing Cook Strait. This is a common (and more affordable) practice, and car-hire companies make it a painless exercise.

There are often cheap deals on car relocation from Wellington to Auckland, as most renters travel in the opposite direction. The catch is that you may have only 24 or 48 hours to make the journey.

PUBLIC TRANSPORT

Metlink (☑ 0800 801 700; www.metlink.org.nz) is the one-stop shop for Wellington's regional bus, train and harbour ferry networks; there's a handy journey planner on their website. You can pay by cash or use **Snapper** (www.snapper.co.nz), an integrated prepaid smartcard. The Snapper fares are cheaper ($1.66 for a one-zone trip as opposed to $2) but the card costs $10, so it's probably not worth purchasing for a short stay.

Bus

Frequent and efficient **Metlink** (p407) buses cover the whole Wellington region, running between approximately 6am and 11.30pm. Major **bus terminals** (Map p388; Lambton Quay) are near the Wellington Train Station, and on Courtenay Pl near the Cambridge Tce intersection. Pick up route maps and timetables from the **i-SITE** (p406) and convenience stores, or online.

Metlink also runs **After Midnight** buses, departing from two city stops (Courtenay Pl and Manners St) between midnight and 4.30am Saturday and Sunday, following a number of routes to the outer suburbs. There's a set $6.50 fare for most trips.

Train

Metlink (p407) operates five train routes running through Wellington's suburbs to regional destinations. Trains run frequently from around 6am to 11pm, departing Wellington Train Station. The lines are as follows:

➡ **Johnsonville** via Ngaio and Khandallah

➡ **Kapiti** via Porirua, Plimmerton, Paekakariki and Paraparaumu

➡ **Melling** via Petone

➡ **Hutt Valley** via Waterloo to Upper Hutt

➡ **Wairarapa** via Featherston, Carterton and Masterton

Timetables are available from convenience stores, the train station, **Wellington i-SITE** (p406) and online. Fares are stage-based; there's a handy calculator on the Metlink site. A Day Rover ticket ($14) allows unlimited off-peak and weekend travel on all lines except Wairarapa.

TAXI

Packed taxi ranks can be found on Courtenay Pl, at the corner of Dixon and Victoria Sts, on Featherston St, and outside the railway station. Major operators include **Green Cabs** (☏ 0800 464 7336; www.greencabs.co.nz) and **Wellington Combined Taxis** (☏ 04-384 4444; www.taxis.co.nz). There are also plenty of Uber drivers in the city.

KAPITI COAST

With long, driftwood- and pumice-strewn, crowd-free beaches, the Kapiti Coast acts as a summer playground and suburban extension for Wellingtonians. The region takes its name from Kapiti Island, a wildlife sanctuary 5km offshore from Paraparaumu.

The mountainous Tararua Forest Park forms a dramatic backdrop along the length of the coastline and has some accessible day walks and longer tramps.

The Kapiti Coast makes an easy day trip from Wellington, though if you're after a few restful days there's enough of interest to keep you entertained.

ⓘ Information

The Kapiti Coast's official visitor centre is the **Paraparaumu i-SITE** (☏ 04-298 8195; www.kapiticoast.govt.nz; Coastlands Mall, Main Rd; ◷ 9am-5pm), at the unappealing, sprawling Coastlands shopping area (www.coastlands.co.nz; banks, ATMs, post office, supermarkets...)

ⓘ Getting There & Away

AIR

Kapiti Coast Airport (☏ 04-298 1013; www.kapiticoastairport.co.nz; 60 Toru Rd) is in central Paraparaumu. **Sounds Air** (p406) and **Air2There** (☏ 0800 777 000; www.air2there.com) fly to Blenheim and Nelson.

BUS

InterCity (p407) coaches stop at the major Kapiti Coast towns. Destinations include Wellington, Napier, New Plymouth, Taupo and Auckland.

CAR & MOTORCYCLE

Getting here from Wellington is a breeze by car: just follow SH1. After Paekakariki the Kapiti Expressway takes over; note, older satellite navigation devices might not include this route, which opened in 2017.

TRAIN

Metlink (p407) commuter trains between Wellington and the coast are more convenient and more frequent than buses. Services run from Wellington to Waikanae (generally half-hourly 5am to midnight), stopping in Paekakariki and Paraparaumu en route.

Three days a week the scenic **Northern Explorer** (p407) train stops in Paraparaumu, heading to Palmerston North (from $59, one hour), Ohakune (from $79, 3¾ hours), National Park (from $79, 4½ hours), Hamilton (from $119, 7¼ hours) and Auckland (from $119, 9¾ hours).

The **Capital Connection** (p407) heads from Palmerston North to Wellington on weekday mornings, returning in the evening; stops include Paraparaumu and Waikanae.

ⓘ Getting Around

BUS

Metlink (p407) runs local bus services around Paraparaumu and Waikanae – they're particularly handy for getting from the railway station to the beach.

TRAIN

Metlink (p407) commuter trains connect Paekakariki, Paraparaumu and Waikanae every 30 minutes from around 5am to midnight.

Kapiti Island

Kapiti Island is the coastline's dominant feature, a 10km by 2km slice that has been a protected reserve since 1897. Predator-free since 1998 (22,500 possums were eradicated here in the 1980s), it's now home to a remarkable range of birds, including many species that are extinct on the mainland.

To visit the island, you must make your arrangements in advance with one of two licensed operators. Remember to reconfirm your arrangements on the morning of departure, as sailings are weather-dependent. All boats depart from Paraparaumu Beach, which can be reached by train.

🏃 Activities

The island is open to day walkers (there are some fab trails here), limited each day to 100 people at **Rangatira**, where you can hike up to the 521m high point, Tuteremoana; and 60 visitors at the **northern end**, which has short, gentle walks to view points and around a lagoon.

☞ Tours

★**Kapiti Island Nature Tours**   ECOTOUR
(📞021 126 7525; www.kapitiislandnaturetours. co.nz; departs Kapiti Boating Club, Marine Pde; transport only $80) 🏆 The *whānau* (family) that runs these nature tours has lived here for eight generations. Day tours ($180 including boat and lunch) look at the island's birds (incredible in range and number), seal colony, history and Māori traditions. Overnight stays (from $384, including boat, meals and accommodation) include an after-dark walk in the bush to spot the rare little spotted kiwi.

Kapiti Explorer   ECOTOUR
(📞027 655 4739; www.kapitiexplorer.nz; departs Kapiti Boating Club, Marine Pde; adult/child return from $75/40; ⊙Sep-May) Transport to and from Kapiti Island, along with guided walks ($12 extra); fares include DOC landing permit.

ℹ Information

More information about Kapiti Island can be found in DOC's *Kapiti Island Nature Reserve* brochure (downloadable from www.doc.govt. nz), or in person at the **DOC Wellington Visitor Centre** (Map p392; 📞04-384 7770; www.doc. govt.nz; 18 Manners St; ⊙9.30am-5pm Mon-Fri, 10am-3.30pm Sat).

Paekakariki

POP 1670

The first stop-worthy Kapiti Coast town you come to heading north from Wellington is cute little Paekakariki, 41km north of the capital. It's an arty seaside village stretched along a black-sand beach, serviced by a train station.

◉ Sights & Activities

★**Queen Elizabeth Park**   PARK
(📞04-292 8625; www.gw.govt.nz/qep; MacKay's Crossing, SH1; ⊙8am-dusk; 🚻) 🏆 One of the last relatively unchanged areas of dune and wetland along the Kapiti Coast, this undulating 650-hectare beachside park offers swimming, walking, cycling and picnicking opportunities, as well as a **tram museum** (📞04-292 8361; www.wellingtontrams.org.nz; MacKay's Crossing, SH1; admission by donation; ⊙11am-4pm Sat & Sun, daily Jan) and **horse riding** (📞06-364 3336; www.stablesonthepark.co.nz; MacKay's Crossing, SH1; pony/horse rides from $25/60) outfit. There are three entrances: off Wellington Rd in Paekakariki, at MacKay's Crossing on SH1, and off the Esplanade in Raumati to the north.

🛏 Sleeping & Eating

Finn's   HOTEL $$
(📞04-292 8081; www.finnshotel.co.nz; 2 Beach Rd; r $145-165; 🛜) Finn's is a flashy beige suit in this low-key railway village, but redeems itself with spacious rooms, big bistro meals, a cafe area, craft beer on tap and an in-house 26-seat cinema. Double glazing keeps the highway at bay.

Beach Road Deli   CAFE $
(📞04-902 9029; www.beach-road-deli.com; 5 Beach Rd; mains $11-17; ⊙7.30am-4pm Tue-Thu, Sat & Sun, to 8.30pm Fri; 🍴) This bijou deli and wood-fired pizzeria, stocked with cheese and home-baked bread and pastries, is heaven-sent for the highway traveller or prospective picnicker. The coffee's good too.

Paraparaumu

POP 25,600

Busy Paraparaumu is the Kapiti Coast's major commercial and residential hot spot. It's a tale of two towns: the main town on the highway, with its deeply unappealing shopping-mall sprawl; and Paraparaumu Beach, with its waterside park and walkway, decent swimming and winning view out to Kapiti Island (island boat trips set sail from here). If you're into craft beer or cars, you're in the right town!

The correct pronunciation is 'Pah-ra-pah-ra-oo-moo', meaning 'scraps from an oven', which is said to have originated when a Māori war party attacked the settlement and found only scraps of food remaining. It's a bit of a mouthful to pronounce; locals usually just corrupt it into 'Para-pa-ram'.

👁 Sights

Tuatara Brewery   BREWERY
(☑04-296 1953; www.tuatarabrewing.co.nz; 7 Sheffield St; ⊙3-7pm Wed & Thu, 11am-7pm Fri-Sun) Visit the oldest and most famous of Wellington's craft breweries at its industrial-estate premises where you can slurp a pint or two and chew some bar snacks (biersticks, nachos, pizza). Book in advance for an enlightening Saturday afternoon tasting experience, matching four beers with canapes ($35).

Southward Car Museum   MUSEUM
(☑04-297 1221; www.southwardcarmuseum.co.nz; Otaihanga Rd; adult/child $18/5; ⊙9am-4.30pm) This huge hangar-like museum has one of Australasia's largest collections of antique and unusual cars. Check out the DeLorean, the German-built 1897 Lux and the 1950 gangster Cadillac complete with bullet holes. The museum is signposted from the expressway.

Our Lady of Lourdes statue   STATUE
(access from 16 Taranaki St) Paraparaumu's oddest claim to fame is surely this 14m-high statue of the Madonna, looming over the town from a 75m-high hill. It was commissioned by the local Catholic priest in 1958 for the 100th anniversary of the Lourdes apparitions. While the statue itself is in good nick, it's reached by a scrappy path through a dishevelled part of town and the 14 *Stations of the Cross* that line the route are in a sorry state of repair.

🍴 Eating

Marine Parade Eatery   CAFE $$
(☑04-892 0098; www.marineparadeeatery.com; 50 Marine Pde; mains breakfast $15-20, lunch $23-25, dinner $27-32; ⊙7.30am-4pm Sat-Thu, to 9pm Fri; 🛜) Affecting something of a Robinson Crusoe look, this fresh-as-a-daisy cafe offers a sophisticated international menu and terrific views of Kapiti Island out the front window. The seafood laksa (coconut noodle soup) is delicious and they also serve chia-seed porridge, bagels, pulled-lamb burgers, coconut-poached chicken and meze platters.

Waikanae
POP 10,600

Beachy Waikanae has long been a retiree stamping ground but in recent times it has transformed into a growing, go-ahead town, bolstered by first-home-buyer flight from unaffordable Wellington. It's a cheery seaside enclave, good for some salt-tinged R&R and natural-realm experiences.

👁 Sights

Hemi Matenga Memorial Park Scenic Reserve   FOREST
(www.doc.govt.nz; off Tui Cres) **FREE** This 330-hectare reserve overlooking Waikanae contains a large remnant of native kohekohe forest. The reserve rises steeply from 150m to its highest point, Te Au (514m), a hike of three to four hours. The **Kohekohe Walk** is also here, an easy 30-minute amble on a well-formed path.

Ngā Manu   NATURE RESERVE
(☑04-293 4131; www.ngamanu.co.nz; 74 Ngā Manu Reserve Rd; adult/child/family $18/8/38; ⊙10am-5pm; 🖼) 🌿 Waikanae's main visitor lure, Ngā Manu Nature Reserve is a 15-hectare bird sanctuary dotted with picnic areas, bushwalks, aviaries and a nocturnal house with kiwi, owls and tuatara. The reserve's endangered long-fin eels are fed at 2pm daily; guided bird-feeding tours run at 11am daily (adult/child $25/10 including admission).

🛏 Sleeping & Eating

Kapiti Gateway Motel   MOTEL $$
(☑04-902 5876; www.kapitigateway.co.nz; 114 Main Rd; unit from $125; 🛜🐾) This tidy and welcoming motel may look old-fashioned from the outside but the rooms have been updated and there's a solar-heated pool, free Wi-Fi and Sky TV. All rooms have at least a microwave and a kettle, and some have full kitchens.

Long Beach   CAFE $$
(☑04-293 6760; www.longbeach.net.nz; 40 Tutere St; mains breakfast $13-24, lunch $17-25, dinner $16-33; ⊙9am-11pm; 🛜🔌🖼) Grab a seat in the large conservatory or the herb garden attached to this attractive, family-friendly cafe-bar. It's a sunny spot for an afternoon wine or craft beer, accompanied by live music on Sundays. The extensive menu includes cooked breakfasts, pizza, pub grub and bistro-style dishes.

THE WAIRARAPA

The Wairarapa is the large tract of land east and northeast of Wellington, beyond the Tararua and Rimutaka ranges. It is named after Wairarapa Moana – otherwise known as **Lake Wairarapa**, translating as 'sea of glistening waters'. This shallow 80-sq-km lake and the surrounding wetland is the focus of much-needed ecological restoration, redressing generations of livestock grazing. Fields of fluffy sheep still abound, as do vineyards and the associated hospitality which have turned the region into a decadent weekend retreat.

In recent years this picturesque slice of New Zealand's rural heartland has gained an unlikely Hollywood connection, with blockbuster movie directors Sir Peter Jackson and James Cameron both putting down roots here.

❶ Getting There & Away

From Wellington, **Metlink** (p407) commuter trains run to Masterton (six times daily on weekdays, twice daily on weekends), calling at seven Wairarapa stations including Featherston and Carterton (though notably not Greytown or Martinborough).

Tranzit Coachlines runs the **InterCity** (p407) service between Masterton and Palmerston North ($21, two hours) five days a week (no Monday or Saturday buses, but two on Friday).

❶ Getting Around

Metlink (p407) bus 200, operated by Tranzit Coachlines, heads from Masterton to Cartertown, Greytown and Featherston seven times on weekdays and three times on Saturdays. All of the Saturday buses continue on to Martinborough, but only one of the weekday services does. On weekdays a further five buses connect Martinborough to the train station at Featherston.

Beyond the main towns, you'll need your own vehicle; many of this area's notable sights are out on the coast and along rural roads. As is often the case, getting there is half the fun: the drive up over the ranges from Wellington is particularly scenic.

Masterton & Around

POP 23,400

The Wairarapa's main hub, Masterton (Whakaoriori) is an unremarkable, unself-conscious little city getting on with the business of life. Nobody was more surprised than the Mastertonians themselves when it was rated New Zealand's most beautiful city in the 2017 *Keep NZ Beautiful Awards*. It does,

OFF THE BEATEN TRACK

RIMUTAKA CYCLE TRAIL

The 115km, three-day **Rimutaka Cycle Trail** (www.nzcycletrail.com/trails/rimutaka-cycle-trail) is one of the Nga Haerenga New Zealand Cycle Trail 'Great Rides'. The trail kicks off at the head of Wellington Harbour before scaling the Rimutaka Ranges, then spilling out around the western end of Palliser Bay.

however, have rivers on two flanks, a lovely central park and some striking 20th-century buildings. Plus there are some interesting natural attractions in the surrounding area.

To the southwest is **Carterton**, one of a clutch of small rural towns punctuating SH2. It boasts by far the best hanging flower baskets of the lot, along with some good second-hand shops, cafes and craft breweries.

◉ Sights

Queen Elizabeth Park　　　　　　PARK
(www.cityofmasterton.co.nz; Dixon St, Masterton) Planted in 1877, Queen Elizabeth Park is perfect for stretching your legs. Walk around the lake, dump someone on the see-saw, see if the little train is running or practise your slip catches on the cricket oval.

Aratoi Wairarapa Museum of Art & History　　MUSEUM
(☑06-370 0001; www.aratoi.co.nz; 6 Dixon St, Masterton; admission by donation; ◷10am-4.30pm) Hushed and refined, this small but splendid gallery hosts an impressive program of exhibitions and events (and has a busy cafe and a shop).

Wool Shed　　　　　　　　　　MUSEUM
(☑06-378 8008; www.thewoolshednz.com; 12 Dixon St, Masterton; adult/child $10/2; ◷10am-4pm) Occupying two historic woolsheds, this baaaa-loody marvellous little museum is dedicated to NZ's sheep-shearing and wool-production industries. Smell the lanolin! It's also a good spot to pick up a home-knitted hat.

⌂ Sleeping

Mawley Holiday Park　　　HOLIDAY PARK $
(☑06-378 6454; www.mawleypark.co.nz; 5 Oxford St, Masterton; sites from $36, unit with/without bathroom from $100/70) ⌘ This amenable, clean campground is spread across the verdant banks of the Waipoua River, just north of the town centre. Units range from basic

WELLINGTON REGION MASTERTON & AROUND

cabins (bring your own linen) to self-contained two-bedroom units.

Cornwall Park Motel MOTEL **$$**
(☑06-378 2939; www.cornwallparkmotel.co.nz; 119 Cornwall St, Masterton; unit from $120; ☎☒) Hide yourself away on the backstreets in this tidy motel. The neat brick units are warm and comfortable, set amongst manicured lawns centred on a large old elm tree.

✖ Eating

★ Clareville Bakery CAFE **$**
(☑06-379 5333; www.theclarevillebakery.co.nz; 3340 SH2, Clareville; mains $6-22; ◷7.30am-4pm Mon-Sat; ◉) Located on SH2 immediately northeast of Carterton, this brilliant bakery-cafe is famous for its sourdough bread, lamb-cutlet pie, open steak sandwich and lavash-style crackers – but everything displayed on the counter is borderline irresistible. There's garden seating, a play area for the kids and regular live-music evenings.

Gladstone Inn PUB FOOD **$$**
(☑06-372 7866; www.gladstoneinn.co.nz; 571 Gladstone Rd, Gladstone; pizza $17-20, mains $27-32; ◷11am-late Tue-Sun; ◉) Gladstone, 18km south of Masterton, is less a town, more a state of mind. There's very little here except a handful of vineyards and this classic old timber inn, haven to thirsty locals, bikers, Sunday drivers and lazy afternoon sippers who hog the tables in the glorious garden bar by the river. There's the odd crafty beer on tap, too.

ℹ Information

DOC Masterton Office (☑06-377 0700; www.doc.govt.nz; 220 South Rd, Masterton; ◷9am-

---

OFF THE BEATEN TRACK

CASTLEPOINT

On the coast 68km east of Masterton, Castlepoint is a truly awesome, end-of-the-world place, with a reef, the lofty 162m-high **Castle Rock**, some safe swimming and walking tracks. There's an easy (but sometimes ludicrously windy) 30-minute return walk goes across the reef to the lighthouse, where 70-plus shell species are fossilised in the cliffs. A one-hour return walk runs to a huge limestone cave (take a torch), or take the 1½-hour return track from **Deliverance Cove** to Castle Rock. Keep well away from the lower reef when there are heavy seas.

4.30pm Mon-Fri) A regional office rather than a visitor centre, but you can still call in for Wairarapa-wide DOC information, including advice on tracks.

Masterton i-SITE (☑06-370 0900; www.wairarapanz.com; 6 Dixon St, Masterton; ◷9.30am-4.30pm) Can sort you out with local information, including a copy of the *Wairarapa Visitor Guide,* and advice on accommodation.

Greytown

POP 2200
The prettiest of several small towns along SH2, Greytown (Te Hupenui) is home to a permanent population of urbane locals and waves of Wellington weekenders. It was the country's first planned inland town: intact Victorian buildings line the main street with interesting historic plaques on many of them (pick up the *Historic Greytown* brochure for a handy map). Within the old buildings you'll find accommodation, cafes, restaurants and some swanky shopping.

In 1890 Greytown became the first town in NZ to celebrate Arbor Day, bequeathing it a legacy of magnificent mature trees. The mountain ash in the grounds of St Luke's Anglican Church is the last survivor of three saplings which mysteriously sprouted after being stolen in 1856 from a delivery carted by hand, over the Rimutakas. Greytown's other historic claim to fame was as the site of a Māori Parliament which held two sessions at nearby Pāpāwai Marae in the 1890s.

◉ Sights

Cobblestones Museum MUSEUM
(☑06-304 9687; www.cobblestonesmuseum.org.nz; 169 Main St; adult/child $7/3; ◷10am-4pm daily Oct-May, Thu-Mon Jun-Sep; ◉) Occupying the site of an old coach stop, complete with its original stables and well-worn cobbled courtyard, this endearing museum comprises an enclave of transplanted period buildings and donated old-time objects, dotted around pretty grounds just begging for a lie-down on a picnic blanket. There's a blacksmiths, a school, a fire station, a church, a wool shed... Wairarapa colonial history in tangible form.

Stonehenge Aotearoa MONUMENT
(☑06-377 1600; www.stonehenge-aotearoa.co.nz; 51 Ahiaruhe Rd, Ahiaruhe; adult/child $10/5, tour $20/5; ◷10am-4pm daily Jan, Wed-Sun Feb-Apr & Sep-Dec, Sat & Sun May-Aug) About 10km east of Greytown in a farmer's backyard, this full-scale adaptation of England's Stonehenge is orientated for its southern hemisphere location on a

grassy knoll overlooking the Wairarapa Plain. Its mission: to bring the night sky to life, even in daylight. The pre-tour talk and audiovisual presentation are excellent, and the henge itself a surreal (and delightfully eccentric) sight.

🛏 Sleeping

Greytown Campground CAMPGROUND **$**
(☑06-304 9387; www.greytowncampground.co.nz; Kuratawhiti St; sites/cabins from $15/65) This simple camping option is scenically spread through Soldiers Memorial Park, 650m from the main street. As well as shady sites, accommodation options include a gypsy caravan, a glamping tent and two handkerchief-sized cabins with bunk beds. Plus there are bush walks, tennis courts and a massive kids' playground nearby.

Oak Estate Motor Lodge MOTEL **$$**
(☑06-304 8188; www.oakestate.co.nz; 2 Hospital Rd; unit from $140; ☎) A stand of gracious roadside oaks and pretty gardens shield this smart complex of red-roofed units at the southern end of town. Choose from studio, one- and two-bedroom options. Expect tasteful interiors and white doves strutting about on the lawns. There's free wi-fi, although the signal is not strong.

🍴 Eating

French Baker BAKERY **$**
(☑06-304 8873; www.frenchbaker.co.nz; 81 Main St; mains $7-16; ☺7.30am-3.30pm) Buttery croissants, tempting tarts and authentic breads – this artisan bakery is le real McCoy. Grab and go from the cabinet, or tuck into a ham-and-cheese croissant, soup or spaghetti bolognese, capped off with a silky flat white coffee.

Saluté TAPAS, PIZZA **$$**
(☑06-304 9825; www.salute.net.nz; 83 Main St; tapas $9-19, pizza $21, mains lunch $18-24, dinner $36-38; ☺noon-late Wed-Fri, 11.30am-late Sat & Sun) A neat red iron-clad house on the main street, Saluté will suit you down to the ground if you like things saucy, succulent, crisp, charred and fried, along with lashings of olive oil and wedges of lemon. For non-sharing types there a few stand-alone mains, and moderately priced pizza is available throughout the day.

🛍 Shopping

Imperial Productions TOYS
(☑06-304 9625; www.imperialproductions.co.nz; 5 McMaster St) A cute old-fashioned shop for a cute old-fashioned town, Imperial sells

WORTH A TRIP

PUKAHA MT BRUCE NATIONAL WILDLIFE CENTRE

About 30km north of Masterton, the 10-sq-km **Pukaha Mt Bruce National Wildlife Centre** (☑06-375 8004; www.pukaha.org.nz; 85379 SH2; adult/child $20/6, incl guided walk $45/25; ☺9am-4.30pm) is one of NZ's most successful wildlife and captive breeding centres. The scenic 1½-hour loop walk gives a good overview. There's also a kiwi house here and a series of aviaries for viewing other native birds. Tuatara are also on show, and the eels are fed daily at 1.30pm. Guided walks depart at 11am and 2pm daily; book in advance.

If you're travelling by campervan, it's possible to book an 'overnight experience' including a night tour, secure park, toilet facilities (no showers) and an unforgettable dawn chorus ($95 per person).

beautiful rendered traditional toy soldiers and other figurines. Keep an eye out for the tiny Māori warriors.

ℹ Information

Greytown Information Centre (89 Main St; ☺2-4pm Fri, 11am-3pm Sat & Sun) This volunteer-staffed centre is housed in Greytown's historic town hall (1869).

ℹ Getting There & Away

The nearest train station is at Woodside, 5km away; Wairarapa Line trains between Wellington and Masterton stop here. Bus 204 heads between Main St and the station ($2, 5 minutes) six times on weekdays and twice on Saturdays.

Metlink (p407) bus 200 operated by Tranzit Coachlines stops at Greytown en route between Masterton ($5, 30 minutes) and Featherston ($3.50, 14 minutes) seven times on weekdays and three times on Saturdays. All of the Saturday buses continue on to Martinborough ($5.50, 49 minutes), but only one of the weekday services does.

Martinborough
POP 1470

Laid out in the shape of a Union Jack with a leafy square at its centre, Martinborough (Wharekaka) is a photogenic town with some charming old buildings, surrounded by a patchwork of pasture and pinstripe grapevines. It is famed for its wineries, which draw in visitors to nose the pinot noir, pair it up with fine food and snooze it off at boutique accommodation.

With most of its cellar doors arranged around the perimeter of the town grid, Martinborough provides a uniquely accessible experience for oenophiles. It's quite possible to walk around the major wineries, but the classic Martinborough sight is of gaggles of merry pedal-powered punters getting ever more wobbly as the afternoon progresses.

◉ Sights & Activities

The most ecofriendly way to explore the Wairarapa's wineries is by bicycle, as the flat landscape makes for puff-free cruising. Rental bikes are comfortable cruisers with saddlebags for your booty. Suffice to say, you ought to pay greater attention to your technique, and to the road, as the day wears on.

Rental outfitters include Green Jersey Explorer Tours (p415), Indi Bikes (☑027 306 6090; www.indibikesmartinborough.co.nz; 1-6 seater $35-190 per day; ☺10am-5.30pm Fri-Sun), Martinborough Top 10 Holiday Park (p415) and Martinborough Wine Merchants (p416).

Martinborough Brewery
BREWERY

(☑06-306 6249; www.martinboroughbeer.com; 10 Ohio St; tasting paddle from $10, tour $5; ☺11am-7pm Thu-Mon Mar-Nov, Thu-Tue Dec-Feb) It's hard to go anywhere in NZ these days and not find a craft brewery bubbling away in the corner. Martinborough is no exception. The brewery counters the town's prevailing wine vibe with its range of meaty brews (dark beers a speciality). Sip a tasting paddle or a pint on the sunny terrace out the front. Brewery tours by arrangement.

Palliser Wines
WINERY

(☑06-306 9019; www.palliser.co.nz; 96 Kitchener St; tasting $5, waived with purchase; ☺11am-4pm) Wines so good, even the Queen has some stashed away in her cellar. A slick outfit, as befitting one of Martinborough's best-known producers.

Martinborough Vineyard
WINERY

(☑06-306 9955; www.martinborough-vineyard.co.nz; 57 Princess St; tasting $5, waived with purchase; ☺11am-4pm daily Oct-May, Fri-Tue Jun-Sep) The first vineyard to plant pinot noir in the region, this vineyard is a local legend with a sterling international reputation.

Margrain
WINERY

(☑06-306 9292; www.margrainvineyard.co.nz; cnr Ponatahi & Huangarua Rds; tasting $5-10, waived with purchase; ☺11am-3pm Sun-Thu, 1-4pm Fri, 11am-5pm Sat) Sip a wide range of high-quality wines at this character-filled cellar door, with a casual on-site cafe overlooking the vines.

Schubert Wines
WINERY

(☑06-306 8505; www.schubert.co.nz; 57 Cambridge Rd; tasting $5, waived with purchase; ☺11am-3pm) Run by German imports who searched for and found the best spot in the world to produce their favourite wine, pinot noir. This compact cellar door is big on personality, with a fine range of wines including the unusual tribianco, a blend of three white wine varieties.

Ata Rangi
WINERY

(☑06-306 9570; www.atarangi.co.nz; 14 Puruatanga Rd; tastings $5, waived with purchase; ☺1-3pm) 🍃 One of the region's pioneering winemakers. Great drops across the board and a cute cellar door, also selling honey and olive oil.

Tirohana Estate
WINERY

(☑06-306 9933; www.tirohanaestate.com; 42 Puruatanga Rd; $1-2 per wine; ☺10.30am-4.30pm Tue-Sun) Head past the popular restaurant to the tasting room hung with swords and guns.

Haythornthwaite Wines
WINERY

(☑06-306 9889; www.ht3wines.co.nz; 45 Omarere Rd; tastings $5; ☺11am-5pm) 🍃 Sustainable, hands-on winery producing complex drops including cherry-like pinot noir and gorgeous gewürztraminer. If the weather's fine, the tasting will be served at the outdoor tables.

Poppies Martinborough
WINERY

(☑06-306 8473; www.poppiesmartinborough.co.nz; 91 Puruatanga Rd; ☺11am-4pm Fri-Tue) Delectable handcrafted wines served by the label's passionate winemaking and viticulturalist duo. Savour their wines alongside a well-matched platter in the stylishly simple cellar.

Coney Wines
WINERY

(☑06-306 8345; www.coneywines.co.nz; 107 Dry River Rd; ☺11am-4pm Fri-Sun Dec-Mar, Sat & Sun Oct, Nov & Apr-Jul) Fingers crossed that your tasting host will be the inimitable Tim Coney, an affable character who makes a mighty syrah and may sing at random. It's also home to the excellent Trio Cafe; bookings recommended.

WAIRARAPA WINE COUNTRY

Wairarapa's world-renowned wine industry was nearly crushed in infancy. The region's first vines were planted in 1883, but in 1908 the prohibition movement put a cap on that corker of an idea. It wasn't until the late 1970s that winemaking was revived, after Martinborough's terroir was discovered to be similar to that of Burgundy, France. A few vineyards sprang up, the number since ballooning to around 30 across the region. Martinborough is the undisputed hub of the action, but vineyards around Gladstone and Masterton are also on the up. Pinot noir is the region's most acclaimed variety, but sauvignon blanc also does well, as do aromatics and syrah.

Wairarapa's wineries thrive on visitors: well-oiled cellar doors swing wide open for tastings. Most wineries charge a tasting fee (although many will waive it if you purchase a bottle); others are free. Some have a cafe or restaurant, while others will rustle up a picnic platter to be enjoyed in their gardens. Winter hours wind back to the minimum.

The *Wairarapa Visitor Guide* (available from local i-SITEs and many other locations) has maps to aid your navigations. Read all about it at www.winesfrommartinborough.com.

WELLINGTON REGION MARTINBOROUGH

⚐ Tours

Green Jersey Explorer Tours   CYCLING
(☑06-306 6027; www.greenjersey.co.nz; 16 Kitchener St; 6hr guided tours incl lunch $120, bike hire per day $40; 🚲) Offers guided tours of three vineyards and an olive grove, including a picnic lunch. Bike hire is also available, as are dedicated family-orientated tours (fewer wineries, more farm animals).

Zest Food & Wine Tours   FOOD & DRINK
(☑04-801 9198; www.zestfoodtours.co.nz; per person incl lunch $595) Exclusive small-group tours (two to four guests) around Martinborough and Greytown, with the focus squarely on quality wine and food. Pricey, but worth it if you want a really personalised experience. The tour starts from the Featherston railway station and includes the train from Wellington.

Martinborough Wine Tours   WINE
(☑06-306 8032; www.martinboroughwinetours.co.nz; per couple incl lunch $575) An upmarket 'Martinborough in a Day' tour for couples, with tastings at five wineries, a bit of history, an olive farm visit and a fine wine-matched lunch. Less fancy half-/full-day tours also available (per person $85).

✹ Festivals & Events

Toast Martinborough   FOOD & DRINK
(☑06-306 9183; www.toastmartinborough.co.nz; Memorial Sq; from $89; ☺Nov) A hugely popular wine, food and music event held on the third Sunday in November; book in advance.

⌸ Sleeping

Claremont   MOTEL $$
(☑06-306 9162; www.theclaremont.co.nz; 38 Regent St; unit from $145; 🖧) A classy accommodation enclave 15 minutes' walk from town, the Claremont has two-storey, self-contained units in great nick, modern studios with spa baths, and sparkling two-bedroom apartments, all at reasonable rates (even cheaper in winter and/or midweek). It's surrounded by tidy gardens with barbecue areas, and they also offer bike hire.

Martinborough Top 10 Holiday Park   HOLIDAY PARK $$
(☑0800 780 909; www.martinboroughholidaypark.com; 10 Dublin St; sites from $42, unit with/without bathroom from $139/80; 🖧) Just five minutes' walk from town, this appealing campsite has grapevine views, shady trees and the town pool over the back fence. Cabins are simple but great value, freeing up your dollars for the cellar door. Good-quality bikes, including tandems and child seats, are available for hire.

Old Manse   B&B $$$
(☑06-306 8599; www.oldmanse.co.nz; 19 Grey St; r $230-255; 🖧) Oozing historic charm, this venerable villa has five en-suite rooms painted in bold colours. Two are larger than the others but they're all a decent size. Plus there's a cedar hot tub in the garden with views over the vines.

Peppers Parehua   RESORT $$$
(☑06-306 8405; www.peppers.co.nz; New York St West; cottage from $272; 🖧🏊) Martinborough's ritziest accommodation comprises 28 free-standing cottages scattered around

an ornamental lake surrounded by vines. All have fully equipped kitchens and open fireplaces, and some have private cedar hot tubs. The complex also includes a tennis court and restaurant.

✕ Eating

Café Medici CAFE $$
(☑06-306 9965; www.cafemedici.co.nz; 9 Kitchener St; lunch mains $9-23, dinner $30-36; ⊗8.30am-4pm daily & 6.30pm-late Fri & Sat) A perennial favourite among townsfolk and regular visitors, this airy cafe has a sunny courtyard and great coffee. Tasty, home-cooked food includes muffins, big brunch dishes such as Spanish eggs, delicious prawn linguine, and Med-flavoured dinner options such as Moroccan lamb tagine.

Pinocchio BISTRO $$$
(☑06-306 6094; www.pinocchiomartinborough. co.nz; 3 Kitchener St; mains $36-38; ⊗6pm-late Wed-Fri) Odd name aside, there's much to love about this upmarket but relaxed little restaurant. Expect modern, produce-led country dishes such as pulled lamb with peas, and their signature confit duck with duck-liver parfait and pumpkin.

☿ Drinking & Entertainment

Micro Wine Bar WINE BAR
(☑06-306 9716; www.facebook.com/microwinebar; 14c Ohio St; ⊗4pm-late Thu-Mon) Moreish little Micro packs a punch with its excellent wine list (mostly local with some far-flung stars), notable craft-beer selection and yummy nibbles. The tasting flights are a good way to sample the vineyards that got away ($20 for five whites, $25 for reds). Catch the sun streetside or head to the courtyard. Vinyl spins on the vintage 1970s stereo.

Circus CINEMA
(☑06-306 9442; www.circus.net.nz; 34 Jellicoe St; adult/child $16/11; ⊗3pm-late Wed-Mon) Lucky old Martinborough has its own stylish arthouse cinema. This modern, micro-sized complex has two comfy studio theatres and a cafe opening out on to a sunny, somewhat Zen garden. Reasonably priced food (mains $22 to $34) includes bar snacks, pizzas and mains with seasonal vegies. Take your wine into the cinema with you.

⛫ Shopping

Martinborough Wine Merchants WINE
(☑06-306 9040; www.martinboroughwinemerchants.com; 6 Kitchener St; ⊗9.30am-6pm) Adjoining the Village Cafe, this large store is an excellent place to buy local wine and maybe taste some, too. They also sell olive oil and chocolate, and rent out bikes ($25/35 per half/full day) for cellar-door adventures.

ⓘ Information

The cheery **Martinborough i-SITE** (☑06-306 5010; www.wairarapanz.com; 18 Kitchener St; ⊗9am-5pm) stocks wine region maps.

Cape Palliser

The Wairarapa coast is rugged, remote and sparsely populated. A trip to the landmark Cape Palliser lighthouse is a must-do if you can spare the time and have your own wheels. From Martinborough, the road wends through picturesque farmland before hitting the coast. This section of the drive is impossibly scenic – hugging the coast, with wild ocean on one side and sheer cliffs on the other. Look for shadows of the South Island, visible on a clear day. If you've got time, it's well worth taking the hike to the Putangirua Pinnacles (p385).

As you approach Cape Palliser (Matakitakiakupe) you'll reach the wind-worn fishing village of **Ngawi**. The first things you'll notice here are the rusty bulldozers on the beach, used to drag fishing boats ashore.

On the way there or back, take a short detour to the crusty waterside settlement of **Lake Ferry**, overlooking **Lake Onoke**. The lake empties directly to the sea through grey, shingled dunes, with big black-backed gulls circling overhead. The **Lake Ferry Hotel** (☑06-307 7831; www.lakeferryhotel.co.nz; 2 Lake Ferry Rd, Lake Ferry; ⊗noon-3pm & 5-9pm Mon-Fri, 11am-9pm Sat & Sun; ☎) has a beaut outdoor terrace upon which to sit, sip and snack on some fish and chips.

◉ Sights

Cape Palliser Lighthouse LIGHTHOUSE
(Cape Palliser Rd) Get a few puffs into your lungs on the 250-step climb to the base of this candy-striped lighthouse (1897). It's a terrific view from up here, and a great place to linger if the wind isn't blowing your eyeballs into the back of your head. The surrounding shoreline is home to a malodorous seal colony, the North Island's largest breeding area for these fellers.

Whatever you do in your quest for a photo, don't get between the seals and the sea: if you block their escape route they're likely to charge you – and they can move surprisingly fast.

Understand New Zealand

New Zealand Today

Despite a decade marred by disasters, including devastating earthquakes and mining and helicopter tragedies, New Zealand never loses its nerve. The country remains a titan on both the silver screen and the sports field, and change is coming in the world of politics...

Best on Film

Lord of the Rings trilogy (2001–03) Hobbits, dragons and magical rings – Tolkien's vision comes to life.

The Piano (1993) A piano and its owners arrive on a mid-19th-century West Coast beach.

Whale Rider (2002) Magical tale of family and heritage on the East Coast.

Once Were Warriors (1994) Brutal relationship dysfunction in South Auckland.

Boy (2010) Taika Waititi's bitter-sweet coming-of-age drama set in the Bay of Plenty.

Best in Print

The Luminaries (Eleanor Catton; 2013) Man Booker Prize winner: crime and intrigue on West Coast goldfields.

Mister Pip (Lloyd Jones; 2006) Tumult on Bougainville Island, intertwined with Dickens' *Great Expectations*.

Live Bodies (Maurice Gee; 1998) Post-WWII loss and redemption in NZ.

The 10pm Question (Kate de Goldi; 2009) Twelve-year-old Frankie grapples with life's big anxieties.

The Collected Stories of Katherine Mansfield (2006) Kathy's greatest hits.

The Wish Child (Catherine Chidgey; 2016) Harrowing, heartbreaking WWII novel; NZ Book Awards winner.

Jacinda Mania

In 2010 she was NZ's youngest sitting MP, by 2017 she was running the country. The swift rise of Jacinda Ardern has been touted as part of a global political shift. Ardern became the youngest ever Labour Party leader in 2017, only a few weeks ahead of the election that propelled her to the role of prime minister at the age of 37 – making her NZ's youngest PM for 150 years. Passionate about climate change, unabashedly feminist and an ardent supporter of gay rights, Ardern's ability to win support with her energetic style was dubbed 'Jacindamania'. The final polls gave Labour a less-than-maniacal 37% of the vote, but resulted in a coalition government led by Labour.

Ardern's articulacy and verve have seen her aligned with other youthful, socially progressive world leaders like Justin Trudeau and Emmanuel Macron, part of a youth-powered political sea change. But Ardern's style remains quintessentially Kiwi: unpretentious and accessible. When an Australian radio journalist sought to fact-check the correct pronunciation of Ardern's name in 2017, he was astonished to be connected with the PM directly, who explained the right pronunciation personally. It's 'AH-durn', if you're wondering.

Overseas Stampede

Being a dream destination isn't all it's cracked up to be, especially when tourist numbers boom and property investors swoop in. Aussie and Asian buyers are increasingly wise to NZ property – some seek holiday homes, others see the far-flung nation as a safe haven from global unrest and nuclear war. Cue a spiralling housing crisis, and the International Monetary Fund (IMF) ranking NZ's housing as the most unaffordable in the Organisation for Economic Co-operation and Development (OECD) in 2016.

The worst effects have been felt in Auckland, home to almost one-third of the country's population. Auckland has struggled to keep pace with demand for housing since the post-WWII housing boom, but in recent years rental rates and house prices have sprinted past local incomes, dashing dreams of home ownership and leaving more New Zealanders homeless. With house prices that grew by 75% within four years, over-subscribed Auckland was named one of the world's least affordable cities. There were signs of a slowdown at the end of 2017, but Auckland Council and the government have scrambled to plan more than 420,000 new dwellings, clamp down on foreign buyers and plug black holes in the construction sector – where a dearth of skilled tradesmen and monopolies on building supplies have helped contribute to eye-watering prices. With Auckland's population expected to increase by one million in the next 30 years, the fixes can't come swiftly enough.

International property purchasers aren't the only ones carving off a little too much of NZ. The issue of managing NZ's increasing number of visitors – now an annual 3.54 million – is high on the agenda, particularly from a conservation perspective. In response to the enormous popularity of the Tongariro Alpine Crossing, DOC has placed a time limit at the car park at the beginning of the track, forcing tourists to use traffic-reducing shuttle services. Meanwhile, tourism hubs like Te Anau, gateway to world-famous Milford Sound, are seeing their peak season start ever earlier, and local grumbles about the numbers of visitors on tramping trails and roads are getting louder. A country beloved for being wild, green and beautiful faces the challenge of keeping it that way, in the face of a tourism stampede.

Never Forget

Kiwi battler spirit has been repeatedly pushed to its limits over the past decade. Christchurch's recovery from the 2010 and 2011 earthquakes suffered a setback when another quake hit in 2016, while earthquakes in Kaikoura in November 2016 rattled road and rail access until repairs were finished at the end of 2017. But NZ doesn't just rebuild, it reinvents: pop-up cafes and restaurants and a shipping-container mall showed how fast Christchurch could dust itself off after disaster. Ensuing years have allowed the bigger post-earthquake projects to take shape, including the Canterbury Earthquake National Memorial, unveiled in 2017.

Another notable memorial remembers the Pike River Disaster in 2010, in which a methane explosion claimed 29 lives – the country's worst mining accident in more than a century. By the wishes of the families of the men killed in the accident, the site of the mine has been folded into Paparoa National Park and their memorial will be a new 'Great Walk', opening in 2018.

POPULATION: **4.83 MILLION**

AREA: **268,021 SQ KM**

GDP GROWTH: **4.1% (2016)**

INFLATION: **1.9% (2017)**

UNEMPLOYMENT: **4.8% (2017)**

if New Zealand were 100 people

65 would be European
15 would be Maori
12 would be Asian
7 would be Pacific Islanders
1 would be Other

where they live
(% of New Zealanders)

65 — North Island
19 — South Island
11 — Australia
4 — Rest of the World
1 — Travelling

population per sq km

NEW ZEALAND   AUSTRALIA   USA

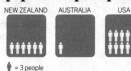

👤 ≈ 3 people

History

Historians continue to unravel New Zealand's early history...with much of what they discover confirming traditional Māori narratives. In less than a thousand years NZ produced two new peoples: the Polynesian Māori and European New Zealanders (also known by their Māori name, 'Pākehā'). New Zealand shares some of its history with the rest of Polynesia, and with other European settler societies. This cultural intermingling has created unique features along the way.

Māori Settlement

The first settlers of NZ were the Polynesian forebears of today's Māori. Archaeologists and anthropologists continue to search for the details, but the most widely accepted evidence suggests they arrived in the 13th century. The DNA of Polynesian rat bones, dated to centuries earlier, has been written off as unreliable (and certainly not conclusive evidence of earlier settlement). Most historians now agree on 1280 as the Māori's likeliest arrival date. Scientists have sequenced the DNA of settlers buried at the Wairau Bar archaeological site on the South Island, and confirmed the settlers as originating from east Polynesia (though work is ongoing to pinpoint their origins more precisely). The genetic diversity of the buried settlers suggests a fairly large-scale settlement – a finding consistent with Māori narratives about numerous vessels reaching the islands.

Prime sites for first settlement were warm coastal gardens for the food plants brought from Polynesia (kumara or sweet potato, gourd, yam and taro); sources of workable stone for knives and adzes; and areas with abundant big game. New Zealand has no native land mammals apart from a few species of bat, but 'big game' is no exaggeration: the islands were home to a dozen species of moa (a large flightless bird), the largest of which weighed up to 240kg, about twice the size of an ostrich...preyed upon by *Harpagornis moorei*, a whopping 15kg eagle that is now extinct. Other species of flightless birds and large sea mammals, such as fur seals, were easy game for hunters from small Pacific islands. The first settlers spread far and fast, from the top of the North Island to the bottom of the

Similarities in language between Māori and Tahitian indicate close contact in historical times. Māori is about as similar to Tahitian as Spanish is to French, despite the 4294km separating these island groups.

TIMELINE	AD 1280	1500–1642	1642
	Based on evidence from archaeological digs, the most likely arrival date of east Polynesians in NZ, now known as Māori.	The 'classic period' of Māori culture, where weapon-making and artistic techniques were refined. Many remain cultural hallmarks to this day.	First European contact: Abel Tasman arrives on an expedition from the Dutch East Indies (Indonesia) but leaves in a hurry after a sea skirmish with Māori.

THE MORIORI MYTH

One of NZ's most persistent legends is that Māori found mainland NZ already occupied by a more peaceful and racially distinct Melanesian people, known as the Moriori, whom they exterminated. This myth has been regularly debunked by scholars since the 1920s, but somehow hangs on.

To complicate matters, there were real 'Moriori', and Māori did treat them badly. The real Moriori were the people of the Chatham Islands, a windswept group about 900km east of the mainland. They were, however, fully Polynesian, and descended from Māori – 'Moriori' was their version of the same word. Mainland Māori arrived in the Chathams in 1835, as a spin-off of the Musket Wars, killing some Moriori and enslaving the rest, but they did not exterminate them.

South Island within the first 100 years. High-protein diets are likely to have boosted population growth.

By about 1400, however, with big-game supply dwindling, Māori economics turned from big game to small game – forest birds and rats – and from hunting to farming and fishing. A good living could still be made, but it required detailed local knowledge, steady effort and complex communal organisation, hence the rise of the Māori tribes. Competition for resources increased, conflict did likewise, and this led to the building of increasingly sophisticated *pā* (fortified villages), complete with wells and food storage pits\. Vestiges of *pā* earthworks can still be seen around the country (on the hilltops of Auckland, for example).

Around 1500 is considered the dawn of the 'classic period', when Māori developed a social structure and aesthetic that was truly distinct, rather than an offshoot of the parent Polynesian culture. Māori had no metals and no written language (and no alcoholic drinks or drugs). Traditional Māori culture from these times endures, including performance art like *kapa haka* (cultural dance) and unmistakeable visual art, notably woodcarving, weaponry and *pounamu* (greenstone).

Spiritual life was similarly distinctive. Below Ranginui (sky father) and Papatūānuku (earth mother) were various gods of land, forest and sea, joined by deified ancestors over time. The mischievous demigod Māui was particularly important. In legend, he vanquished the sun and fished up the North Island before meeting his death between the thighs of the goddess Hine-nui-te-pō in an attempt to bring immortality to humankind.

Enter Europe

The first authenticated contact between Māori and European explorers took place in 1642. Seafarer Abel Tasman had just claimed Van Diemen's Land

1769	1772	1790s	1818–45
European contact recommences with visits by James Cook and Jean de Surville. Despite violence, both manage to communicate with Māori. This time NZ's link with the outside world proves permanent.	Marion du Fresne's French expedition arrives; it stays for some weeks at the Bay of Islands. Relations with Māori start well, but a breach of Māori *tapu* (sacred law) leads to violence.	Whaling ships and seal-hunting gangs arrive in the country. Relations are established with Māori, with Europeans depending on the contact for essentials, such as food, water and protection.	Intertribal Māori 'Musket Wars' take place: some tribes acquire muskets and win bloody victories against tribes without them. The wars taper off, probably due to the equal distribution of weapons.

(Tasmania) for the Dutch when rough winds steered his ships east, where he sighted New Zealand. Tasman's two ships were searching for southern land and anything valuable it might contain. Tasman was instructed to pretend to any natives he might meet 'that you are by no means eager for precious metals, so as to leave them ignorant of the value of the same'.

When Tasman's ships anchored in the bay, local Māori came out in their canoes to make the traditional challenge: friends or foes? The Dutch blew their trumpets, unwittingly challenging back. When a boat was lowered to take a party between the two ships, it was attacked and four crewmen were killed. Having not even set foot on the land, Tasman sailed away and didn't return; nor did any other European for 127 years. But the Dutch did leave a name: initially 'Statenland', later changed to 'Nova Zeelandia' by cartographers.

Contact between Māori and Europeans was renewed in 1769, when English and French explorers arrived, under James Cook and Jean de Surville - Cook narrowly pipped the latter to the post, naming Doubtless Bay before the French party dropped anchor there. The first French exploration ended sourly, with mistrust between the ailing French seamen and Māori, one of whom they took prisoner (he died at sea). Bloody skirmishes took place during a second French expedition, led by Marc-Joseph Marion du Fresne, when cultural misunderstandings led to violent reprisals; later expeditions were more fruitful. Meanwhile Cook made two more visits between 1773 and 1777. Exploration continued, motivated by science, profit and political rivalry.

Unofficial visits, by whaling ships in the north and seal-hunting gangs in the south, began in the 1790s (though Māori living in New Zealand's interior remained largely unaffected). The first Christian missionaries established themselves in the Bay of Islands in 1814, followed by dozens of others - Anglican, Methodist and Catholic. Europe brought such things as pigs and potatoes, which benefited Māori and were even used as currency. Trade in flax and timber generated small European–Māori settlements by the 1820s. Surprisingly, the most numerous category of 'European' visitor was probably American. New England whaling ships favoured the Bay of Islands for rest and recreation, which meant sex and drink. Their favourite haunt, the little town of Kororāreka (now Russell), was known as 'Gomorrah, the scourge of the Pacific'. As a result, New England visitors today might well have distant relatives among the local Māori.

One or two dozen bloody clashes dot the history of Māori–European contact before 1840 but, given the number of visits, interracial conflict was modest. Europeans needed Māori protection, food and labour, and Māori came to need European articles, especially muskets. Whaling stations and mission stations were linked to local Māori groups by intermarriage, which helped keep the peace. Most warfare was between Māori and

---

Abel Tasman named NZ 'Statenland', assuming it was connected to Staten Island near Argentina. It was subsequently named after the province of Zeeland in Tasman's native Holland.

One of the first European women to settle in New Zealand was Charlotte Badger, a convict mutineer who fled to the Bay of Islands in 1806 and refused to return to European society.

1837	1840	1844	1858
European settlers introduce possums from Australia to NZ, creating a possum population boom that comes to threaten native flora and birdlife.	Starting at Waitangi in the Bay of Islands on 6 February, around 500 chiefs countrywide sign the Treaty of Waitangi. NZ becomes a nominal British colony.	Young Ngāpuhi chief Hōne Heke challenges British sovereignty, first by cutting down the British flag at Kororāreka (now Russell), then by sacking the town itself. The ensuing Northland war continues until 1846.	The Waikato chief Te Wherowhero is installed as the first Māori King.

JAMES COOK'S ENDEAVOURS

Countless obelisks, faded plaques and graffiti-covered statues remember the renowned navigator James Cook (1728–79). It's impossible to travel the Pacific without encountering the captain's image and his controversial legacy in the lands he opened to the West.

Cook came from an extremely pinched and provincial background. The son of a day labourer in rural Yorkshire, he was born in a mud cottage, had little schooling and seemed destined for farm work. Instead, Cook went to sea as a teenager, worked his way up from coal-ship servant to naval officer, and attracted notice for his exceptional charts of Canada. But Cook remained a little-known second lieutenant until, in 1768, the Royal Navy chose him to command a daring voyage to the South Seas.

In a converted coal ship called *Endeavour,* Cook sailed to Tahiti and then became the first European to land in New Zealand and the east coast of Australia. While he was there Cook sailed and mapped NZ's coastline in full – with impressive accuracy. The ship almost sank after striking the Great Barrier Reef, and 40% of the crew died from disease and accidents, but somehow the *Endeavour* arrived home in 1771. On a return voyage (1772–75), Cook became the first navigator to pierce the Antarctic Circle and circled the globe near its southernmost latitude, demolishing the ancient myth that a vast, populous and fertile continent surrounded the South Pole.

Cook's travels made an enormous contribution to world thought. During his voyages, Cook and his crew took astronomical measurements. Botanists accompanied him on his voyages, diligently recording and studying the flora they encountered. Cook was also remarkable for completing a round-the-world voyage without any of his crew dying of scurvy – adding 'nutrition' to his impressive roster of specialist subjects.

But these achievements exist beneath a long shadow. Cook's travels spurred colonisation of the Pacific, and within a few decades of his death, missionaries, whalers, traders and settlers began transforming (and often devastating) island cultures. As a result, many indigenous people now revile Cook as an imperialist villain who introduced disease, dispossession and other ills to the region (hence the frequent vandalising of Cook monuments). However, as islanders revive traditional crafts and practices, from tattooing to *tapa* (traditional barkcloth), they have turned to the art and writing of Cook and his men as a resource for cultural renewal. Significant geographical features in NZ bear his name, including Aoraki/Mt Cook, Cook Strait and Cook River, along with countless streets and hotels.

For good and ill, a Yorkshire farm boy remains one of the single most significant figures in shaping the modern Pacific.

Māori: the terrible intertribal 'Musket Wars' of 1818–36. Because Northland had the majority of early contact with Europe, its Ngāpuhi tribe acquired muskets first. Under their great general Hongi Hika, Ngāpuhi then raided south, winning bloody victories against tribes without muskets. Once they acquired muskets, these tribes then saw off Ngāpuhi, but also raided further south in their turn. The domino effect continued to the

1860–69	1861	1863–64	1867
The Taranaki wars, starting with the controversial swindling of Māori land by the government at Waitara, and continuing with outrage over the confiscation of more land.	Gold discovered in Otago by Gabriel Read, an Australian prospector. As a result, the population of Otago climbs from less than 13,000 to more than 30,000 in six months.	Waikato Land War. Up to 5000 Māori resist an invasion mounted by 20,000 imperial, colonial and 'friendly' Māori troops. Despite successes, Māori are defeated and much land is confiscated.	All Māori men (rather than individual land owners) are granted the right to vote.

far south of the South Island in 1836. The missionaries claimed that the Musket Wars then tapered off through their influence, but the restoration of the balance of power through the equal distribution of muskets was probably more important.

The Māori population for 1769 has been estimated at between 85,000 and 110,000. The Musket Wars killed perhaps 20,000, and new diseases (including typhoid, tuberculosis and venereal disease) did considerable damage, too. Fortunately NZ had the natural quarantine of distance: infected Europeans often recovered or died during the long voyage, and smallpox, for example, which devastated indigenous North Americans, never arrived. By 1840 Māori had been reduced to about 70,000, a decline of at least 20%. Māori bent under the weight of European contact, but they certainly did not break.

Growing Pains

Māori tribes valued the profit and prestige brought by the Pākehā and wanted both, along with protection from foreign powers. Accepting nominal British authority was the way to get them. New Zealand was appointed its first British Resident, James Busby, in 1833, though his powers were largely symbolic. Busby selected the country's first official flag and established the Declaration of the Independence of New Zealand. But Busby was too ineffectual to curb rampant colonisation.

By 1840 the British government was overcoming its reluctance to undertake potentially expensive intervention in NZ. The British were eager to secure their commercial interests and they also believed, wrongly but sincerely, that Māori could not handle the increasing scale of unofficial European contact. In 1840 the two peoples struck a deal, symbolised by the treaty first signed at Waitangi on 6 February that year. The Treaty of Waitangi now has a standing not dissimilar to that of the Constitution in the US, but is even more contested. The original problem was a discrepancy between British and Māori understandings of it. The English version promised Māori full equality as British subjects in return for complete rights of government. The Māori version also promised that Māori would retain their chieftainship, which implied local rights of government. The problem was not great at first, because the Māori version applied outside the small European settlements. But as those settlements grew, conflict brewed.

In 1840 there were only about 2000 Europeans in NZ, with the shanty town of Kororāreka as the capital and biggest settlement. By 1850 six new settlements had been formed, with 22,000 settlers between them. About half of these had arrived under the auspices of the New Zealand Company and its associates. The company was the brainchild of Edward Gibbon Wakefield, who also influenced the settlement of South Australia. Wakefield hoped to short-circuit the barbarous frontier phase of settle-

'I believe we were all glad to leave New Zealand. It is not a pleasant place. Amongst the natives there is absent that charming simplicity...and the greater part of the English are the very refuse of society.' Charles Darwin, writing about his 1835 visit to Kororāreka (Russell).

The Waitangi Treaty Grounds, where the Treaty of Waitangi was first signed in 1840, is now a tourist attraction for Kiwis and non-Kiwis alike. Each year on 6 February, Waitangi hosts treaty commemorations and protests.

1868–72	1886–87	1893	1901
East Coast war. Te Kooti, having led an escape from his prison on the Chatham Islands, leads a holy guerrilla war in the Urewera region. He finally retreats to establish the Ringatū Church.	Tuwharetoa tribe gifts the mountains of Ruapehu, Ngauruhoe and Tongariro to the government to establish NZ's first national park.	NZ becomes the first country in the world to grant the vote to women, following a campaign led by Kate Sheppard, who petitioned the government for years.	New Zealand politely declines the invitation to join the new Commonwealth of Australia, but thanks for asking.

ment with 'instant civilisation', but his success was limited. From the 1850s his settlers, who included a high proportion of upper-middle-class gentlefolk, were swamped by succeeding waves of immigrants that continued to wash in until the 1880s. These people were part of the great British and Irish diaspora that also populated Australia and much of North America, but the NZ mix was distinctive. Lowland Scots settlers were more prominent in NZ than elsewhere, for example, with the possible exception of parts of Canada. New Zealand's Irish, even the Catholics, tended to come from the north of Ireland. New Zealand's English tended to come from the counties close to London. Small groups of Germans, Scandinavians and Chinese made their way in, though the last faced increasing racial prejudice from the 1880s, when the Pākehā population reached half a million.

Much of the mass immigration from the 1850s to the 1870s was assisted by the provincial and central governments, which also mounted large-scale public works schemes, especially in the 1870s under Julius Vogel. In 1876 Vogel abolished the provinces on the grounds that they were hampering his development efforts. The last imperial governor with substantial power was the talented but machiavellian George Grey, who ended his second governorship in 1868. Thereafter, the governors (governors-general from 1917) were largely just nominal heads of state; the head of government, the premier or prime minister, had more power. The central government, originally weaker than the provincial governments, the imperial governor and the Māori tribes, eventually exceeded the power of all three.

The Māori tribes did not go down without a fight. Indeed, their resistance was one of the most formidable ever mounted against European expansion. The first clash took place in 1843 in the Wairau Valley, now a wine-growing district. A posse of settlers set out to enforce the myth of British control, but encountered the reality of Māori control. Twenty-two settlers were killed, including Wakefield's brother, Arthur, along with about six Māori. In 1845 more serious fighting broke out in the Bay of Islands, when Hōne Heke sacked a British settlement. Heke and his ally Kawiti baffled three British punitive expeditions, using a modern variant of the traditional *pā* fortification. Vestiges of these innovative earthworks can still be seen at Ruapekapeka (south of Kawakawa). Governor Grey claimed victory in the north, but few were convinced at the time. Grey had more success in the south, where he arrested the formidable Ngāti Toa chief Te Rauparaha, who until then wielded great influence on both sides of Cook Strait. Pākehā were able to swamp the few Māori living in the South Island, but the fighting of the 1840s confirmed that the North Island at that time comprised a European fringe around an independent Māori heartland.

In the 1850s settler population and aspirations grew, and fighting broke out again in 1860. The wars burned on sporadically until 1872 over much of the North Island. In the early years the King Movement, seeking

Maurice Shadbolt's *Season of the Jew* (1987) is a semi-fictionalised story of bloody campaigns led by warrior Te Kooti against the British in Poverty Bay in the 1860s. Te Kooti and his followers compared themselves to the Israelites cast out of Egypt. For more about the NZ Wars, visit www.newzealand-wars.co.nz.

'Kaore e mau te rongo – ake, ake!' (Peace never shall be made – never, never!) War chief Rewi Maniapoto in response to government troops at the battle of Orakau, 1864

1908	1914–18	1931	1935–49
NZ physicist Ernest Rutherford is awarded the Nobel Prize in chemistry for 'splitting the atom', investigating the disintegration of elements and the chemistry of radioactive substances.	NZ's contribution to WWI is staggering: for a country of just over one million people, about 100,000 NZ men serve overseas. Some 60,000 become casualties, mostly on the Western Front in France.	A massive earthquake in Napier and Hastings kills at least 256 people.	First Labour government in power, under Michael Joseph Savage. This government creates NZ's pioneering version of the welfare state, and also takes some independent initiatives in foreign policy.

NEW ZEALAND WARS

Starting in Northland and moving throughout the North Island, the New Zealand Wars had many complex causes, but *whenua* (land) was the one common factor. In these conflicts, also referred to as the Land Wars or Māori Wars, Māori fought both for and against the NZ government, on whose side stood the Imperial British Army, Australians and NZ's own Armed Constabulary. Land confiscations imposed on the Māori as punishment for involvement in these wars are still the source of conflict today, with the government struggling to finance compensation for what are now acknowledged to have been illegal seizures.

to establish a monarchy that would allow Māori to assume a more equal footing with the European settlers, was the backbone of resistance. In later years some remarkable prophet-generals, notably Titokowaru and Te Kooti, took over. Most wars were small-scale, but the Waikato war of 1863–64 was not. This conflict, fought at the same time as the American Civil War, involved armoured steamships, ultra-modern heavy artillery, and 10 proud British regular regiments. Despite the odds, Māori forces won several battles, such as that at Gate Pā, near Tauranga, in 1864. But in the end they were ground down by European numbers and resources. Māori political, though not cultural, independence ebbed away in the last decades of the 19th century. It finally expired when police invaded its last sanctuary, the Urewera Mountains, in 1916.

From Golden Rush to Welfare State

From the 1850s to the 1880s, despite conflict with Māori, the Pākehā economy boomed. A gold rush on the South Island made Dunedin NZ's biggest town, and a young, mostly male population chased their fortunes along the West Coast. Fretting over the imbalance in this frontier society, the British government tried to entice women to settle in NZ. Huge amounts of wool were exported and there were unwise levels of overseas borrowing for development of railways and roads. By 1886 the population reached a tipping point: the population of non-Māori people were mostly born in NZ. Many still considered Britain their distant home, but a new identity was taking shape.

Depression followed in 1879, when wool prices slipped and gold production thinned out. Unemployment pushed some of the working population to Australia, and many of those who stayed suffered miserable working conditions. There was still cause for optimism: NZ successfully exported frozen meat in 1882, raising hopes of a new backbone for the economy. Forests were enthusiastically cleared to make way for farmland.

Revered NZ Prime Minister (1893–1906) Richard 'King Dick' Seddon popularised the country's self-proclaimed nickname 'Godzone' with his famous final telegraph: 'Just leaving for God's own country'.

1936	1939–45	1953	1973
NZ aviatrix Jean Batten becomes the first aviator to fly solo directly from Britain to NZ.	NZ troops back Britain and the Allied war effort during WWII; from 1942 as many as 45,000 American soldiers camp in NZ to guard against Japanese attack.	New Zealander Edmund Hillary, with Tenzing Norgay, 'knocks the bastard off'; the pair become the first men to reach the summit of Mt Everest.	Fledgling Kiwi prog-rockers Split Enz enter a TV talent quest...finishing second to last.

In 1890 the Liberals, NZ's first organised political party, came to power. They stayed there until 1912, helped by a recovering economy. For decades, social reform movements such as the Woman's Christian Temperance Union (WCTU) had lobbied for women's freedom, and NZ became the first country in the world to give women the vote in 1893. (Another major WCTU push, for countrywide prohibition, didn't take off.) Old-age pensions were introduced in 1898 but these social leaps forward didn't bring universal good news. Pensions only applied for those falling within a very particular definition of 'good character', and the pension reforms deliberately excluded the population of Chinese settlers who had arrived to labour in the goldfields. Meanwhile, the Liberals were obtaining more and more Māori land for settlement. By now, the non-Māori population outnumbered the Māori by 17 to one.

Nation-Building

New Zealand had backed Britain in the Boer War (1899–1902) and WWI (1914–18), with dramatic losses in WWI. However, the bravery of ANZAC (Australian and New Zealander Army Corps) forces in the failed Gallipoli campaign endures as a nation-building moment for NZ. In the 1930s NZ's experience of the Great Depression was as grim as any. The derelict farmhouses still seen in rural areas often date from this era. In 1935 a second reforming government took office, campaigning on a platform of social justice: the First Labour government, led by Australian-born Michael Joseph Savage. In WWII NZ formally declared war on Germany: 140,000 or so New Zealanders fought in Europe and the Middle East, while at home, women took on increasing roles in the labour force.

By the 1930s giant ships were regularly carrying frozen meat, cheese and butter, as well as wool, on regular voyages from NZ to Britain. As the NZ economy adapted to the feeding of London, cultural links were also enhanced. New Zealand children studied British history and literature, not their own. New Zealand's leading scientists and writers, such as Ernest Rutherford and Katherine Mansfield, gravitated to Britain. Average living standards in NZ were normally better than in Britain, as were the welfare and lower-level education systems. New Zealanders had access to British markets and culture, and they contributed their share to the latter as equals. The list of 'British' writers, academics, scientists, military leaders, publishers and the like who were actually New Zealanders is long.

New Zealand prided itself on its affluence, equality and social harmony. But it was also conformist, even puritanical. The 1953 Marlon Brando movie, *The Wild One*, was banned until 1977. Full Sunday trading was not allowed until 1989. Licensed restaurants hardly existed in 1960, nor did supermarkets or TV. Notoriously, from 1917 to 1967, pubs were obliged to shut at 6pm (which, ironically, paved the way for a culture of fast,

Wellington-born Nancy Wake (codenamed 'The White Mouse') led a guerrilla attack against the Nazis with a 7000-strong army. Her honours included being the Gestapo's most wanted person and a highly decorated Allied servicewoman, and she was memorialised as 'the socialite who killed a Nazi with her bare hands'.

1974	1981	1985	1992
Pacific Island migrants who have outstayed visas (dubbed 'overstayers') are subjected to Dawn Raids (crackdowns by immigration police). These raids continue until the early 1980s.	South Africa's Springbok rugby tour divides the nation. Many New Zealanders show a strong anti-apartheid stance by protesting the games. Other Kiwis feel that sport and politics should not mix, and support the tour.	*Rainbow Warrior* sunk in Auckland Harbour by French agents to prevent the Greenpeace protest ship from making its intended voyage to Moruroa, where the French government is conducting nuclear tests.	Government begins reparations for land confiscated in the Land Wars, and confirms Māori fishing rights in the 'Sealord deal'. Major settlements of historical confiscation follow.

heavy drinking before closing time). Yet puritanism was never the whole story. Opposition to Sunday trading stemmed not so much from belief in the sanctity of the sabbath, but from the belief that workers should have weekends, too. Six o'clock closing was a standing joke in rural areas. There was always something of a Kiwi counterculture, even before imported countercultures took root from the 1960s onward.

Scottish influence can still be felt in NZ, particularly in the south of the South Island. New Zealand has more Scottish pipe bands per capita than Scotland itself.

In 1973 'Mother England' ran off and joined the budding EU. New Zealand was beginning to develop alternative markets to Britain, and alternative exports to wool, meat and dairy products. Wide-bodied jet aircraft were allowing the world and NZ to visit each other on an increasing scale. Women were beginning to penetrate first the upper reaches of the workforce and then the political sphere. Gay people came out of the closet, despite vigorous efforts by moral conservatives to push them back in. University-educated youths were becoming more numerous and more assertive.

The Modern Age

From the 1930s, Māori experienced both a population explosion and massive urbanisation. Life expectancy was lengthening, the birth rate was high, and Māori were moving to cities for occupations formerly filled by Pākehā servicemen. Almost 80% of Māori were urban dwellers by 1986, a staggering reversal of the status quo that brought cultural displacement but simultaneously triggered a movement to strengthen pride in Māori identity. Immigration was broadening, too, first allowing in Pacific Islanders for their labour, and then (East) Asians for their money.

In 2015 there was a public referendum to decide between five proposed designs for a new national flag, and the winner was a black- and blue-backed silver fern. During a second referendum in 2016, Kiwis decided that on reflection, they preferred the original flag – if it ain't broke...

Then, in 1984, NZ's next great reforming government was elected – the Fourth Labour government, led nominally by David Lange, and in fact by Roger Douglas, the Minister of Finance. This government adopted a more-market economic policy (dubbed 'Rogernomics'), delighting the right, and an anti-nuclear foreign policy, delighting the left. New Zealand's numerous economic controls were dismantled with breakneck speed. Middle NZ was uneasy about the anti-nuclear policy, which threatened NZ's ANZUS alliance with Australia and the US. But in 1985 French spies sank the anti-nuclear protest ship *Rainbow Warrior* in Auckland Harbour, killing one crewman. The lukewarm American condemnation of the French act brought middle NZ in behind the anti-nuclear policy, which became associated with national independence. Other New Zealanders were uneasy about the more-market economic policy, but failed to come up with a convincing alternative. Revelling in their new freedom, NZ investors engaged in a frenzy of speculation, and suffered even more than the rest of the world from the economic crash of 1987.

From the 1990s, a change to points-based immigration was weaving an increasingly multicultural tapestry in NZ. Numbers of incoming Brits

1995	2004	2010	2011
Peter Blake and Russell Coutts win the America's Cup for NZ, sailing Black Magic; red socks become a matter of national pride.	Māori TV begins broadcasting – for the first time a channel committed to NZ content and the revitalisation of Māori language and culture hits the small screen.	A cave-in at Pike River coalmine on the South Island's West Coast kills 29 miners.	A severe earthquake strikes Christchurch, killing 185 people and badly damaging the central business district.

THE CANTERBURY EARTHQUAKES

Christchurch's seismic nightmare began at 4.35am on 4 September 2010. Centred 40km west of the city, a 40-second, 7.1-magnitude earthquake jolted Cantabrians from their sleep, and caused widespread damage to older buildings in the central city. Close to the quake's epicentre in rural Darfield, huge gashes erupted amid grassy pastures, and the South Island's main railway line was bent and buckled. Because the tremor struck in the early hours of the morning when most people were home in bed, there were no fatalities, and many Christchurch residents felt that the city had dodged a bullet.

Fast-forward to 12.51pm on 22 February 2011, when central Christchurch was busy with shoppers and workers enjoying their lunch break. This time the 6.3-magnitude quake was much closer, centred just 10km southeast of the city and only 5km deep. The tremor was significantly greater, and many locals report being flung violently and almost vertically into the air. The peak ground acceleration exceeded 1.8g, almost twice the acceleration of gravity.

In 24 traumatic seconds, NZ's second-largest city had changed forever. The towering spire of the iconic ChristChurch Cathedral lay in ruins; walls and verandahs had cascaded down on shopping strips; and two multistorey buildings had pancaked. Of the 185 deaths (across 20 nationalities), 115 occurred in the six-storey Canterbury TV building, where many international students at a language school were killed. Elsewhere, the historic port town of Lyttelton was badly damaged; roads and bridges were crumpled; and residential suburbs in the east were inundated as a process of rapid liquefaction saw tons of oozy silt rise from the ground.

In the months that followed literally hundreds of aftershocks rattled the city's traumatised residents (and claimed one more life), but the resilience and bravery of Cantabrians quickly became evident. From the region's rural heartland, the 'Farmy Army' descended on the city, armed with shovels and food hampers. Social media mobilised 10,000 students, and the Student Volunteer Army became a vital force for residential clean-ups in the city's beleaguered eastern suburbs.

fell but new arrivals increased, particularly from Asia but also from North Africa, the Middle East and various European countries. By 2006 more than 9% of the population was Asian.

By 2017 NZ had a new face to the world. Helmed by Jacinda Ardern, a coalition government was formed by Labour and NZ First, with support from the Green Party. New Zealand's third woman prime minister is faced with a balancing act between her governing parties while tackling the housing crisis and effecting bigger investment in education and health. It's no wonder that Ardern's ascendancy has been touted as the dawn of a new period of major reform.

The Ministry for Culture & Heritage's history website (www. nzhistory.net.nz) is an excellent source of info on NZ history.

2011	2013	2013	2015
NZ hosts and wins the Rugby World Cup for just the second time; brave France succumbs 8-7 in the final.	New Zealand becomes one of just 15 countries in the world to legally recognise same-sex marriage.	Auckland teenager Ella Yelich-O'Connor, aka Lorde, hits No 1 on international music charts with her mesmeric, chant-like tune 'Royals'.	New Zealand's beloved All Blacks win back-to-back Rugby World Cups in England, defeating arch-rivals Australia 34-17 in the final.

Environment

New Zealand's landforms have a diversity that you would expect to find across an entire continent: snow-dusted mountains, drowned glacial valleys, rainforests, dunelands and an otherworldly volcanic plateau. Straddling the boundary of two great colliding slabs of the earth's crust – the Pacific plate and the Indian/Australian plate – NZ is a plaything for nature's strongest forces.

The Land

New Zealand is a young country – its present shape is less than 10,000 years old. Having broken away from the supercontinent of Gondwanaland (which included Africa, Australia, Antarctica and South America) some 85 million years ago, it endured continual uplift and erosion, buckling and tearing, and the slow fall and rise of the sea as ice ages came and went.

Evidence of NZ's tumultuous past is everywhere. The South Island's mountainous spine – the 650km-long ranges of the Southern Alps – grew from the clash between plates at a rate of 20km over three million years... in geological terms, that's a sprint. Despite NZ's highest peak, Aoraki/Mt Cook, losing 10m from its summit overnight in a 1991 landslide (and a couple of dozen more metres to erosion), the Alps are overall believed to be some of the fastest-growing mountains in the world.

Volcanic New Zealand

The North Island's most impressive landscapes have been wrought by volcanoes. Auckland is built on an isthmus peppered by some 48 scoria cones (cinder cones, or volcanic vents). The city's biggest and most recently formed volcano, 600-year-old Rangitoto Island, is a short ferry ride from the downtown wharves. Some 300km further south, the classically shaped cone of snowcapped Mt Taranaki overlooks tranquil dairy pastures.

But the real volcanic heartland runs through the centre of the North Island, from the restless bulk of Mt Ruapehu in Tongariro National Park, northeast through the Rotorua lake district out to NZ's most active volcano, White Island, in the Bay of Plenty. Called the Taupo Volcanic Zone, this great 350km-long rift valley – part of a volcano chain known as the 'Pacific Ring of Fire' – has been the seat of massive eruptions that have left their mark on the country physically and culturally. The volcano that created Lake Taupo last erupted 1800 years ago in a display that was the most violent anywhere on the planet within the past 5000 years.

You can experience the aftermath of volcanic destruction on a smaller scale at Te Wairoa (the Buried Village) (p321), near Rotorua on the shores of Lake Tarawera. Here, partly excavated and open to the public, lie the remains of a 19th-century Māori village overwhelmed when nearby Mt Tarawera erupted without warning. The famous Pink and White Terraces, spectacular naturally formed pools (and one of several claimants to the title 'eighth wonder of the world'), were destroyed overnight by the same upheaval.

New Zealand is one of the most spectacular places in the world to see geysers. Rotorua's short-lived Waimangu geyser, formed after the 1886 Mt Tarawera eruption, was once the world's largest, often gushing to a dizzying height of 400m.

Born of geothermal violence, Waimangu Volcanic Valley (p319) is the place to go to experience hot earth up close and personal amid geysers, silica pans, bubbling mud pools and the world's biggest hot spring. Alternatively, wander around Rotorua's Whakarewarewa village (p308), where descendants of Māori displaced by the eruption live in the middle of steaming vents and prepare food for visitors in boiling pools.

The South Island can also see some evidence of volcanism – if the remains of the old volcanoes of Banks Peninsula weren't there to repel the sea, the vast Canterbury Plains, built from alpine sediment washed down the rivers from the Alps, would have eroded long ago.

Earthquakes

Not for nothing has New Zealand been called 'the Shaky Isles'. Earthquakes are common, but most only rattle the glassware. A few have wrecked major towns. In 1931 an earthquake measuring 7.9 on the Richter scale levelled the Hawke's Bay city of Napier, causing huge damage and loss of life. Napier was rebuilt almost entirely in then-fashionable art-deco architectural style.

Over on the South Island, in September 2010 Christchurch was rocked by a magnitude 7.1 earthquake. Less than six months later, in February 2011, a magnitude 6.3 quake destroyed much of the city's historic heart and claimed 185 lives, making it the country's second-deadliest natural disaster. Then in November 2016 an earthquake measuring 7.8 on the Richter scale struck Kaikoura – further up the coast – resulting in two deaths and widespread damage to local infrastructure.

Flora & Fauna

New Zealand's long isolation has allowed it to become a veritable warehouse of unique and varied plants. Separation of NZ's landmass occurred before mammals appeared on the scene, leaving birds and insects to evolve in spectacular ways. As one of the last places on earth to be colonised by humans, NZ was for millennia a safe laboratory for risky evolutionary strategies. But the arrival of Māori, and later Europeans, brought new threats and sometimes extinction.

The now-extinct flightless moa, the largest of which grew to 3.5m tall and weighed more than 200kg, browsed open grasslands much as cattle do today (skeletons can be seen at Auckland Museum), while the smaller kiwi still ekes out a nocturnal living rummaging among forest leaf litter for insects and worms. One of the country's most ferocious-looking insects, the mouse-sized giant weta, meanwhile, has taken on a scavenging role elsewhere filled by rodents.

Many endemic creatures, including moa and the huia, an exquisite songbird, were driven to extinction, and the vast forests were cleared for timber and to make way for agriculture. Destruction of habitat and the introduction of exotic animals and plants have taken a terrible environmental toll – and New Zealanders are now fighting a rearguard battle to save what remains.

NEW ZEALAND'S ANCIENT LIZARD

The largest native reptile in NZ is the tuatara, a crested lizard that can grow up to 50cm long. Thought to be unchanged for more than 220 million years, these endearing creatures can live for up to a century. Meet them at **Auckland Zoo** (p75), and other zoos and sanctuaries around NZ.

Birds & Bats

Pause in any NZ forest and listen: this country is aflutter with melodious feathered creatures. The country's first Polynesian settlers found little in the way of land mammals – just two species of bat – and most of NZ's present mammals are introduced species. NZ's birds generally aren't flashy, but they have an understated beauty that reveals itself in more delicate details: the lacy plumage of the rare white heron (kōtuku), the bespectacled appearance of a silvereye, or the golden frowns of Fiordland penguins.

The most beautiful songbird is the tui, a nectar-eater with an inventive repertoire that includes clicks, grunts and chuckles. Notable for the white throat feathers that stand out against its dark plumage, the tui often feeds on flax flowers in suburban gardens but is most at home in densely tangled forest ('bush' to New Zealanders). The bellbird (korimako) is also musical; it's common in both native and exotic forests everywhere except Northland (though it is more likely to be heard than seen). Its call is a series of liquid bell notes, most often sounded at dawn or dusk. Fantails (pīwakawaka) are also common on forest trails, swooping and jinking to catch insects stirred up by passing hikers.

At ground level, the most famous native bird is of course the kiwi, NZ's national emblem, with a rounded body and a long, distinctive bill with nostrils at the tip for sniffing out food. Sightings in the wild require patience and luck but numerous sanctuaries allow a peep of this iconic bird. Look out for other land birds like pukeko, elegant swamp-hens with blue plumage and bright-red beaks. They're readily seen along wetland margins and even on the sides of roads nearby – be warned, they have little road sense. Far rarer (though not dissimilar in appearance) is the takahe, a flightless bird thought extinct until a small colony was discovered in 1948.

And what of the native bats? Populations of both short-tailed and long-tailed bats are declining at frightening speed. DOC is hard at work to protect bats, including ambitious plans to resettle them on predator-free islands. If you spot a bat, count yourself lucky – and consider telling DOC.

B Heather and H Robertson's *Field Guide to the Birds of New Zealand* is a comprehensive guide for bird-watchers and a model of helpfulness for anyone even casually interested in the country's remarkable bird life. Another good guide is *Birds of New Zealand: Locality Guide* by Stuart Chambers.

Trees

No visitor to NZ (particularly Australians) can last long without hearing about the damage done to the bush by that bad-mannered Australian import, the brushtail possum. The long list of mammal pests introduced to NZ, whether accidentally or for a variety of misguided reasons, includes deer, rabbits, stoats, pigs and goats. But by far the most destructive is the possum. At their height, 70 million possums were chewing through millions of tonnes of foliage a year. Following efforts by the DOC to control their numbers, the possum population has almost halved but they remain an enormous threat to native flora (and to bird life...possums prey on chicks and eggs).

Among favoured possum food is the colourful kowhai, a small-leaved tree growing to 11m, which in spring has drooping clusters of bright-yellow flowers (informally considered NZ's national flower); the pohutukawa, a beautiful coastal tree of the northern North Island that bursts into vivid red flower in December, earning the nickname 'Christmas tree'; and a similar crimson-flowered tree, the rata. Rata species are found on both islands; the northern rata starts life as a climber on a host tree (that it eventually chokes).

The few remaining pockets of mature centuries-old kauri are stately emblems of former days. Their vast trunks and towering, epiphyte-fes-

KAURI DIEBACK

Saved from the lumberjacks, the kauri are now under threat from a fungus-like disease known as kauri dieback, which has killed thousands of the trees. Visitors to areas where kauri grow need to do their bit to prevent the spread of spores, which infect the roots of the trees. Clean all your gear and stay on tracks. Keep well away from kauri tree roots. Any footwear or equipment that comes into contact with soil should be cleaned both before and after you leave the area. See www.kauridieback.co.nz for more information.

tooned limbs reach well over 50m high, reminders of why they were sought after in colonial days for spars and building timber. The best place to see the remaining giants is Northland's Waipoua Forest (p176), home to the largest swath of kauri in the country. These mighty trees are under threat from fungus-like kauri dieback disease, so be diligent about following signs that direct you to clean your boots to stem the disease's spread.

Other native timber trees include the distinctive rimu (red pine) and the long-lived totara (favoured for Māori war canoes). NZ's perfect pine-growing conditions encouraged one of the country's most successful imports, *Pinus radiata,* which grow to maturity in 35 years (and sometimes less). Plantation forests are now widespread through the central North Island – the southern hemisphere's biggest, Kaingaroa Forest, lies southeast of Rotorua.

You won't get far into the bush without coming across tree ferns. NZ has an impressive 200 species of ferns, and almost half grow nowhere else on the planet. Most easily recognised are the mamaku (black tree fern) – which grows to 20m and can be seen in damp gullies throughout the country – and the 10m-high ponga (silver tree fern) with its distinctive white underside. The silver fern is a national symbol and adorns sporting and corporate logos, as well as shop signs, clothing and jewellery.

Nature Guide to the New Zealand Forest by J Dawson and R Lucas is a beautifully photographed foray into NZ's forests, home to ancient species dating from the time of the dinosaurs.

National Parks

More than 85,000 sq km of NZ – almost one-third of the country – is protected and managed within parks and reserves. Almost every conceivable landscape is present: from mangrove-fringed inlets in the north to the snow-topped volcanoes of the Central Plateau, and from the forested fastness of the Urewera ranges in the east to the Southern Alps' majestic mountains, glaciers and fiords. The 13 national parks and more than 30 marine reserves and parks, along with numerous forest parks, offer huge scope for wilderness experiences, ranging from climbing, skiing and mountain biking to tramping, kayaking and trout fishing.

Three places are World Heritage Areas: NZ's Subantarctic Islands, Tongariro National Park and Te Wāhipounamu (Southwest New Zealand), an amalgam of several national parks in southwest NZ that boast the world's finest surviving Gondwanaland plants and animals in their natural habitats.

Access to the country's wild places is relatively straightforward, though huts on walking tracks require passes and may need to be booked in advance. In practical terms, there is little difference for travellers between a national park and a forest park, though pets are generally not allowed in national parks without a permit. Disability-assist dogs can be taken into dog-controlled areas without a permit. Camping is possible in all parks, but may be restricted to dedicated camping grounds – check with DOC first.

Environmental Issues

New Zealand's reputation as an Eden, replete with pristine wilderness and eco-friendly practices, has been repeatedly placed under the microscope. The industry most visible to visitors, tourism, appears studded in green accolades, with environmental best practices employed in areas as broad as heating insulation in hotels to minimum-impact wildlife-watching. But mining, offshore oil and gas exploration, pollution, biodiversity loss, conservation funding cuts and questionable urban planning have provided endless hooks for bad-news stories.

Water quality is arguably the most serious environmental issue faced by New Zealanders. More than a quarter of the country's lakes and rivers have been deemed unsafe for swimming, and research from diverse sources confirms that the health of waterways is in decline. The primary culprit is 'dirty dairying' – cow effluent leaching into freshwater ecosystems, carrying with it high levels of nitrates, as well as bacteria and parasites such as E. coli and giardia. A 2017 report by the Ministry for the Environment and Statistics showed that nitrate levels in water were worsening at 55% of monitored river sites, and that urban waterways were in an especially dire state – with levels of harmful bacteria more than 20 times higher than in forest areas. A government push to make 90% of rivers and lakes swimmable by 2040 was met with initial scepticism about the metrics involved, but it's hoped that it will provide an impetus to make NZ's waterways worthy of the country's eco-conscious reputation.

The Department of Conservation website (www. doc.govt.nz) has useful information on the country's national parks, tracks and walkways. It also lists backcountry huts and campsites.

Another ambitious initiative is Predator Free 2050, which aims to rid NZ of introduced animals that prey on native flora and fauna. The worst offenders are possums, stoats and rats, which eat swaths of forest and kill wildlife, particularly birds. Controversy rages at the Department of Conservation's (DOC) use of 1080 poison (sodium fluoroacetate) to control these pests, despite it being sanctioned by prominent environmental groups, such as Forest & Bird, as well as the Parliamentary Commissioner for the Environment. Vehement opposition to 1080 is expressed by such diverse camps as hunters and animal-rights activists, who cite detriments such as by-kill and the potential for poison passing into waterways. Proponents of its use argue that it's biodegradable and that aerial distribution of 1080 is the only cost-effective way to target predators across vast, inaccessible parts of NZ. Still, 'Ban 1080' signs remain common in rural communities and the controversy is likely to continue.

As well as its damaging impact on NZ waterways, the $12 billion dairy industry – NZ's biggest export earner – generates 48% of NZ's greenhouse gas emissions. Some farmers are cleaning up their act, lowering emissions through improved management of fertilisers and higher-quality feed, and major players DairyNZ and Fonterra have pledged support. But when it comes to contributing to climate change, the dairy industry isn't NZ's only dirty habit. New Zealand might be a nation of avid recyclers and solar-panel enthusiasts, but it also has the world's fourth-highest ratio of motor vehicles to people.

There have been fears about safeguarding the principal legislation governing the NZ environment, the 1991 Resource Management Act, in the face of proposed amendments. NGOs and community groups – ever-vigilant and already making major contributions to the welfare of NZ's environment – will find plenty to keep them occupied in coming years. But with eco-conscious Jacinda Ardern leading a coalition government from 2017, New Zealanders have reason to be hopeful of a greener future – Ardern has pledged an ambitious goal of reducing net greenhouse gas emissions to zero by 2050. More trains, 100% renewable energy sources and planting 100 million trees per year...goals worthy of NZ's clean, green reputation.

Māori Culture

'Māori' once just meant 'common' or 'everyday', but Māori today are a diverse people. Some are engaged with traditional cultural networks and pursuits; others are occupied with adapting tradition and placing it into a dialogue with globalising culture.

People of the Land

Māori are New Zealand's *tangata whenua* (people of the land), and the Māori relationship with the land has developed over hundreds of years of occupation. Once a predominantly rural people, many Māori now live in urban centres, away from their traditional home base. But it's still common practice in formal settings to introduce oneself by referring to home: an ancestral mountain, river, sea or lake, or an ancestor.

The Māori concept of *whanaungatanga* – family relationships – is central to the culture: families spread out from the *whānau* (extended family) to the *hapū* (subtribe) and *iwi* (tribe) and even, in a sense, beyond the human world and into the natural and spiritual worlds.

If you're looking for a Māori experience in NZ you'll find it – in performance, in conversation, in an art gallery, on a tour...

> The best way to learn about the relationship between the land and the *tangata whenua* (people of the land) is to get out there and start talking with Māori.

Māori Then

Some three millennia ago people began moving eastward into the Pacific, sailing against the prevailing winds and currents (hard to go out, easier to return safely). Some stopped at Tonga and Samoa, and others settled the small central East Polynesian tropical islands.

The Māori colonisation of Aotearoa began from an original homeland known to Māori as Hawaiki. Skilled navigators and sailors travelled across the Pacific, using many navigational tools – currents, winds, stars, birds and wave patterns – to guide their large, double-hulled ocean-going craft to a new land. The first of many was the great navigator Kupe, who arrived, the story goes, chasing a giant octopus named Muturangi. But the distinction of giving NZ its well-known Māori name – Aotearoa – goes to his wife, Kuramarotini, who cried out, '*He ao, he ao tea, he ao tea roa!*' (A cloud, a white cloud, a long white cloud!).

Kupe and his crew journeyed around the land, and many places around Cook Strait (between the North and South Islands) and the Hokianga in Northland still bear the names that the crew gave them and the marks of their passage. Kupe returned to Hawaiki, leaving from (and naming) Northland's Hokianga. He gave other seafarers valuable navigational information. And then the great *waka* (ocean-going craft) began to arrive.

The *waka* that the first settlers arrived on, and their landing places, are immortalised in tribal histories. Well-known *waka* include *Tākitimu, Kurahaupō, Te Arawa, Mataatua, Tainui, Aotea* and *Tokomaru*. There are many others. Māori trace their genealogies back to those who arrived on the *waka* (and further back as well).

What would it have been like making the transition from small tropical islands to a much larger, cooler land mass? Goodbye breadfruit, coconuts,

> Kupe's passage is marked around NZ: he left his sails (Nga Ra o Kupe) near Cape Palliser as triangular landforms; he named the two islands in Wellington Harbour Matiu and Makoro after his daughters; his blood stains the red rocks of Wellington's south coast.

paper mulberry; hello moa, fernroot, flax – and immense space (relatively speaking). New Zealand has more than 15,000km of coastline. Rarotonga, by way of contrast, has a little over 30km. There was land, lots of it, and a flora and fauna that had developed more or less separately from the rest of the world for 80 million years. There was an untouched, massive fishery. There were great seaside mammalian convenience stores – seals and sea lions – as well as a fabulous array of birds.

The early settlers went on the move, pulled by love, trade opportunities and greater resources; pushed by disputes and threats to security. When they settled, Māori established *mana whenua* (regional authority), whether by military campaigns, or by the peaceful methods of intermarriage and diplomacy. Looking over tribal history it's possible to see the many alliances, absorptions and extinctions that went on.

Histories were carried by the voice, in stories, songs and chants. Great stress was placed on accurate learning – after all, in an oral culture where people are the libraries, the past is always a generation or two away from oblivion.

Māori lived in *kainga* (small villages), which often had associated gardens. Housing was quite cosy by modern standards – often it was hard to stand upright while inside. From time to time people would leave their home base and go to harvest seasonal foods. When peaceful life was interrupted by conflict, the people would withdraw to *pā* (fortified dwelling places).

And then Europeans began to arrive.

Arriving for the first time in NZ, two crew members of *Tainui* saw the red flowers of the pohutukawa tree, and they cast away their prized red feather ornaments, thinking that there were plenty to be had on shore.

Māori Today

Today's culture is marked by new developments in the arts, business, sport and politics. Many historical grievances still stand, but some *iwi* (Ngāi Tahu and Tainui, for example) have settled major historical grievances and are significant forces in the NZ economy. Māori have also addressed the decline in Māori language use by establishing *kōhanga reo, kura kaupapa Māori* and *wānanga* (Māori-language preschools, schools and universities). There is now a generation of people who speak Māori as a first language. There is a network of Māori radio stations, and Māori TV attracts a committed viewership. A recently revived Māori event is becoming more and more prominent – Matariki (Māori New Year). The constellation Matariki is also known as the Pleiades. It begins to rise above the horizon in late May or early June and its appearance traditionally signals a time for learning, planning and preparing as well as singing, dancing and celebrating. Watch out for talks and lectures, concerts, dinners and even formal balls.

Māori legends are all around you as you tour NZ: Maui's *waka* became today's Southern Alps; a *taniwha* (legendary water being) formed Lake Waikaremoana in its death throes; and a rejected Mt Taranaki walked into exile from the central North Island mountain group, carving the Whanganui River.

Religion

Christian churches and denominations are prominent in the Māori world, including televangelists, mainstream churches for regular and occasional worship, and two major Māori churches (Ringatū and Rātana). But in the (non-Judeo-Christian) beginning there were the *atua Māori,* the Māori gods, and for many Māori the gods are a vital and relevant force still. It is common to greet the earth mother and sky father when speaking formally at a *marae* (meeting house). The gods are represented in art and carving, sung of in *waiata* (songs), invoked through *karakia* (prayer and incantation) when a meeting house is opened, when a *waka* is launched, even (more simply) when a meal is served. They are spoken of in the *marae* and in wider Māori contexts. The traditional Māori creation story is well known and widely celebrated.

VISITING MARAE (TRADITIONAL MEETING PLACES)

As you travel around NZ, you will see many *marae* complexes. Often *marae* are owned by a descent group. They are also owned by urban Māori groups, schools, universities and church groups, and they should only be visited by arrangement with the owners. Some *marae* that may be visited with an invitation include: **Koriniti Marae** (Map p262; ☑021 115 1256; www.wrmtb.co.nz; Koriniti Pa Rd; ☺9am-5pm) **FREE** on the Whanganui River Rd; **Mataatua** (p337) in Whakatane; and the *marae* at **Te Papa museum** (p393) in Wellington.

Marae complexes include a *wharenui* (meeting house), which often embodies an ancestor. Its ridge is the backbone, the rafters are ribs, and it shelters the descendants. There is a clear space in front of the *wharenui*, the *marae ātea*. Sometimes there are other buildings: a *wharekai* (dining hall); a toilet and shower block; perhaps even classrooms, play equipment and the like.

Hui (gatherings) are held at *marae*. Issues are discussed, classes conducted, milestones celebrated and the dead farewelled. Te reo Māori (the Māori language) is prominent, and sometimes the only language used.

Visitors sleep in the meeting house if a *hui* goes on for longer than a day. Mattresses are placed on the floor, someone may bring a guitar, and stories and jokes always go down well as the evening stretches out...

The Powhiri

If you visit a *marae* as part of an organised group, you'll be welcomed in a *pōwhiri*.

Outside the *marae,* there may be a *wero* (challenge). Using *taiaha* (quarter-staff) moves, a warrior will approach the visitors and place a baton on the ground for a visitor to pick up, to demonstrate their peaceful intent.

There is a *karanga* (ceremonial call). A woman from the host group calls to the visitors and a woman from the visitors responds. Their long, high, falling calls begin to overlap and interweave and the visiting group walks on to the *marae ātea* (meeting house courtyard). It is then time for *whaikōrero* (speechmaking). The hosts welcome the visitors, the visitors respond. Speeches are capped off by a *waiata* (song), and the visitors' speakers present a *koha* (gift, usually an envelope of cash). The hosts then invite the visitors to *hariru* (shake hands) and *hongi*. Visitors and hosts are now united and will share light refreshments or a meal.

The Hongi

Press forehead and nose together firmly, shake hands, and perhaps offer a greeting such as *'Kia ora'* or *'Tēnā koe'*. Some prefer one press (for two or three seconds, or longer), others prefer two shorter (press, release, press). Men and women sometimes kiss on one cheek. Some people mistakenly think the *hongi* is a pressing of noses only (awkward to aim!) or the rubbing of noses (even more awkward).

Tapu

Tapu (spiritual restrictions) and *mana* (power and prestige) are taken seriously in the Māori world. Sit on chairs or seating provided (never on tables), and walk around people, not over them. The *pōwhiri* is *tapu,* and mixing food and *tapu* is right up there on the offence-o-meter. Do eat and drink when invited to do so by your hosts. You needn't worry about starvation: an important Māori value is *manaakitanga* (kindness).

Depending on area, the *pōwhiri* has gender roles: women *karanga* (call), men *whaikōrero* (orate); women lead the way on to the *marae,* men sit on the *paepae* (the speakers' bench at the front). In a modern context, the debate around these roles continues.

HOW THE WORLD BEGAN

In the Māori story of creation, first there was the void, then the night, then Ranginui (sky father) and Papatūānuku (earth mother) came into being, embracing with their children nurtured between them. But nurturing became something else. Their children were stifled in the darkness of their embrace. Unable to stretch out to their full dimensions and struggling to see clearly in the darkness, their children tried to separate them. Tāwhirimātea, the god of winds, raged against them; Tūmatauenga, the god of war, assaulted them. Each god child in turn tried to separate them, but still Rangi and Papa pressed against each other. And then Tāne Mahuta, god of the great forests and of humanity, placed his feet against his father and his back against his mother and slowly, inexorably, began to move them apart. Then came the world of light, of demigods and humanity.

In this world of light Māui, the demigod ancestor, was cast out to sea at birth and was found floating in his mother's topknot. He was a shape-shifter, becoming a pigeon or a dog or an eel if it suited his purposes. He stole fire from the gods. Using his grandmother's jawbone, he bashed the sun so that it could only limp slowly across the sky, so that people would have enough time during the day to get things done (if only he would do it again!). Using the South Island as a canoe, he used the jawbone as a hook to fish up Te Ika-a-Māui (the fish of Māui) – the North Island. And, finally, he met his end trying to defeat death itself. The goddess of death, Hine-nui-te-pō, had obsidian teeth in her vagina (obsidian is a volcanic glass that takes a razor edge when chipped). Māui attempted to reverse birth (and hence defeat death) by crawling into her birth canal to reach her heart as she slept. A small bird – a fantail – laughed at the absurd sight. Hine-nui-te-pō awoke, and crushed Māui to death between her thighs. Death one, humanity nil.

The Arts

There are many collections of Māori *taonga* (treasures) around the country. Some of the largest and most comprehensive are at Wellington's Te Papa museum (p393) and the Auckland Museum (p73).

For information on Māori arts today, check out Toi Māori at www. maoriart.org.nz.

You can stay up to date with what's happening in the Māori arts by listening to *iwi* stations (www.irirangi.net) or tuning into Māori TV (www. maoritelevision.com) for regular features on the Māori arts. Māori TV went to air in 2004, an emotional time for many Māori who could at last see their culture, their concerns and their language in a mass medium. More than 90% of content is NZ-made, and programs are in both Māori and English: they're subtitled and accessible to everyone. If you want to really get a feel for the rhythm and meter of spoken Māori from the comfort of your own chair, switch to Te Reo (www.maoritelevision.com/tv/te-reo-channel), a Māori-language channel.

At the time of research, production of Māori lifestyle magazine *Mana* (www.manaonline.co.nz) had stopped, but there were hopes of a relaunch down the line.

See Ngahuia Te Awekotuku's book *Mau Moko: The World of Māori Tattoo* (2007) for a close-up of Māori body art, including powerful, beautiful images and an incisive commentary.

Tā Moko

Tā moko is the Māori art of tattoo, traditionally worn by men on their faces, thighs and buttocks, and by women on their chins and lips. *Moko* were permanent grooves tapped into the skin using pigment (made from burnt caterpillar or kauri gum soot) and bone chisels (fine, sharp combs for broad work, and straight blades for detailed work). Auckland Museum (p73) and Wellington's Te Papa (p393) both display traditional implements for *tā moko*.

The modern tattooist's gun is common now, but bone chisels are coming back into use for Māori who want to reconnect with tradition. Since the general renaissance in Māori culture in the 1960s, many artists have taken up *tā moko* and now many Māori wear *moko* with quiet pride and humility.

Can visitors get some work done? The art of *tā moko* is learnt by, and inked upon, Māori people – but the term *kirituhi* (skin inscriptions) has arisen to describe Māori-motif-inspired modern tattoos that non-Māori can wear. *Kirituhi* can be profoundly meaningful and designed to fit the wearer's personal story, but there's an important line in the sand between *kirituhi* and *tā moko*.

Whakairo

Traditional Māori carving, with its intricate detailing and curved lines, can transport the viewer. It's quite amazing to consider that it was done with stone tools, themselves painstakingly made, until the advent of iron (nails suddenly became very popular).

Some major traditional forms are *waka* (canoes), *pātaka* (storage buildings) and *wharenui* (meeting houses). You can see sublime examples of traditional carving at Te Papa (p393) in Wellington, and at the following:

➡ Auckland Museum (p73) Māori Court.

➡ Hell's Gate (p321) Workshop where you can try your hand at woodcarving; near Rotorua.

➡ Putiki Church (p256) Interior covered in carvings and *tukutuku* (wall panels); Whanganui.

➡ Taupō Museum (p277) Carved meeting house.

➡ Te Manawa (p265) Museum with a Māori focus; Palmerston North.

➡ Waikato Museum (p212) Beautifully carved *waka taua* (war canoe); Hamilton.

➡ Wairakei Terraces (p277) Carved meeting house; Taupo.

➡ Waitangi Treaty Grounds (p154) *Whare Rūnanga* and *waka taua*.

➡ Whakarewarewa (p308) The 'living village' – carving, other arts, meeting house and performance; Rotorua.

➡ Whanganui Regional Museum (p254) Wonderful carved *waka*.

The apex of carving today is the *whare whakairo* (carved meeting house). A commissioning group relates its history and ancestral stories to a carver, who then draws (sometimes quite loosely) on traditional motifs to interpret or embody the stories and ancestors in wood or composite fibreboard.

Rongomaraeroa Marae at Te Papa in Wellington, carved by pioneering artist Cliff Whiting, is a colourful example of a contemporary reimagining of a traditional art form. The biggest change in carving (as with most traditional arts) has been in the use of new mediums and tools. Rangi Kipa uses a high-density plastic to make his *hei tiki* (traditional pendants). You can check out his gallery at www.rangikipa.com.

Haka

Haka can be adrenaline-pumping, awe-inspiring and uplifting. The *haka* is not only a war dance – it is used to welcome visitors, honour achievement, express identity and to put forth very strong opinions.

Haka involve chanted words, vigorous body movements and *pūkana* (when performers distort their faces, eyes bulging with the whites showing, perhaps with tongue extended).

The well-known *haka* 'Ka Mate', performed by the All Blacks before rugby test matches, is credited to the cunning fighting chief Te Rauparaha. It celebrates his escape from death. Chased by enemies, he hid himself in a food pit. After they had left, a friendly chief named Te Whareangi

Could heavy metal be the newest form of expressing Māori identity? Singing (and screaming) in Te Reo Māori, Waipu guitar trio Alien Weaponry thrash out songs that narrate the battles of their ancestors.

A conversation starter for your next New Zealand barbecue: would NZ's 2011 and 2015 Rugby World Cup–winning All Blacks teams have been as unstoppable without key Māori players such as Dan Carter, Piri Weepu, Nehe Milner-Skudder and Aaron Smith?

COMMON MĀORI GEOGRAPHICAL TERMS

The following words form part of many Māori place names in New Zealand, and help you understand the meaning of these place names. For example: Waikaremoana is the Sea (moana) of Rippling (kare) Waters (wai), and Rotorua means the Second (rua) Lake (roto).

a – of; **ara** – way, path or road; **awa** – river or valley; **iti** – small; **kai** – food; **kare** – rippling; **kati** – shut or close; **makariri** – cold; **maunga** – mountain; **moana** – sea or lake; **motu** – island; **mutu** – finished, ended, over; **ngā** – the (plural); **nui** – big or great; **o** – of, place of...; **one** – beach, sand or mud; **pā** – fortified village; **poto** – short; **puke** – hill; **puna** – spring, hole, fountain; **rangi** – sky, heavens; **raro** – north; **roa** – long; **roto** – lake; **rua** – hole in the ground, two; **runga** – above; **tāhuna** – beach, sandbank; **tāne** – man; **tapu** – sacred, forbidden or taboo; **tata** – close to, dash against, twin islands; **te** – the (singular); **tonga** – south; **wāhine** – woman; **wai** – water; **waka** – canoe; **wera** – burnt or hot; **whanga** – harbour, bay or inlet; **whenua** – land or country

(the 'hairy man' referred to in the *haka*), let him out; he climbed out into the sunshine and performed 'Ka Mate'.

You can experience *haka* at various cultural performances, including at Mitai Māori Village (p312), Tamaki Māori Village (p312), Te Puia (p307) and Whakarewarewa (p308) in Rotorua.

But the best displays of *haka* are at the national **Te Matatini National Kapa Haka Festival** (www.tematatini.co.nz), when NZ's top groups compete. It's held every two years (and heads to Wellington in 2019).

Contemporary Visual Art

A distinctive feature of Māori visual art is the tension between traditional Māori ideas and modern artistic mediums and trends. Shane Cotton produced a series of works that conversed with 19th-century painted meeting houses, which themselves departed from Māori carved houses. Kelcy Taratoa uses sci-fi, superheroes and pop-art imagery.

Of course, Māori motifs aren't necessarily the dominant features of work by Māori artists. Major NZ artist Ralph Hotere was wary about being assigned any cultural, ethnic or genre label and his work confronted a broad range of political and social issues.

Contemporary Māori art is by no means only about painting. Many other artists use installations or digital formats – look out for work by Jacqueline Fraser, Peter Robinson and Lisa Reihana.

There are some great permanent exhibitions of Māori visual arts in the major centres. Both the Auckland Art Gallery (p67) and Wellington's Te Papa (p393) hold strong collections.

> The first NZ hip-hop song to become a hit was Dalvanius Prime's 'Poi E', which was sung entirely in Māori by the Patea Māori Club. It was the highest-selling single of 1984 in NZ.

Theatre

Powered by a wave of political activism, the 1970s saw the emergence of many Māori playwrights and plays, and theatre remains a prominent area of the Māori arts today. Māori theatre drew heavily on the traditions of the *marae*. Instead of dimming the lights and immediately beginning the performance, many Māori theatre groups began with a stylised *pōwhiri*, had space for audience members to respond to the play, and ended with a *karakia* (prayer or incantation), or a farewell.

Taki Rua is an independent producer of Māori work for both children and adults and has been in existence for more than 30 years. As well as staging its shows in the major centres, it tours most of its work – check out its website (www.takirua.co.nz) for the current offerings. Māori drama is also often showcased at the professional theatres in the main centres as well as the biennial New Zealand Festival (p397). Look out for work by Hone Kouka, Briar Grace-Smith and Mitch Tawhi Thomas.

Contemporary Dance

Contemporary Māori dance often takes its inspiration from *kapa haka* (cultural dance) and traditional Māori imagery. The exploration of pre-European life also provides inspiration.

New Zealand's leading specifically Māori dance company is the Atamira Dance Collective (www.atamiradance.co.nz), which has been producing critically acclaimed, beautiful and challenging work since 2000. If that sounds too earnest, get acquainted with the work of musician and visual artist Mika Torotoro, who happily blends *kapa haka*, drag, opera, ballet and disco. You can check out clips of his work at www.mika.co.nz.

Cinema

Although there had already been successful Māori documentaries (*Patu!* and the *Tangata Whenua* series are brilliant), it wasn't until 1987 that NZ had its first fictional feature-length movie by a Māori writer and director, with Barry Barclay's *Ngati*. Mereta Mita was the first Māori woman to direct a fiction feature, with *Mauri* (1988). Both Mita and Barclay had highly political aims and ways of working, which involved a lengthy pre-production phase, during which they would consult with and seek direction from their *kaumātua* (elders). Films with significant Māori participation or control include the harrowing *Once Were Warriors* and the uplifting *Whale Rider*. Oscar-nominated Taika Waititi, of Te Whānau-ā-Apanui descent, wrote and directed *Eagle vs Shark* and *Boy*.

Ngā Taonga Sound & Vision (www.ngataonga.org.nz) is a great place to experience Māori film, with most showings being either free or relatively inexpensive. It has locations in Auckland and Wellington.

Read Hirini Moko Mead's *Tikanga Māori*, Pat and Hiwi Tauroa's *Te Marae*, and Anne Salmond's *Hui* for detailed information on Māori customs.

Literature

There are many novels and collections of short stories by Māori writers, and personal taste will govern your choices. How about approaching Māori writing regionally? Read Patricia Grace *(Potiki, Cousins, Dogside Story, Tu)* around Wellington, and maybe Witi Ihimaera *(Pounamu, Pounamu; The Matriarch; Bulibasha; The Whale Rider)* on the North Island's East Coast. Keri Hulme *(The Bone People, Stonefish)* and the South Island go together like a mass of whitebait bound in a frying pan by a single egg (ie very well). Read Alan Duff *(Once Were Warriors)* anywhere, but only if you want to be saddened, even shocked. Definitely take James George *(Hummingbird, Ocean Roads)* with you to Auckland's west-coast beaches and Northland's Ninety Mile Beach. Paula Morris *(Queen of Beauty, Hibiscus Coast, Trendy but Casual)* and Kelly Ana Morey *(Bloom, Grace Is Gone)* – hmm, Auckland and beyond? If poetry appeals, you can't go past the giant of Māori poetry in English, the late, lamented Hone Tuwhare *(Deep River Talk: Collected Poems)*. Famously sounding like he's at church and in the pub at the same time, you *can* take him anywhere.

MĀORI CULTURE THE ARTS

The Arts

Māori music and art extends back to New Zealand's early, unrecorded history, but its motifs endure today in diverse forms. European settlers imported artistic styles from back home, but it took a century for postcolonial NZ to hone its distinctive artistic identity. In the first half of the 20th century it was writers and visual artists who led the charge, but in the decades that followed, music and movies catapulted the nation's creativity into the world's consciousness.

Literature

In 2013 New Zealanders rejoiced to hear that 28-year-old Eleanor Catton had become only the second NZ writer to ever win the Man Booker Prize, arguably the world's most prestigious award for literature, for her epic historical novel *The Luminaries* set on the West Coast. Lloyd Jones had come close in 2007 when his novel *Mister Pip* was shortlisted, but it had been a long wait between drinks since Keri Hulme took the prize in 1985 for her haunting novel *The Bone People*.

Catton and Hulme continue in a proud line of NZ women writers, starting in the early 20th century with Katherine Mansfield. Mansfield's work began a Kiwi tradition in short fiction, and for years the standard was carried by novelist Janet Frame, whose dramatic life was depicted in Jane Campion's film of her autobiography, *An Angel at My Table*. Frame's novel *The Carpathians* won the Commonwealth Writers' Prize in 1989. A new author on New Zealanders' must-read lists is Catherine Chidgey, whose heart-rending novel *The Wish Child* (2016) won the country's top fiction prize at 2017's NZ Book Awards.

Less recognised internationally, Maurice Gee has gained the nation's annual top fiction gong six times, most recently with *Blindsight* in 2006. His much-loved children's novel *Under the Mountain* (1979) was made into a seminal NZ TV series in 1981, and then a major motion picture in 2009. In 2004 the adaptation of another of his novels, *In My Father's Den* (1972), won major awards at international film festivals.

The late Maurice Shadbolt also achieved much acclaim for his many novels, particularly those set during the New Zealand Wars. Try *Season of the Jew* (1987) or *The House of Strife* (1993).

MĀORI VOICES IN PRINT

Some of the most interesting and enjoyable NZ fiction voices belong to Māori writers, with Booker-winner Keri Hulme leading the way. Witi Ihimaera's novels give a wonderful insight into small-town Māori life on the East Coast – especially *Bulibasha* (1994) and *The Whale Rider* (1987), which was made into an acclaimed film. Patricia Grace's work is similarly filled with exquisitely told stories of rural *marae*-centred life: try *Mutuwhenua* (1978), *Potiki* (1986), *Dogside Story* (2001) or *Tu* (2004). *Chappy* (2015) is Grace's expansive tale of a prodigal son returning to NZ to untangle his cross-cultural heritage.

Cinema & TV

If you first became interested in New Zealand when watching it on the silver screen, you're in good company. Sir Peter Jackson's NZ-made *The Lord of the Rings* and *The Hobbit* trilogies were the best thing to happen to NZ tourism since Captain Cook.

Yet NZ cinema is hardly ever easygoing. In his BBC-funded documentary, *Cinema of Unease*, NZ actor Sam Neill described the country's film industry as producing bleak, haunted work. One need only watch Lee Tamahori's harrowing *Once Were Warriors* (1994) to see what he means.

The uniting factor in NZ film and TV is the landscape, which provides a haunting backdrop – arguably as much of a presence as the characters themselves. Jane Campion's *The Piano* (1993) and *Top of the Lake* (2013), Brad McGann's *In My Father's Den* (2004) and Jackson's *Heavenly Creatures* (1994) all use magically lush scenery to couch disturbing violence. It's a land-mysticism constantly bordering on the creepy.

Even when Kiwis do humour it's as resolutely black as their rugby jerseys; check out Jackson's early splatter-fests and Taika Waititi's *Boy* (2010). Exporting NZ comedy hasn't been easy, yet the HBO-produced TV musical parody *Flight of the Conchords* – featuring a mumbling, bumbling Kiwi folk-singing duo trying to get a break in New York – found surprising international success. It's the Polynesian giggle-factor that seems likeliest to break down the bleak house of NZ cinema, with feel-good-through-and-through *Sione's Wedding* (2006) enjoying the biggest opening weekend of any NZ film at the time.

Also packaging offbeat NZ humour for an international audience, *Hunt for the Wilderpeople* (2016) and *What We Do in the Shadows* (2014) have propelled scriptwriter and director Taika Waititi to critical acclaim, while *Thor: Ragnarok* (2017) made him a household name – though many argue that the director's star turn as a softly spoken rock creature is the movie's highlight.

New Zealanders have gone from never seeing themselves in international cinema to having whole cloned armies of Temuera Morrisons invading the universe in *Star Wars*. Familiar faces such as Cliff Curtis and Karl Urban seem to constantly pop up playing Mexican or Russian gangsters in action movies. Many of them got their start in long-running soap opera *Shortland Street*.

Visual Arts

The NZ 'can do' attitude extends to the visual arts. If you're visiting a local's home, don't be surprised to find one of the owner's paintings on the wall or one of their mate's sculptures in the back garden, pieced together out of bits of shell, driftwood and a length of the magical 'number 8 wire'.

This is symptomatic of a flourishing local art and crafts scene cultivated by lively tertiary courses churning out traditional carvers and weavers, jewellery-makers, and moulders of metal and glass. The larger cities have excellent dealer galleries representing interesting local artists working across all media.

Traditional Māori art has a distinctive visual style with well-developed motifs that have been embraced by NZ artists of every race. In the painting medium, these include the cool modernism of Gordon Walters and the more controversial pop-art approach of Dick Frizzell's *Tiki* series. Likewise, Pacific Island themes are common, particularly in Auckland; look out for the intricate, collage-like paintings of Niuean-born, Auckland-raised John Pule.

Charles Frederick Goldie painted a series of compelling, realist portraits of Māori, who were feared to be a dying race. Debate over the political propriety of Goldie's work raged for years, but its value is widely

Jane Campion was the first Kiwi nominated as Best Director and Peter Jackson the first to win it. *The Return of the King* won a mighty 11 Oscars in 2004.

The only Kiwi actors to have won an Oscar are Anna Paquin (for *The Piano*) and Russell Crowe (for *Gladiator*). Paquin was born in Canada but moved to NZ when she was four, while Crowe moved from NZ to Australia at the same age.

MIDDLE-EARTH TOURISM

Did the scenery of the epic film trilogy *Lord of the Rings (LOTR)* lure you to Aotearoa? The North Island has most of the big-ticket filming locations, with knowledgeable operators who can take you set-jetting on foot, horseback or by 4WD. Dedicated enthusiasts can buy a copy of Ian Brodie's *The Lord of the Rings: Location Guidebook* for detail on filming locations and their GPS coordinates. Online, DOC has a useful primer (www.doc.govt.nz/lordoftherings).

Matamata, aka Hobbiton Peter Jackson's epic film trilogy *LOTR* put this town on the map and after the filming of *The Hobbit,* the town wholeheartedly embraced its Middle Earth credentials. **Hobbiton Movie Set Tours** (p209) allows you to pose by hobbit holes and enjoy a drink at the Green Dragon Inn.

Mt Ngauruhoe, aka Mt Doom Turns out the one ring to rule them all was forged in Tongariro National Park, in the North Island's youngest **volcano** (p293). Stickler for detail? A few Mt Doom scenes were filmed at Mt Ruapehu (best take a look at both).

Putangirua Pinnacles, aka Paths of the Dead An eerie landscape resembling giant organ pipes, the **pinnacles** (www.doc.govt.nz) FREE were an obvious fit to portray the spooky passage through the White Mountains in *Lord of the Rings: Return of the King*.

Rover Rings (☑04-471 0044; www.wellingtonrover.co.nz; adult/child tours from $95/50) and **Wellington Movie Tours** (☑027 419 3077; www.adventuresafari.co.nz; adult/child tours from $45/30) both offer half- to full-day tours of *LOTR* locations in and around Wellington.

accepted now: not least because Māori themselves generally acknowledge and value them as ancestral representations. In 2016 Goldie's last work became the first NZ painting to be sold for more than $1 million.

Recalibrating the ways in which Pacific Islander and Māori people are depicted in art, Lisa Reihana wowed the Venice Biennale in 2017 with her multimedia work *In Pursuit of Venus*.

Depicting the Land

It's no surprise that in a nation so defined by its natural environment, landscape painting constituted the first post-European body of art. In the late 19th century, John Gully and Petrus van der Velden were among those to arrive and capture the drama of the land in paintings.

Colin McCahon is widely regarded to have been NZ's most important artist. Even where McCahon lurched into Catholic mysticism, his spirituality was rooted in geography. His brooding landscapes evoke the land's power but also its vulnerability. McCahon is widely quoted as describing his work as a depiction of NZ before its seas become cluttered with debris and the sky turns dark with soot.

Landscape photographers also capture the fierceness and fragility of NZ's terrain. It's worth detouring to a few of the country's resident photographers, many of whom have their own galleries (sometimes within, or adjoining their own homes).

Not all the best galleries are in Auckland or Wellington. The amazing Len Lye Centre (p238) – home to the legacy of sculptor and filmmaker Len Lye – is worth a visit to New Plymouth in itself.

Music

New Zealand music began with the *waiata* (singing) developed by Māori following their arrival in the country. The main musical instruments were wind instruments made of bone or wood, the most well known of which is the *nguru* (also known as the 'nose flute'), while percussion was provided by chest- and thigh-slapping. These days, the liveliest place to see Māori music being performed is at *kapa haka* competitions in which groups compete with their own routines of traditional song and dance.

Classical

Early European immigrants brought their own styles of music and gave birth to local variants during the early 1900s. In the 1950s Douglas Lilburn became one of the first internationally recognised NZ classical composers. More recently the country has produced a number of world-renowned musicians in this field, including legendary opera singer Dame Kiri Te Kanawa, million-selling classic-to-pop singer Hayley Westenra, composer John Psathas (who created music for the 2004 Olympic Games) and composer/percussionist Gareth Farr (who also performs in drag under the name Lilith LaCroix).

Tickets for most events can be bought at www.ticketek.co.nz, www.ticketmaster.co.nz or, for smaller gigs, www.undertheradar.co.nz.

Rock

New Zealand's most acclaimed rock exports are the revered indie label Flying Nun and the music of the Finn Brothers.

Started in 1981 by Christchurch record-store owner Roger Shepherd, many of Flying Nun's early groups came from Dunedin, where local musicians took the DIY attitude of punk but used it to produce a lo-fi indie-pop that received rave reviews from the likes of *NME* in the UK and *Rolling Stone* in the US. Many of the musicians from the Flying Nun scene still perform live to this day, including David Kilgour (from the Clean) and Shayne Carter (from the Straitjacket Fits, and subsequently Dimmer and the Adults).

Want something heavier? Hamilton heavy-metal act Devilskin's 2014 debut album hit the top spot on NZ's charts, as did their punchy 2016 follow-up *Be Like the River*. Beastwars, a rasping, trance-inducing sludge metal band from Wellington, is another stalwart of NZ's heavy-metal scene. Meanwhile, hitting the big leagues during tours of North America and Europe, technical death-metal band Ulcerate have risen to prominence as NZ's best-known extreme metal act. We're not worthy.

The TV show *Popstars* originated in New Zealand, though the resulting group, TrueBliss, was short-lived. The series concept was then picked up in Australia, the UK and the US, inspiring the *Idols* series.

Reggae, Hip-Hop & Dance

The genres of music that have been adopted most enthusiastically by Māori and Polynesian New Zealanders have been reggae (in the 1970s) and hip-hop (in the 1980s), which has led to distinct local forms. In Wellington, a thriving jazz scene took on a reggae influence to create a host of groups that blended dub, roots and funky jazz – most notably Fat Freddy's Drop.

The local hip-hop scene has its heart in the suburbs of South Auckland, which have a high concentration of Māori and Pacific Island residents. This area is home to one of New Zealand's foremost hip-hop labels, Dawn

THE BROTHERS FINN

There are certain tunes that all Kiwis can sing along to, given a beer and the opportunity. A surprising proportion of these were written by Tim and Neil Finn, many of which have been international hits. Tim Finn first came to prominence in the 1970s group Split Enz, who amassed a solid following in Australia, NZ and Canada before disbanding in 1985. Neil then formed Crowded House with two Australian musicians (Paul Hester and Nick Seymour) and one of their early singles, 'Don't Dream It's Over', hit number two on the US charts. Tim later did a brief spell in the band, during which the brothers wrote 'Weather with You' – a song that reached number seven on the UK charts, pushing their album *Woodface* to gold sales. Neil has also remained busy, organising a set of shows/releases under the name 7 Worlds Collide – a collaboration with well-known overseas musicians. Tim and Neil have both released a number of solo albums, as well as releasing material together as the Finn Brothers.

In April 2018 Fleetwood Mac announced that Neil Finn would be joining the band, following the unexpected departure of Lindsey Buckingham. Finn, along with Mike Campbell (guitarist with Tom Petty and the Heartbreakers) will replace Buckingham on the band's 2018 tour.

FESTIVALS

Major-league NZ music festivals include **Rhythm & Vines** (p357) in Gisborne and sister festival Rhythm & Alps (www.rhythmandalps.co.nz) in Wanaka. The international alt-rock fest **St Jerome's** (http://auckland.lanewayfestival.com) heads to New Zealand in late January after touring Australia. On Wellington's waterfront in April is **Homegrown** (www.home-grown.net.nz) where you'll catch local talent on five stages. World-music fans flock to the local version of **WOMAD** (p242) in New Plymouth, which features local and overseas acts.

For traditional Māori song, dance, storytelling and other performing arts, check out **Te Matatini National Kapa Haka Festival** (p440); it takes place in late February/early March in odd-numbered years at different venues (it's in Wellington for 2019). In a similar vein, Auckland's **Pasifika Festival** (p83) represents each of the Pacific Islands. It's a great place to see both traditional and modern forms of Polynesian music: modern hip-hop, throbbing Cook Island drums, or island-style guitar, ukulele and slide guitar.

Raid, which takes its name from the infamous 1970s early-morning house raids that police performed on Pacific Islanders suspected of outstaying their visas. Dawn Raid's most successful artist is Savage, who sold a million copies of his single 'Swing' after it was featured in the movie *Knocked Up*. Within New Zealand, the most well-known hip-hop acts are Scribe, Che Fu and Smashproof (whose song 'Brother' held number one on the NZ singles charts for 11 weeks).

Dance music gained a foothold in Christchurch in the 1990s, spawning dub/electronica outfit Salmonella Dub and its offshoot act, Tiki Taane. Drum 'n' bass remains popular locally and has spawned internationally renowned acts such as Concord Dawn and Shapeshifter.

Movers & Shakers

Since 2000, the NZ music scene has developed new vitality after the government convinced commercial radio stations to adopt a voluntary quota of 20% local music. This enabled commercially oriented musicians to develop solid careers. Rock groups such as Shihad, the Feelers and Opshop thrived in this environment, as have a set of soulful female solo artists: Bic Runga, Anika Moa and Brooke Fraser (daughter of All Black Bernie Fraser). New Zealand also produced two internationally acclaimed garage rock acts over this time: the Datsuns and the D4.

Current Kiwis garnering international recognition include the incredibly gifted songstress Kimbra (who sang on Gotye's global smash 'Somebody That I Used To Know'); indie electro-rockers the Naked and Famous; multitalented singer-songwriter Ladyhawke; the arty Lawrence Arabia; and the semipsychedelic Unknown Mortal Orchestra.

R&B singer Aaradhna made a splash with her album *Treble & Reverb*, which won Album of the Year at the 2013 New Zealand Music Awards. When the title track of her album *Brown Girl* was awarded a gong for 'best hip-hop' in 2016, she turned it down saying she'd been placed in the wrong musical category because of the colour of her skin.

Good Lorde!

The biggest name in Kiwi music is Lorde, a singer-songwriter from Devonport on Auckland's North Shore. Known less regally to her friends as Ella Yelich-O'Connor, Lorde was 16 years old when she cracked the number-one spot on the US Billboard charts in 2013 with her magical, schoolyard-chant-evoking hit 'Royals' – the first NZ solo artist to top the American charts. 'Royals' then went on to win the Song of the Year Grammy in 2014. Her debut album *Pure Heroine* spawned a string of hits and sold millions of copies worldwide, while moody follow-up *Melodrama* instantly topped charts in NZ and the US upon its release in 2017.

A wide range of cultural events are listed on www.eventfinda.co.nz. This is a good place to find out about concerts, classical music recitals and *kapa haka* performances. For more specific information on the NZ classical music scene, see www.sounz.org.nz.

Survival Guide

Directory A-Z

Accommodation

The North Island is blessed with great accommodation at every budget level, including excellent holiday parks (fancy campgrounds with tent sites, self-contained cabins, games rooms and often a swimming pool) and some of the world's best hostels. As you'd expect, things are pricier in the big cities of Auckland and Wellington. Motels are the top sleeping choice for most Kiwi families, so you'll find them liberally scattered around all of the main holiday destinations. Hotel accommodation is mainly limited to the bigger cities, with the best range in Auckland and Wellington.

Booking Services

Local visitor information centres around NZ provide reams of local accommodation information, sometimes in the form of folders detailing facilities and up-to-date prices; many can also make bookings on your behalf.

Lonely Planet (www.lonely planet.com/new-zealand/hotels) The full range of NZ accommodation, from hostels to hotels.

Automobile Association (www.aa.co.nz/travel) Online accommodation bookings (especially good for motels, B&Bs and holiday parks).

Jasons (www.jasons.co.nz) Long-running travel service with myriad online booking options.

New Zealand Bed & Breakfast (www.bnb.co.nz) The name says it all.

Bed & Breakfast New Zealand (www.bed-and-breakfast.co.nz) B&B and self-contained accommodation directory.

Rural Holidays NZ (www.ruralholidays.co.nz) Farm and homestay listings across NZ.

Book a Bach (www.bookabach.co.nz) Apartment and holiday-house bookings (and maybe even a bach or two!).

Holiday Houses (www.holiday houses.co.nz) Holiday-house rentals NZ-wide.

New Zealand Apartments (www.nzapartments.co.nz) Rental listings for upmarket apartments of all sizes.

BOOK YOUR STAY ONLINE

For more accommodation reviews by Lonely Planet authors, check out http://lonelyplanet.com/new-zealand/hotels/. You'll find independent reviews, as well as recommendations on the best places to stay. Best of all, you can book online.

B&Bs

Bed and breakfast (B&B) accommodation in NZ pops up in the middle of cities, in rural hamlets and on stretches of isolated coastline, with rooms on offer in everything from suburban bungalows to stately manors.

Breakfast may be 'continental' (a standard offering of cereal, toast and tea or coffee, or a heartier version with yoghurt, fruit, home-baked bread or muffins), or a stomach-loading cooked meal (eggs, bacon, sausages...though with notice, vegetarians are increasingly being well catered for). Some B&B hosts may also cook dinner for guests and advertise dinner, bed and breakfast (DB&B) packages.

B&B tariffs are typically in the $120 to $200 bracket (per double), though some places cost upwards of $300 per double. Some hosts charge cheeky prices for what is, in essence, a bedroom in their home. Off-street parking is often a bonus in the big cities.

Camping & Holiday Parks

Campers and campervan drivers converge on NZ's hugely popular 'holiday parks', slumbering in powered and unpowered sites, cheap bunk rooms (dorm rooms), cabins (shared bathroom facilities) and self-contained units (often called motels or tourist flats). Well-equipped communal kitchens, dining areas, games and TV rooms, and playgrounds often feature. In cities, holiday parks are usually a fair way from the action, but in smaller towns they can be impressively central or near lakes, beaches, rivers and forests.

The nightly cost of holiday-park tent sites is usually $15 to $20 per adult, with children charged half price; powered campervan sites can be anything from a couple of dollars more to around the $40 mark. Cabin/unit accommodation normally ranges from $70 to $120 per double. Unless noted otherwise, Lonely Planet lists campsite, campervan site, hut and cabin prices for two people.

DOC & FREEDOM CAMPING

A fantastic option for those in campervans is the 250-plus vehicle-accessible 'Conservation Campsites' run by the Department of Conservation (DOC; www.doc.govt.nz), with fees ranging from free (basic toilets and fresh water) to $21 per adult (flush toilets and showers). DOC publishes free brochures with detailed descriptions and instructions to find every campsite (even GPS coordinates). Pick up copies from DOC offices before you hit the road, or visit the website.

The DOC also looks after hundreds of 'Backcountry Huts' and 'Backcountry Campsites', which can only be reached on foot. 'Great Walk' huts and campsites are also managed by DOC.

New Zealand is so photogenic, it's tempting to just pull off the road at a gorgeous viewpoint and camp the night. But never assume it's OK to camp somewhere: always ask a local or check with the local i-SITE visitor centre, DOC office or commercial campground. If you are 'freedom camping', treat the area

with respect. If your chosen campsite doesn't have toilet facilities and neither does your campervan, it's illegal for you to sleep there (your campervan must also have an on-board grey-water storage system). Legislation allows for $200 instant fines for camping in prohibited areas or improper disposal of waste (in cases where dumping waste could damage the environment, fees are up to $10,000). See www.camping.org.nz for more freedom-camping tips and consider downloading the free Campermate App (www.campermate.co.nz), which flags drinking-water sources, public toilets, freedom-camping spots and locals happy to rent their driveway to campervans.

Farmstays

Farmstays open the door to the agricultural side of NZ life, with visitors encouraged to get some dirt beneath their fingernails at orchards, and dairy, sheep and cattle farms. Costs can vary widely, with bed and breakfast generally costing $80 to $140. Some farms have separate cottages where you can fix your own food; others offer low-cost, shared, backpacker-style accommodation.

Farm Helpers in NZ (www.fhinz.co.nz) produces a booklet ($25) that lists around 350 NZ farms providing lodging in exchange for four to six hours' work per day.

SLEEPING PRICE RANGES

The following price ranges refer to a double room with bathroom during high season. Price ranges generally increase by 20% to 25% in Auckland and Wellington. Here you can still find budget accommodation at up to $120 per double, but midrange stretches from $120 to $250, with top-end rooms more than $250.

$ less than $120

$$ $120–$200

$$$ more than $200

WWOOFING

If you don't mind getting your hands dirty, an economical way of travelling around NZ involves doing some voluntary work as a member of the international **Willing Workers On Organic Farms** (WWOOF; ☏03-544 9890; www.wwoof.co.nz; ⊙9am-3pm Mon-Fri) scheme. Down on the farm, in exchange for a hard day's work, owners provide food, accommodation and some hands-on organic farming experience. Contact farm owners a week or two beforehand to arrange your stay, as you would for a hotel or hostel – don't turn up unannounced!

A one-year online membership costs $40 for an individual or a couple. A farm-listing book, which is mailed to you, costs an extra $10 to $30, depending on where in the world your mailbox is. You should have a Working Holiday Visa when you visit NZ, as the immigration department considers WWOOFers to be working.

Hostels

New Zealand is packed to the rafters with backpacker hostels, both independent and part of large chains, ranging from small, homestay-style affairs with a handful of beds, to refurbished hotels and towering modern structures in the big cities. Hostel bed prices listed by Lonely Planet are nonmember rates, usually $25 to $35 per night.

HOSTEL ORGANISATIONS

Budget Backpacker Hostels
(www.bbh.co.nz) A network of more than 160 hostels. Membership costs $45 for 12 months and entitles you to stay at member hostels at rates listed in the annual (free) *BBH Backpacker Accommodation* booklet. Nonmembers pay an extra $4 per night. Pick up a membership card from any member hostel or order one online ($50).

YHA New Zealand (www.yha.co.nz) Around 40 hostels in prime NZ locations. The YHA is part of the Hostelling International network (www.hihostels.com), so if you're already an HI member in your own country, membership entitles you to use NZ hostels. If you don't already have a home membership, you can join at major NZ YHA hostels or online for $25, valid for 12 months (it's free for under 18s). Nonmembers pay an extra $3 or more per night. Membership has other perks, such as discounts on some car-hire providers, travel insurers, DOC hut passes and more.

Base Backpackers (www.stayatbase.com) Chain with nine-plus hostels around NZ: Bay of Islands, Auckland, Rotorua, Taupo, Wellington, Wanaka, Queenstown, Dunedin and Christchurch. Expect clean dorms, women-only areas and party opportunities aplenty. Offers a flexible 10-night 'Base Jumping' accommodation package for $289, bookable online.

VIP Backpackers (www.vipbackpackers.com) International organisation affiliated with around 20 NZ hostels (not BBH or YHA), mainly in the cities and tourist hotspots. For around $61 (including postage), you'll receive a 12-month membership entitling you to a $1 discount off nightly accommodation and discounts with affiliated activity and tour providers. Join online or at VIP hostels.

Haka Lodge (www.hakalodge.com) A local chain on the way up, with snazzy hostels in Auckland, Queenstown, Christchurch, Taupo and Paihia. Rates are comparable to other hostels around NZ, and quality is high. Tours are also available.

Climate

Auckland

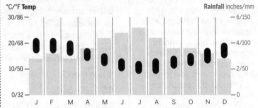

Rotorua

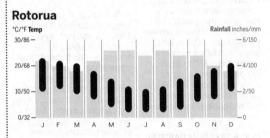

Wellington

Pubs, Hotels & Motels

The least expensive form of NZ hotel accommodation is the humble pub. Some are full of character (and characters); others are grotty, ramshackle places that are best avoided (especially by women travelling solo). Check whether there's a band playing the night you're staying – you could be in for a sleepless night. In the cheapest pubs, singles/doubles might cost as little as $45/70 (with a shared bathroom down the hall); $70/90 is more common.

At the top end of the hotel scale are five-star international chains, resort complexes and architecturally splendorous boutique hotels, all of which charge a hefty premium for their mod cons, snappy service and/or historic opulence. We quote 'rack rates' (official advertised rates) for such places, but discounts and special deals often apply.

New Zealand's towns have a glut of nondescript, low-rise motels and 'motor lodges', charging $90 to $200 for double rooms. These tend to be squat structures skulking by highways on the edges of towns. Most are modernish (though decor is often mired in the early 2000s or earlier) and have basic facilities, namely tea- and coffee-making equipment, fridge and TV. Prices vary with standard.

Rental Accommodation

The basic Kiwi holiday home is called a 'bach' (short for 'bachelor', as they were historically used by single men as hunting and fishing hideouts); in Otago and Southland they're known as 'cribs'. These are simple self-contained cottages that can be rented in rural and coastal areas, often in isolated locations, and sometimes include surf, fishing or other outdoor gear rental in the cost. Prices are typically $90 to $180 per night, which isn't bad for a whole house or self-contained bungalow. For more upmarket holiday houses, expect to pay anything from $180 to $400 per double.

Customs Regulations

For the low-down on what you can and can't bring into NZ, see the New Zealand Customs Service website (www.customs.govt.nz). Per-person duty-free allowances:

➡ Three 1125mL (max) bottles of spirits or liqueur

➡ 4.5L of wine or beer

➡ 50 cigarettes, or 50g of tobacco or cigars

➡ Dutiable goods up to the value of $700

It's a good idea to declare any unusual medicines. Tramping gear (boots, tents etc) will be checked and may need to be cleaned before being allowed in. You must declare any plant or animal products (including anything made of wood), and food of any kind. Weapons and firearms are either prohibited or require a permit and safety testing. Don't take these rules lightly

– noncompliance penalties will really hurt your hip pocket.

Discount Cards

The internationally recognised **International Student Identity Card** is produced by the ISIC Association (www.isic.org), and issued to full-time students aged 12 and over. It provides discounts on accommodation, transport and admission to attractions.

The same folks also produce the **International Youth Travel Card**, available to travellers aged under 31 who are not full-time students, with equivalent benefits to the ISIC.

Also similar is the **International Teacher Identity Card**, available to teaching professionals. All three cards ($30 each) are available online at www.isiccard.co.nz, or from student travel companies like STA Travel.

The **New Zealand Card** (www.newzealandcard.com) is a $35 discount pass that'll score you between 5% and 50% off a range of accommodation, tours, sights and activities. Browse participating businesses before you buy.

A **Budget Backpacker Hostels** (www.bbh.co.nz) membership card costs $45 and entitles you to discounts at BBH member hostels, usually snipping $4 off the price per night.

Travellers aged over 60 with some form of identification (eg an official seniors card from your home country) are often eligible for concession prices.

Electricity

To plug yourself into the electricity supply (230V AC, 50Hz), use a three-pin adaptor (the same as in Australia; different to British three-pin adaptors).

Type I
230V/50Hz

Food

Auckland has New Zealand's most vibrant and exciting dining scene, with numerous top-notch contemporary restaurants and a huge number of good-value ethnic eateries. Wellington comes a close second. While there are good fine-dining places scattered around the other main centres (Whangarei, Hamilton and Taupo have excellent options), more casual dining is the norm. You won't find it hard to find a tasty, family friendly meal almost anywhere.

Being New Zealand, there are world-class cafes in some of the most obscure places, and even the average ones will brew a better coffee than you'll find in most British or American cities.

LGBT Travellers

The gay tourism industry in NZ isn't as high profile as it is in some other developed nations, but LGBT communities are prominent in Auckland and Wellington, with myriad support organisations across both islands. New Zealand has progressive laws protecting human rights: same-sex marriage and adoption by same-sex couples were legalised in 2013, while the legal minimum age for sex between consenting persons is 16. Generally speaking, Kiwis are fairly relaxed and accepting about gender fluidity, but that's not to say that homophobia doesn't exist. Rural communities tend to be more conservative; here public displays of affection should probably be avoided.

Resources

There are loads of websites dedicated to gay and lesbian travel in NZ. Gay Tourism New Zealand (www.gaytourismnewzealand.com) is a starting point, with links to various sites.

Other worthwhile websites include the following:

➜ www.gaynz.net.nz

➜ www.lesbian.net.nz

➜ www.gaystay.co.nz

Check out the nationwide monthly magazine *express* (www.gayexpress.co.nz) for the latest happenings, reviews and listings on the NZ gay scene. New Zealand Awaits (www.newzealand-awaits.com) is a local operator specialising in tours serving LGBT travellers.

Festivals & Events

Auckland Pride Festival (www.aucklandpridefestival.org.nz) Two-and-a-bit weeks of rainbow-hued celebrations in February.

Big Gay Out (www.biggayout.co.nz) Part of the Auckland Pride Festival in February, this flagship day features live music and 'Mr Gay New Zealand'.

Gay Ski Week (www.gayskiweekqt.com) Annual Queenstown snow-fest in August/September.

Health

New Zealand poses minimal health risks to travellers. Diseases such as malaria and typhoid are unheard of, poisonous snakes and other dangerous animals are absent, and there are currently no dangerous insect-borne diseases. The biggest risks to travellers involve exploring the great outdoors: trampers must be clued in on rapid-changing weather and diligent about sharing any plans to visit remote areas, meanwhile drivers must exert extreme caution on NZ's notoriously winding roads.

Before You Go
HEALTH INSURANCE

Health insurance is essential for all travellers. While health care in NZ is of a high quality and not overly expensive by international standards, considerable costs can be built up and repatriation is pricey.

If you don't have a health insurance plan that covers you for medical expenses incurred overseas, buy a travel insurance policy – see www.lonelyplanet.com/travel-insurance. Find out in advance if your insurance plan will make payments directly to providers or reimburse you later for overseas health expenditures. Check whether your policy covers the activities you're planning to do in NZ (eg rock climbing or winter sports) and whether there's a limit on the number of days of cover for the activity.

RECOMMENDED VACCINATIONS

New Zealand has no vaccination requirements for any traveller, but the World Health Organization recommends that all travellers should be covered for chickenpox, diphtheria, hepatitis B, measles, mumps, pertussis (whooping cough), polio, rubella, seasonal flu, tetanus and tuberculosis, regardless of their destination. Ask your doctor for an *International Certificate of Vaccination* (or 'the yellow booklet') in which they will list all the vaccinations you've received.

MEDICATIONS

Bring any prescribed medications for your trip in their original, clearly labelled containers. It is also wise to bring a signed and dated letter from your physician describing your medical conditions and medications (including generic names), and any requisite syringes or needles.

PRACTICALITIES

Newspapers Check out Auckland's *New Zealand Herald* (www.nzherald.co.nz), Wellington's *Dominion Post* (www.stuff.co.nz/dominion-post) or Christchurch's *The Press* (www.stuff.co.nz/the-press).

TV Watch one of the national government-owned TV stations – including TVNZ 1, TVNZ 2, Māori TV or the 100% Māori-language Te Reo.

Radio Tune in to Radio New Zealand (www.radionz.co.nz) for news, current affairs, classical and jazz. Radio Hauraki (www.hauraki.co.nz) cranks out rock.

Weights & measures New Zealand uses the metric system.

Smoking Like much of the Western world, smoking rates in NZ have been on the slide in recent decades. Smoking on public transport and in restaurants, cafes, bars and pubs is banned.

In New Zealand
AVAILABILITY & COST OF HEALTH CARE

New Zealand's public hospitals offer a high standard of care (free for residents). All travellers are covered for medical care resulting from accidents that occur while in NZ (eg motor-vehicle accidents or adventure-activity accidents) by the Accident Compensation Corporation (www.acc.co.nz). Costs incurred due to treatment of a medical illness that occurs while in NZ will only be covered by travel insurance. For more details, see www.health.govt.nz.

The 24-hour **Healthline** (☑0800 611 116) offers health advice throughout NZ (free from local mobile or landlines). Interpreters are available.

INFECTIOUS DISEASES

Aside from the same sexually transferred infections that are found worldwide (take normal precautions), giardiasis is the main infectious disease to be aware of when travelling in NZ.

GIARDIASIS

The giardia parasite is widespread in NZ waterways: drinking untreated water from streams and lakes is not recommended. Using water filters and boiling or treating water with iodine are effective ways of preventing the disease. The parasite can also latch on to swimmers in rivers and lakes (try not to swallow water), or through contact with infected animals. Symptoms consist of diarrhoea, vomiting, stomach cramps, abdominal bloating and wind. Effective treatment is available (tinidazole or metronidazole).

HYPOTHERMIA

Hypothermia, a dangerous drop in body temperature, is a significant risk to travellers in NZ, especially during winter and year-round at altitude. Mountain ranges and/or strong winds produce a high chill factor, which can cause hypothermia even in moderate temperatures. Early signs include the inability to perform fine movements (such as doing up buttons), shivering and a bad case of the 'umbles' (fumbles, mumbles, grumbles, stumbles).

To treat, minimise heat loss: remove wet clothing, add dry clothes with wind- and waterproof layers, and consume carbohydrates and water or warm liquids (not caffeine) to allow shivering to build the internal temperature. In severe hypothermia cases, shivering actually stops; this is a medical emergency requiring rapid evacuation in addition to the above measures.

BITING INSECTS

Wear long, loose clothing and use an insect repellent containing 20% or more DEET to ward off sandflies and mosquitoes, which are particularly common in lake areas and tree-lined clearings. Bites are intensely itchy, but fortunately don't spread disease.

TAP WATER

Tap water throughout New Zealand is generally safe to drink, and public taps with nondrinkable water tend to be labelled as such. However, water quality has faced pollution challenges in some places. Very occasionally, a warning may be issued that tap water must be boiled – your accommodation should inform you if this happens.

PHARMACEUTICALS

Over-the-counter medications are widely available in NZ through private chemists (pharmacies). These include painkillers, antihistamines, skincare products and sunscreen. Some medications, such as antibiotics, are only available via a prescription obtained from a general practitioner. Some varieties of the contraceptive pill can be bought at pharmacies without a prescription (provided the woman has been prescribed the pill within the last three years). If you take regular medications, bring an adequate supply and details of the generic name, as brand names differ country to country.

SURF BEACHES

New Zealand has exceptional surf beaches. The power of the surf can fluctuate as a result of the varying slope of the seabed: rips and undertows are common, and drownings do happen. Check with local surf lifesaving organisations before jumping in the sea, always heed warning signs at beaches, and be realistic about your own limitations and expertise.

Insurance

➡ A watertight travel-insurance policy covering theft, loss and medical problems is essential. Some policies specifically exclude designated 'dangerous activities', such as scuba diving, bungy jumping, white-water rafting, skiing and even tramping. If you plan on doing any of these things (a distinct possibility in NZ!), make sure your policy covers you fully.

➡ Under NZ law, you cannot sue for personal injury (other than exemplary damages). Instead, the country's Accident Compensation Corporation (www.acc.co.nz) administers an accident compensation scheme that provides accident insurance for NZ residents and visitors to the country, regardless of fault. This scheme, however, does not negate the necessity for your own comprehensive travel-insurance policy, as it doesn't cover you for such things as income loss, treatment at home or ongoing illness.

➡ Consider a policy that pays doctors or hospitals directly, rather than you paying on the spot and claiming later. If you have to claim later, keep all documentation. Some policies ask you to call (reverse charges) to a centre in your home country where an immediate assessment of your problem is made. Check that the policy covers ambulances and emergency medical evacuations by air.

➡ Worldwide travel insurance is available at www.lonelyplanet.com/travel-insurance. You can buy, extend and claim online anytime – even if you're already on the road.

Internet Access

Getting online in NZ is easy in all but remote locales. Expect abundant wi-fi in cafes and accommodation in big towns and cities, but thrifty download limits elsewhere.

Legal Matters

If you are questioned or arrested by police, it's your right to ask why, to refrain from making a statement, and to consult a lawyer in private.

Plans are brewing for a referendum on whether personal use of cannabis should be decriminalised, but at the time of writing it was still illegal. Anyone caught carrying this or other illicit drugs will have the book thrown at them.

Drink-driving is a serious offence and remains a significant problem in NZ. The legal blood alcohol limit is 0.05% for drivers aged 20 years and over, and zero for those under 20.

Maps

New Zealand's **Automobile Association** (AA; ☐0800 500 444; www.aa.co.nz/travel) produces excellent city, town, regional, island and highway maps, available from its local offices. The AA also produces a detailed *New Zealand Road Atlas*. Other reliable countrywide atlases, available from visitor information centres and bookshops, are published by Hema and KiwiMaps.

Land Information New Zealand (www.linz.govt.nz) publishes several exhaustive map series, including street, country and holiday maps, national park and forest park maps, and topographical trampers' maps. Scan the larger bookshops, or try the nearest DOC office or visitor information centre for topo maps.

Online, log onto AA Maps (www.aamaps.co.nz) or Wises (www.wises.co.nz) to pinpoint exact NZ addresses.

Money

Credit cards are used for most purchases in NZ, and are accepted in most hotels and restaurants. ATMs are widely available in cities and larger towns.

ATMs & Eftpos

Branches of the country's major banks across both islands have ATMs, but you won't find them everywhere (eg not in small towns).

Many NZ businesses use Eftpos (electronic funds transfer at point of sale), allowing you to use your bank card (credit or debit) to make direct purchases and often withdraw cash as well. Eftpos is available practically everywhere: just like at an ATM, you'll need a PIN number.

Credit Cards

Credit cards (Visa, Master-Card) are widely accepted for everything from a hostel bed to a bungy jump, and are pretty much essential for car hire. Credit cards can also be used for over-the-counter cash advances at banks and from ATMs, but be aware that such transactions incur charges. Diners Club and American Express cards are not as widely accepted.

Money Changers

Changing foreign currency (and to a lesser extent old-fashioned travellers cheques) is usually no problem at NZ banks or at licensed money changers (eg Travelex) in major tourist areas, cities and airports.

Tipping

Tipping is completely optional in NZ.

Guides Your kayaking guide or tour group leader will happily accept tips; up to $10 is fine.

Restaurants The total on your bill is all you need to pay (though sometimes a service charge is factored in). If you like, reward good service with 5% to 10%.

Taxis If you round up your fare, don't be surprised if the driver hands back your change.

Travellers Cheques

Amex, Travelex and other international brands of travellers cheques are a bit old hat these days, but they're still easily exchanged at banks and money changers. Present your passport for identification when cashing them; shop around for the best rates.

Opening Hours

Opening hours vary seasonally depending on where you are. Most places close on Christmas Day and Good Friday.

Banks 9am–4.30pm Monday to Friday, some also 9am–noon Saturday

Cafes 7am–4pm

Post Offices 8.30am–5pm Monday to Friday; larger branches also 9.30am–noon Saturday

Pubs & Bars noon–late ('late' varies by region, and by day)

Restaurants noon–2.30pm and 6.30pm–9pm

Shops & Businesses 9am–5.30pm Monday to Friday and 9am to noon or 5pm Saturday

Supermarkets 8am–7pm, often 9pm or later in cities

Post

The services offered by **New Zealand Post** (✆0800 501 501; www.nzpost.co.nz) are reliable and reasonably inexpensive. See the website for info on national and international zones and rates, plus post office (or 'post shop') locations.

Public Holidays

New Zealand's main public holidays:

New Year 1 and 2 January

Waitangi Day 6 February

Easter Good Friday and Easter Monday; March/April

Anzac Day 25 April

Queen's Birthday First Monday in June

Labour Day Fourth Monday in October

Christmas Day 25 December

Boxing Day 26 December

School Holidays

The Christmas holiday season, from mid-December to late January, is part of the summer school vacation: expect transport and accommodation to book out in advance, and queues at tourist attractions. There are three shorter school-holiday periods during the year: from mid- to late April, early to mid-July, late September to mid-October. For exact dates, see the Ministry of Education website (www.education.govt.nz).

Safe Travel

New Zealand is no more dangerous than other developed countries, but exert normal safety precautions, especially after dark on city streets and in remote areas.

➡ Kiwi roads are often made hazardous by map-distracted tourists, wide-cornering campervans and traffic-ignorant sheep.

➡ Major fault lines run the length of NZ, causing occasional earthquakes.

➡ Avoid leaving valuables in vehicles: theft is a problem, even in remote areas.

➡ New Zealand's climate is unpredictable: hypothermia is a risk in high-altitude areas.

➡ At the beach, beware of rips and undertows, which can drag swimmers out to sea.

➡ New Zealand's sandflies are an itchy annoyance. Use repellent in coastal and lakeside areas.

Telephone

New Zealand uses regional two-digit area codes for long-distance calls, which can be made from any payphone. If you're making a local call (ie to someone else in the same town), you don't need to dial the area code. But if you're dialling within a region (even if it's to a nearby town with the same area code), you do have to dial the area code.

To make international calls from NZ (which is possible on payphones), you need to dial the international access code 00, then the country code and the area code (without the initial '0'). So for a London number, for example, you'd dial 00-44-20, then the number. If dialling NZ from overseas, the country code is 64, followed by the appropriate area code minus the initial '0'.

Mobile Phones

European phones should work on NZ's network, but most American or Japanese phones will not. It's straightforward to buy a local SIM card and prepaid account at outlets in airports and large towns (provided your mobile is unlocked).

Most NZ mobile phone numbers begin with the prefix 021, 022 or 027. Mobile phone coverage is good in cities and towns and most parts of the North Island.

If you want to bring your own phone and use a prepaid service with a local SIM card (rather than pay for expensive global roaming on your home network), Vodafone (www.vodafone.co.nz) is a practical option. Any Vodafone shop (in most major towns) will set you up with a NZ Travel SIM and a phone number (from around $30; valid for 30, 60 or 90 days). Top-ups can be purchased at newsagents, post offices and petrol stations all over the country.

Phone Hire New Zealand (www.phonehirenz.com) rents out mobiles, modems and GPS systems (from $3/10/7 per day).

Pay Phones

Local calls from payphones cost $1 for the first 15 minutes, and $0.20 per minute thereafter, though coin-operated payphones are scarce (and if you do find one, chances are the coin slot will be gummed up); you'll generally need a phonecard. Calls to mobile phones attract higher rates.

Phonecards

New Zealand has a wide range of phonecards available, which can be bought at hostels, newsagents and post offices for a fixed-dollar value (usually $5, $10, $20 and

$50). These can be used with any public or private phone by dialling a toll-free access number and then the PIN number on the card. Shop around – rates vary from company to company.

Premium-Rate & Toll-Free Calls

Numbers starting with 0900 charge upwards of $1 per minute (more from mobiles). These numbers cannot be dialled from payphones, and sometimes not from prepaid mobile phones.

Toll-free numbers in NZ have the prefix 0800 or 0508, and can be called from anywhere in the country, though they may not be accessible from certain areas or from mobile phones. Numbers beginning with 0508, 0800 or 0900 cannot be dialled from outside NZ.

Time

New Zealand is 12 hours ahead of GMT/UTC and two hours ahead of Australian Eastern Standard Time. The Chathams are 45 minutes ahead of NZ's main islands.

In summer, NZ observes daylight saving time, where clocks are wound forward by one hour on the last Sunday in September; clocks are wound back on the first Sunday of the following April.

Toilets

Toilets in NZ are sit-down Western style. Public toilets are plentiful, and are usually reasonably clean with working locks and plenty of toilet paper.

See www.toiletmap.co.nz for public-toilet locations around the country.

Tourist Information

Almost every Kiwi city or town seems to have a visitor information centre. The bigger centres stand united within the outstanding i-SITE network (www.newzealand. com/travel/i-sites) – more than 80 info centres affiliated with Tourism New Zealand. The i-SITE centres have trained staff, information on local activities and attractions, and free brochures and maps. Staff can also book activities, transport and accommodation.

Bear in mind that some information centres only promote accommodation and tour operators who are paying members of the local tourist association, and that sometimes staff aren't supposed to recommend one activity or accommodation provider over another.

There's also a network of Department of Conservation (DOC; www.doc.govt.nz) visitor centres to help you plan outdoor activities and make bookings (particularly for tramping trails and huts). The DOC visitor centres – in national parks, regional centres and major cities – usually also have displays on local flora and fauna.

Travellers with Disabilities

Kiwi accommodation generally caters fairly well for travellers with disabilities, with most hostels, hotels and motels equipped with one or two wheelchair-accessible rooms. (B&Bs aren't required to have accessible rooms.) Many tourist attractions similarly provide wheelchair access, with wheelchairs often available. Most i-SITE visitor centres can advise on suitable attractions in the locality.

Tour operators with accessible vehicles operate from most major centres. Key cities are also serviced by 'kneeling' buses (buses that hydraulically stoop down to kerb level to allow easy access), and many taxi companies offer wheelchair-accessible vans. Large car-hire firms (Avis, Hertz etc) provide cars with hand controls at no extra charge (but advance notice is required). Air New Zealand is also very well equipped to accommodate travellers in wheelchairs.

Download Lonely Planet's free Accessible Travel guides from http://lptravel.to/ AccessibleTravel.

Activities

Out and about, the DOC has been hard at work improving access to short walking trails (and some of the longer ones). Tracks that are wheelchair accessible are categorised as 'easy access short walks': the Cape Reinga Lighthouse Walk and Milford Foreshore Walk are two prime examples.

If cold-weather activity is more your thing, see Snow Sports NZ's page on adaptive winter sports: www.snow sports.co.nz/get-involved/ adaptive-snow-sports.

Resources

Access4All (www.access4all. co.nz) Listings of accessible accommodation and activities around New Zealand.

Firstport (http://firstport.co.nz) Includes a high-level overview on transport in NZ, including mobility taxis and accessible public transport.

Mobility Parking (www.mobil-ityparking.org.nz) Apply for an overseas visitor mobility parking permit ($35 for 12 months) and have it posted to you before you even reach NZ.

Visas

Visa application forms are available from NZ diplomatic missions overseas, travel agents and **Immigration New Zealand** (☑09-914 4100, 0508 558 855; www. immigration.govt.nz). Immigration New Zealand has more than 25 offices overseas, including the US, UK and Australia; consult the website.

Visitor Visa

Citizens of Australia don't need a visa to visit NZ and

can stay indefinitely (provided they have no criminal convictions). UK citizens don't need a visa either and can stay in the country for up to six months.

Citizens of another 58 countries that have visa-waiver agreements with NZ don't need a visa for stays of up to three months per visit, for no more than six months within any 12-month period, provided they have an onward ticket and sufficient funds to support their stay: see the website for details. Nations in this group include Canada, France, Germany, Ireland, Japan, the Netherlands, South Africa and the USA.

Citizens of other countries must obtain a visa before entering NZ. Visitor visas allow stays of up to nine months within an 18-month period, and cost $170 to $220, depending on where in the world the application is processed.

A visitor's visa can be extended from nine to 12 months, but if you get this extension you'll have to leave NZ after your 12-month stay has expired and wait another 12 months before you can come back. Applications are assessed on a case-by-case basis; you may need to provide proof of adequate funds to sustain you during your visit ($1000 per month) plus an onward ticket establishing your intent to leave. Apply for extensions at any Immigration New Zealand office – see the website (www.immigration. govt.nz) for locations.

Work Visa

It's illegal for foreign nationals to work in NZ on a visitor visa, except for Australian citizens or permanent residents, who can legally gain work without a visa or permit. If you're visiting NZ to find work, or you already have an employment offer, you'll need to apply for a work visa, which can be valid for up to three years, depending on your circum-

GOVERNMENT TRAVEL ADVICE

The following government websites offer travel advisories and information on current hotspots:

Australian Department of Foreign Affairs & Trade (www.smarttraveller.gov.au)

British Foreign & Commonwealth Office (www.gov. uk/fco)

Dutch Ministry of Foreign Affairs (www.government. nl/ministries/ministry-of-foreign-affairs)

Foreign Affairs, Trade & Development Canada (www. international.gc.ca)

German Federal Foreign Office (www.auswaertiges-amt.de)

Japanese Ministry of Foreign Affairs (www.mofa.go.jp)

US Department of State (www.travel.state.gov)

stance. You can apply for a work permit after you're in NZ, but its validity will be backdated to when you entered the country. The fee for a work visa can be anything upwards of $190, depending on where and how it's processed (paper or online) and the type of application.

Working Holiday Scheme

Eligible travellers who are only interested in short-term employment to supplement their travels can take part in one of NZ's working holiday schemes (WHS). Under these schemes citizens aged 18 to 30 (occasionally 35) years from 44 countries – including France, Germany, Ireland, Japan, Malaysia, the Netherlands, Scandinavian countries and the USA – can apply for a visa. For most nationalities the visa is valid for 12 months but citizens of Canada and the UK can work for up to 23 months. It's only issued to those seeking a genuine working holiday, not permanent work, so you're not supposed to work for one employer for more than three months.

Eligible nationals must apply for a WHS visa from within their own country. Applicants must have an onward ticket, a passport valid for at least three months

from the date they will leave NZ and evidence of at least $350 in accessible funds for each month of their stay. The application fee is $165 and isn't refunded if your application is declined.

The rules vary for different nationalities, so make sure you read up on the specifics of your country's agreement with NZ at www.immigration. govt.nz.

Volunteering

New Zealand presents an array of active, outdoorsy volunteer opportunities for travellers to get some dirt under their fingernails and participate in conservation programs. These programs can include anything from tree planting and weed removal to track construction, habitat conservation and fencing. Ask about local opportunities at any regional i-SITE visitor information centre, join one of the programs run by DOC (www.doc.govt.nz/getting-involved), or check out these online resources:

➡ www.conservation volunteers.org.nz

➡ www.helpx.net

➡ www.nature.org.nz

➡ www.volunteeringnz.org.nz

➡ www.wwf.org.nz

Women Travellers

New Zealand is generally a very safe place for female travellers, although the usual sensible precautions apply (for both sexes): avoid walking alone at night; never hitchhike alone; and if you're out on the town, have a plan on how to get back to your accommodation safely. Sexual harassment is not a widely reported problem in NZ, but of course that doesn't mean it doesn't happen. See www.womentravel.co.nz for tours aimed at solo women.

Work

If you have been approved for a working holiday scheme (WHS) visa, there are a number of possibilities for temporary employment in NZ. Pay rates start at the minimum wage ($16.50 per hour, at the time of writing), but depend on the work. There's plenty of casual work around, mainly in agriculture (fruit picking, farming, wineries), hospitality (bar work, waiting tables) or at ski resorts. Office-based work can be found in IT, banking, finance and telemarketing. Register with a local office-work agency to get started.

Seasonal fruit picking, pruning and harvesting is prime short-term work for visitors. Kiwifruit and other fruit and veg are harvested from December to May (and other farming work is available outside that season). Fruit picking is physically taxing toil – working in the dirt under the hot sun – turnover of workers is high. You're usually paid by how much you pick (per bin, bucket or kilogram): if you stick with it for a while, you'll get faster and fitter and you can actually make some reasonable cash. Prime North Island picking locations include the Bay of Islands (Kerikeri and Paihia), rural Auckland, Tauranga and the Bay of Plenty, Gisborne and Hawke's Bay (Napier and Hastings).

Winter work at ski resorts and their service towns includes bartending, waiting, cleaning, ski-tow operation and, if you're properly qualified, ski or snowboard instructing.

Resources

Backpacker publications, hostel managers and other travellers are often good sources of info on local work possibilities. Base Backpackers (www.stayatbase.com/work) runs an employment service via its website, while the Notice Boards page on the Budget Backpacker Hostels website (www.bbh.co.nz) lists job vacancies in BBH hostels and a few other possibilities.

Kiwi Careers (www.careers.govt.nz) lists professional opportunities in various fields (agriculture, creative, health, teaching, volunteer work and recruitment), while Seek (www.seek.co.nz) is one of the biggest NZ job-search networks, with thousands of jobs listed.

Try the following websites for seasonal work:

➡ www.backpackerboard.co.nz

➡ www.seasonalwork.co.nz

➡ www.seasonaljobs.co.nz

➡ www.picknz.co.nz

➡ www.pickingjobs.com

➡ www.picktheworld.org

Income Tax

Death and taxes – no escape! For most travellers, Kiwi dollars earned in NZ will be subject to income tax, which is deducted from payments by employers – a process called Pay As You Earn (PAYE).

Income tax rates are 10.5% for annual salaries up to $14,000, then 17.5% up to $48,000, 30% up to $70,000, then 33% for higher incomes. A NZ Accident Compensation Corporation (ACC) scheme levy (around 1.5%) will also be deducted from your pay packet. Note that these rates tend to change slightly year to year.

If you visit NZ and work for a short time (eg on a working holiday scheme), you may qualify for a tax refund when you leave. Lodging a tax return before you leave NZ is the best way of securing a refund. For more info, see the Inland Revenue Department website (www.ird.govt.nz), or call ☎03-951 2020.

IRD Number

Travellers undertaking paid work in NZ (including working holiday scenarios) must first open a New Zealand bank account, then obtain an Inland Revenue Department (IRD) number. Download the *IRD number application - non-resident/offshore individual IR742* form from the Inland Revenue Department website (www.ird.govt.nz). IRD numbers normally take eight to 10 working days to be issued.

Transport

GETTING THERE & AWAY

New Zealand is a long way from almost everywhere – most travellers jet in from afar. Flights, cars and tours can be booked online at lonelyplanet.com/bookings.

Entering the Country

Disembarkation in New Zealand is generally a straightforward affair, with only the usual customs declarations and luggage-carousel scramble to endure. Under the Orwellian title of 'Advance Passenger Screening', documents that used to be checked after you touched down in NZ (passport, visa etc) are now checked before you board your flight – make sure all your documentation is in order so that your check-in is stress-free.

Passport

There are no restrictions when it comes to foreign citizens entering NZ. If you have a current passport and visa (or don't require one), you should be fine.

Air

New Zealand's abundance of year-round activities means that airports here are busy most of the time: if you want to fly at a particularly popular time of year (eg over the Christmas period), book well in advance.

The high season for flights into NZ is during summer (December to February), with slightly less of a premium on fares over the shoulder months (October/November and March/April). The low season generally tallies with the winter months (June to August), though this is still a busy time for airlines ferrying snow enthusiasts.

Airports & Airlines

Auckland is New Zealand's main transport hub. **Auckland Airport** (AKL; Map p68; ☑09-275 0789; www.aucklandairport.co.nz; Ray Emery Dr, Mangere) welcomes flights from all over the world and connects them with domestic flights to all of the major centres. **Wellington Airport** (WLG; ☑04-385 5100; www.wellingtonairport.co.nz; Stewart Duff Dr, Rongotai) has direct flights to and from Australia and Fiji. There are direct flights from the South Island to Auckland, Hamilton, Tauranga, Rotorua, Napier, New Plymouth, Palmerston North, Kapiti Coast and Wellington.

New Zealand's national carrier is **Air New Zealand** (www.airnewzealand.co.nz), with direct flights to and from Australia, the Pacific, Asia and the Americas, and an extensive network across NZ. Numerous international airlines fly into Auckland, but

---

CLIMATE CHANGE & TRAVEL

Every form of transport that relies on carbon-based fuel generates CO_2, the main cause of human-induced climate change. Modern travel is dependent on aeroplanes, which might use less fuel per kilometre per person than most cars but travel much greater distances. The altitude at which aircraft emit gases (including CO_2) and particles also contributes to their climate change impact. Many websites offer 'carbon calculators' that allow people to estimate the carbon emissions generated by their journey and, for those who wish to do so, to offset the impact of the greenhouse gases emitted with contributions to portfolios of climate-friendly initiatives throughout the world. Lonely Planet offsets the carbon footprint of all staff and author travel.

only **Fiji Airways** (www.fiji-airways.com), **Jetstar** (www.jetstar.com), **Qantas** (www.qantas.com.au), **Singapore Airlines** (www.singaporeair.com) and **Virgin Australia** (www.virginaustralia.com) fly into Wellington.

Sea

Ferry Regular ferry services between Wellington and Picton link the North and South Islands.

Cruise Ship If you're travelling from Australia and are content with a slow pace, try P&O (www.pocruises.com.au) and Princess (www.princess.com) for cruises to New Zealand.

Cargo Ship If you don't need luxury, a berth on a cargo ship or freighter to/from New Zealand is a quirky way to go. Freighter Expeditions (www.freighterexpeditions.com.au) offers cruises to New Zealand from Singapore (49 days return) and Antwerp in Belgium (32 days one-way).

Yacht It is possible (though by no means straightforward) to make your way between NZ, Australia and the Pacific Islands by crewing on a yacht. Try asking around at harbours, marinas, and yacht and sailing clubs. Popular yachting harbours in NZ include the Bay of Islands and Whangarei (both in Northland), Auckland and Wellington. March and April are the best months to look for boats heading to Australia. From Fiji, October to November is a peak departure season to beat the cyclones that soon follow in that neck of the woods.

GETTING AROUND

Air

Those who have limited time to get between NZ's attractions can make the most of a widespread (and very reliable and safe) network of intra- and inter-island flights.

Domestic Airlines

The country's major domestic carrier, Air New Zealand, has an aerial network covering most of the country, often operating under the Air New Zealand Link moniker on less popular routes. Australia-based Jetstar also flies between main urban areas. Between them, these two airlines carry the vast majority of domestic passengers in NZ. Beyond this, several small-scale regional operators provide essential transport services to outlying islands, such as Great Barrier Island in the Hauraki Gulf. There are also plenty of scenic- and charter-flight operators around NZ, not listed here. Operators include the following:

Air Chathams (0800 580 127; www.airchathams.co.nz) Flies between Auckland and Whakatane.

Air New Zealand (0800 737 000; www.airnewzealand.co.nz) Offers flights between 20-plus domestic destinations.

Barrier Air (0800 900 600; www.barrierair.kiwi) Flies the skies over Great Barrier Island, Auckland and Kaitaia (and seasonally, Tauranga and Whitianga).

FlyMySky (0800 222 123; www.flymysky.co.nz) At least three flights daily from Auckland to Great Barrier Island.

Jetstar (0800 800 995; www.jetstar.com) Flies from Auckland to Napier, New Plymouth, Palmerston North and Wellington.

Soundsair (0800 505 005; www.soundsair.co.nz) Flies between Wellington and Taupo.

Sunair (0800 786 247; www.sunair.co.nz) Flies to Whitianga from Ardmore (near Auckland), Great Barrier Island and Tauranga, plus numerous other North Island connections between Hamilton, Rotorua, Gisborne and Whakatane.

Bicycle

Touring cyclists proliferate in NZ, particularly over summer. The country is clean, green and relatively uncrowded, and has lots of cheap accommodation (including camping) and abundant fresh water. The roads are generally in good nick, and the climate is usually not too hot or cold. Road traffic is the biggest danger: trucks overtaking too close to cyclists are a particular threat. Bikes and cycling gear are readily available to rent or buy in the main centres, and bicycle-repair shops are common.

By law all cyclists must wear an approved safety helmet (or risk a fine); it's also vital to have good reflective safety clothing. Cyclists who use public transport will find that major bus lines and trains only take bicycles on a 'space available' basis (in cities, usually outside rush hour), and may charge up to $10. Some of the smaller shuttle bus companies, on the other hand, make sure they have storage space for bikes, which they carry for a surcharge.

If importing your own bike or transporting it by plane within NZ, check with the relevant airline for costs and the degree of dismantling and packing required.

See www.nzta.govt.nz/walking-cycling-and-public-transport for more bike safety and legal tips, and the New Zealand Cycle Trail (p32;Ngā Haerenga) – a network of 22 'Great Rides' across NZ.

Hire

Rates offered by most outfits for renting road or mountain bikes are usually around $20 per hour to $60 per day. Longer-term rentals may be available by negotiation. You can often hire bikes from your accommodation (hostels, holiday parks etc), or rent more reputable machines from bike shops in the larger towns.

Buying a Bike

Bicycles can be readily bought in NZ's larger cities, but prices for newer models are high. For a decent hybrid bike or rigid mountain bike you'll pay anywhere from $800 to $1800, though you can get a cheap one for around $500 (but you still then need to buy panniers, helmet, lock etc, and the cost quickly climbs). Other options include the post-Christmas sales and midyear stocktakes, when newish cycles can be heavily discounted.

Boat

New Zealand may be an island nation but there's virtually no long-distance water transport around the country. Obvious exceptions include the boat services between Auckland and various islands in the Hauraki Gulf.

If you're cashed-up, consider the cruise liners that chug around the NZ coastline as part of broader South Pacific itineraries: P&O Cruises (www.pocruises.com.au) is a major player.

Bus

Bus travel in NZ is easygoing and well organised, with services transporting you to the far reaches of both islands (including the start/end of various walking tracks)...but it can be expensive, tedious and time-consuming.

New Zealand's main bus company is **InterCity** (www.intercity.co.nz), which can drive you to just about anywhere on the North and South Islands. **Naked Bus** (☑09-979 1616; https://nakedbus.com) has similar routes and remains the main competition.

Privately run shuttle buses can transport travellers to some trailheads or collect them from the end point of a tramp; advance booking essential.

Seat Classes & Smoking

There are no allocated economy or luxury classes on NZ buses (very democratic), and smoking on the bus is a definite no-no.

Naked Bus has a sleeper class on overnight services between Auckland and Wellington (stopping at Hamilton and Palmerston North) where you can lie flat in a 1.8m-long bed (bring a sleeping bag, pillowcase and maybe earplugs). See http://nakedbus.com/nz/home/sleeper-bus for details.

Reservations

Over summer (December to February), school holidays and public holidays, book well in advance on popular routes (a week or two ahead if possible). At other times, a day or two ahead is usually fine. The best prices are generally available online, booked a few weeks in advance.

Bus Passes

If you're covering a lot of ground, both InterCity and Naked Bus offer bus passes (respectively, priced by hours and number of trips). This can be cheaper than paying as you go, but do the maths before buying and note that you'll be locked into using one network. Passes are usually valid for 12 months.

On fares other than bus passes, InterCity offers a discount of around 10% for YHA, ISIC, HI, Nomads, BBH or VIP backpacker card holders. Senior discounts only apply for NZ citizens.

FlexiPass A hop-on/hop-off InterCity pass, allowing travel to pretty much anywhere in NZ, in any direction, including the Interislander ferry across Cook Strait. The pass is purchased in blocks of travel time: minimum 15 hours ($125), maximum 60 hours ($459). The average cost of each block becomes cheaper the more hours you buy. You can top up the pass if you need more time.

TravelPass InterCity offers six hop-on/hop-off, fixed-itinerary North Island bus passes, from short $125 runs between Auckland and Paihia, to $405 trips from Auckland to Wellington via the big sights in between. See www.intercity.co.nz/bus-pass/travelpass for details.

Naked Passport (www.naked-passport.com) A Naked Bus pass that allows you to buy trips in blocks of five, which you can add to any time, and book each trip as needed. Five/15/20 trips cost $159/269/439.

Shuttle Buses

As well as InterCity and Naked Bus, regional shuttle buses fill in the gaps between the smaller towns. Operators include the following (see www.tourism.net.nz/transport/bus-and-coach-services for a complete list), offering regular scheduled services and/or bus tours and charters:

Go Kiwi Shuttles (www.go-kiwi.co.nz) Links Auckland with Whitianga on the Coromandel Peninsula daily.

Headfirst Travel (www.travel-headfirst.com) Does a loop from Rotorua to Waitomo (with an option to finish in Auckland).

Manabus (www.manabus.com) Runs in both directions daily between Auckland and Wellington via Hamilton, Rotorua, Taupo and Palmerston North. Also runs to Tauranga, Paihia and Napier. Services are offered in collaboration with Naked Bus.

Bus Tours

Clock up some kilometres with like-minded fellow travellers. The following operators run fixed-itinerary bus tours nationwide or on the North or South Islands. Accommodation, meals and hop-on/hop-off flexibility are often included. Styles vary from activity-focused itineraries through to hangover-mandatory backpacker buses.

Adventure Tours New Zealand (www.adventuretours.com.au/new-zealand) Four 11- to 22-day NZ tours of North or South Island, or both.

Flying Kiwi (www.flyingkiwi. com) Good-fun, activity-based trips around NZ with camping and cabin accommodation from a few days to a few weeks.

Haka Tours (www.hakatours. com) Three- to 24-day tours with adventure, snow or mountain-biking themes.

Kirra Tours (www.kirratours. co.nz) Upmarket coach tours (graded 'Classic' or 'Platinum' by price) from an operator with 50 years in the business.

Kiwi Experience (www.kiwi experience.com) A major hop-on/hop-off player with eco-friendly credentials. Myriad tours cover the length and breadth of NZ.

Stray Travel (www.straytravel. com) A wide range of flexible hop-on/hop-off passes and tours.

Car & Motorcycle

The best way to explore NZ in depth is to have your own wheels. It's easy to hire cars and campervans, though it's worth noting that fuel costs can be eye-watering. Alternatively, if you're in NZ for a few months, you might consider buying your own vehicle.

Automobile Association

New Zealand's **Automobile Association** (AA; ☑0800 500 444; www.aa.co.nz/travel) provides emergency breakdown services, distance calculators and accommodation guides (from holiday parks to motels and B&Bs).

Members of overseas automobile associations should bring their membership cards – many of these bodies have reciprocal agreements with the AA.

Driving Licences

International visitors to NZ can use their home-country driving licence – if your licence isn't in English, it's a good idea to carry a certified translation with you. Alternatively, use an International Driving Permit (IDP), which will usually be issued on the spot (valid for 12 months) by your home country's automobile association.

Fuel

Fuel (petrol, aka gasoline) is available from service stations across NZ: unless you're cruising around in something from the 1970s, you'll be filling up with 'unleaded', or LPG (gas). LPG is not always stocked by rural suppliers; if you're on gas, it's safer to have dual-fuel capability. Aside from remote locations like Milford Sound and Mt Cook, petrol prices don't vary much from place to place: per-litre costs at the time of research were hovering above $2.

Hire

CAMPERVAN

Check your rear-view mirror on any far-flung NZ road and you'll probably see a shiny white campervan (aka mobile home, motor home, RV) packed with liberated travellers, mountain bikes and portable barbecues cruising along behind you.

Most towns of any size have a campground or holiday park with powered sites (where you can plug your vehicle in) for around $35 per night. There are also 250-plus vehicle-accessible Department of Conservation (DOC; www.doc.govt.nz) campsites around NZ, priced up to $21 per adult. Weekly campsite passes for rental campervans slice up to 50% off the price of stays in DOC campgrounds; check the website for info.

You can hire campervans from dozens of companies. Prices vary with season, vehicle size and length of rental, and it pays to book months in advance.

A small van for two people typically has a minikitchen and foldout dining table, the latter transforming into a double bed when dinner is done and dusted. Larger, 'superior' two-berth vans include shower and toilet. Four- to six-berth campervans are the size of trucks (and similarly sluggish) and, besides the extra space, usually contain a toilet and shower.

Over summer, rates offered by the main rental firms for two-/four-/six-berth vans booked three months in advance start at around $120/150/230 per day (though they rise much higher, depending on model) for a rental of two weeks or more. Rates drop to $60/75/100 per day during winter.

Major operators include the following:

Apollo (☑0800 113 131, 09-889 2976; www.apollocamper. co.nz)

Britz (☑09-255 3910, 0800 081 032; www.britz.co.nz) Also does 'Britz Bikes' (add a mountain or city bike from $12 per day).

Maui (☑09-255 3910, 0800 688 558; www.maui-rentals. com)

Wilderness Motorhomes (☑09-282 3606; www.wilderness.co.nz)

CAR

Competition between car-hire companies in NZ is intense, particularly in the big cities. Remember that if you want to travel far, you need unlimited kilometres. Some (but not all) companies require drivers to be at least 21 years old – ask around.

INTERNATIONAL RENTAL COMPANIES

The big multinational companies have offices in most major cities, towns and airports. Firms sometimes offer one-way rentals (eg collect a car in Auckland, leave it in Wellington), but there are usually restrictions and fees.

The major companies offer a choice of either unlimited kilometres, or 100km (or so) per day free, plus so many cents per subsequent kilometre. Daily rates in main cities typically start at around $40 per day for a compact, late-model, Japanese car, and from $70 for medium-sized cars (including GST, unlimited kilometres and insurance).

Avis (📞0800 655 111, 09-526 2847; www.avis.co.nz)

Budget (📞09-529 7788, 0800 283 438; www.budget.co.nz)

Europcar (📞0800 800 115; www.europcar.co.nz)

Hertz (📞0800 654 321; www.hertz.co.nz)

Thrifty (📞03-359 2721, 0800 737 070; www.thrifty.co.nz)

LOCAL RENTAL COMPANIES

Local rental firms proliferate. These are almost always cheaper than the big boys – sometimes half the price – but the cheap rates may come with serious restrictions: vehicles are often older, depots might be further away from airports/city centres, and with less formality sometimes comes a less protective legal structure for renters.

Rentals from local firms start at around $30 or $40 per day for the smallest option. It's cheaper if you rent for a week or more, and there are often low-season and weekend discounts.

Affordable, independent operators with national networks include the following:

a2b Car Rentals (📞0800 545 000, 09-254 4397; www.a2b-car-rental.co.nz)

Ace Rental Cars (📞0800 502 277, 09-303 3112; www.acerentalcars.co.nz)

Apex Rentals (📞03-595 2315, 0800 500 660; www.apexrentals.co.nz)

Ezi Car Rental (📞0800 545 000, 09-254 4397; www.ezicarrental.co.nz)

Go Rentals (📞0800 467 368, 09-974 1598; www.gorentals.co.nz)

Omega Rental Cars (📞09-377 5573, 0800 525 210; www.omegarentalcars.com)

Pegasus Rental Cars (📞0800 803 580; www.rentalcars.co.nz)

Transfercar (📞09-630 7533; www.transfercar.co.nz) Relocation specialists with massive money-saving deals on one-way car rental.

MOTORCYCLE

Born to be wild? New Zealand has great terrain for motorcycle touring, despite the fickle weather in some regions. Most of the country's motorcycle-hire shops are in Auckland and Christchurch, where you can hire anything from a little 50cc moped (aka nifty-fifty) to a throbbing 750cc touring motorcycle and beyond. Recommended operators (who also run guided tours) offer rates around $100 per day:

New Zealand Motorcycle Rentals & Tours (📞09-486 2472; www.nzbike.com)

Te Waipounamu Motorcycle Tours (📞03-372 3537; www.motorcycle-hire.co.nz)

Insurance

Rather than risk paying out wads of cash if you have an accident, you can take out your own comprehensive insurance policy, or (the usual option) pay an additional fee per day to the rental company to reduce your excess. This brings the amount you must pay in the event of an accident down from around $1500 or $2000 to around $200 or $300. Smaller operators offering cheap rates often have a compulsory insurance excess, taken as a credit-card bond, of around $900.

Many insurance agreements won't cover the cost of damage to glass (including the windscreen) or tyres, and insurance coverage is often invalidated on beaches and certain rough (4WD) unsealed roads – read the fine print.

See www.acc.co.nz for info on NZ's Accident Compensation Corporation insurance scheme (fault-free personal injury insurance).

Purchase

Planning a long trip? Buying a car then selling it at the end of your travels can be one of the cheapest and best ways to see NZ. Auckland is the easiest place to buy a car: scour the hostel noticeboards. Turners Auctions (www.turners.co.nz) is NZ's biggest car-auction operator, with 11 locations.

LEGALITIES

Make sure your prospective vehicle has a Warrant of Fitness (WoF) and registration valid for a reasonable period: see the New Zealand Transport Agency website (www.nzta.govt.nz) for details.

Buyers should also take out third-party insurance, covering the cost of repairs to another vehicle in an accident that is your fault: try the **Automobile Association** (AA; 📞0800 500 444; www.aa.co.nz/travel). New Zealand's no-fault Accident Compensation Corporation (www.acc.co.nz) scheme covers personal injury, but make sure you have travel insurance, too.

If you're considering buying a car and want someone to check it out for you, various companies inspect cars for around $150; find them at car auctions, or they will come to you. Try Vehicle Inspection New Zealand (09-573 3230, 0800 468 469; www.vinz.co.nz) or the AA.

Before you buy it's wise to confirm ownership of the vehicle, and find out if there's anything dodgy about the car (eg stolen, or outstanding debts). The AA's LemonCheck (09-420 3090; www.lemoncheck.co.nz) offers this service.

BUY-BACK DEALS

You can avoid the hassle of buying/selling a vehicle privately by entering into a buy-back arrangement with a dealer. Predictably, dealers often find sneaky ways of knocking down the return-sale price, which may be 50% less than what you paid, so hiring or buying and selling a vehicle yourself (if you have the time) is usually a better bet.

Road Hazards

There's an unusually high percentage of international drivers involved in road accidents in NZ – something like 30% of accidents involve a nonlocal driver. Kiwi traffic is usually pretty light, but it's easy to get stuck behind a slow-moving truck or campervan – pack plenty of patience, and know your road rules before you get behind the wheel. There are also lots of slow wiggly roads, one-way bridges and plenty of gravel roads, all of which require a more cautious driving approach. And watch out for sheep!

To check road conditions, call ☎0800 444 449 or see www.nzta.govt.nz/traffic.

Road Rules

➡ Kiwis drive on the left-hand side of the road; cars are right-hand drive. Give way to the right at intersections.

➡ All vehicle occupants must wear a seatbelt or risk a fine. Small children must be belted into approved safety seats.

➡ Always carry your licence when driving. Drink-driving is a serious offence and remains a significant problem in NZ, despite widespread campaigns and severe penalties. The legal blood-alcohol limit is 0.05% for drivers aged over 20, and 0% (zero) for those under 20.

➡ At single-lane bridges (of which there are a surprisingly large number), a smaller red arrow pointing in your direction of travel means that you give way.

➡ Speed limits on the open road are generally 100km/h;

in built-up areas the limit is usually 50km/h. Speed cameras and radars are used extensively.

➡ Be aware that not all rail crossings have barriers or alarms. Approach slowly and look both ways.

➡ Don't pass other cars when the centre line is yellow.

➡ It's illegal to drive while using a mobile phone.

Hitching

Hitching is never entirely safe, and we don't recommend it. Travellers who hitch should understand that they are taking a small but potentially serious risk. That said, it's not unusual to see hitchhikers along NZ country roads.

Alternatively, check hostel noticeboards for ride-share opportunities.

Local Transport

Bus & Train

New Zealand's larger cities have extensive bus services but, with a few honourable exceptions, they are mainly daytime, weekday operations; weekend services can be infrequent or nonexistent. Negotiating inner-city Auckland is made easier by Link buses; Hamilton has a free city-centre loop bus. Most main cities have late-night buses for boozy Friday and Saturday nights. Don't expect local bus services in more remote areas.

The only cities with decent local train services are Auckland and Wellington, with four and five suburban routes respectively.

Taxi

The main cities have plenty of taxis and even small towns may have a local service.

Taxis are metered, and are generally reliable and trustworthy.

Train

New Zealand train travel is all about the journey, not about getting anywhere in a hurry. **Great Journeys of New Zealand** (☎0800 872 467, 04-495 0775; www.great journeysofnz.co.nz) operates two routes in the North Island, which are listed below. It's best to reserve online or by phone; reservations can be made directly through Great Journeys of New Zealand (operated by KiwiRail), or at most train stations, travel agents and visitor information centres. Cheaper fares appear if you book online within NZ. All services are for day travel (no sleeper services).

Capital Connection Weekday commuter service between Palmerston North and Wellington.

Northern Explorer Between Auckland and Wellington: southbound on Mondays, Thursdays and Saturdays; northbound on Tuesdays, Fridays and Sundays.

Train Passes

A Scenic Journeys Rail Pass allows unlimited travel on all of its rail services, including passage on the Wellington–Picton Interislander ferry. There are two types of pass, both requiring you to book your seats a minimum of 24 hours before you want to travel. Both have discounts for kids.

Fixed Pass Limited-duration fares for one/two/three weeks, costing $629/729/829 per adult.

Freedom Pass Affords you travel on a certain number of days over a 12-month period; a three-/seven-/10-day pass costs $439/969/1299.

Language

New Zealand has three official languages: English, Māori and NZ sign language. Although English is what you'll usually hear, Māori has been making a comeback. You can use English to speak to anyone in New Zealand, but there are some occasions when knowing a small amount of Māori is useful, such as when visiting a *marae*, where often only Māori is spoken. Some knowledge of Māori will also help you interpret the many Māori place names you'll come across.

KIWI ENGLISH

Like the people of other English-speaking countries in the world, New Zealanders have their own, unique way of speaking the language. The flattening of vowels is the most distinctive feature of Kiwi pronunciation. For example, in Kiwi English, 'fish and chips' sounds more like 'fush and chups'. On the North Island sentences often have 'eh!' attached to the end. In the far south a rolled 'r' is common, which is a holdover from that region's Scottish heritage – it's especially noticeable in Southland.

MĀORI

The Māori have a vividly chronicled history, recorded in songs and chants that dramatically recall the migration to New Zealand from Polynesia as well as other important events. Early missionaries were the first to record the language in a written form using only 15 letters of the English alphabet.

Māori is closely related to other Polynesian languages such as Hawaiian, Tahitian and Cook Islands Māori. In fact, New Zealand Māori and Hawaiian are quite similar, even though more than 7000km separates Honolulu and Auckland.

The Māori language was never dead – it was always used in Māori ceremonies – but over time familiarity with it was definitely on the decline. Fortunately, recent years have seen a revival of interest in it, and this forms an integral part of the renaissance of *Māoritanga* (Māori culture). Many Māori people who had heard the language spoken on the *marae* for years but had not used it in their day-to-day lives, are now studying it and speaking it fluently. Māori is taught in schools throughout New Zealand, some TV programs and news reports are broadcast in it, and many English place names are being renamed in Māori. Even government departments have been given Māori names: for example, the Inland Revenue Department is also known as Te Tari Taake (the last word is actually *take*, which means 'levy', but the department has chosen to stress the long 'a' by spelling it 'aa').

In many places, Māori have come together to provide instruction in their language and culture to young children; the idea is for them to grow up speaking both Māori and English, and to develop a familiarity with Māori tradition. It's a matter of some pride to have fluency in the language. On some *marae* only Māori can be spoken.

Pronunciation

Māori is a fluid, poetic language and surprisingly easy to pronounce once you remember to split each word (some can be amazingly long) into separate syllables. Each syllable ends in a vowel. There are no 'silent' letters.

Most consonants in Māori – *h, k, m, n, p, t* and *w* – are pronounced much the same as in English. The Māori *r* is a flapped sound (not rolled) with the tongue near the front of the mouth. It's closer to the English 'l' in pronunciation.

The *ng* is pronounced as in the English words 'singing' or 'running', and can be used at the beginning of words as well as at the end. To practise, just say 'ing' over and over, then isolate the 'ng' part of it.

The letters *wh*, when occuring together, are generally pronounced as a soft English 'f'. This pronunciation is used in many place names in New Zealand, such as Whakatane, Whangaroa and Whakapapa (all pronounced as if they begin with a soft 'f'). There is some local variation: in the region around the Whanganui River, for example, *wh* is pronounced as in the English word 'when'.

The correct pronunciation of the vowels is very important. The examples below are a rough guideline – it helps to listen carefully to someone who speaks the language well. Each vowel has both a long and a short sound, with long vowels often denoted by a line over the letter or a double vowel. We have not indicated long and short vowel forms in this book.

Vowels

a	as in 'large', with no 'r' sound
e	as in 'get'
i	as in 'marine'
o	as in 'pork'
u	as the 'oo' in 'moon'

Vowel Combinations

ae, ai	as the 'y' in 'sky'
ao, au	as the 'ow' in 'how'
ea	as in 'bear'
ei	as in 'vein'
eo	as 'eh-oh'
eu	as 'eh-oo'
ia	as in the name 'Ian'
ie	as the 'ye' in 'yet'
io	as the 'ye o' in 'ye old'
iu	as the 'ue' in 'cue'
oa	as in 'roar'
oe	as in 'toe'
oi	as in 'toil'
ou	as the 'ow' in 'how'
ua	as the 'ewe' in 'fewer'

Greetings & Small Talk

Māori greetings are becoming increasingly popular – don't be surprised if you're greeted with *Kia ora.*

Welcome!	*Haere mai!*
Hello./Good luck./ Good health.	*Kia ora.*
Hello. (to one person)	*Tena koe.*
Hello. (to two people)	*Tena korua.*
Hello. (to three or more people)	*Tena koutou.*
Goodbye. (to person staying)	*E noho ra.*
Goodbye. (to person leaving)	*Haere ra.*
How are you? (to one person)	*Kei te pehea koe?*
How are you? (to two people)	*Kei te pehea korua?*
How are you? (to three or more people)	*Kei te pehea koutou?*
Very well, thanks./ That's fine.	*Kei te pai.*

Māori Geographical Terms

The following words form part of many Māori place names in New Zealand, and help you understand the meaning of these place names. For example: Waikaremoana is the Sea (*moana*) of Rippling (*kare*) Waters (*wai*), and Rotorua means the Second (*rua*) Lake (*roto*).

a – of
ana – cave
ara – way, path or road
awa – river or valley
heke – descend
hiku – end; tail
hine – girl; daughter
ika – fish
iti – small
kahurangi – treasured possession; special greenstone
kai – food
kainga – village
kaka – parrot
kare – rippling
kati – shut or close
koura – crayfish
makariri – cold
manga – stream or tributary
manu – bird
maunga – mountain
moana – sea or lake
moko – tattoo
motu – island
mutu – finished; ended; over
nga – the (plural)
noa – ordinary; not *tapu*
nui – big or great
nuku – distance
o – of, place of...
one – beach, sand or mud
pa – fortified village
papa – large blue-grey mudstone
pipi – common edible bivalve
pohatu – stone
poto – short

pouri – sad; dark; gloomy
puke – hill
puna – spring; hole; fountain
rangi – sky; heavens
raro – north
rei – cherished possession
roa – long
roto – lake
rua – hole in the ground; two
runga – above
tahuna – beach; sandbank
tane – man
tangata – people
tapu – sacred, forbidden or taboo
tata – close to; dash against; twin islands
tawaha – entrance or opening
tawahi – the other side (of a river or lake)
te – the (singular)
tonga – south
ure – male genitals
uru – west
waha – broken
wahine – woman
wai – water
waingaro – lost; waters that disappear in certain seasons

waka – canoe
wera – burnt or warm; floating
wero – challenge
whaka... – to act as ...
whanau – family
whanga – harbour, bay or inlet
where – house
whenua – land or country
whiti – east

Here are some more place names composed of words in the list:

Aramoana – Sea *(moana)* Path *(ara)*
Awaroa – Long *(roa)* River *(awa)*
Kaitangata – Eat *(kai)* People *(tangata)*
Maunganui – Great *(nui)* Mountain *(maunga)*
Opouri – Place of *(o)* Sadness *(pouri)*
Te Araroa – The *(te)* Long *(roa)* Path *(ara)*
Te Puke – The *(te)* Hill *(puke)*
Urewera – Burnt *(wera)* Penis *(ure)*
Waimakariri – Cold *(makariri)* Water *(wai)*
Wainui – Great *(nui)* Waters *(wai)*
Whakatane – To Act *(whaka)* as a Man *(tane)*
Whangarei – Cherished *(rei)* Harbour *(whanga)*

GLOSSARY

Following is a list of abbreviations, 'Kiwi English', Māori and slang terms used in this book and which you may hear in New Zealand.

All Blacks – NZ's revered national rugby union team
Anzac – Australia and New Zealand Army Corps
Aoraki – Māori name for Mt Cook, meaning 'Cloud Piercer'
Aotearoa – Māori name for NZ, most often translated as 'Land of the Long White Cloud'
aroha – love

B&B – bed and breakfast accommodation
bach – holiday home (pronounced 'batch'); see also crib
black-water rafting – rafting or tubing underground in a cave
boozer – public bar
bro – literally 'brother'; usually meaning mate

BYO – 'bring your own' (usually applies to alcohol at a restaurant or cafe)

choice/chur – fantastic; great
crib – the name for a bach in Otago and Southland

DB&B – bed and breakfast accommodation including dinner
DOC – Department of Conservation (or Te Papa Atawhai); government department that administers national parks, tracks and huts

eh? – roughly translates as 'don't you agree?'

farmstay – accommodation on a Kiwi farm
football – rugby, either union or league; occasionally soccer

Great Walks – set of nine popular tramping tracks within NZ

greenstone – jade; *pounamu*
gumboots – rubber boots or Wellingtons; originated from diggers on the gum-fields

haka – any dance, but usually a war dance
hangi – oven whereby food is steamed in baskets over embers in a hole; a Māori feast
hapu – subtribe or smaller tribal grouping
Hawaiki – original homeland of the Māori
hei tiki – carved, stylised human figure worn around the neck; also called a *tiki*
homestay – accommodation in a family house
hongi – Māori greeting; the pressing of foreheads and noses, and sharing of life breath
hui – gathering; meeting

i-SITE – information centre

iwi – large tribal grouping with common lineage back to the original migration from *Hawaiki*; people; tribe

jandals – contraction of 'Japanese sandals'; flip-flops; thongs; usually rubber footwear

jersey – jumper, usually woollen; the shirt worn by rugby players

kauri – native pine

kia ora – hello

Kiwi – New Zealander; an adjective to mean anything relating to NZ

kiwi – flightless, nocturnal brown bird with a long beak

Kiwiana – things uniquely connected to NZ life and culture, especially from bygone years

kiwifruit – small, succulent fruit with fuzzy brown skin and juicy green flesh; aka Chinese gooseberry or zespri

kumara – Polynesian sweet potato, a Māori staple food

Kupe – early Polynesian navigator from *Hawaiki*, credited with the discovery of the islands that are now NZ

mana – spiritual quality of a person or object; authority or prestige

Māori – indigenous people of NZ

Māoritanga – things Māori, ie Māori culture

marae – sacred ground in front of the Māori meeting house;

more commonly used to refer to the entire complex of buildings

Maui – figure in Māori (Polynesian) mythology

mauri – life force/principle

moa – large, extinct flightless bird

moko – tattoo; usually refers to facial tattoos

nga – the (plural); see also *te*

ngai/ngati – literally, 'the people of' or 'the descendants of'; tribe (pronounced 'kai' on the South Island)

NZ – universal term for New Zealand; pronounced 'en zed'

pa – fortified Māori village, usually on a hilltop

Pacific Rim – modern NZ cuisine; local produce cooked with imported styles

Pākehā – Māori for a white or European person

Pasifika – Pacific Island culture

paua – abalone; iridescent paua shell is often used in jewellery

pavlova – meringue cake topped with cream and kiwifruit

PI – Pacific Islander

poi – ball of woven flax

pounamu – Māori name for *greenstone*

powhiri – traditional Māori welcome onto a *marae*

rip – dangerously strong current running away from the shore at a beach

Roaring Forties – the ocean between 40° and 50° south, known for very strong winds

silver fern – symbol worn by the *All Blacks* and other national sportsfolk on their jerseys; the national netball team is called the Silver Ferns

sweet, sweet as – all-purpose term like *choice*; fantastic, great

tapu – strong force in Māori life, with numerous meanings; in its simplest form it means sacred, forbidden, taboo

te – the (singular); see also *nga*

te reo – literally 'the language'; the Māori language

tiki – short for *hei tiki*

tiki tour – scenic tour

tramp – bushwalk; trek; hike

tuatara – prehistoric reptile dating back to the age of dinosaurs

tui – native parson bird

wahine – woman

wai – water

wairua – spirit

Waitangi – short way of referring to the Treaty of Waitangi

waka – canoe

Warriors – NZ's popular rugby league club, affiliated with Australia's NRL

Wellywood – Wellington, because of its thriving film industry

zorbing – rolling down a hill inside an inflatable plastic ball

Behind the Scenes

SEND US YOUR FEEDBACK

We love to hear from travellers – your comments keep us on our toes and help make our books better. Our well-travelled team reads every word on what you loved or loathed about this book. Although we cannot reply individually to your submissions, we always guarantee that your feedback goes straight to the appropriate authors, in time for the next edition. Each person who sends us information is thanked in the next edition – the most useful submissions are rewarded with a selection of digital PDF chapters.

Visit **lonelyplanet.com/contact** to submit your updates and suggestions or to ask for help. Our award-winning website also features inspirational travel stories, news and discussions.

Note: We may edit, reproduce and incorporate your comments in Lonely Planet products such as guidebooks, websites and digital products, so let us know if you don't want your comments reproduced or your name acknowledged. For a copy of our privacy policy visit lonelyplanet.com/privacy.

WRITER THANKS

Peter Dragicevich

Hitting the road in my home country is always a special treat, especially as it provides the opportunity to spend time with family and friends. Special thanks are due to Christine Henderson for her hospitality in the Far North, Richard King in Wellington and the extended Erceg and Wilson clans in Whakatane, especially Manda and Les Wilson. Thanks too to my sister Joanne Cole for her expert appraisal of the standard of cappuccino in the Bay of Plenty.

Brett Atkinson

Thanks to all of the i-SITE, DOC and information centre staff who helped on the road, especially Glenn Ormsby and Mariet van Vierzen in Kaikoura. Cheers to the innovative chefs and inspired craft brewers of New Zealand for surprises and sustenance, and to Carol for support on occasional beach, island and city getaways. Thanks to my fellow authors, and my appreciation to Tasmin Waby at Lonely Planet for the opportunity to once again explore my Kiwi backyard.

Anita Isalska

Thanks primarily to Jason and Megan Hopper, who took me to the heights of the mountains and let me take them to the depths of Queenstown's basement bars. Gracias to Robyn Columbus Pester for a host of information, and the myriad business operators who answered my many queries along the journey. To my greatest gifts – Kiri and Cooper – a big thanks for rolling with it as ever as I wandered in and out of NZ and our other life.

Sofia Levin

Thank you to my supportive and loving husband, who was left twiddling his thumbs just days after our wedding when I took off for this project; my dear friend Katherine Cameron for constantly checking in on me on the road, you are a fountain of encouragement; and to my two biggest fans – mum and dad.

ACKNOWLEDGEMENTS

Climate map data adapted from Peel MC, Finlayson BL & McMahon TA (2007) 'Updated World Map of the Köppen-Geiger Climate Classification', Hydrology and Earth System Sciences, 11, 163344.

Cover photograph: Lighthouse at Castlepoint, the Wairarapa, Doug Pearson/AWL ©

THIS BOOK

This 5th edition of Lonely Planet's *New Zealand's North Island* guidebook was curated by Peter Dragicevich and researched and written by Peter Dragicevich, Brett Atkinson, Anita Isalska and Sofia Levin. The previous edition was written by Charles Rawlings-Way, Brett Atkinson, Sarah Bennett, Lee Slater and Peter Dragicevich. This guidebook was produced by the following:

Destination Editor
Tasmin Waby
Product Editors Jessica Ryan, Kate Chapman
Senior Cartographer
Diana Von Holdt
Book Designer
Gwen Cotter
Assisting Editors Michelle Bennett, Katie Connolly, Andrea Dobbin, Jennifer Hattan, Helen Koehne, Alexander Knights, Jodie Martire, Lou McGregor, Kristin Odijk,

Monique Perrin, Sam Wheeler, Simon Williamson
Cartographer James Leversha
Cover Researcher
Naomi Parker

Thanks to William Allen, Jennifer Carey, Heather Champion, Daniel Corbett, Joel Cotterell, Jane Grisman, Liz Heynes, Claire Naylor, Karyn Noble, Grant Patterson, Kathryn Rowan, Vicky Smith, Angela Tinson, Tracy Whitmey, Stephan Willemen

Index